PERSPECTIVES ON MODERN CHINA

Studies on Modern China

UNITED STATES ATTITUDES AND POLICIES TOWARD CHINA
THE IMPACT OF AMERICAN MISSIONARIES
Patricia Neils, editor

READING THE MODERN CHINESE SHORT STORY
Theodore Huters, editor

PERSPECTIVES ON MODERN CHINA
FOUR ANNIVERSARIES
Kenneth Lieberthal, Joyce Kallgren, Roderick MacFarquhar, Frederic Wakeman, Jr., editors

MODERNIZATION AND REVOLUTION IN CHINA
June Grasso, Jay Corrin, and Michael Kort

Studies on Modern China

PERSPECTIVES ON MODERN CHINA

FOUR ANNIVERSARIES

KENNETH LIEBERTHAL
JOYCE KALLGREN
RODERICK MacFARQUHAR
FREDERIC WAKEMAN, JR.
editors

THOMAS P. BERNSTEIN
LLOYD E. EASTMAN
MICHAEL H. HUNT
JOYCE KALLGREN
LEO OU-FAN LEE
BARRY NAUGHTON
MICHEL OKSENBERG
DWIGHT H. PERKINS
EVELYN S. RAWSKI
VIVIENNE SHUE
JAMES R. TOWNSEND
JAMES L. WATSON
TU WEI-MING
MARTIN KING WHYTE
ALEXANDER WOODSIDE
MADELEINE ZELIN

An East Gate Book

M. E. Sharpe, Inc.
ARMONK, NEW YORK
LONDON, ENGLAND

An East Gate Book

Avaliable in the United Kingdom and Europe from M. E. Sharpe, Publishers, 3 Henrietta Street, London WV2E 8LU.

Library of Congress Cataloging-in-Publication Data

Perspectives on modern China : four anniversaries
/ edited by Kenneth Lieberthal . . . [et al.].
p. cm. — (Studies on modern China)
Based on papers from the Four Anniversaries China Conference,
held Sept. 10–15, 1989 in Annapolis, Md.
ISBN 0-87332-814-0 (cloth)
ISBN 0-87332-890-6 (pbk.)
1. China—History—Ch'ing dynasty, 1644–1912—Congresses.
2. China—History—May Fourth movement, 1919—Congresses.
3. China—History—1949- —Congresses.
I. Lieberthal, Kenneth.
II. Four Anniversaries China Conference (1989 : Annapolis, Md.)
III. Series.
DS753.84.P47 1991
951′.03—dc20
91-13410
CIP

Printed in the United States of America

The paper used in this publication meets the minimum requirements of American National Standard for Information Sciences—Permanence of Paper for Printed Library Materials, ANSI Z39.48-1984.

ED 10 9 8 7 6 5 4 3 2 1

Dedicated to Lloyd Eastman,
a valued colleague whose lifetime work
exemplifies the spirit of this volume

CONTENTS

PREFACE

KENNETH LIEBERTHAL

DURING the course of the 1980s China began to make rapid strides toward becoming more integrated with the outside world. Domestically, it significantly decentralized its economy, adopted policies that produced major social changes, and began to tinker with the operations of its political system. Culturally, Chinese intellectuals on the mainland began to develop serious discourse with their Chinese counterparts elsewhere, and the cultural scene on the mainland grew more diverse. Television, whose widespread use really began at the start of the 1980s, added a new element to this mix. In sum, a great deal appeared to be changing in China, and these changes were occurring at high speed.

The extent and rapidity of these changes raised serious questions about the forces that were shaping the Chinese society, economy, polity, and sense of place in the world. For many years, the brunt of scholarship on the People's Republic of China had focused primarily on the aspects of that system that were imported from the Soviet Union and from socialist practice elsewhere. Some of the phenomena of the decade of the 1980s suggested the continued salience of China's prewar experience with the United States, Europe, and Japan. And those steeped in Chinese culture and history recognized familiar terrain as they looked at the types of issues that arose concerning questions such as the relationship of intellectuals to the state, the relation of regions to the central authorities, the nature of power in Beijing, and the complex interaction between China and the outside world.

The conveners of the September 10–15, 1989, Four Anniversaries China Conference in Annapolis on which this volume is based—Joyce Kallgren, Kenneth Lieberthal, and Roderick MacFarquhar—felt that the time had come to try to provide more detailed and thoughtful perspective by bringing together a highly unusual mix of people and giving them a somewhat different type of task. Fifty scholars attended this conference to review and discuss sixteen papers that had been distributed in advance of the meeting. The discussion was lively, surprisingly wide ranging, and insightful. Unfortunately, the economics of publication permit us here only to reproduce the papers themselves, along with brief introductions to each section that capture a portion of the issues raised in the discussion.

The conveners asked each paper writer to look back from the year 1989 to the period the writer was considering and to write a paper that analyzed what in retrospect had been the most enduring features of the Chinese system at that earlier time. In many cases, the features that emerged were not ones that analysts of that period alone would have highlighted. The vantage point of 1989 afforded the writers an opportunity to think in broad and systemic terms about the basic features of China. These are not papers that are intended to present the latest research findings on very specialized topics. Rather, they seek to provide perspective on China and its evolution over time.

The conference itself was organized around four periods: high Qing before the Opium War; the May Fourth era; the Maoist era after 1949; and the era of Deng's reforms. Writers about the final period tried to put the Deng era in historical perspective and to identify its future legacy.

The specific paper assignments varied somewhat by the era under consideration, and these are explained in more detail in the introductions to each section. In general terms, the papers concerned the political system; the economic system; the society and culture; and China's interaction with the outside world. This is a "proceedings" volume, and therefore the papers are presented here largely in their original form. Each paper writer was given a brief period in which to make revisions and to make references to other papers and the discussions. All paper writers made at least some changes during the fall of 1989, but the editors did not require that each author make the changes that might have been required had this volume not been proceedings of the conference.

This conference was highly unusual in that it brought together individuals who focus on very different time periods (from high Qing to the present) and who work in different disciplines (anthropology, economics, history, literature, philosophy, political science, and sociology). There was also great diversity in terms of geography, type of institution, and seniority among the participants. Remarkably, discussions flowed easily, and virtually every paper produced lively comments from people whose expertise spanned an array of time periods and disciplines. At one point or another, almost every scholar at the conference heard remarks that challenged some of the fundamental characteristics of "their" China.

We seek to make as much of this intellectual conclave as possible available to a wide audience through the medium of the present volume. We encourage readers to range well beyond their normal sphere of interest in perusing this volume. These papers in their collectivity provide a complex, nuanced, exciting view of a dynamic and in many ways frustrating country.

We wish to thank the Luce Foundation for providing the funding for this conference, and especially Dr. Terrill Lautz at the foundation, who understood the nature of our effort and proved to be flexible and helpful at every turn. We also owe a debt of gratitude to Patrick Maddox of Harvard's Fairbank Center for administrative support for the meeting. Frederic Wakeman of the University of California at Berkeley played an important role in helping us to think through the initial conception of the conference, organizing the papers on the high Qing period, and contributing a paper to the volume itself. We are grateful for his tremendous efforts on behalf of this volume.

Finally, we wish to thank our editors at M. E. Sharpe, Anita O'Brien and Laura Cohn, and express our special thanks to Douglas Merwin. He has over the years been responsible for bringing to press numerous books and journals that have greatly enriched the China field, and we appreciate the enthusiasm and commitment he has shown to this volume.

CONTRIBUTORS

THOMAS P. BERNSTEIN, Political Science Department, Columbia University

LLOYD E. EASTMAN, History Department, University of Illinois

MICHAEL H. HUNT, History Department, University of North Carolina

JOYCE KALLGREN, History Department, University of California, Berkeley

LEO OU-FAN LEE, Literature Department, University of California, Los Angeles

KENNETH LIEBERTHAL, Political Science Department, University of Michigan

RODERICK MACFARQUHAR, Political Science Department, Harvard University

BARRY NAUGHTON, Economics Department, University of California, San Diego

MICHEL OKSENBERG, Political Science Department, University of Michigan

DWIGHT H. PERKINS, Economics Department, Harvard University

EVELYN S. RAWSKI, History Department, Pittsburgh University

VIVIENNE SHUE, Political Science Department, Cornell University

JAMES R. TOWNSEND, Political Science Department, University of Washington

FREDERIC WAKEMAN, JR., History Department, University of California, Berkeley

JAMES L. WATSON, Anthropology Department, Harvard University

TU WEI-MING, Anthropology Department, Harvard University

MARTIN KING WHYTE, Sociology Department, University of Michigan

ALEXANDER WOODSIDE, History Department, University of British Columbia

MADELEINE ZELIN, History Department, Columbia University

PART ONE

1839: THE PROSCENIUM OF LATE IMPERIAL CHINA

FREDERIC WAKEMAN, JR.

IN HIS essay on emperorship, Alexander Woodside urges us to set aside the conventional indictment of despotism as a selfish exercise of power, and to see instead that the perdurance of the imperial institution in China reflected the monarchy's early elimination of feudal rivals. By the eve of the Opium War, there were simply none of the monarchy-limiting forces we are familiar with in European history: aristocrats, municipal oligarchies, corporations, estates, churches. The emperor's own mandarins, meanwhile, were unable to promote an independent bureaucratic conceptualization of the state.

Woodside's main theme, then, is that no one in imperial China could have imagined a "state" as being more than an extension of the personal authority at the "forbidden center" of the empire. "Altogether the Chinese monarchy in 1839 was a despotism locked in a kind of stalemate with a potentially more modern bureaucracy; but it offered very little positive political freedom to its subjects." Thanks to the examination system, moreover, the Chinese monarchy commanded greater elite support and shallower specific loyalties than equivalent European kingships. The emperor owned the empire, and hence only he could effect reform. This created a craving for the achievement of societywide justice "through the impartial leadership of one transcendental figure who ultimately controlled all resources"—a craving for ultimate leadership that could not easily be given up at the end of the ancien régime.

My own essay argues, in fact, that the monarchy's efforts after the Opium War to create a structural alternative to patrimonial leadership not only presaged, but were also linked to, twentieth-century measures to develop a modern system of state control. I believe that we can trace connections betwen the late Qing monarchy's efforts to introduce modern police forces to China, through the Guomindang government's policy of using the police as one of the two "wings" of its rule, directly to the public security system of the People's Republic of China. I argue, furthermore, that the successful construction of this structure has much to do with the current regime's staying power during and after the events of June 1989.

Madeleine Zelin's article about the Qing economy centers on the observation that it was characterized by a high level of output per unit of land thanks to labor-intensive cultivation. Increased overall output—a sixfold increase between 1400 and 1900—came about through land reclamation and the spread of traditional technologies in a "highly fragmented agrarian sector, based on small-scale farm management by tenants and owner-cultivators [that] was supported by a large, bottom-heavy, and extremely lively network of rural periodic markets and market towns."

Manufacturing in the first half of the Qing was mostly cottage industry in rural areas. The rural base of production favored a balanced growth between city and countryside, reinforcing trends toward continued population growth, falling per capital incomes, and a relatively even distribution of wealth among large numbers of economic actors. Those trends in turn led to undercapitalization of enterprises, which perpetuated capital dispersion and prevented China from moving from a highly developed commercial economy to industrial capitalism. State policies facilitated the role of small merchants in commercial networks whose long chains of credit reduced profits at each level. China was thus an empire of middling wealth resting upon a rural production system that increased family income by expanding family size. A production regime that so depended upon the family as a mechanism to pool resources encouraged entrepreneurial attitudes animating rural reform even today.

The importance of the partriarchal family to the economic system of late imperial China is, of course, matched by its centrality to what Tu Wei-ming defines as "the ethicoreligious dimension and the psychocultural dynamics of Chinese society." In his essay, Tu notes how difficult it is for Western scholars—all "children of the Enlightenment"—to sympathize with the hierarchical and authoritarian values of China's shared culture. Even many Chinese intellectuals, who became "themselves children of the Enlightenment with a vengeance" after the May Fourth era, have attacked the subjugation and repression of Chinese authoritarianism.

Tu, however, claims that it is possible to interpret the Chinese perception of the world without being "enslaved in the Enlightenment mentality," thanks in part to the challenge posed by modern East Asian industrialization to the notion that modernization must be defined as Westernization. Also, as global interdependence has increased, the "primordial ties" defining communities have correspondingly strengthened: "ethnicity, mother tongue, fatherland, gender, and religion will continue to define who we are." According to Tu, these are not just reactions to change, but "positive contributions to the meaning of life in an increasingly pluralistic universe."

The Confucian elite on the eve of the Opium War was not—as Woodside would have it—a bureaucratic stratum ideologically dependent upon a despotic emperor. Rather, Tu asserts, Confucian intellecutals "constructed their own cultural identity" by functioning as "communicative teacher[s] in society at large," and were thereby able "to maintain an independent autonomous posture toward the court."

Nonetheless, after 1839 the West overwhelmed the Chinese intelligentsia: the rules changed so radically that intellectuals found themselves "forced to play a game fundamentally unintelligible to them." Many refused to embrace the modern West and its Enlightenment ideology as an intrinsic value. Confucian humanism and the Enlightenment mentality constitute "rival and incompatible value orientations," and attempts to find a higher synthesis repeatedly failed. The ultimate tragedy for twentieth-century intellectuals, Tu concludes, is that their own Confucian humanism was simultaneously ridiculed, and they could neither "tap into their own indigenous resources nor take seriously what the West could offer."

Each of these four essays, then, provides a different historical explanation by way of understanding aspects of contemporary China. Woodside hints at a link between the personalistic rule of Qing emperors and present-day dictatorship, intellectual dependency, and authoritarianism. My essay connects late imperial state-building with Republican and Communist systems of social control. Zelin shows how traditional Chinese modes of agriculture and commerce dispersed capital while creating entrepreneurial habits centered upon a family production regime that still operates in the Chinese countryside. And Tu suggests that the incompatibility between Confucian humanism and Enlightenment thought may explain why Chinese intellectuals feel so ambivalent about contemporary Chinese culture. Taken together, all of the essays share a common interest in decoding patterns of development that help us understand why history weighs so heavily on China today.

1

EMPERORS AND THE CHINESE POLITICAL SYSTEM

ALEXANDER WOODSIDE

The Debate about Emperors in Modern China

A Hobbesian fondness for the rule of a single strongman, as the antidote to conflict and disorder, may well be universal in human politics. The cult of Napoleon in nineteenth-century France, the hopes that Mussolini and Stalin once inspired in their respective countries, and perhaps even the temptations of the "imperial presidency" to very small numbers of Americans, show something of its strength. But because the unity of China was associated with the tradition of a universal monarchy for more than twenty-one centuries (221 B.C.–A.D. 1911), contemporary Chinese thinkers have been particularly sensitive to the supposed "retarding force" of such predispositions in their country.

The courageous political scientist Yan Jiaqi argued in 1980 that monarchism in China habitually meant the deification of the ruler; the periodic slaughter of meritorious ministers below the ruler, whose jealousy of such ministers was preordained; incessant struggles among court factions; and the occasional usurpations of power by eunuchs or by the ruler's relatives, including relatives of his mother or wives. As Yan saw it, all these things had survived after 1949. Mao Zedong's attacks upon rivals like Peng Dehuai and Liu Shaoqi were classic modern demonstrations of the divisive techniques of emperorship. Mao's selection of successors like Lin Biao and Wang Hongwen was entirely similar to the emperors' selection of the crown princes whom they wished to succeed them. Because high positions were held for life in post-1949 China, Chinese political struggles under Communist rule inevitably continued to assume the forms of traditional imperial court politics. The main reason for the survival of this disguised monarchism in contemporary China—the concentration of supreme power in the hands of one person and his secretive courtiers, for life—was said to be the preindustrial nature of the Chinese economy. Because of it, all Chinese revolutions, whatever their intentions, turned into peasant wars. Peasant wars led in turn to the creation of new emperors.[1]

The argument that Mao was an emperor is, of course, a rhetorical one in part. Intended to be disturbing, it nevertheless minimizes awareness of the conscious popular support that Mao's policies might have enjoyed among people other than peasants. But the real curiosity of this debate about the excessive centralization of power in China lies in the fact that it has been going on for such a long time. When a lecturer at the Marxist-Leninist Institute of the Chinese Social Sciences Academy complained in 1980 about China's "pyramidal" leadership structure and the ease with which the top of the pyramid could be appropriated and occupied for long periods by the same small group of people,[2] he followed the footprints of the formidable seventeenth-century philosopher Huang Zongxi (1610–1695). Huang was unfamiliar with the idea of a pyramid; but his denunciation of the emperors' conversion of their empire into an "enormous private estate" that they could pass on to their descendants made the same point. Huang Zongxi had in turn been preceded by Deng Mu (1247–1306), who had criticized Chinese rulers for treating the world as if it belonged to one "fellow." Before Deng Mu there had been thinkers like Bao Jingyan (fourth century A.D.) for whom preimperial antiquity was good precisely because it lacked coercive princes.

The controversy over the nature of political leadership in China thus defies the adage that history proceeds in part by changing the subject, that one day people suddenly realize that the disputes that previously preoccupied and divided them no longer matter so much. The question of the selfishness of the exercise of power at the top of their political system has haunted some Chinese intellectuals for centuries. In our own century, the explanations for what many Chinese clearly regard as a pathological political situation have not changed very much. The last great debate about the survival of despotism in modern China, before the 1980s, occurred forty years ago in the last disillusioning years of Guomindang rule. The vastness of the country's illiterate peasantry received much attention in this debate as well. Apart from the peasants, one writer argued in an important Shanghai periodical in 1947 that democracy was elusive because of China's great size. Western democracy had originated and been renewed in small polities, like the Greek city-states or the thirteen American colonies, where high levels of communal political participation had been possible. Because of China's much bigger scale, poor communications, and low ideological tolerance for the notion of permanent decentralization or disunity, however, the only successful early exercise of a unifying political power, as demonstrated by the First Emperor of the Qin dynasty in 221 B.C., had inevitably rested upon violence and autocracy. The First Emperor's triumphant use of brute force, rather than softer options like negotiated alliances with his competitors, had created a precedent for the construction of Chinese governments from which few succeeding Chinese rulers had been able to break free.[3] This "size" argument remains a staple of the discussions about the lack of democracy in China today,[4] along with the theme that the emperorship is rooted in an unchanged peasant economy.

The first task for any analyst is to try to get the debate under better control. With respect to twentieth-century politics, it is crucial to separate phenomena that may really have change-resistant links to the old emperorship—and that legitimately belong to the "remnants of feudalism" thesis, which Chinese writers, like Soviet ones, greatly abuse—from other phenomena related to the inability of post-1911 Chinese governments to create widespread respect for new institutions quickly enough; their need to legitimize themselves at various levels of the popular consciousness; and their consequent deliberate tactical exploitation of what they imagine to be traditional values, beginning most blatantly with Yuan Shikai in 1915.

It is even more important to grasp the peculiar dynamics of the emperorship that enabled it to survive for so long. The size argument is weakened by the fact that there was little discernible democratic theory in the much smaller city-states that preceded the First Emperor's military unification of China. There was merely an enormously important tradition of political humanism that stipulated that the people were the foundation, but not the masters, of politics and ought to come first. It is true, of course, that fears of the appallingly extended savagery that might accompany Chinese disunity, which were themselves conjured up by the problems of dynastic change in such a large state, did become a growing force in their own right after the empire's genesis. It is difficult to imagine any Chinese emperor voluntarily behaving like the Roman emperor Diocletian, who created a co-emperor and two deputy Caesars to help him govern. But the intelligentsia were equally fearful of the disorder that such a huge polity might permit. In a famous essay on the nature of humankind written in the early 1700s, and much reprinted, Fang Bao divided Chinese history into two periods—the two thousand years before the Warring States and the unification of the empire, and the two thousand years after the Warring States—and warned that the more recent two millennia had been far more full of slaughter and endless military turmoil.

It might seem easier to argue that the emperorship survived by courtesy of an unchanging peasant economy, which ensured the success of a crude state indoctrination process that taught naive peasants obedience to a monarchy. Ann Anagnost's brilliant study of the poor Hunanese peddler who was arrested in China in 1981 for trying to make himself emperor certainly confirms the continued existence of emperor worship in rural China.[5] In fact, the historic emperorship coexisted with different types of economies, even if they were all precapitalist. And although loyalty to the prince was one of the transcendental virtues in Confucianism, the notion that heavy indoctrination, through devices like the exposition of "Sacred Edicts" to villagers, successfully imbued Chinese peasants with a strong fealty to individual reigning emperors, century after century, must also be questioned. As anyone who has ever studied the Chinese countryside knows, Chinese peasants were experts not just at rebellion but at various artful forms of foot dragging; symbolic but not actual compliance; and even the partial appropriation from below of the emperor's assets. (The very hulls of the government grain junks, the emperor's lifeline, expanded illicitly throughout the 1700s, to accommodate the growing quantities of contraband and private cargo shipped by their crewmen and coolies, to the point where the junks could no longer sail the Grand Canal in low-water years.) Even at the best of times, peasant loyalty to existing monarchs was relatively passive. In Russia, great rebels like Pugachev made themselves into reincarnations of specific tsars in order to gain peasant support. Chinese rebels, in contrast, operating in a civilization where bureaucratic and family values were more important and where individual loyalty to specific emperors was consequently weaker, normally confined themselves to invoking much vaguer claims of descent from past dynasties.

Indoctrination itself was administered by the scholar class. They had, in Vivienne Shue's words, a "dual" loyalty to their "home base" and to the "metropolitan bureaucratic culture,"[6] more than to any individual Son of Heaven. Indoctrination accordingly focused Chinese village loyalties upon sages and saints whose connections with actual emperors were tenuous. When inland Anhui primary school pupils, in a rare survey of their attitudes, were asked in 1926 to name the most celebrated figures in Chinese history, the majority named Confucius, Mencius, Zhu Xi, and Laozi; a substantial minority listed mythic emperors such as Yao and Shun and the Yellow Emperor; and only a tiny minority listed two actual rulers, the First Emperor and the founder of the Han dynasty.[7] Such a poll was undoubtedly not very reliable as a free expression of views, but it probably did capture the ambivalence of old-fashion Chinese village schools with respect to historic emperors, and the imitative extension of this ambivalence among the school children being polled.

A real understanding of the long survival of the emperorship in China requires a retreat from the edge of the demonic world in which the discussion is so often located. If some of the ideals and habits of the imperial institution have been difficult for revolutionaries to eliminate, this has been because they stood for virtues as well as vices, in the eyes of the elite as well as of the peasantry. The myth of human perfection for which the emperors were political stand-ins facilitated an anthropocentric humanism in which the elite had a strong investment. This had little to do with the size of the polity or with the credulity of the uneducated. Even at its worst, the tyranny of the emperorship seems to have been the price the Chinese people paid for great political and cultural achievements of other kinds.

The Chinese Emperorship as the Reflection of a Historical Success Story

Two hundred years ago, the Chinese monarchy certainly appeared to be far more the master of its own political system than any equivalent Western kingship was.

Even before the French Revolution, four important forces limited the authority of the European monarchies, with the major exception of the Russian one. These forces were, first of all, powerful hereditary noble families, who believed that they had an inherent right to a share in government; second, the oligarchies of many cities and towns, who had traditions of self-government and political privileges guaranteed them by ancient charters; third, a medley of potentially troublesome representative corporations or institutions, variously called estates or diets or assemblies or parliaments, which thought they had a right to share in legislative and administrative power; and fourth, quasi-autonomous churches with their own governing bodies and a strong potential political influence.

Not one of these monarchy-limiting forces existed in China. There was no strong nobility with hereditary political claims, no chartered self-governing towns, no representative estates or assemblies, and no quasi-autonomous churches. When the famous British diplomatic embassy led by Macartney visited the emperor of China in 1793 and offered him as a gift an English horse-drawn carriage, the high coachman's box on the carriage had to be removed because the Chinese showed "the utmost astonishment" that anyone, let alone a mere coachman, could be placed in a physical position above that of the emperor. The Qianlong emperor's majesty, in fact and in symbol, was far loftier than that of King George III.

Another of the Macartney mission's relatively unsuccessful gifts in 1793 points to the gigantic historical accomplishment upon which this lofty majesty rested. His British visitors also offered Qianlong a volume of portraits of the nobility of Great Britain. They asked a mandarin to write Chinese titles for each of the portraits in the volume. When the mandarin encountered a Sir Joshua Reynolds portrait of a duke who was still a child and was told that the child was a personage of high noble rank by hereditary right, he angrily declined to write any such explanation under the child's portrait. No "little boy" could possess such noble rank, the mandarin asserted; the emperor would think that he was being fooled.[8]

China had an exalted monarchy but no important hereditary aristocracy; Britain had a relatively modest monarchy but a still formidable aristocracy. If one agrees with the modern esteem for meritocracy and for achieved statuses rather than ascribed ones, and with the modern disapproval of "little boys" being powerful aristocrats, in this one important respect China must be regarded as the more progressive state. From the time the First Emperor invented it, the emperorship was associated with the centralization of Chinese government in a politically nonfeudal, nonhereditary, bureaucratic administration. Within the next ten or twelve centuries, the Chinese ruling class came to be recruited through civil service examinations. What this meant was a premodern political system in which great magnates other than the ruler did not have formal hereditary legal and military authority over other people. The contrast is with the legal and the military pluralism of medieval and early modern Europe, as exemplified in the high feudal period by European manorial courts, and by the mobilization by the European magnates of their vassals for military service during the crusades; or in seventeenth-century Europe by the French parlements, and by the armed forces that French nobles still directly commanded at the time of the Fronde aristocratic rebellion in 1648. The mission of unification to which the Chinese emperorship was dedicated could not accept such pluralism.

The difference with the political systems in most of China's Asian neighbors was equally dramatic. In Theravada Buddhist societies like Siam and Burma, for example, the provincial officials whom kings appointed qualified for their positions on the basis of their family status and their inherited networks of clients, not their academic training. They treated their jurisdictions as fiefs or appanages, and they were accordingly said to "eat" their provinces. In China, provincial officials like prefects and county magistrates were literally officials who "knew the prefecture" (*zhi fu*) or who "knew the county" (*zhi xian*), in an intellectual sense, as scholarly outsiders. The contrast between local officials whose chief political activity was supposed to be "knowing" and those whose chief political activity was said to be "eating" illustrates as clearly as anything the gap between a bureaucratizing monarchy and less bureaucratic appanage-distributing ones.

The Chinese monarchy's early elimination of political feudalism, which carried with it the ideological hegemony of scholars rather than aristocrats or merchants, represented the world apogee of bureaucratic state-building until only a few centuries ago. As recently as 1500, up to five hundred governments claimed authority over the people of Europe. But even if large chunks of territory like the Tibetan Jinchuan hill people's domain in northwestern Sichuan were only integrated in any modern sense into the Chinese empire in the 1700s, the real Chinese political equivalents of Europe's Burgundy and Bohemia and Lorraine and Scotland, or the hundreds of German principalities of the Holy Roman Empire, had vanished much earlier.

This was the amazing feat for which the emperorship was the tradeoff. The tragedy was that China's precocious maturity as a centralized monarchical-bureaucratic state required at the outset the bloody-handed engineering of the First Emperor. His militarism and intolerance of rivals set a precedent that traditional Chinese humanism was never entirely able to overcome. The result, to a pessimistic thinker like Liang Qichao looking back in 1904, was something like a marriage between heaven and hell: a civilization where scholars were supreme but where "brute force" was controlled less well than in the West, and where stability, once lost, was regained only through a leadership struggle comparable to the struggle of fighting crickets in a cage, with the fighting coming to an end only when all but one cricket had been killed.[9] Indeed, the more richly developed Confucianism became—the more scholastic, or the more influenced by Buddhist metaphysics—the less capable it seemed to be of working out a legitimate permanent role for military men in the Chinese political system that could control them without abolishing them. Emperors like Qianlong deliberately segregated soldiers from the world of literacy and learning, thus reinforcing their moral marginality. Qianlong explained in 1739 that if soldiers learned to read, they would no longer want to be soldiers.

The axial political problem, as seen from the throne, was the preservation of bureaucratic unity and the prevention of the disguised refeudalization of the empire's administration. This great task—and even by the standards of our own contemporary world, it was a great task—was more important than administrative efficiency. But the lack of administrative efficiency, and certain types of corruption that accompanied that lack, encouraged political habits that are sometimes treated as eternal Chinese traits but were really the price China paid for its size, and for being the world pioneer of a relatively pure postfeudal bureaucratic state. In some respects, the Chinese imperial political system has the same tragic significance in political history that the British industrial economy has in modern economic history: that of the eventual backwardness of the pioneer.

The price that China paid for its pioneering abolition of hereditary political power outside the monarchy was more than just administrative inefficiency, or the overcentralization of power in the emperor. In a society in which there were few precisely stratified laws of clothing and behavior for different social "estates," anyone with the means to do so could—up to a point—try to imitate the standards set by the throne itself. To some extent, the emperors as teacher-rulers were supposed to ensure this. The neo-Confucian philosopher Lu Shiyi (1611–1672) stated that family education must be based upon court education, and that one might even infer the quality and the nature of family education all over China, in a reign period like the one of A.D. 1399–1403, merely by studying the strictness of the court education at the time.[10] Authority in the Chinese empire might be different in scale, but it was not emphatically different in kind. The homespun replication of the monarchical style at different social levels threatened more than efficiency. Wang Tao pointed out in the nineteenth century that the emperorship had encouraged the formation of multiple layers of smaller despotisms within officialdom. In 1920, the famous anarchist Liang Bingxian went beyond even this. Writing about "village revolution" in a short-lived Fujian newspaper, Liang warned that although the last Qing emperor had abdicated, the Chinese revolution had not succeeded because there were a "myriad" of smaller Xuantong emperors scattered throughout China's villages and towns.[11]

In other words, the disappearance of formal hereditary political power meant that feudalism went underground. In compensation, it took the form of what one might call a spiritual micromonarchism, based upon families and big lineages. Big lineages were by no means the norm in traditional China, even south of the Huai River. Emperors nonetheless thought they had to defend themselves against the micromonarchism of lineage leaders bent upon the magnification of their surname-based power. In a definitive case involving the aspirations of large Jiangxi descent groups in 1764, the Qianlong emperor made it clear that the throne could not tolerate the political construction of organized same-surname groups that took whole prefectures as their base, although he would accept such groups whose coverage was smaller than that of a prefecture. When lineage registers were discovered that traced a lineage's ancestry back to the Yellow Emperor or used imperial court terminology to describe the evolution of a lineage, the monarchy burned them, as with the "Chronicles of Succession of the Great Peng Lineage" of 1757.[12]

The proliferation of myriad "local emperors" (as the anarchist Liang called them in 1920), and the imitative universalization of the court ethos among lesser officials and rich commoners, without sumptuary laws of a detailed sort or aristocratic or feudal barrier to restrain this, was still less directly challenging to the authority of the real emperor in Peking than a genuine hereditary nobility would have been. The problem was that it created a society that was also less easy for the central power—any central power—to manage or to mobilize in a crisis.

The Manchu Rulers as the Skillful Inheritors of the Bureaucratizing Monarchy

The Manchu conquest of China in 1644—which was probably carried out by no more than 120,000 Manchu soldiers, plus fewer than 60,000 allied Chinese and Mongols[13]—showed that intelligent outsiders could make the imperial bureaucratic loyalty system work for them, too, while raising more questions about the scope and intensity of the loyalties that the system permitted any emperors to command in hard times. The Manchu emperors themselves had a strong consciousness of being ethnic "others." They linked the question of the survival of their dynastic house to a fear of excessive cultural borrowing, with perhaps much greater theoretical sensitivity than any previous non-Chinese rulers in Chinese history. The Qianlong emperor, for example, was a connoisseur of the politics of even the clothing histories of the former Jurchen (Jin) and Mongol (Yuan) courts. He traced foreign rulers' self-defeating adoption of Chinese clothes back to the foreign Northern Wei dynasty (A.D. 386–535), and demanded that his court scholars investigate the Jurchen emperors' eventual decadence in China as it was related to their acculturation.[14] Whether the Manchu emperors' conservatism in this respect provided a large, and gratuitous, barrier to the modernization through acculturation of the China they led between 1839 and 1911 is less clear. Certainly the Manchu emperors' conservatism also embraced an almost crusading sense of the rightness, and the manifest destiny, of Chinese neo-Confucian philosophy and morality and the classical heritage behind it. Their own different social, linguistic, and religious traditions did not profoundly alter the dynamics of China's bureaucratic state (whose territorial size they vastly expanded) or its monarchy, although Manchu contributions to the statecraft of the empire were fascinating and considerable.

Emperors of China were supposed to try to be sages. The great Han dynasty classicist Zheng Xuan was one of the first to express this thought after the creation of the emperorship, but it followed a more ancient notion of rulers who exemplified "inner sageliness and outer kindliness." The First Emperor's holocaust of classical books ironically gave his successors a matchless chance to stabilize and sanctify the emperorship he bequeathed them, by casting themselves as, first, the restorers and, second, the arbiters of orthodox classical knowledge. This gained them a working political proximity to sagehood. The Han emperors showed how to do it, convening assemblies of despairing Confucian scholars to try to recover all the postholocaust understandings of many scattered texts and systematize their meanings, as at the Stone Channel Pavilion in 51 B.C. and the White Tiger Pavilion in A.D. 79. This early medieval Han paradigm of the emperor as the patron and the expositor of moral and textual knowledge gained strength in succeeding centuries. And for all their fears of becoming too Chinese, the Manchu emperors were brilliant at building upon the ancient Han emperors' traditions of legitimizing imperial power through the promotion and reorganization of classical knowledge. The Qianlong emperor's remarkable "Complete Library of the Four Treasuries" (*Siku quanshu*) project of 1772, through which the emperor employed the cream of the Chinese intelligentsia, is perhaps the best example.[15]

The Manchu emperors, however, ruled Tibet and Mongolia as well as China. One of the great fascinations of their dynasty lies in how they transcended the skill of all previous emperors in carrying out a many-sided religious legitimization of their power that would appeal to diverse constituencies.

In China itself, the cosmological basis of the emperorship in the 1800s continued to be the one essentially provided much earlier by the Han philosopher Dong Zhongshu (second century B.C.). Dong had observed that the Chinese written word for "king" showed three horizontal lines connected by a vertical line. The three horizontal lines represented Heaven, earth, and man, which it was the ruler's duty to connect or "pass through." Such a definition of the ruler did not lend itself to doctrinal limitations. The king, the emperor, harmonized the human world with the much greater order of the universe, was indispensable in providing the means for the moral fulfillment of all his subjects, and was, therefore, the decisive factor in determining whether human affairs would be stable or unstable. The relative balance between the emperor's priestly functions in connecting his subjects to the universe, and his more secular administrative duties as a tax collector, is suggested by the fact that even in the late nineteenth century, the Imperial Observatory—which watched the stars and prepared the calendar—had 211 officials assigned to it, or more than half the total number of officials normally assigned to the Peking ministry in charge of taxes, population, and land, the Board of Finance (362 officials). Dong Zhongshu's theme that a morally exemplary king or Son of Heaven was the key to stability was undoubtedly one elite idea about kingship that really did work its way downward into the popular imagination, where simpler versions of it took root. The Communist revolutionary Peng Pai discovered to his chagrin in the 1920s that the largely illiterate peasants of Haifeng county, Guangdong, thought that there would be no "great peace" (*tai ping*) for China until a "truly mandated Son of Heaven" appeared. But once such a figure did appear, the peasants thought, the effect would be magical. Muskets would fall silent, and he would be immediately enthroned.[16]

The Manchu emperors also claimed to be living incarnations of gods in the eyes of their Tibetan and Mongol subjects. They hardly advertised this claim to the Chinese Confucian intelligentsia, for whom Dong Zhongshu's more religiously modest view of the ruler was enough, and who were conventionally suspicious of Buddhism, Tibetan or otherwise. But since the vision of a polity that took in Tibetans as well as Chinese is one of the most tangible and controversial legacies the Qing emperors have left contemporary China, these emperors' claims to be reincarnations of the Manjusri bodhisattva, the bodhisattva of wisdom, are an important part of their history. The claims helped to make Manchu rule over Tibet far more possible. They were made in 1640, even before the Manchus' conquest of China itself was complete. As recognized reincarnations of Manjusri, the Manchu rulers became, or at least tried to become, "cult objects" among all classes of Mongols and Tibetans. They sponsored their own Buddhist temple complexes at Jehol and Dolon Nor.[17]

It has been suggested, nonetheless, that the general program of the monarchy of China over the centuries was secular and surprisingly modern: the extension of the First Emperor's unifying principles of nonhereditary bureaucratic government. Even in Tibet, the fact that the Manchu emperors were Buddhist monarchs as well as Confucian sages did not make them completely unfaithful to this program. Far from it: Tibet, a theocracy with a powerful hereditary nobility, became the last great theater before the Opium War in which the traditional emperors of China and their agents tried to engage in a limited bureaucratic assault against intermediate group political power of a hereditary nonbureaucratic type. This, at least, is what the only partly realized intentions of Fukangan—the Manchu proconsul and proxy emperor in Tibet after the defeat of a Gurkha invasion of that country in 1792—suggest.

Fukangan set out to make the appointments and promotions of Tibetan officials in Lhasa more impartial, through the introduction of a bureaucratic grades and seniority system that struck at family influence. He tried to deprive the relatives of the incumbent Dalai and Panchen Lamas of all official authority, in a manner that bore at least some resemblance to the First Emperor's attempted repression of aristocratic family power in China. In terms that echo Communist-ruled China's professed horror of Tibetan "feudalism," Fukangan in 1792 denounced the lack of "fairness and justice" associated with the Tibetan nobility's privileged exemption from compulsory government labor. He demanded that all existing Tibetan labor exemption permits be surrendered to him for cancellation;

new ones would be issued on the basis of "meritorious achievements," not heredity. Fukangan also tried to extend the Chinese empire's bureaucratic registers system for Buddhist and Taoist monks to the lamaist monks of Tibet, demanding that the Dalai Lama make written counts—in duplicate—of the staffs of all his monasteries. Fukangan also brought the administration of justice by the senior Tibetan ministers (*kalons*), who had third-grade rank in the general Qing bureaucracy under bureaucratic regulation, to block their arbitrary confiscation of the estates of minor transgressors of the law with whom their families might be feuding.[18]

The result of all this was modest—a political Tibet that was a strange compromise between Tibetan and Chinese imperial views. Commoners were still excluded from officialdom, unlike in China; yet the nobility had at least begun to be bureaucratized. It remained true that the mission of controlling abusive political power of a prebureaucratic kind was a basic part of the traditional emperors' self-image, even in the borderlands. The Qing emperorship in Lhasa publicly stood for "fairness and justice"—whatever the disarray and corruption of the emperors' own entourage back in Peking.

The Stalemate Between the Emperorship and More Independently Bureaucratic Conceptualizations of the State

The coexistence of the Chinese emperorship with the ideal of a nonhereditary political elite was always far from perfect. The possibility that the emperors themselves might refeudalize Chinese politics at the very top, through the granting of important inheritable powers to princely families within the imperial clan, always lay just beneath the surface. It had not irrevocably vanished, as the appanage-like authority of princes in the early Ming dynasty showed. The Aisin Gioro descent group from which the Qing rulers came gave the imperial government of China in the 1800s a core based on personal and kinship ties that was only partly subject to bureaucratic rationalization. In 1846, this imperial "house" or descent group comprised 10,895 members, divided into some 46 lineages and arranged into 12 tiers of nobility.[19]

The size and organization of this descent group symbolized the emperor's extraordinary supremacy over all commoners. He was the only person in China, apart from the official head of the lineage of Confucius, who could unify all his patrilineal kindred, no matter how many, under one administrative agency. In a kinship-oriented society this was an extreme privilege. The size and behavior of the imperial descent group also showed the emperor's immunity to bureaucratic accountability. As courageous reformers like Feng Guifen pointed out in the nineteenth century, members of the imperial house were all on the government payroll, yet their stipends were the only ones not regulated by published quotas. This raised the possibility that uncontrolled, hidden, recurrent increases in such stipends could bankrupt the court.

Significantly, fear of such an outcome was not a new theme for Chinese reformers. In the 1600s, a philosopher like Lu Shiyi had even drawn up charts of the proper ideal organization of the income of the imperial descent group, proposing that rules be introduced to reduce the income of its members by four predictable genealogical stages.[20] This was an attempt to normalize the imperial descent group, to establish the principle that it was not uniquely privileged enough to be allowed to deviate from correct—and accountable—family management. But normalization of the imperial descent group implied normalization of the emperor himself. That meant the transformation of the hybrid monarchical-bureaucratic empire into a less hybrid, more consistently bureaucratic one. The energies and the political basis needed for such a transformation did not exist in China before the Opium War. This does not mean that the rudimentary idea for such a transformation was not there.

That the imperial government had such a primitive, only semibureaucratic core of ten thousand or so imperial kinsmen raises the question as to whether a real bureaucratic state independent of the emperor's wishes and needs had much meaningful existence at all in premodern China. It is not enough to point out that official appointments did not automatically lapse in China when emperors died, the way Burmese administrations had to be effectively recomposed at the moment Burmese kings died. Was Chinese political authority distilled from a relatively immutable respect for certain institutions that emperors only partly controlled, or was political authority effectively personal?

In some ways the emperor's "Inner Court"—which took in the residents of the "forbidden center" of the imperial palaces, and the very privileged officials who were not "forbidden" but invited to enter the palace for audiences—provided the magnetic field for all the rest of the government, both in Peking and in the provinces. The monarchy's dislike of politically expressed particularisms, or politically inspired group formations beyond the central power, made degrees of access to the central power—which was the only meaningful legitimate kind—critical. But even the strongest emperors rationed access to the inner court for practical reasons, not just to preserve an aloof, charismatic majesty. By distributing the privilege of access to their persons arbitrarily and restrainedly, the emperors could try to obtain more total, personal, suprabureaucratic commitments to their policies, from the high officials they did so favor, than they would have been likely to obtain from the masses of careerists in the Outer Court (the rest of officialdom). Hence the rulers continued to invent instruments of more personal rule in the Inner Court, as part of a continuing choreography of officials' access to them in which each individual gate in the palace complex had its own significance. The most famous Qing example was the Grand Council. It began as a secret and obscure "military supplies bureau" inside the Gate of the Imperial Kinfolk in the 1720s, but it soon replaced the older, more distant Grand Secretariat (outside the Gate of Supreme Harmony) as the place where the most important business of the empire was transacted between 1730 and the early twentieth century. But this continuous "repersonalization" of court business by the emperors was really their backhanded tribute to the forces of bureaucratization around them, and the limited nature of the practical loyalties to the throne such forces conventionally encouraged.

The point can be made another way. Bureaucrats themselves viewed audiences with the emperor, not as a transfiguring contact with a semidivine presence, but as part of the promotions lottery. Emperors thus also used the relative "forbiddenness" of their palace to avoid being converted into the mere daily referees of competing *guanxi* networks among their officials. At the height of the White Lotus Rebellion in 1801, the embattled Jiaqing emperor, defensively claiming that he saw as many as a dozen high officials each day, resisted a typical proposal that he admit to his presence all middle-level, on-duty, capital city officials of as low as the fifth bureaucratic grade (out of nine). Such an expansion of access would, the emperor intimated, envelop him in bureaucrats' career intrigues and create a situation "impossible to manage."[21] Bureaucracy, as much as charisma or cosmology, explains the restricted nature of the Inner Court.

The supreme importance of central power, to which all the provinces were theoretically no more than the "outside," external and dependent, suited the interests of many bureaucrats, as well as of the emperor. One central government official reminded a weakening Qing court in 1862 that all periods of prosperity in Chinese history were ones in which the inner government (the center) ruled the outer government (the provinces). Thus, when provincial officials were summoned to Peking and given central government appointments, they called it "ascending to the status of an immortal" (*deng xian*).[22] It was not just the fear of anarchy that buoyed up the centralizing emperorship. Many bureaucrats believed that centralized power was necessary to the discovery and the proper employment of talented people, through the civil service examinations the emperors managed. Delegation of power away from the center raised the issue of who would be the chief examiner. Scholar bureaucrats saw politics itself in terms of empirewide transfers and promotions, not in terms of acquiring local political power formally separate from the center to complement what local economic assets they might have, as if they were a Western-style middle class.

But the absence of any sort of "federal" constitutional basis for government administrative units beyond the center, and the pull of the imperial center as the place where appointments were made, had other consequences. Distance is not just a geographical concept, but a political one. Politically, central and provincial governments were much closer in traditional China than they are in a modern federal republic. There were no strong barriers to corrupt transactions between underlings of the Six Boards in Peking (the famous six ministries of appointments, finance, rites and education, war, justice, and public works, which handled the more ordinary flow of business of the central government) and underlings on provincial governors' staffs. Here the contrast is with the invisible barriers of psychological apartness that exist between the employees of federal governments and the employees of state or provincial governments in a modern republic. In the 1820s, subordinate officials in the provinces engaged in a huge program of collusion with clerks at the Peking Six Boards to collect illicit expense money, called "board dues" (*bu fei*), which they shared among themselves.[23] Heshen, the racketeering Manchu bannerman who became the favorite of the Qianlong emperor between 1775 and 1799, used his closeness to the emperor, and his control of the Peking Board of Finance, to make his henchmen into high provincial officials; he then extracted from the provinces, through them, a stupendous private fortune.

At the same time, because there was no clear division of authority between the central and provincial governments in China, constitutional or otherwise, both central and provincial officials crippled themselves in disputes with each other for which there were few accepted jurisdictional guidelines. This led to losses of power from the system as a whole that more modern governments would not have tolerated. Analyses of this chronic double power loss, as the result of the lack of prescriptive distinctions between the center and the localities, became an obsession with Manchu court reformers like Duan Fang in the early 1900s who wanted to increase the center's powers of resource mobilization.[24]

So put, it seems impossible than anyone in traditional China could have imagined an administrative "state" in practical terms that was more than just an extension of the imperial authority at the "Forbidden Center." Yet there were institutions that commanded loyalties beyond those tendered to individual emperors. It was just that theoretical pictures of the moral indispensability of certain nonimperial parts of the traditional state, whatever the emperor's wishes, centered upon the defense of the permanence of certain types of officials. They did not center upon the defense of the permanence of different levels of government, or different levels of political obligation, as they would have in federal or feudal political systems.

When the early Qing court abolished the medieval position of prefectural judge (*tui guan*), for example, to save payroll expenses, official critics boldly told the emperor that China's "ancient kings" had devised "most fine and subtle laws" for the preservation of the world from heterodoxy. The operation of these ancient laws meant that there were certain types of bureaucrats "whose numbers must not be reduced." The ancient kings were said to have conceived of government as properly divided into two different paths or channels (*tu*) of officialdom. Two channels were the administrative one (which included both the Six Boards in Peking and provincial governors, prefects, and county magistrates) and a countervailing investigative one (which included capital city censors, capital city scrutineers, censors assigned to provincial circuits, and the recently abolished prefectural judges, all of whom were to monitor and criticize the potential misbehavior of officials in the administrative channel). The investigative channel officials, it was argued, were the ones whose numbers were not to be reduced.[25]

This argument did not save the prefectural judges in the 1600s, but its existence did suggest a general consensus that there was a state system that transcended individual dynasties and emperors. Countervailing power was regarded as a necessary part of this system, with which emperors tampered at their own risk. Yet it derived not from "estates" and their representatives, but from bureaucratic "channels." It was valued for its protection of Confucian orthodoxy, not for its protection of individual or group liberties. And its conceptualization by officials themselves betrayed their fear of other officials, rather than just their fear of the monarch, possibly because greater intraclass jealousy existed among Chinese bureaucrats than among European aristocrats.

From the emperors' point of view, such minimal forms of countervailing power were obviously far less fearsome than the fact that, for all the Confucian ideological celebrations of loyalty, the examinations-based bureaucracy fostered a notion of public service that was distinct from the older notion of more personal, feudal service to the king. The rise of the empirewide bureaucracy had devitalized the more feudal personal service ideal in daily practice, without removing it from classical texts. In addition, there was a social or at least psychological tension between many emperors who had inherited their position, and who were not necessarily formidable scholars, and high officials who had earned their positions through educational achievement, and who had richly historical pictures of ideal classical rulers in their heads. The tension could be said to be roughly similar to the more modern one between an ill-educated dictator or president and the bright scientists and technocrats with whom he must surround himself. It inspired the same search for more lowly confidantes with whom the ruler could relax. Few subjects in Chinese history have more intrigued Orientalists, libertarians, and amateur sexual psychologists than the chief group of such confidantes the emperors so often found: the court eunuchs.

Memories of eunuch officials' terrorism and extravagant misrule in the Later Han, Tang, and Ming dynasties generated a universal horror in late imperial China. Chinese writers abhorred the "eunuch problem" in politics so much that they described it in zoological imagery, reducing all the participants to animals. Palace eunuchs who were ascendant became "tigers": creatures with real power. Their ascendancy reduced civil officials to being mere "foxes": creatures who pretended to have power. Present-day Chinese political scientists like Yan Jiaqi still remind their readers of the eunuchs who barred the access of Tang dynasty reformers to the inner palace: the eunuch-controlled palace secretariat of the late ninth century A.D. remains a supreme example to modern Chinese thinkers of the unaccountability of overly centralized power in China.

But eunuch power reflected a trend, as well as the fact that emperors needed managers for the harems that were to provide their successors. Late imperial political theorists were struck by the fact that in early Chinese governments, high officials known as "palace attendants" had shared access to the ruler with eunuchs. As late as the Earlier Han dynasty, the palace attendants who had waited upon the emperor had been virtuous learned literati, drawn often from aristocratic families. But in later Chinese dynasties, the tradition of the non-eunuch palace attendants had disappeared. Access to the "yellow inner doors" of the inner palace had been more and more cut off. The recent dynasty that had best solved the eunuch problem had been (embarrassingly) the non-Chinese Yuan dynasty. For its Mongol emperors had neutralized and supplanted the eunuchs with the *kesig*, a bodyguard of elite hereditary soldiers whose aristocratic chiefs managed the emperors' clothes and food. So wrote Chu Dawen (1664–1743), a studious geographer and military strategist who went so far as to call for a revival of the Mongol *kesig* in eighteenth-century Peking.[26]

Putting this in more modern terms, the declining access to the palace of which the eunuch evil was a symptom signaled the evolution of China's monarchy away from the ideal of the feudal warrior king who had to feast incessantly with his earls and barons and their attendant knights. A high feudal Western ruler like William the Conqueror of England, for instance, could hardly have isolated himself from his liegemen and tenants-in-chief the way the later and weaker Chinese emperors isolated themselves from their bureaucrats. Perhaps an even more telling contrast would be with an early modern European despot like Louis XIV of France. Seeing himself as the first among aristocrats, not as a bureaucratic commander-in-chief, Louis controlled his nobles, not by excluding them from his palace, but by allowing them the ritual privilege of handing him his robe at his daily awakening ceremony. Powerful eunuchs were the more sordid accompaniment of the relative practical decline of the importance of personal loyalty to specific rulers in Chinese politics, thanks to the growing bureaucratic displacement of such loyalties. Because eunuchs supposedly had fewer alternative objects for their loyalty than regular officials with families, they seemed, to weaker and less confident emperors, to be something of an antidote to the relative weakness of common bureaucratic loyalties. There was nothing especially "Oriental" about the eunuchs. The problem did not exist in the more aristocratic social and political world of Japan, or among China's less bureaucratized Asian conquerors. A permanent solution to the eunuch problem within the existing model of kingship, as Chu Dawen saw clearly, required a partial restoration in Chinese politics of more feudal loyalties to the ruler, like those held by the thirteenth-century Mongol palace bodyguard. The early Manchu court, when it revived the eunuch palace directorates of its predecessors, significantly tried to offset them by developing more personal ties with ministers;[27] Manchu emperors could also resolve the loyalty problem by substituting their bondservants for the eunuchs.

Altogether the Chinese monarchy in 1839 was a despotism locked in a kind of stalemate with a potentially more modern bureaucracy; but it offered very little positive political freedom to its subjects. The despotism may have been intensifying; if so, the great landmark of this intensification was, and is, widely believed to have been the first Ming emperor's abolition of the position of chancellor or nonroyal chief executive of the government in A.D. 1380. Most political theorists after 1380 who lamented the disappearance of a nonroyal chief executive for the government were reduced, like Lu Shiyi in the seventeenth century, to requesting that the first board, the Board of Appointments, be exalted above the other five ministries and given more general authority;[28] they evidently did not dare to ask for a return of the chancellor himself. There was a tradition of free speech in Chinese politics, dating back to a more aristocratic age and embodied in such notions as the "honest and sincere mountain and forest scholars" who, as court gentlemen in the Han emperors' entourage, had had the right to rebuke the emperor directly. The Censorate of the 1800s preserved the shadow but not the substance of this notion. Such a tradition of free speech was not part of a widespread religious faith, like the free speech defended by Milton in the *Areopagitica.* This made it difficult to popularize outside the ranks of the more conscientious literati. Demands for its expansion existed, but they were expressed relatively obliquely, as in the proposal the Qianlong emperor dismissed in 1774 to upgrade the head of the Censorate to be the "assistant chancellor" of the government, and to publish a public handbook of the Censorate's rules, thus making it more of an objective ministry and less the personal agency of the emperor.[29] Commoners who described themselves as "sellers of news" (meaning reprints of real or faked court edicts) were ruthlessly suppressed, as in the famous case of Yang Shirong in Anhui in 1774.

But if the monarchy was a despotism that offered little positive political freedom, it also was one with relatively little room to maneuver. By 1839 its capacity for leading the people it ruled in new directions was virtually zero. Even the infamous abolition of the chancellorship had hurt, by reducing the powers of coordination at the top of the government. One has to conclude with this paradox: the Chinese monarchy commanded both greater popular support and shallower specific loyalties than most equivalent European kingships at the peak of their power.

Much of the popular support was provided by the existence of the examination system. It enabled conqueror emperors to convert their newly acquired power into a more peaceful traditional power relatively rapidly. The emperor's role as chief examiner gave millions of people a stake in the emperor system. Belief in even the complex cosmological underpinnings of the emperorship could thus be remarkably self-serving for millions of households, in a way that would not have been true for the theory of the divine right of kings in early modern Europe, which owed what popularity it had essentially to the fear of civil war. In the 1850s, the Taiping peasant revolutionaries' conversion of themselves into kings who offered examinations (with far higher rates of success than the government ones) suggests something of the general popularity of China's examiner monarchs.

Beyond the examinations, most of the poorer intellectuals who ought to have been the monarchy's natural enemies persisted in seeing imperial power as a kind of public trust that was in turn a potential resource for the whole community. Thus, Tang Peng (1801–1844), one of the bright but short-lived young political analysts of the early nineteenth century who were worried about immiseration and runaway upper-class consumption rates, argued in his most famous essay, "Curing Poverty," that all the land in the world belonged to the king, whose "children" the people were. (The notion that all land ultimately belonged to the king could be found in the *Shijing* and antedated the empire.) From this Tang Peng concluded not that the emperor was a tyrant, but that he was the only possible peaceful architect of fine-tuning economic reforms that might return public-spiritedness and greater equality to China.

Alex de Tocqueville once suggested that reformers in prerevolutionary France self-defeatingly accepted the unlimited power of the French despotism, because they had been conditioned to believe that only it could bring a more ideal political system into existence, once its custodians were persuaded to use their power properly.[30] His suggestion is almost certainly more applicable to China in 1839 than to France in 1789. Among some Chinese intellectuals, the emperor's status as supreme landowner could evoke quasi-socialist expectations. Such expectations help to explain the residual strength of monarchism as an idea in China, even after the cosmological affectations of the existing emperorship had withered. The particular theories of Dong Zhongshu about Heaven, earth, mankind, and the emperors could be readily abandoned between 1839 and 1911. The craving for a peaceful achievement of societywide justice, through the impartial leadership of one transcendental figure who ultimately controlled all resources, could not be given up so easily.

The Disappearance of the Emperorship and the Pathos of Twentieth-Century Chinese Political Development

The extravagant expectations that were attached to the monarchy help to explain its downfall, which the Opium War of 1839 initiated. China's opium addiction crisis of the early nineteenth century provoked a court debate about how to deal with it. One can see now that this debate displayed some chilling similarities to the controversy over drugs in Western countries a century and a half later. But it was also one of China's last major culturally autonomous discussions about the general nature of political authority. In the debate, two opposing pictures of the ruler's political responsibilities emerged: a minimalist and realistic one versus a maximalist and idealistic one.

Minimalists, led by officials like Xu Naiji (1777–1839), proposed that the monarchy should simply legalize and tax the drug trade and, in so doing, avoid all conflict with the British. They pointed to the shallowness of the government's technical power: its laws were ineffective, being merely the instruments of private exploitation of local yamen underlings and "rowdies." Since the government could not really suppress the drug trade, they argued, it would be better to acquiesce in the spread of opium, get revenues from it, and punish only scholars, officials, and soldiers who smoked it, while consigning the remainder of the population to the limbo of narcotic addiction. The maximalists, led by officials like Xu Qiu and Lin Zexu, demanded on the contrary that the emperor totally prohibit opium. They denied that the monarchy could limit its moral solicitude exclusively to scholars, officials, and soldiers. In the memorial that ended the debate, Xu Qiu told the emperor that no known "political form" (*zhengti*) in Chinese history permitted a ruler to tolerate, let alone tax, commodities that were thought to harm people.

It is important to remember that the idealistic and maximalist picture of political authority triumphed in the late 1830s. And it did so even though it presented a decaying government with the least comfortable immediate policy options. Its victory inevitably led to events that confirmed the pessimism of its minimalist critics: Commissioner Lin's opium suppression campaign provoked a war with the British that China lost. Thus, the monarchy began its march to its own extinction in 1839 by affirming a morally broad and socially all-embracing view of its responsibilities, rather than the more morally limited and socially confined view that some of its own courtiers recommended to it. Here lies part of the importance of the year 1839 as an anniversary. The lost Opium War implied the undiminished strength of a felt Chinese need for leadership with a broad if not total moral mission, while exposing the hopelessness inherent in the expression of such a need without the invention of a technically much stronger government.

The Chinese monarchy was officially abolished by the Revolution of 1911. The external causes of its demise, between the end of the Opium War and 1911, are well known. But it is impossible not to agree with Marianne Bastid that the monarchy's own internal evolution, conditioned by the downswing of the dynastic cycle, also helped to deflate the grandeur of traditional court institutions.

The Manchu emperors, remaining above the law, could not use it to regulate succession crises among their descendants in any permanent way that would appeal to rational public opinion. After a particularly brutal succession struggle in the early 1700s among many of the twenty surviving sons of the Kangxi emperor, which the Kangxi emperor himself failed utterly to adjudicate, the ruthless victor in the struggle attempted to stabilize future imperial successions by the primitive but wily expedient of having reigning rulers place the names of their chosen political heirs in a sealed box behind a tablet in the Qianqing palace. After 1860, such expedients were not sufficient to block the conquest of real power in the Forbidden City by the empress dowager Ci Xi, one of the former concubines of the Xianfeng emperor. In some of its last years (1889–98), the Chinese monarchy was in fact a duumvirate. The empress dowager made most of the critical decisions with the help of princes allied to her. The man who was the official emperor, after his maturity in 1889, handled only routine business.

The effect of the duumvirate was to make the Chinese political elite more comfortable with the diversity of the powers of the monarchy, and to erode in their eyes the remaining sacredness of the imperial institution. In the debates about the monarchy provoked by the 1898 Reform Movement, "there was hardly ever any question . . . of referring to the cosmological beliefs traditionally associated with the monarchy, and certainly not to the sacred nature of the emperor's person."[31] In the aftermath of such debates, by 1908 the Manchu court had actually accepted a paper declaration of constitutional principles that placed the emperor under the rule of law.

These debates had occurred among the intelligentsia. More humble Chinese workers and peasants, while probably still believing in some sort of monarch as a guarantor of cosmic stability, had never held personal fantasies about the benign sacredness or loving kindness of individual reigning emperors. Because they had never believed that they owed their ruler a personal, specifically religious loyalty, the Chinese emperorship expired more quietly than the Russian monarchy. There was no 1905 St. Petersburg–style "Bloody Sunday" of unarmed proletarian petitioners asking their father the ruler for a redress of grievances and then being gunned down. (What happened in Peking on June 4, 1989, may be the real Chinese parallel to St. Petersburg in January 1905.) The essential passiveness of Chinese popular interest in the monarchical idea at the end of the old order is further confirmed by the disastrous failure of President Yuan Shikai to sustain the curious elective monarchy that he proclaimed in December 1915, as part of an effort to create a stronger central government. Yuan had believed that the Chinese masses were "intensely conservative and monarchical." But popular opposition to Yuan's restored emperorship was certainly more obvious than popular support, and it collapsed in ruins.[32]

The more general political habits the monarchy represented were called into question, but only on a piecemeal basis, before the real emperors left the stage at the end of 1911. What Yan Jiaqi has recently singled out as one of the basic features of China's modern imprisonment in "monarchism"—the lifelong tenure of supreme leaders, and their inability to transfer real power away from themselves—certainly came under attack in the late nineteenth century. In 1890, for example, Tang Shouqian (1857–1917), a secretary to the Shandong provincial governor, published *Wei yan* (Words of caution), which lavishly praised George Washington, a peculiarly radical figure in the Chinese eyes. Washington, Tang noted, had founded a country through war but had then confounded the normal expectations of warlordism by deliberately limiting his own tenure in high office, and by not trying to transfer his power to relatives or descendants. Later revolutions may have made the American one seem relatively tame both to us and to more socially conscious Chinese, yet no world revolutionary figure the Chinese have studied has ever contradicted the First Emperor's paradigm of the conquest and use of power more starkly than George Washington. This may be one reason for the recurrent Americanization of Chinese discourse whenever purely political democracy becomes its major concern. The reigning emperor in the 1890s was asked to read Tang Shouqian's book by his tutor.

In the late nineteenth century overseas Chinese intellectuals also began their long struggle to humanize and transform Chinese politics from the periphery. The theory of the social contract, as elaborated by theorists in Europe from the middle of the sixteenth century, challenged despotic authority in Europe and asserted a popular right of resistance to misbehaving kings there, in ways far more extensive than any known to traditional Chinese political thought. Two influential Hong Kong Chinese writers, He Qi (also known as Ho Kai, 1859–1914) and Hu Liyuan (1847–1916), began to prepare the way for the introduction of contract theory into Chinese politics and apply it to Chinese leaders. In *Xinzheng lunyi* (Proposals for a new government), a tract of 1894, they drew a new picture for Chinese readers of a ruler who receives his power from the people as a trust and must use it to protect their property.[33] Their tract was a distillation but not a rigorous account of Western social contract theory; but such accounts appeared soon after. The earliest Chinese overseas student journal to appear in Japan lost no time in publishing a serial translation of Rousseau's *Contrat social* in 1900–1901.

The traditional emperors had also ruled through fear and murder, as well as through political theory. Scholars loyal to the previous dynasty who failed to accept the Manchu emperors as the architects of the unity among Heaven, earth, and mankind were painfully executed; if they themselves were dead, their grandchildren were exiled, as in the case of Lü Liuliang in 1733. Another overseas Chinese lawyer, the Singapore-born Wu Tingfang (1842–1922), got the desperate Qing court to take him on as legal adviser. He then launched a memorable assault in 1905 upon such phenomena as the emperors' reliance upon judicial torture, slow executions, and the dismemberment of criminals' corpses. This was an enormously important attack upon despotism itself: the late Qing discussion of legal reform that Wu Tingfang helped lead quickly became a bureaucrats' referendum on the character of Chinese political leadership. This was related, as it continues to be today, to the perceived nature of the Chinese people themselves. Wu's political opponents in 1905 asserted that the Chinese people were more unruly than Westerners and would not tell the truth in legal cases without the use of judicial torture. Wu Tingfang scoffed at the idea that the Chinese people were less judicially or politically responsible than Westerners, and he invoked the Hong Kong experience as his trump card. The peaceable behavior of the Chinese people there, under British law, proved that the Chinese were as suited to a humanitarian, torture-free political order as anyone else, Wu concluded.

The issue that Wu Tingfang debated with his opponents in Peking in 1905—how compatible are the Chinese people with less despotic institutions?—has haunted Chinese reformers ever since. In 1989, the brilliant dissident scientist Fang Lizhi was, in a sense, replaying Wu Tingfang's old part when he derided the conservative position in this debate as "the law of conservation of democracy." Such a law "holds that a society's total capacity for democracy is fixed. If there was no democracy to start with, there also will be none later. Nobody . . . has set out to prove this law, because the counterexamples are too numerous. The argument cannot save dictatorship in China; it can only provide us with some comic diversion."[34]

But what is perhaps more pathetic than comic is that surely none of the major twentieth-century leaders of China, at least since 1915, has set out to make himself an emperor. The "classic features" of Chiang Kai-shek's rule have always attracted attention: his sacrifices at the tombs of the Han emperors, his efforts to stimulate sagehood through the presidency of a university and the publication of a textbook.[35] It may nonetheless be worth remembering that the earlier Chiang Kai-shek, in July 1929, made one of the most acute public criticisms of Yuan Shikai's attempted emperorship ever heard in China. Chiang declared that Yuan Shikai's imperial ambitions, to which Yuan had "sacrificed" the Chinese republic, exemplified the traditional individual selfishness of the Chinese people, which the new era of collective organization and political party discipline must overcome. Chiang added that the more junior northern militarists of 1915 had had no alternative but to become Yuan Shikai's obsequious courtiers and join him on his political "road of death," because they had been without a party or an ideology that might shape their relations with a misguided leader more rationally.[36] One could also find anti-imperial elements in Mao Zedong. Although one scholar has caught Mao performing imitations of the emperors' annual plowing ritual as early as 1944,[37] the Mao of that period in Yan'an assured tough-minded Chinese intellectuals, not just gullible Western journalists, that he thought democracy was indispensable as the only known antidote to the stagnation and corruption of government.

Leaving aside the matter of conscious and unconscious hypocrisy, against whose corrosive consequences no politician can be immunized forever, one must recognize that twentieth-century Chinese history has had to carry far too much cargo. That at least is the way it seems to a Qing dynasty specialist.

First, there was the legitimate obsession with political weakness in the face of foreign aggression. When Chen Hansheng, a cosmopolitan economist who had studied at Chicago, Harvard, and Berlin, and had briefly taught American constitutional law at Beida, was asked in 1933 to predict the China of 1953, he wrote that there were just three possibilities: a China that was a total colony; a China whose coastal areas were colonized but whose interior was still independent; and an independent China.[38] Chen had nothing to say about constitutional law; foreign imperialism, not domestic despotism, was for him the chief political problem. Some liberal intellectuals of the 1910s and 1920s, such as Li Jiannong and Gao Yihan, had been preaching the virtues of federalism in China as a means of weakening centralized despotism. They saw stronger provinces as the best means of blocking the usurpation of political authority at the top by "wild-hearted" adventurers in Peking, and they asserted that a federal dispersal of organized political power would also give the Chinese people a better chance to learn how to participate in government. But against the tendency to make the reorganization of Chinese politics a derivative of the concern to resist foreign pressures, the Chinese federalists got nowhere. (Recently Chinese liberals have hoped that the dream of a peaceful reunification with a capitalist Taiwan might put the notion of a less centrally focused Chinese "confederation" back on the agenda.)

Second, there was the intelligentsia's highly responsible desire to free the Chinese people from poverty. This made a narrow focus upon the mechanisms of political choice seem almost reactionary. By 1919, the term Chinese intellectuals were using for "democracy" had changed from the earlier *minzhu zhuyi* (the ideology of rule by the people) to the much broader *pingmin zhuyi* (the ideology of the common people). As the concept of "democracy" became a larger and larger envelope, stuffed with all sorts of economic and cultural and social wishes, the crucial technical matter of how rulers would be chosen became downgraded; the First Emperor's paradigm of empire building harder to discuss; and the desire to believe in some omnipotent architect of economic justice, not completely unlike the imaginary tax-equalizing emperors in premodern utopian thought, all the more difficult to resist.

Third, there was the enormous difficulty of creating broad and stable loyalties to new postimperial institutions. The idea of the political party was, like federalism, a potentially very strong antidote to would-be emperors. But it was also new to China. It had become popular in the West itself only when politics there began to be consciously perceived in contractual terms rather than organic ones. The idea of the political party was popularized in China by Liang Qichao, from about 1900, as one good means of blocking the "private" whims of despotic rulers or stupid princes. But there was a bewildering variety of competing models of what a political party should be. There was the Leninist model of the party as a militarized conspiracy; the Liang Qichao model of the party as a means to an unending political pluralism; the Chiang Kai-shek view of the party as an indocrinative family; and a more general view of the party as a sort of moral overseer, like a more dynamic Censorate. And as Liang Qichao himself warned in 1913, traditional Chinese "gentlemen" intellectuals with a strong individual sense of moral principles would find political parties problematic. They would, specifically, find it difficult to submit to the orders of relatively mundane party leaders, who would require a more regimented obedience than the emperors had because of their parties' daily competition with other parties.

Hence, all the characteristics of the old monarchy have not been purged from the Chinese political system. The lifelong concentration of power in the hands of a few top leaders can be found in countries without powerful monarchical traditions, such as Cuba. So this probably takes its inspiration at least as much from Lenin and Stalin as from Dong Zhongshu. The tendency of a leader like Deng Xiaoping to retire from high office but to continue to exercise supreme power from behind the scenes offers a much purer link to the old emperorship. The Qianlong emperor retired from the emperorship in 1796 but continued to rule until his death in 1799; the empress dowager allowed the mature Guangxu emperor to rule in 1889 only after concluding a backstage agreement with his father and other Manchu princes that renewed her own secret supreme authority. Such maneuvers historically reflected the stalemated monarchical-bureaucratic state. They satisfied the Confucian reverence for old age, but also the bureaucracy's need for a provenly reliable senior promoter and referee of its ambitions. They were and are the clearest example of how personal authority at the very top of Chinese politics can hold its own against more modern forms of institutional authority.

Other legacies of the imperial system are less visible. The traditional monarchy, operating in a politically postfeudal context in which there were no social "estates" or corporations with hereditary privileges, was never able to establish legitimate norms of political decentralization. The difficulty in managing political decentralization, which has continued since 1911, was a reflection more of the imperial institution than of China's size: the Vietnamese, living in a much smaller country, created a province-sized replica of the Chinese imperial system, complete with emperors, examinations, and eunuchs, that carried with it the same continuing failure adequately to legitimate different levels of political obligation. The modern Chinese (and Vietnamese) adoption of the curious Leninist principle of "democratic centralism" has only compounded this legacy.

This is hardly the whole story. The centralizing emperors helped make possible a great achievement: the establishment of the world's first major mandarin tradition in politics, which placed knowledge and scholarship ahead of the hereditary claims of aristocrats. No statebuilders in China have ever succeeded for very long without the cooperation of the intelligentsia. The twentieth century has seen a progressive and dynamic internationalization of the standards of this intelligentsia, and their growing attachment to principles of democracy and science that cannot be controlled from the modern facsimiles of throne rooms. In the long run, the mandarins may well outlast the emperors.

Notes

1. Yan Jiaqi, "Wangguo xunhuan yuanyin lun" (On the reasons for the cycle of kingdoms), in Yan Jiaqi, *Quanli yu zhenli* (Power and truth) (Beijing: Guangming ribao chubanshe, 1987), pp. 82–90.

2. See the remarks of Zhang Xianyang as reported in *Guangming ribao*, October 19, 1980, p. 2.

3. Wu Shichang, "Cong Zhongguo de lishi kan minzhu zhengzhi" (A look at democratic government from the perspective of Chinese history), *Guancha* (The observer), December 27, 1947, pp. 3–5.

4. See, for example, Yu Yingshi, *Zhongguo sixiang chuantong de xiandai quanshi* (A contemporary exegesis of Chinese intellectual tradition) (Taibei: Lianjing chuban shiye gongsi, 1987), p. 34.

5. Ann S. Anagnost, "The Beginning and End of an Emperor: A Counterrepresenta-

tion of the State,'' *Modern China* 11, 2 (April 1985), pp. 147–76.

6. Vivienne Shue, *The Reach of the State: Sketches of the Chinese Body Politic* (Stanford: Stanford University Press, 1988), p. 87.

7. Wang Yankang, ''Gaoji xiaoxuesheng guojia guannian ceyan tongji'' (The statistics of the nation-state conceptualization tests among superior elementary school pupils), *Jiaoyu zazhi* (Educational review) 18, 2 (February 1926).

8. Sir George Staunton, *An Authentic Account of an Embassy from the King of Great Britain to the Emperor of China* (London: Bulmer and Co., 1798), 2:163–64.

9. Liang Qichao, ''Zhongguo lishishang geming zhi yanjiu'' (The study of revolutions from the point of view of Chinese history), in *Liang Qichao xuanji* (An anthology of Liang Qichao), ed. Li Huaxing et al. (Shanghai: Renmin chubanshe, 1983), pp. 420–31.

10. Lu Shiyi, *Sibianlu jiyao* (A summary version of the chronicles of careful thought and clear distinctions), 1:5–5b, in *Lu Futing xiansheng yishu* (The bequeathed works of Lu Shiyi), comp. Tang Shouqi (Beijing, 1900).

11. Liang Bingxian, ''Xiangcun geming'' (Village revolution), in *Wuzhengfu zhuyi sixiang ziliao xuan* (Anthology of materials on anarchist thought), ed. Ge Maochun et al. (Beijing: Beijing daxue chubanshe, 1984), 1:432–33.

12. *Qing Gaozong chunhuangdi shilu* (Veritable records of the Qianlong reign), 542:28–29.

13. Frederic Wakeman, Jr., *The Great Enterprise* (Berkeley: University of California Press, 1985), 1:301–2.

14. *Da Qing Gaozong chunhuangdi shengxun* (Sacred instructions of the Qianlong emperor), 31:11–12b. Earlier Manchu rulers meditated publicly on the same subject, so this was hardly original to Qianlong. Wakeman, *The Great Enterprise*, 1:208–9.

15. The definitive study of this project is R. Kent Guy, *The Emperor's Four Treasuries* (Cambridge: Harvard University Council on East Asian Studies, 1987).

16. Peng Pai, ''Haifeng nongmin yundong'' (The Haifeng peasant movement), in *Di yici guonei geming zhanzheng shiqi de nongmin yundong* (The peasant movement of the first revolutionary civil war period) (Beijing: Renmin chubanshe, 1953), pp. 49–50.

17. See David M. Farquhar, ''Emperor as Bodhisattva in the Governance of the Ch'ing Empire,'' *Harvard Journal of Asiatic Studies* 38, 1 (June 1978): 5–34.

18. Fukangan, ''Cangnei shanhou shiyi shu'' (A memorial about matters related to postwar reconstruction in Tibet), in *Huangchao jingshi wenbian* (A compilation of the statecraft essays of the present court), comp. He Changling (Taibei: Wenhai chubanshe, 1972), 81:15–17.

19. Ju Deyuan, ''Qingdai huangzu renkou chengbao zhidu'' (The system of reporting the population of the imperial lineage of the Qing dynasty), *Lishi dang'an* (Historical archives journal) 2 (1988): 80–89.

20. Lu, *Sibianlu jiyao*, 13:6b–7.

21. *Qing Renzong ruihuangdi shilu* (Veritable records of the Jiaqing reign), 84:9b–11b.

22. Gao Yanhu, ''Qing nei-wai huyong shu'' (A memorial requesting the balanced use of inner and outer government officials), in *Huangchao jingshi wen xubian* (A continuation of the compilation of the statecraft essays of the present court), comp. Sheng Kang (Taibei: Wenhai chubanshe, 1972), 16:25–26.

23. *Qing Xuanzong chenghuangdi shilu* (Veritable records of the Daoguang reign), 42:22–23b.

24. Zhongguo shixue hui (Chinese Historical Studies Association), comp., *Xinhai geming* (The revolution of 1911) (Shanghai: Renmin chubanshe, 1957), 4:33–38.

25. For an example of this type of applied political theory, see Chu Fangqing, ''Cai guan lun'' (On the reduction in numbers of officials), in *Huangchao jingshi wenbian*,

18:7b–8. The author was a high degree-holder and county magistrate.

26. Chu Dawen, "Shizhong zhi zhi" (The post of palace attendants), in *Huangchao jingshi wenbian*, 13:13b–14.

27. Wakeman, *The Great Enterprise*, 2:1013–16.

28. Lu, *Sibianlu jiyao*, 13:4–4b.

29. *Qing Gaozong chunhuangdi shilu*, 963:14–15b.

30. Alex de Tocqueville, *The Old Regime and the French Revolution*, trans. Stuart Gilbert (New York: Doubleday Anchor Books, 1955), pp. 68–69.

31. Marianne Bastid, "Official Conception of Imperial Authority at the End of the Qing Dynasty," in *Foundations and Limits of State Power in China*, ed. S. R. Schram (Hong Kong: The Chinese University Press, 1987), p. 174.

32. Ernest P. Young, *The Presidency of Yuan Shih-k'ai* (Ann Arbor: University of Michigan Press, 1977), pp. 210–40.

33. Their work is discussed—and their conservatism, I think, a bit overemphasized—in Jerome Grieder, *Intellectuals and the State in Modern China* (New York: The Free Press, 1981), pp. 107–9.

34. Fang Lizhi, "China's Despair and China's Hope," trans. Perry Link, *The New York Review of Books*, February 2, 1989, pp. 3–4.

35. John K. Fairbank, *The United States and China* (Cambridge: Harvard University Press, 1959), p. 308.

36. Chiang's speech is reprinted in Gao Jun et al., comp., *Zhongguo xiandai zhengzhi sixiang shi ziliao xuanji* (Anthology of materials on the history of contemporary Chinese political thought) (Chengdu: Sichuan renmin chubanshe, 1984), 1:556–66.

37. Stuart R. Schram, "Party Leader or True Ruler? Foundations and Significance of Mao Zedong's Personal Power," in *Foundations and Limits of State Power in China*, p. 213.

38. Wang Xi and Yang Xiaofo, eds., *Chen Hansheng wenji* (The collected writings of Chen Hansheng) (Shanghai: Fudan daxue chubanshe, 1985), p. 451.

2

THE STRUCTURE OF THE CHINESE ECONOMY DURING THE QING PERIOD
Some Thoughts on the 150th Anniversary of the Opium War

MADELEINE ZELIN

This essay examines some of the major institutional and structural characteristics of the Chinese domestic economy on the eve of the Opium War.[1] As the title indicates, this is a thought piece. An underlying assumption is that the patterns of economic interaction that evolved in China during the late Ming and Qing were not simply representative of an early stage of modern development. Rather, they were the result of a combination of political, institutional, and geophysical factors unique to China. Their interaction determined to a large extent how Chinese people would make their living, organize their markets, and pool their resources. The introduction of Western capital, goods, technologies, and business practices changed the environment within which the workings of the domestic economy were played out. Many of the underlying structures, however, remained intact well into the twentieth century and are important in determining the way the economy of China operates today.

A Brief Overview

By the early 1800s the Chinese economy was one in which a highly fragmented agrarian sector, based on small-scale farm management by tenants and owner-cultivators, was supported by a large, bottom-heavy, and extremely lively network of rural periodic markets and market towns. A high level of output per unit of land was achieved by labor-intensive methods of cultivation, and increased overall output was the result of the spread of traditional technologies and a continuing process of land reclamation. Production of nonagricultural goods was undertaken largely in rural contexts, although a rise in the number of urban handicraft workshops is indicated. Large-scale manufacturing units were rare and limited almost entirely to extractive industries and industries serving the needs of the state.

Within this framework, a number of temporal trends can be detected between the early seventeenth and early nineteenth centuries. Among these is the shift from more extensive to more intensive methods of land and labor utilization, particularly in peripheral regions. This is accompanied by the frequently noted "filling-up" of the internal frontier. The expansion of foreign trade and of marketing activity over this period also resulted in several monetary cycles, the full implications of which have yet to be analyzed. These include a pattern of increasing grain prices quoted in silver in the main southeastern cities from approximately 1780 to 1834, followed by a falling trend until 1850.[2] A similar movement of prices does not appear to have prevailed in peripheral regions and regions that became the main rice exporters of early Qing China. Finally, the Taiping Rebellion (1851–64) initiated a number of changes in demographic and commercial patterns that were not a direct result of foreign trade, but do distinguish the late from the early Qing.

The Agrarian Sector

Several issues have dominated studies of early Qing agriculture. These include the development of output in the face of population increase, changing patterns of land tenure, and the spread of commercial crops and rural by-employments.

New research has done little to alter the conclusions of Dwight Perkins and his team on the question of agricultural output during the Ming and Qing. One reason is undoubtedly the paucity of materials upon which the serious scholar can base estimates of yield on a per unit of land or a per man-hour basis. Perkins's findings are familiar to most students of early modern China. In brief, he estimates a sixfold increase in Chinese population between the fourteenth and nineteenth century. Per capita consumption during this period was maintained by a combination of increasingly intensive farming methods and expansion of cultivated acreage.[3] This was accomplished not by means of technological innovation, but by the spread of the best existing techniques, including deeper plowing, the use of improved and locally specific seed varieties, the movement north of rice cultivation, multiple-cropping regimes, and increasingly meticulous attention to weeding, application of fertilizer, the use of drill sowing in the north and transplanting in the south. At the same time, a shift took place in the pattern of grain supply, with main Ming export regions, such as Anhui and Jiangxi, giving way in the Qing to newly reclaimed lands in Sichuan, Hunan, and Taiwan. Following the model put forward by Esther Boserup, Perkins sees population growth itself as the invisible hand that pushed society to adopt these measures. Under these conditions, long-term increases in per capita output are not expected and indeed are not found.

In a recent book, Chao Kang has attacked the Perkins thesis, claiming diminishing yields per unit of land as early as the late Ming.[4] By contrast, the spread of commercial agriculture and the increasing diversification of cropping patterns have led a small group of scholars in China to postulate rising output of food crops per unit of land and per capita, at least until the nineteenth century.[5] Expansion of the area of specialized cultivation, serving a growing handicraft-processing sector and supported by cheap grain imports from central and western China, was also evident. Cotton, mulberry, sugar cane, tobacco, and tea were widely grown during the Qing. In addition, small areas specialized in plant dyes, fruit trees, pigs, ducks and eggs, and pond-grown fish. In some areas, specialization was quite well advanced. By mid-Qing as much as 70–80 percent of the land in parts of Songjiang fu, Taicang zhou, Haimen ting, and Tong zhou in Jiangsu were planted in cotton.[6] Northern cultivation of cotton, especially in Hebei and parts of Shaanxi and Shandong also grew rapidly, accompanied by the growth of handicraft textile manufacture in these provinces.[7] Cultivation of mulberry, initially concentrated in Zhejiang, Jiangsu, and Guangdong, expanded in Sichuan, Hunan, and Hubei, the main agricultural frontiers of early Qing China. Moreover, the increasingly fine division of labor in the Jiangnan silk industry is underscored by the growing market in mulberry leaves, silkworm eggs, cocoons, mulberry saplings, as well as reeled silk.[8] Fujian and Guangdong, the main sugar cane–producing areas in Ming China, were joined by Sichuan and Taiwan, whose sugar industry underwent extensive development. And the spread of tobacco production in Jiangsu, Zhejiang, and Jiangxi, and later into Shandong, Shanxi, Shaanxi, and Sichuan, inspired periodic panic on the part of officials who feared the consequences of withdrawing so much land from the cultivation of grain.[9]

Despite the elaboration of the marketing system during the Qing, and the ability of some regions to make use of comparative advantage by specializing in textile production, mining, and so on, the vast majority of peasants still produced much of their own food and many of their daily-use items. An admittedly rough calculation based on production and population statistics on the eve of the Opium War finds the percentage of all grain produced that entered the market to be only 10 percent. This figure may be low as it does not include the small amounts of surplus grain routinely sold by peasants at periodic markets.[10] On the basis of early Republican statistics showing commercial crops to have comprised only 17 percent of total acreage, Xu and Wu estimate the early Qing equivalent at approximately 10 percent as well.[11] Perkins estimates that between 20 and 30 percent of all agricultural output was offered for sale prior to 1900.[12]

The second issue is of great interest to students of the revolution inasmuch as concentration of land in the hands of large landowners, and the corresponding immiseration of peasants, is seen by some as a major factor in the Communist Party's success. In fact, the most persuasive evidence now points to a process of land fragmentation and land dispersion in the late imperial period that probably accelerated during the second quarter of the twentieth century.[13] Chao Kang's work using land registers for the Ming and Qing periods demonstrates that, by the Qing, in some regions individual plots were small, that after the initial purchase the rate at which landlords accumulated land was slow, and that the size of landlord estates rarely exceeded several hundred mou.[14] Impressionistic contemporary accounts also speak of the small size of landholdings. Zhang Qian's essay "Beihuang tonglun" notes that in Jiangnan the household with twenty mou would be considered among the upper strata of the rural community, while twelve or thirteen mou would still rank one among those of moderate wealth.[15] This is not surprising when one realizes that even a conservative estimate of per capita arable land for the second half of the Qing was only 2.5 mou.[16]

Data on individual landownership during the pre–Opium War period are rare, and instances in which related economic information is also available are rarer still. Most of the examples we do have suggest, however, that very large holdings during the mid- to late Qing were the product of capital accumulated in noneconomic pursuits.[17] Often at least part of the holdings were cultivated in economic crops. And the owners of such lands were frequently corporate bodies of various kinds.[18] Of particular interest is the appearance of secondary landlordism in regions where profits from agricultural production were high. In parts of Sichuan, merchant investment in rent deposits gave them entree to a rich export rice market through the port of Chongqing.[19] In southern Guangdong, wealthy tenants inserted themselves between producers and landlords to take advantage of the produce of the rich alluvial soils in the Pearl River delta region. Here, profits from cultivation of rice, mulberry, and a variety of other cash crops were large enough to support as many as five layers of "landlords" on one plot of land.[20]

Terms of tenure, cropping regimes, and the degree of reliance on subsidiary occupations varied widely depending on soil and climate, transportation, and proximity to markets.[21] Throughout China, however, the dominant form of land *management* under prevailing conditions of rapidly growing population, land fragmentation, and dispersed ownership was the small family farm.[22] Anthropologists have long recognized that the family was the main economic unit in Chinese society, and it was within the "family firm" that income and expenditure were calculated. By the Qing and probably earlier, this was no longer a self-sufficient economic unit in which the men farmed and the women spun. Susan Greenhalgh divides family mobility strategies into four categories. These include "property accumulation (directed primarily at land), economic diversification (into nonagricultural undertakings), worker dispersal (ideally to higher central places), and family expansion (through the addition of children and formation of complex families)."[23] During the first half of the Qing such activities included merchant sojourning and migration to China's still open internal frontier, a wide variety of cottage-based handicraft activities, the production of commercial crops, occupations as middlemen of different kinds (including peddling in nearby markets), and work in transport.

This brief description of the economic life of the family carries with it no verdict on the welfare of peasants. Insufficient work has been done to determine the real state of peasant livelihood in the Qing, a condition that in any case would have varied greatly by locality. However, the complexity of family mobility strategies may be viewed in the same light as the cropping patterns one sees emerging in late imperial agriculture. On the whole, they represent an intensification of family economic activity to the limits that the traditional commercial economy could accommodate. The economy could accommodate quite a lot, as will be seen. For most peasant families, however, it is likely that all this maneuvering left little surplus for nonessential consumption or savings. What it did do was enable Chinese peasants to stay on the land. From their differing perspectives, Chao Kang, Philip Huang, and Ramon Myers have all shown that, faced with diminishing farm size, the livelihood of the vast majority of peasants was only sustained by the ability to intensify, to turn to subsidiary occupations, and to switch to cash crops.[24] The same pattern of family entrepreneurship is emerging in China today.

One of the most important exceptions to the model of the small family farm is found in the expansion of the agricultural frontier in the first half of the Qing. By the end of the period under study these regions, too, were dominated by small family farms. The process of expansion, however, played a critical role in the development of the Qing economy.

Land reclamation during the early Qing was of three kinds: resettlement of lands abandoned during the wars of the Ming-Qing transition, extension of arable land in already densely settled areas, and expansion into peripheral and mountainous regions.[25] By 1700, large parts of Henan that had been imperial lands in the Ming were being farmed by commoners under the tax classification of *gengming tian.* The resettlement of the Sichuan Basin was not complete until the end of the century. But in both cases, as in the case of the newly created polders in Huguang, or the contiguous field extensions for which there are records in Shandong and Hebei, the dominant form of farm management was still the small owner-cultivated or tenanted farm. In some of the highland and peripheral territories, however, one sees relatively large-scale capital investment in the development of new lands and expansion of the arena of handicraft production. It was here that the availability of New World crops made possible the extension of cultivation to soils that were "too sandy, too acidic, too infertile and drought-prone to have supported settled populations in any numbers in the past."[26]

S. T. Leong's work on the shed people during the Qing provides the most comprehensive introduction to the process of commercial exploitation of highland areas. A large number of these people were pushed by poverty and over-population to migrate to the as yet underdeveloped highland area nearest to their home. And many shed people who moved as part of a commercial venture at times found themselves engaged in subsistence farming of a kind still familiar in highland areas of China today. A substantial portion of this mobile peasant population, however, came to the mountains to man the capitalist enterprises of merchant and rich peasant investors. The areas to which they were drawn tended to be close to high-level marketing systems, particularly south of the Yangzi River, and/or rich mineral, timber, and other natural resources within reach of riverine transport.[27]

In the Lower Yangzi region examined by Anne Osborne one sees numerous examples of large valley-based lineages renting lands to shed people to farm, mine coal, and dig lime. In many instances settlement was arranged by entrepreneurial tenants who paid large rents several years in advance and brought hundreds of peasants to work as subtenants or hired labor. Although the sources do not always indicate where the profits from plantation-style cultivation of maize would come from, it is likely that reclamation of this kind was designed to provide food for miners, tea producers, and handicraft workers, as well as for feeding pigs and making grain alcohol for commercial sale.[28] Fu Yiling's study of the mountainous border region between Shaanxi, Hubei, and Sichuan reveals such a pattern.[29] Here merchants, most of whom appear to have come from Shaanxi, invested in timber lands, iron foundries, paper mills, wood ear and fungus plantations, and salt yards. They put up the capital and hired managers who oversaw the importation of outside laborers, artisans, and transport workers in large numbers. In southwestern Sichuan, merchants invested in large plantations growing wood ears, gill fungus, and various medicinal herbs that were tended by shed people who were also agricultural tenants on the land.[30] The reclamation of alluvial land in the Pearl River Delta region was accomplished largely by local boat people hired by groups of wealthy tenants. Some of these tenants cultivated the land thus produced, using hired labor and direct management, a practice that seems to have continued until the 1930s.[31] As foreign demand for tea expanded, merchant capital also began to play an important role in the development of tea production in northwestern Fujian. Merchants from Canton, Shanxi, and southeastern Fujian organized numerous small and middle-sized tea-processing workshops employing hired labor. At the same time, merchants acting as tenants of local landlords sometimes rented parcels of mountain lands and hired labor to cultivate tea plants.[32] Examples also exist of rich tenants who rented land in these regions and farmed them with hired immigrant labor.[33]

The importance of these lands goes beyond their role as an outlet for surplus population. Indeed, it could be argued that by the time they became critical as a safety valve they no longer played the same role they had played in the early Qing. For many of the handicraft-producing regions of China, the frontier was a major market during the Qing.[34] At the same time, these lands, including the rich rice-growing regions of Huguang and Sichuan, were undertaxed,[35] provided cheap grain for consumption in regions of handicraft specialization,[36] and were an important site for factory-style and plantation-style production of such mountain products as medicinal herbs, bamboo handicrafts, dyes, paper, and tea, as well as salt, iron, and coal. Not everyone went into these regions out of desperation or as the poor tenant of a local landlord. Although most of the investors in highland and cash-crop area reclamation were probably wealthy landowners and lineages from nearby lowland areas, a substantial number appear to have been from among a small number of powerful early Qing merchant groups. These merchants, from Huizhou, Shanxi, Shaanxi, and Canton, also played a dominant role in the development of long-distance commerce and credit institutions in the High Qing.

How much of their wealth derived from exploitation of new opportunities in highland areas, areas of alluvial and lake-bottom reclamation, and the rich paddy lands in Sichuan and Hunan is not known. What is clear is that the boost to the economy provided by these regions during the first half of the Qing was to disappear by the second. As Ho Ping-ti pointed out long ago, by the mid-nineteenth century the Upper Yangzi region was no longer able to absorb large numbers of immigrants. The region that in the twentieth century was to have the densest population in China, was by 1853 no longer a major exporter of grain to the east. And by the end of the Taiping Rebellion, Sichuan was exporting settlers to Jiangnan to repopulate areas devastated by war. It is not insignificant that grain prices in the Upper Yangzi periphery began to rise only in the second quarter of the nineteenth century.[37] From this point on one can assume that the use of hired labor became uneconomical. Yan Ruyi notes that factories were quick to close when the price of maize was too high.[38] In these centers of protoindustrialization, the capital investment in factories was small. The human investment was great. And along with ecological degradation of the highland regions from the turn of the century on, the only lasting legacy of this episode of peripheral colonization seems to have been the relatively high density of population that remained in many of China's remote mountainous areas.

The Early Qing Market Economy

The evolution of the Chinese market economy during the Qing period supported this pattern of rural development. Its main characteristics are widely known from the writings of Skinner, Elvin, Myers, Rowe, Mann, and others. Here I will concentrate on those elements of the commercial economy that contributed to the concentration of population and productive resources within rural areas and facilitated a pattern of dispersed and small-scale production units.

As described by William Skinner, the Chinese market system can be visualized as a nested hierarchy of central places, ranging from rural markets in which peasants changed and borrowed money, bought basic necessities, and sold their handicraft and agricultural produce to higher-level markets in which sophisticated banking and credit institutions and numerous specialists' shops and artisan services could be found. At the apex of this pyramid of central places were regional cities and four central metropolises, most of which served as centers of administration, as well as the apex of a complex commercial network. During the period before the Opium War, the expansion of population, increased commercialization of agriculture, and extrapolation of rural subsidiary occupations led to an increase in the number of markets, particularly at the lower levels of the exchange pyramid. In the most advanced commercial centers of Jiangnan this led to a pattern of permanent market towns (*shizhen*) every three to ten miles.[39]

It is this density of lower-level central places, coupled with a high degree of market integration within regions, that is of most interest here. Gilbert Rozman's comparison of Japanese and Chinese urban development during the eighteenth and nineteenth centuries highlights the greater proliferation of rural markets in China. Comparisons of Chinese urbanization rates in the Song and Qing periods also demonstrate that China's urban population in the later period was far more dispersed among lower order centers of population and exchange.[40] This does not imply the return to a natural economy. Indeed, scholars like Lillian Li, Peter Perdue, and James Lee have utilized grain price series to show a remarkable degree of commercialization and market integration during the Qing, even in areas as remote and late-developing as Gansu and Yunnan.[41] Moreover, studies of a number of regions provide clear evidence of an increase in the number of specialized markets, in the number of market days at periodic markets, and in the number of markets that were permanent centers of exchange.[42]

The world of the Chinese peasant was one in which marketing played an integral part. Skinner's market typology places most peasants within half a day's walk of a standard marketing town and estimates an average of two trips to the market per household per month. The intensity of market involvement for households specializing in handicraft production could be much greater. As Elvin points out, "by the seventeenth and eighteenth centuries it was normal for those who spun or wove cotton in the countryside to make *daily* trips to the market to buy their raw materials."[43]

The proliferation of markets and the role of the peasant in them was in part a function of the overall growth of the economy during the late Ming and early Qing. Nevertheless, grain and other primary products continued to comprise as much as 60 percent of the value of goods entering Qing markets. Manufactures such as raw silk, cotton cloth, and salt, as well as a panoply of local handicrafts, made up the rest.[44] Most of these too, however, were produced in rural contexts. Thus, one of the main characteristics of the Qing market economy was the integration of manufacture and agriculture and the degree to which that economy was driven by individual producers participating in the marketplace on their own behalf, exchanging small amounts of agricultural and handicraft goods.

The Bottom-Heavy Market Structure and Qing Economic Development

The effects on the structure of the economy of a high man-land ratio, family-centered farm management, relatively low land concentration, and a dense, regionally integrated rural marketing system heavily utilized by peasant producers and consumers were numerous. Three of the most important are discussed below.

The Marketplace of Ideas

One of the most useful applications of William Skinner's typology of Chinese urban development has been the analysis of the social dimension of the standard marketing community. While considerable attention has been paid to this unit of social interaction in the formation of marriage alliances, in the spread of "heterodox ideologies," and in the spread of political information, less has been said about the market in its more fundamental role as the place in which economic knowledge is exchanged. *If* the manor was the center for invention and the spread of agricultural technology in the middle period (and there is reason to question this proposition), the market was surely the mechanism through which the best technologies were spread over the succeeding centuries. This was true not only because peasants visited markets with a frequency unusual in other cultures during the same period. It was also a result of the role of subsidiary occupations in the family farms that patronized these markets.

Certainly by the Qing, and probably in earlier periods as well, the most common subsidiary occupation after household spinning and weaving was peddling and porterage. That many peasants were on the road part of the time provided a direct link between producers in different areas. In its most extreme form, peddling was a key factor in the long-distance migration of peasants, as some of their number brought back information on available lands, techniques for planting new kinds of crops, and even the offers of labor bosses organizing teams of workers to migrate to highland reclamation sites. Sojourning merchants and peddlers were among the first extraprovincials to settle in Sichuan. Local gazetteers speak of their role in bringing the knowledge of intensive farming methods to the native population that remained after the devastations of the Ming-Qing transition. Many of these so-called merchants made a bit of money, bought some land, and returned home to Huguang or Jiangxi to bring their families back to Sichuan and their preferred occupation, farming.

The efficiency of the market mechanism in this regard may not have worked to China's long-term advantage. As Perkins pointed out some twenty years ago, the early spread of new seeds, new crops, and better cropping patterns left China by the twentieth century with "no great back-log of advanced but essentially 'traditional' " farming methods with which rapidly to expand production. This was in marked contrast to Japan, where social and political barriers to the spread of agricultural knowledge—not the least of which may have been the underdevelopment of standard marketing towns—left considerable room for the expansion of output without resort to modern and capital-intensive techniques.

It did bequeath a remarkable legacy, however, in the form of knowledge and experience of complex relationships of credit and exchange at the lowest levels of society. By the Qing period, and perhaps earlier, these relationships were often established through the use of written contracts. We will probably never know with certainty why late imperial China, unlike most preindustrial societies, relied so heavily on written legal instruments. Certainly the esteem given the written word in Chinese culture was a factor. The absence of manorial or ecclesiastical law governing economic interaction was another. The tendency of the state to leave the governance of the economy to the private sector, and the willingness of magisterial courts to uphold written agreements, reinforced the propensity to delineate economic and social responsibilities in written form. The development of contractual arrangements in the economy of the Ming and Qing, however, was most directly the result of a convergence of two things: a family system in which all male offspring were entitled to an equal share of family property, and the development of the marketplace as the main arena within which families could compete for scarce resources and a solution to the declining land-man ratio.

Myron Cohen was one of the first scholars to draw attention to the extraordinary role that contract played in late imperial Chinese society. In his words, "all over China, men created, maintained, or severed relationships through contract, which was operative in family life itself as well as in the wider social setting. The use of contract for instrumental purposes must therefore be seen as a fundamental feature of Chinese behavior in general."[45] As Cohen points out, it was common for families to draw up a written agreement to maintain a joint budget and to exploit together the family (*jia*) estate. As economic opportunities expanded and families were forced to intensify their economic activities, such agreements could become extremely complex, taking account of the value and distribution of income from peddling, manufacturing, urban sojourning, as well as farming. Even the appearance of lineage rules that stipulated annual contributions from members who succeeded in obtaining bureaucratic office should be seen as part of this same process. Families also used contracts to divide the *jia* estate and to establish the most efficient mixture of communally and individually held resources.

Even in remote villages during the Qing period, written contracts were used in the hiring of labor, sale and rental of property, distribution of land-use rights, marriage and concubinage, and the sale and indenture of human beings.[46] Societies for the maintenance of irrigation works, embankments and so on also used written agreements to organize investment of cash and labor and the distribution of benefits to large numbers of rural people. Cohen notes that beyond the confines of the village community, ordinary people used written agreements to pool and redistribute resources. The development of partnership contracts provides a prime example of their extension to the world of business.[47] Revolving credit associations were common by the mid-Qing period. Associations or *hui* were also formed to build bridges and schools, endow ferries, and repair roads. The act of joining a guild was a contractual act, entered into by choice and involving the transfer of wealth and the initiation of a new set of social and economic relationships.[48] Even workers entered into such agreements during the Qing. The organization of salt evaporators, known as the Yandigong, is just one example of the use of familiar legal instruments to establish a *hui*, charge dues, and use income to buy land that was managed for the common benefit.[49]

The use of written instruments and participation of so many little people in the marketplace and in itinerant trading encouraged the rise of a whole genre of literature directed specifically at educating people in the practical side of business and trade. Of particular interest are the merchant handbooks that begin to appear in the late Ming. Some, like those described by Timothy Brook, laid out routes and commercial advice for the long-distance merchants whose numbers were increasing from the fifteenth century. Of equal interest are the manuals studied by Richard Lufrano, many of which provided the inexperienced merchant with model contracts, business letters, and other forms of written agreements that could be copied for general use.[50] The publication of books such as these was premised on a growing and literate body of small merchants whose main arena of activity was the lower levels of the marketing hierarchy.

There is now growing evidence that many of the more sophisticated forms of business contracts found in the late eighteenth and nineteenth centuries had their roots in the written agreements described above. The relationship between land tenancy contracts and the development of long-term leases in extractive industries is clear.[51] The process of evolution from one form to the other facilitated the combination of small amounts of capital from numerous sources in the exploitation of coal, salt, and other nonregulated minerals. The written agreements characteristic of the family "firm" also influenced the development of business. The most important institution to grow out of the family economy was the lineage trust. Although the prototype was suggested by Fan Zhongyan in the eleventh century, the practical model for the management of consolidated resources was the household division contract familiar to all Chinese. The maintenance of a portion of household property that was not divided was originally intended to provide income for the performance of religious rites, and in more affluent families, for support of education. Although largely composed of agricultural lands, by the nineteenth century lineage holdings were quite varied and could include shops, fishing rights, and even industrial establishments. In the absence of a corporation law, the lineage trust became an ideal institution for the consolidation of corporate property, and the protection of that property from partition or predation by family members.[52] Moreover, because they grew out of written agreements widely used within Chinese society, the impartible trusts could be applied to small resources as well as large.

The economic impact of these institutions has not yet been systematically explored. The successful lineage trust could provide those with a claim to it with a competitive edge in the marketplace, as well as the more familiar access to education and local prestige. As such it could be a powerful tool for the development of economic resources. In the case of the large lineages of the Pearl River Delta, or the salt merchants of Sichuan, the trust made possible the accumulation of huge fortunes. In the case of the salt merchants, these fortunes were applied to the development of industrial resources on a scale rarely seen in early modern China. Among many of the larger lineages with considerable generational depth, however, the exploitation of neighboring surnames through the lineage trust may have led to little capital accumulation on a per capita basis. In the case of the Pearl River Delta, the concentration of lineage resources in the exploitation of alluvial fields may even have perpetuated the rentier economy and diverted urban commercial capital to rural real estate.[53] In a country where individual fortunes tended to be small, the lineage trust had a very large part to play. Far more needs to be done before we will fully understand the influence that such family-based institutions had on management practices, investment, risk taking, and so on in the early modern economic environment.

The Rural Base of Production

The overwhelming majority of all production, processing, and manufacture during the first half of the Qing took place in rural areas. The factors contributing to the rural base of production were numerous. Although they played a part in its evolution, poor transportation, technological underdevelopment, and rising population alone cannot explain the pattern of household industry that existed in the late imperial period. During the period when the pattern of production one sees in China was evolving, per capita output of food was at least stable, and perhaps rising, with the expansion of grain production in Sichuan, Huguang, and elsewhere supporting increasing specialization in the advanced coastal zones. There was considerable movement of raw materials between regions, although the high costs of transportation did limit the transfer of energy resources. Moreover, as Lillian Li and others have shown, the level of technology and skill involved in the production of many of China's key items of long-distance trade was extremely high. The same can be said of the level of business practice associated with commerce, a point vividly illustrated by both Hao Yen-p'ing and Robert Gardella.[54] One gets closer to an understanding of the factors at work when one looks at the rising man-land ratio in late imperial China, in combination with the market structure, the reservoir of entrepreneurial talent and experience that resided in the peasant community, and the flexible system of credit that supported the economic activities of rural producers.

China on the eve of the Opium War had few manufacturies worthy of the name factory. Those large-scale production units that did exist were often connected to production for imperial use. This was true of the porcelain works at Jingdezhen, as well as the large copper mines in Yunnan, many of which were opened during the Qianlong reign to supply government mints. The most notable exception was the salt factory at Fushun and Rongxian in Sichuan, where by the nineteenth century several hundred firms employed more than 100,000 men. The trend towards privatization of enterprise in the late imperial period, however, had the effect of fragmenting even industries serving the state. The most dramatic example of this process occurred in the silk industry, where the imperial manufacturies turned increasingly to the use of contract labor to produce the silks and brocades used by the court in Beijing.[55]

Thus, most manufacturing was done in small, largely rural workshops or in peasant homes. This form of production dominated the processing of wine, sugar, tobacco, leather goods, oil, iron tools and utensils, and other items of daily use in late imperial China.[56] Cottage industry was also responsible for the majority of silk, cotton and tea, the three most important reprocessed goods in the domestic market. Craig Deitrich has found that during the late Ming and early Qing, nearly four-fifths of all xian gazetteers in a sample he surveyed mentioned the manufacture of cotton cloth in their lists of local products.[57] Likewise, one of the hallmarks of the peasant economy of the Qing period was the spread of Zhejiang-Jiangsu silk culture to nearly every province. In some areas sericulture was practiced for the first time under the Manchu government, while improved techniques reached areas with long traditions of cottage production.[58] In the case of both cotton and silk, the major portion of output was sold in local or regional markets, with the finer cloths being made largely in Songjiang and Suzhou prefectures in Jiangsu.

Despite the preponderance of peasant producers, there was considerable specialization in the production of both cotton and silk. The division of labor between north and south in the production of raw cotton and the commercial production of cotton yarn and cloth is well known. In the silk industry this division was even more finely drawn, some households specializing in the raising of mulberry leaves and silkworm eggs, while others brought in all or part of their leaves to raise silkworms and mature the cocoons. In the late eighteenth century the countryside surrounding Wuqing zhen was replete with households reeling silk yarn, but no one any longer wove cloth. By the early nineteenth century this was also true of peasants in the area of Xiangshan. At the same time, weavers from Wuze, Sheng ze, and Shuanglin zhen made frequent trips to market to purchase small amounts of warp and woof to weave by themselves. In Changshan xian in Shandong, the people were skilled at weaving tussore silk, but all their yarn was purchased from outside. In some more advanced silk production areas there was even a division of labor between those who raised silkworms and those who reeled silk. For example, peasants in Jiaxing specialized in rearing cocoons, which they supplied to household reelers from Huzhou prefecture at least as early as 1800.[59]

The ability of peasants to supply their own raw materials and market the product of their labor, however small the scale of their output, depended on the high density of standard market towns and the system of rural credit available in the late imperial period. Factor markets were well developed, even in the early Qing. Agricultural manuals describe in considerable detail the market in seed, fertilizer, and agricultural labor.[60] In areas of concentrated commercial production, specialized markets were also available to meet production needs and coordinate the output of specialized households. Indeed, some of the best evidence of the tight fit among peasant household production, the market, and rural credit comes from the most advanced regions of handicraft production. In Jiangnan it was quite common for peasants to borrow money from local wealthy households to buy silkworms and to pay back the loan within a few months, after the silk from the resulting cocoons was spun and sold.[61] Brokers and peddlers also provided a form of credit by selling the goods peasants produced on commission, often reaching right into the village to do so. This was true of the boatmen mentioned by Fei Xiaotong in his study of village life in Jiangxi. It was also the function of brokers who went out to sea in boats provided by Ningbo wholesalers to meet local fishermen the moment the daily catch was in.[62] In the tea industry, where much of the output entered the long-distance trade, advance purchase by extraprovincial merchants provided small producers with the capital to tend their tea fields and undertake the initial processing of the tea leaves.[63] Agents such as these were responsible for the survival of the vast majority of peasants producing at low margins and in small volumes throughout the Qing and republic.

Rural credit in preindustrial China was extended in the form of small loans negotiated through contractual arrangements such as the *hui*, the conditional sale of land, indenture, and agreements with usurers. The market town was also the venue for the earliest formal credit organizations. Small private loan offices existed as early as the Yongzheng reign.[64] More important in rural areas were pawnshops. Abe Takeo has estimated that by the mid-eighteenth century there were some nineteen thousand of these firms in China, rising to twenty-five thousand by the early 1800s.[65] Although many were in higher-order central places, there was clearly a large number of pawnshops within easy reach of ordinary rural clients. In more advanced regions pawnshops could play an important role in the intensification of peasant economic activity. As early as the Yongzheng period, Zhejiang Governor-General Li Wei reported that many peasants were choosing not to sell rice in the fall to pay their rents and other obligations. Instead, many pawned part of their harvest, reckoning that the interest they paid to the pawnshop to redeem it would still make it cheaper than the cost of buying rice when they ran out in the spring.[66] There is even evidence that tenant farmers in the vicinity of Wuxi in the late eighteenth century were pawning their rice for less than market value, using the money to engage in petty trading, making a profit from the latter, and still coming out ahead when they redeemed their rice later in the year.[67]

Pawnshops also played a critical role in financing household production. For example, in Yudi xian, the poor pawned their winter clothing to buy leaves to feed their silkworms and redeemed it after the silk was reeled.[68] Peng Ziyi quotes a nineteenth-century source from the Wuxi area that vividly describes the pattern of production and pawning through which peasants in many handicraft-producing areas moved during the year. Here farms were often so small that peasants produced only enough rice to pay the rent, pawn enough grain to redeem the clothing they had previously pawned, and feed the family for the three winter months. In the spring, the whole family would spin and weave cotton yarn and cloth, exchanging the cloth for food to eat. By the fifth month they turned their attention to farming. To have something to eat they pawned their winter clothes in exchange for the rice they had pawned the previous fall. While the rice matured, they returned to their looms, selling their cloth and awaiting the harvest, when the cycle began again.[69] The importance of pawnshops as provenders of cash for rural business activity can be gauged by the high demand for cash that occurred in some regions in February and March at the beginning of the tea season, and in others in April and May when the silk market was at its height.[70]

In contrast to the voluminous evidence of independent peasant handicraft production, there are few examples of putting out in preindustrial China. E-tu Zen Sun writes of independent silk weavers indebted to silk brokers who lent them the money to buy raw materials. Small urban weavers in Nanjing and Suzhou sometimes received their raw materials from the owners of workshops and then paid piece rates based on the quality of the work.[71] A similar process was at work in the calendaring of cotton cloth in Jiangnan.[72] Most producers, however, were independent, purchased their raw materials in rural markets, and sold their products to merchants, peddlers, and brokers who frequented even low-level market towns. As such, the rural-based production regime that so pervaded the Chinese economy of the Qing period was quite different from examples of protoindustrialization in the West. Rarely does one see direct merchant participation in production. Moreover, there is no indication that rural production contributed to a weakening of urban-based guilds and their anachronistic controls on production and distribution. Indeed, as Mark Elvin has argued, it was precisely because of the efficiency of the market mechanism in China that putting out became unnecessary. Only the influence of foreign demand and the difficulties entailed in the transport and marketing of upland products appear to have stimulated direct merchant involvement in manufacture.[73]

The rural base of production allowed a balanced growth between city and countryside and meant that China avoided many of the disruptions that led to a mass exodus of labor to urban areas in other societies during the early modern period. As Philip Huang has shown, the availability of subsidiary income from the marketing of cash crops and handicrafts was a key factor in the perpetuation of China's small-peasant economy.[74] Chao Kang has argued that rising population and the declining man-land ratio made reliance on family-based, as opposed to workshop-based, production inevitable. Once the marginal product of labor fell below the subsistence wage, a situation that Chao feels was reached by the Qing, it became more economical for merchants to contract or purchase goods from household producers than to produce them themselves using hired labor. Surplus labor was thus retained at home, where the peasant and his family were willing to work for less than subsistence wages in order to utilize their residual productivity for whatever return it could bring. This was possible because the equipment needed to produce yarn, cloth, and other handicraft items was relatively cheap, and problems of marketing were solved by the dense network of rural markets in place by the early Qing.

Of course, the threat of underemployment has never been its own solution, and under different conditions one could imagine large numbers of workers migrating to higher-level urban places. It was the combination of factors described above that permitted the particular solution Chao and Huang describe. Its implications will be explored more fully below. In one respect, however, the outcome was clear. Family-based production, mediated by a bottom-heavy marketing system, reinforced the trend toward continued population growth, falling per capita incomes, and a dispersion of national income. This, in turn, contributed to the fragmentation of all economic activity, which was the third main feature of the late imperial economic system.

Fragmentation of Economic Activity

Fragmentation was foremost a response to the dispersion of capital in late imperial China and the facility with which institutional mechanisms were developed to overcome that dispersion. It is a mistake to view this as a sign that the Chinese economy did not generate a surplus.[75] Nor should we necessarily dwell on "culturally motivated" dissipation of that surplus by a dissolute elite, a corrupt bureaucracy, or a high-spending imperial court.[76] More important was the *relatively* even distribution of wealth among large numbers of economic actors, many of whom did utilize the opportunities to multiply their earnings through participation in commerce and through manipulation of China's relatively unregulated preindustrial money market. The reasons for the dispersion of capital will be discussed below. Its manifestations reached into every sector of the economy. In the realm of manufacturing and commerce, the most important were the small scale and undercapitalization of enterprises, and vertical and horizontal fragmentation of the processes of manufacture and distribution. Each of these represents a highly effective accommodation to low levels of original capital accumulation. Together, however, they helped perpetuate the conditions of capital dispersion that led to their rise and hampered China's transformation from a highly developed commercial and handicraft economy to one of industrial capitalism.

Direct evidence of low levels of capitalization are difficult to document, as few company records exist that date from before 1850, and there is little basis upon which to judge the financial needs of a company in late imperial times. A number of Chinese studies have utilized size of workforce to gauge levels of investment. This does not, however, help us calculate the appropriateness of the capital resources of a company to the tasks it sets itself. More useful would be records of company closures, something one rarely finds in the Chinese archives, based as they are on the documents of a state that took little direct role in economic affairs. In the absence of direct evidence, however, indirect evidence does give an indication of some of the problems that undercapitalization could bring.

Shortages of cash to finance trade in an expanding economy were met by the increased used of fiduciary instruments, particularly banknotes issued by *qianzhuang* and remittance certificates issued by *piaohao*. Both were designed to facilitate the transfer of goods and provided merchants with short-term credit and the ability to move funds within cities and along the main routes of long-distance trade. In some areas they became widely used among the general population and could often be seen in purchases of real estate, as well as everyday goods.

As important as their operations were to the fiscal health of the country, the native banks that issued these notes tended to be small, with low capital reserves. Even as late as the 1880s the capitalization of the largest *qianzhuang* in Shanghai was no more than fifty thousand taels, and many had a subscription of no more than twenty thousand taels.[77] Most of these native banks, the main source of loans to Chinese merchants in the financial capital of the Chinese empire, were established using the capital resources of the proprietor(s), an individual, family, or perhaps a few friends and relatives in partnership. Their books were closed at the end of each year, and dividends distributed among the shareholders. Little effort was made to increase their capital reserves by attracting deposits. In the absence of any external controls, the notes issued by these institutions tended to be insufficiently backed by silver reserves, a problem that in the Daoguang period led to frequent bank failures. So serious was the problem that a national debate was launched among high provincial officials over their continued use.[78] Their findings showed banknotes to be an evil that China could not do without.

The weak fiscal foundations of China's main financial institutions limited their ability to support long-term credit, a fact that was brought home dramatically in the late nineteenth century when the failure of client firms lowered trade volume, and the drain of silver to other parts of the country periodically brought down large numbers of Shanghai *qianzhuang*.[79] The fact that 1913 Jiangsu pawnshop regulations (based on Qing practice) contained an item allowing pawnbrokers to suspend business temporarily if their capital subscription fell short of minimum requirements implies that such shortfalls were a frequent occurrence in this sector of the credit industry as well.

Some of the best evidence of undercapitalization comes from the mining industry. The Baxian archives provide a close-up view of the limitations of investment in the coal and iron industry.[80] Most mines in nineteenth-century Baxian were what were locally known as father and son mines, seams exploited by family members as an occupation subsidiary to farming. The relative ease of excavating the horizontal coal seams that dotted the Baxian hillsides and the proximity of the growing city of Chongqing, however, encouraged some larger-scale mining and outside investment. Lease and sale of mining rights became as common as that of cultivation rights, and disagreements over these lands became the second most frequent source of litigation in the magistrates' courts after tenancy disputes.

From the records of these lawsuits one can see several things of importance to the issue at hand. Low levels of savings among the general population meant that partnership was the dominant form of enterprise in the Baxian coal fields as in many areas of the Qing economy. Familiarity with the use of written contracts facilitated the formation of agreements that allowed the pooling of modest resources, even among groups of peasants and landless laborers. Nevertheless, here, as elsewhere, the size of partnerships was extremely small. Altogether there are records of fifty-three partnerships, spanning the period from the late Jiaqing to the early Guangxu reigns. Of these, twenty had only two partners; the mean number of partners was three. Only one partnership, formed in 1875, had as many as eight shareholders, and in this case there is some question as to whether the original two partners were coerced by the other six, many of whom were degree-holders, into granting them shares.[81]

One reason for the small size of partnerships was that, like most forms of handicraft production, it did not take much money to open a coal mine. In Baxian, the average capitalization of a mine that was not dug as a farming sideline was between five hundred and one thousand taels. This compares well with the eight hundred taels Deng Tuo found necessary to open a pit at Mentou gou, near Beijing.[82] The belief that the mine would begin to pay for itself as soon as coal was reached meant, however, that few partnerships anticipated expenses beyond the initial capitalization. In only three of fifty-three surviving partnership contracts did shareholders agree to contribute operating expenses for the mine.[83] Frequent complaints from shareholders in newly opened mines that profits were not being divided indicate that most shareholders expected, and probably required, a speedy return on investment.[84]

The number of bankruptcies recorded in the Baxian archives was in part an indication of the small capital reserves of investors in these mines. Even wealthy developers, however, preferred to suspend operations if anything went wrong. Having put so little into the opening of the enterprise, and with so many alternative outlets for their capital, it was often easier for partners to accept a loss and move on than to attempt to salvage a pit that had encountered even minor problems. Some partnership contracts even stipulated that when the money ran out, any remaining assets would simply be divided and the partnership dissolved.[85]

The Baxian coal industry was a local industry serving local energy needs. Even where the demand was large and government support relatively strong, however, undercapitalization was a major obstacle to mine development. One of the most remarkable accommodations to this problem had its origins in the

Yunnan copper mines. During the second half of the eighteenth century the Qing government encouraged increased copper production by inviting private merchant investment. Despite state subsidies, and a major state contribution to the transport and marketing of copper, investment capital was hard to find. At some mines this led to the so-called brotherhood (*dixiong*) system of labor recruitment. Given the state of mine technology at the time, the largest portion of initial outlay was generally in wages. Under this system, workers received only their subsistence and simple tools until the mine began to produce. Then they received a small share of output, after taxes and other expenses were paid.[86] Workers, in effect, invested their labor as their share in a partnership with mine investors. In this way, many mines were opened for which funds would not otherwise have been found. There is evidence that the practice spread to other provinces as well.

Low levels of capital accumulation were also a factor in the widespread practice of splitting ownership and operation of manufacturing facilities in the Qing and republic. It is not known how far back this practice dates. In the Fu-Rong salt factories in Sichuan, it was not unusual for one investment group to open a well, and another group to rent the finished well in order to pump brine.[87] With the introduction of mechanized pumping, a third group of actual pump owners was often inserted into the production process as well. Iron foundries in Sichuan frequently rented their furnaces to producers who provided their own ore and fuel.[88] In the twentieth century, the uncertainties of the market led many Shanghai developers to build silk filatures and rent them out to entrepreneurs who actually reeled silk.[89] The willingness of the latter to accept such a system of production can be traced to their inability to produce the capital to equip a factory themselves. Most of these operations depended on large infusions of short-term loans for their working capital. Failures, not surprisingly, were common.

Split ownership and operation was just one manifestation of the vertical and horizontal fragmentation of business in the late imperial and early modern period in China. It has already been seen that horizontal fragmentation, or the division of any one phase of production among large numbers of independent producers, was characteristic of Chinese agriculture and the production of silk and cotton thread and unfinished cloth. Horizontal fragmentation was even characteristic of export commodities like tea. In Taiwan and Fujian, most tea farms had between fifty and six hundred shrubs, and even large proprietors like the Lins of Banqiao tended to rent out their shrubs to tenants, rather than grow them as consolidated plantations using hired labor.[90] Under these conditions, the average household could produce no more than 266 lbs. of crude tea a year. According to Gardella, approximately 279 million lbs. of tea were exported from China in 1862–63.[91] Thus, over a million households were involved in the production of tea for export alone.

Vertical fragmentation was also characteristic of most nonagricultural enterprises in the period before the Opium War. Coal mined in the hills surrounding

Chongqing was sold to hundreds of independent peddlers, most of them peasants, who climbed the hills and carried it in baskets balanced on poles, down to riverside coalyards. Here the coal was sold to wholesalers who sold it to boatmen, who marketed it downriver, and to retailers in the city itself.[92] In the silk and cotton textile industries, middlemen also played a major role in linking a highly atomized collection of small producers. Brokers, sometimes dealing with peddlers and not the peasant producer himself, bought raw cotton, cotton yarn, and cotton cloth from peasants who purchased their raw materials from other peddlers and brokers in rural markets. Similar market mechanisms facilitated the movement of silkworms, cocoons, raw silk, and silk cloth along a long marketing chain. Although some large wholesale merchants dealt with millions of lengths of cloth each year, dyeing and finishing were generally contracted to independent artisans and small artisan workshops, often through the mediation of brokers who specialized in these fields. Even references to workshops for the weaving and calendaring of cloth should be treated with caution. As Elvin points out, the premises themselves might be owned by one group of men, who rented them to brokers, who did not employ permanent workers but contracted to individual artisans on a piece-work basis.[93]

The initial processing of tea was undertaken by the primary producer to prevent rapid decay of the tea leaf. The final processing was no less centralized, however. Growers in Fujian brought their tea to over a hundred local, seasonal tea markets, where large numbers of part-time tea brokers bought it and sold it to tea factories. These factories, of which there were hundreds, each "produced only a few hundred chests of tea per year, had little fixed capital investment, and employed fewer than a dozen to several dozen workers."[94] Despite the low levels of investment required by such operations, local production still required annual infusions of working capital, much of which came from the outside, from brokers, warehousers, wholesale merchants, native banks, and later from foreign banks as well.

This degree of fragmentation injected tremendous flexibility into the manufacturing economy. As Chao Kang has demonstrated for cotton textiles, the family firm could respond quickly to market forces. The low costs of equipment, low level of skill required to spin and weave, and availability of raw materials and marketing outlets in nearby market towns meant that a family could devote more or less of its labor to cotton textiles, depending on the return it would bring relative to other forms of productive activity.[95] Indeed, although the impact of competition from machine-made yarn and cloth on the peasant economy of many areas was great, so it seems was the ability of that economy to find other outlets for its labor. This was especially true of areas where the market economy was well developed. Thus, peasants in Jiading may not have been as well off as they were in the Qing, when they planted 30 percent of their land in rice and 70 percent in cotton. By the late 1930s, however, they had made accommodations to new economic circumstances. Now only one-fourth of their land was planted in cotton, but peasants had turned to basket weaving, fishing, cotton weaving, and dressmaking, and they relied far more on consumption and sale of home-grown rice.[96]

The long chain of middlemen and small processors that completed the path from the household economy to the consumer served a similar purpose. Minimum investment in fixed capital allowed money to be drawn out of an industry in years of bad harvests or low demand. Factories, such as they were, opened and closed with great ease in the late imperial period. Hundreds of factories processed tea in late-Qing Fujian, their precise number varying with the state of the market each year.[97] A survey of iron foundries in the Baxian hills shows that few lasted longer than four or five years, and many changed ownership during that time.[98] In the silk and cotton industries, reliance on contractors for dying and finishing meant that no investment had to be made in equipment or in the support of a permanent workforce. In this way, capital was kept liquid and merchants were protected from dramatic swings in market demand.[99]

Nevertheless, this chain of credit, like the long chain of middlemen between producer, processor, and consumer, reduced the profits to be made at each level and helped perpetuate the capital shortage that gave birth to the system at its outset. As will be seen, it also had serious implications for the development of production technology and for China's ability to compete on the international market.

Some Possible Causes and Consequences of China's Domestic Economic Structure

The structure of the Chinese economy during the Qing period grew out of a combination of geophysical, political, and cultural factors. Given the large number of influences on the early modern economy, and their intimate connection with each other, it is often difficult to determine which came first, or which were most instrumental in the formation of the system I have been examining. Several in particular, however, deserve attention because of their implications for today.

China's Natural Endowment

Although culture and politics have shaped even the natural endowment upon which China's economy was built, certain aspects of that endowment are worthy of mention in their own right. The most striking is China's size and the diversity of its climate and natural resources. China found most of what it needed within its own borders. The absence of any political barriers to trade or travel over a large land mass encouraged the development of the commercial economy and the sophisticated banking and credit relationships that supported long-distance trade. Less beneficial was the effect of this continental free-trade zone on invention. As Elvin has noted in the case of cotton, by the early modern period there was no way China could expand national supplies of raw cotton to sufficient levels to stimulate changes in production technology. Domestic production could not be increased without removing land from cereal production. At the national level, the Chinese economy and its existing output were "too big even relative to *world* cotton supplies in the eighteenth century" for imports from the outside to have significantly altered the production regime. At the same time, in China's highly integrated market economy, rapid expansion of output at the local level would have had little impact because local effects were rapidly evened out by interregional trade.[100] Only a big and sudden change could act as a stimulus to major structural transformation of production. The disruption of trading networks as a result of the Taiping Rebellion was one such jolt, but except in the Sichuan salt industry, its impact appears to have been short-lived.[101]

The continental empire also bequeathed to China an internal frontier that it explored in the Qing period with the same sense of manifest destiny that motivated the push across America in the nineteenth century. Although one cannot say what inspires one people and not another to external exploration, it is significant that during the period when western Europe was moving toward the economic colonization of its external world, China was well occupied with the development of its internal frontier. Whereas transoceanic exploration contributed to the great fortunes that fueled Europe's commercial revolution and brought new markets, raw materials, and hard currency to the West, the long-term result of Chinese expansion was the extension of Han settlement, aboriginal warfare, social disruption, and ecological degradation of highland regions.

Labor surplus was not the only factor influencing the organization of production in China. The importance of what might be called fortuitous factors in development cannot be ignored. A far greater proportion of China's land mass is covered by hills and mountains than any of the large nation-states of the Western world. This has implications for agricultural output and for the cost of moving goods from remote regions. The fact that the earliest large deposits of British coal to be mined for a national market were located near the ocean, stands in marked contrast to China's rich endowment of coal and iron in inland and hilly regions far from the centers of early settlement. The ease of mining the latter in horizontal shafts close to the surface discouraged large-scale investment in coal extraction. And the low capitalization of mines discouraged the use of costly modern equipment to salvage mines damaged by flooding or collapse. Likewise, as Lillian Li has pointed out, traditional Chinese sericulture produced a product of as high a quality as anything manufactured in the West. The fragmented Chinese system of household production did not come under serious attack until the appearance of cocoon blight and the need to suit the needs of modern weaving factories made standardization of yarn necessary. Thus, opportunities to improve technologies that in the West had extensive applications in the early stages of industrialization were never taken up in China because their need was not felt.

Of similar importance are the differences between Western mixed agriculture and China's cereal-based economy. Animal husbandry never played an important part in Chinese agriculture. The introduction of scientific livestock management and breeding, however, was one of the main factors in the abandonment of the crofter economy and the introduction of modern consolidated farm management in early modern Europe. The absence of economies of scale in rice agriculture (though not in the development of infrastructures like irrigation) must also have played a part in the fragmentation of Chinese production units and the relatively small involvement of large landowners in estate management. Indeed, agricultural manuals of the late Ming and early Qing urged people to concentrate on the meticulous cultivation of small holdings even before the man-land ratio made this an absolute necessity nationwide.[102]

The Role of the State

The evolution of China's state system has had a profound effect on its economy. It functioned first of all to stabilize the economy, particularly through the operation of the state granary system, which smoothed over seasonal price fluctuations and often circumvented social unrest in time of poor harvests. The efficiency of this system during the early Qing meant there were few mass migrations to the cities by rural poor of the kind seen elsewhere and increasingly in China from the mid-nineteenth century. The dislocations that did occur were over quickly, and populations generally were restored to their place of origin. The notion that the state is ultimately responsible for ensuring public welfare survived the fall of the Qing and plays a powerful role in the political economy of China today. It was in other areas, however, that the state most influenced the shape of the economy as described above.

As is well known, the Single-Whip reforms played an important role in promoting the commercialization of the economy by requiring that most taxes be paid in cash. The Qing insistence on individual household liability for tax hastened further the need for peasants to market their crops. Late Ming and early Qing officials also relied increasingly on paid labor in their yamen, and to carry out state-sponsored relief and construction work. Moreover, although concern about rising population did prompt the Qing to promote regional self-sufficiency in grain, local and provincial officials also approached the problem by promoting the spread of cash crops and cottage industry. While this did not result in technological innovation, it did aid in the diversification of the peasant economy and the expansion of rural subsidiary employments.[103]

Despite these isolated efforts to stimulate economic activity, one of the legacies of political hegemony over a vast empire was declining state intervention in economic affairs.[104] Low levels of taxation encouraged the growth of the private sector. From the Tang period on, the establishment of markets was subjected to little government control.[105] Over the course of the Qing dynasty the number of standard market towns in many counties increased several times, and both merchants and local elites were prompted to establish rural markets as a means to stimulate local economies and ensure prosperity. The fact that the state did not attempt to commandeer the profits of commerce by limiting it to higher-level administrative centers worked in favor of the proliferation of lower-level markets in the late imperial period. Low levels of miscellaneous taxation (*zashui*) and the elimination of the "unloading tax" further encouraged participation in low-level trade. During the early Qing period, state commercial policies were designed to facilitate the role of the peddler and small merchant in the distribution network by posting rates of tax to protect small dealers from the treachery of government personnel, and by exempting those dealing in small quantities of goods from any tax at all.[106]

Although seemingly of minor importance, the state attitude toward usury played a particularly important role in development. On the one hand, by limiting the interest that could be charged by pawnshops, the Qing guaranteed the ability of peasants to obtain the small capital inputs that fueled cottage production. At the same time, the absence of usury laws in general meant that as the man-land ratio rose, the extension of high-cost credit would become a growing industry, absorbing much of the savings of rural elites and providing profits with which the income from investment in production could not compete.

The laissez-faire attitude taken by late imperial governments toward commerce (with the notable exception of salt, taxes on which were the second most important source of state revenue) was matched by its lenient attitudes toward internal migration. Although concerned that mobile populations might be a source of social instability, the state played a major role in facilitating their movement to peripheral regions for reclamation and resettlement. Especially following the *huohao guigong* reforms of the early eighteenth century, areas like Huguang and the southwest were able to provide seed, tools, oxen, and bridging loans to emigrant families from the south and east. Although state encouragement of small owner-cultivator reclamation was sometimes thwarted, policies that deprived people of title to land that was not being farmed did prevent at least some from hoarding wasteland and denying someone else the right to reclaim it.[107]

The state also played an important role in supporting the structures that made the market economy work. Written contracts, and such relationships as partnership, lease, sale, and conditional sale, that they confirmed, would not have worked so well for the redistribution of resources had they not been upheld by the agents of the state. The same may be said of the guilds, whose authority was upheld through petition and government endorsement in higher-level central places. Guilds, too, contributed to the fragmentation of production. Limits on the number of apprentices a shop could employ worked against large-scale production. And although they brought together merchants and artisans for a common cause, their effort to protect their small patch under conditions of increasing competition led to a ludicrous division of the market in many products by the late Qing.[108]

Finally, the dispersion of wealth that characterized the Qing economy was in part a product of government policies that attacked privilege and supported the small taxpaying owner-cultivator. We tend to think of China as a society in which the differentials in wealth between rich and poor were great. In reality, middling wealth was much more typical of the late imperial elite, and in village China the difference between rich and poor could be a matter of a few acres or ownership of a domestic animal or two. The state's attack on the aristocracy in the middle period and on the degree-holding elite and powerful lineages in the Yuan and Ming, and the elimination of the state agricultural sector in the late Ming and early Qing, removed the political supports that sustained a small but enormously wealthy upper class of the kind that survived in Japan and much of early modern Europe. Although not always successful, the early Qing rulers furthered this leveling process by eliminating the tax exemptions and special tax rates of the rich and degree-holding elite, encouraging landlords to pass tax exemptions on to their tenants, and ensuring that famine relief and stabilization grain went to those in need.[109] Where great wealth was allowed to accumulate, the importance of government connections are clear. Among the largest fortunes of the Qing period were those held by the Cohong merchants of Canton, salt merchants, and the so-called Shanxi-Shaanxi group. The first relied for their wealth on monopoly rights to trade with foreigners at Canton, the second on monopoly rights to market salt, and the third, initially on involvement in the government-sponsored tea trade with Russia, and the loan market to officials. Only the last group diversified sufficiently to become an independent economic force.

Rising Population and the Chinese Family System

If state policy provided the preconditions for the dispersion of capital and development of the lower levels of the market hierarchy, the Chinese family system made them the dominant elements in the late imperial economy. Many scholars view the family system as the key to China's rising man-land ratio. The operation of the "family firm" was fundamental to the success of China's flexible rural production regime.

Up to now I have noted some of the effects of population growth on China's economy but have not examined the reasons for that increase in the late imperial period. Several theories have been put forward in recent years. Many scholars have noted the long periods China enjoyed without warfare as a check on population growth. And most agree that by the 1850s, China's overall population was so large that even a demographic blow as severe as the Taiping Rebellion would only take a few decades to recover from. Dwight Perkins and Albert Feuerwerker have stressed the greater potential of Chinese agriculture to accommodate population growth than the dry agriculture of medieval and early modern Europe.[110] The limits of traditional technology's ability to increase output in the latter led to the development of patterns of late marriage and high rates of celibacy that proved a powerful check on population growth down to the nineteenth century.[111] As far as can be determined, throughout history the Chinese encouraged early marriage and high rates of fertility. Family-based religion reinforced these practices. At the same time, the family firm and the opportunities provided by the market economy to intensify nonagriculture as well as agricultural household employments kept people on the farm. The potential to augment family income through an increase in the number of family members working for the firm encouraged high rates of fertility. And the existence of the family as a mechanism for the pooling of resources, however meager, encouraged the entrepreneurial attitudes that pervade Chinese culture and have been seen firing rural reform today.

The manifestations of the family firm in popular culture are numerous. Arkush has shown how peasant proverbs exalt entrepreneurship. Gardella has noted how funeral and marriage customs reveal petty capitalist values. Myron Cohen's studies of family life in both Taiwan and North China demonstrate the importance of family rituals as opportunities to purchase and store up *guanxi* for later use in promoting overall family interests. The popularity of late Ming and early Qing spiritual accounting also demonstrates the influence of notions of profit and loss in everyday social transactions.

The family firm, by providing the part-time labor that served as porters, brokers, peddlers, and handicraft workers, had the greatest impact of any institution on China's early modern development. The flexibility of family-based production militated against the improvement of production technology as much as any labor surplus.[112] The market mechanism it supported, by making it unnecessary for merchants to get involved in production, may have inhibited investment in more complex forms of production in China.[113] The greatest concentrations of wealth in late imperial China lay in the hands of commercial, often lineage-based magnates, merchants from Huizhou, Shaanxi, Shanxi, Guangdong, and Fujian, who bridged the gap between regional systems and dominated interregional trade. Although they did invest to some extent in productive enterprise,[114] their interests remained fundamentally in trade and the institutions that served trade. In that they were not much different from their Western counterparts in the growing Chinese export market centered on Shanghai. The development of commerce thus proceeded further in China than perhaps in any other preindustrial society. But, at least in the Qing period, this development did not produce the basis for modern industrial growth.

Implications for Today

As William Kirby and Thomas Rawski have shown, twentieth-century pockets of development in China can be located. Moreover, the limited progress made during this period in the training of technical and managerial personnel clearly contributed to economic progress in Taiwan in the 1950s and 1960s and to the growth of the mainland industrial economy in the postrevolutionary period. For most of China, however, economic life in the first half of the twentieth century continued to follow the patterns described above. The commercialization of agriculture continued to expand under the influence of increased market opportunities and growing pressure for tax revenue from China's numerous warlord governments. The impact on the economy of foreign trade and treaty ports was also largely in the commercial realm. Although the example of mechanized industry from Western plants stimulated similar efforts by Chinese, problems of undercapitalization and institutional fragmentation meant that most Chinese plants continued to be small and financially insecure. As Hou Chiming has demonstrated, foreign investment in China, too, was largely in trade and contributed little to the development of basic infrastructures for industrial growth. The government's role in this regard was limited as well. Years of warfare, both domestic and foreign, provided neither the atmosphere of political stability nor the opportunity for capital accumulation that a national program of industrialization would have required.

The role of the state in economic development in prerevolutionary China could not have been anything but small. Neither the Qing nor any of its successors in the early twentieth century exercised sufficient control over revenues or human resources to make more than token efforts at state-sponsored economic reform. Where its influence was felt, it was largely negative: in the form of state efforts to collect funds to pay off foreign indemnities and loans and to fund military expansion, in the form of state borrowing and control of the banking industry that stifled private investment, and in the use of inflationary policies as a substitute for genuine income generation. Thus, the ability of the Chinese economy to grow and to meet the consumption needs of a rapidly increasing population must be credited entirely to the resilience and ingenuity of the millions of individuals who manned the private sector.

This pattern was to change with the victory of the Communists in 1949. With the introduction of a planned economy, the state became the key factor in investment, and small-scale, fragmented management gave way to vertical and horizontal integration on a national scale. China's new-found political isolation marked the end of foreign trade as an important element in economic growth. Government policies, such as the compulsory procurement of raw materials and the closure of rural markets, gradually destroyed the handicraft and small-factory production that had been the foundation of the prerevolutionary economy. Although government attitudes toward agricultural sidelines, rural industrialization, and free markets have vacillated over the years, until recently the overall emphasis on state planning and large-scale, urban-centered industrial development has remained intact. Its record in bringing about the one indicator of modernization, sustained rising real incomes, has been poor. At the same time, such policies as those that discouraged birth control and encouraged the irrational expansion of grain crops have greatly accelerated China's population explosion, damaged its productive capacity, and exacerbated basic structural obstacles to balanced industrial growth.

Such comparisons may lead to the false impression that no links exist between the economy of the late imperial period and that of the present Chinese state. Although the state's capacity to intervene directly in the economy has clearly grown during the past forty years, however, it shares with traditional governments certain assumptions that influence both policy and the analysis of how the economy has performed.

Most important is the notion of the state as the protector of the people's livelihood. This is most apparent in the area of food supply. Grain paternalism is a fundamental principle of Chinese statecraft. In the early eighteenth century China had barely recovered from the demographic disaster of the Ming-Qing transition. Yet fears of grain shortages aroused excitement sufficient to block several efforts at fiscal reform and to inspire the aging Kangxi emperor to freeze the head tax at existing levels. The issue of food production has remained an important political tool in the paternalistic Chinese state. In both imperial and modern times, the creation of a sense of crisis in grain output was useful for proponents of conservative economic and social policies. During imperial times the state was seen as having a responsibility to redress, at least in part, the imbalances of output among the provinces. This was accomplished by means of differential taxation, transfers of tax grain and revenue to poorer provinces, and, in times of grain shortage, a variety of policies ranging from direct grain transfers to the encouragement of commercial shipment to deficit areas. At the same time, the state's obsession with grain self-sufficiency resulted in periodic—albeit weakly enforced—bans on grain exports and the production of commercial crops and the victory of those who sought opportunities to profit from the clearance of China's highlands and mountain forests.

The People's Republic has inherited the tradition of grain paternalism. However, its greater ability to influence production—albeit not always in the manner intended—through price fixing and procurement policies has increased even further the influence of politics on cereal output and the usefulness of cereal output to politicians. The environmental consequences of "taking grain as the key link" have been well documented. As Bernstein and others have shown, the famines of the early 1960s were a result of government policies that promoted hoarding and discouraged peasant production. For much of the 1980s the gradual introduction of market incentives seemed to promise a reversal of this trend, and for a brief period China was even exporting grain. Yet the use of grain ration coupons has persisted as both a symbolic and practical tool of social control and a reminder of the importance of the state in assuring food supplies. At the same time, the traditional belief in the responsibility of the state to equalize the distribution of grain has contributed to the polarization between proponents of balanced development and those who see practical advantages in developing the advanced regions first. Finally, during the past two years, the failure of the government to cope with anomalies in the price structure may have resulted in real, though arguably avoidable, shortages. This, in turn, has provided ammunition for those suspicious of reform. Cries of a grain crisis were frequently heard in the months before the political crackdown of June 1989.

Ten years of reform have done much to improve the economic conditions of many of China's people, particularly in coastal regions and in rural areas with convenient links to urban centers. Reassessments of the overall situation during the past few years have revealed, however, contradictions familiar to students of earlier periods—between local and central, inland and coastal, rural and urban, state and private interests. The recent upsurge in small-scale entrepreneurship and the large part it has played in the expansion of China's GDP provides striking evidence of the reemergence of older patterns of economic interaction in response to structural givens that have not changed dramatically despite forty years of Communist rule. The fact that trading has returned as a major occupation of the self-employed adds to the impression that behind the modern industrial projects and joint ventures lies a household economy not dissimilar to that of the prerevolutionary past. Its persistence can be interpreted in many ways. In one sense it is the result of the entrepreneurship inherent in the Chinese family firm (and predictably was accompanied by serious resistance to efforts at population control). Where that entrepreneurship cannot be expressed by obtaining a job for one's children through *guanxi* or by virtue of one's own place within the state sector, it may be secured through the pooling of kinship resources in petty production and trade. It is also the product of a dense rural marketing network that has been allowed to reestablish itself in recent years. The regions that have been most successful in the establishment of small-scale and handicraft industries are, not surprisingly, the same towns whose geographic location and transportation endowment made them centers of trade in the late Qing.[115]

The rapid expansion of such activity has also been possible because it can fill a gap created by decades of repressed consumer demand. The slow growth that China can hope for in domestic purchasing power alone will be insufficient, however, to create the conditions for "modernization" in an economy as vast as China's. It is perhaps for this reason that some of China's leaders have been willing to concentrate on development in a few regions only. It is also for this reason that some economists have placed so much emphasis on the expansion of China's external markets. The result has been the creation of a dual economy. But the diffusion of capital and technology from the advanced to the small-scale sector and the development of small-scale enterprise that serves the advanced and export market have been far greater than in the days of the treaty ports. Perhaps the lesson of history will be that only a combination of both development strategies can serve the economic interests of a country as large, as populous, and as unamenable to centralized direction as China in the modern age.

Notes

1. In highlighting these underlying structures I have made no effort to provide coverage of, or indeed to introduce, much of the extremely interesting work that is now being done on the early Qing economy in China and the West. During the past few years a number of scholars have presented comprehensive summaries of the Chinese economy during the Qing period, which can be consulted by the interested reader. Among them are Albert Feuerwerker, Ramon Myers, and Lloyd Eastman.

2. Hwang Kuo-shu and Wang Yeh-chien. "The Secular Movement of Grain Prices in China, 1763–1910," *Academia Economic Papers* 9, 1 (March 1981): 1–27.

3. Dwight Perkins, *Agricultural Development in China, 1368–1968* (Chicago: Aldine, 1985), p. 37.

4. Chao Kang, *Man and Land in Chinese History, an Economic Analysis* (Stanford: Stanford University Press, 1986), p. 216.

5. See, for example, Gao Wangling, "Guanyu Qingdai Sichuan nongye fazhan" (On the development of agriculture in Qing Sichuan), *Pingzhun xuekan* 1 (1985): 123–37.

6. Gao Pu, "Qing haijiang hemian jianzhong shu" (A request to [encourage] the intercropping of cotton and cereal crops along the coast), *Huangchao jingshi wenbian, juan* 37.

7. Xu Dixin and Wu Chengming, *Zhongguo zibenzhuyi fazhanshi* (A history of the development of capitalism in China) (Beijing: Renmin chubanshe, 1985), pp. 202–3. Sichuan, Anhui, Hunan, and Zhejiang also produced considerable amounts of cotton during the early Qing.

8. Fang Xing, "Qingdai qianqi nongcun shichang de fazhan" (The development of agricultural village markets in the early Qing), *Lishi yanjiu* 6 (1987): 88–89.

9. See, for example, *Daqing shizong xianhuangdi shilu*, Yongzheng 5, 3, *gengyin* (reprint Taiwan, 1964). Hereafter YZ.

10. Wu Chengming, "Lun Qingdai qianqi woguo guonei shichang" (A discussion of our country's internal market during the early Qing period), *Lishi yanjiu* 1 (1983): 99. Wu takes a rather pessimistic view of the extent of commercialization in the late imperial period. He estimates that the long-distance trade in grain was only 21.6 percent of total grain marketed. Moreover, he sees this trade largely in terms of a redistribution between grain-surplus and grain-deficit regions, and not as the result of increased agricultural specialization or handicraft production (p. 103).

11. Their admittedly rough calculation takes note of the fact that the Republican figures include peanuts and soybeans, two crops whose commercial production was largely a twentieth-century phenomenon, and exclude the acreage in mulberry and tea. Xu and Wu, *Zhongguo zibenzhuyi fazhanshi*, p. 214.

12. Perkins, *Agricultural Development*, p. 115.

13. A new analysis of land concentration in the early twentieth century concludes that between 30 and 40 percent of Chinese peasants were landless; landlords and rich peasants owned 50–60 percent of the land, and middle and poor peasants owned the remaining 40–50 percent. Zhang Youyi, "Ben shiji ersanshinian woguo diquan fenpei de zai guji" (A reestimation of the distribution of land in the 1920s and 1930s), *Zhongguo shehui jingji shi yanjiu* 2 (1988): 7.

14. Chao, *Man and Land*, pp. 96–101, 115–28. See also Philip Huang, *The Peasant Economy and Social Change in North China* (Stanford: Stanford University Press, 1986), pp. 103–4.

15. Xu and Wu, *Zhongguo zibenzhuyi fazhanshi*, p. 200. Twentieth-century survey data confirm this pattern. The National Land Commission survey undertaken in the 1930s found the average holdings of landlords to be thirty-four mou, while a survey undertaken

by the Rural Reconstruction Commission noted the average size of landlord property in Jiangsu was fifty-seven mou. Both surveys indicate a tendency for landlords to farm the optimum acreage possible with family labor and to rent the remainder to tenants. Chao, *Man and Land*, pp. 127–28.

16. Xu and Wu, *Zhongguo zibenzhuyi fazhanshi*, p. 200.

17. For example, 48 percent of the managerial landlords in Jing Su and Luo Lun's study originally made their money in commerce or as officials. Jing Su and Luo Lun, *Landlord and Labor in Late Imperial China, Case Studies from Shandong*, trans. Endymion Wilkinson (Cambridge: Harvard University Council on East Asian Studies, 1978), pp. 229–39.

18. Large lineage holdings in the Pearl River Delta region are well known to scholars. Salt merchants' lineages in southern Sichuan accumulated lands throughout the Upper Yangzi region, some of it planted in broad beans and used to feed the large buffalo herds they maintained to pump their brine wells. See Madeleine Zelin, "The Rise and Fall of the Fu-Rong Salt-Yard Elite: Merchant Dominance in Late Qing China," in *Chinese Local Elites*, ed. Joseph Esherick and Mary Backus Rankin (Berkeley: University of California Press, 1990), and Ruby Watson, "Corporate Property and Local Leadership in the Pearl River Delta: 1898–1941," in ibid.

19. Kubota Bunji, "Sinmatsu shiren no daidenko" (Large tenants in late-Qing Sichuan) in *Kindai chugoku noson shakaishi kenkyu*, ed. Tokyo Kyoiku Daigaku Toyoshi Kenkyushitsu (Tokyo: Taian, 1967), pp. 280–81.

20. Robert Eng, "Institutional and Secondary Landlordism in the Pearl River Delta, 1600–1949," *Modern China* 12, 1 (January 1986): 9, 19–24.

21. For general accounts of tenurial relations in the Qing, see studies by Dwight Perkins, Madeleine Zelin, Philip Huang, and Evelyn Rawski, to name a few.

22. Few scholars argue that peasants existed in a state of personal bondage by the Qing period. Indeed, manorialism does not appear to have been the dominant form of agricultural organization even in the Song. See Joseph McDermott, "Charting Blank Spaces and Disputed Regions: The Problem of Sung Land Tenure," *Journal of Asian Studies* 44, 1 (November 1984):13–41. The few examples of managerial landlordism, that is, farming large estates with hired labor, that exist for the Qing are in North China. Philip Huang's detailed examination of managerial farms in the twentieth century concludes that "the managerial mode tended to work best at the scale of 100–200 mou" and that managerial farms showed no pattern of higher productivity than small family farms. Huang, *The Peasant Economy*, p. 169. Chao Kang argues that the small family farms of the Qing period are a retreat from the managerial mode of earlier periods. His analysis, which is not widely accepted, is based on the belief that by the late Ming, the marginal product of labor of Chinese peasants had declined below subsistence, making the use of hired labor uneconomical. Chao, *Man and Land*, pp. 10–12.

23. Susan Greenhalgh, "Family Entrepreneurialism and Economic Development in Taiwan and the People's Republic of China," paper presented to the Annual Meeting of the Anthropological Association of America, Phoenix, November 1988, pp. 6–7.

24. Indeed, Huang has argued convincingly that in twentieth-century Shandong, the smaller the farm, the higher the percentage of its land was devoted to cash crops. Only in this way could one hope to earn sufficient income to live on such a small acreage. Decisions like this held great risks of crop failure, however, leaving the family without income or food crops. Huang, *The Peasant Economy*, pp. 120, 185–201. Not surprisingly, Myers, using the same sources, finds that poorer farmers earned a larger share of their income from nonfarm sources. Ramon Myers in *Cambridge History of China*, ed. John K. Fairbank (London: Cambridge University Press, 1986), 13:255.

25. See Madeleine Zelin, "Government Policy toward Reclamation and Hidden Land

during the Yongzheng Reign,'' ms.

26. Anne Osborne, ''Barren Mountains, Raging Rivers: The Ecological Effects of Changing Landuse on the Lower Yangzi Periphery in Late Imperial China,'' Ph.D dissertation, Colombia University, 1989, p. 158. Maize was particularly well suited to the needs of highland development because of its low labor requirements and its great flexibility as a crop. As Osborne points out (pp. 164–65), it could be planted early or late and needed almost no care until harvested. Even if left on the stalk after ripening, it would not be threatened by severe weather as would other dryland grains.

27. S. T. Leong, ''The P'eng-Min: The Ch'ing Administration and Internal Migration,'' paper presented at the Fifth National Conference of the Asian Studies Association of Australia, Adelaide, May 18, 1984, pp. 4–5. Leong found that ''internal migration as an organized business venture involving a large capital outlay was most common in the highlands of the northern Southeast Coast and of the Lower Yangzi, two of the most commercialized regions, and less so in the Gan Yangzi.'' The development of the upper Han basin of the Middle Yangzi could be accounted for by its rich timber, iron, and other resources.

28. Osborne, ''Barren Mountains, Raging Rivers,'' p. 204.

29. See Fu Yiling, *Ming Qing shehui jingji shi lunwenji* (Collected essays on the socioeconomic history of the Ming and Qing) (Beijing: Renmin chubanshe, 1982), pp. 158–75. This article is based largely on Yan Ruyi's *Sansheng bianfang beilan* and reflects conditions by the early nineteenth century.

30. Yan Ruyi, 9, *shanhuo.*

31. Eng, ''Institutional and Secondary Landlordism,'' p. 19.

32. Robert Gardella, ''The Antebellum Canton Tea Trade: Recent Perspectives,'' *The American Neptune* 48, 4 (Fall 1988): 269.

33. Fu, *Ming Qing shehui jingji shi lunwenji*, pp. 171–72. The government played a small role in expanding grain production through direct investment in grain plantations, largely oriented toward feeding the military. In areas like Jingni, Zhijin, Anxi, and Liuhou, large-scale colony farms were opened utilizing hired labor instead of the traditional allocation of farms to individual tenants. Farm workers were recruited from among Han Chinese migrants, Gansu natives, and from nearby aborigine tribes. Terms of employment were quite good by contemporary standards. Permanent workers were paid two taels a month, in addition to a daily ration of 1.666 pints (*sheng*) of grain per day. Travel expenses were provided for workers brought in from the outside, and all the necessary seed and farming equipment used on the farms were provided by the government. *Gongzhongdang*, Kong Yuqiong, YZ 10,7,23. Within China proper, several areas saw government sponsorship of the transformation of pasture to the cultivation of cereal crops. *Gongzhongdang*, Yungui Governor General Gao Qizhuo, YZ 2,4,19; *Gongzhongdang*, Li Rubai, YZ 5,12,9; *Gongzhongdang*, Shan Wenxiu, YZ 6,7,19. At least part of these lands were drained and irrigation facilities provided at government expense.

34. For example, while the Suzhou-Songjiang region remained the main cotton textile production center for the national market, smaller textile manufacturers in Zhili's Shen independent prefecture and Leting, Yuanshi, and Nangong xian: Shandong's Licheng and Putai xian: Henan's Mengxian and Zhengyang xian: Hubei's Hanyang and De'an: and parts of Sichuan relied for their long-distance trade almost entirely on Manchuria and the northwestern and southwestern frontier. Xu and Wu, *Zhongguo zibenzhuyi fazhanshi*, pp. 280–82.

35. See Zelin, ''Government Policy toward Reclamation,'' for a discussion of hidden land in western China.

36. Hwang and Wang, ''The Secular Movement of Grain Prices,'' p. 18, notes estimates that between sixteen and twenty-seven million *shi* of rice a year were shipped down

the Yangzi during the early eighteenth century, rising to between thirty and forty million in the early nineteenth. A substantial portion of this rice was produced in Sichuan.

37. We do not have the price of maize for the Sichuan prefectures bordering on Shaanxi and Hubei. However, rice, barley, and wheat prices remained relatively stable until the 1820s, when they began to rise. They almost doubled between the 1820s and the 1860s. *Gongzhong zhupi zouzhe*, Yuxue liangjia, Sichuan.

38. Yan Ruyi, 9, *shanhuo*.

39. Fang, "Qingdai qianqi nongcun," p. 85.

40. Chao, *Man and Land*, pp. 49–63, provides a good summary of this literature. He calculates the rate of urbanization in the Song at about 20 percent as compared to about 7 percent in 1820. These figures, of course, mask large regional differences.

41. Perdue has strengthened his price analysis approach with evidence that the Qing government was able to purchase, at Gansu markets, 80 percent of the grain supplies it needed to conduct the northwestern military campaigns of the mid-eighteenth century. Peter Perdue, "The West Route Army and the Silk Road: Grain Supply and Qianlong's Military Campaigns in Northwest China (1755–1760)," ms.

42. See, for example, Fang, "Qingdai qianqi nongcun"; Fan Shuzhi, "SuSong mianbuye shizhen de shengshuai" (The rise and fall of the Suzhou and Songjiang cotton cloth towns), *Zhongguo jingjishi yanjiu* 4 (1987): 57–72; and Gao Wangling, "Qian-Jia shiqi Sichuan de changshi, changshigang jiqi gongneng" (Sichuan markets, marketing networks, and their function during the Qianlong and Jiaqing periods), *Qingshi yanjiuji* 3 (1984): 74–92.

43. Mark Elvin, *The Pattern of the Chinese Past* (London: Eyre Methuen, 1973), p. 270.

44. Wu, "Lun Qingdai qianqi woguo guonei shichang," p. 99.

45. Myron Cohen, "The Role of Contract in Traditional Chinese Social Organization," *VIIIth Congress of Anthropological and Ethnological Sciences*, p. 132.

46. Ramon Myers and Fu-Mei Chan Chen, "Customary Law and the Economic Growth of China during the Ch'ing Period," *Ch'ing-shih wen-t'i* 3, 5 (November 1976): 1–32.

47. For a discussion of the use of written agreements of partnership in the formation of capital in the early Qing, see Madeleine Zelin, "Capital Accumulation and Investment Strategies in Early Modern China: The Case of the Furong Salt Yard," *Late Imperial China* 9, 1 (June 1988): 79–122.

48. Cohen, "The Role of Contract," p. 132.

49. Shu Wencheng et al., "Ziliujing shaoyangongren di hanghui zuzhi—Yandigong" (The guild organization of the Ziliujing salt evaporators—the Yandigong), *Zigong wenshi ziliao xuanji* 12 (1981): 36.

50. Richard Lufrano, "Manuals and Petitions: Commercial Problem Solving in Late Imperial China," Ph.D. dissertation, Columbia University, 1987.

51. See Zelin, "Capital Accumulation," and Madeleine Zelin, "Obstacles to Economic Development: The Mining Industry in Late Imperial Sichuan," paper presented at the Annual Convention of the American Historical Association, New York, December 28, 1985.

52. For a lengthy discussion of the role of lineage estates in the incorporation of business holdings, see Zelin, "The Rise and Fall of the Fu-Rong Salt-Yard Elite."

53. Eng, "Institutional and Secondary Landlordism," p. 31.

54. See Hao Yen-p'ing, *The Commercial Revolution in Nineteenth Century China: The Rise of Sino-Western Mercantile Capitalism* (Berkeley: University of California Press, 1986); Robert Gardella, "The Antebellum Canton Tea Trade" (1988); and Robert Gardella, "Squaring Accounts: Bookkeeping Methods, Accountability and Capitalist Rationalism in Late Qing and Republican China," ms.

55. Lillian M. Li, *China's Silk Trade: Traditional Industry in the Modern World 1842–1937* (Cambridge: Harvard University Council on East Asian Studies, 1981), pp. 48–49.

56. Xu and Wu, *Zhongguo zibenzhuyi fazhanshi,* pp. 329–62, provide an excellent summary of the main areas of specialization in these products, as well as some of the advances in the use of hired labor in the handicraft industry during the Qing.

57. Craig Deitrich, "Cotton Culture and Manufacture in Early Ch'ing China," in *Economic Organization in Chinese Society*, ed. W. E. Willmott (Stanford: Stanford University Press, 1972), p. 111. Deitrich recognizes that this may mask some specialization within each xian, but he feels that most production was still based on the family unit.

58. E-Tu Zen Sun, "Sericulture and Silk Textile Production in Ch'ing China," in ibid., p. 82.

59. Peng Ziyi, "Qingqianqi nongfu fangzhi shougongye" (The early Qing peasant handicraft industry), *Zhongguo jingjishi yanjiu* 4 (1987): 54.

60. For examples see Fang, "Qingdai qianqi nongcun," pp. 89–91.

61. *Xianfeng nanxun xianzhi*, 21, cited in ibid., p. 92.

62. Susan Mann Jones, "Finance in Ningpo: The 'Ch'ien Chuang,' 1750–1880," in *Economic Organization in Chinese Society*, ed. Willmott, p. 69.

63. Gardella, "The Antebellum Canton Tea Trade," p. 269. This practice predated the expansion of overseas trade in tea.

64. Jones, "Finance in Ningpo," p. 63.

65. Cited in T. S. Whelan, *The Pawnshop in China* (Ann Arbor: University of Michigan Center for Chinese Studies, 1979), p. 10.

66. *Yongzheng zhupi yuzhi*, cited in Fang, "Qingdai qianqi nongcun," p. 92.

67. *Qianlong Wujing zhenzhi*, 21, cited in ibid. Seasonal fluctuations in rice prices and the fixed interest rates allowed pawnshops by the government made them useful to speculators in rice. Yang Lien-sheng notes that a person with capital could buy rice for one thousand taels, pawn it for seven or eight hundred, use the money to buy more rice, pawn it, and so on. Later in the year, when the interest was paid, all the rice was redeemed, and it was sold at higher prices, such high profits could be made that the government barred the extension of credit secured by grain to small amounts. Cited in Whelan, *The Pawnshop*, p. 11.

68. *Jiaqing Yudi xianzhi*, 21, cited in Fang, "Qingdai qianqi nongcun," p. 95.

69. Peng, "Qingqianqi nongfu fangzhi shougongye," p. 45. The Qing government played an important role in supporting the pawnshop industry. From the early eighteenth century it deposited large amounts of government funds with them, the interest from which supported famine relief, relief for bannermen, and other state welfare services. The withdrawal of these funds in the nineteenth century, growing competition from *qianzhuang* and Shanxi banks, rural political instability, and "frequent inflation and rural currency devaluation" led to a sharp decline in pawnshop numbers, particularly in rural areas. Whelan, *The Pawnshop*, pp. 11–12, notes that in the 1930s there were only 4,500 pawnshops in China. Moreover, the pawnbroking agencies that largely took their place in rural areas charged much higher interest than their Qing counterparts. What effect this had on peasant livelihood and handicraft industry has never been explored.

70. Whelan, *The Pawnshop*, p. 34.

71. Sun, "Sericulture," pp. 95–96.

72. Dietrich, "Cotton Culture," p. 131.

73. Mark Elvin, "The High-Level Equilibrium Trap: The Causes of the Decline in Invention in the Traditional Chinese Textile Industries," in *Economic Organization in Chinese Society*, ed. Willmott, p. 157. Again, the most notable exception is well salt, produced in Fushun and Rongxian, Sichuan.

74. Huang, *The Peasant Economy*, pp. 191–95.

75. See Carl Riskin, "Surplus and Stagnation in Modern China" in *China's Modern Economy in Historical Perspective*, ed. Dwight Perkins (Stanford: Stanford University Press, 1975), pp. 49–84.

76. Indeed, Thomas Rawski has argued on many occasions that even taking into account the element of corruption, the Qing state never commandeered more than 5 percent of GNP.

77. Hong Xiaguan, "Cong jiedai ziben de xingqi kan Zhongguo zichan jieji de xingcheng ji qi wanzheng xingtai" (The rise of loan capital and the formation and development of the Chinese bourgeosie), *Zhongguo shehui jingji shi yanjiu* 3 (1984): 14, citing an issue of *Shenbao*, dated 1884.

78. Zhang Guohui, "Qingdai qianqi de qianzhuang he piaohao" (Qianzhuang and *piaohao* in the early Qing), *Zhongguo jingji shi yanjiu* 4 (1987): 77–80.

79. Andrea Lee McElderry, *Shanghai Old-Style Banks (Ch'ien-chuang), 1800–1935* (Ann Arbor: University of Michigan Center for Chinese Studies, 1976), pp. 83–90.

80. This discussion is based on my "Obstacles to Economic Development."

81. Baxian 6.6.38818.

82. Deng Tuo, *Lun Zhongguo lishi di jige wenti* (On several questions in Chinese history) (Beijing: Sanlian shudian, 1979), p. 221.

83. Chen Shishun claimed that after he joined with Long Zhangshun and Wu Baiyuan to open a coal mine at Lijia gou, it was agreed that each partner would contribute thirty-six strings of cash each year for operating expenses. Baxian 6.5.4454, dated Tongzhi 5. At the Paotai hou mine established on Linrong shan during the Guangxu period, eight partners shared seventeen of the mine's twenty shares. The profits accruing to the remaining three shares were set aside for the operation of the mine. Baxian 6.6.38818. In the third case, the two partners agreed that if they ran short of funds they would borrow in the name of the partnership. Baxian 6.6.38884.

84. See, for example, Baxian 6.2.7110, 6.2.3721, 6.5.14449, 6.6.38884.

85. See, for example, Baxian 6.5.14456.

86. Wei Qingyuan and Lu Su, "Qingdai qianqi de shangban kuangye he zibenzhuyi mengya" (Early Qing merchant-operated mines and the sprouts of capitalism) (Beijing: Renmin daxue, 1981), pp. 42, 44.

87. Zelin, "Capital Accumulation," pp. 110–11.

88. See, for example, Baxian 6.2.7098 and Baxian 6.2.7102. Both cases date from the early nineteenth century.

89. Robert Eng, *Economic Imperialism in China, Silk Production and Exports, 1861–1932* (Berkeley: University of California Center for Chinese Studies, 1986), p. 71. A similar system existed among Wuxi silk filatures. See Lynda Bell, "From Comprador to County Magnate: Bourgeois Practice in the Wuxi County Silk Industry," paper prepared for the Conference on Chinese Local Elites and Patterns of Dominance, Banff, August 20–24, 1987, p. 30.

90. Robert Gardella, "Peasant Plots and Plantations: Structural Factors in Late Nineteenth Century Competition in the World Tea Trade," paper presented at the AHA Annual Meeting, New York, December 28, 1985, pp. 6–7. According to Gardella, owner-cultivators rarely grew tea on more than 50 percent of their holdings, treating tea culture as a by-employment of crop farming.

91. Ibid., pp. 4, 8.

92. Zelin, "Obstacles to Economic Development," pp. 21–24.

93. Elvin, "The High-Level Equilibrium Trap," p. 165.

94. Gardella, "Peasant Plots and Plantations," p. 8.

95. Chao Kang, *The Development of Cotton Textile Production in China* (Cambridge:

Harvard University East Asian Research Center, 1977), pp. 174–77. Of course, this flexibility was removed when peasants went into debt to large companies for their start-up costs or became bound through exclusive credit and marketing arrangements to large brokerage houses. This, however, tended to occur more in the twentieth century than in the period preceding the Opium War.

96. Fan, "SuSong mianbuye shizhen de shengshuai," p. 71.

97. Gardella, "Peasant Plots and Plantations," p. 8.

98. Zelin, "Obstacles to Economic Development," p. 27.

99. Elvin, "The High-Level Equilibrium Trap," p. 162, makes this point and notes that this also protected merchants from embezzlement by spinners.

100. Ibid., pp. 152–53.

101. For a discussion of the impact of the Taiping on the opening of the Huguang market to Sichuan salt, see Zelin, "Capital Accumulation." William Rowe discusses the destruction of trade guild monopolies in Hankow at this time, but it is not clear that this gave rise to any change in the structure of production in the Middle Yangzi region.

102. Xu and Wu, *Zhongguo zibenzhuyi fazhanshi*, pp. 195–96. An excellent example was Zhang Luxiang's Bunongshu, which says "planting more is not as good as planting a small area well."

103. Peng, "Qingqianqi nongfu fangzhi shougongye," pp. 3–46; Sun, "Sericulture," pp. 82–83.

104. In fact, the relationship between the state and private sector, as between the state center and local government, was more complex than indicated here. Of particular interest is the alternation between attempts to control local fiscal policy and the recognition that local conditions necessitated flexible regulation from below. For a highly provocative examination of the implications of this issue today, see Vivienne Shue, *The Reach of the State, Sketches of the Chinese Body Politic* (Stanford: Stanford University Press, 1988).

105. For an excellent discussion of self-regulation of the commercial economy, see Susan Mann, *Local Merchants and the Chinese Bureaucracy, 1750–1950* (Stanford: Stanford University Press, 1987).

106. For example, peddlers carrying less than 40 *jin* of salt in Sichuan did not require salt certificates. Native customs officials in some areas often let small peddlers pass if the amount of cloth or rice they carried did not equal the minimum tax standard. This is in sharp contrast to Dorothy Solinger's findings that state marketing establishments in the People's Republic routinely denied goods to petty traders.

107. Eng, *Economic Imperialism*, pp. 8–9; *Gongzhongdang*, Oertai, YZ 8,1,13; *Gongzhongdang*, Honan Governor Tian Wenjing, YZ 3,9,11.

108. One example of this fragmentation was the establishment of a Guangdong copper button guild, which fought vigorously throughout the nineteenth century to prevent other merchants from selling similar wares in Chongqing. See Baxian 6.3.10601.

109. For a discussion of the evolution of these policies see Madeleine Zelin, *The Magistrate's Tael: Rationalizing Fiscal Reform in Eighteenth Century China* (Berkeley: University of California Press, 1984).

110. Perkins, *Agricultural Development*; Albert Feuerwerker, "Qing Economic History and World Economic History," paper prepared for the Symposium on the Occasion of the 60th Anniversary of the Founding of the First Historical Archives in China, Beijing, October 7–10, 1985, pp. 12, 15–17.

111. Francesca Bray, *The Rice Economies: Technology and Development in Asian Societies* (New York: Blackwell, 1986), p. 565, notes that even before the spread of rice culture in China, its dry-cereal technology was at a level of sophistication that was unique in the premodern world.

112. As Elvin put it, when demand was high, more peasant labor was drawn into

handicraft production by the higher price their labor could command there than in agriculture. When demand fell, they could divert their labor elsewhere. And since only part of their labor was in any one activity, family income would not be too adversely affected. Because of this flexibility, however, there were no great rewards for inventors of more efficient production technologies. Likewise, there were few penalties in times of poor markets to drive inefficient producers permanently out of business. See Elvin, "The High-Level Equilibrium Trap," p. 162.

113. This argument is also developed in ibid. Chao Kang turns the argument around and says that the fact that peasants in the late imperial period were willing to work for below subsistence wages stifled the development of factory production, even when modern machine methods could be imported and used to raise worker productivity beyond that of peasant producers. Chao, *Man and Land*, pp. 17–19.

114. For example, in mining, in tea plantations, and in the case of the Shanxi-Shaanxi merchants, in Sichuan well salt.

115. One of the most striking success stories has been Wuxi, a major handicraft textile center in the late imperial period. Zigong, in Sichuan, the center of the well-salt industry during the Qing period, has not lacked for entrepreneurship on the part of its people. As its mayor indicated in an interview in May 1989, however, transportation has been a major obstacle to the development of export-oriented industrial projects. Instead, the city has concentrated on industries serving the local market and has tried to capitalize on its fame as a cultural center, in the hope that "consumers" will come to it.

3

MODELS OF HISTORICAL CHANGE
The Chinese State and Society, 1839–1989

FREDERIC WAKEMAN, JR.

> Since the Confucian scholars were constantly proclaiming how the autocrat must rule by benevolence, cultural ritual, and proper decorum, we have been less aware that the autocrat ruled also and more fundamentally by terror and intimidation. . . . Killing had always been the ruler's special recourse to keep the system's many channels working by cleansing them of obstructive persons. Terror could be a lubricant, so to speak, whereas trying to rule by force alone would be fatal and would lose heaven's mandate to rule.
>
> —John K. Fairbank, "Why China's Rulers Fear Democracy"

Rather than attempt to provide a seamless synopsis of the evolution of state-society relationships in China during the last 150 years, this essay will use some of the historiographical models prevalent since 1949 in Western writings on China to analyze changes both in our perception of the modern Chinese revolution and in that process itself.[1] Four sets of patterns will be explored: the development under conditions of oriental despotism of regionalism in the nineteenth century and its evolution into modern warlordism; the restoration of Confucian governance in the Tongzhi period and its reappearance under the Nationalists; the competition between local elites and the state from the late Qing to the early 1950s; and the growing intrusion of state power into societal processes throughout the entire period. The relevance of these historical models, and especially of the fourth set of observations, to the development of the Chinese state's system of social control will be tested by tracing the formation of modern police forces during the twentieth century.

Regionalism/Warlordism/Despotism

Each of these four models locates the beginnings of fundamental change in state-society relations in the period just after the Opium War of 1839–42, when the Taiping Rebellion began to ferment in southern China and then roil up through the Xiang River system to central China in the 1850s. The parallels between this period of peasant rebellion and regional militarism and China a century later first caught the eye of George Taylor in the 1930s, when he was writing about contemporary military conflicts in North China. His work on Qing responses to the Taipings later strongly influenced the group of historians working at the University of Washington in the 1950s and 1960s.[2]

The Modern Chinese History Project carried on by the Far Eastern and Russian Institute of the University of Washington involved an exceptionally coherent group of collaborators. Though the responsibility for each study rested with the author, the projects were advertised as cooperative efforts, and—at least to outsiders—the various conceptual elements of their dominant regionalism model seemed to fit closely together.

Karl August Wittfogel's "oriental despotism" appeared to loom behind the entire structure, one imperial dynast after another participating in a steady growth toward greater and greater autocracy, exacerbated by "conquest dynasties" like the Liao and Yuan but continued by native régimes like the Ming as well.[3] The gentry were no more than a creation of the state, though they did exercise a certain balancing effect thanks to their Confucian pretensions at moral criticism of the throne.[4] Yet they were still essentially an appendage of the monarchy: their lives were dominated by civil service examinations, and their livelihoods were mainly derived from incomes as scholar-officials rather than from more independent sources such as landed rents and fees.[5] Their conquerors, the Manchus, while outsiders from beyond the wall, were aroused into founding the Qing only after being exposed to Chinese political institutions through the Ming frontier banner system.[6]

This essentially changeless history—repetitively nonhistorical by Hegelian standards—was altered by the appearance of the West in 1839. The social and economic consequences of the Opium War, along with the admixture of Chinese millenarian and Christian chiliastic ideologies, produced the Taiping rebels.[7]

The Taiping Heavenly Kingdom in turn represented an entirely novel challenge to the self-maintaining system of Sino-barbarian imperial despotism, and the result was the beginning of a major structural breakdown.[8] The elaborate system of Qing administration, including the "law of avoidance," which prevented officials from serving in their own provinces, was set aside during the emergency. "Militia ministers" (*tuanlian dachen*) like Zeng Guofan were allowed to establish regional armies while acquiring unprecedented control over provincial financial resources they would normally never have been allowed to touch.[9] Protégés of theirs like Li Hongzhang and Zuo Zongtang were able to tap new and more transferable sources of revenue like the Shanghai maritime customs fund or the Shanxi bankers' deposits in order to recruit, train, and equip armies that answered really only to them—provided they remained loyal to the dynasty proper.[10] And members of their secretariats in turn, like Yuan Shikai, were able to go on and create a separate military elite, trained in modern academies, that would constitute the nucleus of the Beiyang warlords in the early years of the twentieth century.

The general drift of this historiographical argument, then, was that the Qing dynasty's response to the challenge of the Taipings had been to permit the rise of regional armies in the 1860s. Though some were disbanded, these military forces—and especially that of Li Hongzhang—remained intact enough during the period of conflict with the West and Japan after the Tianjin Massacre of 1870 to engender and then nurture the Beiyang militarists of the early 1900s. Regionalism spawned warlordism, in other words, and that was the main reason for the fall of the Qing dynasty and ultimately of the imperial system itself.

And of course with the imperial system fell also the traditional Chinese gentry. This disappearance of the last possible counterbalance to the power of the state meant that when central political authority was finally restored through the victory of the Communists, there was absolutely nothing to prevent a Chinese Stalin from appearing in the form of Mao Zedong. Oriental despotism—as unchanging in its ultimate form in China as in Russia—triumphed in 1949, and only a new external challenge, allied with those Chinese forces that could be deemed "free," would put an end to its tyranny.

Confucian Restorations

The Regionalism-Warlordism-Despotism model—at least insofar as it is rendered simplistically above—is too pat. Any single scholar quoted as part of the whole would characterize the entirety as a caricature of his own work. Yet even when considered in all of its various complexities, the regionalism thesis is not nearly as suggestive as the structure of Mary Clabaugh Wright's successive Confucian restorations.

It all began readily enough within the context of the "impact-and-response" learning that Wright acquired in Fairbank's famous seminar at Harvard after the Pacific War. And here too the point of inception was the Opium War and the Taiping Rebellion. The latter was both a familiar phenomenon (An Lushan and Hong Xiuquan were not that far apart, after all) and a novel enough occurrence (Liang Afa's Christian tract was in the end sufficient ideological challenge to inspire a cultural transvaluation) to permit Wright to view the Qing counterinsurgency as both a familiar "restoration" in Tang terms and a new response in Confucian terms. The result was her famous work on the "Tongzhi Restoration," which argued that self-strengtheners like Zeng Guofan were inspired by cultural loyalism to revive the dynasty, and guided by political realism to defend the régime's sovereign interests. They created their own regional bureaucracies, to be sure, but in the end their Confucian conservatism kept them committed to the existing state structure.[11]

There were two consequences to this close identification of the polity with culture. The first was the association of the Sino-Manchu monarchy's very raison d'être with defense of tradition as a whole. This seemed at first a strength, but in the end it turned out to be a fatal weakness. When the imperial state fell, conventional Confucian culture fell with it. Joseph R. Levenson introduced his own Nietzchean variant to this theme: healthy organisms are those that contain a creative tension among their warring parts. The Chinese state had survived for so long after the demise of the medieval aristocracy described by Naito Konan—Levenson believed—precisely because there was a vital tension between the emperor and his scholar-officials.[12] The Taiping emperor's Christian-influenced notion of a transcendental heavenly mandate represented such a fundamental challenge to Confucian ideas of immanent monarchical authority that it threw the Qing emperor and his ministers together in mutual self-defense. Once the gentry found itself in the arms of a monarchy committed to the ironclad defense of traditional values, this critical elite lost all latitude for syncretic adoptions of Western learning. After the failure of the Hundred Days' Reform in 1898, the movement's leader, Kang Youwei, became a champion of the sequestered Guangxu emperor. Each compromised the other, and in the end revolutionaries took the high ground all for themselves.[13]

A second consequence of the identity of polity with culture meant that while the future of traditional culture was fatally compromised after 1911 by its association with the dying ancien régime, conservative political culture remained relatively robust. In her own writing, Mary Clabaugh Wright identified this "muscular Confucianism" in Zeng Guofan's ideology as being present also in the political philosophy of Chiang Kai-shek.[14] Many young political aspirants, including Mao Zedong, admired Zeng Guofan in the early years of the twentieth century. Wright, however, linked both Chiang's counterinsurgency tactics during the Communist suppression campaigns and elements of the New Life Movement in 1934 to Zeng Guofan's influence.[15] Nationalist conservatism was thereby seen as a throwback to Tongzhi restorationism and consequently deemed utterly anachronistic by Wright, who toward the end of her life increasingly identified all of modern Chinese history with a fundamental revolutionary surge that began around the turn of the century.[16]

Wright's preface to *Revolution in China* was written just at a time when Western Sinologists were becoming aware of the importance of the Cultural Revolution. Believing the Cultural Revolution somehow to be connected with the revolutionary movements of the early 1900s, Wright identified a set of new "forces" appearing in China then: women, youth, modern military troops, workers, and so forth. These were the real sources of revolution, not the overseas Chinese conspirators like Sun Yat-sen who only took judicious advantage of the opportunity these forces contributed for a coup de main. Wright's own introduction to, and many of the symposium essays in, *China in Revolution* seriously called into question the prevailing claims of official Nationalist and Communist historiography about Sun Yat-sen's crucial role as "father of the country" during the 1911 Revolution.[17]

Much less obvious at the time than this iconoclastic skepticism about Sun Yat-sen was a new theme of "gentry revolution" that appeared in the Wright volume. The theme was crudely suggested by analogies between the fall of the Manchus and earlier periods of dynastic decline when the scholar-official elite supposedly withdrew its support from the ruling régime.[18] To suggest that the 1911 Revolution was just another instance of the dynastic cycle did this argument no good in most historians' eyes. But there were so many signs of local elite involvement in the revolution—which was coming more and more to appear as a series of provincial secessions from the Center—that the "gentry" thesis imbedded in the Wright model eventually came to have a more lasting influence on later scholarship than either anti-Sun iconoclasm or the "new forces" theme.[19]

Local Elites

De Tocqueville's connection of social revolution with various forms of competition between ruling elites and the modern state has been a major rediscovery of American historical sociology during the past twenty-five years.[20] In Chinese studies this initially appeared to be an effort to combine elements of both those earlier models in research on Cantonese local history that emphasized the tension between prefecture- and county-level officials and the gentry during the Opium War period.[21] The anti-British militia movement of 1839–60 in the Pearl River region simultaneously dissolved this tension and stimulated a primitive class consciousness among poor peasants and across the usual kinship boundaries that had served lineage interests from Ming times on in the delta. But although the Red Turbans were defeated by Viceroy Ye Mingchen in the 1850s in Guangdong thanks to an alliance between the Qing government and powerful local gentry, the latter dominated the forces of order. That is to say, the competition between state and rural elites initially was won by the latter, who proceeded to monopolize local resources and usurp the state's police powers in postbellum Guangdong on an unprecedented scale.[22]

This may have been a useful insight at the time, but the Cantonese case was too limited in historical time and restricted in geographical space to allow historians to extend the model to the rest of China in a more significant sense. A much broader interpretation, arrived at quite independently, was that of Philip A. Kuhn, whose "militarization thesis" became the most frequently cited structural analysis of late Qing history. By closely examining the history of several of the gentry-led militia efforts during the Taiping period, Kuhn was able to show not only that local elites had won back the countryside from the rebels, who were mainly confined to the cities they had conquered in central China in the early and mid-1850s; but also that both sides, rebel and imperial, had experienced a parallel militarization from simple bands or single militia units at the bottom to multiplex regional armies at the top. Moreover, he demonstrated as well that this expansion of extrastate military power was part of a secular process of local informal elite administration that could be traced back to the late eighteenth century, when the formal bureaucratic mechanisms of the state proved insufficient to cope with China's growing population and expanding territory. The militarization of the nineteenth century, in short, was a manifestation of the critical competition between the state and local elites not just for existing resources, but also for new political resources created by demographic need and by foreign competition.[23]

The only obvious defect of Kuhn's analysis, for which he compensated in a second edition of his book, was neglect of ideology. This was amply balanced by its scope, which took in much of the early twentieth century too. In a later piece, Kuhn established the connection between local elite engrossment and the ideology of enlightened self-interest so central to the "statecraft" (*jingshi*) movement after the Opium War. The crucial link, which was provided by Feng Guifen, was the notion of gentry home rule or "local self-government" (*difang zizhi*). As Kuhn showed, this hearkened back to the seventeenth-century ideal of balancing the autocratic power of the "prefectural" (*junxian*) state with the "feudal" (*fengjian*) concerns of enlightened Confucian gentry looking after their own best interests. The local self-government movement that emerged during and after the reforms of the late nineteenth century, however, was neither entirely enlightened nor altogether self-interested. Because of that ambiguousness, which Kuhn detected early on, the phenomenon of local elite home rule has been identified in at least three different guises.[24]

Guises of Gentry Self-Government

The first guise, as suggested by Susan Mann, is benign and affirmative, evoking autonomous municipal government by a responsive set of local leaders seeking to create their own legitimate public sphere of political responsibility. This is the "gentry democracy" that Mark Elvin wrote about in describing the local elite management systems around Shanghai in the early years of this century.[25] Whether influenced by Western chambers of commerce in the treaty ports or appearing as an endogenous phenomenon in Chinese commercial entrepots such as Hankou, these new urban philanthrophies and voluntary associations were usually sponsored by local merchants and guildsmen, and in the aggregate they represented "a gradual popularization of political functions that paralleled (though it lagged behind) the privatization of economic power."[26] They also had rural connections, usually through post-Taiping tax collection agencies that tried to use the new likin revenues to sponsor local reconstruction projects. G. William Skinner notes that such local elite activities were often forbidden by local prefects and magistrates because they encroached upon official prerogatives, even though they represented a reasonably acceptable loyalty to one's native place. Moreover, many rural public service projects were financed in traditionally philanthropic ways by gentry families long known for their Buddhist charity work. Nevertheless, this phenomenon has been identified as a strikingly modern form of elite activism that accompanied the creation of a new sphere of voluntary public service.[27]

The second guise is far less positive, and more in keeping with the autocratic characteristics of the Oriental Despotism model than the putative civil society that some American historians believe was emerging in China toward the end of the nineteenth century. Muramatsu Yuji's masterful study of the Jiangnan bursaries suggested that the post-Taiping settlement in the Yangzi delta entailed a merging of public taxes and private rents so that landlords were able to use the police powers of the state to arrest truculent tenants and enforce their own rent-collection systems.[28] In this guise, local elites actually controlled district governments and eventually shut the central authorities completely out from access to revenue, on the one hand, while exploiting their dependents and subordinates, on the other.[29] At the lowest end of the interface between state and society, in other words, elite dominance weakened the polity and increased the likelihood of social revolution.[30]

In their third guise, local elites were cast as mobilizers of revolutionary movements against the state.[31] Leaders of provincial constitutionalists during the 1911 Revolution, urban reformers like Tan Yankai later sponsored young radicals led by Mao Zedong in a united front against the warlords and imperialists. During this stage of the Chinese revolution, the members of the urban elite and their populist supporters among intellectuals supported peasant movements against local landlords. As the appearance of unitary nationalism gave way to Marxist class struggle, however, the united front within the urban elite sundered. The urban reformers rejected appeals to support the rural poor, and a significant portion of the Communists turned its back upon the cities and took to the countryside. The process described by this third presentation of local elites as political mobilizers therefore followed fairly classic lines: once the social consequences of the revolutionary movement became clear to the privileged, the upper classes recoiled from their alliance with radical youth and betrayed the united front. The Communists, on the other hand, embraced China's rural dispossessed and so in the end triumphed.[32]

As long as the teleology of the Chinese revolution remained alive in the person of Mao Zedong, this third version—theories of peasant nationalism notwithstanding—of the role of local elites tended to prevail among younger Western social historians. And although there were early intimations of the toll inflicted by the Great Proletarian Cultural Revolution, populist sympathies for policies aimed at narrowing the distance between intellectuals and the rural masses also predominated. All of this changed rather rapidly after the death of the Chairman in 1976.

The Power of the Traditional State

Mao Zedong had told André Malraux that he stood "alone with the masses." Nothing was to come between the two entities, least of all a state and party bureaucracy the Chairman himself had helped create. In the aftermath of the Cultural Revolution, which ended decisively with Mao's death, it was not immediately evident that the instruments of the state had managed to entrench themselves so deeply once the initial attack on the "bourgeois headquarters" was thwarted. Rather, a perennial autocratic dream seemed to have been realized. In 1937 the progressive historian Wu Han had had Chiang Kai-shek in mind when he published his biography of the Ming founder, Zhu Yuanzhang. In 1967 the same barbed attack on Mao by historical analogy (*sheying lishi*) cost Wu Han his life. In both cases, nonetheless, the point was clear: China's greatest late imperial autocrat, Zhu Yuanzhang, had in the fourteenth century ruthlessly cleared away the tens of thousands of local elite families—hundreds of thousands of people—who stood between his person and the peasantry from which he had emerged during the plagues, famines, and military apocalypses of the mid-1300s.

Zhu Yuanzhang's image of his empire as a conglomerate of villages over which he alone reigned was one of the pinnacles of Chinese despotism: surely as monarchically egocentric as Qin Shi Huang's vision. But there was a singular and most important difference between the two ruthlessly determined autocrats. Qin Shi Huang's empire was a triumph of bureaucratic centralization at the expense of local customs, parochial privileges, and even native dialects. Zhu Yuanzhang's under-heaven was a much more limited despotism. The Ming ruler's ambition was boundless at a higher and more personal level, centered on his own person and the capital of the realm. When it came to locales, however, his reaction against direct government rule, especially in the lower Yangzi region where the local officials and great families had supported his archrival Zhang Shicheng, was so extreme that he preferred to rely upon informal agents of government even for the important function of tax collection and remission.[33]

The Ming founder's ideal form of local government, then, was a kind of self-administration in which local "tax chiefs" (*liangzhang*) would gratuitously look after tax collection and a few other crucial functions in exchange for direct personal audiences with the emperor and the right to display certain sumptuary privileges. Instead of relying on paid local agents like the Song, the Ming looked to self-supporting tax collectors, on the one hand, and relatively informal mechanisms of control, on the other. The rise of the examination gentry—who eventually were supposed to serve in their own way as informal control agents by transmitting normative "sacred edicts" to the rural population—eventually did in the "tax chiefs." The *liangzhang* were replaced by yamen clerks, lictors (*xunbu*), and runners (*buban*) who squeezed illegal salaries for themselves out of the tax receipts proper. Any effort by the central government to increase quotas only played into the hands of the yamen underlings, which was a crippling burden for the imperial state after the early 1500s. In retrospect, it even seems possible that the Ming dynasty could have survived the economic crisis of the seventeenth century had it been willing to hire more regularly paid personnel to extract a correspondingly greater amount of fiscal resources. Certainly, the agency costs would have been in the régime's favor.[34] But of course the Ming did not survive, though its fiscal system largely did.

The Qing dynasty fell heir to Zhu Yuanzhang's minimalist strategy of local governance.[35] The first two emperors made heroic efforts to gain access to eastern China's economic resources, stifling the prerogatives of the local gentry while encouraging land reclamation, conservancy repairs, famine relief, and tax reform.[36] These efforts largely succeeded, and the Qing state of Qianlong times was the strongest fiscal, military, and political régime in all of premodern Chinese history.[37] But there were few fundamental changes in the taxation system, with the Kangxi emperor freezing land-tax quotas in 1712, and with the Yongzheng emperor's fiscal reforms gradually undermined in the 1740s;[38] private engrossment disturbed the hydraulic system, literally clogging the waterways on which the empire depended for tribute and trade in the 1750s and 1760s;[39] and population growth put the kinds of strains on the state's political resources in the 1770s, 1780s, and 1790s that were earlier described in discussing Kuhn's militarization model.[40]

By the late Guangxu years, after the failure of the Hundred Days Reform in 1898, the accumulated insufficiencies of state power had crystallized into the frustration experienced by the throne—in this case, the Empress Dowager Zixi and her Manchu princely advisers—in failing to reach past provincial officialdom to engage directly with the empire's populace. Determined to bypass these intermediate bureaucratic layers, the monarchy decided to encourage new "pathways of words" to the throne by gingerly supporting a system of advisory councils at the district, prefecture, and province levels to "lend advice." These measures were taken after the dynasty had sent a mission abroad to investigate other monarchies' systems of government, and they represented a last-ditch effort to penetrate society and create a closer bond between the imperial center and the people. But whereas the impulse on the government's side was to integrate top with bottom in order to strengthen its rule, the understanding by local elites was that this would lead to a constitutional convention that would recognize their right to participate in more widely shared political rule. There was thus a basic misunderstanding over the issue of sovereignty—a misunderstanding that eventually led many constitutionalists to support the revolution in 1911.

There were thus two impelling visions about the relationship between state and society—both of which concepts were only recent neologisms in Chinese—

that were coming into conflict in the early years of the twentieth century. One was an *étatiste* drive toward not only recovery of the imperial state's control over its populace, but in addition a much more engaged connection between ruler and ruled. The second, equally fervid, was the desire of local elites to increase their own involvement in local government, whether at the district or provincial level. The struggle over the funding and management of railroads from 1903 to 1910 was precisely a case of these two impulses clashing together.[41] Indeed, one of the major causes of the Revolution of 1911 was the Qing state's dogged determination to assert centralized political authority over increasingly vociferous home-rule elements.[42]

The drive of national political leaders to extend state power down into Chinese society was not blunted by the fall of the dynasty.[43] As Yuan Shikai demonstrated in crushing the "Second Revolution" of 1913, and then in trying to re-create the monarchy, he was thoroughly determined to impose the capital's will upon the provinces.[44] By then, of course, the center could not hold, and Yuan died a comic and maligned figure. But the gradual intrusion of the state into subdistrict administration, tax collection, and law enforcement even at the village level created a new kind of "swing-man" in the form of rural headmen and other local powerbrokers.[45] To examine the connections between these early Republican manifestations of state power and the control systems deployed by the Chinese Communists after 1949, a closer look should be taken at the evolution of the modern Chinese police.

The Modern State and Social Control

One of the most obvious examples of the growth of state power in twentieth-century China was the development of a modern police system, beginning with the establishment by Hunan Governor Chen Baozhen of a special Guards Bureau (Baowei ju) in Changsha during the Hundred Days Reform in 1898.[46] Although the bureau was dissolved along with other local reform-movement institutions after Chen Baozhen was removed from office during the reaction against the Hundred Days, modern police forces reappeared—tellingly enough—under imperialist auspices during the foreign occupation of Beijing after the Boxer Rebellion.[47]

After the Qing court fled to Xi'an, the various nations in the united army of occupation were assigned control over individual sections of the city. The Japanese established military police stations; the other powers set up Public Offices for the Security of the People (Anmin gongsuo), which were meant to handle police work, road repair, and other municipal administrative tasks.[48] When the allied forces withdrew from Beijing in September 1901, the Anmin gongsuo were abolished, but they were almost instantly replaced by a Reconstruction Assistance Patrol Regiment (Shanhou xie xun ying), established along the same lines with Chinese personnel. The Patrol Regiment was in turn the nucleus in

1902 for the Patrol and Construction Department (Gong xun zongchu), which quickly became a model for other police forces in North China.[49]

Yuan Shikai was the leading sponsor of the new European-style police forces of North China.[50] During his tenure as governor-general of Zhili from 1901 to 1907, Yuan began to replace traditional lictors and yamen runners with police patterned after the European and Japanese models that had appeared in occupied Beijing. Yuan began in Baoding, the provincial capital, where, in May 1902, he reorganized five hundred former soldiers for police work, placing them under a Head Bureau of Police Affairs (Jingwu zongju), which also supervised an Academy of Police Affairs (Jingwu xuetang).[51] Once Tianjin was recovered from the allies in September 1902, Yuan made that city his police headquarters, transferring most of the Baoding contingent, along with the new police academy, to Tianjin that fall. The new Tianjin police were amalgamated with the "native police" used by the allied occupiers to form a total force of eighteen hundred men. During the winter of 1902–3 they were supplemented with another thousand fresh recruits from the southern part of the province.[52] Altogether, the modern police forces were meant both to pacify the people and to provide the viceroy's government with a means of bypassing local home-rule interests who until then controlled their own local militia and village braves.[53] The Tianjin police then became a model for the entire province of Zhili, where local police forces were established under the control of a new Ministry of Police, founded in 1905.[54]

In Beijing itself, police reforms were carried out in the spirit of the Meiji Restoration in Japan, where a system of town constables had given way to a metropolitan police force in Tokyo in 1871. The Japanese police (*keisatsu*, which was read in Chinese as *jingcha*) was brought under the Home Department (Naimusho) in 1874 after the police systems of several capital cities of Western countries had been examined; and in the Imperial Rescript of 1881 announcing the future establishment of constitutional government, a modern system of police education was planned, centering upon a police training school set up in Tokyo in 1885. Prussian police officials—Wilhelm Hoehn in the 1880s, Karl Krueger and Edward von Keudell in the 1890s—strongly influenced the curriculum of the police academy, which graduated over a thousand sergeants and inspectors during the six years just before and after the revision of treaties with Japan in 1899 that allowed foreigners the privilege of residing in the interior of Japan. Indeed, one of the aims of training this modern police force was to create a body of educated officials capable of dealing with and protecting the aliens living among them.[55]

Part of the Japanese police officer training program, which included the teaching of English to special officers assigned as interpreters to local police stations, was thus intended to prevent antiforeign incidents from occurring once the foreigners and the Japanese began to comingle. That was one reason why students were sent from China to Japan for police training after the xenophobic

Boxer Rebellion. At the same time, a number of Japanese police specialists—former head inspectors of police stations—were engaged as instructors in China.[56]

The best known of these experts was a "continental adventurer" (*tairiku ronin*) named Kawashima Naniwa who had qualified as an interpreter of Chinese in the Koakai (Rise Asia Society) language school. After the Boxer Uprising he became head of the police in Beijing's Japanese section and then assumed directorship of a school to train Chinese in Japanese police methods.[57]

In 1902 Kawashima submitted a memorandum that constituted the basic document for a program of police reorganization. The rationale for this program was spelled out in the memorandum itself: "There is no country that does not have a police system. It stands as the complement of military strength. One is the preparation for protection against the outside to resist foreign countries in order to protect national interests and rights. The other is an instrument for internal control to restrain the people in order to extend national laws and national orders. These are the two greatest forces of the country and cannot be done without for even one day."[58] In addition to establishing what was to become the ruling metaphor of national political domination—the two wings of army and police protection—during later years, Kawashima's memorandum called for a centralized national police under a police affairs board responsible directly to the emperor and headed by a member of the royal family. Under the board each province was to establish a police affairs yamen, each city and prefecture a police affairs main bureau, each zhou and county a police affairs bureau, and each market, river, and highway a police affairs subbureau. As Kawashima made quite clear, this new Chinese police system was modeled after the centralized police forces of continental Europe, closely resembling above all the police of Holland and of Berlin.[59]

Seeking European wealth and power, the Qing government accordingly decided in 1905 to follow many of Kawashima's proposals by issuing orders to establish training schools for police officials and recruits. On October 8, 1905 a Patrol Constable Board (Xunjing bu) was set up under the presidency of Xu Shichang, then senior vice-president of war; and in 1907, when the Green Standards were abolished, the Xunjing bu was folded into a Board of Civil Administration (Minzheng bu). Within that board all police work was brought under a single Department of Police Administration (Jingzheng si), and it was this department, nearly twenty years later, that would be the key administrative nucleus of Chiang Kai-shek's secret police within the Nationalist Ministry of the Interior.[60]

Despite this immediate administrative connection, it is important to recognize that this first attempt at police modernization around the turn of the century was very different in nature from the modernization program that was undertaken twenty-five years later by the Nationalist régime.[61] The Nationalists' efforts were not only inspired by contemporary examples of police professionalization and technocratic crime fighting in England, France, Germany, and the United States;

they were also directed toward creating an efficient arm of the state, respecting but not responsive to local elites. The late Qing reformers, on the other hand, certainly wished to emulate the police powers of the Meiji state, but they were much more interested in mobilizing core-area elites to transform local government. And those elites in turn were much more concerned with enlarging the "public sphere" (*gong*) of their responsibilities for the defense of domestic law and order than in helping extend the reach of the state beyond the county or prefectural yamen.[62]

Yuan Shikai, on the other hand, continued to use the new police system to displace local elite militia. In Shanghai, for example, the urban gentry had established, on the eve of the 1911 Revolution, a South Market General Works Bureau (Nanshi zong gongcheng ju), which supervised a modern police academy and four precinct stations connected with a merchant militia (*shangtuan*) that by 1911 consisted of three thousand men. These merchant militiamen played a decisive role in the Revolution of 1911 when Chen Qimei attacked the imperial garrison in Shanghai. The reward earned by the local notability as a result of the revolutionaries' victory in November 1911 included the amalgamation of all of the city's police bureaus under an "office of local government" (*zizhi gongsuo*) that was renamed the Municipal Government of Zhabei (Zhabei shizheng ting) and given responsibility for administering North and South Markets by the new republican régime.[63]

Although the gentry's militia survived as a relatively autonomous organization, its municipal police powers were short-lived.[64] In 1913, at the time of the "Second Revolution" when Yuan Shikai extended his domination over central China, the Shanghai Chinese police force was placed under provincial control. A new Songhu Police Prefecture (Songhu jingcha ting) was created directly under the governor's office, and it in turn supervised two subprefectures (*fenting*): one for South Market called Hunan, and one for North Market called Zhabei. The two subprefectures, separated geographically by the International Settlement and French Concession, were linked by the office of the Commissioner for the Songhu Water and Land Police (Songhu shuilu jingcha duban). In 1914, just as Yuan Shikai was reducing the gentry organizations in Shanghai to the role of dike maintenance agencies, absolutely devoid of authority over local police posts, the office of the commissioner was abolished, and the northern and southern subprefectures were combined into a single powerful Songhu Police Prefecture.[65]

In addition to unifying all of the Shanghai police under a single authority, Yuan Shikai attempted to replace its personnel—who came mainly from the Zhejiang-Jiangsu region—with northerners. Yuan appointed as commissioner for the Songhu Water and Land Police Sa Zhenbing, who brought with him more than a hundred police officers from the Beiping-Tianjin area.[66] From this time on there was a strong flavor of the Beiyang warlords' military culture to the Shanghai police force—a flavor that eventually succumbed to local culture in the

1930s. For example, it was common practice early in the Republican period for police commanders to send deputies into Hebei and Shandong to recruit officers and men on the grounds that "Police work in this city is vexatious and troubling. There is the most extreme hardship and toil. Northerners have strong and healthy physiques, so they can endure all this."[67] And later, during the Jiangsu-Zhejiang war of 1924–25, an entire contingent of Beijing policemen was transferred down to Shanghai and remained there once the war was over.[68]

Nationalist Police Reform

After Yuan Shikai's death, a national conference on police affairs was convened in Beijing in April 1917 by the minister of the interior, who brought together higher police officials from the provinces to discuss police training and organization. The following November, as a result, the Ministry of the Interior ordered that the provinces open police training schools. Because of the internecine militarists' wars that broke out that same year, however, central and local governments were too distracted to concern themselves with the details of police administration, and reform efforts lagged. In that respect, the history of the early republic followed the history of the late Qing: despite the promises of centralized authority seemingly guaranteed by the Japanese model and European examples, police control was difficult to impose in China without prior military unification. More effective and lasting police reform had to await the completion of the Northern Expedition and the establishment of a new régime in Nanjing.[69]

The national model for Guomindang police reform in 1927 was the Guangzhou (Canton) Bureau of Public Safety (Gong'an ju)—a title inspired by euphemistic police designations of that period in the United States. The Canton Bureau of Public Safety was established by Su Ge when he put into operation an American system of municipal administration in Guangzhou before the Northern Expedition. After the Nationalists took power, all police departments, except for the metropolitan police headquarters in Nanjing, dutifully changed their name to "bureaus of public safety."[70]

Titular unity nominally entailed administrative unity. In 1928 a national commission of police experts was established, consisting of four capital officials and eight provincial officials under the chairmanship of the director of the Department of Police Administration in the Ministry of the Interior.[71] The following year regulations were promulgated calling for the education of all police officials and recruits; and police academies were established in Zhejiang, Jiangsu, Shanxi, Guangdong, Jiangxi, Hubei, Shaanxi, Shandong, Yunnan, Hebei, Gansu, Zhahar, Qinghai, Fujian, and Guangxi. At the same time the central government decreed that local militia throughout China should be put under official county or municipal authorities.[72] In January 1931 the Ministry of the Interior convened in Nanjing the First National Conference on Internal Affairs (Diyici quanguo neizheng huiyi) to discuss police administration. This was followed in December 1932 by a second conference, consisting of more than one hundred delegates from various cities and provinces who made proposals for the introduction of pension systems for police, the use of new weapons, the hiring of policewomen, and the unification of the fingerprint system.[73]

Throughout this period, the Japanese police system continued to enjoy a high reputation. In 1930 the Ministry of the Interior held an examination to select the ten best graduates from the fifteenth class of the higher police school to attend the police training school of the Ministry of Home Affairs in Tokyo. And that same year the Zhejiang Police Academy sent twenty-one of its best graduates to Japan as well.[74]

But European police forces remained the primary model. In 1929 Wang Darui, one of the members of the national police commission, had taken advantage of attendance at the Fifth International Police Conference in Paris that September to study European police systems. The Viennese police force seemed one of the best systems to copy, and in 1930 the governor of Zhejiang invited Dr. Rudolph Muck and other Austrian police experts to serve as administrative and training consultants. That same year ten members of the graduating class of the Zhejiang Police Academy were sent to Vienna to study, and by 1932 Dr. Muck had become a police adviser to the central government in Nanjing, serving also as a consultant for the reorganization of the Shanghai Public Safety Bureau.[75]

Nevertheless, the influence of continental law enforcement experts on the new Chinese national police system was soon rivaled by that of American police officers.[76] In 1930, for example, the Ministry of the Interior invited Captain A. S. Woods of the Berkeley, California, police department to come to China and serve as an adviser.[77] Woods was asked to help reorganize the metropolitan police of Nanjing because of the Berkeley department's growing reputation as one of the best police forces in the world, thanks to August Vollmer, whose "V-men" were to local police departments as J. Edgar Hoover's "G-men" were to the notion of a national police force.[78]

August Vollmer also held a position at the University of California as Berkeley's first professor of criminology, and it was in this capacity that he trained two Chinese students who were to become Chiang Kai-shek's key police advisers: Feng Yukun and Yu Xiuhao (Frank Yee). After graduating from Berkeley's criminology program in 1932, Feng Yukun returned to China and personally submitted to Chiang Kai-shek a plan for studying the condition of police forces throughout China.[79] Then, after a brief term as the head of Nanjing's traffic division (where he revised the city's traffic regulations), Feng was seconded, in March 1933, to Police Commissioner General Chao Chen's office to serve "as an extra secretary" in the security division.[80] In that capacity Feng introduced a number of American police devices, including the use of radio patrol cars, lie detectors, fingerprinting, police dogs, and so forth. Within twelve months he was invited to serve as dean of police training at the Zhejiang Police Academy.[81]

The Zhejiang Police Academy was one of the premier cadre-training institutions of the new Nationalist régime. It had been founded just after the Northern Expedition by Zhu Jiahua, administrative director of Zhongshan University in Guangzhou who in 1927 was named chief of internal affairs for the newly liberated province of Zhejiang.[82] By the time Feng Yukun became dean, the academy was a model of its kind in Chiang Kai-shek's eyes.[83] Run along military lines, it had several foreign-trained police experts, and Feng was soon joined by his Berkeley criminology classmate Yu Xiuhao.[84] Together the two men forged close ties with the Hangzhou police force, instituted a Berkeley-style beat system of patrolmen, introduced a new cadet system, and added forensic science courses to the school curriculum along with the latest police training methods from the United States of America.[85]

By the fall of 1934 the Zhejiang Police Academy was well on its way to becoming a national institution. In September the faculty learned that in Nanjing the National Police College and the Central Military Academy had been amalgamated into a single institution, leaving the Zhejiang Academy as "the only national police institute in the field," so that the student body was drawn from all over the country, including sergeants from a number of local police forces chosen after a battery of physical and mental examinations such as the U.S. Army Alpha test.[86]

As a national institution, the Zhejiang Police Academy also assumed responsibility for the policing of Lushan, the popular mountain resort in northern Jiangxi where Chiang Kai-shek had his summer residence.[87] Lushan was already being used as a training zone for counterinsurgency forces. The Military Academy Lushan Special Training Unit (Junxiao Lushan texunban) was billeted there, and while some of its graduates were assigned to the anti-Communist investigative unit in the Nanchang garrison, a special cadres brigade was set up by the chief of Chiang Kai-shek's military secret service, Dai Li, to prepare agents for Juntong (Military Statistics Bureau) missions.[88]

During the summer months, the area was overrun with more than twenty thousand visitors and tourists who were easy prey for thieves. It seemed logical, therefore, to give the Zhejiang police cadets a chance to try their hand at practical law enforcement while also beefing up the security of the Generalissimo's favorite mountain spa and showing the foreign-run police in the territory leased by the British at Guling that the Chinese were capable of policing themselves.[89] Their record was so good that the British relinquished their police powers in the leasehold to the Chinese, and the Zhejiang cadets were held up as national models to police officials from other parts of Jiangxi and Hunan. The impressed provincial officials duly returned home in the fall and held competitive examinations to send up to twenty men and women from their own areas to the Zhejiang Police Academy to receive similar training of their own.[90]

The Zhejiang Police Academy was also a top-secret training center for Dai Li's Juntong agents, who were being groomed by Chiang Kai-shek as special cadres to take over local police forces and draw them into his secret police system.[91] Dai Li had seized control of the Zhejiang Police Academy in the summer of 1932, using the authority granted him by Chiang Kai-shek to act as Special Political Officer (Zhengzhi tepaiyuan) for the Zhejiang Police Academy Special Training Section (Texunban).[92]

By 1935, when Chiang Kai-shek announced his decision to merge the Zhejiang Police Academy with the Jiangsu Police Academy to form a new Central Police Academy (Zhongyang jingguan xuexiao), Dai Li's men were in several of the key political training posts, and special clandestine training units were already in place to prepare Juntong personnel for service as Chiang's personal bodyguards, as intelligence agents, and as secret policemen. The texts they studied were translations of Cheka and GPU training manuals provided by Communist defectors.[93]

The Guomindang creation of an elaborate secret service system, which also included Chen Lifu's Central Statistics Bureau (Zhongtong), corresponded to—and dialectically spurred on—counterpart Communist apparatuses. The special services section of the Chinese Communist Party was established in 1928, not long after the party's definitive rupture with the Guomindang. By 1930 there were a number of provincial branches, including those in the various soviets that came under the direction of the Central Office of the Special Service Office attached to the Provisional Central Government of China in Jiangxi. In Nationalist-controlled areas the defection of security chief Gu Shunzhang in 1931 led to enormous setbacks, but the clandestine wing of the party, then under Zhou Enlai's control, recovered from that debacle. Led by Kang Sheng, the Communist secret service eventually left an important legacy for contemporary leaders such as Yang Shangkun and Qiao Shi.[94]

Chiang Kai-shek's decision in 1935 to create a central police training institute stemmed from a wider vision of a countrywide police system that would integrate other systems of local control and stand alongside the army as one of the two critical buttresses of his régime.[95] In his role as president or principal (*xiaozhang*) of the Central Police Academy, Chiang Kai-shek told the graduating seniors of the class of 1937 that "There are two great forces in our country: the army and the police; one is for national defense, and the other is for maintenance of peace. Like a plane, it takes two wings to fly; but because of the complexity of modern police duties and because they are the only public functionaries that are in constant contact with the people, the position of the police is even more important in our society."[96]

In 1936 Chiang summoned a special Conference of Higher Local Administrative Officials (Difang gaoji xingzheng renyuan huiyi) to discuss local police and security problems.[97] The meeting took place within the context of a long-standing debate between officials from the central government and provincial leaders over the retention of the peace preservation corps (*baoandui*).[98]

Provincial officials naturally favored preserving local militia that they themselves funded and controlled, while representatives of the central government opposed the *baoandui* and argued for the creation of regular police departments that would be directed and trained by the new Nationalist government, albeit financed with local resources. After hearing both sides of the argument, Chiang Kai-shek came down on the side of the police.[99]

The Executive Yuan duly approved a proposal that required the provinces to submit plans for police reform according to principles worked out by the Department of Police Administration, which was placed under the direction of Feng Yukun.[100] The latter proclaimed that as of the end of 1936 the peace preservation corps would be abolished and over three years their duties would gradually be taken over by the regular police. As each *baoandui* was dissolved, its budget and arsenal were to be transferred to the county police departments, which would be made as uniform as possible in salary, ranks, and training. To improve the quality of these local police forces, the Department of Police Administration planned to put all recruits through training courses in the provincial capitals and cities, while higher-ranking police officials would all receive educations in the new Central Police Academy. This would also, needless to say, be a further step toward the national integration of public security forces.[101]

The local police regulations of July 25, 1936, raised immediate questions about the relation between these new local police stations and the office of the district magistrate. Was the police station to be entirely separate, or was it to be merged with the magistrate's office under a special police assistant? The Ministry of the Interior could not resolve this question and accordingly asked the Executive Yuan to request instructions from the Committee for National Defense in October 1939. The committee decided in the end to place authority within an adviser's office under the local magistrate, who supposedly retained ultimate police authority.[102]

Meanwhile, there was a furious competition within the security services over control of the central training system, and Juntong chief Dai Li never did win complete authority over the national police force cadres. But he did have his lieutenants in key positions, including the other Berkeley student, Yu Xiuhao, placed in charge of the division within the Police Administration Department that was responsible for police education, fire prevention, foreign affairs, criminal investigation, and "special services." In his letters to August Vollmer, Yu presented their appointments as the triumph of the Berkeley police reform program. "Hereafter," he wrote, "the whole police administration and education will be in the complete control of the V-men."[103] Control was, in fact, to be in the hands of Dai Li's agents, and the years 1936–37 saw the extension of the secret police chief's influence into regular municipal police bureaus—Jiujiang, Zhengzhou, Wuhan, Luoyang—through the manipulation of personnel assignments and of Ministry of Interior training programs.[104]

The Chinese secret service's plan to recruit agents through legal education coincided with the U.S. Federal Bureau of Investigation's police chief training program, and to a certain extent it drew common strength from the "scientific" goal of spreading police professionalism to local law enforcement agencies. Yu Xiuhao reported to Vollmer that from September 15, 1936, on, "high police officers from all parts of China will receive an intensive refresher [*sic*] training in the academy" in Nanjing, while other police officers would be attending a special summer training program at Lushan where the syllabus would be Yu's writings, plus translations of Vollmer's texts on American police systems.[105]

These courses were supplemented by Yu Xiuhao's lecture and inspection trips around the country, as well as by Feng Yukun's frequent public radio broadcasts, "emphasizing the importance of police administration and the need of cooperation from the people."[106] And they accompanied as well moves to introduce the latest American methods for centralizing identification and record-keeping procedures in the Ministry of Interior's police section. Early in 1937, for example, Feng Yukun contacted J. Edgar Hoover to find out how the FBI organized and handled fingerprints, and the Nationalist government began to set up its own Central Finger Print Bureau in Nanjing.[107]

Meanwhile, under Nationalist rule urban police forces in major cities like Nanjing and Shanghai took on a wide latitude of responsibilities for administering public health programs, issuing building permits, collecting and maintaining household registration records, censoring public entertainment, and controlling social mores. The police were given powers of arrest and punishment on the spot for minor infractions, and they routinely collected fines for spitting on the sidewalk, wearing "indecent dress," and exposing too much flesh. This puritanical control of public behavior commenced among urban police forces long before the New Life Movement was actually launched in Nanchang in 1934. Police also unwittingly took part in the creation of a new Republican civic culture by organizing counterdemonstrations to the parades and rallies of the left-wing "reactionaries" (that is, the Communists and progressives opposing the Nationalist revolution) commemorating May 1, May 4, May 30, and so forth.[108]

Simultaneously, new kinds of police organizations were created: Treasury Police to maintain currency controls and enforce state monopolies; Anti-Smuggling Police to curtail smuggling; Railway Police to keep order on trains; Salt Gabelle Police to prevent peasants from making and selling their own salt. Each of these represented new intrusions into Chinese society—intrusions that may have done more to provoke peasant resistance movements than the exploitation of local elites and urban rentiers.[109]

Chiang Kai-shek's plans to train all of the police chiefs of China in the Central Police Academy were thwarted by the War of Resistance.[110] Yet the secret-police system continued to grow for intelligence purposes and because Dai Li was able to effect an agreement with U.S. Navy representatives to create a Sino-American Cooperative Organization (Zhong-Mei hezuo suo). SACO provided FBI and Naval Intelligence instructors to train high-level Juntong agents on the one hand, and regular army, navy, and marines officers to instruct the fifty thousand members of Dai Li's Loyal and Patriotic Army (Zhongyi jiuguo jun) on the other. By the end of the Pacific War, the Military Statistics Bureau of Chiang Kai-shek had about one hundred thousand operatives, making it one of the largest intelligence and secret police organizations in the world at that time.

Police and State Power after 1949

Many police forces turned coat nearly to a man when the Communists won the civil war. Their own control systems—including the Japanese-influenced *baojia* of many Eastern Chinese cities, which operated under the Wang Jingwei puppet government until VJ Day and continued in place under the Nationalist police authorities—had been denounced by the Communists before 1949. The representatives of the new régime, however, were pleased enough to accept the household registries that were simply handed over to them in cities like Shanghai, Canton, and Tianjin.[111] The *baojia* system was abolished in name, but a nearly identical system was set up in its stead in the form of the neighborhood Residents' Committee (Zhumin weiyuanhui) that was directly under the supervision of an increased number of Public Security police outposts (*paichusuo*).[112] In rural areas, the village militia units took over similar *baojia* functions, while regular police duties were performed by the PSB office in the *xian* seat.[113]

Although many of the instruments of state power of the new régime were a legacy of previous governments, one must recognize the utterly novel character of the PRC's social government. Part of its uniqueness was sheerly quantitative, stemming from the massive bureaucratic expansion that took place during the early years of the People's Republic, when the number of state cadres increased from 720,000 in 1949 (constituting 0.13 percent of the population) to 7,920,000 in 1958 (1.21 percent).[114] Part of its novelty was qualitative, reflecting the CCP's interpenetration of state and society via organizational links like the rural militia units, which were both instruments of state control and expressions of local social interests.[115]

Within the public security system itself the Communist Party was of course crucial, and the residents' committees that were established after 1949 worked much more effectively thanks to the techniques learned in the Soviet period and implemented in Yan'an when control was built from the bottom up. In 1952, for instance, a new nationwide system of public security committees was established by organizing groups of three to eleven members in every village, factory, and institution in the country "to organize and lead the masses to help the government and public security organs to denounce, supervise, and control counterrevolutionary elements," and "to protect the state and public order."[116]

Two years later, on December 31, 1954, new regulations were promulgated that formed residents' committees, street offices, and public security substations into a uniform system. City inhabitants were organized into residents' teams from fifteen to forty households. The teams selected one representative each to a general residents' committee overseeing one hundred to six hundred member households. The residents' committee was supposed to undertake public welfare work, reflect the views and demands of residents to local people's councils, mobilize residents to respond to government calls, mediate disputes, and "direct mass security work." Their jurisdiction was congruent with a corresponding public security substation.[117]

The party took a leading role in these organizations; but the coercive muscle of the party was the public security system, which owed a significant degree of its own efficacy to earlier Republican efforts to create powerful state police apparatuses originally modeled on the Bolsheviks' Cheka. It was partly an instrument of their own creation, then, that had been turned upon former Nationalist officials in December 1950 when the PSB requested all people who had held positions with the Guomindang to register in order to "start anew." Four months later, in Shanghai at least, the Public Security Bureau used those registration lists to round up remnants of the former regime for imprisonment or execution.[118]

The crucial difference between the Communists and Nationalists in this respect was thought control. However much Chen Lifu stressed the Three People's Principles, there was simply no comparison between the Nationalist control system's ability to govern thinking and the Communists' ability to force a kind of *xinao* (brainwashing) through struggle sessions, written confessions, cross-checking of police and personnel files, and so on. Even a Michel Foucault would have had difficulty imagining how thoroughly the hegemony of the Communist Party has been imposed upon the Chinese since 1949.[119]

Of course, the CCP also came to power as a military force, and the rank-and-file of the public security forces were originally drawn from regular PLA units toward the end of the civil war. In 1950, under the stimulus of the Korean War, the PLA's Public Security School began to receive thousands of new recruits who had been unable to pass the strict medical requirements of the Aviation and Artillery Schools, the Naval School, and the Armored School.[120] The minister of public security, Luo Ruiqing, was later to serve both as commander of the Public Security Forces and as chief of the army's General Staff.[121] Between 1955 and 1962, however, the PSB was separated from PLA control. Key high-ranking Public Security Bureau officers often had backgrounds as ground forces officers or political commissars in the army, but once in the security services they did not switch back to the military. After 1962, local public security forces were gradually brought back under the control of military regions, with national-level forces ostensibly under the command of Minister of Public Security Xie Fuzhi.[122]

During the Cultural Revolution, both national and local security forces came under severe attack from Red Guards for protecting party powerholders. Actually, the PSB served both sides as political winds shifted. For instance, after the January 1967 "power seizure," when all of the major Chinese leaders except Mao and Lin Biao came under open criticism from the radicals, the Public

Security Bureau helped the Cultural Revolution Small Group arrest leaders of the conservative organizations defending the United Front Department of the Central Committee. Yet a month later, during the "February Adverse Current," the PSB helped in the conservative counterattack.[123] Nonetheless, Mao himself urged his followers to "thoroughly smash the public security procuratorate and justice organs," and by the end of 1967 they were being taken over by military security personnel.[124]

This is not to say that the secret police ceased to be, in their own terrifying way, effective—especially as an instrument in the hands of Kang Sheng and his followers. Millions of people were hauled off to prison and beaten up at the hands of the security organs. In November 1978 at the Central Party School, Hu Yaobang, later the general secretary, described the security organs of that period as "a Gestapo independent of the Central Committee." Although the security organs were supposed to protect the state, he said, under Kang Sheng, "the knife of the organization fell on our own heads rather than the enemy's."[125]

After the Cultural Revolution, when the Public Security Bureau was once more accountable to the party, its personnel launched a campaign to restore the public image of the police and the procuratorate.[126] The campaign stressed both service to the public and protection against social disorder, and it took place within a larger nationwide movement to restore the legal system and inculcate obedience to the criminal and civil codes.[127] The crackdown began on August 25, 1983, when thirty criminals were taken to Workers Stadium in eastern Beijing, paraded before a mass rally, then driven back in town and shot in the back of the head. Weeks later the crackdown was officially announced by the Standing Committee of the National People's Congress, which passed a resolution calling for sterner measures to combat crime.[128]

According to Wang Jingrong, head of the Research Office of the Ministry of Public Security, 5,000 criminals were executed during the next thirteen months as part of a campaign to "educate others."[129] An additional 120,000 people surrendered "to mend their evil ways," and another 70,000 suspected criminals were turned in by ordinary citizens.[130] The authorities subsequently claimed that there had been a major drop in the crime rate from 7 out of 10,000 people in 1982 to 5 out of 10,000 people in 1985.[131] Indeed, the suppression of serious crimes during 1983–85 supposedly brought China's crime rate down to nearly the lowest level since the founding of the People's Republic in 1949.[132] This was also one of the lowest crime rates in the world, and by the end of September 1987 (when the total number of reported crimes in China in the first nine months of that year was about 407,000), Ministry of Public Security spokesmen were attributing the stability of the social order altogether to "the nationwide crackdown on serious crimes, which began in 1983."[133]

The originally high incidence of gang-led crimes had been attributed to propensities for violent behavior acquired during the lawlessness of the Cultural Revolution. Soon, two other causes of crime were identified in the form of foreign "spiritual pollution" and in the spread of commercial exchanges that were part of the economic reforms of the four modernizations.[134] The party leadership was especially offended by the spread of foreign habits and ideas among college youth, and when students demonstrated in December 1986 their disrest was attributed to outside influences. Ruan Chongwu, head of the Ministry of Public Security (MPS), was dismissed the following April mainly because of his lenient treatment of the students at that time. His successor, Zhejiang Party Secretary Wang Fang, claimed that social disorder was being instigated by "antirevolutionaries at home and [through] infiltration and sabotage by hostile organizations from abroad," and additional public security bureaus were soon opened on many campuses around China to "ensure the smooth progress of education."[135] Wang Fang's appointment as minister of public security in 1987, in fact, presaged a dramatic switch in Chinese perceptions of crime and social control. As crime rates suddenly began to rise, public security figures began to worry (in Wang's words at a national conference the following year) that "problems affecting political order may deteriorate to become factors of political instability."[136]

While China's police chiefs warned of turbulent times ahead, the authorities described increasingly frequent attacks on public security organs, whether a police station being razed to the ground in Tibet in October 1987 or another being ransacked by a mob in Guangdong in May 1988. "Some people," said Public Security Minister Wang Fang in September 1988, "regard the beating of public security and judicial cadres and other law enforcement personnel as an act of legitimate defense."[137]

One immediate response on the part of the MPS was to recruit more police officers and agents.[138] While middle and upper cadres among China's 1.2 million policemen went through a program of training in special colleges under the MPS, the police were also given priority in recruiting high school graduates after the national college entrance examinations every year.[139] The best of these were admitted to Public Security University in Beijing to study police management, criminal investigation, law, and crime prevention technology. Competition for admission was keen. In Sichuan, for example, more than one thousand middle school graduates applied to Public Security University, and only twenty were actually enrolled.[140]

Meanwhile, increased market transactions, changing transportation patterns including the acquisition of foreign automobiles, growing migration into the cities by surplus rural labor to work in construction industries or to find jobs in the service sector—all of these placed new burdens on (and created fresh opportunities for) the regular police, who reported a 35 percent increase in serious crimes in the first six months of 1988 over the same period a year earlier.[141]

Household registration picked up as the Public Security Bureau tried to keep track of transient urban populations, which had swollen to more than 50 million by 1988.[142] Free markets had to be licensed and patrolled—activities that led to police corruption.[143] Traffic control demanded increased police supervision and attention.[144] Modernization through a relatively free market economy may have offered elite rural lineages in provinces like Guangdong and Fujian a chance to reassert themselves, and they may also have provided resources for the attainment of a higher degree of local political autonomy, but the process also invited state intervention in new and alarming ways.[145] Paradoxically, the transformation from a centrally planned economy to more of a self-regulating one gave the authoritarian services of the state a much more important role than they enjoyed when the Chairman's ideological campaigns inspired autarchic collective behavior.[146]

As the Public Security Bureau devoted more and more of its personnel's time to social regulation, two new police agencies made their appearance: a paramilitary force designed to counter internal riot and rebellion, and a secret service for counterespionage and control of subversives.[147] The People's Armed Police (Renmin wuzhuang jingcha) was created in March–April 1983 with a mammoth transfer of 500,000 soldiers from the People's Liberation Army, which was removed from internal security duties. Its detachments were supposed to report directly to the public security departments of the local governments, and nationally the PAP (Wujing) came under the Ministry of Public Security. But it also reported directly to the Central Military Commission, which was authorized to take command in the event of an emergency; and it was run as a military institution, observing the same rules and regulations as the PLA.[148]

By 1989 there were over one million PAP troops garrisoned throughout China in newly constructed buildings like the multistoried headquarters bristling with radio antennae in the western Beijing suburb of Haidian. In addition to serving as guards at government ministries, foreign embassies, prisons, and military industrial factories, the Armed Police patrolled frontier areas and handled immigration and passport control.[149] Their men were also supposedly trained in riot control and were thus ready to be used in the event of urban demonstrations. The 27th Army had to be called in to quell the June Fourth Movement, but in Beijing, Shanghai, Chengdu, and Xi'an the Armed Police also had a major role to play in striking out against democracy movement demonstrators.[150]

There was also an expansion of the security services as such after the disbandment of the special unit known as "8341" under the command of Mao Zedong's chief bodyguard, Wang Dongxing. During the Cultural Revolution, Wang Dongxing was placed in charge of the General Office of the Central Committee, which became the party's nerve center to which all foreign intelligence and important domestic documents were sent, and which disseminated all important directives and documents. The General Office essentially replaced the party Secretariat after December 1966, and Wang Dongxing worked through it to place all of the public security organs in China under military control by the following year. In the meantime, his own "8341" unit gathered intelligence on other Chinese leaders, arrested and imprisoned Mao's foes, and acted as the secret service of the central government. "8341" also played a vital role in the arrest of the "Gang of Four" in October 1986.[151]

After Wang Dongxing's political demise, top-level security and intelligence activities had come directly under the control of the Communist Party's Political-Legal Commission (PLC), which had functioned as a "power organ" with hands-on leadership of the security and legal organizations. In 1983 a new Ministry of State Security (Guojia anquan bu) was created and charged with counter-espionage and intelligence-gathering activities. Its minister, Jia Chunwang, reported directly to the PLC, which was replaced late in 1987, at the time of the intensification of public security activities, by a new Political-Legal Leading Group (PLLG). This Central Committee organ, which also supervised the public security organs, the procuracy, and the judiciary, was directed by Qiao Shi, who had been an underground party organizer in Shanghai in the 1940s, and head of the Liaison and Organization departments before and after the Cultural Revolution. Its duties were not altogether clear to outsiders, but later events showed that like the American Federal Bureau of Investigation, it was charged with maintaining surveillance over suspected subversives—including potential dissidents with contacts with the West.[152] The use of electronic monitoring and the impressive tracking of suspects through other police techniques in the days after the Tiananmen Incident are recent evidence of the dominion of the Ministry of State Security over the Chinese.[153]

Together, all three police forces represent the power of the modern Chinese state openly and secretly to exert unprecedented control over its citizens' lives.[154] The regular PSB elements now devote a major part of their resources to normative policing: arresting drug dealers,[155] seizing imported video cassettes, closing down pornographic publishers.[156] They also, together with the other two agencies, have put in place a colossal individual and household control system that by the end of September 1989 will have issued five hundred million electronically coded identity cards to PRC citizens advised to prepare themselves for frequent police verification.[157] Thanks to imported computers equipped with special Chinese software, this new registration system provides the People's Republic of China with the means of totalitarian rule that preceding authoritarian régimes—the late Qing monarchy, Yuan Shikai's abortive republic, the Nationalists' Nanking régime—could hardly have imagined.[158]

Yet all three of those predecessors would have appreciated the drive to acquire such mechanisms. The history of coercion—the rise of the modern police state—thus validates the fourth model of the changing relationship between state and society during the last 150 years. To be sure, it is far from novel (especially after the June Fourth Massacre) to associate Communist Machtpolitik and the leadership's readiness to use force against the populace with the oppressive qualities of the traditional Chinese state.[159] Nor is it uncommon to describe the government that has ruled China since 1949 as representing the growing intrusion of the state into societal processes. But what is less obvious, though just as important to understanding the permanence of this evolution, is the recognition that the intrusion began in the late imperial period, and that it has continued down to the present day. This perdurance lends the modern Chinese state remarkable staying power, despite the chaos of civil war in the 1940s and the turmoil of Cultural Revolution in the 1960s. Even as Communist régimes unravel in the West, it is difficult to imagine the Chinese polity surrendering so readily to anything less than the severest of military and social challenges.

Notes

1. For an excellent discussion of the nature of the contemporary Chinese state-society relationship, see David Mozingo and Victor Nee, "Introduction," in *State and Society in Contemporary China*, ed. Victor Nee and David Mozingo (Ithaca: Cornell University Press, 1983), pp. 17–24.

2. George E. Taylor, "The Taiping Rebellion: Its Economic Background and Social Theory," *Chinese Social and Political Science Review* 16 (1932–33): 545–614.

3. Frederick W. Mote, "The Growth of Chinese Despotism," *Oriens Extremus* 81 (1961): 1–41.

4. In this regard, see the discussion of Jia Yi in Kung-chuan Hsiao, *A History of Chinese Political Thought*, vol. 1, *From the Beginnings to the Sixth Century* A.D., trans. F. W. Mote (Princeton: Princeton University Press, 1979), pp. 473–83.

5. Chang Chung-li, *The Chinese Gentry: Studies on Their Role in Nineteenth-Century Chinese Society* (Seattle: University of Washington Press, 1955), p. xiii; and *The Income of the Chinese Gentry* (Seattle: University of Washington Press, 1962), pp. 196–98.

6. Franz Michael, *The Origin of Manchu Rule in China* (Baltimore: Johns Hopkins University Press, 1942). David Farquhar later showed this to be incorrect in his article, "Mongolian versus Chinese Elements in the Early Manchu State," *Ch'ing-shih wen-t'i* (June 1971): 11–23. More recent interpretations, whether from Frederic Wakeman or Pamela Crossley, suggest the process was complexly intermixed. See, for example, Pamela Crossley, "An Introduction to the Qing Foundation Myth," *Late Imperial China* 6 (December 1985): 13–24.

7. Vincent Y. C. Shih, *The Taiping Ideology: Its Sources, Interpretations, and Influences* (Seattle: University of Washington Press, 1967).

8. Franz Michael, *The Taiping Rebellion: History and Documents* (Seattle: University of Washington Press, 1966–71), 3 vols.

9. Franz Michael, "Military Organization and Power Structure of China during the Taiping Rebellion," *Pacific Historical Review* 18 (1949): 469–83; and "Regionalism in Nineteenth-Century China," introduction to Stanley Spector, *Li Hung-chang and the Huai Army: A Study in Nineteenth-Century Chinese Regionalism* (Seattle: University of Washington Press, 1964), pp. xxi–xliii.

10. Spector, *Li Hung-chang and the Huai Army*, pp. 270–83.

11. Mary C. Wright, *The Last Stand of Chinese Conservatism: The T'ung-chih Restoration, 1862–1874* (New York: Atheneum, 1966), pp. 1–10.

12. Frederic Wakeman, Jr., "A Note on the Development of the Theme of Bureaucratic-Monarchic Tension in Joseph R. Levenson's Work," in *The Mozartian Historian: Essays on the Works of Joseph R. Levenson*, ed. Maurice Meisner and Rhoads Murphey (Berkeley: University of California Press, 1976), pp. 123–33.

13. Joseph R. Levenson, *Confucian China and Its Modern Fate*, vol. 1, *The Problem*

of Monarchical Decay (London: Routledge and Kegan Paul, 1964), pp. 100–116.

14. The term "muscular Confucianism" is from Benjamin Schwartz's *In Search of Wealth and Power: Yen Fu and the West* (Cambridge: Harvard University Press, 1964), pp. 15–16.

15. Mary C. Wright, "From Revolution to Restoration: The Transformation of Kuomintang Ideology," *Far Eastern Quarterly* 14 (1954–55): 525–32.

16. Mary Clabaugh Wright, "Introduction: The Rising Tide of Change," in *China in Revolution: The First Phase, 1900–1913*, ed. Mary Clabaugh Wright (New Haven: Yale University Press, 1968), pp. 1–63.

17. See especially Vidya Prakash Dutt, "The First Week of Revolution: The Wuchang Uprising," in ibid., pp. 383–416.

18. Chuzo Ichiko, "The Role of the Gentry: An Hypothesis," in ibid., pp. 297–317.

19. See especially P'eng-yuan Chang, "The Constitutionalists," in ibid., pp. 143–83.

20. Barrington Moore, Jr., *Social Origins of Dictatorship and Democracy: Lord and Peasant in the Making of the Modern World* (Boston: Beacon Press, 1966); and Theda Skocpol, *States and Social Revolutions: A Comparative Analysis of France, Russia, and China* (Cambridge: Cambridge University Press, 1979).

21. Frederic Wakeman, Jr., *Strangers at the Gate: Social Disorder in South China, 1839–1861* (Berkeley: University of California Press, 1966).

22. Robert Y. Eng, "Institutional and Secondary Landlordism in the Pearl River Delta, 1600–1949," *Modern China* 12, 1 (January 1986): 3–37; Frederic Wakeman, Jr., "The Secret Societies of Kwangtung," in *Popular Movements and Secret Societies in Modern China*, ed. Jean Chesneaux (Stanford: Stanford University Press, 1972).

23. Philip A. Kuhn, *Rebellion and Its Enemies in Late Imperial China: Militarization and Social Structure, 1797–1864* (Cambridge: Harvard University Press, 1970).

24. Philip A. Kuhn, "Local Self-Government under the Republic: Problems of Control, Autonomy, and Mobilization," in *Conflict and Control in Late Imperial China*, ed. Frederic Wakeman and Carolyn Grant (Berkeley: University of California Press, 1975), pp. 257–98.

25. Mark Elvin, "The Administration of Shanghai, 1905–1914," in *The Chinese City between Two Worlds*, ed. Mark Elvin and G. William Skinner (Stanford: Stanford University Press, 1974), p. 250; and "The Gentry Democracy in Chinese Shanghai, 1905–1914," in *Modern China's Search for a Political Form*, ed. Jack Gray (London: Oxford University Press, 1969), pp. 41–65.

26. William T. Rowe, *Hankow: Commerce and Society in a Chinese City, 1796–1889* (Stanford: Stanford University Press, 1984), p. 344. See also Susan Mann Jones, "Merchant Investment, Commercialization, and Social Change in the Ningpo Area," in *Reform in Nineteenth-Century China*, ed. Paul A. Cohen and John Schrecker (Cambridge: Harvard University Press, 1976), pp. 41–48.

27. Mary Backus Rankin, *Elite Activism and Political Transformation in China: Zhejiang Province, 1865–1911* (Stanford: Stanford University Press, 1986), pp. 136–69.

28. Yuji Muramatsu, *Kindai Konan no sosan: Chugoku jinushi seido no kenkyu* (Landlord bursaries of the lower Yangzi delta region in recent times: Studies of the Chinese landlord system) (Tokyo: Kindai Chugoku kenkyu iinkai, 1970), pp. 681–747.

29. James Polachek, "Gentry Hegemony: Soochow in the T'ung-chih Restoration," in *Conflict and Control in Late Imperial China*, ed. Wakeman and Grant, pp. 211–56.

30. Frederic Wakeman, Jr., *The Fall of Imperial China* (New York: Free Press, 1975), pp. 253–54.

31. Joseph Esherick, Jr., *Reform and Revolution in China: The 1911 Revolution in Hunan and Hubei* (Ann Arbor: University of Michigan Press, 1977); Edward J. M.

Rhoads, *China's Republican Revolution: The Case of Kwangtung, 1895–1913* (Cambridge: Harvard University Press, 1975); and Arthur L. Rosenbaum, "Gentry Power and the Changsha Rice Riot of 1910," *Journal of Asian Studies* 34, 3 (May 1975): 689–716.

32. Angus W. McDonald, *The Urban Origins of Rural Revolution: Elites and the Masses in Hunan Province, China, 1911–1927* (Berkeley: University of California Press, 1978).

33. Ray Huang, "Fiscal Administration during the Ming Dynasty," in *Chinese Government in Ming Times: Seven Studies*, ed. Charles O. Hucker (New York: Columbia University Press, 1969), pp. 73–128; and *Taxation and Government Finance in Sixteenth-Century Ming China* (London: Cambridge University Press, 1974). See also Charles O. Hucker, *The Traditional Chinese State in Ming Times (1368–1644)* (Tucson: University of Arizona Press, 1961).

34. William Atwell, "Notes on Silver, Foreign Trade, and the Late Ming Economy," *Ch'ing-shih wen-t'i* (December 1977): 1–33; S. A. M. Adshead, "The Seventeenth Century General Crisis in China," *Asian Profile* 1, 2: 271–80.

35. Joseph Needham and Ray Huang, "The Nature of Chinese Society—a Technical Interpretation," *Journal of Oriental Studies* 12, 1 and 2 (1974): 1–16.

36. Pierre-Etienne Will, "Un cycle hydraulique en Chine: la province du Hubei du XVIe au XIX siècles," *Bulletin de l'école francaise d'extrême Orient* 68 (1980): 261–87; Bin Wong and Peter Perdue, "Famine's Foes in Ch'ing China: Review Article," *Harvard Journal of Asiatic Studies* 43, 1 (June 1983): 291–331; and Jerry Dennerline, *The Chiating Loyalists: Confucian Leadership and Social Change in Seventeenth-Century China* (New Haven: Yale University Press, 1981).

37. Pierre-Etienne Will, *Bureaucratie et famine en Chine au 18e siècle* (Paris: Ecole des hautes études en sciences sociales, 1980).

38. Madeleine Zelin, *The Magistrate's Tael: Rationalizing Fiscal Reform in 18th-Century Ch'ing China* (Berkeley: University of California Press, 1984).

39. Peter C. Perdue, "Official Goals and Local Interests: Water Control in the Dongting Lake Region during the Ming and Qing Periods," *Journal of Asian Studies* 41, 4 (November 1982): 747–66.

40. Susan Mann Jones and Philip A. Kuhn, "Dynastic Decline and the Roots of Rebellion," in *The Cambridge History of China*, ed. John K. Fairbank, vol. 10, part 1 (London: Cambridge University Press, 1978), pp. 107–62; R. Bin Wong, "Food Riots in the Qing Dynasty," *Journal of Asian Studies* 43, 1 (August 1984): 767–88.

41. Tu-ki Min, *National Polity and Local Power: The Transformation of Late Imperial China*, ed. Philip A. Kuhn and Timothy Brook (Cambridge: Harvard University Council on East Asian Studies, 1989), pp. 207–18.

42. Joseph Esherick, Jr., "Review Article: The 1911 Revolution," *Modern China* (1975).

43. P'eng-yuan Chang, "Political Participation and Political Elites in Early Republican China: The Parliament of 1913–1914," *Journal of Asian Studies* 37, 2 (February 1978): 293–313.

44. Ernest Young, *The Presidency of Yuan Shih-k'ai: Liberalism and Dictatorship in Early Republican China* (Ann Arbor: University of Michigan Press, 1977).

45. Philip C. C. Huang, *The Peasant Economy and Social Change in North China* (Stanford: Stanford University Press, 1985); Prasenjit Duara, "State Involution: A Study of Local Finances in North China, 1911–1935," *Comparative Studies in Society and History* 29,1 (January 1987): 132–61; William T. Rowe, "A Note on *Ti-pao*," *Ch'ing-shih wen-t'i* 3,8 (December 1977): 79–85.

46. For the connection between the growth of the nation-state and the formation of modern police systems, see David H. Bayley, "The Police and Political Development in

Europe,'' in *The Formation of National States in Western Europe*, ed. Charles Tilly (Princeton: Princeton University Press, 1975), pp. 328–79.

47. For an enlightening discussion of the establishment of local police in Wuhan during this period, see Rowe, *Hankow: Conflict and Community in a Chinese City*, pp. 283–315.

48. The office chief and upper ranks of the Anmin gongsuo were composed of foreigners, while the cadres were foreign military policemen, and the regular patrolmen were Chinese.

49. Victor Li, ''The Development of the Chinese Police during the Late Ch'ing and Early Republican Years,'' Seminar on Contemporary Chinese Law, Harvard Law School, May 1965, pp. 27–28.

50. Shanghai tongshe, eds., *Shanghai yanjiu ziliao* (Research materials on Shanghai) (Shanghai: Zhonghua shuju, 1936), p. 104.

51. Of course, soldiers had been used earlier in the Qing for police duties. See Narakino Shimesu, ''Shindai ni okeru joshi goson no jian iji ni tsuite'' (Urban and rural public safety during the Qing), *Shicho* 49 (1953): 35–48.

52. Stephen MacKinnon, ''Police Reform in Late Ch'ing Chihli,'' *Ch'ing-shih wen-t'i* 3, 4 (December 1975): 82–83.

53. Stephen R. MacKinnon, ''A Late Qing-GMD-PRC Connection: Police as an Arm of the Modern Chinese State,'' *Selected Papers in Asian Studies,* new series, no. 14 (1983): 5.

54. MacKinnon, ''Police Reform in Late Ch'ing Chihli.''

55. Oura Kanetake, ''The Police of Japan,'' in *Fifty Years of New Japan*, comp. Okuma Shigenobu (New York: E. P. Dillon, 1909), 1: 281–95.

56. Ibid., pp. 294–95.

57. Shen Zui, *Juntong neimu* (The inside story of the Military Statistics Bureau) (Beijing: Wenshi ziliao chubanshe, 1984), p. 3.

58. Li, ''The Development of the Chinese Police,'' p. 33.

59. Ibid., pp. 33–34, 47.

60. Ibid., pp. 6, 38–39; Frank Yee, ''Police in Modern China,'' Ph.D. dissertation, University of California, Berkeley, 1942, p. 29.

61. ''[In Zhejiang around 1911] police functionaries were omnipresent. . . . Local citizens (*gongmin*) repeatedly protested the activity of police assistants (*jingzuo*) who tended to assume the roles of traditional yamen runners, extorting the populace, accepting bribes, and promoting gambling. The problems attendant to this police proliferation became more severe throughout the early Republic.'' R. Keith Schoppa, *Chinese Elites and Political Change: Zhejiang Province in the Early Twentieth Century* (Cambridge: Harvard University Press, 1982), p. 70.

62. ''The politics of the last Qing decade can be viewed in terms of the clash between the continuing mobilization of core-area elites and a new attempt at aggressive state-building by the Qing government.'' Rankin, *Elite Activism and Political Transformation in China*, p. 27. See also Ch'eng I-fan, ''*Kung* as an Ethos in Late Nineteenth-Century China: The Case of Wang Hsieh-ch'ien,'' in *Reform in Nineteenth-Century China*, ed. Cohen and Schrecker, pp. 170–80; and Vivienne Shue, *The Reach of the State: Sketches of the Chinese Body Politic* (Stanford: Stanford University Press, 1988).

63. Zhu Yisheng, ''Shanghai jingcha yange shi'' (History of the evolution of the Shanghai police), *Shanghai jingcha* 1 (1946): 3; Christian Henriot, ''Le gouvernement municipal de Shanghai, 1927–1937,'' doctoral thesis, Université de la Sorbonne Nouvelle, 1983, pp. 19, 22–23.

64. Henriot, ''Le gouvernement municipal de Shanghai, 1927–1937,'' pp. 15–16.

65. Yuan announced in February that local self-government institutions were going to

be abolished. Although he did compromise the following December by promulgating regulations for *difang zizhi* (local self-government), in Shanghai the municipal government (*shizhengting*) became the general office of public works, patrols, and city taxes. Ibid., p. 24.

66. Shanghai tongshe, eds., *Shanghai yanjiu ziliao*, pp. 91, 104.

67. Ibid., p. 105.

68. There were altogether 25 officers, 35 sergeants, and 444 patrolmen. Ibid., p. 104.

69. Frank Yee, "Police in Modern China," pp. 31–32.

70. Ibid., p. 30.

71. Ibid.

72. At the same time, the central leadership of the Guomindang ordered the Ministry of the Interior to take over direct administration of the Capital Police Department in Nanjing. Maryruth Coleman, "Municipal Authority and Popular Participation in Republican Nanjing," paper delivered at the Association for Asian Studies annual meeting, San Francisco, March 27, 1983, p. 5.

73. Yee, "Police in Modern China," pp. 33–34.

74. Ibid., p. 35.

75. Ibid. Muck recommended forming a special foreign affairs police. He also suggested that the Shanghai authorities recruit five hundred policemen from Beiping. Shanghai Municipal Police Files, no. D–3433, April 1, 1932. For the sending of the ten best graduates of the Zhejiang Police Academy to Vienna, see August Vollmer, "Correspondence: Letters from Frank Yee," Bancroft Library, CB-403, letter dated July 25, 1934. Two years later a commission headed by Feng Ti was sent by the Ministry of War to study the police and military systems of England, France, Italy, and Germany; and in 1935, Li Shizhen—eventually principal of the Central Police Academy—was also sent abroad to study the police systems of Europe, the United States and Japan. Gan Guoxun, "Guanyu suowei 'Fuxingshe' de zhenqing shikuang," p. 70. Feng Ti was appointed Chinese military attaché in Berlin in 1936. William C. Kirby, *Germany and Republican China* (Stanford: Stanford University Press, 1984), p. 137.

76. Throughout the early 1930s, however, models of police reform were eclectically chosen from European, Japanese, and American examples. See, for example, Hui Hong, *Xingshi jingcha xue* (Criminal police studies) (Shanghai: Commercial Press, 1936), pp. 2–3.

77. Alfred E. Parker, *Crime Fighter, August Vollmer* (New York: Macmillan, 1961), p. 170; Yee, "Police in Modern China," p. 36.

78. Gene E. Carte and Elaine H. Carte, *Police Reform in the United States: The Era of August Vollmer, 1905–1932* (Berkeley: University of California Press, 1975), p. 3.

79. August Vollmer, "Correspondence: Letters from Feng Yukon," letter dated August 2, 1932.

80. Ibid., letter dated September 12, 1933.

81. Ibid., letter dated March 25, 1934.

82. Zhang Weihan, "Dai Li yu 'Juntong ju' " (Dai Li and the Military Statistics Bureau), *Zhejiang wenshi ziliao xuanji* 23 (1982): 86.

83. Vollmer, "Correspondence: Letters from Frank Yee," letters dated July 25, 1934, and November 13, 1934.

84. Ibid., letter dated May 25, 1934.

85. Ibid., letter dated January 2, 1935.

86. Ibid., letter dated September 10, 1934.

87. Ibid., letter dated July 25, 1934.

88. Huang Yong, "Huangpu xuesheng de zhengzhi zuzhi ji qi yanbian" (Whampoa students' political organizations and their evolution), *Wenshi ziliao xuanji* 11 (1960): 10;

Zeng Kuoqing, "He Mei xieding qian Fuxingshe zai Huabei de huodong" (The activities of the Fuxingshe in North China before the He Mei agreement), *Wenshi ziliao xuanji* 14 (1961): 134; Shen Zui, "Wo suo zhidao de Dai Li," p. 8.

89. Yee, "Police in Modern China," pp. 39–41.

90. Vollmer, "Correspondence: Letters from Frank Yee," letters dated June 30, 1934, and April 6, 1935.

91. Deng Yuanzhong, "Sanminzhuyi Lixingshe shi chugao," p. 155.

92. Zhang Weihan, "Dai Li yu 'Juntong ju' " (The Dai Li I knew), in *Dai Li qi ren* (Dai Li the man), ed. Shen Zui and Wen Qiang (Beijing: Wenshi ziliao chubanshe, 1980), p. 86; Shen Zui, "Wo suo zhidao de Dai Li," p. 8.

93. Zhang, "Dai Li yu 'Juntong ju,' " p. 86; Yee, "Police in Modern China," p. 41.

94. Roger Faligot and Remi Kauffer, *Kang Sheng et les services secrets chinois (1927–1987)* (Paris: Robert Laffont, 1987).

95. Chiang is quoted by Yu Xiuhao as having said: "To establish a country, you first have to establish the police." Yu Xiuhao, *Jingcha shouce* (Police handbook) (Shanghai: Shanghai jingsheng shuju, 1948), preface, p. 1.

96. Yee, "Police in Modern China," pp. 38–39. Chiang also said: "The police must understand that their position in the country is more important than that of the army. The army is only used against the outside to protect the country internationally. The police are used inside to maintain social order within the country and to protect the people's lives and property. Otherwise, social order would not be maintained, the people's lives and properties would not be protected, and the country would then become chaotic." Yu, *Jingcha shouce*, pp. 1–2.

97. Yee, "Police in Modern China," p. 36.

98. He Qideng, "Dangqian zhi jingzheng jigou wenti" (Problems concerning present-day structures of police administration), *Lixing yuekan* 2, 5 (Aug. 30, 1940): 18.

99. Vollmer, "Correspondence: Letters from Frank Yee," letter dated August 6, 1936.

100. Vollmer, "Correspondence: Letters from Feng Yukon," letter dated November 7, 1936. See also the report by Superintendent Tan Shao-liang, Shanghai Municipal Police Files, no. D–7675A, April 2, 1937.

101. Yee, "Police in Modern China," pp. 41–42. In rural areas too poor and remote to afford regular police, law enforcement duties would be assigned to the former *baojia* mutual responsibility units. Vollmer, "Correspondence: Letters from Frank Yee," letter dated May 14, 1937. Six weeks earlier Yee wrote that "Plans have already drown [*sic*] up to transform all the peace-preserving units in the various parts of the country into police, and the central police academy is hurriedly making preparation to give them the necessary supplementary police training in a large scale for a period of three years." Ibid., letter dated March 24, 1937.

102. He, "Dangqian zhi jingzheng jigou wenti," p. 19.

103. Vollmer, "Correspondence: Letters from Frank Yee," letter dated August 6, 1936. See also the letter dated September 10, 1936.

104. Shen, "Wo suo zhidao de Dai Li," p. 8. See also Hung-mao Tien, *Government and Politics in Kuomintang China, 1927–1937* (Stanford: Stanford University Press, 1972), p. 60.

105. Vollmer, Correspondence: Letters from Frank Yee, letter dated September 10, 1936. See also the letter dated October 27, 1936, for plans to train the deans of police schools all around China.

106. Ibid., letter dated January 5, 1937.

107. Vollmer, "Correspondence: Letters from Feng Yukon," letter dated March 23, 1937.

108. Wakeman, "Policing Modern Shanghai."

109. Ralph Thaxton's latest work in progress.

110. "When it comes to discussing lower-level police organizations we cannot help but feel pessimistic." He, "Dangqian zhi jingzheng jigou wenti," p. 20.

111. Ezra Vogel, *Canton under Communism: Programs and Politics in a Provincial Capital, 1949–1968* (Cambridge: Harvard University Press, 1969); Kenneth Lieberthal, *Revolution and Tradition in Tientsin, 1949–1952* (Stanford: Stanford University Press, 1980).

112. "The Public Security Substations are small, local police posts, consisting of a chief, one or two deputies, and several policemen. They are branches of the municipal or *hsien* Public Security Bureaus and are responsible for law enforcement, maintenance of 'social order,' crime prevention, suppression of counterrevolutionaries, direction of Security Committees organized among inhabitants, and welfare work." A. Doak Barnett, *Communist China: The Early Years, 1949–1955* (New York: Frederick A. Praeger, 1964), pp. 322–23.

113. Ibid., pp. 50–51, 203.

114. This expansion was the result of pressure for upward mobility on the part of careerists wanting to "become officials" (*dangguan*). Ying-mao Kau, "Patterns of Recruitment and Mobility of Urban Cadres," in *The City in Communist China*, ed. John W. Lewis (Stanford: Stanford University Press, 1971), p. 106.

115. Nee points to the "mutual dependence of state control and local autonomy" in the militia, which was both "an important instrument of control and mobilization" and—he argues—"a considerable counterbalance to state control." Victor Nee, "Between Center and Locality: State, Militia, and Village," in *State and Society in Contemporary China*, ed. Nee and Mozingo, p. 242.

116. Quoted in Barnett, *Communist China*, p. 51.

117. Ibid., pp. 321–22.

118. The roundup began on April 28, 1951. According to one witness who later fled China, "In Shanghai many public buildings, including two schools, all of which had been taken over by the police weeks before, were used as prisons. One of the execution grounds was near the university. Every day we would see the truckloads of prisoners. While we were in our classes, we would hear the terrible shooting." Robert Loh and Humphrey Evans, *Escape from Red China* (New York: Coward-McCann, 1962), p. 66.

119. "The purpose of the [police substation] system is quite clear: to organize all urban inhabitants and bring them under closer direct control of both the civil administration and the police organs of city governments. There is a deep-rooted tradition in China for the organization of the population in this fashion, but the [new] system . . . appears to be more thorough, and one would guess more onerous, to ordinary people than the traditional pao-chia system the Communists abolished with much fanfare when they took over." Barnett, *Communist China*, p. 323.

120. John Gittings, *The Role of the Chinese Army* (London: Oxford University Press, 1967), pp. 80, 290.

121. After 1959 the public security system was nominally under the leadership of Xie Fuzhi, who was considered ineffective. Before 1966 ultimate decision-making power rested in the five-man Leading Political and Legal Group, which was composed of Xie, Peng Zhen, Luo Ruiqing, Kang Sheng, and Yang Shangkun. Parris H. Chang, "The Rise of Wang Tung-hsing: Head of China's Security Apparatus," *China Quarterly* 73 (March 1978): 130–31.

122. William W. Whitson, "Organizational Perspectives and Decision-Making," in *Elites in the People's Republic of China*, ed. Robert A. Scalapino (Seattle: University of Washington Press, 1972), pp. 401–2.

123. Hong Yung Lee, *The Politics of the Chinese Cultural Revolution: A Case Study* (Berkeley: University of California Press, 1978), pp. 180, 218.

124. Chang, "The Rise of Wang Tung-hsing," p. 131.

125. Tai Ming Cheung, "Big Brother Is Watching," *Far Eastern Economic Review*, November 3, 1988, p. 24.

126. "Credit Goes to Dutiful Procurators," *China Daily*, October 23, 1989, p. 3.

127. An Zhiguo, "Legal Studies: A Nationwide Assignment," *Beijing Review* 28, 51 (December 23, 1985): 4–5. Books and movies featuring heroic and selfless police officers were widely circulated after 1983 when the Public Security Bureau was given the right to try and execute criminals publicly within twenty-four hours of their arrest.

128. "Officers Killed in Line of Duty," *China Daily,* March 13, 1985, p. 3; Michael Browning, "5,000 Executions Called 'Good Lesson,' " *Miami Herald*, November 15, 1984, p. 32A.

129. "It is true that we executed some people in the past year, but it was because in the previous few years we did not do a good job in punishing offenders. Some people who deserved capital punishment were not put to death, and the people were greatly dissatisfied with that." Wang Jingrong, quoted in Browning, "5,000 Executions Called 'Good Lesson,' " p. 32A.

130. Ibid. In 1984 more than 140,000 criminals surrendered to the police and were given lighter sentences according to the traditional principle of "leniency to those who confess their crimes and more severe punishment to those who refuse." Liu Dazhong, "Crime Rate Plummets as Public Back Crackdown," *China Daily*, April 1, 1985, p. 1.

131. From September 1983, when the crackdown began, to June 1985, China registered 750,000 criminal cases, which was a decrease of 34.6 percent over the previous twenty-two months. Wu Jingshu, "Two-Year Crackdown on China's Crime Rate," *China Daily*, December 20, 1985, p. 1. See also "Beijing Crime Rate Has Dropped," *China Daily*, March 20, 1987, p. 3.

132. In 1984 the number of cases reported to the police dropped 15.7 percent to 510,000 as against the previous year. This was close to the average crime rate in the 1950s, about 4 out of 10,000 persons, according to Minister of Public Security Liu Fuzhi. Liu, "Crime Rate Plummets as Public Back Crackdown," p. 1. That is one of the world's lowest crime rates, needless to say. According to figures given at the meeting of the Far East Judicial Seminar held in Beijing on December 19, 1985, the crime rate in France is 3.9 percent; in West Germany, 4.3 percent; in the United States, 4.8 percent; in Britain, 5 percent; in Japan, 1.1 percent; and in China, 0.05 percent. Wu, "Two-Year Crackdown on China's Crime Rate." See also "Tianjin Crime Rate Drops 29 Percent," *China Daily*, May 28, 1985, p. 3; Marvin Howe, "With Few Major Crimes, China's Police Deal with Social Needs," *International Herald Tribune*, December 16, 1985, p. 5.

133. Liu Dazhong, "Nationwide Crackdown on Crime Continues," *China Daily*, October 20, 1987, p. 1. Seventy percent of the crimes were thefts.

134. "Economic Crimes Are Main Target," *China Daily*, March 13, 1987, p. 1.

135. Tai Ming Cheung, "Crackdown on Crime," *Far Eastern Economic Review*, November 3, 1988, p. 23. Hong Kong's *Wenhui bao* reported that in the first six months of 1988, seventy-seven institutes of higher education in twenty-five cities were involved in direct or indirect political protests ranging from putting up big-character posters to demonstrations.

136. Tai, "Crackdown on Crime," p. 23. Political disturbances as such were blamed on rowdy criminal elements, i.e., the Shanghai student protests of December 1986 were attributed to jobless youth. This was at the very least a rhetorical foreshadowing of the "hooliganism" charges leveled by Mayor Chen Xitong at the Tiananmen Square protesters in May and June 1989. See Frederic Wakeman, "The June Fourth Movement in

China," *Items* 43, 3 (September 1989): 57–64.

137. Tai, "Crackdown on Crime," p. 23.

138. "To monitor the growing number of foreigners in the country, the state security organs have had to recruit more and more language students to be trained as tour guides, hotel workers, and as staff in trading companies." Tai, "Big Brother Is Watching," p. 25.

139. Liu, "Nationwide Crackdown on Crime Continues." Police colleges offered short-term courses for directors of police bureaus above county level. Between 1986 and July 1987, about 1,500 police cadres had finished courses on security technology and the law at four police colleges under the MPS. These numbers presumably increased after Wang Fang became minister. Chen Qing, "Police Get Intensive Training," *China Daily*, October 16, 1987, p. 3.

140. Public Security University was founded in 1983. Its curriculum, which was under the supervision of Zhang Guangyi, emphasized physical fitness and skill in boxing, judo, shooting, and driving. Chen, "Police Get Intensive Training," p. 3.

141. Officials reported 72,000 severe crimes during that period, but some believed the figure was actually twice that high. Tai, "Crackdown on Crime," p. 23.

142. Ibid.

143. The Special License Office of the Beijing Police Western District Subbureau, which was established in January 1985, was in charge of registering, administering, and patrolling the more than one thousand hotels, shops, and individual businesses in the district. Only about twenty business licenses a month were granted, causing some merchants to resort to bribery. "Unfortunately, some party officials have not been able to resist temptation." Zhang Jiamin, "Police Praised for Resisting Bribery," *China Daily*, June 7, 1985, p. 3. According to interviews I conducted in Beijing in January 1990, household registration police routinely shake down young Anhui women who have come to the capital to work as domestics.

144. In 1984 there were 750,000 motor vehicles on Beijing's city roads; 548 people were killed and 6,670 were injured in the capital in traffic accidents. "Traffic Death Toll Rises in Beijing," *China Daily*, February 16, 1985, p. 3.

145. For the linkage between a redistributive economy and state power in China, see Mayfair Mei-hui Yang, "The Modernity of Power in the Chinese Socialist Order," *Cultural Anthropology* 3, 4 (November 1988): 408–27.

146. For example, the growth in the numbers of cash-carrying travelling salesman—about 50,000,000 people take a train each day through the country—has meant both an increase in criminal cases on railroads (a 37.1 percent increase between 1987 and 1989) and a rise in the number of railway police (who have to resist the cigarette and cash bribes of people with overweight luggage or illegal goods). Yuan Shuhua, "Railway Police: Safeguards for Passengers," *China Daily*, August 28, 1989, p. 6.

147. Ordinary police were recruited on a much wider basis than before during the winter of 1989–90. Liang Chao, "Beijing to Recruit More Police," *China Daily*, December 7, 1989, p. 3.

148. Tai, "Big Brother Is Watching," pp. 24–25. The dual military and public security chains of command may have been intended to prevent the PAP from developing its own institutional and bureaucratic identity.

149. The PAP was responsible for the Tibetan suppression as well. Ibid., p. 25.

150. Mobile response units were organized in late 1987, modeled on Polish and East German security establishments. Some units received training in Western Germany, it was said, and Chinese security officials also studied in the United States. Tai, "Crackdown on Crime," p. 23. See also "U.S. Cop Tutors Chinese Peers," *China Daily*, March 16, 1989, p. 5.

151. Chang, "The Rise of Wang Tung-hsing," pp. 122–37.

152. On September 8, 1989, Li Peng criticized "a small number of Western countries . . . for stirring up an anti-China current after China put down a counterrevolutionary rebellion in Beijing. We should guard against outside subversion while continuing our contacts with the West." "Li Warns of Outside Subversion in Coping with West," *China Daily*, September 9, 1989, p. 1.

153. The party's International Liaison Department is responsible for foreign intelligence and subversion. Fox Butterfield, "From the Security Apparatus an Obscure Leader Emerges," *New York Times*, June 7, 1989, p. A9; *Beijing Review*, July 10–16, 1989, pp. 22–23, and July 17–23, 1989, p. 24; T. L. Tan, "Profile: Qiao Shi," *Inside China Mainland* (October 1989): 27–28; Tai Ming Cheung, "Big Brother Is Watching," p. 24; Tai, "Security Chief's Rising Star," *Far Eastern Economic Review*, November 3, 1988, p. 24.

154. A new state secrets law, which was supposed to have been promulgated in May 1989, calls for severe punishments to be meted out to those who reveal state secrets. A new State Secrets Bureau was supposed to replace the Central Secrets Commission in order to create a more systematic process of classifying and handling of secret documents. Tai Ming Cheung, "State Secrets Redefined," *Far Eastern Economic Review*, November 3, 1988, p. 25.

155. Chinese police authorities are now engaged in cooperative activities with Interpol and other foreign police agencies to curb the drug traffic out of the Golden Triangle. The MPS has established a special drug force of 1,300 members. Chang Hong, "Nation Vows to Fight Return of Drugs," *China Daily*, October 23, 1989, p. 4.

156. In the two months after August 1989 (when the antipornography drive began under Li Ruihuan) some three million copies of books and magazines that contained "reactionary and pornographic contents" were confiscated. Another nine million copies of books and more than ninety thousand videotapes were taken off the market. "Anti-Porn Campaign Proceeds," *China Daily*, October 18, 1989, p. 3; "Pornography Purge Wins Mass Support," *China Daily*, August 30, 1989, p. 4. I have a "classified" (*neibu*) 125-page list of materials to be censored, issued in October 1989, which includes both pornographic and "bourgeois liberal" titles: *Zhengdun qingli shubaokan ji yinxiang shichang wenjian xuanbian* (A collection of directives on rectifying and cleaning up the market in books, newspapers, and audio-visual materials) (Shanghai: Xinwen chubanshe, 1989).

157. "ID Card Checking Starts Soon," *China Daily*, September 9, 1989, p. 1; Chang Hong, "Inspection of ID Cards Under Way," *China Daily*, September 19, 1989, p. 3.

158. For reports of recent repression, including illegal torture (China signed United Nations instruments in 1986 outlawing torture, and reported 30,000 cases of illegal detention and 202 cases in which policemen raped, beat to death or seriously injured prisoners in 1987), see Jasper Becker, "China Reported to Be Torturing Detainees," *Manchester Guardian Weekly*, July 30, 1989, p. 7; Orville Schell, "Five among So Many," *The Washington Post National Weekly Edition*, August 7–13, 1989, p. 25; Marjorie Sun, "Stories of Repression from China," *Science*, 245: 462; Francis Deron, "Peking Whips Press into Line," *Manchester Guardian Weekly*, August 20, 1989, p. 13.

159. John Fairbank's "final and rather chilling conclusion from the long record of China's history is that no régime in power has ever given it up without bloodshed. Force has been the final arbiter, not Confucian teaching." Fairbank, "Why China's Rulers Fear Democracy," p. 32.

4

THE ENLIGHTENMENT MENTALITY AND THE CHINESE INTELLECTUAL DILEMMA

TU WEI-MING

As children of the Enlightenment, we members of the scholarly community professionally and personally involved in the study of traditional China and its modern transformation inadvertently subscribe to a set of Western cultural assumptions, making a sophisticated appreciation of the process by which China as a civilization-state adapted itself to the impact of the West painfully difficult. Although we rarely engage ourselves in a critical reflection on the Enlightenment mentality, an intellectual effort that has preoccupied some of the brilliant minds from North American and Europe in the last two decades, we are deeply affected by it. For one thing, the conceptual apparatuses we have employed in analyzing China and the symbolic resources we have tapped in interpreting China are Enlightenment in character. In other words, we approach our subject of inquiry from the Enlightenment perspective.

To be sure, any approach we choose to study China is inevitably theory-laden and value-laden; it is naive to believe that we can ever arrive at a totally objective analysis or strictly factual explanation of China and that our interpretation is value-free. We do, however, cherish the view that our analyses, as contrasted with the blatantly ideological accounts of Chinese Marxist historians, are more objective in the scientific sense and that our interpretations, as compared with the highly idiosyncratic views of Japanese Sinological economists, are less biased. We pride ourselves for having been immersed in "disciplines" in the social sciences that are scholarly sound. Quite a few of our claims, such as the origins of the Opium War, the religious aspect of the Taiping Rebellion, the regional basis of the Self-Strengthening Movement, the nature of the 1911 Revolution, the cultural background of the May Fourth Incident, the rise of the Chinese Communist Party, and the elite conflicts in the People's Republic of China, while subject to further evaluation, have been widely accepted as shared knowledge in the international scholarly community. At least, it is arguable that for the last generation China scholars in the English-speaking world have set standards for analyzing and interpreting the major trends in the modern transformation of Chinese civilization.

Our accomplishments notwithstanding, there are blinders in our overall understanding of the ethicoreligious dimension and the psychocultural dynamics of Chinese society. As B. I. Schwartz recently noted, "one of the most intractably problematic aspects of Chinese culture for most contemporary Western scholars has been the perceived role of hierarchy, status, and authority—or to use a harsher 'unmasking' vocabulary, domination, subjugation and repression—not only in the cultural history of Chinese society but even in its shared cultural norms."[1] The reason for this, as Schwartz further noted, is that "most of us are, to a greater or lesser degree, children of the Enlightenment or at least that strain in the Enlightenment which negates and repudiates all ideas and values associated with hierarchy, status, and authority." Despite the fact that the "the theoretical dilemmas concerning the relations of liberty, equality, and democracy to each other have by no means been resolved," dominant Western ideologies, Marxism or liberalism, in attacking the idea of authority from the vantage point of either equality or liberty, shared the Enlightenment orientation.[2] The matter is further complicated by the fact that the post–May Fourth intellectuals in China have been themselves children of the Enlightenment with a vengeance. The iconoclastic attack on Confucianism as the ideology of hierarchy, status, and authority clearly shows that they have fully subscribed to the Enlightenment rhetoric.

Rhetoric

On the occasion of the centenary of the French Revolution, the embodiment of the Enlightenment spirit, there was genuine celebration. The ideals of liberty, equality, and fraternity evoke sensations of progress and rationality, indeed liberation of the human spirit, that all reasonable men must accept as self-evidently true. There was no major debate on the conflict between liberty and equality. There was virtually no concern for clarifying the true meaning of "fraternity," for example, yet how was it to be realized after the ancient regime collapsed? Nonetheless, two hundred years later, the French Revolution has become a story of excess. With the exception of the idealistic Declaration of the Rights of Man, the setting up of the National Assembly, the storming of the Bastille, and the capture and eventual guillotining of the royal family, not to mention the Reign of Terror and war, can no longer generate unqualified admiration. The history spanning a mere decade that witnessed nearly a million killed and that ended with the rise of the dictatorship of Napoleon Bonaparte is hardly glorious. Nevertheless, in the age of reason, every educated person felt indebted to the revolutionary process that brought about many of the political and social changes characteristic of the modern West.

Actually, the modern West has been instrumental in developing from medieval roots the major economic, political and social institutions that define the normative features of the contemporary form of life: market or planned economy, democratic or socialist policy, citizenship, civil societies, professional associations, religious organizations, universities, and so forth. The modern West is neither a territorial concept nor an ethnographic idea, but a shared value. As a value, it has already been deeply ingrained in the collective consciousness of the post–May Fourth Chinese intelligentsia. They think in terms of categories derived from the modern West informed by the Enlightenment. Often they think uncritically, as if these historically determined and culturally conditioned categories were inviolable. Even when they are conscientiously developing their own interpretive stance on what Feng Qi calls "The great debate on past/present and China/West,"[3] they tend to equate the past with China and the present with the West. Although few Chinese intellectuals are acutely aware of their conceptual indebtedness to the modern West, they fully acknowledge that they are the beneficiaries of the Enlightenment world view. The very fact that they use terms such as *zhexue* (philosophy), *kexue* (science), *zongjiao* (religion), *shehui* (society), *zhengzhi* (politics), *jingji* (economy), and *wenhua* (culture) so naturally as if they were indigenously Chinese indicates the degree to which the Enlightenment mentality has penetrated the Chinese mind. This, of course, does not imply that, as children of the Enlightenment, the Chinese intellectuals have transcended their "feudal" past. Far from it, their obsession with China's wealth and power makes their appreciation of the Enlightenment one-sided. As Li Zehou notes, the conflict between enlightenment and the concern for national survival eventually led to the total subsuming of Enlightenment ideas, such as liberty and individual rights, under the rubric of patriotism.[4] Once the survival of China, not only as a civilization-state but also as a unified nation, became an overriding concern, liberal democratic values were either relegated to the background or instrumentalized as expedient means.

Ironically, it was not the Declaration of the Rights of Man (the values of liberty, equality, and fraternity) that truly inspired the Chinese intellectuals of May Fourth. As a patriotic movement, the May Fourth Incident signaled the beginning of a national struggle dominated by the political issue. It was in the political arena, dictated by the orienting question of how to make China wealthy and strong, that the drama of the praxis of the Chinese intellectuals since May Fourth unfolded. Specifically, the Enlightenment symbolized to modern Chinese intellectuals not liberty and human rights as ends in themselves but the "Faustian spirit" unleashed by the social Darwinian quest for superiority. Understandably, the project of the Chinese Enlightenment, as defined by Vera Schwarcz —"liberation from self-repression"[5]—was a two-edged sword. The iconoclastic attack on the Confucian tradition and the concerted effort to establish a truly critically minded humanism are theoretically compatible but, in actuality, represent two conflicting currents of thought. The implications of the legacy of May Fourth—to be the heir of the French Enlightenment and, at the same time, to be the filial son of the "dragon seed" (*longzhong*)—for our attempt to retrieve the process by which Chinese intellectuals responded to the impact of the West is far-reaching. Surely, we must go beyond the Enlightenment mentality to appreciate the Chinese intellectual perception of the world prior to the Opium War, but the task is immensely difficult.

Approach

To be aware that the Enlightenment mentality is in the air and that we, as students of modern Chinese thought, and the contemporary Chinese intellectuals who interpret their own heritage from a presumably internal perspective are both children of the Enlightenment serves as a point of departure for exploring alternative ways of interpreting China's modern transformation since the Opium War. While it is either naive or disingenuous to presume to be able to return to the eve of the Opium War as if nothing had happened, the authentic possibility exists of formulating an interpretation of the Chinese intellectual perception of the world without being enslaved in the Enlightenment mentality. This possibility came into being only in recent decades when the most seminal interpreters of the modern West, such as Talcott Parsons and J. Habermas, showed the desirability and necessity of transcending the Enlightenment mentality in order to understand the complexity of the modern West. Of course, the critical reflection on the Enlightenment legacy by thinkers in North America and Europe provides only one kind of impetus for enlarging the conceptual resources for interpreting the intellectual dynamics of the modern West. The rise of industrial East Asia significantly challenges the widely accepted view that since genetically modernization emerged from the West, structurally modernization must be defined by Westernization. If there are non-Western patterns of capital formation then, by implication, modernization can assume more than one cultural form and the Enlightenment is only historically linked to a particular modality of modernity. As a result, we may approach China's modernization from perspectives compatible with but independent of the Enlightenment mentality. An example to illustrate this observation is in order.

In the 1960s when the structural-function model of modernization dominated the methodological scene, social scientists took it for granted that the developmental patterns in Western European and Northern American societies defined in terms of the Weberian idea of rationalization would eventually spread throughout the world. The influence of the West, hitherto characterized as Westernization, was thought to be global in nature. Thus, "modernization," as a worldwide phenomenon, replaced the parochial term "Westernization" as a universalizable concept. The Enlightenment idea of progress and its subsequent variations of the same theme, be it Darwinian social evolution, Comtean civilizational change, or Marxist historical inevitability, helped scholars of modernization to picture the world in terms of economic, political, and social stages. Rostow's "stages of economic development" and Lerner's "passing of the traditional society" are two obvious examples of how the globe was perceived by the modernists.

The global consciousness that envisioned the power of technology, the inevitable trend of urbanization, the pervasive tendency toward industrialization, and the conspicuous spread of mass communication correctly predicted that the world was shrinking and that the interdependence of nation-states would become a lived reality. However, they totally failed to see that, as the world shrank and the nation-states became interdependent, the primordial ties that for centuries defined the boundaries of human community became strengthened rather than weakened. It has become abundantly clear as we move toward the twenty-first century that ethnicity, mother tongue, fatherland, gender, and religion will continue to define who we are. Actually, the modernization process seems to have underscored their importance not merely as reactions to change but also as positive contributions to the meaning of life in an increasingly pluralistic universe. The nation-states themselves are subject to constant reevaluation; their survivability and continuous flourishing depend, in a large measure, on their ability to harmonize their primordial ties. From this postindustrial, or even postmodern, perspective, the type of comparative civilizational analysis under the influence of the Enlightenment mentality is no longer adequate. As we examine the Chinese intellectual outlook on the world since the Opium War, we must also critically reflect on our own value assumptions.

Context

The Chinese empire on the eve of the Opium War, far from collapsing of its own weight, was still an ordered universe with a flourishing economy, an accountable bureaucracy, a stable society, and a worried but by and large supportive intelligentsia. Surely, the apex of the Qing dynasty under the rulership of Qianlong, which witnessed the unprecedented expansion of the territorial and demographic bases of China, had long passed. The empire was certainly in a period of decline, but the process was gradual, and no signs of a total disintegration were clearly visible.

Unlike France at the time of the revolution, the imperial household in China never produced the likes of a despised King Louis XVI and his wife Marie Antoinette, even though the Daoguang emperor was weak and ineffectual. The Manchu empire had lost much of its vitality, but it was not propped up by a system that inspired little confidence in the people. Since there was no privileged nobility mercilessly taxing the peasantry, despite corruption of the officialdom and rampant rebellious activity, the empire was not threatened by a simmering revolution. The phenomenon of outraged professional classes fulminated by sarcastic writers in a united front against the establishment was totally absent. There were no vociferously protesting people led by political agitators to challenge the legitimacy of the regime. The authorities were able to keep law and order, and the country was not at all on the verge of turmoil.

In the perspective of the enormous dynamism exhibited in Western Europe and North America in the first decades of the nineteenth century, the history of China in the comparable period was uneventful. Yet, the impression of China in a state of stagnation as a result of its own self-imposed isolation is misleading. The rise of the modern West, a sort of out-of-control juggernaut symbolized by the French Revolution, requires more explanation in human history than the seeming steady-state of the Manchu empire does. If we assume that the post-Enlightenment developments in the West define not only historically but also structurally what modernity entails, we can easily see that Qing China failed miserably to prepare itself for the inevitable process. As Donald Shively wittily notes, the Tokugawa Shogunate did not know that it was preparing Japan for modernization;[6] and the Manchu dynasty was never ready for the impact of the West. A macroscopic survey of the psychocultural dynamics of Chinese society with particular reference to the ethicoreligious dimension of the intelligentsia should make the point clear that, while the study of China's response to the West helps us to understand "Confucian China and its modern fate,"[7] it inadvertently undermines the cultural resources mobilized by the intellectual elite for spiritual self-definition as well as for understanding the outside world.

China, under the Qing, was socially highly stratified and yet quite fluid. Despite role differentiation, governed principally by status rather than class, upward and horizontal social mobility was common. If we use the French model as a guide, there was no counterpart to the three estates. The clergy, nobility, and Third Estate, consisting of the remaining sections of society, were all absent. Instead, the imperial household, aided by a relatively meritocratic officialdom, which, in turn, was supported by the gentry, ruling over a massive population composed mainly of the peasantry. Strictly speaking, the people, wrongly labeled as the undifferentiated masses, included not only the peasant but also the artisan, merchant, soldier, and a variety of legitimate and illegitimate occupational groups. The intelligentsia, the local literati as well as scholar-officials, though not necessarily well-to-do, was politically influential and socially prestigious.

The society was hierarchically organized, but it was definitely not "feudalistic" in the European sense. The gap between city dwellers and rustic peasants in the countryside was not pronounced. Whether or not we accept Fritz Mote's assertion about the urban-rural continuum,[8] the phenomenon of the Parisians or the people (traders, craftsmen, shopkeepers, laborers, and the poor) taking to the streets without involving the gentry and the peasantry is unimaginable. While there were occasional riots in the major cities, the lynchings and lootings characteristic of the sporadic outbursts of the urban poor were rare. Rebellions in traditional China were frequently occasioned by peasant unrest led by disgruntled gentry. The intelligentsia, as the most articulate minority, normally provided ideological and administrative support for the court. Even in extraordinary circumstances they did not deliberately alienate themselves from the ruling elite. The gentry—the local literati and the scholar-officials—in late imperial China, though like the nobility in status and the clergy in influence, was a uniquely Sinic phenomenon, for it provided the necessary linkage, the communicative network, between the court and the populace at large.

The gentry in the sociopolitical sense or the intelligentsia in the ethico-religious sense provided ideological and administrative leadership in society with virtually no appeal to brute force. As civilians, they did not have direct access to the military. Their style of governance, in both theory and practice, was predicated on the persuasion of a common discourse, a discourse defined in terms of well-established rituals (*li*). The following observation by Benjamin Schwartz, commenting on the assertion that "the Confucian texts regarded hierarchy, status, and authority not only as a necessary but even as a good aspect of a harmonious society (and a harmonious family)," is pertinent: "Here I am reminded of the depiction of the ancestral ceremonies of aristocratic families in the *Book of Odes* where everyone from the main familial participants to the humblest ceremonial functionaries play their duly assigned roles with the utmost dignity and decorum. The important thing is not whether the role played is august or humble but that one plays one's part in the beatitude of the entire august ceremonial pageant."[9] The intention of the gentry to rule by ritual, if not by virtue, suggests that the Qing empire maintained domestic peace by the mechanism of what E. P. Thompson calls "symbolic control." The presence of a constant threat of physical coercion notwithstanding, it was ritual rather than law that preserved order among the populace.

The authority of the intelligentsia was essential for the successful exercise of "symbolic control." Although the influence and prestige of the intellectual as individuals and as a collectivity were sanctioned by the court and legitimized by the emperor, the relationship between the intelligentsia and throne was reciprocal. The widely publicized ritual of kowtow may have given the impression that the supremacy of the emperor as the Son of Heaven was never challenged, and that the scholar-official was always submissive in front of the awesome imperial presence. Whether or not the idea of reciprocity, as we understand it, was ever practiced, the sources of the intellectual's authority made it possible for him to maintain an independent, autonomous posture toward the court.

The first source of authority for the intelligentsia was the cumulative tradition. For the sake of convenience, we may characterize this as the authority of the past. The scholar-official, seasoned in classical studies, was self-consciously a cultural transmitter who was obligated either by a sense of mission or by "professional" necessity to breathe vitality into the moral codes embedded in the great books. To the local literati and scholar-officials, ideas such as humanity (*ren*), rightness (*yi*), propriety (*li*), wisdom (*zhi*), and truthfulness (*xin*) were not dead letters but living messages for conducting proper life in a civilized society. They could be manipulative, for example, imposing moral codes on the unsuspecting populace while devoting themselves to the pursuit of private interests; they could also be deficient in critical self-awareness, for example, perfunctorily assuming the role of moralizer without themselves being seriously involved in personal cultivation, but they were inescapably trapped in the linguistic game of cultural transmission. Indeed, they were responsible for making the core values of the cumulative tradition coherent, dynamic, and persuasive.

Actually, from the Son of Heaven to the commoner, every living soul in China proper self-consciously or inadvertently took part in the cumulative tradition. It is tempting to find a monocausal reason for this seemingly unique cultural phenomenon. The peculiarity of the Chinese ideographs seems to provide the logical explanation except that no matter how important a value literacy was in traditional China, the majority of those who actively participated in the cultural transmission—peasants, artisans and merchants—were by and large illiterate and thus did not have mastery over the ideographs. It should also be mentioned that if we do not confuse high literacy with cultural sophistication, we should notice that some of the most sophisticated cultural transmitters were actually illiterates—for instance, the mothers of great writers, thinkers, scholars, and statesmen.

The availability of numerous morality books (*shanshu*), the popularity of novels and fiction, and the omnipresence of dramas, operas, and other theatrical performances in the countryside may give the impression that the medium is the message, but the content clearly suggests that what the people of all stations of life were exposed to and what the Four Treasures (classics, history, philosophy, and literature) contain actually belong to the same linguistic universe with varying degrees of cultural sophistication. In other words, the marginal intellectuals who bridged the gap between the cultural elite and the people were more than conduits of the core values of the cumulative tradition, for they actively participated in shaping their contents without losing sight of their general spiritual orientation.

The arguments that the central government, supported by a powerful bureaucracy, was instrumental in standardizing the ideology and that the market towns with their elaborate commercial networks provided the information channels for transmitting shared ideas do not at all undermine the assertion that the core values of the cumulative tradition were the immediate and ultimate concerns of the intelligentsia. Furthermore, the intelligentsia did not passively respond to the institutional constraints; they created infrastructures so that what they cherished spread to all strata of society. As they constructed their own cultural identity, they saw to it that it was open enough to accommodate the ruling minority, on the one hand, and the populace, on the other.

To the scholar-official and the local literatus, the core values of the cumulative tradition were neither abstract ideas nor private beliefs but the "wellspring and live water" that enable a society to become a moral community and a civilization. The intellectuals were intensely interested in the actual process by which these core values became embodied in the lives of ordinary men and women. It is idealistic, if not naive, for us to accept the claim that the exemplary teaching of the educated elite is all that is needed for the people to get the message and behave accordingly. It is beyond dispute that the intellectuals' preoccupation with orthodoxy (the correct common creed) was inseparable from their desire to engender orthopraxy ("correct practice"). In this sense, "people practice it daily without knowing why"[10] clearly indicates that they already know how to do it. From behavior, attitude, and belief to enlightened communal critical self-consciousness, the degrees of refinement are numerous, but the visible signs of correct practice are the minimum requirements for acceptable behavior. This is the grammar of action underlying ritual practice. To ensure that ritual practice was routinized in the full life cycle of each person in China proper, the mechanism of "symbolic control" was implemented by formal organizations such as community compacts and community schools and by informal institutions such as occasional meetings, clan instructions, group readings, and public lectures.

Understandably, the second source of authority for the intelligentsia was social practice. Unlike the Greek philosopher or the Hebraic prophet, the Chinese intellectual realized his calling by serving as the conscience of the people.[11] It is inconceivable that the Chinese intellectual, by a deliberate choice, alienated himself from the people in the street or that he, as the vehicle of a revealed truth, rose about the multitude. Instead, either as scholar-official or as local literatus, the Chinese intellectual found his worth as a man among men constantly in touch with the secular affairs of the mundane world. If the messages he delivered did not strike a sympathetic chord among the people, it was a major challenge to his leadership. Inherent in the structure of his role as a cultural transmitter, he functioned as a communicative teacher in the society at large. Actually, as a teacher, oral persuasion was often more important than making pronouncements in writing. The true teacher was as much an audience as a speaker. Etymologically, the sage reveals himself in audio perceptions. The importance of the "ear" and the "mouth," as contrasted with that of the "eye," suggests the power of orality in cultural transmission. As the voice of the people, the intellectuals were supposed to speak on their behalf.

The third source of authority for the intelligentsia came from heaven. Since "heaven sees as the people see and heaven hears as the people hear," the transcendent referent was in fact rooted in popular sentiment. The appeal to heaven, however, provided Chinese intellectuals with a leverage against the tyranny of the people. They could resist the temptation of joining the revolt of the masses, as in the French Revolution, by observing the direction of the mandate of heaven in a long-term perspective. Surely, as an integral part of the ruling minority, or at least as members of the cultural elite, there was a built-in conservatism in the Chinese intelligentsia. Unlike their counterparts in tsarist Russia, who were under the strong influence of the French Enlightenment and thus automatically adversarial to the political establishment, Chinese intellectuals considered themselves responsible not only for the well-being of Chinese culture but also for the stability of the political order. After all, the meaning of "carrying on the Way on behalf of heaven" implies that they helped the central government to maintain peace and harmony on this earth.

Nevertheless, the evocation of heaven engendered symbolic resources that could not be totally politicized. Dong Zhongshu's theory of mutual responsiveness between heaven and man was originally not intended to be a religious justification for the transcendent power of the autocrat. It was meant to be a divine sanction against monarchic excesses. Even when it was used to justify the supremacy of the monarch, it never turned into a pretext for imperial infallibility. The repeated practice of the emperor in issuing edicts of self-criticism in response to natural calamities, which was often accompanied by a request for new ideas and therefore was an opportunity for scholar-officials to speak with candor on national issues, indicates that heaven could be on the side of the intelligentsia. In fact, the indigenous idea of *geming* (change of mandate) is predicated on the belief that "the mandate of heaven is not constant" and that, in both theory and practice, no human being, not even the Son of Heaven, can embody the divine right to rule. The fallibility of the monarch makes it imperative that the intelligentsia speaks out as the voice of the people on behalf of heaven.

This leads us to the final source of authority for the intelligentsia: conscience. The classical observation that "the commander of the three armies can be replaced but the will of a commoner cannot be snatched away" makes it abundantly clear that there is in China the strong belief that the will power of the individual is mightier than any coercive force in shaping behavior. The Chinese intelligentsia, immersed in the most comprehensive self-cultivation philosophy in human history, took it for granted that what they did in the private domain of their homes was politically consequential and cosmically significant. They also took it for granted that the communal critical self-consciousness they possessed enabled them to go beyond personal and collective interests. Accordingly, they could represent the "great interest" (*dali*) of the nation and act impartially in tone with the "hearts of the people" (*minxin*). Despite manipulation, distortion, and failure, this faith in the salvific power of the intellectual conscience remained strong.

While studies of the political function of officialdom staffed by scholars and the social role of gentry composed of literati are informative, an overview of the self-definition of the intelligentsia helps to identify the ethicoreligious dimension of the Chinese intelligentsia not as a superstructure but as the meaning-given value system that makes sense to them and us of the world view underlying the Chinese orthopraxy as well as orthodoxy. The authority of the Chinese intellectual, derived from multiple sources in culture, society, religion, and psychology, brings understanding to the context in which the impact of the West was perceived.

Dilemma

The story of the unprecedented erosion of Chinese cultural identity, as Chinese intellectuals tried desperately to cope with the Western impact since the Opium War, is well known. Wei Yuan's recommendation that China learn Western superior technology to manage the West, Zeng Guofan's concerted effort to strengthen China's military and industrial capacity on the Western model, Zhang Zhidong's slogan of combining Western function with Chinese substance, and Chen Xujing's advocacy of wholesale Westernization, spanning two generations, vividly chronicle the radical change of the self-image of the Chinese intelligentsia: from the master of the Middle Kingdom to the slave of the West. The wealth and power unleashed by the Enlightenment and the Industrial Revolution overwhelmed the Chinese intelligentsia; the rules of the game were so radically changed that they found themselves forced to play a game fundamentally unintelligible to them.

The explanatory model built around the Middle Kingdom syndrome hides as much as it reveals. It is a truism that the Chinese intelligentsia took China to be the center of the civilized world. Yet, the Manchu dynasty, as a multilingual and multi-ethnic state, had ample experience of moving from the periphery to the center. The collective historical memory of the Jurchens and the Khitans, not to mention the Mongols, provided enough lessons for Chinese intellectuals to appreciate the danger of marginalization and the trauma of national subjugation. After all, Wang Fuzhi had agonized over the plight of a conquered people,[12] and Gu Yanwu had borne witness to the extremities of the collapse of an entire civilization, which he characterized as the "loss of all under heaven" (*wang tianxia*).[13]

To say that China was isolated in the sense that it somehow lacked exposure to the outside world was tantamount to asserting that Europe and a significant part of Russia or the North American continent was cut off from the rest of humanity; this may have been true at a certain juncture of global history, but China had assumed preeminence in a complex international community for centuries. The structure of peaceful coexistence among North, East, and Southeast Asian states based on an elaborate ritual carefully constructed by the Chinese court gives ample testimony to the flexibility and durability of the tribute system. Culturally, the Buddhist conquest of China and the Chinese transformation of Buddhism, arguably the most spectacular indigenization of a foreign religion in human history, clearly show that the Chinese intelligentsia had an enormous capacity to absorb alien modes of thought and styles of life.

To characterize the Western challenge as the combination of the Mongol invasion and the Buddhist conquest/transformation compressed into one generation may convey the "shock," but not the profundity, of the impact. It took the

Chinese intelligentsia two generations to realize the full impact of the Western challenge; yet, to this date, some of the most influential Chinese minds still have difficulty comprehending the West in terms of symbolic resources other than wealth and power. Unlike India, China never experienced full-blown colonialism firsthand. Ironically, while British colonialism did not break the backbone of Indian spirituality (nor did it totally decenter Indian cultural identity), semicolonialism seems to have turned the Chinese intelligentsia into totalistic iconoclasts chronically suffering from an identity crisis since the naval disaster with Japan in 1894.

To compare Japan's speedy modernization with China's lack of response to the Western impact in the last century may help to illuminate the process by which an East Asian state in the periphery transcended its own cultural limitation while massively mobilizing its indigenous symbolic resources for a fundamental transformation of society; it does not throw enough light on the Chinese case. The cost that Japanese intellectual leaders such as Fukuzawa Yukichi willingly paid for playing the social Darwinian game was never fully comprehended by the Chinese intelligentsia. Even if Zeng Guofan, and for that matter Kang Youwei and Liang Qichao, had fully comprehended how much was really needed for China to join the family of nations defined in social Darwinian terms, they would not have recommended a total restructuring of the value system to accommodate it.

Li Hongzhang's shocking realization that, in less than a generation, Japan had not only learned the rules of the Western game but also managed to act like a full-fledged imperialist power, may have made the path of restoration obsolete, but it did not fundamentally change the Chinese value orientation. There was no reference to a redefinition of Chineseness as a precondition for political reform. When Chinese intellectuals became acutely aware that economic and political restructuring inevitably led to social and cultural change, they still cherished the hope that the value system defining their Chineseness and their pivotal role in its creative transformation would not be altered. Despite their totalistic iconoclastic attack on the Confucian tradition, the May Fourth Westernizers were, without exception, obsessed with Chinese culture. Although their optimism that the feudal past could be thrown away like an external cloth-wrapper by an act of their collective will superficially resembled the deep-rooted faith in the perfectibility of human nature by self-effort in classical Confucian thought, the majority of the Westernizers in the humanities and the social sciences made their scholarly contributions in Sinological studies. Even though they openly criticized the ills of the feudal past, they devoted their time and energy to studying it. Some of them even fully acknowledged their indebtedness to the tradition and culture that made China poor and weak.

The Levensonian dichotomy—emotional attachment to China's history and intellectual commitment to Western values—accurately identifies the phenomenon of a divided loyalty in the mind of modern China. The reason for this, however, can hardly be described in terms of a split between emotion and intellect; the conceptual apparatus premised on the irreconcilability of history and value cannot quite come to grips with the complexity of the issue. The heart of the matter seems to lie in the inability or even conscious refusal of the Chinese intelligentsia to embrace fully the modern West, specifically the Enlightenment ideology, as an intrinsic value. Even though they were overwhelmed by the wealth and power of the Western developmental model fueled by the Faustian spirit to explore and conquer, they did not feel the need to probe deeply into the value system that made it possible. To be sure, they were fully convinced that learning from the modern West was a precondition for national survival and that traditional Confucian culture offered little guidance for China to cope with the emerging world order, but they perceived the Western impact and the Chinese predicament mainly in instrumental and utilitarian terms. To them, the correct ideas (orthodoxy)[14] and correct practice (orthopraxy) remained authentically indigenous; the modern West symbolized the triumph of instrumental rationality that was, in principle, incapable of either justifying ultimate ends or accommodating ethics of intention.

Genetically, the Chinese intellectual conception of the brave new world, symbolized by the wealth and power of the modern West, was conditioned by the carriers of Western civilization: diplomats, teachers, merchants, soldiers, and evangelists. Chinese gentry in the nineteenth century had virtually no exposure to the free markets, legal courts, mainline churches, liberal colleges, industrial plants, or government agencies in the West. Those who traveled abroad, notably Kang Youwei and Liang Qichao, were significantly affected by the Chinatown mentality in North America. They were perhaps impressed more by the power relationships, including racial discrimination, than by the civil societies in the United States. Intent on absorbing Western "superior technology" at minimum cost in the shortest period, they were immune to the depth of Western spirituality that made the Enlightenment truly inspirational. Among the difficulties the Chinese intellectuals had in understanding the modern West, three distinctive values merit special attention.

The Individual Self

The Enlightenment assertion, implicit in virtually all declarations of human rights, that the individual qua individual has inalienable rights, and that individualism as the doctrine of protecting the dignity, autonomy, and independence of the private person is a hallmark of the liberation of the human spirit, has never been fully appreciated by the Chinese intelligentsia. The Confucian idea that selfhood, as a center of relationships, realizes itself in communal participation has so much dominated the Chinese discourse on self and society that individualism is often misunderstood as self-centeredness.[15] As the crisis of national survival intensified, the demand for heroic sacrifice became more and more compelling. Any discussion of the liberal creed, such as the legal protection for privacy, appeared to be selfish.

Civil Society

Similarly, the emergence of the theory and practice of society based on a multi-centered structure of power with competing interest groups constantly challenging the legitimacy of the central government[16] has never taken root in the Chinese intellectual consciousness. It was much easier for the Chinese scholar-official to accept the persuasion of concepts such as the "general will" and "social engineer" than to appreciate the potency of notions such as society is mightier than the state. Society as contract, government as a necessary evil, law as the court of appeal for the benefit of the people, and private property as a legitimate right were all alien to the value system of the Chinese intelligentsia. Despite their willingness to learn from the modern West, they never gave up their deep-rooted convictions: society as a moral community, government as exemplary leadership, law as a mechanism of control, and property, in the last analysis, as public.

Radical Transcendence

Although the Enlightenment is supposed to have been against clericalism and thus antireligious, much that the age of reason cherished as secular values was traceable to Judeo-Christian origins. The idea of God, the Creator, as totally beyond human comprehension may have been under a great deal of critical scrutiny, but the belief in human fallibility was never seriously challenged. The psychology of suspicion, the concern that any institution artificially constructed is flawed, remained strong. From the transcending perspective, the mechanism of check-and-balance is absolutely necessary, for any man-made structure is devoid of ultimate legitimacy. On the contrary, Chinese intellectuals were committed to a world view defined in terms of immanent transcendence.[17] To them, the cumulative tradition, as an organic process of human interaction, was a natural outgrowth of the civilized form of life. The hierarchy, status, and authority inherent in society were not artificially constructed as reflections of the power struggle of competing interest groups. Rather, they represented the dynamic order of things. The order might change over time; with proper "social engineering," or the art of statecraft, it could even be reordered, but society would remain hierarchic, status-conscious, and receptive to authoritarian leadership.

Implications

Confucian humanism, as a defining characteristic of Chinese culture, and the Enlightenment mentality, as a dominant intellectual habit of the modern West, are to a significant extent rival and incompatible value orientations. Since there is no adequate neutral conception available, repeated attempts to find a higher synthesis have failed. For generations, Chinese intellectuals have tried to adapt themselves to the Western model. Having come to the realization that Confucian humanism and the Enlightenment mentality are incommensurable, an overwhelming majority of the most articulate modern Chinese intellectuals made an existential decision to opt for "wholesale Westernization." Unfortunately, the Enlightenment mentality as they perceived it could not adequately compete with the value system they had already internalized as standards of judgment. Their misreading of the Enlightenment mentality as the path to wealth and power was further confounded by their insistence that a totalistic iconoclastic attack on Confucian humanism was a precondition for national survival. As Confucian humanism (their own value system) became ridiculed and the Enlightenment mentality (the value system they were determined to import) became instrumentalized, they could neither tap into their own indigenous resources nor take seriously what the West could offer.

The Enlightenment mentality may have created all the major spheres of values for the modern West and, by implication, for the rest of world to emulate, but the same mentality also may have brought humanity to the brink of self-annihilation, including the destruction of the entire ecosystem. As some of the most brilliant minds in the West are wrestling with the question of how to transcend the Enlightenment mentality without abandoning its rational heritage, the *Problematik* of the Chinese intellectual struggle is historically significant.

Notes

1. Benjamin I. Schwartz, "Hierarchy, Status and Authority in Chinese Culture: Some Reflections on Modern Western Attitudes," ms., p. 1.

2. Ibid.

3. Feng Qi, *Zhongguo gudai zexua luoji fazhan* (Shanghai: Renmin chubanshe, 1985), vol. 1, preface.

4. Li Zehou, "Qimeng yu jiuwang," in his *Zhongguo xiandai sixiangshi lun* (Beijing: Dongfang, 1987), pp. 7–50.

5. Vera Schwarcz, *The Chinese Enlightenment: Intellectuals and the Legacy of the May Fourth Movement of 1919* (Berkeley: University of California Press, 1986), pp. 2–3, 94–144.

6. I have confirmed through personal correspondence Professor Shively's remark, which is well-known among his students in Tokugawa history. For his interpretive position on this matter, see Donald Shively, ed., *Tradition and Modernization in Japanese Culture* (Princeton: Princeton University Press, 1971), preface.

7. Joseph Levenson, *Confucian China and Its Modern Fate* (Berkeley: University of California Press, 1968).

8. F. W. Mote, "The City in Traditional Chinese Civilization," in *Traditional China*, ed. James Liu and W. Tu (Englewood Cliffs, NJ: Prentice-Hall, 1970), pp. 42–49.

9. Schwartz, "Hierarchy, Status and Authority in Chinese Culture," p. 3.

10. This idiomatic expression is comparable to *Zhongyong*'s idea that we all eat and drink, but few of us really know the taste. *Zhongyong*, chap. 4.

11. Tu Wei-ming, "The Structure and Function of the Chinese Intellectual in Ancient China," in *The Origins and Diversity of Axial Age Civilizations*, ed. S. N. Eisenstadt (Albany: State University of New York Press), pp. 360–73.

12. Wang Fuhi, "Huangshu," in *Chuanshan yishu*, 35.

13. Gu Yanwu, *Rizhi lu*, 13, under the item ''Zhengshi.''

14. I am indebted to Woody Watson for contrasting these two terms. My interpretive stance, however, is significantly different from his behaviorism.

15. Tu Wei-ming, "Embodying the Universe: A Note on Confucian Self-Realization," *World and I* (August 1989): 475–85.

16. For a recent discussion on civil society, see John Keane, ed., *Civil Society and the State* (London: Verso, 1988). I am also indebted to Edward Shils for his essay "What Is Civil Society?" submitted to the conference on Europe and the Civil Society, Institute Für Die Wissenschaften Vom Menschen (Vienna), Castel Gandolfo, Italy, August 1989.

17. Tu Wei-ming, *Ruxue disanqi fazhan de qianjing wenti* (Taipei: Lianjing, 1989), pp. 165–211.

PART TWO

MAY FOURTH ANNIVERSARY

RODERICK MACFARQUHAR

When the Four Anniversaries China Conference was in the embryo stage, we ruled out a state-of-the-art research conference, and we obviously could not plan for a heat-of-the-moment conference like that held in Chicago in 1967 to assess the eruption of the Cultural Revolution. Rather, we hoped by juxtaposing key markers in modern Chinese history, and by bringing together scholars from different disciplines, to provoke reassessments of and dialogues on broad themes.

As it turned out, the tragedy of Tiananmen Square gave our deliberations unexpected immediacy. More importantly, it underlined the enormous difficulties that the Chinese have encountered in their efforts to transform their traditional society to fit into the wider context of the modern world. During the 150 years covered by the conference, the Chinese people have endured successive massive upheavals, some the product of foreign aggression, others the result of domestic failures, like the events of June 3–4, 1989.

The fifty days of the 1989 prodemocracy movement created new anniversaries that may one day be celebrated in Beijing. The period also encompassed one of the most protean anniversaries of twentieth-century Chinese history: the seventieth anniversary of the May Fourth Movement.The patriotic upsurge of 1919 was the student-led protest against what was seen as the spineless acquiescence of the Chinese delegation to the Versailles Peace Conference in the award of former German concessions in China to Japan. That May Fourth Incident gave its name to the broader and lengthier process of cultural renewal which followed hard upon the collapse of the last empire in 1912.

This anniversary had to be reexamined in the context of the Western impact, which had been of increasing importance from the Opium War of 1839–42. The May Fourth Incident was specifically a reaction to yet another instance of foreign aggrandizement at the expense of China; the May Fourth Movement, with its twin slogans of science and democracy, was an attempt to grapple with the implications of Western military and industrial superiority for Chinese culture. The May Fourth anniversary had, therefore, also to be considered in the light of the efforts of Mao after the 1949 Communist revolution, and Deng from his opening up (*kaifang*) in 1979, to reshape China. What had been the dreams and dilemmas of the May Fourth generation, and how had they fared?

Lloyd Eastman argues that May Fourth was a reaction to the "political" impotence of the Chinese state. After 1949, the Chinese state was rebuilt under Mao and demonstrated enormous political power. But the demonstrations of the spring of 1989, and the inability of the Deng regime to end them except by force, indicated that politically the Chinese state was again impotent. The Chinese polity was in danger of militarization once more, a legacy if not a replication of the warlord era against which the May Fourth Movement was also a protest.

China's international impotence was, of course, central to the May Fourth Movement, and Michael Hunt suggests it led to the emergence then of a "three worlds" view: a preoccupation with imperialism; the concept of a special relationship with the Soviet Union; and a belief in the unity of weak and oppressed peoples. As he explains, that legacy is now "largely spent." Yet Communist leaders cannot seem to break away from old categories, as the attempt to assign blame for the events of 1989 on Western, particularly American, ideological infiltration indicates. At that time they also hinted that if the West persisted in criticism, they could turn back to their ideological allies in the Soviet Union.

But if Lenin's revolution seemed to promise a valuable ally and model for China's struggle against imperialism, Gorbachev's revolution and its repercussions in Eastern Europe must underline for Beijing's beleaguered leaders that they are running out of acceptable friends. Moreover, convenient foreign scapegoats may obscure but cannot eliminate the urgent need for domestic change.

For the May Fourth generation, as Evelyn Rawski reminds us, its radical social agenda was a key to modernization, and indeed formed the basis of CCP policies after 1949. Yet the family system, described as the "source of all evil" seventy years ago, has demonstrated not merely enormous resilience but also unexpected compatibility with modernization, both on the mainland and in Taiwan. Indeed, social engineering by the Communist state has proved less lasting than seemed likely in the years immediately after 1949. The May Fourth demand for mass literacy is closer to achievement, and its impact suggests that state provision of services to society is the more effective way of bringing about social change.

But in 1989, as in 1919, the state is deeply conservative, attempting to marginalize the intellectuals demanding reform and to suppress the students who act as their shock troops. Yet there is perhaps a fatal flaw in the intellectuals' commitment to social change. As Leo Lee suggests, they have always seen themselves as part of the leadership of the process, subjects in relationship to the objects of change, the "people." They abdicated from a truly pluralistic position, never demanding the full implementation of the May Fourth call for democracy.

If the events of the Beijing Spring of 1989 mean anything, it is surely that, seventy years after the May Fourth Movement, democracy in the broadest sense can no longer be treated as a notional terminus *ad quem*, but has rather to be an essential ingredient of the process of societal change. Otherwise the Chinese may be condemned to further defeats and setbacks on their long march to modernity.

5

THE MAY FOURTH MOVEMENT AS A HISTORICAL TURNING POINT Ecological Exhaustion, Militarization, and Other Causes of China's Modern Crisis

LLOYD E. EASTMAN

The May Fourth Movement in both its major manifestations—the New Culture Movement and the student demonstrations—was a reaction to the political impotence of the Chinese state.[1] In 1915, Chen Duxiu had called for a thorough transformation of China's culture and values. This was because, following the manifest failure of the republican institutions that had been established after the 1911 Revolution, he despaired of political action as a means of revitalizing and strengthening the nation. Later, during the May Fourth Incident in 1919, the students rose in protest not only against the decisions of the imperialist powers at the Versailles Peace Conference, but also against the betrayal of the nation by a weak and corrupt warlord regime in Peking.

The May Fourth Movement, in fact, occurred at a time (1915–23) when the power of the Chinese state was at its nadir. It is appropriate, therefore, that now, while we are commemorating the seventieth anniversary of the May Fourth Movement, we reflect briefly upon the causes of China's modern crisis and upon the efforts that have been made to resolve that crisis.

Symptoms of the Chinese empire's decline first became evident during the late eighteenth century. During the preceding hundred years, the Qing dynasty had attained the peak of its imperial power and grandeur. The empire had expanded to its furthest frontiers ever, the country was at peace, the population was growing, and China was the cynosure of the Asian world. From about the 1770s and 1780s, however, Chinese power and prestige dwindled until, by the late 1800s, much of the world looked upon China as a political corpse upon which ravenous imperialists could feed with impunity.

Why does a great nation or civilization decline? Some of the world's preeminent historians—among them Edward Gibbon, Oswald Spengler, Arnold Toynbee, and Paul Kennedy—have pondered this question, each offering his own distinctive explanation. That such notable students of the past have arrived at no consensus should instill in us a considerable diffidence as we search for the causes of China's slide into political impotence and economic want. That the explanation is not monocausal, however, seems patent. Rather, four major historical forces seemingly conjoined to bring about China's modern crisis.

Those four forces—the depletion of the nation's economic resources, weakening of the ruling dynasty, rising levels of militarization in society, and pressures of Western and Japanese imperialism—are analytically distinguishable. Yet they are so closely intertwined that it is frequently impossible to ascertain which force was cause and which was effect.

Crisis in the Ecosystem

By the late eighteenth century, China's growing population was imposing heavy strains upon a deteriorating ecology. From about 65–80 million people at the beginning of the Ming Dynasty (1368–1644), the population of China had grown to roughly 450 million by 1850. The population of the empire in the mid-nineteenth century was, therefore, approximately six times that of four hundred years earlier.

Initially, the effects of this population growth were invigorating. More people meant more labor power to clear forests and create new fields, to expand the irrigation networks, and to help in the labor-intensive tasks of rice-paddy agriculture. More people also meant increased consumer demand, which stimulated the growing commercial sector.

By the latter decades of the eighteenth century, however, this phase of expansion had reached the point of diminishing returns. No longer did additional labor power produce commensurate increases in economic output. More serious was the fact that much of China's natural resources were being squandered. Waves of migrants moved from the densely settled regions of the east into the hitherto sparsely populated uplands and mountains elsewhere in the empire. In those frontier regions, they cleared the land for agriculture, but with no thought for the morrow. Forests were ravaged, leading to erosion on a massive scale. Fertile topsoils were thus washed downstream, where the silt settled to the bottoms and outlets of rivers, lakes, reservoirs, and canals. The result was increased frequency of flooding in times of rain and severe water shortages in times of drought. An index of this change is the fact that, during the Song dynasty, areas along the Huai River suffered a major flood only once every 30 years, but during the Qing dynasty they flooded once every 5.3 years.[2]

By the last quarter of the eighteenth century, the pressures of overpopulation were being felt throughout the empire. Prime farmland even in South and West

China, in the provinces that had been the primary targets of immigration during the preceding century, was in short supply; unemployment levels were rising; the general standard of living was declining.

Sensitive observers now had a sense of foreboding. The scholar Hong Liangji, for instance, wrote two essays in 1793 that were astonishingly similar in purport to Thomas Malthus's *Essay on the Principle of Population*, published five years later. In those essays, Hong warned that the human population was increasing faster than the food supply. "The population within a hundred years or so," he wrote, "can increase from fivefold to twentyfold, while the means of subsistence, due to the limitation of the land area, can increase only from three to five times."[3] As a result, he warned, many, especially the poor, would die of disease, hunger, and cold, whereas among those who survived, the rich would become richer and the poor would become even hungrier.

With the passing years, the situation worsened. By 1820, the brilliant essayist Gong Zizhen warned that, because of worsening economic conditions since the late eighteenth century, "The provinces are at the threshold of a convulsion which is not a matter of years but a matter of days and months."[4] Thirty years later, on the eve of the Taiping Rebellion, the French missionary Abbé Huc poignantly described the condition of the Chinese people: "il y a encore ce qu'on pourrait appeler le pauperisme fixe et permanent, qui, comme une lèpre incurable étend ses ravages sur la nation tout entière."[5]

Indeed, the signs of social distress and political discontent were to be seen everywhere. Bands of beggars, fleeing conditions in the villages, flooded the cities demanding alms; bandits and pirates plied their trades virtually at will; and, perhaps most ominous of all, political rebellion became pandemic.

A different perspective on the long-term, secular decline of Chinese civilization has been provided by Prof. S. A. M. Adshead of the University of Canterbury in New Zealand.[6] Adshead argues that China by the mid-seventeenth century was in the grips of a severe energy crisis as a result of centuries of deforestation. China had once enjoyed ample supplies of wood and timber, even in what is now the nearly treeless plains of the north. By the mid-seventeenth century, however, the more densely populated areas of the nation suffered a severe wood shortage. High transportation costs prevented the extensive use of coal; China was thus forced to adopt what Adshead calls "a low-energy pattern of ecology."

This increasing use of low-energy methods of production was evidenced, for example, in the manufacture of salt. In earlier days, salt manufactories had relied largely on wood as fuel for dehydrating the salt brine. As wood came in short supply, and was thus more expensive, the salt producers shifted to reliance on solar heat, despite the fact that the salt thus produced was of an inferior quality. Other heavy industrial users of fuel at this time were metal smelters, porcelain and glass manufacturers, and brick kilns, the development of which was retarded by the fuel crisis.[7]

Adshead speculates that in earlier times—say, in the time of Marco Polo—China had surely used more energy per person than did Europe. But in 1800, China was using only about one-half as many energy units per capita as were Europeans. The available evidence suggests, therefore, that the energy crisis was a significant cause of China's decline, both absolutely and relative to Europe.

It is sad to contemplate that this ravaging of the environment by an expanding population was not inevitable, as shown by the experience of Japan. By the mid-seventeenth century, deforestation of the Japanese islands had proceeded so far that, as Conrad Totman writes, "Japan today should be an impoverished, slum-ridden, peasant society subsisting on a barren, eroded moonscape characterized by bald mountains and debris-strewn lowlands." Regenerative forestry during the Tokugawa period preserved Japan's ecosystem, however, and even today the country is wrapped in lush, verdant forests.[8] China did not benefit from such enlightened policies.

Crisis in the Political System

The economic effects of ecological exhaustion, and the social-political problems that resulted from it, were exacerbated by the growing ineffectiveness of government. This deterioration of administration was attributable in part to the seemingly inexorable workings of the dynastic cycle. Chinese historians had long believed that each dynasty, initially vital and efficient, eventually became self-indulgent, corrupt, and ineffective. Certainly, this appeared to be true in the Qing dynasty. Since the latter years of the Qianlong reign (the late eighteenth century), and through the reigns of each of the succeeding emperors, imperial leadership had been weak. During the same period, the civil administration was fraught with factional struggles, corruption, and inefficiency. Heshen—the young Manchu nobleman who during the last decade of Qianlong's reign became the emperor's favorite (some said his lover)—has been especially blamed for the corruption, demoralization, and factionalization of the bureaucracy.

A factor other than the dynastic cycle, however, was involved here. For, with the rapid growth of the population, and with the spread of banditry, feuding, and rebellion, the size and methods of the bureaucracy did not change in response to the changing conditions and challenges. Whereas in, say, the 1680s a bureaucracy of about 20,000 civilian officials had administered a nation of 125 million people, in 1800 the same-sized bureaucracy was expected to govern a population that was not only much larger (totaling about 300 million) but also far more restive and needful of social services than in earlier times. Many tasks of government were, consequently, simply neglected. Overworked magistrates ignored the activities of bandit gangs and secret societies in their areas of jurisdiction as long as those activities did not attract the attention of higher authorities in the government. Because reports of social unrest in an official's area of jurisdiction resulted in demerits on his personnel record, the official also had a special interest in ignoring social unrest if at all possible. And with the dynasty experiencing fiscal difficulties, even the central administration discouraged local initiatives. An official in the 1840s observed that "State ministers hint that flood, drought, and bandits are not to be reported, in order to save the emperor trouble and to save the limited revenue, which is not permitted to be used for such trifles."

The seriousness of this condition of administrative atrophy is suggested by the fact that the existence of the Society of God Worshippers—what was to become the Taiping Heavenly Kingdom—was not reported to Peking until 1851. This was seven years after the society was first organized and a time when the future rebels numbered upward of twenty thousand well-armed adherents.

The exhaustion of the ecology and the weakening of government contributed to the outbreak in the mid-nineteenth century not only of the Taiping Rebellion, but also of the Nien and Moslem Rebellions. Other forces were at work, however, that added to the crisis at the time of the May Fourth Movement.

A Third Source of Crisis: Increased Levels of Militarization

The May Fourth Movement took place in a context of warlordism. The provinces by 1919 were dominated by military strongmen who collected and dispersed revenues, dispensed a rough justice, and waged war in total disregard for the so-called central government in Peking. Farther down the political hierarchy—and particularly in the peripheries of the major regional systems—local elites, commanding a few dozen rifles and perhaps a machine-gun, held sway over their villages and often preyed on their neighbors. Just five or six years after the collapse of the Qing dynasty, then, China's traditional political system had disintegrated, and a new formal structure of administration had yet to be erected in its place.

The increasing influence in society of military activities, organizations, personnel, and values—a process that was in full flower during the warlord period—had initially appeared as a response to worsening social disorder during the late eighteenth and early nineteenth centuries. For, as the economic crisis worsened and as the Qing imperial state weakened, secret societies proliferated, salt and opium smuggling spread, and tax-resistance movements and tenant unrest became common. Yet the traditional mechanisms of control were no longer effective. Local leaders themselves took the initiative, therefore, in forming local militia and fortifying their villages with defensive walls. Not infrequently these armed units, whose original purpose was to defend their own villages, themselves turned to banditry and aggression against their neighbors. By the 1840s, and reaching a peak during the period of the Taiping Rebellion (1851–64), local society throughout the country, in both north and south, was in a state of armed turmoil.[9]

During the Taiping Rebellion, too, regional leaders such as Zeng Guofan, Zuo Zongtang, and Li Hongzhang organized much larger, regional armies when it became evident that the regular armies of the dynasty, the Banners and the Army of the Green Standard, were incapable of resisting the rebel forces. These regional armies foreshadowed the warlordism at the time of the May Fourth Movement, for they were personal armies, loyal primarily not to the dynasty but to their commanders, and ruled their provinces virtually without the let or hindrance of the imperial authorities in Peking. By contrast with the May Fourth era, however, the central government retained sufficient prestige that the empire did not break up into autonomous and warring regional powers.

The level of militarization declined following the suppression of the great midcentury rebellions. Social order was partially restored, the role of personal armies was at least partially diminished, and civilians regained control of the bureaucratic apparatus. Yet the incidence of local violence—in the forms of banditry, secret-society uprisings, and feuding—never returned to the pre-Taiping levels. And the sudden reappearance, after the collapse of Yuan Shikai's government in 1916, of all the former features of militarization—regional and personal armies, domination of local administrations by military men, and village defense forces organized and controlled by local elites—strongly suggests that the process of militarization had only been in temporary remission during the three to four decades preceding the warlord era, 1916–28.

Foreign Pressures

The effects of the foreign presence in China during the nineteenth and early twentieth centuries—what is often called "imperialism"—is a topic of intense controversy. Many nationalistic Chinese have attributed all of China's social, political, and economic difficulties during the nineteenth and twentieth centuries to foreign exploitation. The fact is, however, that the several sources of China's decline are closely interconnected, and it is extraordinarily difficult to sort out the specific consequences of the foreign presence. Probably imperialism did less damage to China's domestic economy than the critics have claimed. Nonetheless, it is manifest that the foreign presence did impose heavy pressures on the political system, thus adding momentum to the general process of political and economic decline.

The two areas where foreign pressures most affected the political system were the finances and the legitimacy of the government. After each of the wars that the Qing dynasty fought with and lost to the foreign powers between 1839 and 1900, indemnities were exacted. Initially the amounts of these indemnities were relatively modest. The indemnity exacted by Britain after the Opium War, for instance, amounted to but 21 million taels. After the Sino-Japanese War of 1894–95, Japan ultimately received an indemnity of 230 million taels. And then, only five years later, after the Boxer fiasco, the eight allied powers received a financial settlement of 450 million taels.

The burden of these payments upon the Chinese government is suggested by the fact that the indemnity of 1895 amounted to about one-third of Japan's gross national product. This contributed significantly to Japan's modernization effort, paying, for example, for the expansion of that country's railway, telephone, and telegraph systems. It also enabled Japan to create a domestic iron and steel industry.[10] At the time of the Revolution of 1911, China's foreign debt was a staggering 900 million taels. Expenditures of the dynasty had also risen sharply because, being thrust into the international arena, it was forced to undertake expensive reforms of the governmental administration, army, and educational system. The result was to bankrupt the dynasty. As Putnam Weale was to observe, "During the Revolution the one decisive factor was shown to be almost at once—money, nothing but money."[11]

As the foreigners heaped humiliations upon China, moreover, the ineptitude and self-serving of the dynasty's rulers became progressively obvious to the Chinese people. By 1911, the dynasty had lost all moral credibility. By exacerbating the Chinese government's political and fiscal difficulties, therefore, imperialism contributed importantly to the collapse of the dynasty.

The May Fourth Movement: The Chinese Polity at Its Nadir

As a result of China's worsening political impotence and economic scarcities, not only the Qing dynasty, but the entire two-thousand-year-old imperial system, had lost legitimacy. When the revolutionaries seized power in 1911–12, therefore, they faced the task of establishing, virtually from scratch, a wholly new political and administrative structure.

Leaders of the revolution drew inspiration for their new government from the West, especially from the liberal, republican institutions of France and the United States. Thus, the new regime possessed a full panoply of democratic features, such as a constitution, representative assemblies, separation of governmental powers, and political parties.

These republican institutions were fragile, however, because few Chinese truly understood or were committed to the values of Western liberalism. Concepts such as the protection of individual rights, tolerance of minority opinions, or restrictions on the chief executive's authority were alien to Chinese political traditions. They were contrary, also, to the most deeply embedded Chinese social and behavioral patterns—such as unqualified respect for paternal authority and the subordination of the individual to the larger social group. In fact, the leaders of the new republic who created these liberal republican institutions had not been attracted to liberalism per se. Rather, they were attracted to the prospect, first, that liberal republican institutions would provide China the national solidarity needed to resist foreign imperialism. Second, they anticipated that the system of representative assemblies would provide a means for them to maintain the social-economic interests of themselves and the gentry class.

Both these goals were to be frustrated during the presidency of Yuan Shikai.

For Yuan was more concerned to centralize state power than he was to protect gentry interests. And the new government was no more capable of resisting foreign pressures than had been the old dynasty.

The revolutionary republican government thus had no true constituency: not President Yuan Shikai, who was neither a revolutionary nor a republican; not the gentry, who now realized that their local interests were actually threatened by the Republican government; and not, of course, the common people, most of whom were still essentially apolitical. Thus, after Yuan Shikai's abortive effort in 1916 to displace the republic with a new dynasty (Yuan died that same year), the central government virtually ceased to function. The republican institutions in Peking remained in place, at least nominally, but in the provinces there was an almost complete political vacuum. Thus began the era of warlordism, during which society and politics became dominated by the military.

Such was the political setting of the May Fourth Movement. It marked the lowest point of China's political life in recent times: governmental institutions were in shambles; the nation's weakness served as an open invitation for foreign intervention; and, most dispiriting to Chinese patriots, all attempts to rejuvenate the nation, whether through reform or revolution, had ended disastrously.

As noted in the title of this essay, the May Fourth Movement represented a turning point in China's modern history. In using the term "turning point," I am, of course, speaking metaphorically, for history is process and is rarely subject to sharp zigs and zags. Nonetheless, signs of momentous change did become evident during the May Fourth Movement.

In the first phase of the movement, from 1915 until May 4, 1919, the dominant mood was still extreme pessimism regarding the condition and future of the nation. Chinese confidence and pride were at low ebb. This was the emotional culmination of the entire process of decline since the late eighteenth century. Intellectual leaders at the time, such as Chen Duxiu, Hu Shi, and Li Dazhao, now felt utter despair. Attempts at military and political reform during the final fifty years of the dynasty had, they felt, all been for naught. Even the revolutionary creation of a new political structure, modeled on those of the leading states in the West, had only resulted in increased tyranny and foreign insult.

They concluded, therefore, that the cause of China's debility lay deeper than questions of political institutions or leadership. Instead, declared Chen Duxiu and his fellow writers in *New Youth* magazine, the problem lay in the debilitating effects of China's traditional culture. They thus renounced political involvement and dedicated themselves to achieving the transformation of China's traditional society and cultural values, replacing them with the democratic values and scientific outlook of the West.

But the transformation of the nation's culture, even if possible, would have required generations. In the atmosphere of supercharged nationalism of 1919, few educated Chinese had the patience to wait so long for national regeneration. This was not a time for cool logic, but a time for action. Action, in this context, meant political action. Following the May Fourth Incident, therefore, in the second phase of the May Fourth Movement (1919–23), *New Youth*'s agenda of cultural transformation was ignored, and there began a fervent search for political solutions. Now virtually every current of political philosophy and ideology found adherents: anarchism, guild socialism, syndicalism, Deweyian concepts of democracy, and, yes, Marxism.

The intellectual and political debates during these years were, of course, an important part of the history of the May Fourth Movement. In the final analysis, however, armed force, and not ideas, had the most immediate effect on Chinese politics. Politics had become militarized, and without military backing, ideas died aborning. Or, as Mao Zedong was to phrase it, "Power grows out of the barrel of a gun."

Militarization in the Post–May Fourth Period

This militarization of politics was a natural consequence of warlordism, which was now in full sway. Following the collapse of Yuan Shikai's government in 1916, contests for power were determined not by popular elections nor by debates in representative assemblies, but by the threat or actual use of military force. Civilian bureaucracies were tools of the militarists, employed in large part to raise revenues for the armies.

The transition to militarized politics was exemplified during the 1920s by Sun Yat-sen and the Guomindang. Sun was essentially a man of ideas. Although he was not a profound thinker, he had gained his position of leadership through his articulation of a revolutionary ideology and his personal charisma, rather than through organizational or military talents. During the era of warlords, however, this put him at a disadvantage. In 1917, for example, he had established a revolutionary government in Canton, but his position there was wholly dependent on the support and good will of several regional militarists. That support was evanescent, however, and twice in the ensuing six years he was forced to flee Canton as a result of disagreements with his military backers.

These experiences instilled in Sun the realization that he could attain his revolutionary goals only if he possessed a military force that was loyal to and dependent on him alone. One of the first results of his alliance with Russia, negotiated in 1923, therefore, was the creation of the Whampoa Military Academy and an army controlled by his party, the Guomindang.

When Sun died in March 1925, the Guomindang was still essentially a civilian-dominated political movement. But in the struggle for Sun's mantle of leadership, each of the civilian candidates—Liao Zhongkai, Hu Hanmin, and Wang Jingwei—lost out, one after the other, to the commandant of the Whampoa Academy, Chiang Kai-shek.

By schooling and inclination, Chiang was a soldier. Trained in a Japanese military academy, he understood the use of military force far better than did his civilian competitors for leadership of the party. He rose to leadership within the Nationalist movement, and made the Nationalist regime preponderant in national politics, because of his mastery of the techniques of using military force in support of political goals.

The militarization of politics within the Nationalist movement was evident, however, in ways other than simply Chiang Kai-shek's strategies of overcoming his rivals. For the very structure and values of the Guomindang and the government fell under the influence of the military. This was evidenced, in part, by the predominance of military officers in key posts within the regime. It was also evident in the expressed goals of the regime. In 1934, for instance, Chiang launched the New Life Movement with the purpose of fundamentally transforming and strengthening the nation. The sources of inspiration for this movement were diverse; Confucianism, Christianity, fascism, and the Japanese samurai code of Bushido all commingled within the movement. But the essence of the New Life Movement was nothing more nor less than the values of military life as Chiang understood them. "What is the New Life Movement that I now propose?" Chiang asked rhetorically. "Stated simply," he replied, "it is to thoroughly militarize the lives of the citizens of the entire nation so that they will cultivate courage and swiftness, the endurance of suffering and a tolerance for hard work, and especially the habit and ability of unified action, so that they will have the habit of and capacity for sacrifice for the nation."[12] The military ethic was thus implanted at the very core of Chiang's regime.

Mao Zedong, like Chiang Kai-shek, rose to a position of leadership because he, too, was able to adapt his political strategies to the militarized milieu of the 1920s and 1930s. The Communist Party, following its founding in 1921, was a quintessentially civilian organization, the leadership consisting of youngish intellectuals, many of whom had been swept into the political current by the nationalistic passions of the May Fourth Movement. The cofounders of the party, Chen Duxiu and Li Dazhao, had been leaders of the May Fourth Movement, and in 1921, at the ages of forty-two and thirty-two respectively, were considered elder statesmen. Most other founding members, such as Mao Zedong and Zhang Guotao, were still in their twenties.

The top leaders of the Communist Party during the first decade of its existence—Chen Duxiu, Qu Qiubai, Li Lisan, and Wang Ming—were civilians by both training and outlook. The advice given to the Chinese Communists by representatives of the Russians—whether it was from Stalin in Moscow or from the Russian advisers serving in China—was also premised on the orthodox Marxist assumption that the leading force of the revolution must be the industrial proletariat operating from an urban base. The leaders of the party were not, to be sure, totally uninterested in the use of armed force—as was evidenced by Qu Qiubai in the Autumn Harvest Uprisings of 1927, and by Li Lisan's plan of revolutionary insurrection in 1930. But always they insisted that military actions were but a subordinate aspect of an essentially urban and proletarian revolutionary strategy.

It was Mao Zedong who, even though he had received no military training, eventually devised a revolutionary strategy emphasizing the role of an army operating in a rural environment. After the Autumn Harvest Uprisings in 1927, for instance, he had established a revolutionary base in the remote mountains of Jiangxi Province, where he made no attempt to maintain close ties with the revolutionary movement in the cities. He premised that, because China was in a warlord situation, his rural revolutionary base could survive for a relatively long time. The leadership of the Communist Party disagreed, however, criticizing him for "military adventurism." Indeed, during his rise to power from 1927 to 1935, Mao was in official disfavor fully three-fourths of the time. Meanwhile, the party leadership that was supported by Russia, led by Wang Ming, was attempting to organize and agitate among the industrial workers in Shanghai. As a result of Nationalist repression, however, Wang Ming's efforts were a total failure.

Meanwhile, Mao Zedong's guerrilla army continued to grow, and during the Long March, in 1935, he was recognized as the supreme leader of the party. Thereafter, down to the final victory over the Guomindang in 1949, the army was a primary instrument in Mao's revolutionary strategy.

Despite the importance of the army in Mao's revolutionary struggle, the Communist movement was never as thoroughly militarized, in terms of either personnel or values, as was the Guomindang. Mao had remarked in 1938 that "Our principle is that the Party commands the gun, and the gun must never be allowed to command the Party."[13] This principle was not always evident during the years of revolutionary struggle in the 1930s and 1940s, when virtually the entire top leadership of the party assumed some form of military command. Even after "Liberation" in 1949, the military continued to play a leading role. Military committees wielded supreme authority over four of the six major administrative regions of the nation. (North and Northeast China, which had fallen to the Communists earlier than the four regions farther south, were administered by civilian "people's governments.") Even at the local levels, administration was directed by Military Control Commissions, which were composed of officers of the People's Liberation Army.

But Mao had not abandoned his principle that the party should command the gun. Even as early as 1951, as the regime consolidated its control throughout the nation, civilian cadres took over local and regional administrative functions from the People's Liberation Army. The shift to civilian rule was also evident in the central organs of the government and party where, by 1956, civilians outnumbered representatives of the People's Liberation Army by a ratio of three to one. By the mid-1950s, therefore, civilian control of the military seemed unchallengeable.

During the Cultural Revolution, however, the relationship was suddenly reversed completely. The party apparatus was now virtually dismantled and governmental offices operated under the supervision of military control committees. Even during the period 1968–71, when civilian institutions were being rebuilt, military officers still occupied the majority of the top party and government posts and constituted 46 percent of the party's major policy-forming body, the Central Committee.

After the downfall of Marshal Lin Biao in 1971, however, civilian dominance over the military was reasserted, and the army was again reduced to the subordinate role that it had held prior to the Cultural Revolution. Yet the events of the student protests and the Tiananmen Massacre in May and June 1989 revealed that he who controls the military also controls the regime. Thus, although it has for several years appeared that one of the important historical contributions of the Communists was to eliminate the last vestiges of warlordism, the army has obviously not been displaced as a player in the game of Chinese politics.

Imperialism in the Post–May Fourth Period

Since the May Fourth Movement, the Chinese have rid themselves of foreign exploitation and imperialistic pressures. As the Chinese people proudly proclaim, they "have stood up." Already during the late 1910s and early 1920s, in fact, imperialism began to retreat before the rising tide of Chinese nationalism. Tariff autonomy, for instance, was fully restored to China in 1933; the Nationalist government regained control of the Maritime Customs, the Post Office, and the Salt Revenue Administration. In 1943, the last remaining provision of the unequal treaties, extraterritoriality, was eliminated. Japanese aggression in the 1930s and 1940s marked a monstrous resurgence of imperialism, but the end of World War II saw imperialism retreating not just in China but throughout the world. Today, under the Communists, China enjoys the same freedom from foreign pressures as does any other major world power.

Continuing Problems: Political

Of the four historical forces that had brought China to a political nadir during the period of the May Fourth Movement, therefore, one (imperialism) has been eliminated and one (the militarization of society) has been reduced. What of the other two: political weakness and ecological exhaustion?

Since the May Fourth Movement, the Chinese have experienced great difficulty in reestablishing an effective political system. The Nationalists, seizing power in 1927–28, were the first political force to confront this task. Almost immediately, however, they encountered many of the same problems—corruption, factionalism, and administrative atrophy—that had crippled the Qing dynasty in its waning days. Moreover, the age-old tradition of governmental authoritarianism persisted, providing historical confirmation once again of the truth of Lord Acton's dictum, "Power corrupts, and absolute power corrupts absolutely.'' The causes of the Nationalists' defeat in 1949 were, of course, highly complex. The Nationalists' failure to create an effective administration that was responsive to the needs of the people, however, contributed importantly to the Communist victory.

Although the Communist regime is frequently called ''totalitarian''—a term that implies effective administration as well as absolute political control—it too has encountered many of the same problems of administration as did the Nationalists. Bureaucracy, with all its administrative pathologies, continues to vitiate the best-intentioned policies of the leadership; local bureaucrats often continue to ignore the directives and policy initiatives of the central government; and corruption, nepotism, and back-doorism are still pervasive.

The government's response to the Tiananmen demonstrations of May and June 1989 tragically revealed that traditional-style authoritarianism and opposition to political pluralism still reign supreme. Moreover, the auguries for the future of Chinese politics are not favorable. True, many observers are now saying that the genie of democracy, which was let out of the bottle in the student protests of 1989, will inevitably transform the dynamics of Chinese politics. But the history of the present century argues for a less optimistic prediction. Despite the repeated revolutions since 1911, despite the May Fourth Movement and other demonstrations calling for democracy and political reforms, and even despite the several constitutions and legal codes that seemingly provided a foundation for democracy and the rule of law, traditions of self-serving bureaucracies and closed authoritarian regimes have persisted virtually unchanged. Deng Xiaoping and Li Peng, on the one hand, and Yuan Shikai and Chiang Kai-shek, on the other, have more in common than one would expect merely by comparing their ideological commitments. For, in fact, they have each been profoundly traditional in their political behavior. Probably, therefore, as Chen Duxiu and Hu Shi proclaimed in 1917, true political reform can be attained only by means of a thorough social-cultural-psychological transformation. The present generation of student leaders may represent the fruit of such a transformation. But the persistence throughout the course of the past eighty years of the same behavioral traits among the bureaucrats, and of the autocratic tendencies of political leaders, does not instill optimism that even members of this younger generation of Chinese, when they become older and leaders of the Chinese nation, will provide more effective or democratic rule.

Continuing Problems: Ecological

But perhaps the gravest problem confronting China today—the one that, for the long term, overshadows all other problems—is the persistence, and indeed the acceleration, of ecological deterioration. Despite roseate reports in the media, both Chinese and foreign, that the Communists have accomplished miracles of reforestation, pest control, improved farm yields, and the like, the alarming fact is that China suffers terribly and increasingly from damage to its environment.[14]

The claims regarding the greening of the nation by means of massive tree plantings in cities, rural areas, and forest regions, for instance, are actually belied by widespread and increasing deforestation during the past forty years. Maoist efforts to increase grain production led to the clearing of millions of acres of forest land. The demands of industrialization—for building material, fuel, and paper—have likewise taken a terrible toll. A recent survey by the Ministry of Forestry reveals that timber consumption has increased from 196 million cubic meters in 1976 to 344 million cubic meters in 1988. This consumption of the nation's forests exceeds official estimates of the natural growth rate by 100 million cubic meters.[15]

The widespread deforestation, in conjunction with poor soil management, has exacerbated the problem of soil erosion. The topsoils of the loess highlands in the northwest and of the Yangzi drainage area are being washed into the rivers at the rate of billions of tons a year. Erosion in Sichuan and Guizhou was not a serious problem before 1949, but recent deforestation in those mountainous provinces is causing the loss of more than 250 million tons of topsoil each year—the annual loss being equivalent to nearly five inches of topsoil from an area of 400 square miles. In many regions of those provinces, erosion has stripped away the thin layers of surface soil and left only barren patches of rock. The result, of course, is that the productivity of the farms thus affected is greatly reduced. Furthermore, the eroded soil settles in the rivers, lakes, and reservoirs downstream, thus raising water levels, blocking outlets, and reducing storage capacity, all of which worsens the destructiveness of flooding and the ravages of drought.

Pollution is another major problem. There exist few studies of the effects of air pollution, although every visitor to China soon becomes keenly aware of the soot and sulfur dioxide spewed out by the millions of low-efficiency coal and charcoal burners used for cooking and, in the north, for heating. Industry is an even greater source of air pollution, in part because coal, which is a relatively "dirty" fuel, now provides the bulk of the nation's primary energy (70 percent, by comparison with about 20 percent from crude oil, and 7–8 percent from natural gas and electricity). Energy use in China, moreover, is inefficient, fully 70 percent of the burned fuels being wasted and thrown into the air as emissions of pollutants—a figure 50 percent higher than in Europe and twice as much as in Japan.

Even more distressing is the pollution of the nation's water. Shanghai, for example, discharges 5 million tons of waste every day, only 4 percent of which is sanitized in water treatment plants. All of this discharge is dumped into the Huangpu River, which is the city's principal source of drinking water. Elsewhere in China, the situation is little better. In fact, only 10 percent of the waste water discharged by the nation's cities is treated, so that every major river in the country is seriously polluted. China's burgeoning industries similarly discharge enormous volumes of pollutants into the country's water supply. Even in the rural areas, the rivers, ponds, and wells that provide peasants their drinking water are badly polluted both by the discharges from the 400,000 or so small rural factories and by the leakage of toxic materials from chemical fertilizers and pesticides.

Finally, it is shocking to learn that, despite the population explosion in China, the available farmland has been declining both qualitatively and quantitatively. Improper irrigation practices, the increased use of chemical fertilizers in place of organic fertilizers, the failure to rotate wet and dry crops, and the reduced planting of green manure and legume crops have all contributed to a significant deterioration in the quality of the country's prime farmland. In Hunan, as much as 40 percent of the farm area has turned into boggy soil, which reduces the air content of the soil and its ability to absorb nutrients. In other regions, increases in the saline content of the soil is reducing crop yields. In recent years, moreover, much of the land opened to cultivation has been in hilly or sandy areas where productivity is low and where erosion easily washes away the topsoil.

At the same time, large amounts of the country's prime arable land are being removed from cultivation. Between 1952 and 1979, for example, while the nation's population shot upward by two-thirds, 100,000 square miles of arable land were being taken from farm production and used for factories, residences, and roads. Despite land reclamation programs, therefore, the amount of arable land per person declined by half during that twenty-seven-year period.[16] This trend has undoubtedly gained momentum since 1979.

The second phase of the May Fourth Movement was a time of exuberant optimism, bringing to mind Wordsworth's lines regarding the French Revolution: "Bliss it was that dawn to be alive, But to be young was very heaven." Indeed, in 1919 and 1920, China's youth were convinced that they could remake the nation by laying the foundations for political democracy, economic prosperity, and social equality.

China's condition did, in fact, begin to improve during and after the May Fourth Movement. The Nationalists and Communists, in turn, began the process of recreating a political structure, and the swelling emotions of nationalism forced imperialism to retreat.

Yet, viewing the May Fourth Movement in historical perspective is a sobering experience. The Chinese people have too often suffered terribly since those heady and hopeful days in 1919. China's rulers, regardless of party affiliation, have too often been an authoritarian lot, treating rivals and ordinary citizens despicably. The tasks of developing the economy—not only an economy that is industrially advanced, but even one that feeds the people adequately—have been more than daunting. The continuing deterioration of the ecosystem, a process that was clearly evident in the late eighteenth century but has gained momentum in recent decades, augurs poorly for the future. China desperately needs creative solutions and imaginative leadership. All too frequently, however, the ideals of reformers and revolutionaries alike have foundered on the hard realities of corruption, self-serving, petty politicking, and tyranny.

Notes

1. Professors Ch'i Hsi-sheng and Joseph W. Esherick served as discussants of this paper at the conference. Their critiques were most helpful in revising the manuscript for presentation here. I am also indebted to professors Peter C. Perdue, Evelyn S. Rawski, and Thomas G. Rawski for providing me with references to valuable materials that I used in revising the manuscript.

2. An excellent case study of ecological and political changes during the period discussed here is Peter C. Perdue, *Exhausting the Earth: State and Peasant in Hunan, 1500–1850* (Cambridge: Harvard University Council on East Asian Studies, 1987). See also Kang Chao, *Man and Land in Chinese History: An Economic Analysis* (Stanford: Stanford University Press, 1986), pp. 201–8.

3. Paraphrase by Ho Ping-ti, *Studies on the Population of China, 1368–1958* (Cambridge: Harvard University Press, 1959), p. 271.

4. Ibid., p. 273.

5. Quoted in George E. Taylor, "The Taiping Rebellion: Its Economic Background and Social Theory," *Chinese Social and Political Science Review*, 16 (1932–33): 560.

6. This and the next paragraph are based on S. A. M. Adshead, "An Energy Crisis in Early Modern China," *Ch'ing-shih wen-t'i* 3, 2 (December 1974): 200–228.

7. Li Bozhong, "Ming-Qing Jiangnan gongnongye shengchan zhong de ranliao wenti" (The fuel problem in industrial and agricultural production in Jiangnan during the Ming and Qing Dynasties), *Zhongguo shehui jingji shi yanjiu* (Research on Chinese social and economic history) 4 (1984): 34–49.

8. Conrad Totman, *The Green Archipelago: Forestry in Preindustrial Japan* (Berkeley: University of California Press, 1989), p. 1.

9. The starting point for an understanding of the early course of militarization in Chinese society is Philip A. Kuhn, *Rebellion and Its Enemies: Militarization and Social Structure, 1796–1864* (Cambridge: Harvard University Press, 1970).

10. Peter Duus, *The Rise of Modern Japan* (Boston: Houghton Mifflin, 1976), p. 142.

11. B. L. Putnam Weale, *The Fight for the Republic* (New York: Dodd, Mead, 1917), p. 19.

12. Chiang Kai-shek, "Xinshenghuo yundong zhi yaoyi" (The essential meaning of the New Life Movement), in *Jiang Zongtong sixiang yanlun ji* (The collected thoughts and speeches of President Chiang), 12: 68.

13. Mao Zedong, "The Question of Independence and Initiative within the United Front," in *Selected Works of Mao Tse-tung* (Peking: Foreign Languages Press, 1965), 2: 224.

14. This section is based primarily on Vaclav Smil, *The Bad Earth: Environmental Degradation in China* (Armonk, NY: M. E. Sharpe, 1984). See also Baruch Boxer, "China's Environmental Prospects," *Asian Survey* 29,7 (July 1989): 669–86.

15. *China Daily*, July 28, 1989, p. 3.

16. Nicholas R. Lardy, *Agriculture in China's Modern Economic Development* (Cambridge: Cambridge University Press, 1983), p. 3.

6

THE SOCIAL AGENDA OF MAY FOURTH

EVELYN S. RAWSKI

The May Fourth Movement of the late 1910s and early 1920s[1] aimed to create a "new citizen" in order to build the foundations for a new nation-state. Before Chinese could concentrate their energies on public affairs, they had to be freed from their prior loyalties to parents and family; their intellectual horizons had to be raised from the local and personal realm to that of the nation. Preaching in favor of "Mr. Science" and "Mr. Democracy," the New Culture activists denounced Confucianism, traditional religious beliefs, China's family system, and the subordination of women. The iconoclastic thrust of the movement was supplemented by a response to the new social tensions accompanying the emergence of an industrial working class in cities like Shanghai. New interest in mass mobilization spurred language reforms to enlarge communication with Chinese of different social classes, attempts to organize and educate workers, and experiments in rural reconstruction. The leaders of this first cultural revolution were to be youth, an inversion of the traditional Chinese age hierarchy.

Seventy years after the May Fourth Movement, the aspirations of the May Fourth youth, a group that included Mao Zedong and other future leaders of the Chinese Communist Party, provide a window through which one can evaluate contemporary conditions in the People's Republic of China. As will be seen, the CCP's social agenda was fundamentally shaped by May Fourth. The May Fourth demands for social change themselves originated in reformist visions of the 1890s. When one looks at the implementation of the May Fourth social agenda in the context of modern Chinese history, one sees continuities that span the 1949 boundary separating the Republican and PRC periods.

This essay is organized into several sections. In the first, I examine the origins of the May Fourth goals in the radical visions of Chinese thinkers at the turn of the century. I then turn to look at historical trends on the major social reforms that were espoused by the Nationalists during the Nanking decade (1927–37) and in the CCP-held areas from the 1930s on: mass education, class equality, gender equality and the attempt to abolish the family system. Finally, I compare the implementation of the May Fourth social agenda in the People's Republic with that of the Guomindang-dominated Republic of China.

The Social Agenda

Demands for female emancipation and the destruction of the Chinese family system did not begin with May Fourth but went back to at least the late 1890s, when writers like Kang Youwei and Tan Sitong attacked the oppression of the Confucian social bonds and the subordination of women. Kang Youwei's utopian society was one in which the institutions that subordinated women would be eliminated. Both Kang and his student Tan Sitong asserted that the unequal status of men and women in traditional China was a violation of the universal moral law. According to Tan Sitong, the martyr of the 1898 Reform Movement, the Buddhist scriptures affirmed the fundamental equality of men and women; a symptom of how far Chinese society had deviated from this innate human condition was the prevalence of "lust" as the primary kind of interaction between men and women. In *On Benevolence*, Tan discussed in detail the reforms that would be necessary before Confucian sexual repressions could be eliminated and the sexual discrimination between men and women abolished.[2] Women's innate mental capacities were equal to those of men; if they were given equal opportunity, their contribution to society would be comparable.[3] The liberation of women would require abolition of the family and the marriage institution: Kang suggested that in the utopian age, men and women could cohabit on the basis of renewable one-year contracts. The weakening of the family institution was desirable not only because the family bond was the cause of personal suffering, but also because "the family institution tends too easily to become the focus of loyalty of the individual person at the cost of the solidarity of the larger society."[4]

Kang's vision of a utopia was one in which territorial states would give way to a universal welfare state caring for the citizen "from cradle to grave."[5] He was looking beyond nationalism, yet many of his assumptions concerning the political powers of the universal state were congruent with the May Fourth drive to create a modern nation-state in China. For example, his advocacy of women's emancipation rested not only on moral grounds but also on the premise that women would then be free to contribute their talents to Chinese society.

Kang Youwei's Confucian commitments make it surprising that his major intellectual bedfellows were anarchists, who abhorred Confucianism and set out to destroy it.[6] For the anarchists, free association among free persons was the prerequisite for a good society. Like Kang, anarchists believed that tradition must be destroyed: they may have been the first to call for a "Confucius revolution."[7] The family served "as an instrument for the production of selfishness" and should be abolished, along with marriage and the Confucian Three Bonds.[8] Like Kang, the anarchists would also have abolished the state, which they regarded as the greatest source of oppression.

The social agenda set by the late Qing reformers on women's issues was only partially fulfilled. The radical demands for abolition of marriage and the family voiced by the late Qing reformers and the anarchists were never seriously adopted by either the Chinese Communist Party or the Guomindang, both of which enacted laws to protect women's rights within marriage and to legislate for the equal rights of women with respect to education, jobs, and political participation. The legislation was one thing; implementation was another. Neither party put a high priority on attacking the structural causes of the continuing second-class status of women. The CCP's first priority was the eradication of class inequality, and women's issues subsequently took a backseat to the drive for eradicating class inequality.

Kang Youwei's utopian vision of a "universal moral community"[9] required that all barriers creating divisions among people be abolished, and that included class. For Kang, the three main victims of Chinese social inequality were slaves, outcasts, and women. While Kang held that class inequality was a violation of the moral law and should be abolished, he did not believe that the division of humans into separate occupations was itself an evil if private property were abolished and replaced with a system of public ownership and control in agriculture, industry, and commerce.[10]

Chinese radicals initially had difficulties in adopting class analysis and fitting it into the Chinese context. The class categories did not fit in easily with traditional views of stratification,[11] and the image of a society torn by internal conflict was diametrically opposed to the perceived need to create nationalist unity. From Liang Qichao to Sun Yat-sen, early twentieth-century reformers and revolutionaries explicitly rejected class struggle: China's main problem was not economic inequality, but poverty. Many May Fourth activists were attracted to socialism but rejected Marxism precisely because of its emphasis on class struggle, seeking instead corporatist or syndicalist socialist solutions to the conflicts between an emergent laboring class and the capitalists. It was not until the Comintern's direct participation in the creation of Communist cells in China that Chinese intellectuals decisively switched their allegiance to Marxism and to the Marxist emphasis on class struggle as the primary political item on the revolutionary agenda.[12] The major turning point in the identification of class equality as a priority in social engineering was thus 1920.

During the twentieth century Chinese leaders have attempted to meet a new goal, that of mass literacy. Almost all of the reform proposals from the late nineteenth century on have included a generous component of education. For Liang, writing in 1896–97, education, or the lack of it, was the fundamental cause of the oppression of women. Without schooling, women were unable to earn their own livelihoods and became parasites on men; the subordination of women was the outcome of their economic weakness. Liang argued that the way to "enrich China and strengthen the military" was to emancipate women by providing them with education and freeing them to work.[13] Education, broadly conceived, was also the most fundamental means of creating the "new citizen" who would be equipped with the values and attitudes that were needed to create a popularly based constitutional government.

Education is clearly correlated with economic development. One might argue that the historical advances in literacy found in both the People's Republic of China and the Republic of China on Taiwan would have occurred even without the inspiration of the May Fourth leaders, who recognized its importance for political modernization. Liang's interest in cultural transformation led him to involve himself in the dissemination of information through publications to an expanding audience. For the May Fourth activists, mass education was a fundamental goal in the drive to create a new modern Chinese culture. Anarchists, Marxists, and anti-Communist liberals like Hu Shi who quarreled over other political issues could agree on this item, and so could the Nationalists and Communists. During the 1930s, when the Guomindang initiated a "New Life Movement," education was still the means by which the new citizen was to be created. Mao's speeches from the 1940s pointed to the need to attack the problem of ignorance and backwardness among China's people. In post-1949 China this emphasis on the transformative power of education has led to the Maoist notion that education or "remolding" can create the correct class consciousness even in persons of the wrong class origin. Education has thus been seen as crucial for political, social, and economic reasons.

Mass Literacy

Movements to expand mass literacy in the 1920s were led by individuals with a diverse spectrum of philosophical and political positions.[14] The American influence was represented by leaders like Jimmy Yen, a Yale graduate whose Thousand Character Movement, begun in 1922, was first sponsored by the YMCA. Tao Xingzhi, a graduate of Columbia University's Teacher's College and student of John Dewey, pioneered in "living" education at Xiaozhuang, a village near Nanjing, where he taught that society was a classroom and sought to combine teaching, learning, and doing into one educational process. Adult education was also part of the Confucian-inspired rural reconstruction project in Zouping County, Shandong, led by Liang Shuming. The ideas of these educational pioneers influenced the CCP-sponsored efforts before 1949 in rural areas. In Jiangxi Mao used a wide variety of materials and the "little teacher" system that had been touted by Tao to run night schools and spare-time schools for adult illiterates. Basic literacy was also a goal of the "mass line" in education during the Yan'an period.

The drive for mass education engendered proposals on changing the nature of the written language. In contrast to the more radical proposals of the 1920s and 1930s that would have completely supplanted Chinese characters with an alphabet, PRC leaders adopted more moderate measures to reduce the number of Chinese characters in use and to simplify characters by reducing the number of strokes needed to write them. These reforms have become politically contentious: during 1957, character reform was one of the issues on which the "rightists" accused the CCP of autocracy; during the thaw after the Great Leap Forward, some writers focused on the confusion created by the arbitrary introduction of simplified characters; during the Cultural Revolution, hatred of the phonetic alphabet (pinyin) resulted in Red Guards tearing down pinyin street signs. Since the Cultural Revolution, this relatively moderate reform program has itself encountered severe popular resistance, and the most recent (1977) list of over eight hundred simplified characters has not been widely adopted.

Both the Guomindang and the Chinese Communist Party also advocated the unification and standardization of the national language—a policy that has been resisted by dialect speakers. Because character reform is linked to speech reform and the replacement of dialects with the national language, Putonghua, character reform has clear implications for increased political centralization and the weakening of regional loyalties. The current stagnation of language reform in the People's Republic thus reflects an unwillingness on the part of the CCP leadership to confront the regional, minority, and cultural identity issues that have blocked further advances in writing reform.

From 1949, the PRC government attacked illiteracy on two fronts. A school system was consolidated and pushed into rural areas; enrollments were greatly expanded. By 1976, 96 percent, and by 1988, 97.1 percent, of school-age children were attending primary school.[15] These attendance rates masked significant problems. First, they masked persistent urban-rural and regional disparities in schooling, disparities that worsened in the 1980s with the post-Mao reforms. Some parents took their children out of school in response to new economic opportunities created by the reforms while others dropped out because they were unable to pay the school and book fees. The education minister Li Tieying estimated in 1989 that approximately one-third of the students only attended elementary school, another third went on to lower middle school, and only 30 percent were able to go on to higher middle school. The average length of schooling was less than five years.

Adult education was another priority in the post-1949 period. Periodic campaigns focused on providing a minimal education to China's adult illiterates. In 1956 this was defined as recognition of 2,000 characters for workers and 1,500 characters for peasants. The most recent statistics on illiteracy and semiliteracy provided by a 1 percent sample survey conducted in 1987 indicated that less than 27 percent of Chinese aged twelve and older were semiliterate or illiterate.[16] The national average masks tremendous regional disparities, with literacy rates ranging from less than 30 percent for Tibet to over 86 percent for the province of Liaoning.

Further statistics provide us with information to assess the timing of the literacy gains made since 1949. These appear in table 1, which shows a steady improvement in literacy among successive birth cohorts during the twentieth century. The regular progression of the literacy rates by age group suggests a long-term trend toward a steady improvement in Chinese literacy that transcends the 1949 boundary and the catastrophes of the war with Japan (1937–45) as well as the civil war (1946–49). The same long-term trend appears in recent studies of female literacy in different regions.[17] Although the literacy rates of birth cohorts who reached school age before the establishment of the People's Republic of China might also have been raised by the adult literacy campaigns that were conducted after 1949, one can question whether campaigns of such limited efficacy (by the testimony of the PRC authorities themselves) could by themselves produce such a regular statistical pattern.

The figures in table 1 also show the perceptible improvement of educational opportunities for Chinese who came of school age after 1949. Surprisingly, these figures do not reflect dramatic upheavals like the Great Leap Forward (1958–62) and the Cultural Revolution (1966–68), although the "bad years" of 1959–61 and the post-Mao reforms adversely affected school enrollments.[18] The period after the most violent phase of the Cultural Revolution had ended was also the period when there was another large advance in mass literacy.

Class Inequality

The development of demands for class equalization was closely linked to the growth of the Chinese Communist movement and to Mao Zedong, who refined the Chinese vocabulary of class and from the 1930s experimented with different tactics of class struggle.[19] By 1956, most obvious class distinctions in Chinese society had been eliminated with land reform and agricultural collectivization and the transition to state ownership of industrial enterprises, but as in the Soviet Union a new privileged stratum of military officers, cadres, and intellectuals appeared. Class remained an important issue in both the Cultural Revolution and the debate on a "new class" theory of socialism in 1975–76.[20]

Mao and his colleagues focused on the elimination of class as the primary item on their revolutionary agenda. During Mao's lifetime, the gap between rich and poor within a village and within urban areas probably narrowed significantly. China enjoyed much greater equality on these measures than many other developing societies, but the policies of the regime ignored the widening gap in inequality among different rural localities and between rural and urban dwellers that had come about during the twenty years from 1956 to 1976.[21] Estimates of the gap between per capita incomes in rich and poor agricultural regions range from 11 : 1 on up; estimates of the ratio of urban to rural incomes from 3 : 1 up

Table 1

PRC Literacy Rates by Age Group (1987)

Age (*sui*)	Percent literate	Year born	Year first entered school
1–14	92.7	1973–77	1979–83
15–19	91.9	1968–72	1974–78
20–24	91.2	1963–67	1969–73
25–29	86.5	1958–62	1964–68
30–34	79.8	1953–57	1959–63
35–39	75.0	1948–52	1954–58
40–44	72.1	1943–47	1949–53
45–49	50.8	1938–42	1944–48
50–54	47.4	1933–37	1939–43
55–59	38.2	1928–32	1934–38
60–64	31.9	1923–27	1929–33
65+	21.3	before 1923	

Source: State Statistical Bureau, Department of Population Statistics, *Zhongguo 1987 nian 1% renkou chouyang diaocha ziliao* (Materials from China's 1987 1 percent sample population survey), national volume (Beijing: Zhongguo tongji chubanshe, 1988).

to 6 : 1.[22] Statistics on educational attainments show obvious differences in literacy rates among regions, and those on female education indicate that the urban-rural divide favoring urban dwellers has never been eliminated.[23]

The CCP's deemphasis of the old class labels since Mao's death has occurred as the economic reforms have stimulated anxiety in China about the emergence of increasing gaps between rich and poor. Available measures lend weight to this concern. Even though decollectivization was first carried out in poorer agricultural regions that also benefited from the loosening of restrictions on migration to cities,[24] recent statistics show that rural industry, the primary source of affluence for many rural localities, has been most conspicuous and most successful in the suburban belts of China's major metropolises and in the regions that have traditionally been the most commercialized. Figures on the wealthiest townships and villages in 1985 show that they are clustered around Beijing, Shanghai, Tianjin, and in coastal provinces like Jiangsu and Zhejiang.[25] These wealthiest townships and villages are very scantily represented in provinces like Gansu, Yunnan, and Guizhou, areas that together with most of Northwest China suffered a declining agricultural output per capita in relation to the national average between 1957 and 1979.[26]

In short, the same localities that lagged behind agricultural development during Mao's lifetime—those with poor access to fertile land, water, urban markets, and industrial outputs—are still lagging behind the national growth trends in the post-Mao period. It is also possible that these rural-rural inequalities have increased rather than declined. The World Bank reported in 1985 that while its own figures did not indicate such a trend, there were "some unfortunate consequences for inequality" in the sharp decline in rural cooperative medical insurance financed from collective welfare funds, and in declines in primary and secondary school enrollments of women. Both declines were especially notable in the poorer localities, suggesting that the "safety net" protecting the living standard of China's poorest households was shrinking.[27]

According to official statistics, the post-Mao period has seen a decline in the ratio of urban to rural incomes, but abundant statistical data in the 1980s confirm the persistence of inequalities between urban and rural areas, among different regions, and between generations.[28] Income inequalities in the countryside influence access to reproduction: the strong tendency for women to "marry up" means that households in poor localities have greater difficulty in attracting brides, a difficulty that will be exacerbated by female infanticide.[29] One recent study indicates that fertility and female literacy continue to vary systematically with the core-periphery dichotomy posited by G. W. Skinner's regional systems framework.[30] Despite the narrowing of urban-rural differences in literacy, the return of entrance examinations, keypoint schools, and the other pre–Cultural Revolution educational policies[31] continue to perpetuate significant inequalities in access to higher education.

Gender Inequality

The first phases of the movement dealt with the elimination of customs like footbinding, which had been attacked by Kang Youwei and Liang Qichao. The first antifootbinding society organized by Kang (1892) had a male membership; male reformers, officials, and foreign women led these efforts in the late Qing, which culminated in the 1900 edict banning footbinding.[32] This ban did not meet with quick compliance, particularly outside the big cities, and movements to abolish footbinding and female infanticide in rural China continued into the May Fourth Movement.

Women were not permitted to vote in the nationwide elections of 1918. While women's rights groups formed from 1911 on did lobby specifically for the vote, the "Manifesto of *New Youth Magazine*" (1919) stopped short of advocating universal suffrage for males, much less females.[33] The suffrage was achieved quickly. The KMT Provisional Constitution for the Tutelage Period, passed in 1931, guaranteed equal rights to women, as did the Constitutional Program adopted in the Kiangsi Soviet the same year.[34] Demands for freedom of marriage choice (and the right to divorce), property rights, the right to hold office, the right to obtain an education and to work were supported by the Guomindang and the Chinese Communist Party, and enshrined in law from the 1920s on.[35]

The implementation of legislation affecting women was considerably delayed, particularly in the contentious area of women's property rights in marriage. Through the twentieth century, traditional marriage exchanges—the bride price (monetary and commodity gifts presented by the groom's family to the bride's family) and dowry (goods, including money, brought by the bride into marriage for the benefit of the new conjugal unit)—have persisted, while feminists have asserted such principles as the freedom of marriage choice, the right to divorce, and the bride's property rights over the dowry and her own earnings, all of which are at odds with traditional practices. The legislation enacted by CCP-controlled bodies has wavered in its support of the feminist position, with the most radical provisions favoring women being enacted by CCP-controlled bodies before 1949. As an example one can compare the 1941 Jin-Cha-Ji Draft Marriage Regulations, which provided that property owned before marriage and one's wages were the exclusive party of the individual and not common property, with the clause in the 1950 Marriage Law, continued in the 1980 Marriage Law, that declared that all property was held in common after marriage.[36]

The CCP position on women's issues from the 1920s was based on Marxist orthodoxy, which emphasized class rather than gender struggle (Johnson 1983). Despite adopting (from 1922) manifestoes that supported universal suffrage, protection for female labor, and abolition of legislation restricting women's rights, the CCP viewed women's rights groups with some reserve as "bourgeois" and elitist in their membership and character. The CCP position, as articulated by Mao Zedong, was that women's rights would come with the general victory. During the 1930s, however, the CCP's program supporting feminist issues was at its high point.[37] Marriage regulations were passed granting women freedom of marriage and divorce, equal pay for equal work, property rights after divorce, and equal rights to land allocations in land reform. CCP labor codes had provisions for paid maternity leave and nursing facilities for mothers. Women were also encouraged to participate in the local soviets.

According to some writers, the massive resistance of poor peasant males to feminist goals caused the party to backtrack from its stated platform.[38] Gender equality directly conflicted with the values held by the poor peasant males who were the target of CCP recruitment; during the war against Japan and the civil war, family harmony was a slogan of the women's movement and the party concentrated on bringing women into the labor force "on a broader basis than before."[39]

With the establishment of the People's Republic of China in 1949, the CCP initially supported a return to a broader agenda. The 1950 Marriage Law and the 1953 campaign to popularize this law, however, met with great resistance on the local level, particularly in rural areas, and they were not aggressively followed up in subsequent years. Indeed, during the Cultural Revolution years, feminist issues were again attacked as "bourgeois" and the primacy of class struggle reaffirmed. Instead, the CCP fell back on the orthodox position that gender equality would only be achieved with the economic transformation of the country. The state concentrated on bringing more women into the labor force; by the early 1970s, perhaps 70 percent of working-age women participated in collective labor.[40]

In the years after Mao's death, women's issues were again brought to public attention. The Women's Federation was revived, and its journal published articles concerning the continuing problems young women faced in asserting their right to free choice in marriage, free divorce, and work rights. The freedom experienced by the young women who roamed China as Red Guards during the Cultural Revolution was replaced by a reassertion of traditional parental controls over their lives, while many of those women found themselves still single and rapidly devalued on the marriage market. Arranged marriages continue to be common in village China; payments of a bride price are more open than ever before and lead to violent resistance to divorce by husbands who claim that they have "paid" for their wives.[41]

The CCP drive to recruit women into the workforce was replaced in the early 1980s by discussions that moved in the opposite direction. Some writers said that the proper place for women was the home; the building of a socialist spiritual civilization depended on mothers. Women's biological inferiority, according to other accounts, meant that they should not be employed at physically taxing jobs. Reforms aiming at decentralization of job placement of college graduates showed employers routinely discriminating against hiring women.[42]

To what extent have demands for gender equality been met? China's record of achievement is not very different from other countries in the socialist and capitalist worlds; in short, women who "hold up half of heaven" continue to fall well short of achieving equal power and status.[43] Women's right to inherit property from their natal families was affirmed in the 1930 Civil Code of the Nationalist government and in PRC laws but meets continued resistance in rural China,[44] where persistent traditions of exogamous marriages mean that daughters will leave their natal villages when they marry. Despite advances in terms of women's access to education, jobs, and freedom of marriage choice, women continue to be underrepresented in top decision-making posts, underpaid, and bear a heavier workload than their male counterparts.

Table 2, which presents data on literacy rates among men and women, underlines the continuing bias against women in access to education. At every age level, women are more likely to be illiterate or only semiliterate. This gap between male and female literacy is "unusually great" in comparison with other Asian societies, and even in comparison with Muslim societies in Asia and the Middle East.[45] At the same time, the figures support the long-term trend toward elimination of illiteracy that was the main theme of table 1 and show a narrowing of the gender gap in literacy over time, as well as the improvement in access to education for the three youngest female birth cohorts (those born since 1963), who entered school at the end of the Cultural Revolution. Like table 1, the

Table 2

PRC Literacy Rates by Sex and Age Group (1987)

Age (*sui*)	Literate males (%)	Literate females (%)
12–14	96.1	89.1
15–19	95.6	88.0
20–24	93.2	86.3
25–29	94.7	78.0
30–34	90.7	66.4
35–39	87.3	62.0
40–44	85.7	57.4
45–49	77.3	43.0
50–54	67.2	26.2
55–59	59.1	15.7
60–64	52.4	10.9
65+	40.5	5.6

Source: State Statistical Bureau, Department of Population Statistics, *Zhongguo 1987 nian 1% renkou chouyang diaocha ziliao*, table 5-9, p. 172.

figures in table 2 show that advances in female literacy begun in the 1930s were notably accelerated in the post-1949 period. Female educational attainments fell in rural areas during the "bad years" of 1959–61 and in the post-Mao reform period.[46]

China is now a country that can do more than provide its citizens with minimal literacy. Table 3 points to the increased access to higher education that women have come to enjoy over time, although the figures indicate a relative decline in female university enrollments in the last decade. At every level, including primary school, women have been systematically underrepresented, and the degree of underrepresentation increases with the level of schooling. The power of this gender bias, which is especially strong in rural China, is underscored by the statistics presented in table 4, based on a 1 percent sample survey of China's population, which compare male and female illiteracy and semiliteracy in the agricultural workforce.

Like women in many other countries, urban women in China have made greater status advances than rural women.[47] Urban women have much more education than their rural counterparts.[48] With the overwhelming majority of urban women now working, the former contentious relationship with mothers-in-law has been softened as the latter perform many domestic tasks and child care. Scarce housing has led some couples to choose the more comfortable (for women) domestic environment of matrilocal residence. Pension benefits at work dampen anxiety about security in old age.

The PRC government's espousal of birth control, an issue first raised in 1922

Table 3

Educational Achievements of Women in the People's Republic

Year	Primary school	Middle school	University
1954	33.3	25.1	26.3
1964	35.0	34.3	25.7
1974	43.7	38.1	33.8
1984	45.4	38.8	28.1

Source: Zhongguo jiaoyu nianjian 1949–1981 (Chinese education yearbook, 1949–81) (Beijing: Zhongguo baike chubanshe, 1981).
Note: Figures are expressed as a percentage of women in the student body.

Table 4

Levels of Educational Attainment in China's Agricultural Labor Force Based on 1 Percent Population Survey, 1987

Educational level	Males	Females
University[a]	0.02	0.003
Higher middle school	5.65	2.63
Lower middle school	34.44	20.44
Primary school	77.69	58.71
Illiterate or semiliterate	20.63	41.29

Source: State Statistical Bureau, Department of Population, *Zhongguo 1987 nian 1% renkou chouyang diaocha ziliao*, table 6-16.
Note: The sample population totaled 4,017,837.
[a]This category includes those with any university attendance in addition to university graduates.

when Margaret Sanger visited China and spoke at Peking University on "The What and How of Birth Control,"[49] does not seem to have enhanced women's status. Birth control campaigns based on delayed marriage, birth spacing, and fewer children occurred in 1956–58, 1962–66, and the 1970s, but had minor effect on fertility in rural areas until the mid-1960s. During the 1970s, rural China experienced "the most rapid fertility decline on record for any large population."[50] Since 1979, when the government instituted a policy of one child per family, there were large increases in the use of abortion as a means of birth control, and reports of female infanticide.[51]

Destruction of the Family System

"The Chinese family and clan system was the basis of despotism" and "the source of all evil," proclaimed writers in the magazines of the May Fourth Movement.[52] Here, too, their attacks on the family echoed the views of Kang Youwei, who believed that the family would disappear in the utopian age. Kang, a man who personified the Confucian virtues of filial piety, came to denounce the family as a source of personal suffering for its members that "perpetuated inequality."[53]

Despite the vigor of the May Fourth attack on the family and the campaign in the early 1950s against the extended family, the patrilineal family institution has never been the object of a concerted mass campaign in the People's Republic. Feminist scholars have ascribed the CCP reluctance to alter the traditional Chinese family to two factors: the traditional family-based values of the poor peasant males who formed the core of the CCP's rural support, and the government's reliance on the family to provide welfare services and stability in rural life during periods of rapid political and economic change.[54] During the 1950s, when collectivization took away the family's role in farm management, restraints on urban migration supported its continuing importance in daily life.[55] Peasants repudiated attempts during the Great Leap Forward to substitute domestic services with communal kitchens and nurseries, and the family survived into the 1970s. Since Mao's death and decollectivization, the family has regained its traditional function as a unit of production. Its raison d'être has thus been strengthened more than at any point since the early 1950s.

The family is still responsible for providing for its members. The 1980 Marriage Law states that children have the duty to support not only their parents but also their grandparents.[56] Newlyweds still tend to reside within the compound of the groom's father. Despite recent advocacy for reform,[57] marriage for many Chinese continues to be patrilocal. The repercussions of these traditional practices are most evident in the countryside. In many cases, because of Chinese rules concerning surname exogamy, marriage required that the bride move out of her natal village. Exogamous marriages and patrilocality produce parents who continue to devalue their daughters, who will not provide them with long-term support, and value their sons, who will be with them through old age.

Comparison with Taiwan

The depth and periodization of China's achievements in fulfilling the social agenda set by May Fourth reveals processes of historical causation on several levels. In areas like the achievement of basic literacy and equal access of women to education, the statistics depict long-term shifts that predate the establishment of the People's Republic of China. Expansion of education was a specific goal of the PRC, but its realization was hampered by shortages of funds. Gender inequality, another long-espoused goal of the CCP, has not been emphasized during much of the period since 1949. By contrast, the CCP's attack on class inequality was swift and accomplished early through land reform and the transfer of industrial enterprises to state ownership. The party did not focus on the broader issue of inequality among regions and between town and countryside, and these inequalities probably widened over the first three decades of Communist rule. Economic reforms put in place in the 1980s have had the largely unintended consequence of narrowing urban-rural inequalities while perhaps increasing intravillage inequality.

It should come as no surprise to discover that the People's Republic of China has not achieved full class and gender equality; in this respect China is no worse than other socialist countries and slightly better in some areas than the capitalist countries in the world.[58] How does the record of the PRC on these social issues compare with the achievements of the Nationalist government on Taiwan?

The KMT government that has ruled Taiwan since 1945 is, like the CCP, a child of the May Fourth Movement. Although Chiang Kai-shek's education and outlook predated May Fourth, many of his colleagues—perhaps most prominently Dai Jitao—not only were active participants but also were sympathetic to the anarchist positions voiced during May Fourth.[59] As noted earlier, Guomindang legislation adopted many of the same feminist platforms taken up by the CCP.

In 1945, when the Nationalist government took over Taiwan from the Japanese, the island was a predominantly agrarian economy. After 1949, the Nationalists carried out a program of land reform that not only distributed land to peasant cultivators but also, according to some arguments, created such small landholdings that many farm children had to seek their livelihood away from farming. Taiwan chose an export-oriented strategy of development that focused on the use of cheap female labor and foreign investment. Economic growth accelerated in the late 1960s and continued in the 1970s and 1980s, to produce today a country whose per capita income and other economic measures are typical of modern industrialized economies.[60] Educational statistics for the Republic of China indicate that here, too, Taiwan is more advanced than the PRC. Under Japanese colonial rule, Taiwanese probably had better access to primary schooling than their mainland counterparts. This is suggested by the relatively low illiteracy rates found in Taiwan in the early 1950s, which can be compared with the much higher rate of illiteracy in China in 1949. A comparison of figures for 1952, when slightly over 42 percent of the population was illiterate, and 1986, when 8 percent was illiterate, shows that Taiwan virtually eliminated illiteracy during its postwar economic development.[61] By 1983, enrollment in primary school was almost universal (99.8 percent), and the majority (86.6 percent of boys, 87.5 percent of girls) were continuing their education in lower middle schools.[62] With low tuition, education in the Republic of China has been a channel of upward mobility that is open to a large portion of the population.

To what extent has Taiwan embraced goals of class equality? Although the Republic of China never attacked the institution of private property and thus the foundations of class, historical events have tended to diminish the gap between rich and poor that is characteristic of most capitalist countries. During the colonial period (1895–1945), Japanese monopolized the top governmental and economic positions. At the end of World War II, there was a small business elite on Taiwan whose wealth was derived primarily from banking and other business activities, and a larger group of small-scale and middle-scale entrepreneurs. The Nationalist government of Chen Yi, governor from 1946–47, attacked the economic position of this Taiwanese elite through expropriation. A major purge of the Taiwanese educated elite occurred in 1947, as a result of the February uprising against KMT rule; ten thousand to twenty thousand individuals were arrested and detained.[63] Relatives of those implicated in the uprising were barred from government service, which included teaching. This purge is said to have destroyed the educated Taiwanese middle class,[64] while land reform, carried out in the 1950s, substantially reduced the power of Taiwanese landlords.

Meanwhile, the mainlanders who accompanied the Guomindang when it moved its national government to Taiwan were unable to bring all of their assets with them. According to one author, "most of the class interests adhering to the Nationalist state were sheared off by the move to Taiwan, which principally included government officials, parliamentary representatives, and military personnel."[65] Although we lack a statistical measure of the degree of income inequality in Taiwan in the late 1940s, it is therefore likely to have been significantly smaller than the income inequality of the Nanking period (1927–37). Taiwan's postwar economic growth has been characterized by a plethora of small family firms, and this had a positive effect on income distribution.

Studies of income differentials in Taiwan show that Taiwan's economic development from the 1950s to the late 1970s was associated with increasing income equality.[66] A comparison of the Gini coefficients, one measure of income inequality, shows slightly less inequality for Taiwan (Gini coefficient = .30 for Taiwan in 1978; .33 for China in 1979), suggesting that there was no significant difference in income distribution between these two countries. Another measure of income distribution, the share of income received by the poorest 40 percent of families, is somewhat higher in Taiwan (22.7 percent) than in China (18 percent).[67]

Taiwan and the People's Republic are at very different stages of economic development, with significantly different systems for provision of goods and services. In both societies, the family development cycle plays an important role in determining household income. What happens if the effect of the family development cycle on income inequality is examined?

Susan Greenhalgh has argued persuasively that income inequality in Taiwan is not the product of a hardened class structure but instead reflects the movement of households through the family developmental cycle.[68] Similar arguments suggest that the family developmental cycle accounts for half of the rural intra-village income inequality in the PRC and a "substantial" part of intra-urban income differentials.[69] The family developmental cycle, however, cannot account for the growing regional inequalities in today's China. As noted earlier, these regional income inequalities in the PRC stem from disparities in resource endowments—human capital, infrastructure, access to markets, and productive capacity—that are not easily overcome. One can thus argue that Taiwan has made substantial gains in eliminating barriers to income mobility that yet remain in the PRC.

A number of studies show that women in Taiwan, like their mainland sisters, entered the labor force in increasing numbers during the postwar period. By 1980, 39 percent of working-age women in Taiwan had joined the labor force.[70] The discrepancy between female and male wages also fell and daughters were given more schooling. Wage earning seems to have enhanced the mobility of young women, but it has not released them from their subordinate status in family strategies, which through the early 1980s continued to dictate the actions of sons and daughters.[71]

The traditional extended family is very much a part of Taiwan's rural scene today. In fact, the extended family form may have become more popular as economic development provided increased options for rural people.[72] The joint family has flourished because it offers conjugal households savings in living expenses and taxes; provides the domestic services of the mother-in-law to young housewives who can work outside the home; and increases the economic potential and security of the conjugal units.[73] As one scholar has noted, "China's traditional family system has tremendous capacities for effective resource mobilization and entrepreneurial expansion. There is no doubt that this family system played a crucial role in Taiwan's rapid and equitable development."[74]

Comparison of the degree to which the May Fourth social agenda has been implemented in the capitalist environment of Taiwan and the socialist society of China underlines the common experience that the Guomindang and the Chinese Communist Party shared in their early years. Both Taiwan and China have significantly expanded mass education and mass literacy. Both countries eliminated the power of local landlords through land reform. Taiwan has also been able to achieve economic growth and significantly reduce income inequalities at the same time. Comparison of available measures indicates that Taiwan has matched (and perhaps outdone) the PRC in achieving a broadly based distribution of income, even though the Nationalist government on Taiwan has never committed itself to the kind of class equality espoused by the CCP. Conversely, the failure of the PRC to create a more egalitarian society points to the complexity of economic development and the consistent urban bias of PRC policies.[75] In the PRC, the poorest 40 percent of the population reside in the countryside.

The continued subordination of women in both the People's Republic of China and the Republic of China underlines the inability of different political systems at different levels of economic advance to achieve full gender equality. The vitality of the family system in both countries today suggests that the May Fourth leaders and Kang Youwei were apparently wrong about the family as an obstacle to modernization. The parallels between the renascent family in the PRC and the elaborated family in Taiwan testify not only to the flexibility of this institution, but to the likelihood that it will survive when many other elements in Chinese society have passed away.

Notes

1. Historians sometimes distinguish between the Nationalist movement of May 4, 1919, which protested the Peking government's pro-Japanese stance at the peace negotiations at Versailles, and the broader New Culture Movement, which began ca. 1915 and extended into the early 1920s. In this essay, "May Fourth" refers to the New Culture Movement.

2. Kazuko Ono, *Chinese Women in a Century of Revolution*, ed. Joshua A. Fogel (Stanford: Stanford University Press, 1989), pp. 36–38.

3. Hao Chang, *Chinese Intellectuals in Crisis: Search for Order and Meaning, 1890–1911* (Berkeley: University of California Press, 1987), pp. 60–61, 91; Kung-chuan Hsiao, *A Modern China and a New World: K'ang Yu-wei, Reformer and Utopian, 1858–1927* (Seattle: University of Washington Press, 1975), pp. 446–49.

4. Chang, *Chinese Intellectuals in Crisis*, p. 61.

5. Ibid., p. 63.

6. Or perhaps not so surprising: see Martin Bernal, *Chinese Socialism to 1907* (Ithaca: Cornell University Press, 1976), pp. 25–30, on Kang's knowledge of socialism.

7. Arif Dirlik, *The Origins of Chinese Communism* (New York: Oxford University Press, 1989), p. 77.

8. Ibid., p. 78.

9. Chang, *Chinese Intellectuals in Crisis*, p. 59.

10. Ibid., p. 60.

11. Philip Kuhn, "Chinese Views of Social Classification," in *Class and Social Stratification in Post-Revolution China*, ed. J. L. Watson (Cambridge: Cambridge University Press, 1984), pp. 16–28.

12. Dirlik, *The Origins of Chinese Communism*.

13. Ono, *Chinese Women*, pp. 26–28.

14. Evelyn S. Rawski, *Education and Popular Literacy in Ch'ing China* (Ann Arbor: University of Michigan Press, 1979), pp. 167–73.

15. *Renmin ribao* (People's daily), overseas edition, November 6, 1989, p. 4.

16. State Statistical Bureau, *Zhongguo tongji nianjian 1988* (Chinese statistical yearbook 1988) (Beijing: Zhongguo tongji chubanshe, 1988), table 3-14.

17. William R. Lavely, "The Spatial Approach to Chinese History: Illustrations from North China and the Upper Yangzi," *Journal of Asian Studies* 48, 1 (1989): 100–113; William R. Lavely, Xiao Zhenyu, Li Bohua, and Ronald Freedman, "The Rise of Female Education in China: National and Regional Patterns," paper presented at the annual meeting of the Population Association of America in New Orleans, 1988.

18. Lavely et al., "The Rise of Female Education."

19. Stuart Schram, "Classes, Old and New, in Mao Zedong's Thought," in *Class and Social Stratification in Post-Revolution China*, ed. Watson, pp. 29–55.

20. Richard C. Kraus, *Class Conflict in Chinese Socialism* (New York: Columbia University Press, 1982).

21. Carl Riskin, *China's Political Economy: The Quest for Development Since 1949* (New York: Oxford University Press, 1987); Martin K. Whyte, "Social Trends in China: The Triumph of Inequality?" in *Modernizing China: Post-Mao Reform and Development*, ed. A. Doak Barnett and Ralph N. Clough (Boulder: Westview Press, 1986), pp. 103–23.

22. Thomas G. Rawski, "The Simple Arithmetic of Chinese Income Distribution," *Keizai kenkyu* 33, 1 (1982): 21; Riskin, *China's Political Economy*, pp. 232, 234; Whyte, "Social Trends in China," p. 109.

23. Lavely et al., "The Rise of Female Education."

24. Whyte, "Social Trends in China."

25. *Zhongguo xiangzhen qiye guanli baike quanshu* (Encyclopedia on enterprise management in China's townships and villages) (Beijing: Nongye chubanshe, 1987), appendix 4, table 9.

26. Riskin, *China's Political Economy*, p. 229.

27. World Bank, *China: Long-term Development Issues and Options* (Baltimore: Johns Hopkins University Press, 1985), p. 30.

28. Martin K. Whyte, "Inequality and Stratification in China," *China Quarterly* 64 (1975): 648–711; Whyte, "Destratification and Restratification in China," in *Social Inequality: Comparative and Developmental Approaches*, ed. Gerald D. Berreman and K. Zretsky (New York: Academic Press, 1981), pp. 309–36; Whyte, "Social Trends in China."

29. Lavely et al., "The Rise of Female Education."

30. Lavely, "The Spatial Approach to Chinese History."

31. Suzanne Pepper, "Chinese Education After Mao: Two Steps Forward, Two Steps Back and Begin Again?" *China Quarterly* 81 (1980): 1–65.

32. Elisabeth Croll, *Feminism and Socialism in China* (London: Routledge and Kegan Paul, 1978), pp. 45–50.

33. Tse-tung Chow, *The May Fouth Movement* (Cambridge: Harvard University Press, 1960), pp. 174–75.

34. Andrew Nathan, *Chinese Democracy* (Berkeley: University of California Press, 1986), p. 90.

35. Chow, *The May Fourth Movement*, p. 258; Kay Ann Johnson, *Women, the Family and Peasant Revolution in China* (Chicago: University of Chicago Press, 1983); Rubie S. Watson, "Women's Property in Republican China: Rights and Practice," *Republican China* 10, 1a (1984): 1–12.

36. Jonathan K. Ocko, "Women, Property, and Law in the PRC," in *Marriage and Inequality in Chinese Society*, ed. Rubie S. Watson and Patricia B. Ebrey (Berkeley: University of California Press, 1991).

37. Johnson, *Women, the Family, and Peasant Revolution.*

38. Ibid.; Judith Stacey, *Patriarchy and Socialist Revolution in China* (Berkeley: University of California Press, 1983); Margery Wolf, *Revolution Postponed: Women in Contemporary China* (Stanford: Stanford University Press, 1985).

39. Jackal (1981), p. 84.

40. Johnson, *Women, the Family, and Peasant Revolution*, p. 169.

41. Emily Honig and Gail Hershatter, *Personal Voices: Chinese Women in the 1980's* (Stanford: Stanford University Press, 1988).

42. Ibid.

43. Martin K. Whyte, "Sexual Inequality under Socialism: The Chinese Case in Perspective," in *Class and Social Stratification in Post-Revolution China*, ed. Watson, pp. 198–238.

44. Johnson, *Women, the Family, and Peasant Revolution*, pp. 110–12.

45. Nick Eberstadt, "Material Poverty in the People's Republic of China in Interna-

tional Perspective,'' in U. S. Congress, Joint Economic Committee, *China's Economy Looks Toward the Year 2000. Vol. 1: The Four Modernizations* (Washington, DC: Government Printing Office, 1986), pp. 185–86.

46. Lavely et al., ''The Rise of Female Education.''

47. Wolf, *Revolution Postponed*; Whyte, ''Sexual Inequality under Socialism.''

48. Lavely et al., ''The Rise of Female Education.''

49. Chow, *The May Fourth Movement*, p. 258.

50. William R. Lavely, ''The Rural Chinese Fertility Transition: A Report from Shifang Xian, Sichuan,'' *Population Studies* 38, 3 (1984): 365.

51. H. Yuan Tien, ''Abortion in China: Incidence and Implications,'' *Modern China* 13, 4 (1987): 441–68.

52. Chow, *The May Fourth Movement*, p. 185.

53. Hsiao, *A Modern China and a New World*, p. 451.

54. Johnson, *Women, the Family, and Peasant Revolution*; Stacey, *Patriarchy and Socialist Revolution*; Wolf, *Revolution Postponed.*

55. Elisabeth Croll, *The Politics of Marriage in Contemporary China* (Cambridge: Cambridge University Press, 1979).

56. Wolf, *Revolution Postponed*, p. 208.

57. Johnson, *Women, the Family, and Peasant Revolution*, pp. 197–99.

58. William L. Parish, ''Destratification in China,'' in *Class and Social Stratification in Post-Revolution China*, pp. 84–120; Whyte, ''Sexual Inequality under Socialism.''

59. Dirlik, *The Origins of Chinese Communism.*

60. In 1986 per capita income in Taiwan was approximately US $3,000, at a point when per capita income in the PRC was an estimated US $400. Harold C. Hinton, *East Asia and the Western Pacific 1987* (Washington, DC: Stryker-Post, 1987).

61. Republic of China, Council for Economic Planning and Development, *Taiwan Statistical Data Book 1987* (Taipei, 1987), table 2-4b.

62. *Zhonghua Minguo Taiwan diqu guoli tongji zhipiao* (Republic of China, Taiwan national statistical indicators) (Taipei: United Daily, 1985), table 4.4.

63. George H. Kerr, *Formosa Betrayed* (Boston: Houghton Mifflin, 1965), p. 310.

64. Hill Gates, *Chinese Working-Class Lives* (Ithaca: Cornell University Press, 1987), pp. 45–48.

65. Edwin A. Winckler, ''Elite Political Struggle, 1945–1985,'' in *Contending Approaches to the Political Economy of Taiwan*, ed. E. A. Winckler and Susan Greenhalgh (Armonk, NY: M. E. Sharpe, 1988), p. 153.

66. Shirley W. Y. Kuo, *The Taiwan Economy in Transition* (Boulder: Westview, 1983).

67. Ibid., table 6.1; World Bank, *China: Socialist Economic Development* (Washington, DC: International Bank for Reconstruction and Development, 1983), table 3.21.

68. Susan Greenhalgh, ''Is Inequality Demographically Induced? The Family Cycle and the Distribution of Income in Taiwan,'' *American Anthropologist* 87, 3 (1985): 571–94.

69. Riskin, *China's Political Economy*, p. 235; T. Rawski, ''The Simple Arithmetic of Chinese Income Distribution,'' p. 20.

70. Kuo, *The Taiwan Economy in Transition*, table 5.2.

71. Lydia Kung, *Factory Women in Taiwan* (Ann Arbor: UMI Research Press, 1983); Susan Greenhalgh, ''Sexual Stratification: The Other Side of 'Growth with Equity' in East Asia,'' *Population and Development Review* 11, 5 (1985): 263–314.

72. Gallin and Gallin (1982).

73. Rita Gallin, *Rural Industrialization and Chinese Women* (East Lansing, MI: Michigan State University Working Paper, 1984).

74. Greenhalgh, ''Sexual Stratification,'' p. 306.

75. T. Rawski, ''The Simple Arithmetic of Chinese Income Distribution,'' pp. 17–19.

7

MODERNITY AND ITS DISCONTENTS
The Cultural Agenda of the May Fourth Movement

LEO OU-FAN LEE

My current research on the cultural legacy of the May Fourth Movement—and for that matter, of twentieth-century Chinese culture—can be characterized as variations on an amorphous theme: that of modernity. However complex or problematic its theoretical underpinnings, the word has certainly come into intellectual fashion in post-Mao China, in part because it is semantically linked with the word "modernization," which has been further canonized in the official Four Modernizations. In contemporary Chinese literature, the word "modernism" (*xiandai zhuyi*) has been a subject of heated debate (as it was in Taiwan in the 1970s) and a catch-all phrase comprising various new artistic trends derived from a resurgent craze for Western literature among the post-Mao generation of young writers and critics.

It would be convenient to dismiss all such talk of Chinese "modernism" and "postmodernism" as irrelevant echoes of a new Western craze. It is also tempting—an approach one should resist—to consider such literary and artistic manifestations merely "superstructural" products of a modernizing society (Taiwan) or ideological byproducts of new government policy (PRC). I would argue, however, that the roots of these recent "modernisms" can be traced to a new mode of historical consciousness that began to emerge after the turn of the century and became firmly anchored in the intellectual discourse of the May Fourth era. This new historical consciousness, based on a new conception of time and human progress, has tended to dominate the general outlooks of Chinese intellectuals of different political persuasions; it has also served to inspire new forms of literary creation that have come to be known, since the Literary Revolution of 1917, as New Literature.

In this essay I shall first try to apply the concept of modernity as a new mode of historical consciousness, which in my view tended to shape the cultural creativity of the May Fourth period. In the second part, I concentrate on literature and trace the literary implications of modernity. The third part turns to the problem of May Fourth intellectuals and their self-appointed role as agents of enlightenment on behalf of modern culture, together with some latter-day assessments of their role.[1]

Historical Consciousness

I begin with a question from a May Fourth stance. Much, of course, has been said about the iconoclastic side of the conspicuous antitraditional ideology of the May Fourth intellectual revolution. But in what ways did the May Fourth generation, and their predecessors, attempt to define their difference from the past and articulate a new range of sensibilities that they would consider "modern"?

In the popular May Fourth parlance, to be "modern" means above all to be "new" (*xin*), to be consciously opposed to the "old" (*jiu*). The proliferation of journal titles and terms composed of the word "new" was striking, from Liang Qichao's "New People" (*Xinmin*) and Chen Duxiu's "New Youth" (*Xin qingnian*) to such prevalent compounds as "New Tide" (*Xinchao*), "New Literature and Art" (*Xin wenyi*), "New Life" (*Xin shenghuo*), "New Society" (*Xin shehui*), and "New Epoch" (*Xin shidai*). This intellectual posture of newness does not by itself represent anything new, for in traditional China there were indeed recurrent debates between "new" and "old"—or between "moderns" and "ancients"—in matters related to scholarly texts as well as governmental policy. What makes for the qualitative difference in the May Fourth formulation is rather its implicit equation of newness with a new temporal continuum from the present to the future. In other words, the notion and value of "newness" are defined in a context of unilinear time and a unilinear sense of history that is characteristically untraditional and Western. The most eloquent manifestation of this new historical consciousness was the notion of "epoch" (*shidai*)—the heightened awareness that China had entered into a "new epoch" of world history that rendered its destiny no longer separate but an integral part of mankind. Thus one finds in this new historical outlook an emphasis on, even a mystical apotheosis of, the moment "now" as the pivotal point marking a rupture with the past and forming a progressive continuum toward a grandiose future.

In a pioneering paper on "Chinese Intellectuals' Notion of 'Epoch' in the Post–May Fourth Era," Lung-kee Sun traces the first signs of this "advent of modernity" in the late Qing Self-Strengthening Movement. Xue Fucheng, for instance, assessed his own time as marking the end of China's isolation and the "dawn of an epoch of association among nations."[2] Both Xue and Wang Tao considered these changes irreversible, regardless of human wishes. By 1895, Kang Youwei and Yan Fu had fully embraced this unilinear thinking about time and history coupled with "an almost mystical faith in progress." As several recent studies have pointed out, this conception of history represents a drastic departure from the traditional cyclical view, a view shaped by the alternation of the "Five Elements" and the Confucian notions of dynastic cycle and *yi zhi yi luan*—a period of order, then one of chaos. Kang's famous three-stage theory of the ages of "decay and chaos," "rising peace," and "universal peace," though based in part on the Gongyang and Liyun texts of his New Text Confucianism, is altogether a forward-looking prophetic vision of history moving in a "unilinear, irreversible process of evolutionary development."[3] This view, according to Chang Hao, is less indebted to these ancient Chinese texts, whose seemingly linear view is nevertheless "couched within a larger cyclical framework" than to "the Western view of history, which is a process of unilinear development in both its secular and religious guises."[4] For this essentially Western scheme, Kang was indeed influenced by Yan Fu as well as by publications of some Christian missionaries, such as Timothy Richard and Young Allen. Yan Fu stated categorically in 1895:

> The greatest and most irreconcilable difference between Chinese and Western thinking is that the Chinese love the past and neglect the present, while the Westerners strive in the present to surpass the past. The Chinese believe that to revolve from order to disorder, from ascension to decline, is the natural way of heaven and of human affairs. The Westerners believe, as the ultimate principle of all learning and government, in the infinite, daily progress, in advance that will not sink into decline, in order that will not revert to disorder.[5]

Insofar as the primary sources for this unilinear view are Western-derived, the translations and writings of Yan Fu occupied a place of seminal significance—in particular, his introduction of what has come to be known as social Darwinism. It is commonly assumed that the Darwinian and Spencerian principles of "natural selection" and "survival of the fittest" lent themselves not only to a nationalistic imperative for China to strive for survival but to increased emphasis on human progress as a key component of this new vision of history based on evolutionism.

It may be worth noting that "the term 'evolution' plays very little part in all of Darwin's own writing: it is not used, for instance, in the first edition of *The Origin of Species*. The connection between Darwin's theory of 'natural selection' and traditional arguments about 'organic evolution' was made explicit only subsequently." As Stephen Toulmin has argued, the indiscriminate application of Darwin's "science" to the other realms has led to a "conception of Evolution as Cosmic Progress—revealing a universal and irreversible direction of historical development in the natural and human worlds."[6] This confusion in nineteenth-century Western thought between evolution as a biological or zoological theory and evolutionism as a doctrine of historical and cosmic progress gave

Darwinism a much broader meaning and appeal in modern European thought. Yan Fu, through his effective interpretations of Spencer and Huxley, further popularized this confusion in his own country.

It can be argued that Yan Fu's interpretation purposefully hinges on such a confusion. In his 1895 essay on the "Origins of Power" (*Yuanqiang*), he briefly describes Darwin's theory only to demonstrate its relevance to the human world because "human beings are but a species of animals." He then applauds Herbert Spencer for having developed a grand system that comprised all and for having used the evolutionary theory to "explicate affairs of human ethics and government." It was precisely in establishing such an analogy between the animal and human realms that Yan was able to decry the deterministic implications of Darwin's theory. Without human intervention, the Darwinian idea of progress could only lead to scientific fatalism determined by such "objective" elements as heredity and environment which "replaced conscious, logical choice as the main determinants of human action."[7] Yan Fu's reading of social Darwinism thus represents a reversal of this fatalistic tendency (which was also observable in nineteenth-century European thought) by asserting the central importance of human volition in both individual and collective forms. Benjamin Schwartz, in his classic study of Yan Fu, has specifically pointed to Yan Fu's interest in "the Faustian-Promethean exaltation of energy and power both over non-human nature and within human society." As he commented: "What interests Yan Fu here is not so much the Darwinian account of biological evolution qua science, even though science is a cherished value. It is precisely the stress on the values of struggle—assertive energy, the emphasis on the actualization of potentialities within a competitive situation."[8]

Subsequent Chinese writings, all influenced by Yan, tended to expand the scope of his view. Evolutionism had entered the May Fourth ideological discourse as a central component through the writings of Chen Duxiu, Lu Xun, and others. In Chen's famous plea to youth, he incorporated a great deal of social Darwinian rhetoric and considered "progressivism" to be one of the five cardinal characteristics of New Youth. In another well-known article lauding "The French and Modern Civilization," he included evolutionism as one of the three major French contributions and paid special tribute to Lamarck. Before he was converted to Marxism, Chen had become a true believer in historical progress. The imprint of this new outlook is clearly seen in Chen's proclamation of a "twentieth-century consciousness" in an essay called "The Year 1916":

> The epoch in which you are living, what epoch is this? It is the beginning of the sixteenth year of the twentieth century. The changes of the world are evolutionary, different from month to month, year to year. The shining history is unfolding faster and faster. . . . To live in the present world, you must raise your head and proudly call yourself a person of the twentieth century, you must create a new civilization of the twentieth century and not confine yourself

> to following that of the nineteenth. For the evolution of human civilization is replacing the old with the new, like a river flowing on, an arrow flying away, constantly continuing and constantly changing.[9]

This positive conception of the new epoch represents a clear affirmation of a new historical consciousness that focuses on the present as a dynamic flow of progressive change—a temporal scheme of the succession of centuries, instead of dynasties, that includes China in the mainstream of world history. Interestingly, exactly seventy years later (1986) in post-Mao Beijing, the idea of "twentieth-century consciousness" was once again hoisted by three young Beida leaders as the guiding concept of their massive project to rewrite the history of modern Chinese literature, as they attempted to bring Chinese literature to reenter the world.[10]

As the word *jinhua* (evolution), literally "progressive transformation" became part of the modern Chinese vocabulary, replacing the less frequently used *yanhua* or *tianyan* (as used in Yan Fu's translation of Huxley's *Evolution and Ethics*), more scholarly or semischolarly writings on evolution also became available, which both gave a fuller history of the Darwinian strains than Yan Fu had done and extended the concept of evolution, in fact, to philosophical discussions of "cosmic progress." Although the rich literature on this subject awaits more in-depth study, my preliminary research has revealed that not only did some of the most renowned thinkers—Zhang Dongsun, Zhang Junmai (Carson Chang), and Li Shichen among them—write extensively about evolution, general treatises, popular pamphlets, scholarly texts, and translations were also published in the 1920s and 1930s. As Bonnie McDougall has discovered in the case of some general literary histories about Western literature and literary theories,[11] most of these general philosophical writings are based, in part or in whole, on such English-language Western books as Thilly, *History of Philosophy*; Perry, *Philosophy of Recent Past and Present Philosophical Tendencies*; Elliot, *Modern Science and Materialism*; Joad, *Introduction to Modern Philosophy*; Marvin, *History of European Philosophy*; and Külpe, *The Philosophy of Present* [*sic*] *in Germany.*[12] All of these presumably included chapters on evolution. A translation of Walter Libby's *Introduction to Contemporary Civilization* had a first chapter titled "The Idea of Progress." There was also a hundred-page pamphlet on "Evolution and Eugenics" (Jinhua lun yu shanzhong xue) cowritten by Chen Changheng and Zhou Jianren (Lu Xun's third brother) in the popular series "Dongfang wenku" published by the *Dongfang zazhi* (Eastern miscellany) of the Commercial Press.[13]

Another piece of clear evidence of the stirrings of this new mode of historical consciousness was the effusive usage of the word *shidai* (epoch). As documented by Lung-kee Sun, the term—perhaps of Japanese origin—was first introduced in the decade before the founding of the Republic, and by around 1927 it had become a catchword especially among radical intellectuals. Of its various usages when first introduced, "shidai's most important connotation came to be 'the present time' or 'our time,' always with the implication that it is a time of breathlessly rapid changes and incessant innovation."[14] The present epoch was, almost by definition, a "new" era radically different from all past periods, bringing "new tides" that could not be resisted. This sentiment was expressed eloquently in Luo Jialun's manifesto for the *Xinchao* (New tide) magazine. Accordingly, an individual living in this new epoch must seek to comprehend it: "Know your shidai" became a clarion-call. The words of the radical poet (later Trotskyite) Wang Quqing were typical: "Know your shidai! Your shidai—that is the present developmental stage of society you are living in—foredains what you should do, and whence to start."[15] Thus the new consciousness of time also carried with it an imperative of timing: one would "lag far behind" the time if one were not vigilant; therefore, one should continually move forward with time and even "push it forward." For some young writers, the battle between the old and the new easily took on a radical imperative: "The old writers, lagging behind shidai, are in no position to shoulder the responsibility of expressing shidai's life. This responsibility can only fall upon the shoulders of new writers, because the latter have a genuine feel for the life of the shidai!"[16]

This familiar configuration of concerns tended to produce a new personality type that Thomas Metzger has aptly called "the zealously ideological, heroic self." To varying degrees, this "heroic self" was basic not only to leftist radicalism and Maoism but also to modern revivals of Confucianism and the Sun Yat-sen–Chiang Kai-shek ideology of the Guomindang. Metzger gives six characteristics to this new vision:

> First, the self is armed with a doctrinal system that explains the laws of the cosmos and history and fixes the goal of life. Second, one is filled with a fiery, selfless determination to "struggle" for this goal. Third, thus determined, one is with "the people" or with the people's "real" desires. . . . Fourth, in this struggle, perceived historical tendencies constitute a "tide" filled with "power" and moving irresistibly toward ego's goal. Fifth, in this light, the key problem is fusing ego's heroic spirit with this powerful historical tide [by] translating an inner vision into the outer world.[17]

Finally, this heroic type, whether on the currently winning or losing side, "habitually expressed great optimism about the imminent change for the better in world affairs." Of these six characteristics, one might add, at least four of them concern themselves with the new consciousness of history treated above. It was only with the awareness that China had entered a new epoch and was going through epoch-making transformation that a new "philosophy of life" based on energy and optimism was possible. The social-political contents of the various "doctrinal systems" or philosophies of life did indeed vary a great deal, as Metzger has pointed out, but still a common "structure" or mode of thinking existed among modern Chinese intellectuals.

On the more popular level, this new consciousness had infused the urban world of commercial consumption and set a glamorous foreign-flavored lifestyle favored by bourgeois urbanites and writers. Shanghai, with its large and prosperous foreign concessions, became the center of this "modern" universe. As its chic Chinese transliteration indicates, the term *modeng* meant to be "à la mode," to acquire a fashionable veneer and taste. The adjective "romantic," which I used in my early book, *The Romantic Generation of Modern Chinese Writers*,[18] to characterize this new urban literary temper in the May Fourth era, does not do full justice to either the urban milieu in which such a temper was produced or the temporal frame in which it was manifested. The treaty-port cities, particularly Shanghai, constituted a "specialization" of "modernity"—a configuration of space that crystallized the present moment, a self-contained world that was cut off and set apart from the traditionalism of the surrounding countryside. The journey of the progressive writers from the countryside to the city took on the added meaning of a temporal journey from a point of the traditional past to arrival at the modern present. Although advancing in time and joining the twentieth century in spirit, modern Chinese intellectuals during the 1920s and 1930s were not entirely comfortable with the concomitant problem of spatial change—not only in terms of the urban-rural split but also with regard to the greater realization that with the twentieth century China had become "one nation among many." In this regard, the vulgar Darwinian phrase "survival of the fittest" came as much to haunt as to elevate their spirits because either the jungle image of competition in the raw (hence the domination of physical prowess) or the ideological canvas of imperialism (military and political power) posed a direct external threat. This shared sense of threat and anxiety, as is well known, lay at the core of their fervent nationalism.

Thus, "modernity" in China was loosely defined as a mode of consciousness of time and history as unilinear progress, moving in a continuous "stream" or "tide" from the past to the present; it also contained the valorized notion of the present as a new "epoch" not only unprecedented and qualitatively different from previous eras but better, which leads prophetically to a purposeful future. The influence of Darwinian strains of evolutionary thought in China led to the emergence of this new perception. Its dynamism was manifested especially among May Fourth and post–May Fourth Chinese intellectuals in an outlook of the ego's active fusion with the forward tide of history.

Literature

It is not surprising, in view of the close interaction between modern Chinese thought and literature, that on the literary scene of the 1920s and 1930s, the terms *shidai* and *xiandai* (with connotations of both modern and contemporary) were prevalent and used almost interchangeably. So, too, were such related phrases as *shidai xing* ("epoch" quality or the nature of the present era), *shidai gan* (sense of the epoch or temper of the age), *chaoliu* (tide or current) and *sichao* (currents of thought) or *wenyi sichao* (currents of literary thought). Some of these terms came from the introduction or partial translations of the works of Taine (time, environment, temper of an age), George Brandes (who wrote, among other books, *Main Currents of 19th-Century Literature*), Kuriyagawa Hakuson, and others. Titles of novels, stories, and literary journals often carried the words *shidai* or *xiandai.* For instance, one of the most fashionable literary figures in the Shanghai literary world, Ye Lingfeng, wrote a long popular novel, *Shidai guniang* (A girl of the times), worked as editor in the *Xiandai Shuju* (Modern Bookstore) and edited a journal titled *Xiandai xiaoshuo* (Modern fiction).

Inevitably, two ideas began to take hold: the view, first raised by Hu Shi, that each epoch had its own literature and the slogan adopted by many writers that "literature must reflect its own time." Both ideas obviously were derived from an acute time-consciousness that inclined toward the present moment. Lung-kee Sun has indicated that in Hu Shi's own textual scholarship the word *shidai* was used in a neutral sense (and it did not figure prominently in Dewey's thought), but it soon took on a "contemporary" meaning as "modern era."[19] By the end of the 1920s, both this modern-oriented notion of *shidai* and the idea that "literature must reflect its own time" had entered into the "revolutionary" vocabulary of the radical writers on the leftist front, although the concept did not originate with Marx and perhaps owed more to Belinsky.

The infusion of these ideas into literary discourse has had profound consequences. For the close connection between New Literature and the new consciousness of time and history created a Chinese matrix of literary modernism that diverged significantly from the fundamental tenets of European modernism. The intellectual issues involved are extremely complex since, as is well known, the mercurial nature of modernism in the West has been "an ever-renewed cause for debates and discoveries."[20] Despite divergences of opinion, however, there is at least agreement among Western scholars that modernism does or did exist (depending on one's periodization between modernism and postmodernism) and that, moreover, the term covers a wide range of historically related movements from roughly 1890 to 1930: impressionism, postimpressionism, expressionism, cubism, futurism, symbolism, imagism, vorticism, dadaism, surrealism.[21] Most scholars also agree that "one of the defining features of this modernism has been the breaking down of traditional frontiers in matters of literary and cultural concern."[22] Thus there is at least a superficial ground for comparison with the Chinese May Fourth Movement.

My earlier formulations of the emergence of a new sense of time among Chinese intellectuals since the late Qing and especially during the May Fourth period bear striking resemblances to the post-Renaissance view in the West. As Matei Calinescu, a leading scholar of Western modernism, has aptly described it: "Modernity was conceived of as a time of emergence from darkness, a time of awakening and 'renascence,' heralding a luminous future.'' ''Man was therefore to participate consciously in the creation of the future: a high premium was put on being with one's time and not against it, and on becoming an agent of change in an incessantly dynamic world.''[23] The ''modern'' outlook of May Fourth intellectuals also evinced some strong traces of what Calinescu calls the ''bourgeois idea of modernity,'' which may be regarded as a direct descendent of the post-Renaissance view buttressed by ideas of Enlightenment and the development of the Industrial Revolution: ''the doctrine of progress, the confidence in the beneficial possibilities of science and technology, the concern with time . . . the cult of reason, and the ideal of freedom defined within the framework of an abstract humanism, but also the orientation toward pragmatism and the cult of action and success.''[24]

However, as Calinescu argues, at some point during the first half of the nineteenth century ''an irreversible split occurred between modernity as a stage in the history of Western civilization—a product of scientific and technological progress, of the industrial revolution, of the sweeping economic and social changes brought about by capitalism—and modernity as an aesthetic concept.'' The gap widened in the course of the century, and the relations between the two modernities became ''irreducibly hostile.'' The modernity as aesthetic or cultural concept, ever since its beginnings in romanticism, had inclined toward radical antibourgeois attitudes. ''What defines cultural modernity is its outright rejection of bourgeois modernity, its consuming negative passion.''[25] Its negativity lay in its profound disillusionment with the positive notions of reason and progress, which in its process of ''embourgeoisement'' had turned into ''vulgar utilitarianism'' and ''the philistinism of middle-class hypocrisy.''

Thus, the various movements associated with modernism, all derived from this aesthetic modernity, point to an artistic stance that subverts realism and humanism, the two cardinal tenets of nineteenth-century historical modernity. It is also ''antihistorical'' in the sense that this modern sensibility ''tends to see history or human life not as a sequence, or history not as an evolving logic; art and the urgent now strike obliquely across. Modernist works frequently tend to be ordered, then, not on the sequence of historical time or the evolving sequence of character, from history to story, as in realism and naturalism; they tend to work spatially or through layers of consciousness, working towards a logic of metaphor or form.''[26]

If one looks at the Chinese literary scene at the time when these variants of modernism reached a height in Europe, shortly after the First World War, about the same time as the May Fourth Movement, it is obvious that the Chinese counterpart differed. To be sure, some vague notions of aesthetic modernism also found its way into certain literary journals. The phrase ''art for art's sake'' was consciously adopted by the early Creationists, albeit given a more positive and dynamic twist to the original meaning of Gautier's notion of ''l'art pour l'art.'' In the mid-1920s, Baudelaire became one of the most frequently translated

French authors in China. What may be termed the postromanticist tendency for the artist to define a subjective realm of imagination as both a more private and more profound "reality" can also be found in the works—and artistic proses—of some Chinese writers in the early 1920s: not only the famous Yu Dafu, but also the lesser known Feng Naichao, Lin Ruji, Yu Gengyu, and Fang Weide, and even Lu Xun.

The crucial point of difference, however, is that these Chinese writers did *not* choose (nor did they feel the necessity) to separate the two domains of historical and aesthetic modernity in their pursuit of a modern mode of consciousness and modern forms of literature. There was *no* discernible split; on the contrary, humanism and realism continued to hold sway. The majority of writers, perhaps buoyed by their new historical consciousness, were eager to create realistic narratives that incorporated the unilinear sequence of historical time or the evolving sequence of character. The gingerly attempts of a few "romantic" or "neoromantic" authors mentioned above to give some symbolic shape to the undulating "waves" of the private psyche were also made within the conscious framework of the modern "tides" of history.

Looking at the Chinese literary imagination from a European perspective, one can state the most obvious: the new consciousness of history—or more specifically, of the new mode of evolutionary thinking about time and history—had penetrated into Chinese discourses of literature as well. Bonnie McDougall's research on the early introduction of Western literary theories into China has revealed that Chinese writers relied heavily on a number of English textbooks of literary history that adopted an evolutionary scheme of progressive stages: from classicism, romanticism, realism, naturalism, to "neoromanticism."[27] Influenced by the concept of evolution, Chinese writers and critics (from Liang Qichao, Chen Duxiu, Hu Shi to Mao Dun) came out in favor of realism and naturalism. Mao Dun, for instance, who was fully aware of some of the avant-gardist trends in Europe which had moved beyond realism—particularly symbolism, expressionism, and futurism (which he discussed in learned essays)[28]—stopped short of embracing these "avant" trends. In an announcement published in the *Xiaoshuo yuebao* in 1920, Mao Dun stated that contemporary Chinese literature had developed only to the point between classicism and romanticism, and in this "order of evolution" Chinese literature could not "leap to the sky in one step." Despite his considered effort to separate aesthetic concerns from the temporal, he nevertheless concluded that Western works of realism and naturalism must be introduced first for emulation.[29]

Why did modern Chinese writers embrace this Western type of modernity without developing a hostile attitude toward it in their conceptions of art and literature? Perhaps it would help, to answer this central question, to put both sides—the West and China—in their historical contexts. One reason, it might be argued, why the two modernities became "irreducibly hostile" in the West starting in the first half of the nineteenth century is that the first kind of modernity, as epitomized in the industrial revolution, was actually taking place, giving Western writers and artists something very real—and from their vantage point very negative—to react against. More specifically, the benefits and the evils of the industrial civilization were fully manifested in the urban middle class, with its taste of philistine vulgarity due to the accumulation of money. In China, however, in the 1920s and 1930s modernity was largely an unrealized idea rather than a tangible reality. Insofar as Chinese intellectuals experienced the "modern world" as an objective reality, it was in the guise of the modernity of other societies (the countries of Europe and the United States, and to some extent Japan). Since this modernity was introduced into China in the form of (or at least in close conjunction with) imperialism, the Chinese felt that they, too, had to have it in order to arrest imperialism's impact. Chinese intellectuals and creative artists, in other words, did not have the luxury enjoyed by their Western counterparts of adopting a hostile stance toward modernity.

On a deeper level, it may be noted that one of the central intellectual "fountainheads" of Western modernism—a theory that radically altered the way in which Western artists and writers envision reality—did not have the same effect in China. Despite its early introduction in China in 1913,[30] the theory of Freud, unlike that of Darwin and Bergson, failed to make profound inroads into Chinese literary thinking and practice. To be sure, there were again some isolated examples of Freudian influence, such as Lu Xun's prose poetry collection *Yecao* (Wild grass) and some early crude stories written by Guo Moruo, both employing dream devices. But with a few notable exceptions (to be discussed later), most modern Chinese writers did not embrace the Freudian insight of the unconscious as a deeper structure of reality, as they later embraced, quite fervently, the Marxist concepts of social class and historical materialism as objective and "scientific" laws governing the outer reality. This apparent lack of separation between the two realms of the conscious and the unconscious perhaps reflects a holistic frame of thinking derived from the largely holistic tradition of Chinese philosophy,[31] a conception that sees the world as a "whole" in which boundaries between external and internal reality are intentionally or unintentionally blurred. More specifically, it can also be argued that the external demands of the era—unceasing social and political turmoils—were such that modern Chinese writers turned their obsessions outward: they could ill afford to indulge in introspective psychoanalysis. Consequently, the most notable tendency of Western modernistic literature—the purposeful break with external reality and the incessant probing of the inner, fragmented psyche through a comparably fragmented system of language (hence the technique of "stream-of-consciousness")—did not really catch on among Chinese writers, in spite of their fairly up-to-date knowledge of such new Western samples.

If one looks further into literary sources of Western modernism in addition to Freud, however, one would be amazed to find that almost the entire gallery of major writers associated with various strains of European modernism—from

Baudelaire, Verlaine, Rimbaud, Wilde, Beardsley, and Schnitzler, to Yeats, Joyce, Eliot, Hemingway, Faulkner, Amy Lowell, W. H. Auden, and Gertrude Stein—were known in China from the late 1920s, chiefly through a number of literary journals, all published in Shanghai. This special urban milieu, with its foreign concessions, provided a window for recent literary trends in the international arena. It was in this setting that some Chinese writers began to read about these modernist authors in some of the well-known Western literary journals they were able to find, or even subscribe to, in a few Shanghai foreign bookstores: *Vanity Fair, Harper's, The Dial, The Bookman,* and *Living Age* in English and *Lettre Français* and *Le Monde* in French.[32] Some of the articles from these foreign journals were translated, together with photographs or cartoons, which the trend-conscious Chinese writers reproduced in their own journals: Shi Zhicun's *Xiandai*, Ye Lingfeng's *Wenyi huabao* (Literary pictorial), Shao Xunmei's *Jinwu yuekan* (Golden house monthly, modeled consciously after the celebrated *Yellow Book* in England).

This body of information remains little explored by Chinese scholars, who until recently considered it "decadent," hence immoral and not in tune with the ethical-progressive "temper" of the period as contained in the dominant tenet of realism. On the other hand, if one examines closely the artistic stances of these men and their journals, it is not surprising that they were groping toward a certain "modern aesthetic" that they would like to articulate in opposition to the theory and practice of realism as propagated by the leaders of the May Fourth Movement. In a sense, they may be considered China's pioneer literary modernists, whose literary opinions bore a certain affinity to the Western counterparts they promoted, though their creative work did not entirely reach the artistic frontiers of the Western avant-garde. This literary phenomenon, situated in Shanghai in the 1930s, remains little known and deserves close study by literary scholars.

As Mao Dun's famous novel *Midnight* illustrates, Shanghai in the 1930s was a veritable island of tangible modernity and also a bastion of foreign imperialist presence. Given this conjunction, it was no wonder that most Chinese writers who resided there developed, like Mao Dun, an ambivalence toward this largest treaty port: they fully enjoyed—and indeed marveled at—the modern conveniences and material comforts Shanghai's concessions provided. At the same time, they also regarded the city a center of capitalist exploitation and debauchery.

Raymond Williams has described the history of English literature as a transition in setting from the pastoral "knowable communities" of the countryside to the "city of light and darkness."[33] If the city had indeed become the only possible habitat and artistic universe for all European modernists, one can never cease to be amazed that the same urban transformation did *not* exactly take place in modern Chinese literature, despite the literary efforts of Shi Zhicun and his friends. For all its dynamism and allure, the modern city of Shanghai paled in moral and ideological significance against the massive countryside, the rural world that most Chinese writers affirmed as the genuine reality that their realistic writing must aspire to reproduce or recapture. The urban style of Chinese modernism in prose and poetry remained, as it were, in isolated splendor for about two decades (from the mid-1920s to the mid-1940s) and thereafter declined, to be overtaken by the triumphant power of the countryside, the Communist revolution. The predominantly rural modes of social realism and socialist realism held sway in China for more than half a century. It was only after 1976, with the death of Mao and the downfall of the Gang of Four, that the city reemerged as the central place for a younger generation of radical-modernists: since 1985, some young poets and critics in Shanghai—Wu Liang, Zhang Xiaobo, and others—have begun to develop a new "urban consciousness" (*chengshi yishi*), a purposeful reaction against the countryside.

This rapid survey of the urban-rural interaction in modern Chinese literature suggests that the European experience of artistic modernism was not fully duplicated in China, although some measure of urban-based and Western-inspired avant-gardist experimentation was achieved. Marxist scholars would perhaps attribute this to the economic fact that early twentieth-century China had not reached the stages of "high capitalism" and "late capitalism" that presumably provide the infrastructure for high modernism and postmodernism. I have tried to argue that it was, ironically, historical modernity—the new mode of temporal consciousness that privileges and valorizes the present—together with its optimistic vision that does not allow for a full-fledged disillusioned reaction against it in the form of artistic modernism. If one brings in the case of Soviet Russia, the comparison is further complicated by the phenomenon of Russian futurists and constructivists who believed, also optimistically, in the capacity of modern art to express the infinite potentialities of the future world—a modernist stance that did not take root in China. Nor was modernity seen as so threatening to the native human essence that, as the Japanese thinker Takeuchi Yoshimi argued, it must be "overcome." Even such a rural nativist as Shen Congwen had stopped short of advocating total resistance to what he considered to be the inevitable tide of modernization.

What distinguishes some writers from the zealously heroic intellectuals (and revolutionary romantics) described earlier lies perhaps in a certain degree of ambiguity in the former's self-image. On the one hand, these writers shared the grand historical vision of the intellectual zealots in the public arena. On the other hand, however, they differed from the zealously ideological type in their lack of a sustained optimism due to certain private doubts and wavering about the "present."

Lu Xun, the foremost modern Chinese writer by his public renown, also exemplifies this ambiguity in the most anguished way. His entire outlook, it can be argued, hinges on an unresolved tension between his unequivocal support of all the enlightened "modern" causes of the May Fourth Movement and the incessant pessimism that haunts his private psyche with regard to the ultimate meaning of life. Thus, he openly voiced his belief in evolutionism while at the same time refusing to fuse his self with the onward positive tide of history: he would lose himself, as the recurring image of the shadow in his prose poetry suggests, in a dark void of the present. It is this type of uncertainty that provides the inner resources for a more subjective mode of aesthetic expression. In this sense, Lu Xun may be considered a great "modernist" in a unique way: unlike most of his contemporary "modernists" who were either heroic zealots or tender-hearted humanists, Lu Xun has made a creative paradox out of the double meaning of modernity.[34]

Modern Chinese Intellectuals: Knowledge and Power

Lu Xun's case may indeed be unique. His creative enactment of this double—and conflicting—meaning of modernity marks him both as a highly individualistic artist and a leading member of the May Fourth intelligentsia. On the other hand, most other writers did not seem to share Lu Xun's agony, nor did they sense any conflict between the roles of artist and intellectual. As I have argued above, modernity in the form of a new historical consciousness had so dominated the May Fourth generation that their intellectual discourse does not allow much room for the kind of abstract or existential meditations on the meaninglessness of the world or of the human individual. The self is never alone, but enveloped in the "reality" of history. In the words of Li Dazhao, "reality is dynamism; life is transformation" since the human subject, "this I and life of mine, forever follows the current of life and the torrent of the great age, to be thereby amplified, continued, transformed, and developed."[35] Thus the aspirations of May Fourth intellectuals concerning both cultural change and their own role in the society and polity of the time were likewise influenced by this shared historical consciousness.

Lin Yusheng has argued that the mode of thinking of May Fourth intellectuals is essentially "culturalistic-intellectualistic"—that is, that their frame of mind is anchored in the belief that change in ideas must take precedence over change in society and polity.[36] I would like to add that since this mode of thinking was, as Lin also argued, both derived from tradition and coupled with the crumbling of the traditional world order, their views of society and polity were rather complex. It is clear that in this new frame of mind society and polity were no longer integrated in one order but rather bifurcated. For the more radically minded, society was seen as pitted against a warlord-dominated state and their own role as critical intelligentsia was to serve as spokesmen (or women) for society. As Lu Xun's numerous stories and essays have shown, however, Chinese society itself was itself ridden with ills and the manifest purpose of the new literature and new culture was to change and reform society.

What was to be done? It would seem that the slogan "new culture" became the crucial component in this agenda of societal change, but its meaning remained amorphous. As the veteran literary journalist Cao Juren recalls, "generally speaking, the new literary movement was part of the new culture movement, but what after all is new culture? Our impressions at the time were extremely fuzzy."[37] A small publisher in Shanghai called itself the "New Culture Bookstore" and opportunistically published four volumes of "discussions of the problem of new culture" and two volumes of "commentaries on new literature"; the material was drawn largely from the handouts from the Chinese literature class at Cao's own normal school.[38] Another advocate of reform prescribed three priorities: freedom in thought and speech, education, and journalism. A literary critic, Xie Liuyi, championed the cause of "aesthetics of life" and cited examples of William Morris, Russell, and Carpenter as advocates of the aesthetics of labor.[39] Perhaps the dominant view in this reformist frame of thinking was that of science as an instrument of enlightenment and a totem of Western civilization.

Ever since Chen Duxiu erected the image of his two famous teachers, Mr. Democracy and Mr. Science, the terms had become catch-all phrases that remained ill-defined. Leaving aside the issues concerning democracy (the subject for another lengthy paper), I am prepared to argue that science fits perfectly the new ethos of modernity because of its aura of rationality and progress. The works by Charlotte Furth and Daniel Kwok have already fortified this argument. At the same time, the popular view of science in the May Fourth period went far beyond the scholarly or disciplinary boundaries of what is now known as natural and social sciences. As popular knowledge, science was the spirit of the modern era and the signal of the historical tide; it carried all the allure of a brave new world ushered in by the twentieth century. In the repository published by the Commercial Press, "Dongfang wenku," a series of four volumes were devoted to accounts of diverse "scientific" subjects under the title of *Kexue zazu* (Miscellaneous collections on science): the archaic-sounding word *zazu* was derived directly from the title of a traditional collection of bizarre and fantastic tales, *Youyang zazu*. Even a glance at the titles in the table of contents, which mix knowledge with wonder, serves to confirm this impression: "The Unimaginable New Discoveries in Astrology," "The Structure of Atom," "Einstein's Theory of Light and Energy Being Pulled by Gravity Confirmed," "Strange Reptiles," "Four-Legged Birds," "Experiments in Longevity," "General View of Freud's New Psychology," "The Machines That Record Thought," "New Cures for Tuberculosis," "New Windmills," "Automatic Stamp-Vending Machines," "Long-distance Cannons," "Monorail Railways," "Bicycles on Water," and so forth.[40]

Obviously, in the popular May Fourth view, science expanded the horizons of knowledge and would soon establish a new world order beyond the traditional confines of the Middle Kingdom. On the other hand, for all of Hu Shi's advocacy of the "scientific method," Western science as a full-fledged academic discipline of pure research did not receive much attention. Thus, in the May Fourth period this "undisciplined" knowledge was considered both an instrument of social reform and a system of new values presumably earmarked for a new society—the former utilitarian (or "useful" for society), the latter a matter of moral faith. As Yan Bofei has argued in a recent article, science had assumed a new form of authoritarianism that comprised the modalities of both Western rationality and traditional Chinese moral faith: scientism became, in fact, ideological truth, and the "scientific method" a kind of empiricism with a strong utilitarian bent toward social practice. Consequently, the May Fourth elevation of science has left a dubious legacy: as a new deity it ceased to be true knowledge; its powers of intellectual enlightenment proved faulty and limited.

In a seminal article titled "Dual Variations on Enlightenment and National Salvation," the renowned PRC scholar Li Zehou presents a dual thesis on the May Fourth Movement. He argues that the May Fourth Movement comprised two different, but mutually interactive, components: the New Culture Movement, and the patriotic anti-imperialist student movement. The task of enlightenment was undertaken by two modes of action: individual rebellion and the many "societies" (*she*) and "study associations" (*xuehui*) organized by younger members of the May Fourth generation. Despite their amorphous objectives, these societies all shared "a common inclination, that is, a kind of pragmatic yearning and search for a new ideal society or social ideal."[41] Both modes of action, grounded in cultural and social concerns, proved to be deficient, and the majority of May Fourth intellectuals reverted to politics and adopted the revolutionary practice of Marxist revolution. What makes this familiar argument distinctive is Li's underlying injunction that the revolutionary imperative of national salvation had eclipsed the demands for enlightenment, and the intellectuals themselves, who first embodied the task of enlightenment, were engulfed and "conquered" by the collective objective of national salvation. Consequently, the May Fourth Movement was, in a sense, an abortive revolution because its intellectual goal of enlightenment remains unrealized.

Another renowned scholar and literary theorist, Liu Zaifu, argues in an important article that the "loss" of the enlightenment spirit was closely connected with the changing roles of the modern Chinese intellectuals: "As the subject of the Literary Revolution, the intellectuals in their historical role as agents of enlightenment not only enlighten other people but also affirm themselves—that is, to affirm a self as an individual of the new century, an intellectual in a modern sense endowed with independent character and spirit, and no longer as a scholar-official subservient to the imperial court or to a certain political structure."[42] Liu further states that the May Fourth writers viewed themselves as "bodies of light who can illuminate and awaken other people. Thus they practiced enlightenment through their own works. Their task was not so much the dissemination of knowledge as the illumination of an inner spirit and an inner dignity, the development of a consciousness of modern life, morality, and culture based on science and democracy.''[43] In Liu's assessment, the May Fourth intellectuals were definitely the ''subject'' in relation to the ''object'' they wished to enlighten, the people. Intellectuals also positioned themselves as a historical vanguard. But their role was reversed by the Communist revolution: the intellectual reformers and enlighteners became themselves the objects of thought reform, whereas the peasant masses had become the subject. The further reversal of roles in the post-Mao era, which positively reestablished the position of the intellectuals, is cause for clear-headed self-reflection: Liu argues that Chinese intellectuals should relinquish the role of prophet and savior and rather consolidate themselves as a self-conscious group.

Both Li and Liu are acknowledged leaders of the most recent movement of ''cultural self-reflection'' (*wenhua fansi*). Their views are worth noting because they represent a position favored by younger intellectuals that places culture above politics. They would like to return to the spirit of May Fourth—intellectual enlightenment—and continue with its unfinished task. In my view, however, this solution is not so simple because the dilemma is not so much between enlightenment and national salvation as about the notion and practice of enlightenment itself. If we adopt Liu Zaifu's argument, it is obvious that the definition of enlightenment also involves a subject-object relationship with the people. One of the cardinal themes of modern Chinese intellectual history and literature is how generations of intellectuals since Liang Qichao attempted to represent the ''people'' and articulate their voice. The notion of a ''modern culture'' in the May Fourth context evokes the image of an urban-rural gap: the intellectuals in the cities wished to throw some light on the rural populace who, in Lu Xun's famous metaphor, slept in an ''iron house'' without windows about to suffocate to death. For all their role reversals, Chinese intellectuals have not bridged such a gap, in my opinion, by destroying the iron house. The peasant masses remain largely silent and refuse to join the intellectual discourse.

If, as Liu Zaifu suggests, intellectuals should be more self-conscious and return to a collective self-redefinition, it would seem that this task is equally unfinished.

In a devastating article commemorating the seventieth anniversary of the May Fourth, the young scholar Gan Yang has put the entire Chinese intelligentsia to task by citing the works of Foucault and Deleuze. The problem with intellectuals, according to Gan Yang, lies precisely in that they wish to speak for others and to speak the truth to others who have not seen the truth. ''But the intellectuals suddenly discover today that, first, the masses no longer need the intellectuals to speak for them'' and, second, their own discourse is part of a power system.[44] Thus, Gan Yang, echoing Foucault, argues that intellectuals should no longer place themselves on a high plateau vis-à-vis other people but rather analyze seriously and critically how their knowledge has become a constituent element of a new power system. ''The greatest lesson for Chinese intellectuals of the past hundred years,'' in Gan Yang's view, ''lies perhaps in this: they have always and everywhere put top priority on society, nation, people, country, but have never dared with sufficient courage to bring up individual freedom as the first principle.''[45] The self, in other words, was never separated from the societal whole in the May Fourth discourse of new culture, which remains monological. Even the notion of personal liberation was still considered part of a societal rebellion against tradition.

Gan Yang's critique raises a number of intriguing issues. Chinese enlightenment, in Gan Yang's view, forms a value system as monolithic faith because it always inclines to seek a ''final solution.''[46] It is not sufficiently pluralistic so that personal liberty and the inherent worth of the individual as a value can be placed as a basic condition. In his fervent espousal of pluralism, Gan Yang has not delved into the implications, other than power, of May Fourth culture. Granted the premise that no knowledge is value-free, one can still argue that excessive values have been placed on the notion of ''new knowledge'' as an essential part of ''new culture.'' As my brief discussion of science has indicated, perhaps the aspirations of national salvation turned science into another form of ''utility.'' For that matter, it would seem that Western knowledge, since the mid-nineteenth century, had never become really ''essence'' in China, and even the excessive craze for Western knowledge in the May Fourth period was utilitarian in the sense that it served the purposes of a collective quest for a new Chinese society and nation. The phenomenon fits a new slogan recently coined by Li Zehou (as an intentional reversal of the late Qing parlance): ''Western essence for Chinese utility.''

I am basically in agreement with Gan Yang but would push his argument even further. In my view, Chinese ''modernity'' as formulated in the May Fourth cultural agenda is monological because it contains a strain of linear historicism that sees world history as moving in one direction toward a better future. Since May Fourth intellectuals, with the exception of a few tormented writers, do not wish to separate themselves from this ''historical tide'' (which to them signified ''modern civilization''), they also deprived themselves of a true pluralistic position of multiple roles and multiple choices. If the culture of modernity ultimately entails a kind of cultural pluralism—before we confront the further implications of fragmentation and relativism of a ''postmodern'' era—then indeed the Chinese project is unfinished. The spate of commemorative articles and books on the May Fourth legacy in the wake of the ''cultural self-reflection'' movement testifies to the seriousness of the effort, which alas is being suppressed once more by the political forces of anticultural barbarism.

Notes

1. The first two parts of this essay are the abridged and revised version of another paper I wrote for a volume of scholarly essays presented to Benjamin Schwartz and edited by Merle Goldman and Paul Cohen, *Ideas Across Cultures* (Cambridge: Harvard University Council on East Asian Studies, 1990).

2. Lung-kee Sun, "Chinese Intellectuals' Notion of 'Epoch' (*Shidai*) in the Post–May Fourth Era," *Chinese Studies in History* 20, 2 (Winter 1986/87): 44.

3. Hao Chang, *Chinese Intellectuals in Crisis: Search for Order and Meaning, 1890–1911* (Berkeley: University of California Press, 1987), p. 52. See also James Reeve Pusey, *China and Charles Darwin* (Cambridge: Harvard University Council on East Asian Studies, 1983), pp. 15, 37.

4. Chang, *Chinese Intellectuals in Crisis*, p. 52.

5. Quoted in Pusey, *China and Charles Darwin*, p. 51.

6. Stephen Toulmin, *Human Understanding: The Collective Use and Evolution of Concepts* (Princeton: Princeton University Press, 1972), pp. 321–22.

7. Yan Fu, "Yuanqiang" (Origins of power), in *Yan Jidao xiansheng yizhu* (Posthumous writings of Yan Fu) (Singapore: Nanyang xuehui reprint, 1959), pp. 98–99. See also H. Stuart Hughes, *Consciousness and Society* (New York: Vintage Books, 1958), pp. 38–39.

8. Benjamin Schwartz, *In Search of Wealth and Power* (Cambridge: Harvard University Press, 1964), p. 46.

9. Chen Duxiu, *Duxiu wencun* (Surviving writings of [Chen] Duxiu) (Hong Kong: Yuandong reprint, 1965), 1:41.

10. The three Beijing University scholars are Chen Pingyuan, Qian Liqun, Huang Ziping; their symposium, "Ershi shiji Zhongguo wenxue" (Twentieth-century Chinese literature), was first serialized in *Dushu* 1–3 (January–March 1986). It was later published as a book, *Ershi shiji Zhongguo wenxue sanren tan* (The symposium of three on twentieth-century Chinese literature) (Beijing: Renmin wenxue chubanshe, 1988).

11. See Bonnie McDougall, *The Introduction of Western Literary Theories into Modern China, 1919–1925* (Tokyo: The Center for East Asian Cultural Studies, 1971), chap. 1.

12. These titles are taken from Chen Zhengmo, *Xiandai zhexue sichao* (Currents of contemporary philosophy) (Shanghai: Shangwu, 1933).

13. Chen Changheng and Zhou Jianren, *Jinhua lun yu shanzhong xue* (Evolution and eugenics), Dongfang wenku no. 50 (Shanghai: Shangwu, 1923).

14. Sun, "Chinese Intellectuals' Notion of 'Epoch,' " p. 52.

15. Ibid.

16. Ibid., pp. 65–66.

17. Thomas A. Metzger, "Comments on Leo Ou-fan Lee's Paper at the Breckinridge Conference on Individualism and Holism," ms. pp. 5–6. I am grateful for these comments.

18. Leo Ou-fan Lee, *The Romantic Generation of Modern Chinese Writers* (Cambridge: Harvard University Press, 1973), chaps. 2, 14.

19. Sun Lung-kee, personal letter to the author dated January 13, 1988. I am much indebted to his research and insight.

20. Monique Chefdor, Ricardo Quinones, and Albert Wachtel, eds., *Modernism: Challenges and Perspectives* (Urbana: University of Illinois Press, 1986), p. 1.

21. Malcolm Bradbury and James McFarlane, eds., *Modernism 1890–1930* (New York: Penguin, 1976), p. 23.

22. Ibid., p. 14.

23. Matei Calinescu, *Faces of Modernity: Avant-Garde, Decadence, Kitsch* (Bloomington: Indiana University Press, 1977), pp. 20, 22.

24. Ibid., p. 41.

25. Ibid., pp. 41, 44.

26. Bradbury and McFarlane, *Modernism 1890–1930*, p. 50.

27. McDougall, *Western Literary Theories*, chap.1.

28. See a recent collection of Mao Dun's critical essays, *Mao Dun wenyi zalun ji*

(Miscellaneous essays on literature by Mao Dun) (Shanghai: Shanghai wenyi chubanshe, 1981), vol. 1.

29. Ibid., pp. 6–8.

30. The first Chinese introduction of Freud, published in *Dongfang zazhi* in December 1916, was a translation of a popular piece by a certain Dr. H. Addington, "The Marvels of Dream Analysis" from an American journal, *McClure* (November 1912). Since the piece was in the spirit of popular science, not strictly speaking a scholarly treatise (as Freud himself intended his theory to be), the Chinese version seems well in line with the emergent temper of introducing Western knowledge as a way to modernity. The subsequent Chinese discussions of Freudian theory generally followed this mode of popular inquiry without delving seriously into the aesthetic implications of the Freudian notion of the subconscious on modern literature. For this I am indebted to the research of my student Mr. Jicheng Lin.

31. See Donald Munro, ed., *Individualism and Holism in Chinese Thought* (Ann Arbor: University of Michigan Press, 1986).

32. The information is based on my extensive interviews with Shi Zhicun and Xu Chi, poet and essayist, in China in 1986.

33. Raymond Williams, *The Country and the City* (New York: Oxford University Press, 1973), chaps. 16, 19.

34. For a fuller discussion, see my book, *Voices from the Iron House: A Study of Lu Xun* (Bloomington: Indiana University Press, 1987).

35. Li Dazhao, "Jin" (Present), quoted in Cao Juren, *Wentan wushi nian* (Fifty years on the literary scene) (Hong Kong: Xin wenhua chubanshe, n.d.), p. 107.

36. Yü-sheng Lin, *The Crisis of Chinese Consciousness: Radical Anti-Traditionalism in the May Fourth Era* (Madison: University of Wisconsin Press, 1979), chap. 1.

37. Cao, *Wentai wushi nian*, p. 109.

38. Ibid.

39. Yang Duanliu, "Zhongguo gaizao de fangfa" (The ways of reforming China), in *Zhongguo gaizao wenti* (The problems of reform in China), Dongfang wenku no. 15 (Shanghai: Shangwu, 1923), pp. 7–20; Xie Liuyi, "Shehui gaizao yundong yu wenyi" (Social reform movements and literature), in *Jindai wenxue yu shehui gaizao* (Modern literature and social reform), Dongfang wenku no. 62 (Shanghai: Shangwu, 1923), pp. 8–11.

40. See the table of contents of *Kexue Zazu* (Miscellaneous collection on science), 4 vols., Dongfang wenku no. 58 (Shanghai: Shangwu).

41. See Li Zehou, *Zhongguo xiandai sixiang shilun* (Treatises on the modern intellectual history of China) (Beijing: Dongfang chubanshe, 1987), p. 21. The article is included on pp. 7–49. Li's framework may have been influenced by the work of Vera Schwarcz, *The Chinese Enlightenment: Intellectuals and the Legacy of the May Fourth Movement of 1919* (Berkeley: University of California Press, 1986).

42. Liu Zaifu, "Wusi wenxue qimeng jingshen de shiluo yu huigui" (The loss and return of the enlightenment spirit in May Fourth literature), in *Wusi: Duoyuan de fansi* (May Fourth: pluralistic reflections), ed. Lin Yü-sheng et al. (Hong Kong, Sanlian shudian, 1989), p. 95.

43. Ibid., p. 97.

44. Gan Yang, "Ziyou de linian: Wusi chuangtong de queshi mian" (The concept of liberty: A lacuna in the May Fourth tradition), in *Wusi: Duoyuan de fansi*, ed. Lin, p. 64.

45. Ibid., p. 64.

46. Ibid., p. 71.

8

THE MAY FOURTH ERA
China's Place in the World

MICHAEL H. HUNT

Today, outside China no less than in, May Fourth is thought of almost exclusively in terms of politics, society, and culture, while its links to Chinese foreign affairs attract limited attention. Those links are intimate and important and deserve serious scrutiny.

It is, to begin with, a commonplace that the May Fourth Movement was set off by a decision reached at the Versailles conference on April 30, 1919, a decision that bitterly disappointed Chinese patriots. They had hoped to see the Shandong concession that Japan had seized from Germany at the beginning of World War I returned to China. It was, after all, a claim based on justice and reenforced by China's reentry into the war on the Allied side in 1917. Woodrow Wilson's repeated professions of sympathy and friendship for China and his blueprint for a new international system characterized by equality among all nations and respect for the principle of self-determination offered grounds for hope that China's claim would be honored.

But Britain, France, and Italy had stood by their secret 1917 agreements recognizing Japan's hold on Shandong. Wilson, the prophet of the new international order, had failed to hold his ground. The arguments of the Chinese delegation (representing the Canton regime as well as that in Beijing) had proven unavailing. News that the Allies had left Japan in control was, one Peking University graduate later recalled, a great shock. "We at once awoke to the fact that foreign nations were still selfish and militaristic and they were all great liars."[1]

This shock ignited the organized protests. Early in the afternoon of May 4, three thousand students from thirteen colleges and universities in Beijing gathered in front of Tiananmen, denouncing the Shandong decision. Their manifesto, drafted for the occasion by Luo Jialun, warned that the loss of this territory carried China an important step toward annihilation. It called on all citizens "to strive to secure our sovereignty in foreign affairs and to get rid of the traitors at home.''[2] Those traitors were Cao Rulin, Zhang Congxiang, and Lu Congyu, all high-ranking pro-Japanese officials. The protestors marched through the central city to Cao's house. They set the house on fire and beat Zhang, who had been found within it. Police, finally abandoning their benevolent neutrality, arrested thirty-two students.

Their comrades continued to organize and agitate, while demonstrations spread to more than two hundred other cities. Another round of arrests in early June only served to broaden the base of support for the protest. So great did the popular pressure become that the Beijing government was forced on June 10 to announce the resignation of the three traitors. On June 28 the Chinese delegation refused to sign the Versailles treaty sanctioning the give-away of Shandong, and the Beijing government reluctantly went along.

It is also widely understood that the May Fourth Movement derived much of its impetus from the long-mounting crisis in China's foreign relations. The students who went into the streets on May 4, 1919, could look back on eighty years of defeats and the steady decline of their country's standing in the world. The Opium War and the imposition of the first of the unequal treaties was followed by the loss of dependent states along the periphery, the deep incursion of foreign economic and cultural influence, and the repeated use of force and threats of force to guarantee foreigners their newly won dominance. Chinese policy makers had alternately responded with a stubborn policy of military resistance and diplomatic delay; bold initiatives in education, technology, commerce, and finance to make China stronger; desperate reliance on popular support; and expedient attempts to align with sympathetic foreign powers. All these strategies had failed, leaving patriots in ever deeper despair.

The outbreak of World War I along with rampant political factionalism and the devolution of power under the Republic allowed Japan to tighten its grip on China. It seized Germany's Shandong concession in 1914 and followed in 1915 with a collection of twenty-one demands designed to extend greater control over China's administration, economy, and territory. Finally, in 1917 and 1918 it granted political loans to the financially strapped government of Duan Qirui to ensure its dependency. These loans cleared the way for agreements strengthening Japan's claim to Shandong and extending broad rights for Japanese forces to operate in China (nominally in joint opposition to the Bolshevik threat). This aggressive Japanese policy and the supine attitude of the Beijing government had already provoked public demonstrations and boycotts between 1915 and 1918.

While the impetus, both immediate and long-term, supplied by foreign crisis to the May Fourth Movement is clear, the legacy of May Fourth to China's subsequent foreign relations is a good deal less clear. A foreign relations field in flux offers no ready generalizations.[3] A number of possibilities suggest themselves, though they are not all equally convincing.

One possibility is to be found in that era's appeal to Chinese to cultivate a new spirit and style in all aspects of their national life. Chen Duxiu's well-known call to youth in 1915 urged them to break with the outlooks of a bankrupt past. That meant being "self-reliant," "progressive," "enterprising," "cosmopolitan," "utilitarian," and "scientific." Only a vigorous and forward-looking China could construct a new and more favorable relationship with the world. In 1919, in the wake of the May Fourth experience, Chen as well as Li Dazhao made much of the need for self-reliance.[4]

But these vague hopes invested in a psychological transformation had at best a subtle influence whose long-term significance would be hard to trace and harder still to appraise. Vera Schwarcz has even suggested that the iconoclastic and cosmopolitan outlook of some May Fourth activists set them at odds with those emphasizing national salvation and left them uncomfortable with sharply nationalistic foreign policies.[5] In any case, the May Fourth era's call for new values was not ground breaking but echoed a call for a "new citizen" heard during the late Qing from Liang Qichao and others.

A second possibility would be to highlight the rising spirit of patriotism evident in May Fourth. It prompted demands for the recovery of lost territory and the abrogation of unequal treaties that gave foreigners their privileged standing in China. These demands, widely endorsed in the May Fourth era, would command the attention of the Chinese state from the 1920s to the 1950s.

But this concern with redeeming losses and bringing the foreign presence under control was hardly new in 1919. The push to preserve territory had already been going on full tilt during the late Qing, and the campaign against the unequal treaties had also figured prominently during the dynasty's last decade. It is not clear what May Fourth activists added to this well-established set of concerns.

A third foreign relations perspective on May Fourth would stress its contribution to popular mobilization in the name of national survival. At first, students and teachers wrote about China's crisis to arouse their fellow citizens; they carried their message to the streets of Beijing, Shanghai, and other cities; and they attended the meetings of merchants and other groups to press for support in the form of resolutions, sympathy strikes, and boycotts. By degrees other urban Chinese—journalists and other writers, workers, clerks, merchants, industrialists, and even government employees—came to the support of the movement.

On the other hand, it is hard to see May Fourth as a watershed in popular mobilization. The nineteenth century is replete with instances of resistance and protest set off by foreign invasion or disruption of local society. From the turn of the century, mobilization took on a pronounced urban and more "enlightened," self-consciously nationalist character.[6] This was first evident in the popular opposition to the continued Russian occupation of the Northeast (Manchuria) in 1903, the 1905 anti-American boycott protesting immigration restrictions, the rights-recovery movement widespread at the provincial level, and boycotts aimed against the Japanese in 1908 and 1915. May Fourth built on an already rising level of political awareness and in turn helped set the stage for the still more powerful demonstrations of the 1920s.

The final and most promising line of inquiry is to see May Fourth as the time when a new scheme for interpreting international affairs took shape, a scheme that might for shorthand be called a "three-worlds" view. That view was most clearly articulated, enthusiastically embraced, and consistently held by the nascent Chinese Communist party, though it also exercised a strong influence over the Nationalist party in the 1920s. It served to define the world scene and China's place in it. By looking at the emergence of this influential set of ideas in the May Fourth era, we gain a strategic vantage point for considering how Chinese have in this century both retained and reshaped their imperial heritage.

In July 1922, in the immediate wake of the May Fourth era, the Second Congress of the recently founded Communist party issued a document that assembled the separate elements of the three-worlds view into one integrated appraisal of world affairs and Chinese foreign relations.[7] One world belonged to imperialism, which had since 1839 steadily preyed on China. The second was given over to the Soviet Union, whose Bolshevik revolution offered a model and created a supporter for China in the battle against world capitalism. The third was made up of the national revolutionary movements that had sprung into existence since World War I and that shared China's commitment to the overthrow of imperialism and feudalism.

This May Fourth reconceptualization of international affairs, fusing the older spirit of patriotism with a more cosmopolitan outlook on the world, would prove durable. It would last into the 1950s and to some extent even beyond. This durability can be explained in part by the character of the ideas themselves. They built on and were congruent with already extant notions. The constituent elements were flexibly linked together in a self-reenforcing system of thought. And each of these elements contained some ambiguity that gave them broad political appeal under a variety of circumstances.

The elements in the three-worlds view would stand in a strikingly stable relationship to each other. The first world of imperialism and the second of the Soviet Union would dominate, while the third world of fellow revolutionaries would occupy a place of secondary importance. This was already reflected in the Communist party's 1922 formulation. It gave highest priority to battling the imperialists, especially Britain and the United States. Good Sino-Russian relations, including formal recognition of the USSR, came next on the list of ten practical concerns then entertained by the party. Attention to the revolutionary movements of colonial and semicolonial peoples was relegated to ninth place.[8]

At the heart of the May Fourth outlook on the world was a picture of China beleaguered by imperialism, which in its most general sense described a condition of foreign economic exploitation and political and military domination suffered by China and other weak countries under the boot of the stronger states of Europe, the United States, and Japan. The concept had a dual appeal: it offered a systematic explanation for the workings of the international system then tormenting China, and it served as a politically effective rallying cry for Chinese deeply aggrieved by foreign encroachment and abuse. Already in the 1920s the Communist and Nationalist parties, and even at times the warlord governments in Beijing, had embraced the concept and used it to mobilize popular support against Japan, Britain, and the missionary enterprise. Anti-imperialism persisted in the resistance to Japan over the following decade and a half, in the cold war struggle against the United States, and finally (in the strangest turn of all) in the opposition in the 1960s and 1970s to Soviet hegemonism.

Imperialism proved an easy concept to embrace in part because it raised to a new level of conceptual sophistication an older picture of the world dating back at least to the first contacts with Westerners along the coast and perhaps even before then, to long experience on the inner Asian frontier. Chinese observers of the early Canton trade regularly commented on the foreigners' dependence on Chinese goods. The resulting conception of foreigners gave prominence to their economic activity and needs, even their greed and obsession with commerce. The conflicts of the nineteenth century added to this notion the image of foreigners as beasts with rapacious natures ready to devour China and the Chinese. The deepening foreign economic and cultural penetration evoked yet another facet to the picture of foreigners as people able to turn the loyalty of Chinese. The behavior of "rice Christians," treaty port merchants, youths who went abroad to study, and even high officials tainted by daily contact with foreign envoys all served to support this view of betrayal from within so popular with foreign policy militants.

The observations on foreigners also gave rise to a more self-confident view of international relations that was also to find its way into later notions of imperialism. The greed and rapacity of foreigners offered a handle that might allow Chinese to manipulate them. The "barbarians" could either be tamed by satisfying their hunger or pitted against one another by manipulating their greed. This notion that contradictions existed among the powers and gave rise to competition for international advantage informed even early attempts at "barbarian management" and saw further development as Li Hongzhang, Yuan Shikai, and other late Qing officials battled to defend China's frontiers and blunt foreign penetration. A special favor granted to one demanding power might appease its greed and lead it to resist other, still more rapacious powers.

There was yet another, ambivalent reaction to foreign powers that would find a place in later views of imperialism. Late Qing students of the world were fascinated by the strength and prosperity of Western countries and especially by the science and technology that allowed them to work economic and military miracles. But the very societies that worked these miracles were also marked by glaring deformities. Their political life was driven by repellent opportunism and self-interest. Religious superstition was incredibly widespread. Individualism and egalitarian behavior led to a lamentable "anarchy" in situations that called for a sense of ethics, ceremony, and mutual obligation. Chinese observers were left with the puzzle of how to explain economic success in societies gone so obviously wrong in other respects. Imperialism would offer a way for some out of their perplexity, reconciling the materially attractive to the morally repugnant.

These various preoccupations and convictions about foreign societies and international behavior were incorporated into the Chinese understanding of "imperialism" (*diguozhuyi*), a term that politically engaged intellectuals began to embrace around the turn of the century. They were, however, far from agreeing on its specific meaning. The reason is simple. They combined the older perceptions of foreigners in a variety of ways, and they made different uses of the socialist and other literature on imperialism that was reaching them mainly through Japanese translations.[9] The divergent understandings of imperialism that resulted served in a sense to update an older argument between militants determined to turn back the foreign threat and moderates given to temporizing in foreign affairs the better to concentrate on a long-term strategy of internal strengthening. By 1905–7 those persistent differences were reflected in a debate between reformers and revolutionaries that turned in part on the significance each assigned imperialism and the most appropriate response to it.[10]

Speaking for the former outlook, Liang Qichao saw imperialism as a formidable threat. Arising from foreign economic needs, it was having a destructive impact on China. By 1902, Liang had identified the economic process in the advanced capitalist countries that impelled them to find and control foreign markets. Plagued by the threat of overproduction, which trusts could no longer control, the imperialists had turned to China. They used their excess capital to bring the Chinese government under their sway. This influx of foreign money also carried the danger of enslaving the Chinese economically and replicating the social ills already evident in capitalist countries. Chinese had to unite against this threat, Liang contended, not turn against one another in revolutionary violence that would only create new opportunities for further imperialist gains.

Hu Hanmin, responding for the revolutionaries, played down the imperialist danger consistent with the priority the United League (Tongmenghui) placed on the overthrow of the Manchu dynasty in favor of a republic. This close associate of Sun Yat-sen disagreed with Liang on the two key issues of enduring significance. First, foreign capital and trade were not inherently dangerous to China. Trade could be mutually beneficial, and a China that could not (according to Hu's calculations) generate internally the capital needed to create a modern industry had to look abroad for financing. Second, Hu rejected the economic interpretation of imperialism. Chinese had to bring the foreign presence under control and reclaim lost rights, but this was a political problem that could be resolved through a negotiated readjustment of Sino-foreign relations. The high costs to both Chinese and foreigners of a prolonged conflict left as the only reasonable course economic cooperation and political accommodation between China and those now prone to imperialist behavior.

Sun and his aides in the Nationalist party retained views through the 1910s and into the early 1920s consistent with the position that Hu Hanmin had staked out.[11] Imperialism was fundamentally a political phenomenon and by no means an inevitable stage in the development of capitalism. Imperialism stood, in their view, for those conditions of domination and abuse that arose from inequalities of power among states. The strong, driven by a nationalist dread of insecurity or the desire for aggrandizement, would lord it over the weak, seizing their territory, interfering in their politics, and exploiting their economy. But the imperialists, guided by political calculation, could be reasonable. As long as aggression remained a paying proposition, they would persist. If, on the other hand, the dominated fought back and thereby raised the cost, then the imperialists would begin to retreat from untenable positions. Just as Sun saw imperialism as a political phenomenon, he saw its antidote in political terms. If China could become strong and united, then it would not only survive but flourish. It would "no longer be humiliated and partitioned by other nations" but rise to the ranks of the world's great powers.[12]

Sun and his immediate associates rejected the view that the economic drive of the imperialists was inherently dangerous. Once the Chinese state could regulate and police foreign enterprise, the former imperialists could be made to serve China's economic development, while earning a reasonable profit for themselves. Sun cited the developmental experience of Japan as well as the countries of North and South America to support this view that foreign investment could be beneficial if properly controlled. In any case, China had no other road to rapid industrialization. "Everywhere in China, production is not yet developed, our people are unemployed . . . ; if we can introduce foreign capital, create employment, then Chinese need no longer be hired laborers for others, while our domestic production will be greatly multiplied."[13]

This conception of imperialism gave Sun and other Nationalist leaders, long frustrated in their pursuit of power, a valued degree of political flexibility in dealing with the powers. By thinking of the links between imperialism and capitalism as loosely drawn, Sun embraced a relatively moderate appraisal of the foreign presence. A cooperative, open-door foreign policy could contribute to China's modernization and defense. Sun's position had the practical virtue of signaling an interest in accommodation to powers who continued to exercise considerable influence in Chinese politics and hence over the fate of Sun's movement. It also served to sanction the concessions to foreigners that Sun had made a political stock-in-trade. To win fresh resources to overcome his domestic rivals, Sun regularly held out the promise of some economic contract or advantage to be granted once his movement had gained power. Knowing that the political enemy, imperialism, could be made into an economic friend made such seemingly opportunistic attempts to buy foreign support more defensible.[14]

The Nationalist party's conception of imperialism, never theoretically or systematically developed, pointed in different directions through the 1920s. During the period of alliance with the Communists, the Nationalists stressed the dangers of foreign economic control and the betrayal by warlords and others who served as foreign tools. They also gave greater play to imperialism as a target of mass mobilization. All that changed after Jiang Jieshi (Chiang Kai-shek), Sun's successor as head of the Nationalist party, turned on his Communist allies in 1927 and completed the Northern Expedition in 1928. He was thereafter to play down mass movements as an instrument of foreign policy and to conciliate the Western powers the better to pursue state-building and limit Japanese demands. This gradualist and accommodating approach, restraining even the campaign to end the unequal treaties, reflected a conception of imperialism consistent with Sun's. The left wing of the party attacked Jiang for his caution, but even those critics, who appear to have been prompted less by conviction than by political advantage, accepted the idea that China could gain economically by cooperating with the powers.[15]

May Fourth contributed to the appeal of the alternative, economic conception of imperialism promoted earlier by Liang Qichao. Outrage provoked by the Shandong decision prepared intellectuals for the radical critique of a Western-dominated international system. The Allies operated, according to Li Dazhao, by the rules of "a robber's world," one in which China could expect no justice. Even China's professed friends were hypocrites. Woodrow Wilson talked of self-determination and then betrayed that principle and China's hopes.[16]

Following this visceral reaction against yet another foreign policy defeat, contact with fragments of the Marxist-Leninist canon and with Communist International (Comintern) envoys helped deeply disillusioned Chinese to repackage old ideas about the economic nature of imperialism into a new, seemingly scientific analysis. By 1922 the Communist party had taken as its own a thoroughgoing, theoretically grounded economic conception of imperialism. The major capitalist countries, "tortured under the pressure of a small minority of bankers and entrepreneurs," were plagued by overproduction. "Hoping to escape from the fire of social revolution," they had to look abroad and "rob the resources and labor of the colonies and weak nations." China had become a joint colony of all the powers and was suffering acutely from economic exploitation and oppression as well as social and political division. Not until imperialism was overthrown would it be possible for the Chinese people to reach their goal of "equality and self-determination."[17]

This Communist view of imperialism was in two crucial respects at odds with Sun's. First, imperialism was not accidental or contingent behavior but the inevitable result of capitalist development. It was not the expression of political calculation or nationalist impulses but the consequence of economic maldistribution that left no solution to mature capitalism but to turn to foreign markets for relief from domestic crisis. Second, imperialism was especially pernicious because it divided and degraded the Chinese people. No accommodation of the sort that Sun envisioned was thinkable. The source of this conviction appears to have been patriotism and a deep-seated aversion to the foreign impact in Shanghai and other large treaty ports. Foreigners dominated the economy and exploited Chinese workers, leaving the many in squalor while a few enjoyed great wealth. Foreigners controlled the local government. Foreigners ran the modern schools. Chinese merchants, students, politicians, and warlords all flocked to embrace foreign ways and accept foreign direction. How could China gain the unity that Sun advocated if the imperialists continued to seduce some Chinese and set them against their compatriots battling foreign domination?

By mixing patriotism (perhaps even xenophobia) with Marxism-Leninism, this Communist view created an internal tension. The received, orthodox Marxist view held that imperialism served an important historical role. By tearing down feudal institutions and values, it prepared the way for a more economically advanced, capitalist China. Only through the destructive effects of imperialist penetration would it be possible to progress to the next stage. But so economically and politically destructive was this process, so socially divisive and personally humiliating were its effects, and so feeble were its measurable contributions to China's progress that members of the fledgling Communist party found it nearly impossible to sit with arms folded while imperialism wreaked havoc all around them. The result was that party members found themselves condemning and trying to frustrate the very force that theoretically at least was their country's and movement's best long-term hope.[18] Dominant figures in the Communist party at heart wanted progress without pain, at least not pain inflicted by foreigners.

The effort to grasp and popularize an economic conception of imperialism was to span several generations. Immediately following the May Fourth demonstrations, Marxist study groups sprang up in Shanghai, Beijing, and other cities. After its founding the Communist party continued the educational effort as party members attended schools in China and the Soviet Union, and party publications reached a broader audience. Though no major translation or treatment of Lenin's *Imperialism* appeared until 1925, party journals devoted a good deal of attention to it. For example, *Xin qingnian* (New youth) between 1921 and 1926 devoted approximately 45 percent of its articles to Lenin's notion of imperialism, either as a theoretical construct or as a way of understanding China's problems.[19] Despite the repression that followed the violent split with the Nationalists, an abundance of writings on imperialism continued to appear in the late 1920s.[20] The United Front policy in the latter part of the 1930s made possible another, better-coordinated campaign to introduce imperialism, this time with a Stalinist gloss (focusing on the threat to the Soviet Union and stressing the imperialists' struggle to stave off economic crisis),[21] while party schools in base areas, especially Yan'an, indoctrinated cadres, including patriotic students carried there by the rising anti-Japanese tide. Another concerted educational effort was made after World War II. Publications at first carried forward the Stalinist orientation, but increasingly they reflected a Maoist one (with its focus on China and its stress on popular resistance).[22] Finally, following the party's seizure of power in 1949, the theme of imperialism found a prominent place in school texts at all levels.

The idea of imperialism was not only a staple for the party faithful; it had long been an important part of the intellectual diet of its leaders. The policy results are, however, difficult to define with assurance or accuracy, at least until more policy sources become available.[23] From what we do know, it would appear that Communist policy has not been as rigid in its approach to the great powers as might have been expected from the pronouncements of the keepers of ideological orthodoxy. Mao Zedong appears to have moved toward a favorable appraisal of the capitalist powers and especially the United States in the late 1930s and 1940s. In the late 1970s Deng Xiaoping embraced an open-door policy premised on the notion that economic relations with the imperialists could benefit China. Even today with the term "imperialism" out of favor, the party is still torn between two distinct understandings of how to deal with the capitalist world. While still fighting the insidious political and cultural effects of foreign contacts ("bourgeois liberalism"), it continues to hope to exploit the economic advantages to be derived from those contacts.

The second of the essential elements making up the May Fourth view on the world was the belief in a special relationship with the Soviet Union. This special Soviet status stood in a reciprocal relationship to the idea of imperialism. The leaders of the new Russia had broken with their own country's aggressive past and with the community of imperialist states by announcing they were setting their foreign relations on a new footing. Important Soviet initiatives throughout the 1920s reflected this new anti-imperialist turn of policy. The advantageous place the Soviet Union had gained in the minds of revolutionaries was, in turn, to promote an understanding of imperialism consistent with Soviet orthodoxy. As the new Rome of the international Communist movement, Moscow was in a position to interpret the doctrine of imperialism in ways favorable to Soviet interests.

The development of this special relationship marked a sharp historical turn for China and Russia. Czarist policy toward the Qing had been characterized by opportunism and betrayal. While pretending to mediate between China and threatening Anglo-French forces, Russia had at midcentury extracted sweeping territorial concessions. In the mid-1890s Russia gained a foothold in the Northeast and then expanded it as the price for moderating Japanese demands and for granting China an alliance. The Boxers gave the czar's forces an excuse for the brutal occupation of all of the Northeast, and even after Japan had curbed the Russian appetite and limited Russian influence to the northern portion of the Northeast, Russia stubbornly held on, striking a cynical deal with

Japan to hold off Chinese claims. If Russian policy thereafter grew milder, it was not because of a change of heart but because of growing internal unrest from 1905 and the distraction of the struggle against Germany after 1914.

The powerful appeal of the Bolshevik revolution pushed to the background, for a time at least, accumulated Chinese resentment and suspicion. For May Fourth intellectuals the Bolshevik revolution was, to begin with, a beacon of hope in dark times. Li Dazhao described it in December 1918 as "the revolution of the twentieth-century type" that would sweep aside the "things that are the vestiges of history—all the emperors, warlords, aristocrats, bureaucrats, militarists, and capitalists." Impatient with China's seeming immobility and backwardness, the revolutionary upsurge in Russia showed how much could be accomplished in a short time. Writing in 1920 from London, Zhou Enlai reported that only such a swift, insurrectionary assault could be "effective in thoroughly cleaning out old abuses." Just as the Renaissance, the Reformation, and the French Revolution had propelled the West to the front ranks of civilization, so the explosion in Russia heralded an age of social revolution in which China would advance. Mao Zedong concluded in 1920 that Russia had become "the number one civilized country in the world" and that Chinese should see the importance of "helping Russia in the completion of its socialist revolution."[24]

The Bolshevik revolution also exercised a strong appeal as an anti-imperialist force aligned with revolutionary movements everywhere. Immediately following the October revolution, Trotsky had in the name of the new Bolshevik regime denounced the secret treaties concluded by the Allies and endorsed the principle of self-determination. This sweeping proclamation became more credible with the issue of the Karakhan manifesto in March 1920. It set the Soviet Union on record as ready to renounce all czarist privileges and interests in China and to abrogate all secret and unequal treaties. Karakhan urged the Chinese people to "understand that their only allies and brothers in the struggle for freedom are the Russian workers and peasants and their Red Army."[25]

By the 1920s the Soviet Union had begun to command respect as the fountainhead of revolutionary doctrine and as a model of revolutionary practice. By study and emulation, Chinese might match the achievements of the Communist party of the Soviet Union and the new Soviet state. Here was an appealing source of guidance and support for Chinese in despair over the defects in their own culture and at odds with hostile imperialist powers. Here was a strategy for gaining power and dramatically transforming a country that was, like Russia, agricultural, poor, mired in tradition, and only recently rid of monarchy. Finally, here was hope that China might jump from feudalism to socialism with no or only a brief pause at the degrading capitalist stage.

Drawn by the favorable possibilities in China, emissaries sent out by the newly established Comintern did missionary work. They came to preach the word, hand out literature to the curious and discontent, and draw potential converts into the bands of the faithful. Gregory Voitinsky arrived in early 1920, followed by Maring (Hendricus Sneevliet), Michael Borodin, M. N. Roy, Pavel Mif, and Otto Braun. They and the publications they carried with them began to define the Bolshevik program and describe its implementation. Chinese radicals struggled to master the holy books and the Soviet-supplied exegesis for them.[26]

Though Communists and even for a time Nationalists brought enthusiasm and high expectations to the Sino-Soviet relationship, unsettling questions about the relationship prompted by the practical experience of dealing with the Soviet Union kept arising. Just how reliable was Moscow as a supporter of China's anti-imperialist revolutionary struggle? Had the USSR set aside its own traditional interests in China, especially along the border? Could its doctrine be imported into China intact and applied wholesale without significant adjustment to Chinese conditions and attitudes? Indeed, just how appropriate was the Soviet Union as a model for Chinese to study and emulate?

The Nationalists offered a lukewarm endorsement of the special relationship. Sun Yat-sen turned to the Soviet Union in 1923 for want of alternative sources of foreign support. Even so, he resisted the full embrace of the Comintern (though for some within the party even his cautious approach carried him too close). He took its material aid and accepted its advisers, who tried to help him transform the Nationalist party along Leninist lines. But the Soviet Union did not become his model, nor did Marxism-Leninism become his faith.

Jiang Jieshi shared Sun's view that the Comintern was a tool to serve his practical political needs. Despite his suspicion of the Red menace and his 1927 break with both foreign and native-born Bolsheviks, he did not embark on a simple ideological crusade. The weakness of the Nationalist regime as it struggled against its enemies at home and abroad left little room for such an indulgence. In fact, Jiang pursed a complex three-sided approach to the USSR. It was a presence along the border in Mongolia, Xinjiang, and the Northeast that needed to be managed and where possible neutralized. It was, moreover, a source of support against Japan that took on added importance in the late 1930s as Jiang's German connections began to fray. It was, finally, the apparent master of the Chinese Communists and hence might be induced to leash the latter.

The special relationship with the Soviet Union thus became the exclusive property of the Communists after 1927. The 1922 party congress had already set the tone. As world capitalism tottered, "Soviet Russia of the workers and peasants" stood firm, "the marvellous cornerstone of the world's revolutionary labor[ing] mass." The October revolution had ignited the struggle of the proletariat throughout Europe, in the United States, and even in Japan, and it had given impetus elsewhere in the world to the rise of national revolutionary movements. But as the Soviet Union gave, so should it receive. As "the forerunner in the emancipation of all oppressed nations," it deserved the protection of the awakening masses in China no less than elsewhere.[27]

Despite this and later equally emphatic endorsements of the special relationship, it is difficult to know how the party privately assessed the USSR as a supporter and model. This is an issue still wrapped in controversy in part because it became entangled in cold war polemics over the monolithic nature of world communism and in part because the historical sources needed to arbitrate it are kept locked in Chinese archives by leaders who are concerned about the practical consequences of a candid look at the Sino-Soviet past.

The safest generalization would for the moment seem to be that hardheaded revolutionaries felt a growing ambivalence about the relationship. Due weight had to be given to an accumulating debt for ideological inspiration, material support, and political guidance. That debt was particularly heavy for the 1920s. The Soviet Union had supplied its Chinese clients operating funds, offered refuge to ill and exhausted cadres, provided schooling, served as a clearinghouse for news and intelligence, and perhaps most important of all, gave hope for ultimate success as they endured hard times from 1927 onward.

But the questions that Sun and Jiang had faced, the Communists had also ultimately to confront. Some party leaders had difficulty with the advice of their Comintern advisers—their insistence on an intimate alliance with the Nationalists, their call for reliance on the Nationalists' left wing and an insurrectionary strategy in Canton following Jiang's blow against the party in April 1927, and their imposition of young and inexperienced Soviet-trained party members into top leadership posts. Late in the decade, some cadres could not see how defense of the Soviet Union against war initiated by the imperialists would advance China's revolution, and thus they became tongue-tied when obliged to explain publicly this internationalist obligation.[28]

Doubts grew stronger in the 1930s as the party itself became more self-reliant. Otto Braun insisted on a strategy of static defense when Jiang attacked the Jiangxi Soviet in 1934–35. The resulting defeat set the Communists off on their Long March ordeal. The shifting and self-interested stance of Soviet policy through the rising international tensions of the 1930s and the ensuing world war produced uneasiness in Yan'an that ground away at residual deference and admiration, while Stalin's postwar suspicions of the Chinese revolution, dalliance with the Nationalists, and limited material and diplomatic support left Communist leaders painfully uncertain about their standing and his intentions. Mao later recalled that during the Civil War Stalin "took us half seriously, half skeptically. When we won the war, Stalin suspected that ours was a victory of the Tito type, and in 1949 and 1950 the pressure on us was very strong indeed."[29]

The 1950s seemed to remove serious doubts about the Sino-Soviet relationship. An alliance concluded in 1950 guaranteed China's security. After Stalin's death the Soviet Union took the final step toward liquidating its position in the Northeast and Xinjiang. Throughout the decade, Soviet aid and advice proved important in China's economic and military modernization, while economic, educational, and cultural exchange drew the two countries still closer together.

But even these halcyon days were not free of tensions. Mao's visit to Moscow in 1950 revealed a striking lack of rapport with Stalin and served to highlight the cultural and intellectual gulf separating these two internationalist comrades.[30] Mao later began to nurse doubts about the Soviet economic model and then the Soviet Union itself as a backsliding socialist state intent under Khrushchev on seeking an accommodation with the United States. Thus, the special relationship had begun to fray by the late 1950s. The anti-Soviet polemics of the 1960s and the resulting policy of opposition to hegemony snapped the bond between the two countries and dealt a heavy blow to this key element in the May Fourth outlook.

The transition from a special to an ordinary relationship between China and the Soviet Union was not easy. Though they confronted the strains, misunderstandings, and territorial rivalries that are commonplace in international affairs, the memory of cooperation, friendship, and support made those difficulties hard to face and manage, not to mention resolve. The Chinese Communist party had been like a child in need of family support and guidance if it were to survive and develop, but by the 1950s it aspired for opportunities outside the folds of the family. The paternal embrace, once supportive, was now deeply irritating, while a lack of recognition of the former dependent's achievements evoked feelings of anger and rejection. Today, with the long estrangement ending, China and the Soviet Union are moving toward a more ordinary relationship. But good memories of earlier family ties persist along with the bad ones associated with recent quarrels, and together they will undoubtedly complicate whatever new relationship China seeks to build with the Soviet Union.

The last and least important of the May Fourth triad was a belief in the unity of the weak and oppressed. Looking out on a world, and especially an Asia, dominated by Europeans, North Americans, and Japanese, Chinese of the May Fourth era felt a bond with "the weak and small nations" (*ruoxiao minzu*). They all had a common goal—liberation from foreign control and the elimination of the internal obstacles to justice and development. By banding together, these countries might compensate for their individual weakness and through international solidarity hasten an end to their oppression. "It is no longer valid," Mao Dun wrote in *Dongfang zazhi* (Eastern miscellany) in April 1920, "to think in terms of one particular people's progress. All must assist one another in their development of civilization." Writing that same year, Mao Zedong argued for transcending a narrow patriotism and "helping Korea toward independence, helping Southeast Asia toward independence, and helping Mongolia, Xinjiang, Tibet, and Qinghai toward autonomy and self-determination."[31]

This identification with the weak and oppressed took two main forms, to each of which was attached an important qualification. One was the generalized identification with countries dominated by Western power, especially but by no means exclusively those countries in Asia.

The origins of this first view can be traced back to the turn of the century when Chinese observers of international affairs had begun to find ample and disturbing parallels between their own condition and that of other peoples pressed to the edge of extinction by the great powers. Turkey was Europe's sick man, whose internal turmoil had left it easy prey. Egypt revealed the dangerous political consequences of letting foreigners seize financial control. Poland was a sad illustration of the perils of territorial dismemberment at the hands of cynical statesmen. The Philippines was a reminder of the universal abuse conquerors heaped on their subjects. Other subjugated peoples—Jews, Irish, and American blacks—received sympathetic treatment. Their doleful fates served as a cautionary tale to rouse Chinese patriots.

This community of the oppressed was not in the post–May Fourth Chinese conception entirely egalitarian. China was not simply one ordinary member; it was, rather, by virtue of its size, population, cultural heritage, or revolutionary experience, a special country. It could play any of a variety of prominent roles. It could stand simply as an inspiration to others locked in similar struggles. It could be a repository of experience for younger political movements to study. It could assume a vanguard role in a pan-Asian or even global struggle against foreign domination. More ambitious still, it could be the fountainhead of a strategy of revolution or development suitable for copying by others. Most ambitious of all, it could serve the role of patron supplying material assistance and detailed advice.[32]

This concern with the weak and oppressed took a second, more concrete form—with those peoples occupying China's territorial periphery. Like the Chinese, they lived under feudal conditions and suffered from imperialist penetration and manipulation. They too needed revolution and deserved self-determination.

The sense of solidarity in this case was even more strongly qualified. An abstract feeling of sympathy collided with the far stronger spirit of patriotism. Patriotic Chinese had rejected and at times even reviled the Manchu dynasty, but at the same time enthusiastically embraced and defended with remarkable tenacity the territorial boundaries carried to new limits by their conquerors. Chinese, in effect, made the Qianlong emperor (1736–96) one of the fathers of their country. The great military campaigns launched during his rule brought striking gains to the empire all along the inner Asian frontier. Those acquisitions in Xinjiang, Mongolia, and Tibet all contained weak and oppressed peoples.

Chinese were caught in a bind. They could not surrender the territorial patrimony handed down from the Qing without also renouncing the dream of restoring China to a place of power, security, even greatness in the world. But they could not deny irredentist forces without also undermining their broad principle of solidarity with such weak and oppressed peoples.

The best way out of this contradiction was to claim for Chinese (meaning the Han) a position of superiority over ethnic and national groups along the border. From that position, Chinese leaders could pronounce with assurance that liberation and self-determination would inevitably result in the incorporation of minority peoples into a greater China. The process by which this was supposed to occur should be familiar to Americans from their own history. A policy of attraction—of drawing ''backward'' peoples into the cultural and economic folds of the advanced—was in theory the mainstay. But to ensure the process was not disrupted by chauvinistic or other regressive elements, time-honored techniques were employed. Armed forces were kept at the ready; a political strategy of divide-and-rule was often effectively brought into play; and Han frontier settlement was tolerated and sometimes encouraged.

The tension between this new-found sense of solidarity and an older sense of patriotism and superiority is evident in the outlook of Sun Yat-sen and Jiang Jieshi. Already in the 1910s Sun had stressed China's unity with Asian revolutionary movements, and this feature of his thinking had become more marked under the influence of the Comintern in the 1920s. Even so, Sun insisted that China had a role to play as inspiration, model, and even protector and teacher for fellow Asians.[33] Notions of solidarity became even more problematic when Sun and later Jiang had to deal with China's own border peoples. The Nationalists remained resolutely imperial in their territorial claims. Sensitive to the charge of having a double standard, Sun sought to distinguish China's expansion in Asia from modern imperialism. China had exercised its influence through the cultural appeal of the ''kingly way'' (*wangdao*), whereas imperialism advanced through ''military conquest and hegemony'' (*badao*). The distinction among peoples now living in China would gradually disappear, Sun contended, and all would become part of ''a single cultural and political whole.'' Jiang went a step further and claimed that in effect a problem did not exist because minority peoples came from the same stock as the Han.[34]

The Communist party was even more emphatic and tenacious in support of the internationalist vision of a community of the abused, but here too that vision was joined to pretensions to superior standing. Once more we can turn to the pronouncement of the Second Congress where the party position was clearly staked out. It identified the ''movement of national revolution'' as one of two great forces for change. Together with ''the [proletarian] revolutionary movement'' led by the Soviet Union, it would sweep away imperialism and capitalism. The Great War and the example of the Russian Revolution had already spurred to resistance the oppressed nations of India, Egypt, Ireland, and Korea as well as China.[35]

As the party gained in strength and found a more Chinese voice, it began to lay claim to leadership of the gathering revolutionary force in Asia. A 1939 statement by Zhang Hanfu made China's resistance war ''a glorious example'' and ''the harbinger and vanguard'' for others also struggling to achieve liberation and independence. Neighbors could draw on China's ''experience and lessons.'' Zhang Ruxin writing in 1941 located the Chinese Revolution at ''the core of the national revolution struggles of all the oppressed peoples of the East'' and placed the Chinese Communist party in ''the forefront of the revolutionary movements of colonial and semicolonial areas.'' In 1945 Liu Shaoqi attributed to the "Thought of Mao Zedong" the power to help in "the cause of the emancipation of the peoples of all countries, and of the peoples of the East in particular."[36]

Pre-1949 party discussions on the future of border areas similarly qualified support for self-determination, autonomy, and liberation with claims to standing as big brother if not parent. Peoples along the periphery would have the right to decide their own future as long as they chose some form of federation with China. The 1922 party congress had set the pattern. It explicitly identified the peoples of Mongolia, Tibet, and "Turkistan" as participants in the global struggle for self-determination. Set off from China proper by race and economic conditions, "they should organize three autonomous nations." But at the same time the Congress made clear that these peoples would ultimately become part of "the China Federal Republic, which will then be the real union of nationalism."[37]

Early party statements on the border areas contain apparent anomalies. The Communists gave formal support in the 1920s for the independence of Outer Mongolia, and they recognized in 1928 and after that the struggle of Taiwan's weak and oppressed people was distinct from China's. In both instances expediency goes far toward explaining the Communist stance. A weak and dependent party had to accept the Soviet position on Mongolia in the 1920s, even though it caused members and sympathizers visible unease. On Taiwan the party was limited by Comintern guidelines that put colonies under the jurisdiction of the Communist party in the metropolis. Taiwan's Communist party (formed in 1928) thus functioned as a branch of the Japanese Communist party and lay beyond the purview of the Chinese Communists.[38]

In the early 1930s party leaders generally skirted the question of China's territorial claims and gave minorities the unqualified right to secede. But once in Yan'an the Communists began to resolve any doubts about their adherence to traditional territorial claims just as they began to stake out their position as a leading revolutionary movement. As early as 1936 Mao had privately indicated that although Xinjiang, Tibet, and Mongolia (including Outer Mongolia) could enjoy autonomy, they would still be federated with China. He made the point formally in 1938. In 1941 the party claimed Taiwan as part of China.[39]

The views on the weak and oppressed that had emerged before 1949 continued to be heard thereafter. The People's Republic reiterated its loyalty to that global community but simultaneously advanced claims to prominence in it. As early as 1951 Lu Dingyi publicly contended that leaders of revolutionary movements could learn from Mao the importance of applying Marxist-Leninist theory to the particular conditions under which each operated.[40] The Sino-Soviet split and the continuing tensions with the United States raised this community of weak and oppressed to a new level of importance in the 1960s and 1970s. The struggling countries of Africa, Latin America, and Asia along with American clients seeking greater independence (chiefly Western Europe and Canada) constituted an "intermediate zone." By bringing these countries of the second and third worlds together, China could create a powerful new international united front against the two imperialist superpowers.[41]

China's claim to solidarity with and leadership in the global community of the oppressed has proven since 1949 more than simple posturing. The People's Republic has provided material assistance and educational opportunities that were, especially in the 1950s and 1960s, large in proportion to the resources at hand. Moreover, in Korea between 1950 and 1953 and in Vietnam during the 1960s, internationalist commitments, strongly reenforced by patriotic impulses, carried China even further—to a heavy investment in life and treasure to help resist American aggression. For example, in October 1950 Mao privately justified intervention as a step undertaken to defend the Korean revolution and prevent the Americans from running "wild to the detriment of East Asia."[42]

But China has also set limits that make its actual assistance seem small compared with sometimes flamboyant rhetoric. It has not offered wholesale or indiscriminate support to revolutionary regimes or insurgent movements.[43] Its regional ambitions have thrust it into bitter conflicts with India and Vietnam, both important members of that community to which China claims to belong. Finally, its strong commitment to its own economic development has led recently to bids for international loans and markets that crowd out others in the developing world.

Closer to home, in the border areas, the abstract commitment to solidarity and self-determination began to give way even before 1949 to a policy of control and assimilation foreshadowed by previous party pronouncements. After 1949 no less than before, it was hard to imagine allowing a minority population that was only 6 percent of China's total to decide the future of over half the land area at China's disposal. Arguing against such a course were Han feelings of cultural superiority, the pressing claims of frontier defense, the attractions of underpopulated and resource-rich territories, and the association of national greatness with the integrity of inherited territorial limits. In 1951 Communist authorities asserted their authority in Tibet, bringing to an end four decades of virtual independence for that region. Elsewhere—in Inner Mongolia, the Moslem Northwest, and Xinjiang—the party denied self-determination and instead vindicated long-standing imperial claims (even while Mao issued warnings against Han chauvinism).[44] Only Outer Mongolia and Taiwan eluded the grasp of the People's Republic. Continuing repression in Tibet and Xinjiang reflect the high priority still accorded defense of the empire handed down from the high Qing.

How should one appraise the three-worlds view that is May Fourth's foreign relations legacy, and how does one account for its demise?

From a broad historical and comparative perspective, it would be fair to credit the May Fourth generation with boldly confronting some of the classic questions already glimpsed earlier in the Qing and recurrent in the foreign policy of every nation. How does the international system work, and how do forces dominant within it shape, even distort, weaker members? Where in a treacherous world may reliable allies be found, and how much confidence can be placed in them? Finally, how should foreign policy serve those aspirations that define a nation's character?

The May Fourth response to these questions served well for a time, but the ideology it gave rise to was by degrees undercut by the internal contradictions which the three-worlds view harbored from the outset. The contradictions grew more acute, particularly for the Communist party as it gained its footing and confidence in the late 1930s and 1940s and then gained state power in 1949. With the establishment of the People's Republic, the anxiety over China's survival that had energized the May Fourth generation also faded, and dreams of greatness could enjoy a revival.

The notion of imperialism, the most durable if the least ground-breaking of the May Fourth elements, left Chinese divided on the practical question of whether they could extract economic benefits from international capitalism without also running the risk of ideological contamination and social division. The answer differed, depending on how one appraised the powers' motives (were they political or economic?) and the powers' social and economic impact on China (was it malignant or benign or at least potentially benign?). For Chinese who no longer think of themselves as victims of international politics and who instead increasingly seek to project their power at least regionally, the guiding concerns of the doctrine of imperialism are irrelevant if not potentially embarrassing.

The admiring view of the USSR did for a time minimize frictions on a long and troubled border and blanket historical memories of a long and troubled relationship, and thus helped unite people of different backgrounds in a common enterprise. China and especially the Communist party gained much from the ties with the USSR, but the relationship also created on the Chinese side strategic and ideological constraints and a sense of dependency that gave rise to deep and ultimately explosive strains. An ideology that made the relationship with the USSR special could dampen but not eliminate conflicts of interest. Palmerston's dictum that nations have no permanent friends, only permanent interests, proved in the long run correct.

The identification with the weak and oppressed, perhaps least significant of the May Fourth elements, proved problematic at two levels. First, while in rhetoric solidarity remained important, it was given a hierarchical twist by patriotic impulses and Chinese pretensions to regional power status. Second, expressions of solidarity have proven even emptier when measured against performance in China's border areas. The tempting conclusion to draw is that China, while proclaiming its solidarity with the weak and oppressed, has demonstrated in practice that it is a multinational empire hostile to self-determination and that, in addition, it may have more to gain through economic, military, scientific, and cultural relations with its former nemesis, the capitalist world.

The May Fourth legacy is now largely spent. China has arrived at one of those transitional points when fundamental questions about its place in the world demand fresh answers. When and how those answers will appear and what form they will take, are a good deal less clear.

Notes

I owe special thanks to Steven Levine for his thoughtful comments on an earlier version of this paper.

1. Quotation from Chow Tse-tsung, *The May Fourth Movement: Intellectual Revolution in Modern China* (Cambridge: Harvard University Press, 1964), p. 93.

2. Quotation from ibid., p. 106.

3. The old response paradigm seems outmoded, while the imperialism paradigm is slipping even in its stronghold in China. On the state of the field, see Paul Cohen, *Discovering History in China: American Historical Writing on the Recent Chinese Past* (New York: Columbia University Press, 1984); Jin Liangyong, "Jianguo yilai jindai Zhongwai guanxishi yanjiu shuping" (A review of post-1949 research on the history of modern Sino-foreign relations), *Jindaishi yanjiu* (Studies in modern history), no. 3 (May 1985): 193–214; and Michael Hunt, "Meiguo guanyu Zhongguo duiwai guanxishi yanjiu wenti yu qianjing" (The study of the history of Chinese foreign relations in the United States: problems and prospects), *Lishi yanjiu* (Historical studies), no. 3 (1988): 150–56 (trans. Yuan Ming).

4. Chen Duxiu, *Duxiu wencun* (Surviving writings of [Chen] Duxiu) (Hong Kong: Yuandong reprint, 1965; originally published 1922), 1:1–10; Deng Ye, "Shilun wusi houqi Chen Duxiu shijieguan de zhuanbian" (An exploration into the changes in Chen Duxiu's world view late in the May Fourth period) in *Chen Duxiu pinglun xuanbian* (A selection of critical essays on Chen Duxiu), ed. Wang Shudi et al. (Zhengzhou: Henan renmin chubanshe, 1982), 1:380; and Yuan Qian et al., comps., *Li Dazhao wenji* (Collected works of Li Dazhao) (Beijing: Renmin chubanshe, 1984), 2:3.

5. Vera Schwarcz, *The Chinese Enlightenment: Intellectuals and the Legacy of the May Fourth Movement of 1919* (Berkeley: University of California Press, 1986).

6. Charlotte Furth makes this point in "May Fourth in History," in *Reflections on the May Fourth Movement: A Symposium*, ed. Benjamin I. Schwartz (Cambridge: Harvard East Asian Research Center, 1972), p. 60.

7. I refer to the "manifesto" of the Second Congress but see also the "decisions," both in C. Martin Wilbur, *The Communist Movement in China: An Essay Written in 1924 by Ch'en Kung-po* (New York: Columbia University Press, 1966), pp. 105–19.

8. "Jiaoyu xuanchuan wenti yi jue'an" (Resolution on the question of educational propaganda) dated from 1922, in *Zhongguo gongchandang xinwen gongzuo wenjian huibian* (A collection of documents on Chinese Communist party journalism), comp. Zhongguo shehui kexueyuan xinwen yanjiusuo (Beijing: Xinhua chubanshe, 1980), 1:2–3.

9. Harold Z. Schiffrin, *Sun Yat-sen and the Origins of the Chinese Revolution* (Berkeley: University of California Press, 1970), chap. 10. Documentary materials compiled in China over the last decade may help shed some additional light on this process of intellectual transmission. See, for example, *Shehuizhuyi sixiang zai Zhongguo de chuanbo* (The propagation of socialist thought in China), 3 vols. (Beijing: Zhonggong zhongyang dangxiao keyan bangongshi, 1985).

10. The following account draws from Martin Bernal, *Chinese Socialism to 1907* (Ithaca: Cornell University Press, 1976), pp. 142–47; Li Yu-ning, *The Introduction of*

Socialism into China (New York: Columbia University Press, 1971), pp. 10–14; and Michael H. Hunt, *The Making of a Special Relationship: The United States and China to 1914* (New York: Columbia University Press, 1983), pp. 258–66.

11. This discussion relies on A. James Gregor and Maria Hsia Chang, "Marxism, Sun Yat-sen, and the Concept of 'Imperialism,' " *Pacific Affairs* 55 (Spring 1982): 54–79.

12. Sun quoted in ibid., p. 72, n. 54.

13. Ibid., p. 69, n. 43.

14. This opportunism is an important theme in C. Martin Wilbur, *Sun Yat-sen: Frustrated Patriot* (New York: Columbia University Press, 1976).

15. Edmund S. K. Fung, "The Chinese Nationalists and the Unequal Treaties 1924–1931," *Modern Asian Studies* 21 (Oct. 1987): 793–819; and Edmund Fung, "Anti-Imperialism and the Left Guomindang," *Modern China* 11 (January 1985): 39–76. See also P. Cavendish, "Anti-Imperialism in the Kuomintang 1923–8," in *Studies in the Social History of China and South-east Asia*, ed. Jerome Ch'en and Nicholas Tarling (Cambridge: Cambridge University Press, 1970), pp. 23–56.

16. Zhu Jianhua and He Rongdi, "Shilun Li Dazhao de fandi sixiang" (An exploration of Li Dazhao's anti-imperialist thought) in *Li Dazhao yanjiu lunwenji* (A collection of research papers on Li Dazhao), ed. Han Yide and Wang Shudi (Shijiazhuang: Hebei renmin chubanshe, 1984), 2:515–29; Deng, "Shilun wusi houqi Chen Duxiu," pp. 381–83.

17. Wilbur, *The Communist Movement*, pp. 105–6, 110.

18. I draw on Arif Dirlik, "National Development and Social Revolution in Early Chinese Marxist Thought," *China Quarterly*, no. 58 (April–May 1974): 286–309, which makes this point in relation to the debates of the late 1920s.

19. This calculation is from Lawrence Sullivan and Richard H. Solomon, "The Formation of Chinese Communist Ideology in the May Fourth Era: A Content Analysis of *Hsin ch'ing nien*," in *Ideology and Politics in Contemporary China*, ed. Chalmers Johnson (Seattle: University of Washington Press, 1973), p. 154. Ke Bainian, writing under the pseudonym Li Chunfan, supplied the first translation of Lenin under the title *Diguozhuyi qianshuo* (An elementary introduction to imperialism) (Shanghai: Xinwenhua, 1925). Zhang Jinglu, "Liening zhuzuo Zhongyiben nianbiao" (A chronology of works by Lenin translated into Chinese) in his *Zhongguo chuban shiliao (bubian)* (Historical materials on Chinese publishing [supplement]) (Beijing: Zhonghua, 1957), p. 455. For an outline of a party curriculum from the mid-1920s giving imperialism a prominent place, see C. Martin Wilbur and Julie Lien-ying How, eds., *Documents on Communism, Nationalism, and Soviet Advisers in China, 1918–1927: Papers Seized in the 1927 Peking Raid* (New York: Columbia University Press, 1956), pp. 131–33.

20. See, for example, Ma Zhemin, *Guoji diguozhuyi lun* (On international imperialism) (Shanghai: Kunlun, 1929), and the more mechanical treatment by Wu Junru, *Diguozhuyi duiHua sanda qinlue* (Imperialism's three great aggressions against China) (Shanghai: Minzhi, 1929). A new translation of Lenin's imperialism also appeared in 1929 under the title *Diguozhuyi lun* (On imperialism). Produced by Yi Liji, it was to be revised and reprinted in 1937 and again in 1948 and 1949.

21. From a large literature intended for popular consumption, see the books by Guo Moruo, Qian Yishi, Zhang Bi, Zhang Hanfu, Zhang Qinfu, and Zhang Jianfu, and above all Liu Shi's *Jietou jianghua* (Street talk) (privately printed [distributed by Shenghuo], 1936). Some of these appeared in the series "Shijie zhishi congshu" (Series on world knowledge).

22. These trends are evident in the volumes that appeared in the series "Shehui kexue" (Social science) between 1946 and 1948.

23. For a helpful guide to changing assessments, see Fudan daxue lishixi Zhongguo

jindaishi jiaoyanzu, comp., *Zhongguo jindai duiwai guanxi shiliao xuanji (1840–1949)* (Selected historical materials on modern China's foreign relations [1840–1949]) (Shanghai: Renmin chubanshe, 1977), vol. 2. These must be supplemented by a wealth of new materials (most of it limited to "internal use") that have appeared over the last decade. These are discussed in Michael H. Hunt and O. Arne Westad, "The Chinese Communist Party and International Affairs: A Field Report on New Sources and Old Problems," *China Quarterly*, no. 122 (June 1990): 258–72.

24. Quotations from *Li Dazhao wenji,* 1:602, 603; Zhongguo geming bowuguan, comp. *Zhou Enlai tongzhi ju Ou wenji xubian* (A supplement to the collected works from comrade Zhou Enlai's period of residence in Europe) (Beijing: Wenwu chubanshe, 1982), p. 71; Stuart Schram, "Mao Tse-tung's Thought to 1949," in *Cambridge History of China*, ed. John K. Fairbank and Albert Feuerwerker (Cambridge: Cambridge University Press, 1986), 13:802; and Mao to Cai Hesen, December 1, 1920, in *Mao Zedong shuxin xuanji* (Selected letters of Mao Zedong), comp. Zhonggong zhongyang wenxian yanjiushi (Beijing: Renmin chubanshe, 1983), p. 3.

25. A translation of the manifesto is in Allen Whiting, *Soviet Policies in China, 1917–1924* (New York: Columbia University Press, 1954), pp. 269–71. The quotation is from p. 271.

26. Arif Dirlik, *The Origins of Chinese Communism* (New York: Oxford University Press, 1989); and C. Martin Wilbur and Julie Lien-ying How, *Missionaries of Revolution: Soviet Advisers and Nationalist China, 1920–1927* (Cambridge: Harvard University Press, 1989).

27. "Decision" of the Second Party Congress, in Wilbur, *The Communist Movement,* pp. 111, 118.

28. See the resolution on propaganda work (bearing a date on the seal of June 25, 1929) issued by the Second Plenum of the Sixth Central Committee, in Zhongguo shehui kexueyuan, comp., *Zhongguo gongchandang xinwen gongzuo,* 1:45.

29. *Selected Works of Mao Tse-tung* (Beijing: Foreign Languages Press, 1961–), 5:304.

30. See the suggestive account by Mao's interpreter, Shi Zhe, "Beitong Mao zhuxi fangSu" (Accompanying Chairman Mao to the Soviet Union), *Renwu* (Personalities), no. 5 (September 1988): 5–21.

31. Quotations from Irene Eber, "Images of Oppressed Peoples and Modern Chinese Literature," in *Modern Chinese Literature in the May Fourth Era,* ed. Merle Goldman (Cambridge: Harvard University Press, 1977), p. 132; and *Mao Zedong shuxin xuanji*, p. 3. Eber offers a suggestive examination of themes in literature that mirror nicely political commentary.

32. Steven M. Goldstein suggests these distinctions in "The Chinese Revolution and the Colonial Areas: The View From Yenan, 1937–1941," *China Quarterly,* no. 75 (September 1978): 595–96.

33. Fung, "The Chinese Nationalists," p. 800. For a detailed contemporary survey building on Sun's general views, see Li Zuohua, *Shijie ruoxiao minzu wenti* (The problem of the world's weak and small nations) (Hankou: Baihe, 1928).

34. June T. Dreyer, *China's Forty Millions: Minority Nationalities and National Integration in the People's Republic of China* (Cambridge: Harvard University Press, 1976), pp. 16–17.

35. Quotations from Wilbur, *The Communist Movement*, p. 110.

36. Quotations come in order of appearance from Goldstein, "The Chinese Revolution," pp. 603, 611, 596. Goldstein points out that Comintern statements can be found that sanctioned at least the Chinese claims to offer inspiration and example.

37. Wilbur, *The Communist Movement,* p. 113.

38. Frank S. T. Hsiao and Lawrence R. Sullivan, "The Chinese Communist Party and

the Status of Taiwan, 1928–1943,'' *Pacific Affairs* 52 (Fall 1979): 446–67. On Outer Mongolia, see *Xiangdao zhoubao* (Guide weekly), no. 147 (March 17, 1926): 1358; no. 148 (April 2, 1926): 1388–90; no. 149 (April 13, 1926): 1402–4; and no. 184 (January 21, 1927): 1952.

39. Mao reportedly chafed over the surrender of China's claims to Outer Mongolia in the Nationalist-Soviet treaty of 1945. Dreyer, *China's Forty Millions,* pp. 63–64, 67, 70; and Stuart R. Schram, ''Decentralization in a Unitary State: Theory and Practice, 1940–1984,'' in *The Scope of State Power in China,* ed. Stuart Schram (London: School of Oriental and African Studies, 1985), pp. 81–83.

40. Goldstein, ''The Chinese Revolution,'' p. 619.

41. See Stuart Schram, *Chairman Mao Talks to the People: Talks and Letters, 1956–1971* (New York: Pantheon, 1975), pp. 170, 180–81, 189; and King C. Chen, *China and the Three Worlds: A Foreign Policy Reader* (White Plains, NY: M. E. Sharpe, 1979), pp. 3, 39–44.

42. Quote from Chai Chengwen and Zhao Yongtian, *KangMei yuanChao jishi* (A record of resisting America and aiding Korea) (Beijing: Zhonggong dangshi ziliao chubanshe, 1987), p. 56.

43. Peter Van Ness, *Revolution and Chinese Foreign Policy: Peking's Support for Wars of National Liberation* (Berkeley: University of California Press, 1971).

44. For details, see Dreyer, *China's Forty Millions,* pp. 79–91.

PART THREE

THE PRC'S FIRST FORTY YEARS

JOYCE KALLGREN

Of the four anniversaries around which this conference was organized, perhaps the best known and most easily accepted as an important date for non-Chinese scholarly audiences would be the fortieth anniversary of the establishment of the People's Republic of China.

It is not surprising that the fortieth anniversary of the People's Republic should attract political and scholarly attention. An anniversary—especially of each decade—seems to be important not only to individuals but also to nations. Organizers plan commemorative events and also pause to assess the past and consider future goals.

With respect to the People's Republic, planning for programs, festivals, and parades on the occasion of the fortieth anniversary was well underway by the fall of 1988. Moreover, events in late 1988 and even early 1989 engendered cautious optimism about the state of the nation in contrast to conditions some forty years earlier. Since 1949, some would argue, the Chinese people had been satisfactorily progressing toward building an industrial state. To be sure, the agenda for political change was less clearly drawn and the assessment of its progress less certain. But in terms of international recognition, and to a considerable degree as measured by conventional indices of the quality of life, progress had been made. Differences arose over how much of this progress preceded the death of Mao, and how much could be attributed to the more recent reform efforts.

In this context and atmosphere, the four authors of the essays in this section together with one of the conference organizers met to discuss the issues for discussion in papers. On the basis of that meeting, and of informal conversations over the next eight months, the essays in this section were written. Though written from the perspective of 1989—that is, a forty-year experience—the manuscripts focused primarily on the period of Maoist leadership. Analysis of the decade of the post-Mao reform was left to authors of the fourth-anniversary manuscripts.

The reader will discover that certain themes found in earlier portions of this volume recur with heightened emphasis in the essays in this segment. Moreover, a review of assessments made in 1979 shows that the themes selected in 1989 had often been foreshadowed ten years earlier. But in 1989 the experience of recent changes allowed those themes to be redrawn more sharply and refined in the light of a decade's experience. In this light, the essays in part three link the traditional and modern periods of China history and politics with the most recent decade's developments.

An important theme common to pre- and post-1949 China is the ongoing tension between the state and society. It underlies many of the observations of the four essays that follow. It was an important achievement of Mao Zedong to extend the power of the state throughout the land in the post-1949 decade. Did the state's political power remain constant, increase, or diminish throughout the thirty-year period examined here?

Vivienne Shue addresses the expansion of power but cautions of the need for more care in analysis. She ultimately refines and limits the more common view about the increase of state power through the use of "paradoxes" that show both the strength and limitations of the state.

Thomas Bernstein and Martin Whyte speak of the party and society—examining the efforts of Mao to control the state and society through the party. They draw our attention to a companion set of developments. First, they recognize the extraordinary personal power of Mao himself, and the capacity of the party and state to regulate and shape the lives of Chinese citizens. Bernstein addresses the matter of the Maoist leadership. After noting Mao's position as paramount leader, Bernstein examines both the problems that such a dependence upon a paramount leader causes and Mao's serious policy errors, and why others in the leadership didn't try to restrain him. The question, a central one in Chinese affairs, can be traced back to an assessment of imperial leadership in the time of the dynastic state. It also points to the contemporary unstable situation in which current Chinese leaders share power. Bernstein shows the reader that the leaders in the Maoist era were convinced that they needed Mao and would not take the risk involved in replacing him. Such a question is relevant to the 1990s.

Barry Naughton, in his economic analysis, speaks of the state more in its economic than its political role. He writes of the achievements of the Chinese state in its first few steps toward industrial development. He refines the assessment of the first decade by reminding us of the contributions of the Soviets. Although he records the limitations and failure of Chinese development, he also observes that by the end of thirty years, China was operating in a "totally different universe of possibilities." On balance, though, his judgment stresses the heavy burdens that economic errors had brought the Chinese. In a number of respects, his analysis of the difficulties faced by the Chinese prepares the reader for observations of the essays in part four with respect to economic innovation.

One outcome of the expansion of the power and effectiveness of the state was the decline of the domain of Chinese society, the arena in which smaller units—the clan, lineages and villages, the family, and individuals—might act with relative independence. The state and the Communist party seemed to exercise increasing control. Whyte focuses upon Chinese society, chronicling the growth and strength of the state: its reach and capacity to intervene not only in politics and economics but also through effective organizational structures into many of the interstices of individual life. He makes the reader aware how such power affected the outlook and commitment of individuals, examining the costs of developing and sustaining the powerful state not only in terms of the decline in consumption and living standards but also in the decline in the vitality and work ethic of Chinese men and women. Thus, Whyte sets forth, as do his three colleagues, the problems that the post-Mao reforms would address.

Taken together, the four essays in part three set out the competing and conflicting themes of centralization versus decentralization, of the relationship between state and society, and show how the policies developed from them—sometimes carried to extremes in the aftermath of a long and costly civil war—were initially greeted with enthusiasm, then grudgingly observed, and finally opposed, thus making the nation-state responsive to and welcoming of the changes in the post-Mao period.

9

POWERS OF STATE, PARADOXES OF DOMINION China 1949–1979

VIVIENNE SHUE

Most historians and students of comparative politics are inclined nowadays to the view that the *real* victories of the Chinese Communist revolution are to be measured more in terms of "state building" than in terms of "building socialism." The fundamental historical significance of the revolution is lodged not so much in the specific political programs or in the soaring social aspirations of the Marxian ideology its leaders proclaimed, but in the raw and simple fact that final military victory by the revolutionists in 1949 put an end at last to China's prolonged national nightmare at the edge of anarchy. Against the sorry backdrop of a century's dynastic decline, civil war, and social decay, the victory of the People's Liberation Army finally swept from the stage all the frowsy remnants of the old regime. The Communists' triumph brought peace at last, national reunification, and a mandate to govern. The social catharsis of a brutal and protracted revolution cleared the way, in short, for the winning party to rebuild the state.[1]

For over one hundred years, no state authority had managed to stand firm on the seeming quicksand of Chinese society. It took the revolution to lay a new social foundation. And the state that was erected upon that fresh foundation soon came commonly to be regarded as one of the most centralized, penetrating, and imposing states holding sway in the modern world.

It was a state designed very deliberately in the *modern* image. Its sovereignty, enshrined in a written constitution, was conceived as absolute and indivisible. Its power was imagined to be the transcendent expression of the will of the collective citizenry, the force and product of the wishes of the whole of the Chinese people. Its territoriality was clear and distinct, with but few significant exceptions, actually encompassing the entire expanse of the old imperial realm. And the new state, a vociferous if callow actor also on the international stage, bound itself by solemn oaths never to rest until its national sovereignty over all Chinese irredenta was restored. Within its borders, the state's monopoly on the legitimate means of coercion was quite promptly made complete. The newborn state issued laws and decrees crafted, on the modern model, to be nonarbitrary yet entirely impersonal. It established rules, specified procedures, and commanded obedience from citizens and officials alike, obedience monitored and enforced by its own administrative, jural, constabulary, and penal institutions, all rapidly and fully elaborated after 1949. The new state also associated itself, in principle at least, with the modern ideals of rational bureaucratic decision making, economic planning and social engineering, meritocracy, public education and political participation, science, secularism, and the general demystification of social relations, both public and private.

Since this was to be a state with enormous responsibilities, it would naturally require both mighty power to command and firm leadership or guidance. The Communist party, then conceived as fused *with* the people and as the leading element *of* the people, was also therefore to be fused with the state and would lead the state. Patterned in part on the Lenin-Stalin model of the Soviet Union and in part on the apparatus and the ethos of China's own imperial past, the infant party-state had all the makings of a modernized autocracy.

This, of course, is precisely what it did become. Over the ensuing decades, the party-state was labeled and analyzed variously by scholars and journalists—as a totalitarian system, an authoritarian regime, or a dictatorship of the proletariat. Generally speaking, there were few who saw cause to question the patent truth that state power in postrevolutionary China was consolidated quickly and subsequently grew to awesome, even fearful, proportions.

From the vantage point of 1989, however, it may be worth another look back at the nature, evolution, and limits of party-state power in China, before the current era of "reform." The best of the many recent sociological, historical, and political studies concerned with theories of the state and with state-society relations have been elaborating and confirming for us what we probably should have known all along: that states everywhere, but especially perhaps in the Third World, can be "strong" and "weak" at the same time; that even the strongest of states, while dependably capable in some respects, can be astonishingly impotent in others; and that societies, especially those that are caught up in the processes of development, are by no means necessarily passive and cannot be regarded as merely acted upon by their states, but must be conceived instead as interacting continually with state actors and state institutions to produce an array of more and less "statist" outcomes.[2]

We now, so lately witnesses to spontaneous marches, hunger strikes, and other impressively peaceful popular demonstrations, and witnesses also to government intimidation, official murder, and Beijing's vain and cowardly attempts at a coverup, may have acquired a newly accented taste for reassessing the strengths and the weaknesses of the Chinese state. Whatever else still remains obscure to our vision, surely recent events have made it intensely plain to all of us that an intimate, and doubtless painful, knowledge of what the Chinese state under Mao both could and could not do has fatefully shaped the choices of action that men like Deng Xiaoping and Li Peng came to believe were the only ones left to them in 1989.

State Goals

To attempt an assessment of any given state's strengths and weaknesses, accomplishments and failures, or capabilities and performance, it seems best to begin with what we think we know about the goals of states generally in the modern world. Here there is plenty of conceptual help to be found in the recent explosion of comparative politics scholarship concerned with state theory, state building, and state-society relations. This is a refreshingly eclectic and wide-ranging literature that has, nonetheless, yielded considerable consensus in the specification of a set of essential goals that must generally be pursued by modern states. Prominently listed in such a set one can usually find the goals of autonomy, revenue expansion, security, hegemony, and, when possible, legitimacy.[3] A state's ability to attain the first four of these goals is widely thought also to rest on the relative development of its capacities of penetration and control. That is, a state's capacity to reach into social groups and organizations with its messages, regulations, and demands, and its capacity to enforce those regulations and demands, are each factors that in large part determine that state's overall ability to attain its goals of relative autonomy, enhanced revenues, national security, and ideological hegemony. Furthermore, it is widely believed that a state's capacity to attain the fifth major goal—the goal of legitimacy—in turn depends in large part on its performance in regard to the first four. This short list of states' goals, supplemented by the two familiar notions of penetration and control, are the basic concepts that I will deploy to orient the general consideration of the evolution of state power in China between 1949 and 1979.

Autonomy

Modern states seek to maximize their autonomy, both domestically and internationally. To put this in a somewhat less reified formulation, state actors and agents seek to establish and refine institutions and routines of governance that give them the greatest possible independence of action. They aim to reduce their dependence—economic, military, and otherwise—on alien states and agents in the international arena. And they prefer domestic arrangements that allow them to "rise above" the mere representation and pursuit of the specific interests of any given segment(s) of society, so that they may pursue instead the interests of the state itself, which are customarily, if not always convincingly, conceived as coincident with the "general interest" and the "public welfare."

The ideal of absolute state autonomy seems not any more, if it ever was, actually attainable in either the domestic or the global arena. But modern states can and do differ dramatically in just how close they come to this ideal; and any given state apparatus, as it evolves over time, may go through periods of relatively greater and relatively less autonomy of action. Bearing this potential variability in mind, we might readily surmise that the postrevolutionary Chinese state came closest to the ideal of autonomy, on both the domestic and international dimensions, sometime during the decade of the 1950s.

Once established, the young People's Republic was not even accorded diplomatic recognition by many of the world's leading powers. Excluded from the United Nations, under a crippling trade embargo, and denied development aid and assistance by members of the Western alliance and by the many smaller states held in the thrall of that alliance during those early years of the cold war, China seemed to many destined to enter the Eastern bloc and assume the role of Soviet minion. Now, of course, it is understood that the Sino-Soviet relationship was actually troubled and uneasy from the start. China's trade with the Soviet Union did grow steadily in the first half of the decade, but steps toward genuine economic integration had not proceeded very far before Soviet credits were suspended in 1957.[4] Although China's leaders acquired a certain amount of Soviet aid at the beginning, without which "China's tempo of industrialization in the 1950s would have been considerably slower," the Chinese leadership never seemed to feel either economically dependent or militarily much fettered by Russian interests and concerns in the Asian theater of the then hazardous global confrontation with the West. From the Korean War to the Taiwan Straits crisis, the Chinese state clearly charted its own course in international conflicts and other tests of resolve.

Isolated and vulnerable as it was, it did not enter readily into relations of economic or security dependence or countenance compromises to its autonomy in calculating its own options and interests in world affairs. By the end of the decade, with the impending rupture in relations with the Soviets, the Chinese state indeed stood very much on its own and unsupported in a dangerous world.

On the domestic scene, the autonomy of the Chinese state also seemed at its peak during the first decade. The revolution had discredited and finally destroyed what remained of the erstwhile socioeconomic elites of China. Land reform, collectivization, and the nationalization of industry and commerce decimated the propertied, bureaucratic, and business classes, depriving them not only of their former wealth and political influence but also of the last shreds of their public dignity. Chinese society was literally turned upside down in the early days of the People's Republic. The poor and the lowly were exalted, redefined now as the only dependably healthy, creative, and progressive elements of society. The previously proud and accomplished were reconceived as reactionary elements, class enemies, and traitors to the nation. The party-state presided as the social slate was wiped quite clean.

It would be an exaggeration to say that Chinese society was entirely remade during the 1950s; but there is no doubt that it was thoroughly reconfigured. In that process of structural and moral reformation, it was the party-state that was defining all the terms and making all the rules. The Chinese state thus enjoyed, for a short period, an extraordinary degree of autonomy vis-à-vis entrenched social elites. In that thin atmosphere of revolutionary purity and austerity, the old social elite was consciously reconceived as the enemy, and the new social elite was yet to be made. Not in any way beholden for its power to the vested interests of the past, nor yet penetrated, captured, compromised, or coopted by newly rising social subgroups with agendas of their own, the party-state of the 1950s was an unusually free agent as it set out to execute its quotidian responsibilities in policy formulation and implementation. This relative autonomy, this freedom from social compromise, imparted to almost all the new state's early actions an enormous ethical clarity.

The state manifestly pursued the good; virtue reigned. Many Chinese, who were later to suffer the personal anguish of political disillusion, can still to this day vividly recall the purity of those young truths and common convictions. Such a pristine condition could not naturally last long. A new elite was straightaway found to be materializing. A robust "new class," clutching a disproportionate share of social esteem, political influence, and material benefits, arose, not surprisingly, in and around the party-state apparatus itself. This, the "Red aristocracy"—child of the union of revolution and rule—clung with cocky confidence to its vested interest in the social structural status quo and in the exaltation of "revolutionary virtues," quickly becoming convenient moral certitudes.

By the early 1960s, Mao Zedong could be heard darkly warning complacent cadres against permitting the party-state to betray its mission by falling captive to the mean and narrow interests of the very social elite it had itself spawned. His unlooked-for musings along these lines were met at first with various forms of incomprehension and self-defense. Then again, in the Cultural Revolution, Mao made repeated and increasingly risky attempts to give emphatic voice to the aspirations of the gathering underclass. Thus, he apparently hoped to galvanize what he always believed was the "basically good" and proletarian party-state against its own threatening tendencies to see and to serve elite interests first. But even the shocks and strains of the Cultural Revolution were not enough to disentangle the skeleton of state from the determined embrace of its youthful and muscular social elite. The two, ineluctably, had been fused into one body. So, all the misguided attempts of the Cultural Revolution "to change the human soul" and to revive the reign of virtue notwithstanding, it became sadly obvious to all that the crystalline moment of uncompromised truth in power, the brief period of the "relative autonomy" of the revolutionary state, was already past.

In sum, the revolutionary party-state's early autonomy allowed it to restructure society and redefine social values in ways that were later, quite paradoxically, to set severe limitations on its own freedom of action and response in the face of shifting social needs and demands. The Chinese experience suggests that even for the freshest and strongest of states, autonomy is not only something to be analyzed as "relative"; it tends to be transient as well.

Revenue

The better to pursue all their other goals, modern states must seek to secure and to expand their sources of revenue. This is even more intensely true, perhaps, for states in the Third World that take state investment for rapid, guided economic development as their foremost task and as the ultimate touchstone of their own legitimation. As Young has summarized the historical record, "From the birth of the modern state, the relentless search for money has been a constant theme of statecraft and the pivot for a ceaseless struggle with civil society, anxious to limit state extraction."[5] This is an area, once again, in which the postrevolutionary Chinese state evidently experienced its most arresting success and development in its earliest years. The collectivization of agriculture and the nationalization of industry and commerce in the first half of the decade of the 1950s gave the state unprecedentedly penetrating access to all the major product- and revenue-generating components of the national economy. This penetration and control, coupled with the generally improved health of the economy in what was after all a period of postwar boom and recovery, brought nothing short of windfall profits into state coffers.

State budget revenues climbed dramatically during the 1950s, both absolutely and as a proportion of gross domestic product. Reported at just 6.5 billion yuan in 1950, total state budget revenues had soared to 54.2 billion in 1959. The government's major sources of revenue shifted tremendously over that period as well, away from direct taxes on agriculture and toward higher levies on industry and commerce along with direct collection of profits from state-run enterprises. Income from industrial and commercial taxes and profits rose from 49 percent of total state budget receipts in 1950 to 91 percent by 1959. As the state exercised its control over the national budget, it opted for heavy investment and little encouragement for consumer or luxury goods production. The rate of gross investment consequently mounted sharply during the early years, staying above 20 percent for the whole of the First Five-Year Plan period.[6]

This was a pace and a pattern that could not possibly be sustained. Whereas total state budget revenue had been multiplied more than eightfold in the first decade, it took another two decades for it to double just once more.[7] Even more indicative of the leveling-off of state control in the financial sphere, state revenues as a proportion of total national income stood at 32 percent in 1979—exactly the percentage they had maintained on average for the period of the First Five-Year Plan![8] The state's share of the national product did not expand much after the first decade.

In the realm of revenue expansion, however, as in the matter of autonomy, it was the very scope of the state's initial victories that seemed paradoxically to sow the seeds of later problems and limitations. Expanded state control of revenue had come only with expanded state control over investment, profits, trade, prices, and wages. These controls tended, in turn, to drive initiative and competitiveness out of the system, replacing them with inefficiency and poor consumer services, disincentives to labor and declining productivity, chronic product and investment imbalances, and most of the other familiar vices of central planning and the command economy. The practice of directly collecting the profits of state enterprises and treating them as state revenue was especially important in eliminating the prod of profit from the conduct of business in most of the nation's large industrial and commercial firms, thus effectively stifling experimentation, innovation, and most of the other forms of risk taking that can serve as correctives to lost opportunity and waste. Had the state managed to attain secure control over its revenue base only by means that would inevitably slow down the engine of economic growth that generated the revenues?

By the end of the first decade, the Chinese economy was about to encounter a series of complex and dire setbacks. The gross miscalculations of the Great Leap Forward were to leave Chinese planners and people with a tragically slow climb back up to pre-Leap economic performance levels. No sooner had this arduous task been accomplished than the violence and disruptions of the early years of the Cultural Revolution intervened again to hinder overall progress toward development. Yet as recent research has confirmed, even during the Cultural Revolution, and in the face of the unrelenting population pressures of the period, China's general economic growth performance remained quite respectable, if no longer as spectacular as it had been in the 1950s. As Prime explains:

> National income, China's measure of total net output value, grew at an average annual rate of 6.9 percent between 1966 and 1975. This rate of growth was below the 8.9 percent rate of the First Five-Year Plan when China received substantial Soviet aid, as well as the 14.7 percent of the 1963–1965 period, when the economy was recovering from the Great Leap Forward. Growth during the Cultural Revolution, however, was slightly higher than the 6.6 percent average annual growth for the thirty-three years between 1953 and 1985. . . . Thus, far from being a total economic disaster, there were substantial increases in production capacity and output during the Cultural Revolution period.[9]

Yet the continuing struggle to achieve these good growth results caused other distortions to take firmer and firmer hold of the state-planned economy. The accumulation rate was kept high—too high, considering the country's many urgent needs for social expenditure. The division of the national income between accumulation and consumption gave over 27 percent to accumulation in 1965, following the recovery from the Leap. It rose to more than 30 percent in 1966 and stayed over 30 percent for the entire decade of the 1970s.[10] Personal income and consumption stagnated. Most of this intensive, state-mandated reinvestment went into productive units, especially and disproportionately into heavy industry. Little was left for other vital segments of the economy, such as light industry, housing, transport, education, or health. To help persuade the Chinese public to continue curbing its consumption and leisure, the party-state promoted unstinting labor, frugality, austerity, and self-sacrifice as social values all through the 1960s and 1970s. The state-planned economy did go on registering respectable rates of growth, then, but only at the cost of demanding more and more labor from the people while insisting that they be prepared to live on indefinitely in bleak and strenuous poverty. Resentment against the state's exorbitant extractions mounted as the promise of a better life for all faded from view. Economic "growth," as people know and governments often forget, is not all that is meant by economic "development."

In sum, the postrevolutionary state quickly and surely attained the essential goals of revenue expansion and control, but in its very success it laid the foundations in certain institutions, routines, and operating assumptions for its later relative inability, despite great effort, to promote satisfactory development.

Security

Modern states aim to be prepared to counter all perceived threats both domestic and international, to the security of their rule. Internationally, they establish and cultivate military, intelligence, and diplomatic means to protect the national security. Domestically, they seek to routinize the authority of their regimes through public ceremonies, pledges of due process, and a host of customary formalities intended to forestall sudden shocks to regime integrity and safety. They also deploy police, secret police, administrative controls over the population, and political and other surveillance networks to defend their government against sabotage, overthrow, and sometimes even against generalized political opposition or public ferment that might potentially destabilize their rule. Over the course of its first thirty years, the postrevolutionary Chinese state also demonstrated some impressive strengths in protecting its security, but its development in this regard did not follow a trajectory very similar to the patterns explored above where autonomy and revenue were concerned.

Domestically, extensive efforts were made during the early 1950s to establish a system of control along Soviet lines. Those efforts were credited with little success, however, and after 1955, as Schurmann observed,

> Soviet-type patterns of control were abandoned, and, indeed, reversed. Instead of the continued elaboration of bureaucratic systems of control, a process of gradual reduction in the power of these control organizations began. . . . This decline was part of a general shift from a system of parallel bureaucracies on the Soviet model toward a system of Party-dominated lateral integration.[11]

This approach was to prove far more effective, ultimately giving the Chinese state its reputation for comprehensive surveillance, attempts at thought control, and other politicized intrusions into the private lives of individuals and families.

Neighborhood security groups, mandatory public health inspections, regular political study sessions at the work unit, secret dossiers on all citizens, tight restrictions on travel, residence, and job mobility, political mobilization campaigns aimed against enemies of the party and the state, and canons of party discipline that called upon citizens to spy and to inform on one another—all these techniques and others were vigorously deployed to intimidate and discipline the hapless Chinese citizen. Periodically, throughout the 1950s, 1960s, and 1970s, the whole party propaganda apparatus and the public security apparatus appeared to be seized by paroxysms of suspicion about the activities of spies, traitors, and class enemies. Where security was concerned, the watchful state's ability to penetrate the basic units of society was menacingly obvious.

For the most part, serious threats to state security from domestic groups were by these means averted or suppressed. Opposition and resistance were expressed primarily through passive means and by various forms of evasion or deceit. Occasional job actions or peasant boycotts and demonstrations did present overt if localized challenges to state authority. But these were generally quickly and decisively put down. Only the secessionist rebellion in Tibet required the state to use significant military force against its own people.

This subdued situation prevailed only, of course, until the onset of the Cultural Revolution when the leaders of state declared their intention deliberately to discard social peace and security in favor of social revolution. Millions of youths, mobilized as Red Guards, took to the city streets to make trouble of all kinds. Local power seizures and counterseizures proliferated. Authorities and officials of all levels and functions were divided into warring camps and factions. It was a period of tenuous state security at best, when the party itself was under vehement attack and the apparatus of state was gravely weakened by purges, suspensions, and the dispatch of key cadres to the countryside for labor and thought reform. Public opposition and dissent, so long and so assiduously contained, now blared incongruously from every street corner. The military was repeatedly called in to restore order, only to become embroiled itself in the power struggles underway everywhere.

The Chinese government had been widely regarded in the early 1960s as a once-revolutionary Marxian regime, now securely in the seat of power, and making its dreary way toward political routinization. By the end of the decade it revealed itself, instead, to be riven with factional strife and with fundamental ideological disagreement. Without means for the genuine expression of popular sovereignty, and with its colossal failure even to institutionalize viable procedures of civilian rule and succession at the top, it began to look increasingly like any garden variety twentieth-century dictatorship in which the military frequently intervenes. Ensuing reports of purges and attempted assassinations prolonged the period of profound state insecurity beyond the days of violence in the streets. The general atmosphere of doubt and disarray in the state apparatus endured late into the 1970s. When the "Gang of Four" were finally arrested in something like a palace coup, the world gaped in disbelief at the ease with which the heirs apparent to all the awesome authority of the People's Republic of China could be toppled.

The international security of China has also had an episodic history, with periods of surprising danger and vulnerability. Unlike the Soviets, the Chinese did not find the means to modernize their military. Despite their pride-driven pursuit of a credible nuclear capability, they never resolved to keep up with the military technology of the developed nations of the world. This fact of technological backwardness and relative military weakness contributed, perhaps, to the prudence China's leaders tended to display in involving themselves in international conflicts. Also important, of course, was the fact that China never really assumed membership in a stable international alliance. Its several brief adventures in international conflict, confined generally to its borders and adjacent regions, also therefore never seemed to be driven by considerations of global power balance, but tended instead to be derived from conditions quite immediate and ad hoc.

Involvement in the Korean War, and the various mobilizations of resources and sentiment it justified, probably assisted the infant state in the consolidation of its power and authority at home. Other border conflicts—with India in the early 1960s, and with the Soviet Union in 1969—were contained. Chinese civilian and military leaders were always very careful to signal their intentions of keeping their armed conflicts restrained, even when they protested that surrender was not negotiable. While they were still declaring world war to be inevitable, the Chinese swung toward the West in the early 1970s, and this marked their first foray into superpower balancing. It was a limited but shrewd move that carried few risks for them. In retrospect, it would appear at least marginally to have improved the security of the nation, perhaps the world. Yet, by the end of the decade of the 1970s, Chinese state leaders had allowed themselves to be provoked into a bloody and embarassingly botched conflict with the Vietnamese. This episode revealed to other powers quite starkly once again the relative weakness of the Chinese military and the unpreparedness of the state to safeguard its international security.

In sum, the Chinese state's record of accomplishment, in its pursuit of the goal of domestic and international security over the first three decades, was decidedly mixed. A single trend is hard to discern. It is not at all clear that the state was stronger in this regard at the end of the period than it had been at the beginning. And a good case might well be made for thinking it was weaker.

Hegemony

Modern states seek ideological "hegemony" as Gramsci used the expression; they attempt to set the terms—both empirical and normative—in which most public issues are conceptualized and discussed in society, and they seek to dominate that public discourse, driving it in directions that suit both their short-term policy goals and their long-term state-building ambitions. They utilize all the informational, educational, scientific-technical, ceremonial, and artistic resources at their command to promote their vocabularies and systems of meaning, their messages and preferred interpretations, among the people. Existing social groups, whose historical roots and whose very raison d'etre are most often to be found in dramatically different universes of moral meaning, may be bombarded with state-originated "informational" and "educational" messages in a calculated effort to integrate those groups and their individual members more securely into the officially countenanced social cosmos and conception. Hegemony is thought to be achieved when all the various groups in society are in fact constrained publicly (and to a certain extent also even privately) to conceptualize and express their own interests and aspirations in terms acceptable to and validated by the holders of power. If ideological hegemony is achieved, then, even the very interests and ideals that individuals and social groups are able to pose for themselves, or imagine for their future, are heavily bounded and determined by the preconceptions and limits of the hegemonic discourse that is available for them and others in society to employ.[12]

There can be little doubt that the postrevolutionary state in China achieved a high degree of success in pursuing the goal of ideological hegemony. In fact, the whole realm of propaganda and what was referred to as "thought work" received unusually heavy emphasis, even for a socialist state, in China under Mao. Several factors contributed to this propensity to prefer tight control of the political and social discourse. In part it was attributable to the special requirement that Marxism-Leninism as a social philosophy has imposed upon itself—to be popularly understood and accepted as not only useful but also historically true. "Reeducation" of the masses properly to understand their own history has thus been a familiar part of the Marxist-Leninist project, wherever it has been undertaken. Also, in the case of China, certain traditional ways of thinking about government, politics, and popular motivation—especially those deriving from the Confucian philosophy and its precepts on statecraft—tended to legitimize and support the party-state's drive to achieve a more perfect public harmony through societywide unanimity of thought and purpose. Finally, it cannot be forgotten, Mao Zedong's personal proclivity to stress the power of human thought and will in the making and the changing of history and social reality focused both great weight and great promise on "thought work" and the conscious remolding of people's attitudes and beliefs.

The Chinese people thus were made to endure long periods of intense party-state propaganda barrage, recurring demands that they publicly confess and vow to rectify even the pettiest examples of their own incorrect thinking, and demands also that they criticize and ostracize others—friends, colleagues, and family members—whose thoughts and behavior fell outside the officially accepted bounds. Besides propaganda there was, especially during Mao's later years, a stupendous state-coordinated effort to "purify" and "proletarianize" Chinese culture in virtually all of its means of expression. Most obvious, of course, was the repeated pummeling and purging of China's intellectuals, on grounds that they remained unreconstructed carriers of the old culture and vectors of various bourgeois disorders.

Other known or suspected sources of heterodoxy were purged as well, however. Organized religious practice was banned for all practical purposes, and popular religion, ridiculed as mere superstition and a waste of good money, was sharply restricted if not quite annihilated. The popular arts were also subjected to the party-state's passion for purification. Literary works were heavily censored; those not portraying a sufficiently proletarian spirit became unavailable to the reading public, and their authors were dismissed from their posts or otherwise punished. Even music that was deemed "old-fashioned," "foreign," or otherwise insalubrious was not broadcast on the state radio network. At the height of the pressure, during the Cultural Revolution, only a handful of revolutionary operas and musical works, which embodied the inspirational values and approved political messages of the party-state, were permitted to be performed throughout China. The virtual isolation of the Chinese people from other countries and cultures of the world at that time made the tasks of moral and cultural domination all the easier for the state to attempt. All human knowledge, even modern science itself, became subject to the party-state's "revolutionary" revalorization. "Good" science was that which yielded use-value for the people and for production; "bad" science was that which yielded only knowledge for its own sake and ran the risk, therefore, of appropriation by the forces of reaction in society.

The discourse about political and social life in China was most plainly dominated by the hegemonic ideology of the state—often even to the edge of absurdity. Current information disseminated through the state-run news media was highly controlled and cast always in terms of social values and political analysis that fit the prevailing preoccupations of the discourse of state. Ordinary people were certainly affected in their daily life by this powerful effort to change their thinking. There is little doubt that, in part at least, most people did come to identify themselves and to relate to one another in the highly charged moral, social, and political categories—such as "poor peasant," "rich peasant," "rightist," and "ruffian"—that were promulgated and made potent by the state.

Still, hegemony too has its practical limitations. Social groups in the thrall of a state-dominated discourse may, it is true, be constrained to employ the official moral lexicon as they justify and pursue their own goals and interests; but in doing so they may also and just as clearly engage in struggle for control over the real meaning of the words they and all other social groups are compelled to use.[13] On occasion, the social struggle waged for power over and within the terms of the official discourse can become so intense that the official moral vocabulary itself loses coherence and integrity. The combat for control over meaning can alter meaning; and those who conduct that combat may (intentionally or unintentionally) mock the official discourse, even as they present themselves as its most faithful practitioners.

China's Cultural Revolution provided daily examples of this sort of hegemonic deterioration. All parties to the factional strife that dominated the politics of the entire period adhered determinedly to the vocabulary of Marxism–Leninism–Mao Zedong Thought. Indeed, they glorified Mao's every utterance, memorized long passages from the sacred texts of the revolution, and vowed constancy to its principles and purposes at every opportunity. Nonetheless, these same groups and factions gave widely divergent, even diametrically opposed, interpretations to those texts and sayings; each group reading (not to say twisting) the party-state's messages to suit its own needs in the otherwise unrestrained social competition of the times. Who will ever forget those days when "ultra-left" really meant "ultra-right," and when every newspaper, tabloid, and big-character poster talked about "sham revolutionaries and traitors" and sported headlines such as, "WHO ARE THE REAL 'MONSTERS,' 'FREAKS,' AND 'SCABS'?"

There were many accidental casualties in the Cultural Revolution, and the credibility, viability, and applicability of the party-state's own ideological and moral lexicon were certainly among them. The social struggle itself, ostensibly conducted strictly within the boundaries of the state's own ruling discourse, actually challenged, distorted, and ultimately undermined the ideological hegemony that the party-state earlier had labored so intently to press into the popular mind.

The limits of the Maoist party-state's ideological hegemony have more recently been revealed to us in other ways as well. The last decade has seen the reemergence of many old values, attitudes, popular beliefs, and social practices previously excoriated and maligned by the authority of the revolutionary party-state. The alacrity with which so many people in China have resumed acquisitive and entrepreneurial attitudes and values during the last decade of "reform," for example—attitudes and values hitherto associated most directly with all the reactionary evils of bourgeois-capitalism—certainly suggests that three decades of the party-state's nearly incessant anticapitalist propaganda did not manage to expunge such inclinations from many hearts and minds. The widespread return of young and old alike to both organized and popular religious practice all over China during the last decade likewise suggests the failure of the secular state's protracted efforts to erase "silly myths and superstitions" from the people's consciousness.[14]

The swift resurfacing of family and traditional life-cycle ceremonials, of pilgrimages and propitiatory offerings to the gods, of shamanism, fortunetelling, spirit chasing, and the like—as if these practices and the values associated with them had never been officially disparaged and suppressed—is especially revealing of the limits of party-state hegemony. For these popular practices evince a belief in another world, another realm of experience, which lies beyond the power of the very secular science of the socialist state even to comprehend. The millions of people who, we now know, continued to harbor religious beliefs and convictions throughout the Mao years were not just disagreeing with some of the party-state's propaganda messages; they were conceiving of quite a separate sphere of knowledge and reality, one simply not akin to, and certainly not subject to, the sort of reality and knowledge so aggressively purveyed by the state.

This is not to suggest that the ideological hegemony achieved and sustained by the party-state through the first thirty years of rule did not have dramatically deep and lasting effects on the thoughts and behavior of almost all Chinese citizens. It is only to note the resilience, in the face of protracted propaganda barrages, of alternative discursive traditions concerning social organization, morality, human values, and the meaning of life. Alternative beliefs—even alternative cosmologies—endured in the mind, under cover as it were, to provide order and meaning again when the discursive hegemony of the party-state faltered.

In sum, the Chinese state's experience provides us with some perplexing contrasts in its pursuit of ideological hegemony. Few other modern states have tried harder or more consistently to set the terms of social discourse than the postrevolutionary Chinese state. And few, perhaps, have done more to penetrate popular thought, and to monitor and control popular behavior. Yet the very ideological hegemony of the party-state left the social struggles of the 1960s unresolved and unresolvable in its own terms, thus creating the conditions for widespread and ever more corrosive alienation, cynicism, and other forms of popular disbelief to fester. By the end of the 1970s then, the way was clearly open for alternative moral discourses, some of which had been sheltering there in the social underbrush all along, to emerge once more as a newly renovated public philosophy was being called for and was fashioned. The ideological hegemony of the postrevolutionary Chinese party-state, long thought to be all but impregnable, was looking rather frayed and wearing very thin by the late 1970s.

Legitimacy

Modern states need to develop and maintain an appropriate level of legitimation for their rule. Although a monopoly over the legitimate means of coercion in society can be regarded as the sine qua non of effective state sovereignty, constant reliance upon coercion to ensure popular compliance is not only an inefficient and expensive strategy, but probably ultimately a self-defeating one. "Rulers," as Young observes, "find their tasks simplified if volitional compliance supplants fear-driven obedience."[15] Since citizens are more apt to make voluntary sacrifices for governments they regard as rightfully governing, modern rulers try to garner and sustain popular faith in and support for their regimes. They may do this by means of constitutions or covenants, by their establishment of consultative procedures or participatory institutions, by means of popular education or indoctrination, and especially by means of their effective maintenance of social order and their manifestly good management of the national economy.

How legitimate any government actually is, is unfortunately a highly subjective matter. Popular legitimacy may be thought of as a function of the difference between a citizenry's reasonable expectations about state performance and its actual beliefs about how that state is performing. Gauging a state's legitimacy, therefore, means getting somehow inside the private thoughts of ordinary citizens. Since reliable attitudinal survey research for China between 1949 and 1979 does not exist, there will never be much that can be said with empirically supported certainty about the postrevolutionary state's accomplishments or failures in pursuit of the goal of legitimacy during that period. However, perhaps surprisingly, given the rather mixed and muddy state performance profile sketched out in this discussion so far, the great mass of the anecdotal data that we do have—from émigré interviews, eyewitness accounts, personal memoirs, and the like—clearly indicates that the postrevolutionary state enjoyed an extraordinarily high and wide measure of legitmacy during its first thirty years.[16] If one insists on speculating—and that, as I have said, is all that one can do—on how and why the party-state managed so long to preserve so much of its popular legitimacy despite all, one must look again at a few general features of the system and the situation.

The postrevolutionary state certainly did everything it could from the start to set the Chinese people's expectations of its rule at a very high level. It pledged itself to bring about sweeping changes in society, to revive and reorder the economy, and to set the nation on a course toward prosperity, modernity and authentic democracy. In the first decade, the changes actually wrought by the regime were epochal indeed. Through the swift accomplishment of most of its initial programs to foster economic growth, greater equality, and socialist transformation, the new state fairly earned the faith of many.

By the time of the post–Great Leap disaster, however, when the early brilliance should have begun to tarnish, the party-state had already achieved such strict control over information and its circulation in society that much of the brutally bad news simply failed to be reported to the people at large. Party-state control and censorship of the media played a major role in this, of course. But equally important may have been the fact that by then the basic internal structure of Chinese society itself had become exceedingly segmented, even parcelized.

By the early 1960s, through the institutionalization of the unit (*danwei*) as the all-purpose primary urban social component; through the promotion of people's communes as comprehensive, self-reliant, and highly self-contained units of rural life and production; through the universally administered household registration system and other strict controls on population mobility; and through heavy state regulation of trade, commerce, and other natural forms of lateral social and economic exchange and integration, the Chinese people at large were already increasingly coming to find their lives bounded and confined in highly segmented, small, and quite discrete cells of social organization.[17] Networks of personal, professional, or other relationships that traditionally in the past had helped to span and connect such cells in Chinese society were becoming increasingly difficult to sustain. There was, therefore, a growing shortage of operative formal and informal networks through which popular reservations and apprehensions, private doubts, dissenting views, or indeed any information that could challenge the state's sanitized versions of events might flow.

Without the reality checks that easy access to national, regional, or even county or citywide information networks might have afforded them, there must have been relatively few people (including most cadres and officials) in China who could have known for certain when the state lied. The bigger the lie, perhaps, the smaller the risk of informed social contradiction. The trend toward social cellularization, plus strict state censorship and monopoly of the news media, plus the personally experienced recent history of authentic party-state achievements left much of the population believing lies in the 1960s and 1970s. The popular legitimacy of the party-state was apparently quite effectively, if only temporarily, preserved by these means.

The Cultural Revolution, in this as in so many other domains, was to mark something of a turning point, however. Not only did new networks of lateral social integration arise with the mobilization of all segments of the population to take part in the movement, but the party-state itself started speaking openly to the people with more than one voice. Many voices emanated from the heretofore seemingly so solidary party-state; and they made devastating charges of corruption and deceit against one another. Different official and quasi-official news vehicles took different sides in the struggle and slandered each other as viciously and as often as they were able. Novel sources of information proliferated—the big-character posters, unstructured mass gatherings of all sorts, handbills, Red Guard newspapers, and the never-silent loudspeakers—and these nearly drowned citizens in a tidal wave of turbulently contradictory information on an overwhelming range of public issues.

The very fitness of the party to govern was subjected to searing public scrutiny, and clearly the state suffered numerous bruising blows to its authority over the crooked course of the Cultural Revolution. Finally, the personal prestige of Mao Zedong, Zhou Enlai, Lin Biao, and a few other men was made the unsatisfactory substitute for regime legitimacy. Political stability was not the result. Nor did this device help in any way to stem the forlorn flow of popular political sentiment away from social idealism toward cynicism.

When Mao finally died in 1976 and the little-known Hua Guofeng moved to arrest his closest allies, the "Gang of Four," and then had himself named party chairman in Mao's place, we may well imagine that regime legitimacy was left hanging by a slender thread. In the utter absence of credible governmental alternatives, however, this thread was to hold. Gestures were made to procedural justice—the ''Gang'' would be tried in a court of law; a new constitution would be drafted right away. Gestures were made also to the principles of fairness and representativeness—those who had been tainted by the toxins of the ultraleft would be given an opportunity to examine their consciences and to mend their ways; Deng Xiaoping, twice-banished leader of the ''loyal opposition,'' would be restored to office. Finally, gestures were made to resuming progress once again toward the core and sacred goals of national wealth and power—an ambitious program of industrial, agricultural, scientific, and military modernization was announced. By such means, and at a most precarious pass, the interim ruling group set about the tasks of bracing the fractured foundations of party-state legitimacy.

In sum, with the partial evidence available to us, one can at least dimly trace an evolutionary trajectory with respect to party-state legitimacy that is not unlike the patterns already sketched for other state goals discussed above. Early reserves of revolutionary state legitimacy were great indeed, but they were gradually diminished, through the 1950s, by policy error and patent injustice. Amazingly, however, in the 1960s and 1970s, what residual popular faith and goodwill did remain to the regime were risked repeatedly in social upheaval and were finally exhausted by elite power struggles fraudulently conducted in the name of revolution. The members of China's governing coalition at the end of the decade of the 1970s, having seen so much hard-won state legitimacy already squandered, must have been acutely aware of their need to restore what they could. This surely is part of the reason they came to believe that there was a mandate for bold reforms.

State Organization and State-Society Relations

An exploration of a state's performance in the pursuit of some of its ''goals,'' such as the five goals just considered, cannot alone provide a fully satisfying basis upon which to draw robust conclusions about a state's capacities overall. Judgments about the relative strengths or weaknesses of states must be made with reference to many other questions as well. In particular, much more systematic consideration would have to be given to relevant changes in the internal organization of the state itself, as well as to the changing nature of state-society interactions.

In the Chinese case, for example, troubling questions and tensions about the proper location of authority within the state structure were never fully resolved.[18] Discussions and resolutions concerning the desirable degree of centralization or decentralization of power formed a recurring leitmotif in China's postrevolutionary politics. Besides the systemic tensions inherent in central-local divisions of power, there were also strains traceable to the ministry-by-ministry (or other *xitong*-by-*xitong*) divisions of functional responsibility, administrative oversight, and policy initiative. Structural characteristics such as these, giving rise to the push and pull of central-local bargaining, administrative poaching, and other familiar forms of bureaucratic politics, all naturally were to leave their marks on overall state strength and capacity. Political factionalism, cadre careerism, and other forms of competition and segmentation internal to the party-state apparatus could also be seen alternately accelerating or impeding state responsiveness and performance. All the many case-specific factors such as these would need to be weighed in the balance if one were to derive a fully discriminating evaluation of the powers of state in postrevolutionary China.

Similarly, social structural changes, whether abrupt or gradual, and the effects these changes had on the nature of state-society interactions, would need to be considered much more substantively. Such complex processes as the heightening of individual class identification and the deepening of social cellularization may initially have been "caused" (or anyway abetted) by the state, but they in turn obviously had the power to "affect" the state in the exercise of its capacities as well. Social cellularization tended to enhance the salience of localistic and other parochial sentiments that frequently came between the (perfect) design and the (imperfect) implementation of state policy. Cellularization may also have enhanced the salience and the serviceability of *guanxi* networks and other dubious adaptations to scarcity that again compromised the state's capacity to govern impartially and with popular support.[19] Whether a state is reaching or not reaching its essential "goals" is a matter that can only be judged in full knowledge of all the past and present mutually conditioning interactions that transpire between state and society.

Such an enquiry cannot be attempted here. By reflecting briefly on what fragmentary insights have emerged from this essay's more modest focus on state goals, however, we may hope to bring to light one or two working hypotheses with which eventually to address that much larger analytical task.

State Strengthening and Reform

As this essay has endeavored to illustrate, by the late 1970s it did appear, however counterintuitively, that the Chinese party-state was pursuing a number of its essential goals with less effectiveness than it had shown in the 1950s. In this limited sense, then, it may serve some constructive purpose to offer the hypothesis that at the end of the seemingly strong, certainly austere, and avowedly authoritarian reign of Mao Zedong, China's powers of state were, paradoxically, "weaker" than they had been at the beginning.

In the early 1950s, the party-state that Mao was building, riding the wide crest of the wave of social revolution, patently scored high on every dimension surveyed here; on state autonomy (vis-à-vis both international forces and domestic social elites), on revenue generation, on state security (internal and external), on national ideological hegemony, and most plainly on regime legitimacy. By 1979, despite all the challenging upheavals of the Cultural Revolution, the state apparatus remained captive to a clearly identifiable and very determined social elite—

an elite ironically created by the early revolutionary state itself. Domestic state autonomy was thus much constrained. By 1979, central state revenue portions had long since ceased to expand as the planned economy had long since failed to generate the generous surpluses that were expected. By 1979, state security was in violent and visible jeopardy, with the PLA pathetically embroiled in a losing war against Vietnam and with domestic public security forces tracking underground organizations and arresting political dissidents in several cities. By 1979, the previously unchallenged national hegemony of Mao Zedong Thought was already unraveling under pressure from those both in and out of power. And state legitimacy was so suspect that the Deng Xiaoping regime resolved to rest its own claims to just rule on distancing itself from the policies and the personalities of the past, exposing to public view as many of the old regime's crimes and stupidities as it could uncover or invent.

The post-Mao leadership's all too keen awareness of these very worrisome symptoms of state weakness must be recognized, further, to have been an important factor in their collective decision to embark upon a program of wholesale reform. Central to their strategy, in carrying out reform, was no simple-minded antistatist intention to limit excessive government regulation. In fact, they made no secret from the start of their determination to use reform as a means to renovate and restore the already sorely compromised authority and the partially paralyzed powers of the party-state. Reform of the bureaucracy along meritocratic lines, if carried out successfully, could be expected to yield more, not less, relative autonomy for the state. Reform of the economy along market lines showed promise not of diminishing but of enlarging the state's potential revenue sources. And so on. With hopeful expectations such as these, and with their own intimate and painful knowledge of just how poor state performance had been in the recent past, the post-Mao leadership was impelled toward reform.

This is why it was so mistaken for so many, both inside and outside China, to allow themselves to fall into the habit of thinking that statism and reform, like oil and water, could not be mixed. After the many grisly reminders of 1989, perhaps, none of us will again be so likely to forget how often "state strengthening" and "reform" have been well blended in the political history of China.

Notes

1. This kind of argument has been made with greatest clarity in Theda Skocpol, *States and Social Revolutions* (Cambridge: Harvard University Press, 1979). For a recent discussion of the need to focus again on the "socialist content" of the post-1949 Chinese political experience, however, see "Politics, Scholarship, and Chinese Socialism," in *Marxism and the Chinese Experience*, ed. Arif Dirlik and Maurice Meisner (Armonk, NY: M. E. Sharpe, 1989), pp. 3–26.

2. For one stimulating recent work addressing these important theoretical questions, see Joel S. Migdal, *Strong Societies and Weak States* (Princeton: Princeton University Press, 1988).

3. My selection of these goals for this discussion is loosely adapted from a list given in Crawford Young, "The African Colonial State and Its Political Legacy," in *The Precarious Balance: State and Society in Africa*, ed. Donald Rothchild and Naomi Chazan (Boulder: Westview Press, 1988), pp. 25–66. (I am grateful to Catherine Boone for bringing this valuable source to my attention.) The notes to Young's essay are also useful in providing readers new to the "state theory" literature with an introduction to many of its important works.

4. This discussion is based on Carl Riskin, *China's Political Economy* (New York: Oxford University Press, 1987), p. 76. Riskin observes further that "During the bitter dispute that raged between the two countries in the early 1960s, China rushed to repay its debt early, and did so in 1965."

5. Young, "The African Colonial State," p. 363.

6. Riskin, *China's Political Economy*, pp. 71, 73. According to Riskin, the total state budget revenues rose from 22 percent of GDP in 1952 to 29 percent in 1957.

7. Total state budget revenue in 1979 was just 110.3 billion yuan. (*Statistical Yearbook of China, 1985* [New York: Oxford University Press, 1985].)

8. Riskin, *China's Political Economy*, p. 363.

9. Penelope B. Prime, "Socialism and Economic Development: The Politics of Accumulation in China," in *Marxism and the Chinese Experience*, ed. Dirlik and Meisner, p. 139.

10. Ibid., p. 143.

11. Franz Schurmann, *Ideology and Organization in Communist China* (Berkeley: University of California Press, 1966), p. 314.

12. This assertion applies to modern liberal states as well as to authoritarian systems, even though the intensity of the effort and the techniques employed in the pursuit of hegemony do differ from state-type to state-type and, of course, from state to state. For illuminating explorations into this aspect of the Gramscian notion of hegemony, see Raymond Williams, *Marxism and Literature* (Oxford: Oxford University Press, 1977), and David Laitin, *Hegemony and Culture: Politics and Religious Change Among the Yoruba* (Chicago: University of Chicago Press, 1986).

13. This is one of the basic insights, elaborated with great care, in James C. Scott, *Weapons of the Weak* (New Haven: Yale University Press, 1985).

14. As Watson's essay in this volume suggests, however, folk knowledge and beliefs that have survived the Maoist era cannot be assumed to have come through unscathed. Some have suffered what might be regarded as an erosion of their original richness. Others have clearly been modified and adapted to changing circumstances created by the experiences of state socialism. For more on the dynamic relationship between folk culture and state ideological hegemony in China, see Helen F. Siu, "Socialist Peddlers and Princes in a Chinese Market Town," *American Ethnologist* 16, (1989):195–212; and *Agents and Victims in South China* (New Haven: Yale University Press, 1989).

15. Young, "The African Colonial State," p. 32.

16. Most individual citizens who have commented report that they personally did believe in their government and that they actually had immense faith in and respect for the party, the PLA, and Mao and other state leaders, even well into the period of the Cultural Revolution. This remained true even for many thoughtful individuals who were themselves victimized by the political system in place. See, for example, Yue Daiyun and Carolyn Wakeman, *To the Storm* (Berkeley: University of California Press, 1985).

17. This process of social cellularization is discussed in much more detail than is possible here in Vivienne Shue, *The Reach of the State: Sketches of the Chinese Body Politic* (Stanford: Stanford University Press, 1988), esp. chap. 4. As argued there, the trend toward exaggerated social segmentation or parcelization, already visible in the

1960s, was nonetheless much intensified during the 1970s.

18. And indeed, in a recent review of the issue, Paul Cohen has concluded "that the very size of the Chinese polity renders it improbable that . . . the tension between centralizing and decentralizing forces can ever be permanently relaxed" ("The Post-Mao Reforms in Historical Perspective," *Journal of Asian Studies* 47, 3).

19. These necessarily brief speculations are developed further in Shue, *The Reach of the State*, chap. 4.

10

THE PATTERN AND LEGACY OF ECONOMIC GROWTH IN THE MAO ERA

BARRY NAUGHTON

From the beginning of China's contact with the West, the overwhelming need for economic development has been recognized by virtually all Chinese leaders and intellectuals. The Communist party and the Guomindang struggled to the death but shared remarkably similar visions of the state accelerating and guiding the economic development process. This consensus was not unique to China, of course, and images of the heroic struggle for economic construction echo through the domestic propaganda of Korea, the Soviet Union, and many other developing countries. But for better or worse, it was the Communist party in China that actually laid the framework of institutional change and accelerated industrialization, and accomplished the first stage of a fundamental and inevitable historical transformation. How does one evaluate the achievements and shortcomings of that effort? Was the Chinese development strategy under Mao a success or a failure? What was the legacy left to post-Mao China?

Simply by asking these questions, one implicitly raises another: Was the economic performance of Maoist China really as bad as one would conclude from the ritual condemnations of that era that regularly accompany discussions of today's China? There appears to be a fundamental contradiction between the overwhelmingly negative appraisal of the Chinese economy pre-1978 and an overall growth performance substantially more impressive than any other low-income nation. Is it possible to resolve this contradiction? In this essay, I address these questions through a discussion of economic strategies followed and results achieved in China during three different subperiods: the 1950s, dominated by Soviet assistance and advice; the Great Leap Forward (overlapping at first with the previous period) and its catastrophic aftermath; and a third period beginning around 1964 and extending past the death of Mao. Examining different aspects of the very different experiences in these periods, I make inferences about the success or failure of the development effort in each.

Chinese development policy after 1949 includes major success and disastrous failure. The initial accomplishment—establishing institutions to increase saving and successfully investing in accelerated economic growth—was remarkable. This success was aided—indeed made possible—by tremendous Soviet assistance. The 1950s created a legacy that was overwhelmingly positive for economic growth in the medium run, while also containing some potentially serious problems. Subsequently, rather than addressing these problems, policy shifted and was instead dominated by the Great Leap Forward, the split with the Soviet Union, and a progressive militarization of the Chinese economy. The short-run result was disastrous and, after recovery, was followed by a progressive deterioration of the planning capabilities of the economy, and a massive waste of resources. These negative policies resulted in only a modest deceleration of the economy initially, because of the built-in momentum created in the 1950s, but gradually eroded the foundations upon which growth was built. The result for the entire 1952–78 period was a respectable growth of output, combined with massive waste of the fruits of growth and a surprisingly negative legacy to the inheritors of the economy post-Mao.

In an essay of this sort, it may be worthwhile to declare biases and briefly sketch the perspective on the economic development process that informs the discussion. I see economic development as being dominated by a process of accumulation of capital—not just physical capital but also, and even more importantly, the "human capital" of technical, administrative, and entrepreneurial skills. There are long time lags in the development process: creation of new capital enhances productivity not only in the present but also for a long time into the future. Moreover, enhanced human skills increase productivity not only by making workers more productive in ordinary tasks, but also by giving society as a whole better problem-solving skills that are useful in meeting the new challenges that inevitably arise. The experience of other East Asian economies since World War II demonstrates that countries that invest steadily in human skills and physical capital can experience gradual acceleration of economic growth over an extended period, and economic transformation that is remarkably rapid by historical standards. While China is held back by the existence of regions with poor transportation and populations with limited land and skills, still, everything about the post-1949 record indicates that China is also capable of accelerating growth to very high levels if it can persevere in policies that will steadily accumulate beneficial effects.

In spite of the generally superior efficiency of markets in matching present needs and available goods, governments can intervene very effectively in the development process when they take steps to accelerate the accumulation of physical and human capital. The government can do that by creating an environment that rewards private individuals for those investments, or it can organize the investments itself. There may be some losses in efficiency when the government intervenes, but if planning is done well, those losses will be overwhelmingly outweighed by the benefits of increased capital accumulation and growth. If, however, planning is not done well, it can create staggering losses that more than offset the benefits of increased investment. Moreover, as economies become more complex, the task of planning becomes increasingly complex and harder to do well. Thus, at some point, China would probably have found it necessary to institute economic reforms with a greater role for the market, regardless of its experience with planning. In the actual case, though, China's experience with central planning failed not because of some inherent flaw to planning, but because China failed to do it properly.

In the following, I concentrate mainly on development strategy and the growth of industry, and largely neglect agriculture. Agricultural growth has been slow enough to act as a brake on overall development, but rapid enough to satisfy most basic needs. One's assessment of agricultural performance depends largely on the extent to which one views agriculture as being fundamentally constrained by limitations on land, water, and fertilizer, or whether one believes that better incentives and organizations would permit peasants to find ways to surmount these limitations. I am not an expert in this area, and I have nothing useful to add to the existing literature.[1] The neglect of agriculture may also be justified because Chinese development strategy customarily has given greatest importance to industrialization. Indeed, one of the themes of the following is that not just industrialization, but also industrialization for the purpose of military strength, was one of the major driving forces of Chinese economic strategy through much of this period, and that this objective distorted the entire pattern of development. Perhaps this is not surprising, for the initial consensus for economic development among leadership elites was always linked and subordinated to the need to build a strong nation. Nation building in an era of nuclear superpowers has imposed a huge burden on Chinese development.

Comparative Growth Performance

A baseline for consideration of economic growth can be drawn by examining changes in national income per head. Constant fluctuation in China's economy makes choosing end points difficult (there are no "normal" years), but comparing two "peak" years, 1953 and 1978, official Chinese data on net material product—a version of national income—indicate average annual growth of 6 percent. Population growth was almost exactly 2 percent per annum, and so net material product per capita grew at 4 percent annually. Comparison with other developing countries is given in table 1. While not as good as superstars like Korea, China's overall performance is quite strong, arguably better than a country like Brazil, which grew faster but accumulated a large debt. Moreover, China

Table 1

Growth of National Income Per Capita

Country	Percentage
China: NMP 1953–78	4.0
Others: GNP 1960–80	
India	1.4
Pakistan	2.8
Indonesia	4.0
Thailand	4.7
Brazil	5.1
Korea	7.0

Sources: China 1988 Statistical Yearbook, pp. 52, 97; World Bank, *World Development Report 1982*, pp. 110–11.

grew much more rapidly than other low-income countries, such as India and Pakistan.

China's official figures overstate the growth performance somewhat. The methodology used overstates growth rates because the definition of national income used and the Chinese price structure both give a large weight to the rapidly growing industrial sector, and a small weight to slower-growing agriculture and services. Chinese practice of linking successive growth indexes instead of revaluing all output in a consistent price basis also leads to some overstatement. An attempt to adjust fully for these problems might lead to a per capita growth figure closer to 3 percent than 4 percent. Such a correction is not attempted here. It would be tedious and sensitive to a number of assumptions; moreover, sustained growth over 3 percent per year would still be quite a successful performance, beyond any other low-income country, and result in more than a doubling of output per head over a twenty-five-year period. The fundamental question with regard to China's performance is not whether output has grown rapidly—it has—but rather whether growth rates approached their potentials, whether a healthy foundation was laid for future growth, and whether the fruits of growth were distributed in a reasonable fashion.

The Early Achievement

It is now common to look back on the 1950s as a kind of "golden age" of China's development, and this was in fact a period of remarkable achievement. In this achievement, the assistance of the Soviet Union played an indispensable role. The accomplishment can be summarized into two categories: (1) the establishment of a mechanism to increase saving and investment; and (2) effective policies to allocate that investment (including the creation of institutions that could be used to make allocation decisions).

Increasing Saving

The most fundamental task required to accelerate economic growth is to increase investment. There are several ways to do this: some countries rely on foreign investment to increase the supply of savings available domestically; some rely on gradually increasing private domestic saving. Planned economies are distinctive in relying almost entirely on domestic savings that are controlled directly by the government and channeled through the government budget. In China, the new leadership was able to take advantage of the economic recovery brought about by the restoration of order after 1949 to push up saving: production revived while living standards remained low. During the chaos of war and inflation, the terms of trade had moved against agriculture. Disruption of links with the city meant that industrial goods had become expensive relative to agricultural goods: about 20 percent more expensive than in the 1930s.[2] Simply by preventing living standards from rising too quickly—by preventing the terms of trade from swinging back toward agriculture—the government was able to capture much of the increment to production. In essence, this was done by keeping prices of industrial products relatively high while costs fell as production revived. When high-priced industrial consumer goods were sold to the population, the profits and taxes earned flowed into the state budget. The government was able to do this because it exerted monopoly control over the commercial system and could thus dictate prices both of agricultural procurement and of industrial sales.

This is the standard fiscal system of Soviet-style economies: but whereas in the Soviet Union these financial relationships were obtained by a traumatic spoliation of the peasantry, they appeared in China "naturally" as the outcome of economic recovery. The Soviet Union had lacked control over the commerce system before collectivization, and thus resorted to quasi-military methods and dramatic inflation in order to push up the national rate of saving. In China (as in the Eastern European countries) such drastic measures were unnecessary. Moreover, since the Chinese government gained control of the commerce and price systems early on, it was able to use those systems to facilitate agricultural collectivization, rather than using collectives as the immediate instrument for augmenting state revenues. Chinese collectivization was carried out smoothly primarily because, unlike their Soviet predecessors, the Chinese had already established a network of state-controlled institutions in the countryside. Virtually all agricultural trade was controlled by the supply and marketing cooperatives, which had over 30,000 rural branches (about 15 per county); while rural credit cooperatives had been established in over 80 percent of rural townships, and indeed incorporated 60 percent of total rural households were members of credit coops. Indeed, by the time of collectivization, the government had run training courses for half a million accounting personnel in the countryside, providing a source for coop personnel with at least rudimentary training.[3] These conditions were decidedly lacking in the Soviet Union. Of course, redistributive land reform made it easier to keep average rural living standards growing at only moderate rates, because expropriation, relative equality, and a measure of income security all made the majority more satisfied with the growth that existed.

In the fiscal system that was created, most of the tax revenues of the government (and consequently most of the financial resources for investment) were accumulated within the industrial sector. Some direct taxes were also levied on the agricultural sector, but the burden of "forced saving" or taxation on the rural sector was primarily felt indirectly, in the form of low procurement prices for agricultural products. Peasants were required to deliver their output to the state at prices below those that would have prevailed if free market exchange was in operation, a type of unequal exchange that socialist economists refer to as the "scissors gap."

The existence of the "scissors gap" is sometimes treated as a sign of "urban bias." But here one must be careful. In an underdeveloped country, in which 80 percent of the people are rural residents, the burden of increased domestic saving inevitably falls predominantly on rural residents. There is simply no other adequate source of savings. The crucial point is not that the burden of saving and financing government services falls on rural people, but rather that agriculture becomes nonlucrative relative to other types of productive activity. It is a type of activity, rather than a category of person, that is disfavored by such a policy. As a result, when individuals have control over resources (including their own labor power), they seek to channel those resources away from agriculture and into other types of activity—such as industry—where they can earn higher incomes.

While agricultural production was disfavored, industrial production was privileged. The vast bulk of state revenues were generated within industry and appeared sometimes as taxes and sometimes as profit, which were then remitted directly to the state budget. The absolute level of profitability of industry, ultimately determined by the markup over cost on goods sold to households for consumption, was maintained high by the "scissors gap." By 1957, 50 percent of government revenues were generated within industry, and by 1964, more than 70 percent, a number that has been at least maintained since.[4] This system also had a high buoyancy. Revenues were collected within industry: as industry grew more rapidly than national income as a whole, the rate of revenue collection, and thus the national saving rate, tended to rise. The nation was thus launched onto the path of economic development, with economic growth leading to higher saving and investment that could in turn fuel further growth.

Investment Allocation

It is not enough to generate saving: the saving must be channeled into appropriate investments. This was also done during the 1950s. The creation of new physical capital, particularly in industry, was strikingly successful. During the rehabilitation of the national economy, investment was concentrated on the Northeast ("Manchuria"), which received about 25 percent of total investment. The substantial legacy of Japanese heavy industrial plants formed a basis for development and practically demanded a concentrated response. By 1952, the Northeast had surpassed the peak output levels obtained under the Japanese and was accounting for almost 40 percent of total industrial output. The First Five-Year Plan followed with an emphasis on a group of 156 large projects imported from the Soviet Union. These projects were given top priority that led to quick results: the average completion time for these projects was only 3.6 years, substantially above the subsequent performance of the Chinese economy.[5] Mistakes were made: overall strategy neglected the potential of Shanghai and other coastal economic centers, and some of the large inland plants turned into huge white elephants. The steel mill at Baotou and the dam at Sanmenxia would rank well up on a global list of costly fiascos. Yet, in spite of the failings, overall assessment of this investment program must be overwhelmingly positive. A remarkably comprehensive heavy industrial base was created in a very short time. This was a "big push" industrialization, but a big push was precisely what the Chinese economy needed for the rapid creation of new industrial sectors. Moreover, this big push was accompanied by rising living standards.

The investment in human capital was, in some ways, even more important. It was characteristic of the 1950s that large-scale investment in physical capital was accompanied by large-scale creation of institutions to develop human capital. Networks of keypoint universities and research institutes were founded, and there was widespread establishment of training and vocational schools. Skilled manpower to operate every aspect of the economic system was developed based on the Soviet experience. An estimated 38,000 scientists, technicians, and workers were trained in the Soviet Union between 1950 and 1960, while 11,000 Soviet experts came to work in China. The really striking thing about the development of human capital during this period was how pervasive it was. Skills were being developed simultaneously at nearly every level of expertise, and through nearly all available channels. Training of scientists and administrators was matched with training of workers and technicians; knowledge was transmitted through blueprints and designs, as well as training and on-site advisers. A rough match between the supply of skills provided and the demand for skills was assured by the pervasive Soviet role on both sides of this equation.[6]

Thus, one can go back to the 1950s and see that the indicators of growth were very good. Even more striking is the fact that the conditions for future growth were also improving. New industrial capacity was just beginning to be brought on stream; newly trained people were just taking up new jobs. Indeed, most of the actual increase in output through 1957 was wrung out of plants that already existed in 1949, and the Soviet-aided projects were just beginning to contribute.[7] A virtuous cycle had been created, based on three factors. First, there were time lags before investments already made could be brought to peak efficiency. Second, the investment rate was on a natural escalator that would expand the future flow of investments. Third, investments had been made in depth, particularly in engineering capacity and educational institutions that would allow China to begin creating more of its own capital and augmenting its own human skills.

The Soviet Role

There is a frequent tendency in the China field to play down the importance of Soviet assistance in the 1950s. Writers often stress the small size of direct Soviet aid, and the fact that it was in the form of loans rather than outright grants. Obviously, the bitterness felt by the Chinese after the Sino-Soviet split also contributed to numerous statements minimizing the importance of Soviet assistance. But these views are completely untenable. The successful Chinese accomplishment during the 1950s would have been inconceivable without the substantial assistance of the Soviet Union.

First, the sheer magnitude of the Soviet presence is such that if one judges the Chinese economy to have been a success in the 1950s, one must inevitably accord the Soviet Union a significant part of the credit. About 50 percent of industrial investment during the First Five-Year Plan was either for equipment imported from the USSR and Eastern Europe or for domestic projects that directly supported the Soviet plants. A large proportion of new industrial capacity created during the First Plan period came directly from the imported plants, with 58 percent of new rolled steel capacity and 40 percent of new electrical capacity directly from those imports.[8] Moreover, these plants were accompanied by blueprints and technicians, amounting to one of the largest transfers of technology in world history. Generally speaking, there were no industrial secrets between "fraternal socialist" countries, and the complementarity of Soviet equipment, training, and technical assistance was of incalculable value.

Moreover, imports of machinery were actually accelerating through this period: according to figures compiled from international trade statistics, China imported U.S. $2.2 billion worth of machinery from the Soviet Union and Eastern European countries through 1957, but U.S. $2.55 billion in 1958–61.[9] Since it would certainly take at least one to three years from the time of importation to full capacity operation of these projects ("ramping up"), Soviet bloc equipment was making a direct contribution to Chinese output growth well into the 1960s. During the Great Leap Forward, despite the madness of backyard steel mills, a substantial proportion of increased output came from the large Soviet-supplied plants coming on stream. Although uncertainties of valuation make precise figures impossible, as late as 1965, at least one-third of the total machinery installed in Chinese industry had been imported from the Soviet Union or Eastern Europe.[10]

The Soviet Union made a fundamental contribution in another way, beyond the huge direct contribution to China's industrial development. This was the enormous savings in time and expense made possible by the provision of a complete development model. In the first place, the prestige of the Soviet model permitted the Chinese leadership quickly to reach a consensus on development policy and avoid political conflict and experimentation. China, like Eastern Europe, was able to avoid the costly and generally inflationary period when revolutionary success is followed by economic fumbling and bitter experience with unrealistic policies. Debate over economic strategy was postponed until late 1955 or 1956, by which time several years of substantial economic successes had already been recorded. Moreover, the nature of Soviet across-the-board aid permitted rapid progress in several areas simultaneously. While economic planners were being trained, direct Soviet assistance allowed the drafting of the first plans to proceed quickly: as one well-known Chinese economist put it, the First Five-Year Plan was drawn up "half in Beijing and half in Moscow." While the institutions to manage a planned economy were being created, an investment program centered on a limited number of attainable but crucial projects was already underway. While technicians were being trained, Soviet designs could be used for the construction of new plants. Economic construction could begin at the same time as the building of an administrative structure and the training of a skilled manpower base, rather than waiting until after these had been accomplished. Since mass development of human skills was combined with the revolutionary removal of entrenched social obstacles to development, the result was extremely rapid progress. This remarkable record of progress on virtually all fronts simultaneously could not conceivably have occurred without Soviet help.

Some Ambiguities of Early Success

One can unequivocably judge the first period of Chinese development as a success, but the legacy of that success was not entirely unambiguous. On the positive side, a substantial economic and technological dynamism had been imparted to the Chinese economy. A whole set of new technologies, just being mastered, were now available to serve as starting points for domestic technological development. Indeed, through the 1970s, in a vast range of fields from rockets to accounting, Chinese developments can be traced back to a Russian origin. This technological capability was another kind of capital stock that would contribute to future development.

On the negative side, the successes of the First Five-Year Plan were taken somewhat for granted in China and were attributed to the superiority of socialist development strategy and the natural talent and industriousness of the Chinese people. The catastrophe of the Great Leap Forward was wrought by leaders who were blind to the magnitude of the accomplishment during the early part of the 1950s, since they failed to appreciate how difficult that achievement had really been: in some ways the successes were "too easy." Moreover, the growth through 1957 had been accompanied by a progressive increase in the level of planning and degree of state control of the economy. It was easy to attribute success to the fact of planning and the fact of state control, rather than to the amount of expertise that was brought to bear on economic decision making. In fact, both increased steadily during this period, but whereas in the preceding paragraphs I have attributed success to the increase in expertise and physical investment, the Chinese quite naturally tended to attribute success to the increasingly socialistic nature of the economy.

Yet to a large extent, the economy that functioned during the 1950s was a mixed one. Private industry grew until socialization in 1956, and even state-run factories had a great deal of freedom. Machinery enterprises, for example, were able to sell a portion of their above-plan output, contract bank loans that were repayable within a year, and hire new workers independently as long as they were within their wage bill limits.[11] There was much talk of central planning, but precisely because of the difficulty of erecting a comprehensive planning structure, the existing organizations didn't try to do too much. Central planning focused on the large-scale investment projects and not much else; a small-scale unplanned sector persisted through much of the period. Because it was easy to recognize limitations to the planning process, the system had a lot of flexibility. The combination of maximum expertise concentrated on a few large-scale state projects and maximum flexibility to the remainder of the economy is probably close to optimal. But the lessons of the First Five-Year Plan were certainly not seen in that way by Mao or most others in the Chinese leadership.

Finally, there were a number of difficult problems related to the nature of the system the government had created to increase national saving and pump it into industrial investment. I mentioned above that government manipulation of prices was used to privilege industry, enhancing profitability within industry and using this as the predominant source of government revenues. Within a totally centralized economy, such a system would not make much difference: the government, having arbitrarily defined prices to accumulate profits in industry, would simply appropriate those profits to itself. But to the extent that there is any freedom of movement or autonomous control over productive resources in the economy, those resources will tend to be drawn into industry, as those who control resources attempt to reap some of the excess returns generated in that sector. Industry will exert a powerful attractive force, as long as the government can maintain higher returns in industry than in other sectors.

It is worth stressing how peculiar this fiscal system is. The state, in theory, owns all the land and mineral resources in the country; has control over international trade and domestic commerce; and manages every sector directly or indirectly. Yet the state "chooses" to set a zero rental rate on land; a zero price for mineral deposits; a zero personal income tax; very low customs duties; and low prices for the products of agriculture, transportation, construction, and commerce. This makes the state almost entirely reliant on industry, which becomes the sole sector that is rich and powerful. In the short run, the system succeeds in increasing saving, but in the long run it creates a stunted fiscal structure, in which all the aspirations of the state are made dependent on what is essentially a single source of tax revenue. The ideological priority given to industry and industrial workers is thus matched by the financial priority given to industry, at the cost of a substantial distortion to the incentives created within the system.

The maintenance of a rich industrial sector inevitably implies a relatively poor rural economy. To some extent, rural collectives were designed to enforce this poverty, because of their role in ensuring compulsory deliveries of agricultural products, guaranteeing the profitability of industry and the supply of revenue to the government. Yet while collectives are useful in extracting a surplus from rural areas, the state monopoly on commerce is more fundamental in this respect, and Chinese collectives were not nearly as closely identified with the extractive function as were Soviet cooperative farms. More essential is the importance of collectives in compensating for the enforced poverty of rural areas by providing an alternative way to tax the agricultural population directly for the provision of social services. Without industry, the rural areas are fiscally poor, generating no revenues directly. The collectives permitted the creation of a demonetized administrative structure. In particular, social services were provided largely through defining certain activities as worthy of workpoints, and supplementing this from rural industrial profits and selective fiscal subsidies. This aspect of the rural economic system achieved substantial successes. By 1975, this system provided 85 percent of the rural population with some kind of basic medical insurance; enrolled 121 million children in elementary school; and provided moderate welfare benefits to a substantial part of the low-income population. As a result of these measures and the general increase and equalization of food availability, life expectancy at birth had increased from forty to sixty-five years during the period under consideration here. This put China well ahead of other poor nations, and ahead of some middle-income nations like Brazil.[12] A centrally mandated, nonmonetized program of self-taxation in rural areas spread social services widely at minimum administrative cost. However, this system was inseparable from the collective organization of agricultural production, and the failure to create a broadly based system for financing rural services was to create difficulties later on.

The Great Leap Forward

The Great Leap Forward was a period of drama and conflict, of bizarre ideology and shifting policy. China tried to do everything at once: while "walking on two legs" was one of the slogans of the day, "walking on fourteen legs" would be more accurate. Even as investment soared, consumption also grew rapidly during 1958–59, as peasants moved into high-income jobs in cities or rural industry. Besides leaps in material production, there were "leaps" in the production of poetry and short stories, and a massive establishment of nurseries, kindergartens, and, of course, the famous rural dining halls. Naturally this maelstrom of activity encourages a multiplicity of interpretations. Nevertheless, from an economic standpoint, the essential content of the Great Leap Forward is very simple indeed: an excessively rapid pace of industrial development drew productive resources—especially manpower—into industry from other sectors. Agriculture in particular was starved of labor power and other productive resources, while exactions on agriculture increased to feed the new industrial workers. Bad weather may have contributed to problems but was not the primary cause. Food production plummeted, and mass starvation followed. In the aftermath of the crisis, industry was chopped back to release resources (manpower) back into agriculture. Although many foolish things were done in industry, the crisis was one of food availability that resulted from the crippling of agriculture. Bland statements about resource flows are not quite appropriate to the Leap: the country went crazy smelting steel and generating electricity, creating a vast industrial conflagration that sucked in everything, leaving the farmers hungry, thirsty, and gasping for breath.

Delusions and politics were both important causes of the Great Leap Forward, but there was also an important economic dynamic at work. The decentralization of management control enacted in November 1957 gave a free hand to local party and government officials to engage in industrialization schemes. Given the fiscal system described above, where returns were maintained artificially high in industry and low in agriculture, local officials naturally responded to these incentives by mobilizing resources under their control into industry. Having created a distorted fiscal system based on rich industry/poor agriculture, China's leadership discovered that decentralization of economic authority led to a rush into industry, regardless of the original intention of the decentralization. A built-in instability to the economy was thereby revealed, one that was of course greatly intensified by the instability in central policy created by leadership conflict. Future policy would have to devise some way to control that built-in instability.

After years of secrecy, the fundamental tragedy of the Leap has been disclosed. Thirty million died as a direct result of starvation or indirectly as a result of famine-induced susceptibility to disease. Certain provinces were particularly hard hit: in Sichuan and Guizhou, over 5 percent of the population died during 1960; total excess mortality over the period was about 11 percent of the population in Sichuan, 6 percent in Guizhou, 4 percent in Gansu.[13] We don't know how to incorporate suffering on this scale into an assessment of economic development. Nor does one know how to evaluate the Chinese leadership's response. Through early 1959, in spite of numerous mistakes and delusions, the responses seem flawed but human; after summer 1959 and through virtually the end of 1960, the response seems inhuman and criminal. None of this fits into a rational assessment of accomplishments and shortcomings.

The Break with the Soviet Union

China broke with the Soviet Union in the ideological, military, diplomatic, and economic realms. Rarely in history does one observe such a thorough reversal of relations between two countries in such a short period. This break naturally had profound repercussions in every aspect of China's economic and development policy. Did China, however, ever break with a Soviet model of development? This question has never been adequately answered in the China literature, largely because a proper answer requires a thorough reevaluation not just of Chinese development strategy, but also of Soviet policy under Stalin and Khrushchev. The Chinese did not break with a static "Soviet model." Rather, they broke with the contemporaneous Soviet Union onto which they projected many evils, and which they identified with domestic Chinese policy positions. But there had been substantial change in economic strategy in the Soviet Union in the 1950s and early 1960s, and changes in the way in which previous Soviet experiences were evaluated. That spirit of change, identifiable with Khrushchev, ultimately failed to reshape the Soviet economic system into a qualitatively different system, but nonetheless informed Soviet attitudes and the opinions of Soviet advisers in China during this time. It was with that attitude of critical reappraisal and eclectic pragmatism that Mao broke.

After the break with the Soviet Union, China's economic experience diverged significantly from what it had been prior to the break, and from some Soviet precedents. Moreover, those changes were substantial enough to create differences in the way the system operated and the level of performance of which it was capable. Do those differences cumulatively amount to something worth being labeled a "model of development"? No. Which was more important: the deviations from a Soviet "model," or the direct impact of the rupture with the Soviet Union? Unquestionably, the direct impact of the rupture was more significant.

The New Course

At first, during the early 1960s, Chinese economic policy was overwhelmingly dominated by the need to organize recovery from the post-Leap catastrophe. But as China did recover, eventually a new economic strategy was developed that guided Chinese economic development through 1978. Economic strategy during the 1950s had been dominated by the fact of Soviet guidance and assistance: the changes in economic strategy from the early 1960s were dominated by the need to adjust to the rupture with the Soviet Union and the attendant hostility between China and the USSR. This assertion should not be understood in an overly simple or mechanical fashion. It is not the case that every aspect of Chinese economic strategy after the 1960s was inevitably dictated by the break with the Soviet Union; rather, it is that most aspects of that strategy can be understood as logical extensions of, or sometimes radical responses to, the conditions given by the rupture with the Soviet Union.

In particular, three fundamental interrelated changes run through Chinese economic strategy after 1964. Chinese economic strategy became (1) militarized; (2) technologically isolated; and (3) decentralized, with a deterioration in central capabilities. Militarization was a response to the loss of the Soviet Union as an ally, and the gradually increasing danger of overt conflict with the Soviet Union. Technological isolation was, of course, a result of the abrupt cutoff of the inflow of Soviet technology, combined with China's continuing hard-line position vis-à-vis the capitalist powers. Decentralization has been interpreted in the literature as part of a "populist," antibureaucratic, and perhaps prorural development pattern. That view is no longer tenable, but a degraded central government role is nonetheless an important characteristic of this period. The reduced central government role is best seen as an outgrowth of the preceding factors: decentralization represented the specific means by which the Chinese militarized their economy, and responded to a general regression in technical and administrative capabilities.

Militarization

During 1964–65, China underwent an unprecedented mobilization of resources for military purposes. This mobilization was caused by the general deterioration of China's international relations and catalyzed by the American decision to start bombing North Vietnam, using the Gulf of Tonkin incident as a pretext. The most important part of this mobilization was the decision to give priority to a vast program of inland industrial construction called the "Third Front." This huge investment program initially drew the bulk of China's industrial investment into development of industries in China's Southwest, especially Sichuan and Guizhou. The bulk of the investment was not in military industry per se, but rather in the entire range of heavy industrial goods: coal mines, steel mills, and machinery enterprises in particular. Factories were purposely dispersed into remote mountainous locations in order to be able to survive a large-scale assault on China.[14]

In this initial form, the Third Front strategy was not one of decentralization, but it envisaged an objective that was highly compatible with decentralization. That is, the objective was to create regional industrial systems that had the potential of surviving and operating independently in the event of a catastrophic attack on coastal China, with subsequent "decapitation" of the central government and occupation of advanced coastal production bases. Subsequently, in 1969–70, a second phase of the Third Front construction program was explicitly linked to notions of independent industrial systems to be created in a number of different regions. At that time, central government policy, highly influenced by Lin Biao, called for the construction of ten independent regional economies, each of which would be able to survive a national military catastrophe.

The year 1965 also saw the creation of an expanded military industrial system within the national planning system. This took the form of a panoply of military machine-building ministries, numbers two through seven. At the same time, after the success with building an atomic bomb (exploded in 1964), the decision was made to proceed with high-priority development of long-range missiles, and the new Seventh Ministry of Machine Building was organized to pursue that objective, which obtained its first substantial success in 1970.[15] Organizationally, this represents only a modest development of a Soviet-style military industrial complex. Nor was the apparent commitment of resources that great. The Chinese claim that only about 5 percent of industrial investment over the 1949–80 period went into military industry.[16]

The militarization was in fact pervasive. First, the massive commitment of resources to the Third Front for national defense reasons came in addition to—and not instead of—large-scale military expenditures of the traditional kind, so that the military burden was simply that much greater. Second, although the overt outlay for military industries does not seem great, the true costs were much greater. For example, in an account of the development of China's aeronautics industry, reference is repeatedly made to the valuable contributions of numerous civilian plants, to the organization of cooperative groups of civilian ministries, and to the contribution of the Chinese Academy of Science. It is clear that the developers of China's missile force had access to virtually every resource in the economy, and most of these resources were contributed for the good of the nation, rather than purchased. Thus, when the same source asserts that China's missile development cost "13 percent of Japan's outlays on aeronautics, and one-half of 1 percent of the United States'," one can be sure that his accounting is less than comprehensive.[17] The monetary figures in no way reflect the contribution of scarce technical skills and precision machinery, which were unavailable to the rest of the economy

Technological Isolation

In the early 1960s, China's ability to import technology was crippled both by the rupture with the Soviet Union, and by the permanent shift in the availability of agricultural surplus, which required that China use foreign exchange to import food. The impact of the Soviet withdrawal has traditionally been described by the Chinese in a certain formulaic way: the Soviets walked out, taking their blueprints with them, dealing a sharp setback in a time of great difficulty; however, through diligent self-reliance, we were able to overcome these problems. In other words, the impact was intense in the short run, but modest in the long run. Although this formulation accurately reflects some of the psychological trauma of the early 1960s, as an economic statement, it is precisely backward. In fact, the short-run impact of the withdrawal of Soviet technicians was virtually nil: the post-Leap crisis was based in agriculture and food supply, and investment projects around the country had to be shut down in any case. But the long-run impact was very great. Instead of Chinese technological capabilities being continuously broadened and strengthened by a steady inflow of Soviet technology, those capabilities were basically frozen. The stock of domestic technological capacity from that moment on was roughly unchanged, indeed began to depreciate almost immediately. Of course, that capability was not frozen at a zero level: an impressive domestic technological capability had already been created, and China immediately put that capability to work solving crucial problems. But the process by which that capability was being continuously strengthened came to a drastic halt.

Some of the more pressing problems created by the rupture with the Soviet Union were solved in nearly heroic fashion: the steel industry learned to make hubs for railroad cars, and the machine tool industry successfully produced drill bits for oilfields.[18] Of the sixty-six large-scale Soviet-aided projects still under construction, about a third were abandoned, and two-thirds eventually completed. Moreover, a new technology-import program was begun almost immediately. A Japanese vinylon plant was imported to Beijing in 1963, and Austrian and West German plants imported for the steel industry. This import program involved only U.S. $300 million, so it was only about one-tenth the size of Soviet imports during the 1950s, and as a result had to be selective. Generally, single exemplars of a given technology were imported, and the choices were made well, despite substantial military emphasis. Some major successes were involved, including the importation of basic oxygen technology from Austria, but only a third of the importation program could be carried out before ties were disrupted by the Cultural Revolution.[19]

In a different international environment, such a program of selective technology import, combined with continuous study of developments in world science and technology and scrupulous copying of imported plants could have been the centerpiece of a program that would have continued to expand and deepen China's technological capabilities.[20] But this did not occur. Instead, centrally orchestrated campaigns were used to solve crucial problems. Some were key bottlenecks in economic development, such as those mentioned above: but perhaps more important was the mobilization of scientific and industrial design resources for military purposes. High-tech resources went overwhelmingly into the nuclear and aeronautics programs, stretching existing capabilities to the limit; ordinary industrial design resources went overwhelmingly into the construction of Third Front plants under difficult conditions. In these circumstances, there was little in the way of technology resources available to augment the stock of technological capabilities (through selective importation and training of new technicians), nor was there much application of technology to the continuous upgrading of technique within the ordinary industrial sector.

Part of this was because of the tremendous impact of the Cultural Revolution on the educational system. Part, however, was the result of a more or less conscious development strategy. When Zhou Enlai outlined in 1965 the long-term development strategy that would lead to the "Four Modernizations," he called explicitly for a fifteen-year period of expansion of a self-sufficient industrial system, followed (in 1980!) by a renewed opening of the economy and a drive to reach advanced world levels. In other words, China would gamble that it had imported sufficient Soviet technology to permit the expansion of a "basic" industrial sector and would concentrate its efforts on producing more of these medium-tech products. Technological development would be concentrated on the defense-related nuclear and aeronautics programs (this is unstated but is deducible from actions). Of course, such an approach is highly compatible with the continued drive for quantity targets characteristic of Soviet-type economies, exemplified in the Chinese slogan "take steel as the key link." Moreover, given China's uncompromising ideological stance and the impact of the Cultural Revolution, it probably also reflects a realistic appraisal of China's access to international technology.

Where the strategy was profoundly unrealistic was in its neglect of the importance of continually building technological capabilities. Even to "stand still," as it were, to maintain a homologous relation between technology and economic development, it is necessary to continue to invest in technical capabilities. This is so first because technical capacity decays, through obsolescence and human aging, and second because as economies (and factories) grow in size, and natural resources must be sought in increasingly inaccessible and dispersed locations, new demands are placed on designers. Thus, the country that is borrowing technology finds itself in a position where it must not simply diffuse new techniques and machinery, but must also adapt, expand, and improve those techniques, simply to maintain a process that has already been put in motion. In nuclear and aeronautics fields, China, by concentrating its technological resources, was able to do precisely that, building upon Soviet technology. But what of the ordinary industrial sectors? Here is an assessment of technological progress during that time in design of electric power generation equipment:

> The large-scale 125,000-, 200,000-, and 300,000-kilowatt large-scale thermal generators were all designed by simply enlarging the pre–Cultural Revolution 50,000- and 100,000-kilowatt generators, and lacked the indispensable basis in experimentation and testing. In addition, because we overemphasized creating small and light generators, safety margins were eroded; and this combined with shoddy manufacturing processes and slipshod inspection to create many quality and reliability problems. . . . Even though one has now [1984] spent a lot of time and money improving these designs, there are still a lot of fundamental problems of quality and capability that one has been unable to solve.[21]

Similar realities emerge in the steel industry: a few crucial technical problems were solved, and the basic oxygen technique was successfully introduced from abroad. But the simplest and most basic technological capacities not only did not increase, they declined. Utilization coefficients of blast furnaces, a good technological indicator of a production process that should be fairly fully mastered, declined significantly after 1965 and remained low until 1978.[22] Technological progress was similarly slow or nonexistent in many industrial sectors.

Decentralization and Deteriorating Central Capabilities

During 1969–70, China implemented a radical program of decentralization. The roots of this decentralization can be discerned in the two previous characteristics of post-Leap strategy. The decentralization was founded not on an attempt to make industrial management more efficient or responsive (by allowing local control), but rather on an attempt to make it independent and survivable. To this end, ten economic regions were outlined that were to construct independent industrial systems. Most were multiprovince cooperative regions, but smaller independent systems were to be built in Shandong, Xinjiang, and Fujian-Jiangxi.[23]

Alongside this strategy and the associated Third Front construction, an attempt was made to put all economic planning on a regional basis. Control over the vast majority of enterprises was decentralized to provinces and below; provinces were given contractual responsibility for most of their budgetary revenues and investment; additional financial resources were made available for enterprises and local governments. In addition, the system of material balance planning, the heart of the Soviet-style planned economy, was restructured to put it on a regional basis as well. Central planners, for a brief period, became responsible only for transferring blocks of resources between provinces, without attempting to compile a detailed "balance sheet" of individual suppliers and users. Thus, the basic planned industrial economy, focusing on the largest enterprises, was restructured and placed on a regional basis.[24]

At the same time, localities were given control over an autonomous, small-scale industrial sector outside the control of the standard planned economy. Centering on the "five small" rural industries, a local industrial sector was fostered in which the output and financial resources belonged solely to the localities. County and commune-based industries grew extremely rapidly, fed not only by the reinvestment of locally generated revenues, but also by generous commitments from the central government. While the large-scale economy was being restructured to give it more of a decentralized mode of management, a separate small-scale economy, minimally subject to any centralized management, was growing to account for a significant minority of industrial production.

The management of and relationship between the different parts of the industrial system were never successfully specified. The large-scale decentralization of large enterprises was often formalistic: complex enterprises were remanded to local governments that did not have the expertise to manage them by central ministries that did not wish to surrender control. Often the ministries maintained control over decisions about inputs and output, while financial resources accrued to local governments. More crucial was the failure to develop a planning system that made sense. The system of transferring blocks of resources between provinces lasted for only a few years, but no clear alternative was successfully developed. Chinese planning, in relation to its Soviet model, became coarse, incomplete, and inconsistent. It was coarse in the sense that only a relatively small number of materials were allocated by planners; incomplete, because with local industry under local control, central planners never had a monopoly over even the output of the most crucial sectors; and inconsistent because planners were often allocating only a portion of needed resources, requiring local bodies to supplement those allocations by "mobilizing" local resources.

Thus, it was not simply that the decentralization of 1969–70 was an "administrative" rather than an "economic" decentralization. This administrative decentralization was distorted by two forces, one that affected the demand for decentralization, and one that shaped the supply. On the demand side, the purpose of the decentralization was to make regions potentially survivable on an autarkic basis, but only in the event of war: before war started, or if there was no war, central government direction could be as or more effective. There was no demand for an effective middle ground of decentralization that could work in the present. On the supply side, there was no coherent effort to build in partially decentralized mechanisms of coordination of the myriad economic tasks that were taking place in the present. There was no development of central government skills to manage the new coordination tasks that would be required by a decentralized mechanism. On the contrary, the central government's ability to exert specific, detailed control over the economy was slowly ebbing away, undermined by the erosion of skilled manpower and administrative skills, by the focus on military and difficult interior construction tasks, and by the abrupt political changes that kept the central government in turmoil. Such skills were, if anything, even less available at the local level. Particularly given that inputs of technical and managerial personnel per unit of output were declining through this period, the process of spreading coordination and control decisions out to a larger number of people must have meant a decline in the quality of those decisions.

Yet it was essential to maintain certain types of control over the economy. The lesson of the Great Leap Forward revealed, above all else, that one type of control was indispensable. It was essential never to allow an uncontrolled flow of manpower out of the agricultural sector. To carry out a decentralization, the system had somehow to be immunized against the distorted incentives created by the rich industry/poor agriculture syndrome. Since the center did not have the ability to manage directly, or even specifically monitor, individual investment and production decisions, it was forced to impose a series of three crude controls on the development process. The first of these was autarky itself: regions had to be approximately self-sufficient in food. Mandated self-sufficiency, while originating in military imperatives, was the one way to ensure that local government constraints replicated those on the central level, and ensure that local governments had an interest in keeping the population down on the farm and producing grain. The second control was the prohibition on profit seeking and production of consumption goods. Backed up by the continuing monopolies the central government had over grain and cotton, the government was able to force local industrialization into a heavy-industry mode that replicated central government priorities.[25]

The third control probably had the most impact, and also differentiates China most clearly from the Soviet Union: this was the virtually complete control over population movement and the absence of a labor market. During the 1950s, China had been a society in motion. Migration and urbanization were both significant. Even during this period, it was clear that the wages and benefits provided to urban workers were far above those available to rural residents, and there was tension associated with the pace of new hiring and migration to urban areas. The legal framework for population control was laid in 1958 but immediately became a dead letter, for the Leap was of course accompanied by an even vaster movement of the population than before. After the Leap, the priority was again on population movement, but this time it was a compulsory ejection of population from the cities in the wake of disaster. Thus, it is only from the mid-1960s that population immobility became a regular characteristic of Chinese society. From the mid-1960s, the preexisting legal restrictions on migration became effective in practice, and changing of jobs within the urban sector virtually disappeared. The social controls prevented the contradictions and failings in the economic management system from leading directly to economic chaos or disaster, but they had extremely negative social consequences that became effective immediately and, in the long run, had very negative economic consequences as well.

The impact of autarky-based decentralization is especially clear in the province of Shandong, which was a focus of such policies and thus suffered and benefited disproportionately. Shandong also graphically illustrates the way the autarkic impulses in industrial and agricultural policy came together. Instructed to build a "small third front" in the mountainous interior of the province, Shandong enjoyed a high level of investment support from the central government throughout the 1970s. Shandong built a medium-sized steel mill costing half a billion yuan that accumulated operational losses of 200 million yuan over the next ten years. Railroads were built through the center of the province, linking power plants and machinery and military enterprises. A series of duplicate automobile plants were intentionally created to maximize "survivability." These investments produced few valuable assets: during the entire period 1966–75, only 9 of 46 large projects begun were completed, and only 7,000 of the 13,500 small projects.[26] Nor did the generosity with which government investment was lavished on the province have any beneficial effects for the average resident. Despite a substantial natural comparative advantage in production of economic crops such as cotton, peanuts, and tobacco, the province was instructed to become self-sufficient in grain production. This objective was ultimately achieved, with great fanfare, in the early 1970s, at substantial cost to living standards. When household surveys were resumed in 1978, they revealed that rural incomes in Shandong were 25 percent below the national average, although the province was well above average both in the 1950s and subsequently in the 1980s. The costs of national development policies were reflected in a particularly concentrated form in Shandong.

Costs

Militarization, technological isolation, and administrative devolution led to enormous waste. Some of the stories of wasted investments would be comical if they did not represent such a heavy burden on a poor country. For example, during the Third Front period, twenty electric power plants were built underground or in caves, representing hundreds of millions of yuan in excess costs.[27] Over a billion yuan was spent on a large-scale integrated steel mill at Jiuquan in Gansu, a plant that has yet to produce anything other than a modest quantity of pig iron. These examples could be multiplied many times. By the end of the 1970s, Chinese planners were struggling to get hundreds of unworkable, misdesigned, or incomplete projects into production. It is frequently held that one indicator of inefficiency in the Soviet Union is the large volume of uncompleted construction, which typically amounts to between 70 and 85 percent of the value of the annual flow of new investment. In China, in 1977, the stock of uncompleted construction projects amounted to 210 percent of the value of that year's capital construction, or 80 billion yuan. In other words, two full years worth of investment was "in the pipeline," making no contribution to current production.[28]

Rather than multiplying examples of this sort, I have made an effort to bring together some aggregate figures on the uses to which output was put. At the beginning of this essay, it was established that output had grown fairly rapidly, with the unstated presumption being that rapid growth of output provided more resources for consumption and productive investment. Is it possible that the inefficiencies and distortions of the system could be so great that they could cancel out a substantial part of the growth of output? To answer this question I have assembled data on three uses of output that are of particular interest:

1. Worthless output: This consists of products and investment projects that were officially declared to be worthless and written off the books. This is pure waste.

2. Increased stockpiles and incomplete construction: Every economy builds up a certain volume of stockpiles and work in progress as part of ordinary economic activity. However, these items are much larger in socialist economies, and especially much larger in Maoist China, than in other economies, relative to

national income. While stockpiles cannot be considered pure waste, they represent the volume of resources tied up in the operation of the system, and thus neither available for consumption nor ready to be brought to bear as new productive assets. They might be used in the future, but they are making little contribution in the present.

3. Military expenditure: The data consist of current military expenditures through the budget, as well as investment in military facilities and industries. All nations make military expenditures; moreover, investments in military industries may create technological and physical assets of value to the civilian economy. However, China's very large commitment to the military during this period ensured that a substantial portion of output was initially channeled into military uses with little productive application to the economy.

Minimum values for resources expended in these three categories are presented in table 2, all drawn from Chinese sources. The total value is 733 billion yuan. A significant portion of this total represents waste, either because output was unusable, or because it was tied up as excess inventories. The entire value, however, represents resources that were not available to increase consumption but had not yet created new productive assets through the investment process. Temporarily, at least, these resources were not contributing in productive ways to the civilian economy. Moreover, this is a minimum figure, because it omits a number of categories for which data are lacking, including inventories and uncompleted construction of nonstate-owned units, unnecessary excess costs associated with Third Front projects that were completed, and costs imposed on civilian enterprises for military and Third Front tasks. The aggregate number given in table 2 is a lower bound estimate of resources channeled into uses with very low contribution to production development or consumption.[29]

The number 733 billion yuan is very large, too large to be understood directly. To what should this number be compared? One could compare it to total cumulative output (net material product) for all years from 1953 through 1978: that amounted to 4,000 billion yuan. These nonproductive uses amount to 18 percent of everything that was produced from 1953 to 1978. However, one can derive a more interesting number by considering only that part of cumulative output that was created by economic growth. Let us consider that part of output that was the result of increased output per capita. Consider the following thought experiment. In 1953, total NMP was 70.9 billion, or just over 120 yuan per capita. If there had been no economic growth (no increase in output per capita), the economy would still have been larger in subsequent years because of population growth. If we account only for population growth and inflation (calculated according to official Chinese price indices), with real output per head unchanged, then total output (net material product) in 1978 would have been 129 billion yuan. Because actual output per head more than doubled during this period, actual output in 1978 was 301 billion, so 172 billion was the result of economic growth. For each

Table 2

Economic Growth and Its Uses (in billion yuan)

Cumulative output resulting from growth in output per head 1953–78	1,400
Selected uses of output	
Worthless output	
Value of stockpiles written down	
1962–63	30+
1973	5
Written-off construction projects	
1953–78	50+
Increased stockpiles and construction	
State enterprise inventories increase, 1952–78	268
Uncompleted construction	80
Military	
Budget military outlays	257
Investment in military industry	17
Military and civil defense investment	26
Subtotal	733

Sources: Write-offs are estimates based on Xu Yi, *Caizheng yanjiu* (Fiscal research), no. 4 (1981): 8, and Yang Song, *Jinrong yanjiu* (Financial research), no. 6 (1981): 26. Written-off construction projects comes from Han Shuanglin and Li Cai, "The Impact of Construction Costs on Investment Efficiency," in *Jiben jianshe touzi xiaoguo yanjiu* (Studies of the effectiveness of capital construction investment), ed. Xue Baoding et al. (Beijing: Zhongguo jingji chubanshe, 1987), p. 272, who also cite an alternative estimate of 94.2 billion in such losses between 1953 and 1980. State stockpiles ("working capital subject to norms") and budget military outlays from *1988 Tongji nianjian* (Statistical yearbook), pp. 34, 754. Investment in military industry from Yang Yonglian, *Zhongguo junshi jingjixue gailun* (Outline of China military economics) (Beijing: Zhongguo jingji chubanshe, 1988), pp. 148, 243; military investment is derived by comparing two series of capital investment, the smaller of which is described as "not including military and civil defense investment," in *Jiben jianshe gongzuo shouce* (Capital construction work handbook) (Beijing: Zhongguo jianzhu gongye chubanshe, 1983), p. 378.

year from 1954 through 1978, one can calculate in this way the total output that was due to growth in real output per capita. If one then sums the values for each year, we obtain the total cumulative value of output that was the result of economic growth (increased output per capita). That sum amounts to 1,400 billion. Obviously, this is the maximum accomplishment one can attribute to the economic development strategy that was followed. At a minimum, 733 out of this 1,400 billion, more than half of the additional output created by economic growth between 1953 and 1978, was either wasted outright, spent on the military, or tied up by the inefficiencies of the economic system. Significantly, less than half of increased output went to consumption or new productive resources.

The Collapse

After the death of Mao, China's leaders did not automatically turn to a program of economic reform. Quite the contrary, they initially believed that, having rid China of the Gang of Four and other leftists, they could reestablish a centralized program of investment and reconstitute the favorable conditions that had seemed to prevail during the First Five-Year Plan. Instead of receiving technology from the Soviet Union, they would purchase advanced technology from capitalist countries, using revenues from China's rapidly expanding surplus of petroleum. A central plan would ensure rapid incorporation of this technology and acceleration of growth.

Ultimately this program failed, and the reason for its failure is rather simple. China simply did not have, at that time, the in-depth planning, administrative and technical personnel and research in place to coordinate such a large-scale program. This became apparent during 1978 through two events. The first was the unseemly unraveling of the technology import program, and the second was the collapse of petroleum development. The import program was based on the grandiose Ten-Year development plan, centering around the construction of 120 super large-scale projects. But in contrast to the priority construction projects of the First Five-Year Plan, these projects were selected more or less at random, as goals, not as detailed proposals. Feasibility studies were never carried out for any of the projects. Nevertheless, different sections of the bureaucracy began signing expensive contracts with foreign parties, committing to 22 large-scale projects, costing 13 billion U.S. dollars, mostly in the last part of 1978. In the meantime, the petroleum resources on which those imports were based simply were not materializing. Petroleum production reached 100 million metric tons in 1978, but plateaued at that level, as China drilled several million meters of new oil wells during 1977 and 1978, but did not discover a single new producing well. Plans had been moving ahead to construct a large-scale natural gas pipeline to transport Sichuan natural gas initially to Hubei and Hunan, and eventually all the way to Shanghai. Huge investments were made on the basis of this project, but it was discovered in 1978 that there simply wasn't enough exploitable natural gas in Sichuan to supply such a pipeline. Thus, in both petroleum and natural gas, the fundamental work of developing future reserves to come on stream to supplement current production had not been done.[30]

These simultaneous developments could be seen as very bad luck but were not really accidental. Fundamentally, they reflect the erosion of skills and planning work that had taken place in China. The gradual depletion of technical skills and the subordination of available skilled manpower to military tasks and the maintenance of simple production had placed the entire economic system at increasing risk. Without the reserves of planning (problem-solving) ability and without flexibility in the economy, it was inevitable that new challenges would severely strain that economic system. There was a certain poetic justice in the fact that the crisis came because reserves had not been located and verified in what had been the most striking success story during the Mao years, the petroleum sector. This is an apt metaphor for the gradual exhaustion of reservoirs of capabilities in the face of increasingly formidable challenges which can be observed in many sectors of the Chinese economy.

Legacies

By 1978, the development strategy followed in the People's Republic had failed. In an immediate sense, the failure was due to the deterioration in planning, administrative, and technological capacity; to militarization; and to the astonishing waste and inability to solve immediate problems. Yet at the same time, the fact that one can document both reasonably robust growth and astonishing levels of waste and nonproductive expenditure shows that the underlying conditions for economic growth were quite strong.

The legacy is an ambiguous one. First, the People's Republic did accomplish, in however flawed a fashion, the initial phase of industrialization of the Chinese economy, creating a substantial industrial and technological base that simply had not existed before. By the late 1970s, China was operating in a totally different universe of possibilities than it had been in the early 1950s. The industrial capital stock was about twenty times as great in 1978 as it had been in 1952. Second, the rural services infrastructure had insured a significant building of human resources at the base levels: the overall population was much healthier, better fed, and more literate than in the early 1950s. One should bear these major accomplishments in mind.

On the other side, the legacy of problems was surprisingly heavy. Most important was the deterioration in China's technical and administrative capacity that had been allowed to take place since the 1960s. This is true from a technical, managerial, or administrative standpoint. While the demands on the administrative structure increased, the capabilities of that administrative structure declined until the system nearly collapsed. The legacy was not only that adequate skills were not available to run the economic system that had been in place during the early 1970s, but also that the skills, creativity, and insight needed to reorient the economy, import new technologies, convert production methods, and strategize future development were in critically short supply. The reorientation of national policy after 1978 made it possible to begin rebuilding those skills: but in contrast to the 1950s, immediate decisions about economic strategy and tactics had to be made before those skills could possibly be rebuilt. Strategizing about economic development and training people to strategize about economic development had to be done simultaneously, and the dual task has proven to be extremely difficult.

Second, an enormous amount of worthless capital stock had been created. Misguided investment decisions have created industrial plant, especially in the

Third Front, that will never be productive. Such capacity is actually worse than worthless, because interest groups have been created which seek to perpetuate state support for those deficit units. The result is a steady drain on the economy. In fact, China depleted its precious stock of human skills and ran down its existing assets in order to build up a new physical capital stock of limited value. In a sense, much of the investment of the Cultural Revolution period had simply been used to convert valuable capital into worthless capital. This is occasionally true literally, as in those cases where productive factories were moved from coastal locations into the Third Front, where they were unable to produce effectively and were eventually left to rust. In this way, spinning gold into flax, China's investment policies during these years created almost as many liabilities as assets. Moreover, many of the assets that were created were fairly specific and could not easily be converted to alternative uses.

Third, an excessively simple and rigid set of regulations underlay much of the operation of the government and economy. A complex of four interlocking elements—price controls, profitable industry, restrictions on mobility, and nonmonetized social services in the countryside—ensured that local and national economies continued to function. These elements allowed a highly simplified administrative structure to carry out many tasks: while this was in a sense economical, it resulted in an administrative structure that was ultimately so overburdened with multiple tasks that it had no flexibility. When changes were made in the organization of agricultural production from 1981, the entire complex of rural services collapsed in most parts of the country. The introduction of modest amounts of economic freedom into the system quickly eroded the government's fiscal base, with dire consequences to every aspect of the economy. After ten years of reform, the government has been unable to carry out fiscal and price reforms.

Finally, China entered the post-Mao era without a clear analysis of its situation, or the nature of its economic system. The traumatic character of relations with the Soviet Union caused an inability to analyze the Soviet model and its legacy, and the ways in which China had diverged from it. Reformers were happy to blame the problems in the economy on the Soviet model, while those targeting the deterioration of skills were inhibited from pointing out the favorable aspects of the Soviet legacy in earlier years. The result was a pervasive tendency to treat China as a highly centralized economy that needed, above all, decentralization: a prescription that was quite wide of the mark.

Thus, by the end of 1978, the legacy must be judged to be largely negative. Things actually were as bad as Chinese economists liked to say: the economy had been brought to "the verge of collapse." This negative assessment rests on the judgment that economic development, though reasonably rapid, had not brought substantial benefits to the population in terms of consumption, nor had it laid a healthy foundation for future growth. Ironically, the exception to this generalization is probably in the countryside, where the creation of a broad base of simple skills and a healthy population laid the foundation for a spurt of agricultural and other economic growth in the countryside after 1981. In the countryside, the fundamental investments in human capital had been made, and so the next stage of growth could take place. In industry and public administration, on the other hand, disinvestment in human capital had been occurring. This was particularly telling, for this is one area where vigorous state action strategizing and implementing economic reform was most needed. A thorny knot of problems had been created by low efficiency in many sectors of the economy, distortions of the fiscal and administrative systems, and large amounts of worthless or deficit capital. China's governmental organs had to resolve immediate crises, develop new strategies for growth, and work out the first stages of economic reform—and all these needed to be done while experts were being trained or retrained and institutions were being rebuilt. The difficulty—the near impossibility—of these tasks has repeatedly threatened to overwhelm the economic reform process since 1978, and resulted in repeated crises that keep erupting despite the remarkable progress that has been made.

Notes

1. For the period through 1978, see Nicholas Lardy, *Agriculture in China's Modern Economic Development* (New York: Cambridge University Press, 1982). One part of the story is updated in Bruce Stone, "Developments in Agricultural Technology," *China Quarterly*, no. 116 (December 1988): 767–822.

2. Given the disruption of the period, there were large regional variations in prices, and the national average is only an approximation. State Statistical Bureau, *Zhongguo maoyi wujia tongji ziliao (1952–1983)* (Trade and price statistical materials) (Beijing: Zhongguo tongji chubanshe, 1984), p. 423; for detailed discussion, see Luo Gengmo, ed., *Xin Zhongguo ruogan wujia zhuanti shiliao* (Several specialized historical materials on prices in new China) (Changsha: Hunan renmin chubanshe, 1986 [1965]), esp. pp. 27–40.

3. Liu Suinian and Wu Qungan, *Zhongguo shehui zhuyi jingji jianshi* (An outline history of China's socialist economy) (Harbin: Heilongjiang renmin chubanshe, 1985), pp. 119–20; Vivienne Shue, *Peasant China in Transition* (Berkeley: University of California Press, 1980), gives a detailed description of the way these institutions were used to push and pull peasants into producers' collectives.

4. *Zhongguo caizheng tongji 1950–1985* (China fiscal statistics 1950–1985) (Beijing: Zhongguo caizheng jingji chubanshe, 1987), p. 38.

5. Wei Jingtao, Li Yangju, and He Xiaojun, "Strengthen Keypoint Construction," in *Jiben jianshe touzi xiaoguo yanjiu* (Studies of the effectiveness of capital construction investment), ed. Xue Baoding et al. (Beijing: Zhongguo jingji chubanshe, 1987), pp. 169–70.

6. Leo Orleans, "Scientific and Technical Manpower," *Science and Technology in the People's Republic of China* (Paris: OECD, 1977), p. 107; Roy Grow, "Soviet Economic Penetration of China, 1945–1960," in *Testing Theories of Economic Imperialism*, ed. S. Rosen and J. Kurth (Lexington, MA: D. C. Heath, 1974), pp. 261–81.

7. On the importance of the industrial legacy from pre-1949 China, see Thomas Rawski, *China's Transition to Industrialism* (Ann Arbor: University of Michigan Press, 1980).

8. Chen Huiqin, "A Preliminary Analysis of the Economic Efficiency of Imported Technology over 30 Years," *Gongye jingji guanli congkan* (Digest of industrial economic management), no. 5 (1981): 44–54.

9. U.S. Central Intelligence Agency, *Foreign Trade in Machinery and Equipment since 1952* (Washington, DC, January 1975), p. 1.

10. Chen Huiqin, "A Preliminary Analysis," discussing import of industrial technology, says China bought U.S. $2.7 billion of equipment from the USSR and East Europe during the 1950s. Converting through rubles into yuan at an ultimate exchange rate of 3.6 to 1, this would amount to 9.7 billion yuan. The 1985 industrial census recorded a total of 12.5 billion yuan worth of imported equipment from before 1970 still in use in China's large industrial plants, which is about right, given the additional import during the 1960s of equipment from the West and Eastern Europe. Total industrial capital stock in 1965 was 104 billion yuan, of which no more than one-third would be machinery.

11. Gu Jiaqi and Wang Shiyuan, "A Retrospective and Prospective of the Evolution of the Management System in the Machinery Industry," *Zhongguo jijie dianzi gongye nianjian 1986* (Yearbook of the machinery and electronics industry in China) (Beijing: Jijie gongye chubanshe, 1986), p. I-14.

12. Reconstructed estimates of life expectancy are from Judith Banister, *China's Changing Population* (Stanford: Stanford University Press, 1987), p. 116. See also World Bank, *China: The Health Sector* (Washington, DC: IBRD, 1984), p. 155.

13. Basil Ashton et al., "Famine in China, 1958–61," *Population and Development Review* 10, 4 (December 1984): 613–45; Thomas Bernstein, "Stalinism, Famine, and Chinese Peasants: Grain Procurements during the Great Leap Forward," *Theory and Society* 13, 3 (May 1984): 339–77. Data on individual provinces are my own rough calculations from the volumes in the series *Zhongguo renkou* (China population) (Beijing: Zhongguo caizheng jingji chubanshe, 1988): *Sichuan fen ce*, p. 120; *Gansu fen ce*, pp. 141, 143; *Guizhou fen ce*, p. 148.

14. Barry Naughton, "The Third Front: Defence Industrialization in the Chinese Interior," *China Quarterly*, no. 115 (September 1988): 351–86; Yan Fangming, "A Review of Third Front Construction," *Dangshi yanjiu*, no. 4 (1987): 70–73, 69.

15. Gu and Wang, "Retrospective and Prospective of Machinery Industry," p. I-15; Zhang Zhuo, ed., *Dangdai Zhongguo de hangtian shiye* (Aeronautics in contemporary China) (Beijing: Zhongguo shehui kexue chubanshe, 1986), pp. 32–42.

16. Yang Yongliang, *Zhongguo junshi jingjixue gailun* (Outline of China military economics) (Beijing: Zhongguo jingji chubanshe, 1988), pp. 148, 243.

17. Zhang, *Dangdai Zhongguo de hangtian shiye*, pp. 508, 511.

18. One engineer, Shen Hong, successfully designed the processes for producing railroad hubs, 4.2-meter-thick steel-rolling mills, and 12,000-ton forging equipment, the latter two with important military applications. See "Inventors Shen Hong, Yuan Longping and Xu Jinhang Receive Awards from a United Nations Organization," *Yangcheng wanbao* (Guangzhou evening news), September 28, 1985, p. 1.

19. Chen, "A Preliminary Analysis."

20. This would be close to the most successful programs of technological development in semi-industrialized countries. Those programs generally rely on significant import of technology (about 50 percent of total S&T expenditures) combined with large-scale training of technical manpower, only subsequently investing in large-scale domestic research. See Robert Evenson, "Technology, Productivity Growth, and Economic Development," in *The State of Development Economics: Progress and Perspectives*, ed. Gustav Ranis and T. Paul Schultz (Oxford: Basil Blackwell, 1988), pp. 486–527.

21. Li Daigeng, *Xin Zhongguo dianli gongye fazhan shilue* (Outline history of the

development of the electric power industry in the new China) (Beijing: Qiye guanli chubanshe, 1984), pp. 272–73.

22. Roger Cliff, "Technical Change in China's Iron and Steel Industry, 1949–1986," Master's Thesis, University of California, San Diego, 1989, p. 44.

23. Wang Haibo, *Xin Zhongguo gongye jingji shi* (History of the industrial economy of new China) (Beijing: Jingji guanli chubanshe, 1986), pp. 348–49.

24. A concrete and concise account of this is provided by ibid., pp. 367–78.

25. Christine Wong, "Ownership and Control in Chinese Industry: The Maoist Legacy and Prospects for the 1980s," U.S. Congress Joint Economic Committee, *China's Economy Looks Toward the Year 2000* (Washington, DC: GPO, 1986), 1:589.

26. Zhao Jian and Liu Kexun, *Jingji yanjiu ziliao* (Economic research materials), no. 7 (1981):4–5; *Zhongguo gangtie gongye nianjian 1986* (Steel industry yearbook) (Beijing: Yejin gongye chubanshe, 1986), pp. 545–48; *Shandong shengqing* (Shandong provincial conditions), pp. 429–40; Zhao Hong and Xiong Zhaoxiang, "Prospects for Development of the Auto Industry," *Caizheng yanjiu ziliao* (Fiscal research materials) 90 (1981): 26–30.

27. Li, *Xin Zhongguo dianli gongye fazhan shilue*, pp. 222–23, 378–79.

28. Ding Hua and Wu Xingguo, "Rectify the Orientation of Capital Construction, Raise Economic Efficiency," *Jingji yanjiu*, no. 1 (1982): 49; Mark Harrison, "Investment Mobilization and Capacity Completion in the Chinese and Soviet Economies," *Economics of Planning* 19, 2 (1989): 65–66.

29. I believe that the data on written-off and incomplete construction projects apply only to nonmilitary investment, since data on military investment are reported through separate statistical channels. If this is not the case, then table 2 includes some double-counting in the form of military and military industry investment that was incomplete or written off. A maximum estimate of possible double-counting in that case would be about 8 billion yuan, which should then be deducted from the total. This adjustment would not significantly affect the argument here.

30. See Wang, *Xin Zhongguo gongye jingji shi*, pp. 403–6; Wei et al., "Strengthen Keypoint Construction," pp. 171, 180; According to Kim Woodard, "five of the six large field complexes in the northeast corridor reached maturity in the late 1970s." "Development of China's Petroleum Industry: An Overview," in *China's Petroleum Industry in the International Context*, ed. F. Fesharaki and D. Fridley (Boulder: Westview, 1986), p. 99.

11

STATE AND SOCIETY IN THE MAO ERA

MARTIN KING WHYTE

In some ways the Communist victory in 1949 represented the launching of a dramatic effort to transform the relationship between state and society in China. Yet in very basic respects 1949 symbolizes the failure of attempts to transform that relationship in even more fundamental ways, and the formation of a system that had strong echoes in China's imperial past. The contest between Western-oriented reformers and revolutionaries during the early decades of the twentieth century, a contest eventually won by revolutionaries in the CCP, is usually portrayed as a debate over how thoroughly to change the nature of the Chinese social order, with revolutionaries determined to go much further. Yet the events and trends of the post-1949 period, and particularly those of the post-Mao reform era, force us to rethink our ideas and categories. The reformers who lost the contest advocated ideas and institutions that posed a more fundamental threat than did those of the CCP to the basic operating principles that had governed the state-society relationship in China for centuries.[1]

State and Society in Late Imperial China

The imperial system, whose collapse gave rise to the contest between reformers and revolutionaries in the twentieth century, was based in theory, if not in reality, on a totalistic logic.[2] Society was conceived of as a vast human hierarchy in which each individual had a place, with interpersonal ties to parents, children, siblings, teachers, students, employers, employees, and so forth knitting the hierarchy together and providing solidarity and constraints. It was the duty of the state and its officials to proclaim a set of official values that would regulate all social relationships, with rule conceived of as much in terms of preaching and setting moral examples as of administration.

To be sure, the state lacked the personnel and resources actually to control and regulate all social relationships, but autonomous groups that existed at the grass roots were expected to pay homage to official values, and heterodox local groups or those that simply grew too strong were potential targets for official suppression. In a frankly utopian conception of the state-society relationship, it was assumed that if every individual could be firmly incorporated into binding social ties, with orthodox values spread and assimilated by all, social harmony and prosperity would reign. There was no place in this conception for ideas dear to the Western liberal tradition—the individual pursuit of self-interest as a good in itself, the "market place of ideas" as a source of social dynamism, or politics as centered on the competition among autonomous interest groups. In the Chinese imperial tradition these Western notions were seen as profoundly threatening and disruptive, for if individuals, groups, and ideas were allowed to develop independently and compete for influence without state guidance and control, the result could only be chaos.

Several clarifying observations should be made about this claim that the imperial Chinese state was based upon a dominating totalistic vision. First, this claim does not imply that official orthodoxy was unchanging. Major new cultural influences, such as Buddhism, were incorporated into (and later partially expunged from) the imperial orthodoxy, and successive dynasties and rulers devoted considerable energy to compiling new codifications of basic moral texts and sacred edicts to set the tone for the whole society.[3] Thus, China's rulers saw the orthodox tradition "as not something wholly fixed in the remote past but susceptible of later expansion . . . as living and growing, rather than static."[4] What was important was not that official moral standards remain fixed, but that the state retain control over the process of determining what kinds of thinking and behavior were acceptable.

A second and perhaps even more important point to make about this totalistic vision was that it was an ideal that never came close to being realized. Given the very limited human and financial resources of the imperial bureaucracy, as well as the poverty and illiteracy of much of the population, China's rulers could have no illusions about fully translating this vision into grass-roots reality. Throughout the imperial period, ordinary Chinese had substantial autonomy from the state in how they ordered their lives—for example, in where they lived, how they made a living, when they married, and what pleasures they sought in their free time. The imperial state also tolerated a wide range of heterodox beliefs and activities—secret societies, spirit diviners, sectarian religious cults, and so forth—even though it would have preferred a more orderly and uniform social world. Furthermore, it is probably the case that the ability of the state to dominate society weakened over the dynasties and centuries, as the dismantling of direct imperial control over most land and other resources and the growth of population, markets, and heterogeneity in society made attempts to impose imperial orthodoxy increasingly difficult.

What is striking, however, is the fervor with which imperial rulers and their advisers continued to pursue the unrealizable goal of total dominance over society. Social problems and even natural disasters tended to be blamed on incorrect thinking due to insufficient guidance in orthodox values, and elites down through the centuries devised ingenious mechanisms for imposing their orthodoxy on the most distant corners of their complex realm, in spite of the limited resources of the state. Official canons and texts were not simply compiled but disseminated, through both formal mechanisms, such as in village schools and through the *xiangyue* lectures that were supposed to be held in towns throughout the realm twice a month, and also in more popularized versions, such as by rural storytellers and local operas. Even at the end of the Qing the influence of this effort was widely visible, as the following excerpt from Guo Moruo's memoirs makes clear:

> Lecturers on the *Sacred Edict* [of Kangxi], who told stories about loyalty, filial piety, and fidelity from the morality books, often came to our village. . . . This type of simple storytelling was a form of entertainment that people in the villages liked to listen to very much. They would stand before the platform of the *Sacred Edict* and listen for two or three hours. The better storytellers could make the listeners weep. It was easy to make the villagers cry; all you had to do was draw out your voice a bit at the sad parts and add a few sad sobs. Before I had begun my schooling, I was already able to understand the morality books of these lecturers on the *Sacred Edict*.[5]

Even though China's rulers could have no doubt about their inability to realize their totalistic vision, this did not lead them to stop trying or to accept a pluralistic definition of the good society. A characterization of the People's Republic of China as "a political system in which government officials consider anything outside of their control to be unorthodox and deviant"[6] applies as well to imperial China, even at the end of the dynastic period. The fact that this vision was unrealizable does not mean that it had no impact at all. Arguably, the degree to which the imperial Chinese state achieved cultural and moral dominance over society was greater than in many other agrarian states and ancient civilizations, even though this dominance was always very far from total. Furthermore, many highly detailed attempts to regulate the behavior and thinking of the ordinary population in the Mao period have clear precedents in the imperial period. To select one trivial example, the imperative of adopting short and straight hair during the Cultural Revolution, which achieved such uniformity of "proletarian" coiffures, harkens back to the demand by the Manchu rulers of the Qing that Chinese men keep their hair long and bound in a queue. China's imperial rulers seemed persuaded that even an unrealizable totalistic vision would help them maintain the orderliness of Chinese society.

When social and political chaos did follow in the wake of the demise of the imperial system in 1911, Chinese politicians and intellectuals agonized over the causes and the solutions. Oversimplifying the nature of this debate and the political struggle that ensued enormously, two quite different agendas for change emerged. Those usually referred to as reformers developed a fundamental intellectual challenge to the imperial system and Confucianism and advocated the construction of a new social order along more pluralist lines. The state would provide a legal framework within which a society based upon the rule of law rather than of men would be built. The myriad new forms of group life and associations that had sprung up in the vacuum left by the fall of the dynasty would be regulated by this new legal framework, but they would no longer have to pay homage to a uniform set of official values. Individuals would be at least partially released from the stultifying constraints of ancient traditions and hierarchical families, and from their vitality and competition would come national creativity and growth. These ideas were central themes during the May Fourth Movement, although even then they had to compete for popular influence with more totalistic world views—either of a new revolutionary order or of a revived neo-Confucian society.

For complex reasons, the advocates of a more pluralistic China lost out in this competition for influence long before 1949. Many such reformers hoped to realize their agenda through the Nationalist regime, but when that regime descended into familiar authoritarian patterns, not to mention ineptitude and corruption, they found little room there for their ideas. Some bravely (or foolishly) held out hopes for a "third path" (neither Nationalist nor Communist) that would lead China to a form of modern nationhood based upon laws, markets, and competition. This advocacy of a third path, however, became a minor note in a political scene increasingly dominated by competition between the Nationalists and the Communists.

To a considerable extent the reformers were discredited by social developments in the years between 1911 and 1949. The governmental weakness, social conflict, poverty, and moral confusion of that period seemed to many Chinese to provide graphic evidence of the wisdom of the basic principles of the late imperial system—China needed a strong state proclaiming and enforcing a uniform set of values if chaos was to be avoided. The Nationalist regime tried and failed to provide the needed societal unity, and so this task was left to the Chinese Communists. China's pluralist reformers failed in their attempt to set China's political agenda in the first half of the twentieth century, and during the Mao period their ideas would become even more irrelevant.

Social Transformations in the 1950s

Upon victory the CCP set out to engineer a social revolution, but at the same time it established a state-society relationship that was in basic respects much less revolutionary and more "traditional" than would have been the case if the reformers had won. To justify this argument more clearly, I need to specify what was novel and what was traditional in the social change program carried out by the CCP after 1949.

The revolutionary aspects of the CCP transformation of society initiated after 1949 are fairly familiar. A foreign doctrine (Marxism-Leninism) and organizational system (the Leninist-Stalinist party-state) was adapted to Chinese conditions and forcefully extended over China's social landscape. The existing amalgam of traditional Chinese and Western-influenced (and in some cases Western-owned or controlled) organizations and institutions was repudiated, new institutions based primarily upon Soviet models were implanted, and China's citizens were subjected to intensive thought reform and political study in an attempt to develop support for the new values and institutions. Doctrines of class struggle and slogans calling for military-like assault on objectives replaced reverence for harmony and moderation. Socialist transformation eliminated the petty capitalism that had been the basis of China's economy for centuries and instituted centralized control and planning over all sectors of the economy. Subsequent campaigns were launched designed to create new momentum in socioeconomic and ideological transformation and to reduce further the influence of traditional Chinese and Western ideas and practices. In these and other ways, the impact of the changes introduced by Mao and his colleagues was truly revolutionary, and Chinese society had a very different face and feel in the 1960s and 1970s than it had possessed in the decades preceding 1949.

Less well appreciated, however, are the ways in which the new system built after 1949 had deep resonance with traditional Chinese ideas and institutions. Before 1949 some commentators argued that Soviet ideas and institutions were so profoundly alien to Chinese traditions and sensibilities that the CCP could not possibly triumph nationally. When this prediction failed, some observers remained undaunted, arguing instead that the CCP's victory was only partial and temporary, and that enduring Chinese ways would resurface eventually, with society "casting off" the alien, Soviet-inspired institutions and values. Because this sort of argument continues to have considerable currency and provided what now appears to be unwarranted optimism about the prospects for fundamental changes after 1978, I wish to be quite clear about why I reject it in favor of a view that stresses the substantial congruence of traditional Chinese imperial and Soviet assumptions about the state-society relationship.

Wherein lies the resonance between the imperial tradition and the new system built by Mao? Even though the content of the ideas involved and their specific organizational forms are quite different, the fundamental premises behind the late imperial Chinese polity and Marxism-Leninism-Maoism correspond to a remarkable degree. Both conflict dramatically with the basic assumptions of China's Westernizing reformers and of contemporary Western societies.

In late imperial China, as I have pointed out, society was conceived of as a giant human pyramid knit together by individual social ties and obligations, with rulers and officials proclaiming and enforcing a cultural and ideological orthodoxy designed to maintain social order and avoid chaos. In Marxism-Leninism-Maoism, society is conceived of instead as a single, well-regulated factory controlled by a plan. The implications of these two images are much the same. There is one correct way for society to be organized. It is a fundamental responsibility of rulers to proclaim and enforce that correct way. Citizens should, through some combination of indoctrination, organization, and coercion, be induced to subordinate themselves to the needs and goals of the social groupings to which they belong, and these in turn should be subordinated to the goals and orthodoxy proclaimed by the state. In both conceptions autonomous individuals, self-conscious interest groups, and competing ideas and values are seen as threats to the political and social order.

The nature of the danger posed by autonomous individuals, groups, and ideas is somewhat different in these two world views (neo-Confucianism and Marxism-Leninism-Maoism). In traditional Chinese thinking, the failure to maintain the dominance of orthodox ways threatened social chaos, economic decline, and perhaps the fall of the dynasty. In Marxism-Leninism-Maoism the same failure threatens to undermine the pursuit of socialism and communism and perhaps even to lead to counterrevolution. In spite of some differences on this and other points, there is a fundamental congruence on the nature of the proper state-society relationship. In both world views the state should dominate society and should coopt, replace, or control grass-roots social groups to prevent autonomous forms of social life and culture from emerging and gaining influence.[7]

While late imperial and Maoist China shared a basic commitment to state domination over society, the reality on the ground was fundamentally different. As already noted, the late imperial state lacked the resources and ability actively to penetrate and control grass-roots social life and had to use a variety of indirect means to try to sustain state dominance. This effort often failed, leaving considerable power over grass-roots social life in the hands of groups and organizations that were substantially outside of state control—lineages, secret societies, religious sects, and so forth. Through its successful nationwide conquest of power and the use of Leninist-Stalinist organizational principles and modern instruments of rule, Mao and his colleagues were able to realize a more complete, although never total, state dominance over society. Indeed, one might say that only after 1949 did the imperial totalistic dream come close to being realized.

The specific measures taken to transform grass-roots social life in China after 1949 reflect a creative combination of Soviet and traditional Chinese organizational ideas. The story of how Soviet-style organizations were implanted in the 1950s is fairly familiar. Foreign ownership and control of property and organizations in China were eliminated. State monopolies over key sectors of the economy—foreign trade, banking, rail and air transport, domestic trade in vital commodities, and so forth—were established early on. A variety of preexisting organizations, such as secret societies and religious sects, were suppressed, while others were coopted or replaced by new organizational forms. With socialist transformation in 1955–57, state monopoly control over the economy was completed, with the exception of small remnants of private enterprise and trade. State monopoly control extended not only to the economy, but also to the mass media, the educational system, and in general to all forms of organizing and influencing the population. Familiar Soviet-style "transmission belt" organizations were formed to assist the CCP in establishing state dominance—the Communist Youth League and the Young Pioneers, the Women's Federation, official trade unions, writers' and artists' associations, "patriotic" religious organizations, "democratic" parties, and so forth.[8] By the time socialist transition had been completed, the process of transforming a chaotic and heterogeneous society into new organizational forms dominated by the state had been accomplished.[9]

The predominantly Soviet-inspired organizational transformation of the 1950s is only part of the story, however. The CCP leaders made creative additions to their Soviet organizational models, producing patterns of grass-roots social organization that went beyond those found in the Soviet Union. They adopted a combination of household registration, migration controls, and rationing that was designed not only to keep track of the population, nor simply to inhibit migration into the largest cities (as in the Soviet Union), but to inhibit all movement upward within the entire urban hierarchy and to make it possible to "mobilize" people to accept downward movement within this hierarchy. They implemented a form of socialism that involved more direct bureaucratic allocation, and less use of markets, than was the case in the Soviet Union. This distinction was visible not only through the extensiveness of rationing of food and consumer goods in China after the 1950s, but also in the attempt virtually to eliminate the labor market and voluntary job changes. The result was a system in which people were locked into assigned jobs and housing, unless of course the authorities decided to reassign them bureaucratically.[10] These innovations in social organization and control at the societal level were matched by novel features in the way the population was organized at the grass roots. Because the latter mechanisms differ in fundamental ways between urban and rural areas, it is necessary to describe these two sectors separately.

Two mutually reinforcing grass-roots social-control systems were developed in China's cities in the 1950s: those centered around work units (*danwei*) and those organized in residential areas. The virtual elimination of labor markets by the end of the decade meant that urbanites found a form of "permanent employment" in their danwei, and in the environment of shortages and rationing that developed, employees became very dependent upon goods and services made available through their places of work. Work units in many instances provided housing, nursery schools, health clinics, dining halls, and recreational facilities, and they distributed ration coupons and scarce goods to employees. They supervised the leisure-time activity of their members, ran local cleanliness campaigns, organized innoculation drives against diseases, mobilized their flock to guard against crime dangers, mediated interpersonal and marital disputes, and screened applications for marriages and divorces (and eventually for childbearing). They regularly organized mandatory political study sessions for employees and required the latter to submit to criticism and self-criticism rituals, and they occasionally extended these activities to dependents of employees as well. The bureaucratic overseers in such urban work units had no clear limits on what activities and thoughts of employees (and family members) they could supervise and control.

In urban neighborhoods not attached to particular work units the second leg of the urban social control system prevailed. Residents' committees (incorporating 100–800 neighboring households) and residents' small groups (overseeing 15–40 households within a residents' committee) provided services to residents and supervised their lives. As with work units, these state-mandated neighborhood organs ran cleanup campaigns and innoculation drives, established first-aid clinics and nursery schools, organized anticrime meetings and citizen patrols, mediated interpersonal and marital disputes, and gave approval for marriages and divorces (and later, for childbirth as well). They also organized residents not involved in outside work units for regular political study and mutual criticism meetings in an effort to make sure that there were no "blank spots" in society that didn't received the party's latest messages. Many urban families, of course, fell under both urban grass-roots social-control systems and had two separate sets of bureaucratic overseers.[11] So in addition to the Soviet-style organizations that replaced or preempted voluntary associations and secondary groups, a highly intrusive and penetrating system was constructed designed to maximize official control over primary groups at the urban grass roots.

The rural grass-roots organizational system was designed with similar goals in mind, although the specific organizational forms it took were different in crucial ways. Land reform and collectivization eliminated lineages, religious sects, and gentry-dominated voluntary associations from control over rural social life, and a unitary organizational model was implemented in their stead—first the agricultural producers' cooperatives of 1955–58, and then the rural people's communes.[12] As noted earlier, migration restrictions were fairly effective in stemming migration from rural areas into the cities after the 1950s (and prior to the reform era), and most peasants remained locked into their native villages. (The major exception was women, who usually moved at marriage into their husbands' homes, often in different villages, but were then locked into residence in their new locales.) Centralized quota and price setting and state and commune regulation of economic life in general eliminated much of the autonomy of peasant farming while also placing limits on rural incomes. A set of new rural organizations—CCP, Communist Youth League, Women's Federation, rural people's militia, and brigade and team leadership groups, was constructed to oversee the lives of peasants, and to some degree political study, supervised leisure-time activities, wired broadcasting networks, and other means were used to influence rural ideas and behavior.

Even though the basic goal of securing state dominance of grass-roots social life was as visible in rural as in urban China, such dominance was more difficult to achieve. APCs and communes were collective, rather than state, enterprises, and this meant (among other things) that peasants were not eligible for the guarantees and benefits received by state employees, but saw their incomes rise and fall depending upon local conditions and their own efforts. In most locales and time periods, there was also a larger remnant of a private economy remaining than in the cities, in the form of private plots and markets, household handicrafts, and the private financing and construction of housing. These differences produced a situation in which peasants were not as totally dependent for their livelihoods as were urbanites upon the state or their immediate work unit (the team-brigade-commune, in the case of peasants).

Other features distinguished the setting in rural China at the grass roots. More rural people were illiterate, much work took place in dispersed locales, and farming alternated between back-breaking seasonal peaks and off-season lulls. These features made it harder to organize rural than urban residents for after-hours political study and similar activities, and passive lecturing to the inattentive was more common than active involvement by peasants in discussion and mutual criticism. Perhaps the major difference between city and countryside was that in rural areas the new organizational systems were built on top of preexisting villages and kin groups. Thus the grass-roots enforcers of state policies were not paid bureaucrats, as in the city, but kinsmen and lifelong neighbors whose livelihoods were dependent upon the peasants they were assigned to lead.[13] Although state dominance and control over rural social life increased immeasurably after 1949, it still remained short of the levels achieved in the cities. Peasants had no more freedom to leave or change their lot in life than did urbanites, but they at least enjoyed a partial buffer from state intrusion and control that enabled them to preserve more cultural autonomy in some areas of their lives, such as in celebrating weddings, festivals, and funerals.

The way in which the state-society relationship was structured in the People's Republic after 1949 displayed, as already noted, a number of important additions and innovations in comparison with the Soviet model upon which it was primarily based. In the USSR there was less of a thorough effort to eliminate markets in jobs, housing, and the distribution of consumer goods than in Mao's China, and Soviet citizens were less fully dependent upon their immediate bureaucratic superiors for meeting their basic needs than were their Chinese counterparts. As noted earlier, Soviet citizens have been generally freer to change jobs and places of residence than have Chinese.[14]

In addition, a sharper distinction has been made in the Soviet Union between the party and its immediate transmission belt organizations, on the one hand, and the ordinary population, on the other, in terms of the effort to develop political study, mutual criticism, and organizational discipline. As a result, ordinary citizens in the USSR are less often and less mandatorily subjected to intensive efforts to shape their activities and thinking through such routines. In a related vein, the effort to regard intimate patterns of personal life, such as marriage, divorce, and childbearing, as targets for state intervention has been much more extensive in China than in the USSR. De facto, then, Soviet citizens have enjoyed wider areas of at least somewhat autonomously regulated private life, with state control experienced as more external and less a part of the fabric of grassroots social life, in comparison with the situation in China.[15] This contrast between China and the USSR reached an extreme during the Cultural Revolution, when attempts to monitor and control styles of dress, cultural life, and thought reached their peak.[16] Through such contrasts we can see that in the Mao period (and even before the break with the Soviet Union in 1960), the CCP went considerably beyond the Soviet model in the attempt to achieve state dominance over all of social life. I would argue that this more ambitious attempt in China to penetrate and control society at the grass roots can be explained by the way in which the CCP combined mutually reinforcing features of their Marxist-Leninist and traditional Chinese heritages. What I have termed the totalistic vision inherent in late imperial Chinese statecraft provided the fundamental rationale for these innovations.[17]

State and Society in the Late-Mao Period

For the most part the state-society relationship I have been describing was consolidated by the end of the 1950s. What was the impact of subsequent events and campaigns in the Mao era, and particularly of the Cultural Revolution, on this system? I contend that in its essential elements this organizational system endured until Mao's death (and to a considerable extent it endures to this day), although the intensity of efforts to regulate all corners of social life fluctuated. For the most part these fluctuations were keyed to China's political campaigns with, for example, remnant private enterprise, autonomous social groups, and heterodox cultural products restricted sharply during the Great Leap Forward, allowed to revive somewhat during the succeeding crisis period, and then falling under attack again in the socialist education campaign after 1962.

The impact of China's most tumultuous campaign, the Cultural Revolution, is a different and more complex story. If one considers the period of the mass movement itself (1966–68) and the remainder of the Cultural Revolution decade (1969–76) separately, quite different trends in the state-society relationship are apparent. While the intent of Mao Zedong and other radicals was clearly to cleanse society of remnant bourgeois and "feudal" influences and thus produce social life more fully congruent with Maoist orthodoxy, the actual impact of the mass movement was quite contradictory. The campaign stimulated young participants to suppress heterodox cultural practices and influences, such as Western dress and coiffure, traditional Chinese art, ancestor worship, and contacts with overseas relatives. However, at the same time the existing organizational structures, from the Chinese Communist Party down to lowly urban residents' committees, were attacked and either made inoperative or at least much less effective. As a consequence, Red Guards and rebels as well as nonparticipants were to a considerable extent released from the tight bureaucratic controls that had shaped their lives and thinking. Many people traveled freely around the country, some engaged in free-flowing debates, others were confined to "cowsheds" and forced to reexamine their lives, and many simply tried to stay out of the way and puzzle out what was happening to their society.

For much of the population, a campaign intended to purify society and subordinate it more fully to the pursuit of the Maoist vision resulted instead in a degree of relatively autonomous social interaction, exchanges of ideas, and independent, critical thinking that was unprecedented in the post-1949 period. From the outside China did not look, in 1966–68, like a place in which the seeds of the reemergence of civil society were being planted, but in retrospect the temporary dismantling of the system of bureaucratic regulation of social life so laboriously constructed in the 1950s may have been a pivotal event that prepared the way for the popular demands for democratic reform and cultural freedom that have been such a prominent feature of the post-1976 period.

The remaining years of Mao's rule, from 1969 to 1976, may be viewed as akin to trying to put Humpty Dumpty back together again. The elaborate system of bureaucratic controls over grass-roots social life was reconstructed, if anything in a more intrusive and rigid way (with further efforts to inhibit market transactions, individual choice, and autonomous social interaction). The reconstructed Humpty Dumpty had cracks, however, and it soon became apparent that society was not as effectively dominated by the state as had been the case prior to the Cultural Revolution. Flaws and internal contradictions existed within China's post-1949 organizational system, and the Cultural Revolution accentuated these and added new fissures. At this point it makes sense, then, to shift to an attempt to assess the strengths and weaknesses of the state-society relationship in the Mao period in general.

Problems Spawned by Mao's Pursuit of Totalistic State Control

I have argued that in the Mao era an attempt was made to establish a thoroughgoing state dominance over society, using organizational ideas drawn both from Leninism-Stalinism and the Chinese imperial tradition. In essence Mao wanted a form of socialism in which all social groups and activities would be part of the planned state political economy, and in which individual choice, market distribution, and independent social groupings would play no role. In spite of Mao's well-known animus toward bureaucracy, his ideas implied the creation of one of the most bureaucratized social orders in human history.[18] This uniform social order was to be guided by official interpretations of Marxism–Leninism–Mao Zedong Thought, and the attempt to subordinate all of social life to that orthodoxy represented a continuation of an age-old dream of Chinese rulers.

In many ways, Mao and his colleagues were successful in realizing their objectives. A powerful state machinery was built that controlled grass-roots society throughout the realm as never before. National unity, a growing stature of China in world affairs, and a mobilized population replaced the weak central control, ineptitude, and social problems of the Nationalist era. Major changes in social organization were pushed through successfully, and it became possible to call out huge numbers of people in drives to eliminate diseases, foster literacy, and build up the national economy. China had become a different social order from the one that prevailed prior to 1949, and on the surface a very successful one, in terms of the ability to mobilize popular energies to confront the nation's problems.[19]

These successes, however, must be balanced against inherent problems within the new social system. One problem was simply the inherent impossibility of realizing the totalistic vision shared by Mao and his imperial predecessors. Ideally, all groups and individuals were supposed to be subordinated to the official organizational system and cultural orthodoxy, so that there would be no autonomous social relations and ideas to interfere with popular responsiveness to regime goals. In reality, even in the "high tide" periods of campaigns, much social life remained outside of full or effective state control, and considerable popular energy was expended avoiding or subverting bureaucratic controls.

One of the gaps in the organizational system was that most basic group, the Chinese family. In spite of periodic pronouncements that seemed to foreshadow attempts to "destroy" the family or to require that popular loyalties be given to the party and Mao, rather than to kinsmen, the net effect of trends in the Maoist era was probably to strengthen family ties and solidarity.[20] In addition to the family, most individuals were enmeshed in extended kinship ties, friendships, former schoolmate relationships, and in bonds with workmates, neighbors, and leisure time groups (e.g., practising taijiquan, raising songbirds, etc.). It was impossible for the state to monitor and control interaction in all of these dispersed social networks and solidary families.

The effect of such remaining elements of fairly autonomous social relations was to promote what has been called "political diglossia," which is a fancy way of saying that individuals voiced official rhetoric and slogans on public occasions in their work and residential collectives while using a completely different type of language and sentiments in private conversations with intimates. These private conversations were often quite apolitical, but nonetheless they served to reinforce the sense that public discourse was induced and artificial. In the right circumstances these intimate, unsupervised social ties could provide a sounding board for grumbling, rumors, and political heterodoxy that undermined the persuasive power of the state's messages. When this happened, popular discontent might build up, even as an appearance was maintained of nearly unanimous popular support for official policies.

The success of elites in controlling public displays of opinion was such that they might fool themselves about the degree of popular support for their policies. When circumstances changed, due to a factional struggle at the top or a dramatic change in the official "line," mass anger and contentiousness might burst into the open. The result was a volatility in Chinese politics that presented a constant threat to order-minded leaders. As R. H. Tawney observed about an earlier era, "Political forces in China resemble Chinese rivers. The pressure on the dikes is enormous, but unseen; it is only when they burst that the strain is realized."[21]

The combination of less than fully effective control over social ties and interactions and a highly dependent population facing severe shortages produced other built-in problems in this organizational system. As it became clear to subordinates that the benevolence of the state and of immediate bureaucratic superiors was not a reliable guarantee that their needs would be met, they resourcefully tried to find ways to "work the system" or "beat the system." Since control over the essentials of life was monopolized by bureaucratic gatekeepers who operated with considerable personal discretion, a competitive effort by subordinates to manipulate personal ties in order to get their needs met was inevitable. Again the organizational features imported from the Soviet Union and behavioral tendencies with deep roots in traditional Chinese culture reinforced one another, producing an infestation of Chinese organizational life with *guanxi* networks.[22]

When, through increases in scarcity, bureaucratic arbitrariness, or other factors, the reliance on such personal-favor networks became paramount, as appears to have happened toward the end of the Mao era and early in the reform era, the effect was to undermine further the state's efforts to gain popular acceptance of its view of the world. Subordinates increasingly recognized that the official "rules of the game" were a sham and that one had to manipulate personal ties in order to survive or get ahead. They also recognized that the people in the best position to manipulate such ties and gain personal advantage were the bureaucratic gatekeepers themselves. Such a system of totally bureaucratized distribution had inherent dangers for elites. If this system could have produced a reliable and satisfying flow of goods and services to all segments of the population, then it might have contributed to state dominance over society. Since it is inherently difficult to maintain such reliable and equitable paternalism, however, the eventual outcome was increasing cynicism and hostility toward the system. In a nearly totally state-dominated society, dissatisfaction with one's lot in life is not likely to be attributed to fate, the failings of the market, or one's personal deficiencies. A state that promises too much to its population is courting political disaster.

A further built-in weakness of the Maoist organizational system stemmed from its very success in mobilizing popular energies. The entire logic of the organizational system was premised on the effort to overcome potential resistance to official goals and campaigns in order to maximize popular participation and enthusiasm. By suppressing discordant views and objections and manipulating consent and enthusiasm, this system was able to launch misguided campaigns that caused immense popular suffering and damage to the nation, the prime example being the Great Leap Forward. The observation of a Soviet scientist who was in China at the time of the Leap conveys the problem succinctly: "One can compare the manner in which Mao governs China to the way in which a drunken bus driver would conduct his crowded bus along a precipitous and curving mountain road. The number of passengers who realize the danger grows with each passing moment, but no one dares to push the driver out of the way and take over for himself the responsibility of guiding the vehicle to safety."[23] The effect of the organizational system was to make the entire population subject to the whims of a small elite, and in some cases of the paramount leader. If one could always count upon the leader or leaders being all-wise and benevolent, then this system might have been acceptable, but as the example of Mao Zedong shows quite vividly, in the hands of a misguided or vengeful leader, the results could be disastrous.

The same problem was duplicated on a smaller scale at lower levels in the organizational system, and particularly within individual work units and neighborhoods. The degree of dependence on one or a few leaders was so extreme that subordinates were often reduced to sycophancy. In the terminology of Albert Hirschman, subordinates had the ability neither to "exit" (to another job and residence) nor to exert "voice" (by protesting and organizing against the acts of superiors) but were forced to rely on ingenuity in displaying "loyalty."[24] The result was that superiors were able to cultivate bands of submissive supporters, but the innovative and politically conscious activists supposedly desired by Mao were hard to find. Given the power that superiors had over their flocks, and the degree of personal arbitrariness with which that power was exercised, the result was often not benevolent paternalism, but venal manipulation of power for personal advantage and spiteful mistreatment of those who had offended the leader and his (or her) cronies.[25]

The inability of subordinates to organize and defend their interests and the near impossibility of leaving meant a danger of being confined to a political purgatory in which they had to continue to work alongside of individuals who had denounced and tormented them over the years and campaigns. In this regard, as well as in terms of frustration at unmet state promises, Chinese organizational life could take on a pressure-cooker form. Suppressed animosities and rivalries could build up over time, ever threatening to produce open and vicious interpersonal conflict if the organizational situation changed.

Such features of organizational life in the Mao period have been seized upon by reform-era critics as evidence of China's "feudal legacy." In one sense this term is quite apt, for through the attachment of peasants to the land and workers and employees to their work units, and the granting of practically unbridled power over such rural and urban domains to individuals in reward for political loyalty, Mao and his followers created something like a form of socialist feudalism.[26] In another sense, however, the term "feudal legacy" is quite misleading, since what is implied is that the organizational forms and behavioral tendencies involved are direct inheritances from the imperial period. This implication is misleading because no such rigid, patrimonial system existed in the late imperial era, a period when markets, individual mobility, and relatively autonomous associational life were pervasive (despite the best efforts of imperial rulers). It required the creative building upon both Leninist-Stalinist and imperial Chinese legacies that occurred under Mao (as described in this essay) to create "socialist feudalism." The roots of this particularly rigid social form are to be found mainly in developments of the 1950s, rather than in earlier centuries and dynasties.

An additional major defect in the way the state-society relationship was organized under Mao is that the resulting system was not very successful in producing and delivering goods and services. Mao did not feel that a tradeoff had to be made between socialist purity and economic efficiency. Instead he assumed that by constructing a more consistently socialist system, in which maximum popular efforts could be mobilized and given central guidance, optimal economic results would be produced. The reality was often far different. The economy failed to grow fast enough to provide expanding employment opportunities, necessitating divisive mobilizations to settle urban educated young people in the countryside. The inefficient, production-oriented state economy failed to produce enough food, housing, and consumer goods to satisfy popular demands, resulting in stagnating or even declining consumption levels for significant portions of the population. The effort bureaucratically to plan and coordinate the entire economy led to imbalances and bottlenecks, while in local production units the result was often poorly motivated workers and low levels of technical innovation. In general the economic results of the system did not match the increasingly intense mobilizations of labor power carried out in their pursuit.

Both the failure of consumption standards to keep up with popular aspirations and the lack of control over their own work situation and income experienced by rural and urban laborers produced something quite different from the desired enthusiastic and innovative work force.[27] The problem was not simply the absence or weakness of material incentives, but the fact that subordinates did not have the autonomy to respond creatively to their work environment. The inappropriateness of such a bureaucratized system was most apparent in fields requiring initiative and flexible responses (e.g., farming or creative intellectual work), somewhat less visible in areas like manufacturing and services, and least problematic in routine activities subject to simple coordination, such as construction.

It was unrealistic to assume that a paternalistic state that planned production for an entire populace, with that populace undistracted by concern for selfish gain, would produce optimal results. The result can be characterized more accurately as a rigid, bureaucratic (and quasi-feudal) organizational machinery that was increasingly riven by factional conflict, personal favoritism, and interpersonal tension. The Maoist state was unable to inspire the best efforts or even meet the basic needs of many members of society.

Conclusions

I have argued that in the Maoist era, elites, influenced by traditional Chinese totalistic ideals and equipped with Soviet organizational forms and modern technology and communications, attempted to create an extreme degree of state domination over society. Their goal was not only to end China's considerable political and social chaos, but to make the country economically strong and to construct socialism and communism. The main features of the new state-society relationship were consolidated by the end of the 1950s, but an even more "purified" state-dominated system emerged in the wake of the Cultural Revolution. This social order could boast considerable successes in realizing cherished national goals of achieving political unity, economic construction, and popular mobilization, and also in regard to more concrete objectives, such as controlling inflation, combatting diseases, and spreading health care and schooling. Over time, however, and particularly in Mao's final years, a number of serious problems that were inherent in this organizational system became increasingly apparent, not only to outside observers, but increasingly even to members of the elite.

In the post-Mao era, serious efforts have been made by China's reformers to deal with these problems, first by retreating from some of the more extreme practices introduced during the Cultural Revolution decade, but eventually by tinkering with the basic features of the system that was constructed during the 1950s. Efforts to foster marketization, personal choice, material incentives, and cultural diversity and to pursue legal and civil service reforms (and even to debate broader political reforms) were intended to address the defects of the rigidly bureaucratic social order inherited from Mao. Yet it would be misleading to regard these changes as a process by which a modern, rational set of organizational practices was being proposed to replace an irrational and outmoded set. It would also be inaccurate to see those who resist such reforms as motivated purely by a Neanderthal effort to hold onto their power. What is involved is tradeoffs more than progress. The reforms carried out since 1978 have had a real impact, in terms of addressing some of the defects discussed above. They have reduced interpersonal tensions within organizations, fostered individual initiative and incentives, reduced the extreme dependence of subordinates somewhat, and made possible greater cultural creativity and diversity. However, by shifting the major engine of societal dynamism from state-mobilized mass energies to decentralized and competitive individual, family, and community initiatives, these reforms weaken the state's ability to maintain the dominance of official values. By so doing they appear to threaten the state's ability to mobilize uniform efforts in favor of national goals or even to maintain some of the fruits of past mobilizations.

As the state has stepped back from an effort minutely to control daily social life in most realms (a key exception being birth control), a variety of phenomena that elites and many ordinary citizens find undesirable (e.g., gambling, inflation, stealing of crops, student demonstrations) have reemerged along with more desirable ones (e.g., improved food supplies, a more lively cultural realm). As a result, movement even a short distance along the continuum from total state domination toward a civil society only loosely regulated by the state has produced elite conflict. In this conflict the conservatives can argue that the reforms undermine the very considerable accomplishments of the state-dominated social order. In advancing this argument they can draw on powerful sentiments in favor of public order and strong central control and against diversity and chaos, sentiments that are grounded in both Marxism–Leninism–Maoism and in the Chinese tradition.

The "liberals" or more ardent reformers, in contrast, in advocating such things as individual rights, interest groups, and the free competition of ideas, are proposing a more revolutionary agenda. Some liberals have tried to argue that the organizational forms and practices they advocate have some grounding in the Chinese tradition, but such efforts seem forced and unconvincing. If such reformers argue, however, that their agenda should be adopted because it will make China more similar to the capitalist West, they leave themselves politically vulnerable. Such arguments are still highly problematic in a culture formed through a fusion of Marxist-Leninist and neo-Confucian world views, traditions that are both profoundly hostile toward Western, "bourgeois" ways and pluralist values. Perhaps eventually this revolutionary effort to shift away from total state dominance will reemerge and be victorious. The tragic events of the Beijing Spring indicate that, for now, the effort to renounce a totalistic vision of the proper Chinese political order has failed once again.

Notes

1. Of course, one may legitimately ask whether the reformers would have had the ability and political will to push through the sorts of changes dictated by the logic of their position. I do not mean to argue here that if the Western-oriented reformers had won the contest, China would, in fact, be some sort of liberal, pluralist society today.

2. I use the term totalistic to indicate an assumption that the state should totally dominate social life, with orthodox moral views and cultural values, as defined by the state, being used to judge popular thinking and behavior. Alternative terms, such as "totalitarian," might be used to convey this idea, but they contain too many specific meanings drawn from the European experience that are not fully applicable to China.

3. For a discussion of this process in the Ming, see in particular John Dardess, *Confucianism and Autocracy* (Berkeley: University of California Press, 1983). For the extensive efforts during the Qing to develop an orthodoxy based upon the sacred edicts of the Kangxi emperor and commentaries upon them, see Victor Mair, "Language and Ideology in the Written Popularizations of the Sacred Edict," in *Popular Culture in Late Imperial China,* ed. D. Johnson, A. Nathan, and E. Rawski (Berkeley: University of California

Press, 1985). My discussion of the imperial roots of these totalistic assumptions owes a great deal to discussions with my colleague, Donald Munro, and he has been an invaluable guide to sources such as these that illustrate these assumptions.

4. Quotation from Wm. Theodore de Bary, *Neo-Confucian Orthodoxy and the Learning of the Mind-and-Heart* (New York: Columbia University Press, 1981), p. 165.

5. Quoted in Victor Mair, "Language and Ideology in the Written Popularizations of the Sacred Edict," in *Popular Culture in Late Imperial China,* ed. Johnson, Nathan, and Rawski, pp. 354–55.

6. Perry Link, Richard Madsen, and Paul Pickowicz, "Introduction," in *Unofficial China*, ed. P. Link, R. Madsen, and P. Pickowicz (Boulder: Westview Press, 1989), p. 2.

7. Or, to put the matter in the terms of the neo-Marxist terminology that is currently fashionable (with its roots in the writings of Gramsci), the state should maintain not only political, but also cultural, "hegemony" and prevent the emergence of a "civil society" standing apart from the state and its orthodoxy.

8. The term transmission belt, drawn from the Soviet literature, conveys the idea that the primary goal of these organization involved transmitting the policies of the party to selected subgroups of society, rather than serving the interests of those subgroups and pressuring the party. Democratic parties were not part of the Soviet experience after the break with the left socialist revolutionaries, but became a common feature in the new power structures established in Eastern European countries after 1945.

9. This generalization applies to the dominant Han Chinese portion of the People's Republic. A degree of greater organizational pluralism and weaker state control of grass-roots social life persisted in some minority nationality regions into the 1960s. The story of what happened in such regions will not be dealt with in this essay.

10. One can debate whether the differences from the Soviet Union here are qualitative or merely quantitative. The USSR has a population registration system, it has regulations that (fairly ineffectively) inhibit migration into the largest cities, and at times significant subgroups have been coercively resettled in less desirable locales. However, migration in general is not controlled in the USSR to the extent it is in China, most goods can be purchased by all who have the cash to pay for them, and in most nonwartime periods voluntary changes of jobs and residences have been possible. Of course, the population situation is very different in the Soviet Union, with the major concern having been how to stimulate people to leave the rural sector, rather than, as in China, how to keep them down on the farm.

11. Actually, there could be more than two. A family might have both spouses and perhaps other members employed outside and supervised by different *danwei,* one or more children in school and supervised by the authorities there, and Grandma submitting to the oversight of the local residents' committee. In addition, employed people not living in danwei housing would be caught up in some of the activities supervised by the residents' committee, such as local cleanliness campaigns, even if the primary supervision of their political study and other activities came from their work units.

12. In addition, there were state farms in small numbers from the 1950s onward, which constituted a sort of hybrid of rural and urban organizational forms.

13. The heads of urban residents' committees were not paid bureaucrats, but rather local residents appointed to these posts by the authorities and given only modest "cost of living supplements." Unlike rural grass-roots cadres, they were not linked by kinship to those they led, and their livelihood did not depend upon the motivation and efforts of people in the neighborhood. In terms of their degree of loyalty to the state versus to those they led, residents' committee officers were in an intermediate position between cadres in state units and team and brigade cadres.

14. In this and other comparisons some degree of oversimplification is required, with

variations in time and space not considered. For example, after 1940 government decrees made it illegal for Soviet citizens to change jobs, and these restrictions remained in effect for some years after the end of World War II, even though they were not always enforced. Certainly, rationing of food items and consumer goods has been intermittently applied in the USSR and persists in the Gorbachev era. Nonetheless, the claim made here is that such phenomena were not so pervasive and constant, and thus not such a part of the basic system of organization in the USSR, as they were in China.

15. Perhaps nowhere is this contrast so apparent as in the Soviet countryside, where weak organizational roots of the CPSU and the failure to develop primary party units in most *kolkhozy* until the 1950s contributed to the external and violent nature of the collectivization drive carried out in the 1930s.

16. Parallels are sometimes drawn between China's Cultural Revolution and Stalin's "great purge" of 1936–39. During the height of the Stalinist terror, however, there was never the sort of minute effort to organize and restrict popular cultural and social life that was to occur in the Cultural Revolution. Again in this comparison the contrast between external and official control and penetrating grass-roots internal control is visible.

17. More specific ways in which traditional Chinese social control practices, such as the *baojia* mutual surveillance groups and the *xiangyue* moral lecturer system, contributed to the grass-roots social control system in the PRC have been noted by a number of scholars. See the discussion in my book, *Small Groups and Political Rituals in China* (Berkeley: University of California Press, 1974).

18. Elsewhere I have noted that Mao's ideas led to extreme bureaucratization in a structural sense, even though the specific content and functioning of the resulting organizations was supposed to be nonbureaucratic. See my article, "Who Hates Bureaucracy? A Chinese Puzzle," in *Remaking the Economic Institutions of Socialism,* ed. V. Nee and D. Stark (Stanford: Stanford University Press, 1989).

19. As a testimonial to this fundamental change, the negative stereotypes used in regard to China shifted from stressing a population immune to mobilization to one that was overmobilized—from a "sheet of loose sand" to an "empire of blue ants."

20. This generalization oversimplifies a complex and controversial reality, and an entire research program would be needed to specify for whom, under what conditions, and when family ties of various kinds were weakened or strengthened. But clearly legal obligations to support aged relatives, enforced population immobility, and the declining ability to rely on primary ties outside of the family gave ties within the immediate family a continuing power and priority for most Chinese.

21. R. H. Tawney, *Land and Labor in China* (New York: Harcourt and Brace, 1932), p. 161.

22. That such features do not owe their origins solely to the Chinese tradition becomes apparent when we consider the endemic nature of similar tendencies in Stalin's Soviet Union. For example, Soviet industrial enterprises were forced to rely on special "procurers" (*tolkachi*) who cultivated personal ties and networks with favors and payoffs (*blat*) in order to gain the supplies and outlets needed to keep the system running. Such illicit dealing in the USSR is termed operating "on the left" (*na levo*), while in China it is called going by the back door (*zou hou men*).

23. Mikhail Klochko, *Soviet Scientist in Red China* (New York: Praeger, 1964), pp. 211–12. Of course, at the elite level Peng Dehuai did try to draw attention to the dangers, but the way in which he was purged and the campaign against "rightist sympathizers" launched after his downfall acted precisely to keep the brakes from being applied in time to avoid calamity.

24. Albert Hirschman, *Exit, Voice, and Loyalty* (Cambridge: Harvard University Press, 1972).

25. For a vivid account of such a corrupt local ''independent kingdom'' extending into the post-Mao period, see Liu Binyan, *People or Monsters* (Bloomington: Indiana University Press, 1983). For the best treatment of the sort of imposed dependency created by the Maoist organizational system, see Andrew Walder, *Communist Neo-Traditionalism* (Berkeley: University of California Press, 1986).

26. The parallels with ''true'' feudalism of the Western sort can be taken further. One of the most interesting and unusual practices that flourished in the late-Mao period and into the reform era was the *dingti* system, by which urbanites could retire and have a job in their work unit (but not necessarily the same job that they had held) given to a son or daughter. A system of job inheritance developed that seems rather incompatible with socialism or with modern labor allocation practices in general. This *dingti* system was denounced and curtailed in the 1980s.

27. These motivational problems existed even in the 1950s, but they were exacerbated by decisions to freeze bonuses and promotions and restrict or eliminate private earning opportunities that were carried out in the 1960s and 1970s.

12

CHINESE COMMUNISM IN THE ERA OF MAO ZEDONG, 1949–1976

THOMAS P. BERNSTEIN

The CCP as the Country's Ruling Institution, 1949–1976

In the late 1940s and early 1950s, the Chinese Communist Party (CCP) astonished the world with its capacity for effective governance. Having won the Civil War, the party leaders moved swiftly to restore order, instituted centralized control over China for the first time in nearly a century, and established China as a credible great power in East Asia by fighting the United States to a standstill in Korea. They succeeded in rapidly rehabilitating the war-torn economy, and in embarking on ambitious programs of industrialization and socialist transformation.

The effectiveness of the party and its ruling elite was based first on an impressive degree of unity, cohesion, and capacity to cooperate. The top leaders were in the prime of life. The average age of the regular members of the Seventh Central Committee in 1945 was forty-seven years. The leaders were confident and dynamic. They were sure that they would be able to find the answers to their country's immense problems. They had accumulated decades of experience not just in fighting but also in governance. They had a theory in which they believed, which they had learned to apply to Chinese realities, even as they were committed to learn from the Soviet Union and benefit from Soviet assistance and guidance.

Second, their effectiveness was based on organizational skills, which they had learned in the long years of revolution, and which codified in principles such as that of the mass line, had been taught and disseminated within the party, the army, and its ancillary organizations. As a result, the rapid expansion of organizations became possible when the mainland as a whole came under Communist control. The party itself grew in size from 1.2 million members in 1945 to 4.5 million in 1949, and to 10.7 in 1956. Skill in establishment of mass organizations, in mobilization, and in waging of mass campaigns enabled the Communists rapidly to absorb the newly occupied areas of the South and the cities from which they had been isolated for twenty years. Skills long developed in united front work were used to elicit cooperation from and establish control over vital groups, particularly students, intellectuals, and businessmen. The CCP systematically penetrated to the grass roots, recruited activists, set up local organizations, and launched campaigns to shake up and destroy real or presumed opposition, securing unprecedented control from Beijing down to the villages and urban neighborhoods.

A third source of effectiveness was mass support, based to a large extent on performance. In the first several years of rule, the Communists brought peace and order; ended runaway inflation; cracked down on rampant corruption (there was widespread admiration for the puritanical dedication of party and army cadres); eliminated various social evils, abuses, and pathologies associated with the old society; redistributed property; and increased living standards, mobility, and security. To a significant degree, the CCP was able to convert support earned on the basis of performance into more lasting legitimacy. The Communist leaders were able to imbue the country with a sense of purpose and cohesion based on national and socialist ideals, the latter undoubtedly accepted by a portion of the population, particularly young people. It was able to secure substantial popular acceptance of its policies and the sacrifices that they might entail, but it enjoyed the legitimacy to obtain willing sacrifice, whether it be for the war in Korea or for socialist causes. The CCP, however, also relied on open coercion to deal with class enemy groups and on an array of pressures, persuasion, and disguised coercion to deal with suspect middle groups, such as intellectuals and "patriotic" businessmen.

The reform group that came to power in 1978 was in a very different situation. The ruling groups of both 1949 and 1978 faced immense problems, but the one of 1949 could look back on a morale-boosting record of great, even miraculous, achievement. In 1978, CCP leaders could look back on great achievements in the first eight years of party rule, but since then, on a record of self-inflicted wounds. They spoke of "ten lost years," of "ten years of catastrophe," or even of twenty years of leftism. A county party secretary told me in 1985 that policies in agriculture had been correct from 1949 to 1955, had been in error from 1955 to 1978, and had been correct again since 1978, thus writing off twenty-three years of PRC rural history. Major opportunities to make progress had been lost, immense human and material resources wasted, and modernization slowed. While China was hung up with Great Leaps Forward and Cultural Revolutions, other nations had passed it by. The dazzling record of the "five tigers" of East Asia contrasted painfully with China's inefficient, high-cost progress.

By the time of Mao's death, popular support had to a significant degree eroded. Popular hostility to the radicals then in power had manifested itself in mass demonstrations on Tiananmen Square in April 1976. Undoubtedly the public viewed post-Mao leaders as a distinct improvement over the Gang of Four, but the reformers who gained power in 1978 knew well that they faced major problems of securing support and legitimacy. Chen Yun, a prestigious party elder and planner, now back in power, thought that if the agricultural situation was not improved, "branch party secretaries will lead their teams to go begging in the cities." Before Liberation, peasants had joined the revolution because they were hungry. But thirty years after Liberation, there was still hunger in the villages.[1]

More generally, living standards had stagnated for about two decades. Support could no longer be gained by conjuring up visions of a glorious future, as once had seemed possible during the heyday of Maoist mobilization in 1958 ("three years of hardship, one hundred years of happiness"). Since then, the ideology had lost much of its appeal. Not only had the promises of a glorious future not materialized, but ideological ideals had been devalued and debased by relentless political manipulation, endless political campaigns, struggles, and abrupt line changes. Both within and without the party, people suffered from ideological burnout. Mass support could only be gained, as in 1949, by performance, that is, by raising people's living standards. The CCP had lost the authority to ask for sacrifice. The country's disillusionment with causes seems to have applied even to national ones, as shown by the apparent lack of popularity of China's brief Vietnam War in 1979, in evident contrast to the Korean War.[2]

The elite's confidence in socialism had been shaken by the mid-1970s. Where there was certainty in the early 1950s, there was doubt in the late 1970s. Reformers realized that many ideological axioms would have to be reexamined and that experimentalism—"practice is the sole criterion of truth"—would have to be the order of the day. Fundamental questions about the nature of capitalism and socialism had to be asked, and many of the accepted verities of the old belief system jettisoned. Concepts that had long been treated pejoratively—markets, private entrepreneurship, foreign investment—had to be rehabilitated. In the early 1950s the superiority of socialism was accepted as axiomatic within the CCP. But in the late 1970s and 1980s, there were widespread doubts on this score and hence about socialism's basic claim to legitimacy, which rested, as Lenin had said, in the capacity of socialism to outperform capitalism.

Political Instability

The contrast between the time around Liberation and the time around Mao's death reflected the impact of two decades of the radical policies of the Great Leap Forward and the Cultural Revolution. It also reflected growing rather than declining political instability, and decreasing rather than increasing institutional coherence of the party.

During the thirty-odd years between the establishment of the PRC and the onset of the post-Mao reform period, the Chinese Communist Party did not manage to become a stable ruling institution. One indicator of this was the question of succession. China's founding revolutionary elite remained in power, and the issue of succession, both to the elite as a whole and to the individual leader, was not resolved; indeed, it was the source of enormous conflict. The senior leaders of the party in the 1950s and 1960s had founded the movement in the 1920s. But the rising average age of the leadership—the Central Committee regulars averaged 46.8 years in 1945 and 53 in 1956—was an indicator of the slow rate of promotion of younger leaders into the top ranks. Some were promoted at the second session of the Eighth Congress in 1958, but Mao's fears that regular mobility through the hierarchy would lead to a decline of revolutionary fervor led him to search for alternative solutions by the recruiting of "revolutionary successors," steeled in the "storms of mass struggle." Mao's approach only provoked conflict, eventually leading to the purge from various political bodies of "mass representatives" who had emerged during the Cultural Revolution. With the arrest of the relatively young Gang of Four and their supporters in 1976, and later, with the purge of the Maoist "Whatever Faction," the average ages of the Politburo and Central Committee members rose as power continued to be held by the founding Long March generation. Most of those who were in power in 1978 or, having been rehabilitated, returned to power, had thus held leading posts long before 1949 and therefore in the early 1950s. Many were in their seventies or eighties. The problem of rejuvenating the elite had to be left to the 1980s.

As of 1976, the CCP had to find successors for the entire ruling elite, but it also had to find a successor for the supreme leader. Mao Zedong had occupied that position since 1935, and more firmly since 1943. He occupied the party's highest individual position, chairman of the Central Committee, an unusual personal position among Communist parties, which, as Bialer notes, lack a formal "leadership principle," in contrast to German National Socialism.[3] Mao was also the personal head of the armed forces by virtue of his chairmanship of the party's Military Affairs Commission, which he held from 1935 on, the year of his rise to supreme power. He also was state chairman until 1959 and was a member of the Standing Committee of the Politburo. His unrivaled stature as the nation's supreme leader, however, was based more on personal power and personal qualities, real or attributed, than on institutions.

The succession issue was raised already in 1956. Chairman Mao, anxious to avoid the power struggles that followed the death of Stalin, devised the idea of withdrawing to the "second front" of decision making. This would enable his lieutenants, especially Liu Shaoqi, his long-established successor, to gain experience in taking charge of day-to-day affairs, allowing the Chairman to focus on long-term issues. Mao became disillusioned with Liu, who was the most important victim among the top leaders of the Cultural Revolution purges. He then picked Lin Biao, the minister of defense, but turned against Lin when he felt threatened by his growing military power. The rift between Mao and Lin culminated in a failed coup attempt in 1971. A few years later, Mao apparently thought of Wang Hongwen as a possible successor. Wang, a young Shanghai radical and a member of the Gang of Four, rose like a helicopter to the top but also displeased the aging Chairman, apparently for lack of competence. Mao thus turned on each successor, but he finally filled the vacuum shortly before his death by designating Hua Guofeng as his successor ("with you in charge I am at ease"). A long-time Hunan first party secretary, Hua lacked the power base of more senior leaders, even though he held more top positions in the years from his elevation in 1976 to his fall in 1980–81 than any other leader in the history of the PRC. He was easily removed by Deng Xiaoping, demonstrating that office counted for little as compared to personal authority and personal power bases, especially ties to the military.[4]

Mao's search for successors caused China to join a select group of Communist states, such as North Korea and Romania, characterized by "socialism in one family," in which relatives play major roles in the leadership.[5] In China, Mao's wife, Jiang Qing, rose to Politburo membership during the Cultural Revolution, as did Lin Biao's wife, Ye Qun. Mao's nephew, Mao Yuanxin, acquired a great deal of power in the mid-1970s as the gatekeeper to the increasingly feeble Chairman. (Since 1978, a number of children of top leaders have themselves gained leading posts, though not at the top.)

A second issue was intraparty decision making. The CCP was in principle organized along Leninist lines of democratic centralism and was not accountable to anyone, including its own members. Nonetheless, intra-elite decision making had been characterized in the 1940s and early 1950s by adherence to unwritten rules of procedure concerning free debate and discussion within the ruling Politburo. But a decline in adherence to such norms occurred as Mao became increasingly arbitrary and tyrannical in the late 1950s and 1960s.[6]

A major watershed in this respect was the Lushan Plenum of 1959. On that occasion, Peng Dehuai, the minister of defense, criticized Mao's Great Leap Forward as well as his increasingly arbitrary decision-making style of bypassing regular party institutions. In 1955, Mao had forced through collectivization, and he had stopped attending Politburo meetings in early 1958, coming only to those he wished to address. In speaking out, Peng exercised his prerogative as a Politburo member, but Mao treated Peng's critique as a right-opportunist challenge to his position and pressured the meeting into purging Peng. Peng's criticism thus ended in a victory for Mao but led many in the leadership to conclude that he had been treated unfairly and that the party's norms had been violated. In early 1962, Peng sought rehabilitation since his 1959 views on the errors of the Leap had been fully vindicated, but Mao resisted, leaving key elite members with a sense that a breach of propriety had not been corrected.[7]

In the 1960s, what procedures there were ultimately gave way to Mao's increasingly intense preoccupation with fundamental issues of substance, namely, revisionism and revolution. A post-Mao critique claims that adherence to democratic centralism would have prevented the Leap from being launched: it would have forestalled the antirightist campaign that followed on Peng's purge in 1959, thereby preventing the disastrous revival of the Leap. In this view, the Cultural Revolution itself could and would have been stopped:

> In February 1967, so many Politburo members, vice-ministers, and comrades of the Military Affairs Standing Committee came forward to oppose the "Great Proletarian Cultural Revolution." I think that if the Politburo had convened a meeting according to the normal principle of democratic centralism to discuss whether or not the "Great Cultural Revolution" should be conducted and how it should be conducted, the mistake could have been corrected in good time.[8]

In the late 1940s and early 1950s, the Chinese leaders succeeded in maintaining a degree of unity that distinguished them favorably from the purge-ridden Soviet Union. Few violent purges occurred in the 1950s, one of the most important being that of Gao Gang in 1953. But beginning in the late 1950s, especially in 1959, as exemplified by the Peng affair, intra-elite tensions rose, culminating in the massive purges of the Cultural Revolution, and in cycles of purge and rehabilitation thereafter. In the 1960s, factional strife pitted Lin Biao, the minister of defense who had replaced Peng Dehuai, together with Jiang Qing and various radicals, against the party establishment. From 1969 and 1971, Mao himself was engaged in a struggle with Lin Biao, his "closest comrade in arms," which, as noted, culminated in an unsuccessful coup, including a plot to assassinate Mao. In the 1970s, the radical Gang of Four fought the moderate group around Premier Zhou Enlai and the rehabilitated Deng Xiaoping. These struggles led to sharply increased turnover rates among the ruling elite. Whereas virtually all members of the Seventh Central Committee of 1945 were reelected to the Eighth in 1956, two-thirds of the Eighth were not to be found on the Ninth in 1969. About 28 percent of the members of the Ninth Central Committee failed to make it to the Tenth, elected in 1973, while 38 percent of the members of the Tenth failed to win reelection to the Eleventh in 1977. After years of internecine strife, the rise to power of Deng's reform coalition in 1978 signified the promise of the reemergence of a reasonably cohesive ruling group. In 1979 and 1980, however, conflict with competing groups, including Hua's "Whatever Faction" and the "Small Gang of Four," was in progress, and deep cleavages within the reform coalition opened up as well in the 1980s. The years of stable, unified leadership from the mid-1940s to the mid-1950s appear thus to have been an exception to a pattern of a high level of intra-elite conflict in the 1930s, particularly prior to 1935, and from the late 1950s on. Third, the impressive organizational cohesion of the Communist party as a whole gave way to severe cleavages. Party membership grew from 5.6 million members in 1950 to 10.6 million in 1957, and to 39 million in 1977. Apart from the proposition that party office meant power, control, and special privileges, it was hard to conclude in

1978 that the party had the capacity to provide dynamic and forward-looking leadership. Its once renowned mobilizational capacities had declined. The party as a whole was riddled by factionalism and by personal relations.[9] As Sullivan writes:

> Perhaps most disturbing was the party secretaries' weak identification with the "corporate" order of the party. Despite efforts since the 1940s to instill party members with an organizational loyalty transcending individuals, many party members below the central level failed to distinguish between institutional and personal authority. "Individuals equated themselves with the party or were even above the party . . . some party secretaries behaved like heads of families."[10]

The Leninist model of the impersonal cadre devoted to principled implementation of party policy was just that, a model. To be sure, the extent to which the party had ever lived up to the ideals of the Leninist party should not be exaggerated. Factions and personal relations had always played a role in party politics and were not simply a product of the leftist era. Factional affiliations of high-level officials can be traced to the early days of the party and army. Reliance on personal ties and networks had deep roots in Chinese culture. But there is little doubt that the disruption of organizations during the Cultural Revolution resulted in sharply increased reliance on factional and personal ties, which became essential sources of security in an era of organizational disruption, chaos, and conflict.[11]

The party was to a significant degree fragmented along generational lines. Layers of status and experience differentiated those whose seniority dated to the Long March or before from those who had joined during the War of Resistance and the Liberation War. The formative experience of all these groups had been politicized armed conflict, whereas that of those who joined between 1949 and 1966 was construction. But the formative experience of those who joined in the Cultural Revolution era—fifteen million between 1969 and 1976—was again a version of revolution. Doubts naturally arose as to the loyalty of the Cultural Revolution recruits to the reformist cause. Further cleavages separated those who had been purged and then rehabilitated from the survivors and the beneficiaries of upheaval.[12] Revitalization of the party into a coherent instrument of the will of the top leaders was a formidable task facing the post-Mao leadership.

Fourth, the CCP did not succeed in incorporating technical talent into the party, a crucial issue for a ruling party engaged in a massive industrialization effort. Not only had the Cultural Revolution caused an overall acute shortage of educated manpower, but the party had failed to find a legitimate place for the experts within its ranks. In contrast, other Leninist states had managed to incorporate the technically trained even during the stage of mobilization and all-out transformation, when Leninist parties tend to adopt exclusionist attitudes toward society.[13] In the 1930s, Stalin abandoned class labels and sponsored the recruitment and advancement of those with technical higher education, provided they were loyal to him.[14] But by the time of Mao's death, the CCP had not managed to make such a technocratic transition. Recurring, intense anti-intellectualism expressed itself in political suspicion and persecution of intellectuals from the old society. During the Cultural Revolution, this hostility extended to the "spiritual aristocrats" of good class background who had been trained since 1949, some in the Soviet Union.

By the time the reformers came to power, the country's small but vital technically trained elite was still to a significant degree excluded from legitimate political participation. The party still faced the task of promoting to positions of power those who combined leadership ability with knowledge of technology.[15] This task applied to the central leadership and to the party as a whole. Thus, in the early 1980s, a pathetic 4 percent of the roughly 40 million party members had attended higher schools and 13.8 percent had been to senior middle or specialized secondary schools. Some 42 percent had gone to primary school, and 10 percent were illiterate, a reflection of the fact that half the party members were peasants.[16]

Fifth, the party's relations with the military became more rather than less stable. To begin with, given the nature of the revolution, there was little differentiation between the party and army in the 1930s and 1940s. The building of a civilian party differentiated from a professional military subordinate to the civilian party was a task that got underway in the early 1950s. Even then, the military in China retained a major voice in politics: 19 percent of the Central Committee members elected in 1956 came from the military. But in the 1960s, this voice gained greatly in strength. In 1963 and 1964, Mao called on the military to serve as a national model for revolutionary revitalization. He was impressed by the way the PLA under Lin Biao had recovered politically from the Leap disaster. He also called on the civilian party and government agencies to establish PLA-style political departments, often staffed by demobilized army cadres. During the Cultural Revolution he relied on the army to provide overall control and support while the paralyzed civilian party was being purged. In 1969, when 45 percent of the Central Committee membership elected at the Ninth Congress came from the military, Mao himself began to worry that the army had grown too strong and that the principle that "the party commands the gun, the gun must never command the party" was in jeopardy This precipitated the conflict with Lin Biao, whom he purged in 1971.[17]

In late 1973, Mao forced through an abrupt transfer of the commanders of the key military regions. This demonstrated that local military commanders, who had long been in office and whose power greatly increased during the Cultural Revolution, could still be controlled by the center, or rather by Chairman Mao as their personal commander. But the task of reducing the army's role in politics had by no means been completed by the time of his death or by 1978. Army leaders played a central role in the purge of the Gang of Four and in the return to power of Deng Xiaoping.[18] Compared to the 1950s, the army was still over-represented on the Central Committee, accounting for about 32 percent of the members.

All in all, the CCP entered the post-Mao era, when major new challenges of governance would arise, as a severely damaged institution, a sharp contrast to the state of the party in 1949, when it took over the country.

Extremism with Chinese Characteristics

What had gone wrong with China's attempt to build socialism? Post-Mao critics in China blamed leftist or ultraleftist mistakes. These included pursuit of unrealistic goals, adventurism, subjectivism, voluntarism, disregard of objective conditions, and misestimation in the 1960s of the nature and extent of class struggle, especially within the party. Aside from blaming the villains—Lin Biao, the Gang of Four, and a few others—critics assigned Chairman Mao primary responsibility for pushing the leftist line.[19]

Leftist radicalism does indeed serve as an explanation of the political, economic, social, and cultural disasters that befell China between 1958 and 1976. But at least some of the problems summarized in the preceding section were not unique to the leftist period in China but arose during the stage of mobilization or of radical social and economic transformation in other Marxist-Leninist states as well. It is no accident that in the reform eras of the Soviet Union, China, and other Communist countries undergoing reform, deep regret has been voiced that moderate approaches to socialist transformation were abandoned early on. In Russia, in the view of some, if only the New Economic Policy of the 1920s had not been abandoned, and if only Bukharin's nonviolent, reconciliationist, and cooperative approach to socialism had been followed, the country could have been spared much agony. Similarly, Chinese intellectuals have suggested that the country would have been immensely better off had there been no premature transition to socialism and had New Democracy, with its emphasis on united fronts and partnership between state and private enterprise, been maintained.[20] Wistful might-have-been images of "socialism with a human face" contrast with the harshness of the approaches actually adopted by Stalin from 1928 on and imitated in various ways later in China, Eastern Europe, Cuba, and Vietnam.

The transformative policies of Stalin, Mao, and others entailed pursuit of several goals, namely, those of rapidly remaking entire societies, not only to develop or modernize them, but to build new, socialist, and ultimately communist societies populated by selfless people. Because of their scope and ambition, these goals deserve the label totalitarian. To pursue them, the leaders of the party-state and its instrumentalities necessarily accumulated immense political, bureaucratic, and economic power. This power was not constrained by institutions or law, or by alternative coordinating mechanisms such as the market, nor was it accountable to social interests. (An illustration of this point was the Chinese ruling elite's determination and capacity to exploit the peasants on behalf of the goal of industrialization, even though this elite had come to power by mobilizing peasant support, and even though the bulk of the party members were peasants.[21])

The power that the ruling elites exercised was not total, in that there were limits to the extent to which societies and individuals could be mobilized, limits to organizational effectiveness, and limits to availability of resources that could be deployed. Moreover, with the passage of time, bureaucratic and local interests posed constraints of variable intensity. But in some of its manifestations, the power exercised by Marxist-Leninist systems could be remarkably totalitarian, as witness the tight control over individual lives exercised through the Chinese system of urban units. Most important, the structure of power opened the way to the exercise of supreme and arbitrary power by individual leaders.[22]

How power was used was to some extent a matter of choice. In principle, power could be used prudently. Goals could be pursued in a balanced, moderate, circumspect way. There was room for choice on the part of the decision-making elite. Some leaders or policy currents in these regimes stood for a measured, reasonable process of guided change, even within the framework of the total transformation that differentiated their goals from those of the NEP or New Democracy.[23] In China, Chen Yun's policies in the later 1950s were a good example of this preference for relative moderation.[24] Some leaders opted for more moderate approaches, either because they believed that extreme methods were appropriate only for the early stage of revolutionary transformation or because they learned from the costs of extremist ones. Liu Shaoqi's stance in 1956 and from 1960 on approximated this pattern. Conflict between more moderate and more extreme policy currents could be found in both Stalin's Russia and Mao's China. Whether or not the political process yielded restrained policy outcomes was a key determinant of the outcome of the transformative enterprise. But given the goals, given the available means, and given supreme leaders such as Mao, the forces favoring advance without restraint often prevailed.

Developmental, Utopian, and Political Goals

The desire to speed up the rate of development, to attain breakthroughs and quick results, was widely found in Marxist-Leninist systems (and of course is not exclusive to them). It was characterized by impatience, a sense of urgency, a search for shortcuts, a sense that time was running out, and that it was essential to catch up with and surpass the advanced states.[25] The urge to catch up not only was designed to demonstrate the superiority of socialism, but was a product of the siege mentality in which Marxist-Leninist elites live. Their universe was populated by domestic and external enemies. Stalin's 1931 speech, in which he invoked past defeats and linked the future survival of the Soviet Union to maximum speed of construction, was perhaps the most famous articulation of this point.[26] For China, the U.S. threat in its various forms was a reality and helped spur the development effort. Stalin in 1931 had given his country ten years to prepare for imperialist attack. Mao in early 1956 gave his country "twelve years to basically complete industrialization" since the "American troop disposition does not appear organized for fighting a war." But a year later China's threat perception increased sharply and contributed to the accelerated efforts of the Leap.[27] From 1955 on, Mao promoted the acquisition of a nuclear capability, for without atomic and hydrogen bombs, "others don't think what we say carries weight."[28]

The quest for rapid development often led to abbreviation of targets—for example, to demands that the Soviet First Five-Year Plan be completed in four years or the Chinese Second in two or three. It often led to enormous rates of resource mobilization, such as to investment of 20 or 30 percent of the national product, or even 45 percent in China during the Leap year of 1959. Heavy industry had absolute priority, resulting in major sectoral imbalances. Because of the relentless emphasis on speed, life in a Communist state in the throes of rapid industrialization campaigns was one of storming of targets, shock work, labor heroes, and the strains and stresses of coping with overextension. A climate of militance and military language prevailed: "There are no fortresses that Bolsheviks cannot conquer." Because construction goals took on a sacred character, cautionary expertise was often treated as antisocialist subversion, resulting in adoption of crackpot schemes. Great achievements and great failures could result. Usually the costs were high.

In China, the temptation to speed up was enhanced by the country's distinctive capacity to launch mass campaigns and movements. Campaigns enabled Chinese leaders to make maximum use of their organizational assets and skills by mobilizing the population for a variety of purposes, including development projects. The campaign approach was rooted in guerrilla war, which required that higher-level directives be kept flexible in order to maximize local initiative and flexibility. Such tactics differed from the much tighter control preferred in the Soviet Union, where distrust of spontaneity prevailed.[29] During Chinese campaigns of socialist construction, an atmosphere of all-out advance was generated, together with a mindset of "better left than right" (*ning zuo wu you*), meaning that lower-level cadres were afraid to slow down the advance lest they become vulnerable to charges of rightism. Under such conditions, unleashing of campaigns often led to overresponse. Thus, collectivization was completed in 1956, at least four years ahead of schedule. Campaigns generated momentum that could resemble an avalanche, as when "ninety million peasants went into battle" in 1958 to produce steel, only to turn out junk.[30] To be effective, campaigns had to be curbed from the top down, since only an authoritative top leader could impose restraint without becoming vulnerable to attack for slowing down the march to the future. At key points, Mao's orientation, however, was to "let them go ahead'' (*rang tamen gan*) and to override the voices of caution.

Massive breakthrough projects such as the Leap won out not only because those opposed were silenced. Organizational interests played a role in generating elite support. Liu Shaoqi and Deng Xiaoping supported the Leap in 1958 in part because the party's role greatly expanded during the Leap, the implementation of which was largely in the hands of the provincial and local party organizations, rather than in the hands of central government agencies. But the dream had its own potency. As Deng Xiaoping put it in his *Selected Works*:

> It should not be said that Comrade Mao Zedong was the only one who erred. Many comrades in the party leadership were also wrong. The Great Leap was the overheated idea of Comrade Mao Zedong, but were we not too overheated? Comrade Liu Shaoqi, Comrade Zhou Enlai, and myself did not oppose it. Comrade Chen Yun kept silent. . . . The error of the party leadership was not the error of one person; it was our collective responsibility.[31]

But it was China's tragedy that the top dreamer ''did not foresee'' that ''coal and iron cannot walk by themselves; they need vehicles to transport them.''[32] The lack of even the most elementary knowledge—top leaders evidently hoped and believed that agricultural yields could increase ten- or a hundredfold in one year, Mao proposing that as a result of these increases, one-third of China's arable land could henceforth be left fallow—greatly compounded the effect of the massive antirightist campaign of 1957, when China's experts were crushed.[33]

Yet the dream persists, even in rationalized form. The urgent desire to speed up development continues to be found in China today, in the reform era. Output is supposed to be quadrupled by the year 2000, if not before. China's leaders encouraged the breakneck growth of local industry, regardless of its distorting effect. Li Peng's government ''Work Report'' in April 1989 criticized overeagerness for results, the excessive scale of construction, blind expansion, focus on growth rates, and persistence of extremely high investment rates.[34] The urge to leap forward thus appears to be a constant; the extent of the extremism with which leaders pursued it was a variable.

As for utopian goals, Marxist-Leninist systems normally envisaged a two-stage strategy of building socialism first and communism later, based on the successful creation of the necessary material conditions. The urge to accelerate development was sometimes accompanied by the urge to speed up the transition to the communist future. This urge was rooted in impatience to break decisively with bourgeois values thought contemptible, and in the belief that progressive production relations could speed up the growth of productive forces. Utopian impulses were often nurtured in order to garner the developmental benefits of idealistic dedication, willingness to sacrifice and to bear hardship for the cause. The utopian urge also came from a romantic longing to recapture the past, as in the case of the Maoist effort to replicate the dedication and community spirit of the Yan'an period. In China and Cuba in the 1960s, the impulse to implement utopian ideas was also rooted in a critique of the Soviet Union, which was criticized to be building the new society on the sands of capitalist motivations. Prolonged efforts to incorporate egalitarian or other utopian values into current practice always proved costly, however, and hence were always ultimately abandoned by Marxist-Leninist states.[35]

In the Soviet Union, utopian policies were pursued during War Communism, to some extent during the First Five-Year Plan period, and briefly under Khrushchev. The Chinese pursuit of utopianism stood out for its duration, scope, and impact.[36] It included the attempted leap into communism of 1958, with its large communes, free supply for peasants, and mess halls. Although at the Wuhan Plenum in late 1958 Chinese leaders disavowed immediate entry into communism, extraordinarily ambitious time frames of only a few years for the transition continued to be set. "Winds of communism" continued to blow, revived as a result of the Peng purge in July 1959 and the consequent antirightist campaign, and lasting until the Great Leap Forward was called off. The Cultural Revolution decade saw major efforts to promote wage equality, educational equality, and intravillage equality. Policy was not consistent, but periodic "radical winds" sought to give these and related policies a push.[37]

The Maoist case was in sharp contrast to that of Stalin. In 1931, Stalin decided that because egalitarian pay did not work, egalitarianism was a petit bourgeois deviation from Leninism.[38] The Soviet Union under Stalin came to have a highly differentiated wage system. Stalin also aligned his regime with the aspirations for upward mobility of the educated, ultimately dropping class criteria for admission to higher schools and to the party. Although Mao could be caustically critical of excessive egalitarianism, as in the Zhengzhou speeches of early 1959, his goal was to reduce differentials, not widen them.[39] He favored some wage equalization, crusaded during the Cultural Revolution against the "spiritual aristocrats" produced by the higher schools, and created a political climate in which advocacy of differentials was essentially subversive. As Marxist-Leninist states, both Russia and China were susceptible to pressures in favor of egalitarianism, but in the Soviet Union, Stalin imposed restraint from above.[40] As the authoritative interpreter of the doctrine, Stalin was able to steer Russia into a socially conservative direction.

Since Mao opted in favor of utopian policies and rarely spoke for restraint, there was no authoritative barrier to leftism, and "better left than right" attitudes often prevailed. The campaign style sharply exacerbated the consequences of this mentality, since it vested power with locals to compete with one another in pushing goals as far leftward as possible, while those lagging were vulnerable to charges of rightism. Mao, as Joseph notes, sympathized with leftist errors, even when he criticized them. Leftism was a mistake of excessive revolutionary enthusiasm; rightism, on the other hand, a subversive mistake of line. Leftists were "staunch and steadfast, and devoted to the party, only their approach shows leftist one-sidedness."[41] Interestingly, the official 1981 evaluation of Mao takes a similarly sympathetic viewpoint: "Chief responsibility for the grave 'Left' error of the 'Cultural Revolution,' an error comprehensive in scope and protracted in direction, does indeed lie with Comrade Mao Zedong. But, after all, it was the error of a great proletarian revolutionary."[42]

In the PRC, it is worth noting, acceptance of the Soviet model provided a temporary restraint on utopianism. What the Chinese had adopted in the early 1950s was a Stalinist model from which various leftist policies had been purged, since in the Soviet view they had not. Chinese acceptance of the model as authoritative meant, for example, that rural communes were not set up during the collectivization campaign of the First Five-Year Plan, since the Soviet Union had rejected communes as inappropriate. It was only when the Chinese abandoned the established Soviet model as authoritative that communes were promoted.[43]

As for pursuit of political goals, the concentration of power and the lack of accountability created the possibility for top leaders to stage political upheavals that went beyond what is considered normal in Marxist-Leninist systems, normal being the standards established by Lenin himself. The normal exercise of power included the right to use violence against class enemies, especially in the initial stage of takeover and revolutionary consolidation. The presumption that enemies lurk about meant that the Communist elite lived in a world of "we versus they" or Lenin's *kto kogo* (who prevails over whom). This mentality may well persist. In China recently, the we versus they world view came to the surface, when Deng Xiaoping told his military audience on June 9, 1989, after the Tiananmen Massacre, that "we must always remember how cruel our enemies are."[44] Still, once the major class struggles were won and the major social transformations accomplished, a more inclusionist attitude was often adopted, as exemplified by Chinese policy in 1956 and early 1957, or by Hungary's Kadar, who in 1962 proclaimed that "he who is not against us is for us."

Extremism in this context meant going beyond accepted assumptions about the use of violence. Stalin and Mao did this to extraordinary degrees in the Great Purge and Cultural Revolution, both characterized by orgies of violence against Communists labeled as class enemies and hence subject to repression in the name of the revolution. There was no barrier to this application of definitions to those who had hitherto been part of the system. Safety for even highly placed officials could at best be found if a skillful court politician, such as Zhou Enlai, pleaded with Mao to exempt a particular individual from Red Guard persecution.[45]

Mao's political extremism did not just consist of terrorizing the party in new ways in order to preserve or expand his power. His assault on the party was rooted in deeper concerns. Mao was concerned with the self-serving bureaucratic tendencies of a ruling party not accountable to the public. He thus raised an issue that came to the fore in the wake of de-Stalinization in the Soviet Union and Eastern Europe and that has been a core reform issue ever since. Mao raised it in the mid-1950s, when he worried about the party's "divorce from the masses," which in his view had contributed to the Hungarian and Polish upheavals in 1956. In February 1957, in the first version of his speech on contradictions among the people, Mao had given support to assertiveness from below, including strikes and disturbances, on the ground that such pressure would help the party overcome bureaucratism.[46] Mao's experiment with stimulating critical participation from below backfired during the Hundred Flowers of May 1957, when students and intellectuals criticized the party monopoly. The result was the fierce antirightist purge of the intellectual community.

How to check bureaucratization, corruption, and special privilege returned to Mao's agenda in the 1960s. One reason was that cadre conduct in the countryside had degenerated in the wake of the Leap. Between 1962 and 1965, disputes flared up over the form that the socialist education campaigns should take, designed to revitalize the party and reinspire the peasants.[47] Mao favored extensive mass participation in the rectification of village party cadres. By 1966, he concluded that the normal mechanisms of intraparty rectification could no longer insure the party's purity at any level. He mobilized the Red Guards to shake up the party from without. The Cultural Revolution did not, however, yield any lasting institutional solution for the problem of party accountability. Early in the Cultural Revolution, Mao had rejected experiments with truly radical organizational alternatives modeled on the Paris Commune of 1871, when he criticized the Shanghai Commune on the grounds that leaders could not be dispensed with. All that Mao could come up with was the doleful prospect of cultural revolutions every seven or eight years. Thus, Mao raised a problem central to rule by Marxist-Leninist parties but found only destructive solutions.

Party Leaders and Their Chairman: Tying Down a Loose but Indispensable Cannon

China suffered immense disasters as a result of the Great Leap Forward and the Cultural Revolution.[48] The Great Leap Forward gave rise to an unprecedented famine and a severe economic depression; the Cultural Revolution to chaos, disruption, terror, and the degrading of institutions, notably the party. Mao Zedong did not act alone in devising the Great Leap Forward or the Cultural Revolution. But Mao undoubtedly bore a major share of the responsibility for the disasters of the leftist era. Without Mao, it is scarcely imaginable that they could have happened, or at least not for as long as they did. The fact that only his death opened the way to a fundamental change in course demonstrates this point. But if Mao was responsible for so many disasters, why did the other leaders of the party let him get away with it? Why was he not stopped?[49] His subordinates, after all, were powerful and authoritative personalities in their own right, with long records of bold deeds and great achievements. Why, to quote Lucian Pye, did "China become a nation of Jonestowners, as one element after another self-destructed while singing praises to the glory of the one who might have been judged its tormentor?''[50]

The question arises not only because of the enormous damage that Mao-inspired adventures such as the Leap or the Cultural Revolution did to the country, but because they also weakened national security. As Nelsen notes: ''From August 1967 through September 1968, China was probably less able to defend herself than at any time since the national disasters which followed the Great Leap Forward.''[51] Defense capabilities were sapped and such enormously difficult tasks as building nuclear weapons and missiles made infinitely more daunting by the Leap and the Cultural Revolution.[52]

Efforts to Restrain Mao

Mao's lieutenants did seek to restrain him. As the frequency of Mao's misjudgments, errors, and failures rose, and as the quality of his performance declined, the central leaders made efforts to curb him. They made efforts to reduce his influence and sought at times to bypass and ignore him. But on the whole, these efforts were ineffective. If anything, they merely provoked him to suspect plots and to counterattack.

The first such attempt took place in 1955 and sought to prevent Mao from speeding up the pace of collectivization. But this failed as Mao counterattacked with charges of right opportunism. Mao succeeded in forcing through the collectivization of agriculture and promoting ''rash advance'' in the economy as a whole in the first half of 1956. In June 1956, however, top-level officials such as Zhou Enlai, Li Xiannian, and others combined to call a halt to rash advance.[53] At the Eighth Congress of the CCP held in September, changes in the party leadership and constitution apparently sought to reduce Mao's capacity for independent initiatives. Khrushchev's attack on the Stalinist ''cult of the personality'' at the Twentieth Congress of the CPSU earlier that year provided the legitimation. One step was to omit the Thought of Mao Zedong from the new party constitution. Another was to dilute Mao's control over central party institutions. Mao remained as chairman of the Central Committee but lost the right to chair a greatly strengthened Secretariat. Four vice-chairmen of the Central Committee were elected, evidently to balance Mao's solo status as chairman. The party constitution also contained a provision for an ''honorary chairman,'' hinting at Mao's retirement. LaDany notes that the ''bitter medicine administered to Mao was so sweetly coated that the curtailment of his power was barely noticed.''[54]

Mao's power was not in fact curbed. Mao continued to seize the initiative, as when he promoted the Hundred Flowers and the Great Leap Forward. In late 1958, during the first limited retreat from Great Leap Forward extremism, it was announced that Mao would step down as state chairman, but this had been agreed upon and was not a demotion. At the Lushan Plenum in July 1959, he was criticized by Peng Dehuai, but except for damage to his reputation, Mao emerged victorious.

The Leap collapsed in the summer of 1960 and compelled China's leaders, Mao included, to order a drastic retreat. Mao evidently suffered a significant loss of prestige among segments of the public. Satirical allegories about Mao appeared in a Beijing journal, which depicted him as an overambitious megalomaniac, or so the Cultural Revolutionists charged.[55] There are even some reports that during the famine peasants cursed his name, a contrast to the apparently more normal peasant view of Mao as the founding emperor who had given them land.[56] In the aftermath of disaster, his subordinates attempted to curb their chairman by restoring collective decision making, so as to reduce the possibility of adoption of ill-considered initiatives. Thus, the "fine traditions" of inner-party democracy, collective leadership, and democratic centralism were to be revived. At the seventh-thousand-cadre meeting in January 1962, Liu Shaoqi offered stinging criticisms of the errors made by the Center, dwelling at length on the need to restore party norms as a major corrective.[57] Deng Xiaoping said that democratic centralism included "the policies of blaming not the speaker but being warned by his words," an apparent reference to Peng Dehuai. Deng also quoted Mao on upholding the "style of humility and prudence." In the past few years, he said, "some of our comrades have abused the people's trust," causing discontent; "serious shortcomings in party leadership" had appeared.[58] Mao Zedong gave his endorsement to democratic centralism but stressed that "true proletarian centralism" was essential to preventing China from turning into a bourgeois dictatorship, such as Yugoslavia.[59]

The more orderly decision-making process of the post-Leap era included the convening of meetings with broadened participation, including that of experts. The more informal meetings that Mao had dominated in the late 1950s "were replaced by larger, more formal central work conferences attended by regional generalists and by high-ranking specialists from the ministries, the Central Committee departments, and the Secretariat. . . . Policy was now made in forums at which Mao's influence was substantially restricted or so he would later complain."[60] The Chairman still had to approve Politburo documents before they were circulated, since they were issued in the name of the Central Committee, of which he was chairman. But this apparently did not apply to documents issued by the Secretariat, which under Deng Xiaoping had became a powerful institution.[61] Mao's anger—vented in complaints publicized during the Cultural Revolution about "emperors" making arbitrary decisions or Deng having treated him like the dead father at his funeral—was apparently rooted in the greater autonomy of the Secretariat. It was used on behalf of recovery measures. Having been in charge of the Leap, party leaders had perforce come to be in charge of managing the recovery, a task that had a sobering impact upon them.

Organizational measures served to "patch up the rather tattered decision-making apparatus within the party'' but did not solve the fundamental problem, which was the absence of ''effective institutional curbs on Mao's power.''[62] Despite efforts to constrain him, and despite his own, voluntary retreat to the second front, Mao retained the power to intervene decisively. In 1961 he had accepted the policies of retreat, but by 1962, he contested pessimistic economic assessments that called for continuation of such emergency measures as household farming, which had proven effective remedies in famine-stricken areas.[63] At the Beidaihe Conference and at the Tenth Plenum, Mao decisively rejected further retreat, telling the Central Committee ''never to forget class struggle.'' His ''commanding presence'' enabled him to silence opposition and lay down a harsher political line, and to repudiate the policies of the head of the Secretariat's Rural Work Department, Deng Zihui, as well as those of Chen Yun. Household contracting was outlawed. At the same time, a compromise was reached in that the production team, the lowest level of the three-tiered commune structure, was named as the unit of distribution, rather than the more ''progressive'' brigade. This was part of a more general compromise package according to which class struggle should not be pursued to the exclusion of all else, and the major recovery policies were to remain.[64]

Henceforth, revolutionary fundamentalism coexisted with moderate policies. The combination was inherently unstable. It enabled emerging radicals to charge betrayal, that is, to say that policies were red in form but white in essence. Party leaders in charge became vulnerable on a wide range of concrete policy issues of being inadequately responsive to the Chairman's line, even when they tried hard to carry out his wishes. The cleavage between fundamentalist and pragmatic political orientations was compounded by the effects of Mao's retreat to the second front. Having chosen not to grapple with the concrete emergency issues of Leap recovery and of the long-term problems of concrete policy, Mao began to suspect that his colleagues were isolating him for nefarious purposes. As he put it in October 1966 after launching the Cultural Revolution: ''I put too much trust in others. It was at the time of the Twenty-three Articles that my vigilance was aroused. I could do nothing in Peking; I could do nothing at the Centre. Last September and October I asked, if revisionism appeared at the Centre, what could the localities do? I felt my ideas couldn't be carried out in Peking. Why was the criticism of Wu Han initiated not in Peking but in Shanghai?''[65]

Mao's subordinates might seek to adopt decision-making processes that reduced Mao's role, or they might advance policies with which he disagreed, but for the most part they were not willing directly or openly to confront, challenge, or criticize him.[66] Individuals have attested to this. Bo Yibo wrote in 1988 of a speech that he gave at Lushan in which he supported Mao against Peng: ''When I review it today, there were still some words contrary to my convictions in my speech at that time. This is something for which I cannot excuse myself and for this I still have a guilty conscience.''[67]

At the seven-thousand-cadre conference in early 1962, Peng Zhen ''could not bring himself to confront Mao . . . directly.''[68] Peng Zhen and Chen Yi reportedly were bold in raising delicate matters with the Chairman, but not in challenging a firmly articulated view. Zhou Enlai could remonstrate with Mao and had a keen sense of timing in knowing when to approach the great man. Teiwes concludes that ''Based on extensive interviews, it is my belief that Deng Zihui was virtually the only leader who could continue to argue his case once Mao had made a forceful decision.''[69] On the whole, leaders ''recognized that Mao could make serious mistakes and thus might try to vitiate his initiatives through bureaucratic devices, [but] none had the courage (or gall) to question directly Mao's fundamental evaluation of the current situation and the priority tasks of the Party.''[70]

Two important exceptions to the general pattern of unwillingness to challenge Mao directly need to be noted. One occurred during the ''February Adverse Current'' during the Cultural Revolution in January and February 1967. This was a dramatic confrontation between members of the Military Affairs Commission and vice-premiers, who were trying to call a halt to the Cultural Revolution or at least to preserve the army's integrity, and radical leaders, notably Jiang Qing, Zhang Chunqiao, Chen Boda, and Kang Sheng, bent on ever widening the purge, including to the military. In his memoirs, Marshal Nie Rongzhen writes of the disruption of social order, the drop in production, the paralysis of organs, the cruel overthrow of old cadres. ''We absolutely could not agree to this.'' Radicals, supported by Lin Biao, sought to carry the Cultural Revolution into the PLA, causing armed struggle and severe damage to defense capabilities. The nuclear test site that Nie oversaw had been disrupted; a rocket scientist was being driven insane by relentless Red Guard persecution. ''The motherland was in a state of danger. . . . Any party member could not but give this deep thought, and worry about the country's future.''[71]

Nie and other writers on the period depict the deep outrage felt by the veteran leaders, who had devoted their lives to the cause, and who now saw the world that they had built in decades of bitter fighting torn down by radical upstarts.[72] Feelings of hatred and anger boiled to the surface at a series of enlarged meetings of the Standing Committee of the Politburo and of the Military Affairs Commission, at which the establishment leaders and the radicals faced one another, pounding on the table, shouting and cursing. Nie quotes Ye Jianying as charging the radicals with plunging the party, the government, and the factories into chaos. But that wasn't enough: now they were after the army. But if the army is plunged into chaos, what will maintain the dictatorship of the proletariat? ''Can fellows like Kuai Dafu—a radical student leader—command the military?''[73]

During one of the mid-February meetings, Vice-Premier Tan Zhenlin summoned up his courage to ask Mao that the Cultural Revolution be stopped. According to a recent account, he first assured the Chairman that he had never opposed him since Jingangshan and then went on as follows:

> I have come to the conclusion that if the Cultural Revolution is not stopped, there will be no peace for the party, the nation, the army, or the people! I, Tan Zhenlin, am ready to risk life, jail, and party membership to fight it to the better end!
>
> Mao pushes a tea mug to one side, as if pushing aside an annoying obstacle, and gives Tan Zhenlin a sharp, ice-cold look. Then he turns to look at the military leaders who wait silently for his response. His look is as merciless as a blade. "Is this what you all think?"
>
> Meeting Mao's look, Nie Rongzhen recklessly walks up a step and says huskily: "Chairman, we ask that the question of the Cultural Revolution be voted on in the Political Bureau."
>
> Marshal Nie stands straight in front of the Chairman, four steps away. Every muscle in his body is tense, his uniform is soaked with sweat.[74]

According to this account, the challenge made Mao uneasy. He responded by saying that he needed time to think. The radicals present charged that the proposal represented a "dangerous countercurrent." Zhou Enlai quietly advised Mao to end the meeting. In the end, Mao turned against the military leaders, and Tan Zhenlin and others were subjected to mass struggle but not destroyed.

The second case of direct opposition was Lin Biao's coup attempt in 1971, which apparently was the only plot ever hatched from within the elite to kill Mao Zedong. As noted earlier, Lin had accumulated much power in the course of the Cultural Revolution. Mao worried about his dominant position, complaining that party committee decisions were being referred to military commanders for discussion and approval. Lin sought to enhance his position still further by reviving the state chairmanship while nudging the Chairman into a position of impotent sagehood. Mao countered with maneuvers to revive the civilian party and with attacks on Lin allies. Mao, a skillful political infighter, whittled away at Lin's power during a year of political maneuver by "throwing stones, mixing sand, and digging up the cornerstone."[75] In desperation, Lin and his son Liguo plotted to assassinate the Chairman. An indictment of Mao, drawn up by Lin Liguo, charged Mao, code-named "B-52," with being a ruthless tyrant. The indictment appears to have been plagiarized from Khrushchev's 1956 speech denouncing Stalin's crimes:

> Today he uses sweet words and honeyed talk to those whom he entices, and tomorrow he puts them to death for some fabricated crimes. Those who are his guests today will be his prisoners tomorrow.
>
> Is there a single political force which has been able to work with him from beginning to end? . . . His few close comrades-in-arms or trusted aides have also been sent to prison by him. Even his own son has been driven mad by him. He is a paranoid and a sadist.[76]

So confident was Mao of his invulnerability that after Lin's death the indictment was circulated in the party. Yet in the wake of the Lin Biao affair in 1971,

Mao's authority suffered a major blow. How could the Great Helmsman have so misjudged the character of his "closest comrade-in arms" and designated successor? Judging by the reports of Chinese students then in the countryside, the Lin coup was a watershed in Mao's authority among the young, who had followed him blindly only a few years previously.

Mao's Power and Authority

Despite challenges such as those of the "February Adverse Current" and Lin Biao, Mao remained the country's supreme leader until his death. Why was he so invulnerable? One set of reasons emerges from some of the preceding quotations: Mao was a tough, ruthless, and skillful opponent, whom one did not cross lightly. The penalties could be formidable. Long before the Cultural Revolution, with its many elite deaths, those who disagreed with cherished policies found themselves removed from power. The courageous party agricultural expert Deng Zihui was twice purged for questioning Mao's policies. Peng Dehuai's purge in 1959 was perhaps the most celebrated case of someone on whom Mao turned, believing Peng had plotted against him rather than simply putting forth his views. During the Cultural Revolution, Mao proved willing to see long-time allies such as Liu Shaoqi killed. The prospects of having to face disgrace, end of career, penalties inflicted on family, and worse were undoubtedly compelling deterrents to risking a challenge.

Moreover, Mao was a brilliant political tactician. He could adopt disarming tactics of making a timely self-criticism; he could retreat when necessary, as in agreeing to the military demand for an order protecting the PLA from the Cultural Revolutionaries. He could devise deadly stratagems to trap an opponent. His skill in counterattack and intimidation were major factors in reducing the likelihood of direct challenge. Causing Mao to believe that his power was being challenged was, in other words, a highly risky business, since Mao was willing to deploy the full arsenal of tools with which ruling dictators maintain their power.

A second, even more important reason, for Mao's invulnerability was his authority. Even before his deification during the Cultural Revolution, he was in a class by himself. He was the Chairman. His subordinates reported to him (*huibao*). He was surrounded by an aura of exceptionality. He inspired awe, deep respect, and obedience, especially among the military. (Suo Guoxin describes a Mao reception for the marshals during the Cultural Revolution, at which the marshals took notes as if they were cadets.[77])

Mao's authority was based on his achievements as the leader of the Chinese revolution and as the nation's leader. Mao had, after all, led the revolutionary struggle. He had worked out an unorthodox strategy and had established himself as the main theorist, conceptualizer, strategist, and tactician of the movement. Under his leadership, victory against remarkable odds had been achieved. The elite's reliance on Mao had paid off. Mao had been right, not only against Chinese rivals, but even against Stalin himself, who advised the Chinese Communists not to push to full victory but stop at the Yangzi, lest the United States intervene. As a result, "They thus developed a sacred awe and admiration for him. It was not only fear of the man at the top that led them to consent to his most irrational moves; it was an almost superstitious belief that in the long run Mao was always right."[78]

Second, Mao's authority came from his status as the nation's leader. He was the founding father of the New China and the symbol of the nation's revival: "The Chinese people have stood up." He represented the yearnings of Chinese for national unity and greatness. It was Mao who decided to stand up to the Americans in Korea against the advice of others, and it was his judgment that was correct. It was Mao who decided that China must have nuclear weapons. It was Mao who was the prime mover in resisting Soviet guidance ("why can't we innovate?") and in shaking off dependency on the Soviets. And it was Mao who held up China's greatness by receiving President Nixon in Beijing.

Because of his achievements and his demonstrated greatness, his subordinates were willing to give Mao the benefit of the doubt. They suspended judgment even in the face of troubling evidence that things were not going as they should. One source of continued belief in Mao was that in the past he had been right, especially if one took the long view and did not get hung up on minor shortcomings. If one didn't understand the Chairman's purposes right away, in the long run they had always become clear. Faith in the Chairman's superior wisdom and knowledge was apparently widespread. Peng Dehuai held this belief. Zhang Wentian, purged with Peng at Lushan, commented at a meeting before Mao counterattacked, "Mao is a wise man. Chairman Mao is the only one of us who knows Chinese history."[79] In January 1967, Zhu De, the old commander-in-chief of the PLA, tried to make sense of the Cultural Revolution, using this line of reasoning:

> Like many other marshals and generals, Zhu De firmly believed in Mao Zedong's ability to arrive, through scientific analysis, at the only correct way out of complex and confusing situations, while others are still in a daze. Mao had absolute authority in his mind. "Losing confidence in the Chairman is tantamount to losing one's life support." Confronted by the present chaotic situation, Zhu De habitually turns to this belief. However, the incredible things that have happened in the Cultural Revolution so far have brought many doubts. He has tried to suppress these doubts. He still believes that in the immediate future, in just a few months, Chairman Mao will once again prove that he is correct and the situation will miraculously clear up. "It cannot be otherwise," Zhu De reminds himself. He already feels the relief.[80]

With this mindset, Zhu was putty in Mao's hands. Mao told him that the Cultural Revolution "is unprecedented in history. Some things will be unpleasant . . . but I firmly believe that its orientation is correct. Some comrades in the armed forces cannot understand it right now. This is regrettable. Please help them."[81] Mao succeeded in winning Zhu over, but Zhu later met with the other marshals, learned more of the damage being done to the PLA, and again became convinced of the need for restraining action. He then joined others in cajoling Mao into approving the eight-point order to this effect.

A third reason for Mao's invulnerability, it may be surmised, was that his colleagues could not do without him, despite the erosion of his authority as disaster followed on disaster. No doubt, his subordinates would have much preferred him to be less disruptive; yet it is likely that they were afraid that ousting the Chairman or publicly criticizing him would endanger the stability of the regime. Maintenance of the supreme personal symbol of the Communist system was evidently thought of as essential. Thus, after the Great Leap Forward, steps were taken so that "Mao's own responsibility was carefully shielded to protect his legitimacy." Mao's self-criticism of June 16, 1961, in which he talked about his mistakes and shortcomings was apparently not circulated to the provinces, Mao's own wishes notwithstanding.[82] Even victims of Mao's unjust wrath acquiesced in the maintenance of his prestige. Thus, Peng Dehuai promised Mao after the Lushan Plenum in 1959 that he would not commit suicide, which in the Chinese cultural context would have caused Mao badly to lose face, recalling the celebrated suicide of Qu Yuan in the fourth century B.C., who gave his life to protest the ruler's failure to take his advice.[83] The other generals, too, as MacFarquhar notes, consistently sought to safeguard Mao's reputation.[84]

De-Maoization after his death confirms the point that his colleagues needed him. To be sure, to legitimate and implement the reforms, his successors had to criticize Mao in public. But they evidently felt that depriving Mao of his authority was an extremely delicate matter. Consequently, de-Maoization turned into a carefully orchestrated striptease in which the Chairman was deprived not of all his clothes but only of those that in the reformers' eyes no longer fit. Mao's status as the founding father was left intact, for fear that otherwise, the entire Communist enterprise might have collapsed. Khrushchev, as has often been noted, could attack Stalin because he had Lenin to fall back on; but in China, Mao combined the roles of Lenin and Stalin. He was both the revolutionary founder and the state builder. His authority had to be sustained in a way that Stalin's did not.

The dependence of his subordinates on Mao for supreme guidance helps explain one of the more anomalous aspects of Mao's role, namely, their acquiescence in Mao's remaining above the battle long after he had come to lead the radical faction.

In the pre-1966 period, for instance, struggles were waged between the party establishment and Mao's surrogates—Minister of Defense Lin Biao, who led the military challenge to the civilian party, and the radical intellectuals around Jiang Qing and Chen Boda, who challenged the propaganda and cultural apparatus.

Although Mao was in fact the leader of the radical forces, he was largely immune from direct challenge. Complex bureaucratic battles were fought, in which the civilian party sought to minimize Lin Biao's intrusion into the civilian sector, while the propaganda and culture establishment sought to protect themselves from Jiang Qing's initiatives. Yet in these struggles, the antiradical participants evidently accepted the role of Mao as the supreme arbiter, despite his obvious partisanship.

During the "February Adverse Current," Mao played this dual role of supreme leader and factional boss in truly dramatic circumstances. The leaders of the military and governmental establishment, having raised the specter of the country's collapse, refrained from blaming the Chairman for the catastrophic situation, as if it weren't perfectly obvious that it was Mao who had enabled the radicals to rise to power in the first place. Mao is depicted in their writings as one to whom it is possible to appeal, who is open to persuasion, who might intercede in particularly awful cases of persecution, and who might have been deceived by the machinations and slanders of the leftists. He is in a class apart from the detested radicals. He appears in the role of a mediator during the confrontations between the military and vice-premiers and the radical leaders. At one point, Mao chairs a session at which Foreign Minister Chen Yi, a Politburo member and PLA marshal, and Zhang Chunqiao, one of the newly risen Gang of Four, square off. Mao intervenes: " 'Please let's end this friction. Chen Yi, you are right from your standpoint, and Zhang Chunqiao is right from his standpoint. Let's talk it over calmly, without hurting each other.' Mao's voice is calm and even, giving no indication of whose side he is on."[85] Chen Yi and the others appear to accept the legitimacy of this mediating posture, not noting or not daring to note the obvious, namely, that Zhang Chunqiao attended this meeting only by the grace of the Chairman.

In the 1970s this pattern of battle continued between the moderate Zhou-Deng group and the radicals. Mao continued to play the role of supreme arbiter above the battle. He gave some support to this group and some to that, and he served as a last court of appeal. From his point of view, playing off factions against one another maximized his power. What is puzzling is not why Mao chose to use such tactics, but why the moderates acquiesced in them, since they stacked the game against them.

Their acquiescence can be explained by fear of Mao, by his authority, but also, it would seem, by their need of him.

Reliance on a personal ruler probably met Chinese cultural expectations. The Chinese elite may well have believed that a supreme personal ruler, embodying the virtues and capabilities of a founding emperor, was necessary to meet the needs of a peasant society with a two-thousand-year-long imperial tradition. Long before the Mao cult took on its totalistic proportions, PRC symbols had in fact linked the person of Mao with the institution, as in the phrase, "under the leadership of Comrade Mao Zedong and the party Center," as if institutional abstractions were not enough. It is noteworthy that after the Leap, when there was an effort to reassert the institutional authority of the party, this custom continued, perhaps even in intensified form. The speeches by Liu Shaoqi and Deng Xiaoping at the seven-thousand-cadre conference of 1962, which emphasized democratic centralism, nonetheless constantly stressed the personal leadership of Chairman Mao.[86] Post-Mao writers on patriarchy (*jiazhang zhidu*) criticized the behavior of party secretaries, who acted as local autocrats and emperors, emulating the supreme one. They traced this to the expectations of Chinese society, and to their own "feudal" assumptions as to what leadership was all about.[87]

Why Cultural Revolution?

If Mao was in fact invulnerable—if at most his policies could be questioned or his influence indirectly circumscribed—why did he launch the Cultural Revolution? One reason is that what matters in politics is perceptions. Mao appears to have thought that his power, influence, and authority had been reduced far more than was actually the case. But even if Mao had come to this conclusion, what evidently mattered most of all for him were the great ideological purposes of the antirevisionist struggle. For his revolutionary goals to be attained, he needed more power. He needed to emancipate himself from any and all constraint, real and imagined, and this is what he evidently sought to accomplish in the Cultural Revolution.

To this end, Mao pursued a three-pronged strategy. First, he asserted his authority as a theorist, that is, as the discoverer of the principle of continuing the revolution under the dictatorship of the proletariat. He laid claim to the status of chief theoretician of the antirevisionist camp, who had raised Marxism-Leninism to new heights.

Second, Mao built up his cult. A cult of Mao had existed since 1943 but it was modest in scope compared to that of the Cultural Revolution.[88] During the Cultural Revolution the cult of Mao took on unprecedented qualitative and quantitative dimensions. Mao became the "great teacher, great leader, great supreme commander, and great helmsman." He was the "reddest red sun that shines most brilliantly in our hearts." The country was saturated with his *Quotations* and his Thought was elevated above the party. Mao became infallible, and the country was run on Fuhrerist principles. Mass worship of the Chairman took on religious and ceremonial forms, as peasants bowed to the Chairman's picture and performed loyalty dances.[89] Accusations of having questioned or doubted his words were treated as sacrilege and exposed the individual in question to persecution by fanatics.

Third, Mao set his personal leadership against that of the party in an unprecedented way. Before the Cultural Revolution, Mao had shown disregard for the party institution by bypassing regular party meetings and violating party procedures. He had also sponsored the rise of the military as an alternative institution providing leadership. During the Cultural Revolution, Mao sponsored an outright assault on the party institution itself, consisting not only of the dragging out of individual "capitalist roaders" but of rebel "power seizures" of party committees. These hitherto sacrosanct centers of the party's authority became discredited and paralyzed, their authority usurped by various outside groups. Mao did not, to be sure, intend to destroy the party. He ordered the process of rebuilding to start in 1967 and purged Lin Biao in order to regain control over the military.

Mao did not succeed in his enterprise. He had to call it off lest full-scale civil war break out. Still, he remained supreme, and by the time of his death the Chinese political system had become even more personalized than it had already been. But Mao's supremacy was more nominal than real, not only because of his growing decrepitude, but also because during the Cultural Revolution, power had fragmented. A process of dispersion had taken place. Mao ended up with unchallenged personal power but with less real control. He left his successors the task of rebuilding the party, and he left them the task of coming to grips with the role of the dominant leader.

Notes

I am grateful to Harry Harding and David Zweig for their comments, as well as for points raised by other participants in the Four Anniversaries Conference. This paper was also given at the Fall Regional Seminar of the Berkeley Center for Chinese Studies in September 1989. I would like to thank Kenneth Jowitt for commenting.

1. Chen Yun, "Tiaozheng guomin jingji, jianchi an bili fazhan" (Adjust the national economy; persist in developing according to proportions), March 21, 1979, *San zhong chuan hui yilai* (Since the third plenum) (Beijing: Renmin chubanshe, 1982), 1:74. See also Zhai Yuzhong et al., "Peng Da Jiangjun hui guxiang" (General Peng returns home), *Xinhua yuebao wenzhai ban* (April 1979): 146.

2. Chinese students abroad have reported on the unpopularity of the Vietnam War and of efforts to stay out of the army.

3. Seweryn Bialer, *Stalin's Successors* (Cambridge: Cambridge University Press, 1980), p. 31.

4. For analyses of the succession problem, see Frederick C. Teiwes, "Mao and His Lieutenants, " *Australian Journal of Chinese Affairs* 19/20 (January 1988); Roderick MacFarquhar, *The Origins of the Cultural Revolution*, vols. 1 and 2 (New York: Columbia University Press, 1974, 1983); Kenneth Lieberthal, "The Great Leap Forward and the Split in the Yenan Leadership," chapter 7, in *The Cambridge History of China*, ed. Roderick MacFarquhar and John K. Fairbank (Cambridge: Cambridge University Press, 1987), 14:293–359; and Roderick MacFarquhar, "The Succession to Mao and the End of Maoism," ms., 1989.

5. Cf. Kenneth Jowitt, "Soviet Neotraditionalism: The Political Corruption of a Leninist Regime," *Soviet Studies* 35, 3 (July 1983): 275–97.

6. See Frederick C. Teiwes, *Leadership, Legitimacy, and Conflict in China* (Armonk, NY: M. E. Sharpe, 1984).

7. For a thorough and dramatic description and analysis of the Peng affair, see MacFarquhar, "High Noon at Lushan," *The Origins of the Cultural Revolution,* chap. 10.

8. Wang Renzhong, "Unify Thinking, Conscientiously Rectify Party Work Style," *Hongqi*, no. 5, March 1, 1982, FBIS: China, no. 55, March 22, 1982, p. K17.

9. For a stinging indictment, see *People's Daily* commentator, June 24, 1980, FBIS: China, no. 126, June 27, 1980, pp. L7–9.

10. See Lawrence R. Sullivan, "The Analysis of 'Despotism' in the CCP, 1978–1982," *Asian Survey* 27, 7 (July 1987): 807.

11. Cf. William L. Parish, "Factions in Chinese Military Politics," *China Quarterly*, no. 56 (October–December 1973): 667–99.

12. For extensive analysis, see Hong Yung Lee, *From Revolutionary Cadres to Party Technocrats in Socialist China* (Berkeley: University of California Press, forthcoming), parts 2 and 3.

13. On the issue of inclusion, see Kenneth Jowitt, "Inclusion and Mobilization in Marxist-Leninist Political Systems," *World Politics* 28, 1 (October 1975): 69–96.

14. See Sheila Fitzpatrick, "Stalin and the Making of a New Elite," *Slavic Review* 38, 3 (September 1979): 377–402.

15. This issue is dealt with at length in Lee, *From Revolutionary Cadres to Party Technocrats.*

16. Ibid., chap. 10.

17. See Michael Y. M. Kao, ed., *The Lin Piao Affair: Power, Politics, and Military Coup* (White Plains, NY: International Arts and Sciences Press, 1975).

18. According to MacFarquhar, the military agreed to their reduced role in politics as part of a bargain that brought Deng Xiaoping back to power. Deng joined the Military Affairs Commission and became PLA chief of staff. See MacFarquhar, "The Succession to Mao and the End of Maoism," p. 54

19. See *Resolution on CPC History (1949–81)* (Beijing: Foreign Languages Press, 1981) for the official evaluation of Mao.

20. The forthcoming book on Wugong by Edward Friedman, Paul Pickowicz, and Mark Selden seeks to show that an indigenous, cooperative, participatory form of semi-socialism, based on the market and on private property, emerged during the Anti-Japanese War but began to be crushed by dogmatic policies enforced from the top down as early as 1944.

21. On this point, see Yang Jianbai and Li Xuezeng, "The Relations between Agriculture, Light Industry, and Heavy Industry in China," *Social Sciences in China*, no. 2 (1980): 182–214.

22. This point was made as early as 1903 by Leon Trotsky, when he predicted that Lenin's model of the party would lead to gravitation of power into the hands of a single leader. See Bertram D. Wolfe, *Three Who Made a Revolution* (Boston: Beacon Press, 1948), p. 253.

23. See Werner Hahn, *Postwar Soviet Politics* (Ithaca: Cornell University Press, 1982).

24. See Nicholas Lardy and Kenneth Lieberthal, eds., *Chen Yun's Strategy for China's Development: A Non-Maoist Alternative* (Armonk, NY: M. E. Sharpe, 1983); and Dorothy J. Solinger, *Chinese Business under Socialism: The Politics of Domestic Commerce, 1949–1980* (Berkeley: University of California Press, 1984), chapter 2.

25. Cf. Kenneth Jowitt, "Time and Development under Communism: The Case of the Soviet Union," in *Temporary Dimensions of Development Administration*, ed. Dwight Waldo (Durham: Duke University Press, 1970).

26. Josef Stalin, *Works* (Moscow: Foreign Languages Publishing House, 1954), 13:40–41.

27. Steven M. Goldstein, "Sino-Soviet Alliances: 1937–1962," in *Patterns of Cooperation in the Foreign Relations of Modern China*, ed. Harry Harding (forthcoming), pp. 18, 29.

28. Quoted in John W. Lewis and Li Xuetai, *China Builds the Bomb* (Stanford: Stanford University Press, 1988), p. 36

29. In his memoirs, Marshal Nie Rongzhen describes the incomprehension of Soviet military advisers when faced with the flexible style of the Chinese commanders in using initiative to carry out orders, a style that was at the heart of the campaign approach, whether civilian or military. See *Nie Rongzhen huiyi lu* (The recollections of Nie Rongzhen) (Beijing: Jiefangjun chubanshe, 1984), 2:730–31.

30. Mao Zedong, "Speech at the Lushan Conference," July 23, 1959, in *Chairman Mao Talks to the People*, ed. Stuart Schram (New York: Random House, 1974), pp. 131–46. Mao defended himself but admitted to having caused "chaos on a grand scale."

31. *Selected Works of Deng Xiaoping* (Beijing: Foreign Languages Press, 1984), p. 260.

32. "Speech at the Lushan Conference," in *Chairman Mao Talks to the People*, ed. Schram, p. 142.

33. See "Talks at the Beidaihe Conference (Draft Transcript)," in *The Secret Speeches of Chairman Mao*, ed. Roderick MacFarquhar et al., Harvard Contemporary China Series, no. 8 (Cambridge: Harvard University Press, 1989), p. 432.

34. *Renmin ribao*, April 6, 1989.

35. The major analysis of this subject is Richard Lowenthal, "Development versus Utopia in Communist Policy," in *Change in Communist Systems*, ed. Chalmers Johnson (Stanford: Stanford University Press, 1971), pp. 33–116.

36. See Lowell Dittmer, *China's Continuous Revolution: The Post-Liberation Epoch, 1949–1981* (Berkeley: University of California Press, 1987).

37. See David Zweig, *Agrarian Radicalism in China, 1968–1981* (Cambridge: Harvard University Press, 1989). Ill-conceived Maoist egalitarian policies, however, increased rather than decreased inequality. Cf. Carl Riskin, *China's Political Economy: The Quest for Development since 1949* (New York: Oxford University Press, 1987), chap. 10.

38. Stalin, *Works*, 13:58–60.

39. "Mao Tse-tung: Speeches at the Chengchow Conference," *Chinese Law and Government* 9, 4 (Winter 1976–77).

40. See Sheila Fitzpatrick, ed., *Cultural Revolution in Russia, 1928–31* (Bloomington: Indiana University Press, 1978).

41. William Joseph, *The Critique of Ultra-Leftism in China, 1958–1981* (Stanford: Stanford University Press, 1984), pp. 55, 244. At the 1962 seven-thousand-cadre meeting, Liu Shaoqi opposed treating leftist mistakes merely as an error of method. See *Liu Shaoqi zhuanqi* (Collected works of Liu Shaoqi) (Beijing: Renmin chubanshe, 1985), 2:427–28.

42. *Resolution on CPC History*, p. 41

43. The Great Leap Forward, however, was inspired by Khrushchev's own leap into communism.

44. *South China Morning Post*, June 20, 1989.

45. Cf. Teiwes, "Mao and His Lieutenants."

46. "On the Correct Handling of Contradictions among the People (Speaking Notes)," February 27, 1957, in *The Secret Speeches of Chairman Mao*, ed. MacFarquhar et al., especially pp. 170–77.

47. See Richard Baum, *Prelude to Revolution: Mao, the Party, and the Peasant Question, 1962–66* (New York: Columbia University Press, 1975).

48. "Loose cannon," used in the heading above, is also Lynn T. White's term. See his *Policies of Chaos: The Organizational Causes of Violence in China's Cultural Revolution* (Princeton: Princeton University Press, 1989), p. 9.

49. The question of why Mao was not stopped has agitated post-Mao reformers. For a

thoughtful analysis of their views, see Sullivan, "Analysis of Despotism," pp. 800–821.

50. Lucian Pye, *The Mandarin and the Cadre: China's Political Cultures*, Michigan Monographs in Chinese Studies no. 59 (Ann Arbor: Center for Chinese Studies, University of Michigan, 1988), p. 157.

51. Harvey Nelsen, *The Chinese Military System* (Boulder: Westview Press, 1977), p. 137.

52. Lewis and Li, *China Builds the Bomb*, provide rich material on the impact of upheaval on the nuclear weapons project.

53. See MacFarquhar, *The Origins of the Cultural Revolution*, 1:chap. 7.

54. Laszlo LaDany, *The Communist Party and Marxism, 1921–1985: A Self-Portrait* (London: C. Hurst, 1988), p. 217.

55. Lieberthal, "The Great Leap Forward and the Split in the Yenan Leadership," in *The Cambridge History of China*, ed. MacFarquhar, 13:320; and Timothy Cheek, "Deng Tuo: A Chinese Leninist Approach to Journalism," in *China's Establishment Intellectuals*, ed. Carol Hamrin and Timothy Cheek (Armonk, NY: M. E. Sharpe, 1986), pp. 109–10.

56. Reported by a Chinese dissident scholar who was in Anhui and the Shanghai suburbs during the famine.

57. *Liu Shaoqi zhuanji*, especially p. 355.

58. "Deng Xiaoping's Speech at the Enlarged Central Work Conference (February 6, 1962)," *Renmin ribao*, overseas ed., February 16, 1987, FBIS: China, no. 31, February 17, 1987, pp. K1–14.

59. Schram, ed., *Chairman Mao Talks to the People*, p. 167.

60. Harry Harding, *Organizing China* (Stanford: Stanford University Press, 1981), p. 185.

61. Lieberthal, "The Great Leap Forward," p. 354.

62. Ibid., pp. 362, 328.

63. In 1989, part of a speech by Deng Xiaoping given in 1962 was published, in which he supported household contracting as a remedy to the crisis. See *Nongmin ribao*, August 2, 1989, FBIS: China, no. 171, September 6, 1989, pp. 28–30.

64. Lieberthal, "The Great Leap Forward," pp. 331–35.

65. Schram, *Chairman Mao Talks to the People*, p. 270. The Twenty-three Articles were the last of a series of programs for the socialist education campaign, about which Mao, Liu, and Deng had disputed with Peng Zhen. The issues were how far to carry the purge of rural cadres, how far to rely on outside work teams, and to what extent to rely on the poor and lower-middle peasants. See Baum, *Prelude to Revolution*. See also Pitman B. Potter, "Peng Zhen," in *China's Establishment Intellectuals*, ed. Hamrin and Cheek, pp. 37–38.

66. In the realm of foreign policy, where a harsh revolutionary line together with the break with the Soviet Union increased Chinese isolation and vulnerability, a policy derisively labeled the "three conciliations and one reduction" was proposed in 1962. The formula meant conciliation of imperialism, revisionism, and reaction, that is, the United States, the Soviet Union, and India, and less support for revolution. See Steven Goldstein, "Sino-Soviet Alliances, 1937–1962," pp. 41–42.

As the United States escalated its war in Vietnam, disputes about united action with the Soviet Union also broke out. Cf. Harry Harding and Melvin Gurtov, *The Purge of Lo Jui-ch'ing* (Santa Monica: Rand Corporation, 1971).

67. Bo Yibo in *Renmin ribao*, October 23, 1988, FBIS: China, no. 216, November 8, 1988, p. 39.

68. Lieberthal, "The Great Leap Forward," pp. 327–28.

69. Teiwes, "Mao and His Lieutenants," pp. 14–15, and accompanying notes.

70. Lieberthal, "The Great Leap Forward," p. 328.

71. *Nie Rongzhen huiyi lu*, p. 853. The reference to the mad scientist is in Suo Guoxin, *1967 nian de 78 tian "Er Yue Niliu" jishi* (Record of the 78-day "February Countercurrent" in 1967) (Changsha: Hunan wenyi chubanshe, 1986), p. 49. An abridged English translation of this work is in *Chinese Law and Government* 22, 1 (Spring 1989).

72. For another such perspective, see Tie Zhuwei, *Chen Yi Yuanshai zai "wenhua da geming" zhong—shuang zhong se yu nong* (Marshal Chen Yi during the Cultural Revolution: When frost is thick, the colors become richer) (Chengdu: Jiefangjun chubanshe, 1986), pp. 106–11, 120–26.

73. *Nie Rongzhen huiyi lu*, p. 854.

74. Suo Guoxin in *Chinese Law and Government*, p. 82.

75. "Throwing stones" meant adding critical remarks to reports, "mixing sand" meant adding members to the Military Affairs Commission, and "digging up the cornerstone" meant reorganizing the Beijing Military Region. See Kao, *The Lin Piao Affair*. See also LaDany, *The Communist Party of China*, pp. 335ff.

76. "Struggle to Smash the Lin-Ch'en Anti-Party Clique's Counterrevolutionary Coup," part 2, CC-CCP Chung-fa no. 4, 1972, in Kao, *The Lin Piao Affair*, pp. 89–90.

77. Suo Guoxin in *Chinese Law and Government*, p. 71.

78. LaDany, *The Communist Party of China*, p. 252.

79. Ibid., p. 251.

80. Suo Guoxin in *Chinese Law and Government*, pp. 40–41.

81. Ibid., p. 44.

82. Lieberthal, "The Great Leap Forward," p. 321; and "Zai guangda de zhongyang gongzuo huiyi shang de jianghua" (Speech at the enlarged central work conference), January 30, 1962, in *Mao Zedong sixiang wansui* (Taibei: N.p., 1969), p. 406.

83. "Mao Zhuxi yu Peng Dehuai tongzhi de tanhua (zhailu)" (Chairman Mao's talk with Comrade Peng Dehuai, excerpts), September 23, 1965, in *Peng Dehuai zishu* (Peng Dehuai's own account) (Beijing: Renmin chubanshe, 1981), p. 288.

84. MacFarquhar, "The Succession to Mao," p. 114.

85. Suo Guoxin in *Chinese Law and Government*, pp. 81–82.

86. See notes 46 and 47.

87. Sullivan, "The Analysis of 'Despotism' in the CCP," pp. 806–7.

88. Xu Jianhua, "Comrade Mao Zedong: From Opposing the Personality Cult to Accepting It," *Gongren ribao*, Feburary 1, 1985, FBIS: China, no. 31, February 2, 1985, pp. K3–4.

89. See Richard Madsen, *Morality and Power in a Chinese Village* (Berkeley: University of California Press, 1984).

PART FOUR

THE DENG ERA

KENNETH LIEBERTHAL

The Deng Xiaoping era poses special problems for this volume, as the papers in this section have been written while this era is still in progress. This has, moreover, been a period of remarkably wide-ranging efforts to effect fundamental change in the Maoist system that existed as of the mid-1970s. Driven by a crisis of confidence among the populace, recognition of tremendous progress in the other countries of East Asia, and fear of military threats from the north and the south, Deng sought in the late 1970s and early 1980s to encourage far-reaching reform of the Chinese system. To this end, he nurtured the political ascendancy of individuals who wished to move China far away from its Maoist precepts.

The resulting reform effort lacked a coherent strategy. Indeed, it was marked by tremendous experimentation and a spirit, as the Chinese put it, of "crossing a river by feeling for stones on the bottom." Many diverse strands fed into the "reform" movement. These included substantial erosion of the role of the state plan in the economy, numerous policies to "open up" the country both internationally and domestically, and various initiatives to bring younger people into responsible political positions and to encourage greater flexibility and liveliness in the political system.

It is not possible to assess the long-term effects of these many policy innovations as of 1989. Indeed, the violent suppression of the Tiananmen demonstrations on June 4 and challenges to many of the reform policies by hard-line leaders in the wake of that tragedy provided the writers of the papers in this section with a sharp reminder of the dangers in making firm statements about the impact or permanence of various measures in China. Against this background, two of the paper writers (James Townsend and James Watson) seek to put the reform policies in historical perspective, while the other two writers (Michel Oksenberg and Dwight Perkins) analyze, respectively, the key political and economic policies and their likely effects.

Professor Townsend's essay puts the "open" (*kaifang*) policy squarely into its historical context in terms of its substance, driving forces, and effects. He finds that the current effort at kaifang differs in important ways from those of its predecessors during the past century. The Deng era kaifang, for example, has been implemented by a Chinese state that enjoys full sovereignty. Perhaps in part for this reason, by most measures the current kaifang policy has not been as extensive as were its earlier counterparts, and it also is fairly modest when compared to the "openness" of various other countries.

Townsend's analysis identifies the types of contention that arise among the various agents of a kaifang policy, and in so doing he elucidates the types of obstacles this policy encounters in the short term. But his historical overview shows that there are forces (such as overseas Chinese) that support kaifang over the long term, and this historical analysis thus makes Townsend quite sensitive to the long-term durability of the "open" policy of China.

While James Townsend's historical focus highlights long-term continuities, James Watson's concentration on cultural identity tends to emphasize the tremendous gulf between the culture of the younger generation of urban Chinese and that of their predecessors. Professor Watson uses analysis of death rituals to illustrate his thesis that orthopraxy (adherence to correct practice) more than orthodoxy (acceptance of correct beliefs) provided the glue that held together traditional China. Immersion in common folk traditions buttressed this Chinese cultural identity. But those raised in China after the antisuperstition campaigns of the early 1950s, according to Watson, have been raised without this cultural integument. The Communists made concerted efforts to undermine China's rich folk tradition and to attack the ritualistic practices that had been so important to cultural identity.

Given this cultural disruption, Professor Watson notes that it is not surprising that the students in 1989 turned to foreign political rituals and symbols to highlight their sentiments during the democracy movement demonstrations. Urban Chinese youths simply no longer share the indigenous cultural identity that formerly was so central to the concept of being "Chinese." The situation in the Chinese countryside remains somewhat more traditional, as more of the traditional folklore and orthopraxy survive there than in the cities. Chinese society is thus no longer characterized by a common sense of being "Chinese," and this represents a sharp break with history. Professor Watson does not suggest that the Communist reform leaders have begun to make progress in forging a Chinese cultural identity.

Dwight Perkins directs his attention to the sphere that formed the centerpiece of the reform effort—the economic arena. He finds, in a balanced and thoughtful analysis, that the reforms produced significantly faster growth for the Chinese economy, with important positive spinoffs for the standard of living of the people of China. He also demonstrates that the reforms have made what are almost certain to be lasting changes in, for example, the distribution of labor among sectors and the relationship of the domestic economy to the international economic arena.

Professor Perkins argues that it would be very difficult to reverse fundamentally the key economic reforms that have occurred since 1978. Should the political leaders prove determined to do so, moreover, they would incur a very high price for their policies. The growth rate of the Chinese economy would slow significantly, and the leaders would face a major crisis in trying to absorb new labor into productive jobs over the coming decade. Given that the reforms have diffused knowledge of urban and foreign standards of living throughout Chinese society, moreover, the pressures for a better diet and for other components of a higher living standard will remain an important force in the political and economic systems.

While Dwight Perkins's analysis of the economy highlights the benefits of reforms and the costs that will be paid should they be abandoned, Michel Oksenberg seeks to provide a multifaceted assessment of the lasting effects of the reforms in the political system. Professor Oksenberg identifies the major accomplishments, failures, and memorable events of the era and then reviews a broad array of specific reform policies. In his final section, he tries to reflect on how the Deng era policies affected the people from whom the next generation of Chinese officials will come.

Professor Oksenberg's presentation conveys the complexity of the Deng era. This period produced major changes in the political system and in the relationship between the polity and the population. It resulted in major changes in the demographic distribution of the population, the nature of political exhortation to which citizens were exposed, the relationship of Chinese to the international arena, and so forth. In some ways, Oksenberg finds, the Chinese were pulled both toward their past (their historical roots) and toward their future by the reforms. But when summing up this wide-ranging overview, Professor Oksenberg's overall conclusion is a sober one: that the legacy of the Deng era seems highly uncertain.

These papers as a group show both that the Deng era reforms resonated in many ways with China's past, and that they marked departures that introduced significant changes into China. While the reforms produced remarkable material results, they have left a far less certain legacy in the mentality of the rulers and ruled alike. Almost certainly, China will find it impossible to revert to a Maoist or pre-Gorbachev Soviet-type system for a sustained period of time—the reforms have introduced too many elements that will make any such wholesale reversion highly unstable. But these papers also provide ample warning that China's future course has not yet been set, and that there is probably little consensus within the country about the key characteristics that the society and polity should embody.

13

THE DENG ERA'S UNCERTAIN POLITICAL LEGACY

MICHEL OKSENBERG

What is likely to be the enduring political legacy of the Deng Xiaoping era? What political developments occurred in China during the 1980s that are likely to persist or affect the country's path in the next century? These questions, explored in this essay, would be difficult to answer under any circumstances, but they are particularly perplexing in the aftermath of the student-led demonstrations that swept Beijing and other cities in April, May, and June 1989 and that engendered a massive crackdown.

At this writing in late 1989 and early 1990, Eastern European countries and the Soviet Union are in the midst of transforming their previous Leninist political systems, and while the outcome of those unprecedented changes is unclear, they dramatically reveal a new lesson: Leninist systems are not necessarily enduring. In the light of the demonstrations in Beijing, many foreign and Chinese observers who yearn for a democratic China now believe that the Chinese system is on its deathbed, while others see in the crackdown and its numbing effect the continued strength of the Leninist state.

This essay seeks insight into the Chinese future, and more specifically the Deng era's impact upon it, by pursuing four different inquiries or approaches to the topic. It first probes the record of the Deng era. What were the political achievements, failures, and searing events for which the decade will be remembered, and what is the balanced assessment? Will the era be recalled more for its political successes or its blunders and lost opportunities? Next, the essay identifies the major trends of the era, several of which began before Deng's ascent to the pinnacle of power, and asks which of these trends are irreversible and which might be halted by determined leaders during Deng's waning years or in the post-Deng era. Then, the essay analyzes the specific political reforms undertaken in the 1980s. These were more extensive than many observers appreciate, although they did not transform the fundamental nature of the system. This section asks: Do the reforms lay the basis for a system transformation? What reforms are likely to endure, and what could be easily swept aside by leaders determined to restore the pre-Deng system? The final section reflects on how the Deng era affected the individuals from whom the next generation of officials probably will come. What lessons did China's future political leaders and bureaucrats learn in the 1980s that will shape their views of governance?

I tried to think through each inquiry without preconceptions, if that is possible. Before embarking upon the task, I had hoped that perhaps one or two of the four approaches would, at best, yield firm conclusions or, at worse, narrow the range of possibilities. But each led to the same conclusion: the legacy of the Deng era seems highly uncertain. The range of possible developments after Deng in the coming decade is wide indeed. Why this is so merits reflections prior to plunging into the essay.

In the mid-1970s, on the eve of Mao's passing, A. Doak Barnett assayed the achievements and failures of the Mao era and looked to the Chinese future after Mao. He called his assessment *Uncertain Passage*.[1] I had fastened upon the same word—uncertain—only to recall the title of the Barnett volume. Despite his title, Barnett argued that the imperatives confronting Mao's successors would impel them to jettison many of the radical policies of the Cultural Revolution and propel them toward a more pragmatic course, including expanded economic and intellectual relations with the outside world. What was uncertain to Barnett was how Mao's successors would manage the transition to a less ideological era.

Although in important respects the situation in the late Deng era is different, in some respects it is the same. Deng, as Mao, has botched the management of his succession. Unbridled factional strife again characterizes elite politics. Power at the top continues to inhere in individuals rather than formal position. The military, as in the mid-1970s, evidently will play a crucial role in the succession. Power appears to have gravitated to the provinces due, in part, to the political weakness in Beijing. Many in the populace appear cynical about their political system. Once again a political upheaval in the capital—the Beijing spring of 1989 and its tragic ending—has dealt a body blow to the system and traumatized the leaders, as did the 1971 Lin Biao affair and the Tiananmen incident of April 1976.

Perhaps the same cautious optimism that Barnett evidenced is still warranted. The same underlying factors that prompted Deng Xiaoping to embark upon economic and political reform and upon his opening to the outside world are still powerfully at work. Although the organizational and ideological instruments for integrating the Chinese polity have been losing their effectiveness, powerful new mechanisms are arising to sustain the unity of the country. Its growing economic interdependence and the telecommunications and transportation transformations are slowly creating national economies and cultures as never before.

At the same time, the role of the military and the appropriate zoning of decision-making authority within the vast state apparatus remain major problems, as they have been for over a century. The similarity in the political problems that China confronted at the ends of the Mao and Deng eras, as well as in the late Qing and the Republican eras, raise profound questions about China's capacity to develop an institutionalized political system at the apex, a point that Lucian Pye has stressed repeatedly.[2] And one wonders whether and how China will ever create a system that enables the populace meaningfully to participate in their governance.

The uncertainty at the end of the Deng era seems greater than at Mao's end. The uncertainty of the mid-1970s involved the future direction in which the nation would move economically and culturally. After a decade of political turmoil of the Cultural Revolution and its aftermath, however, both the leaders and the populace thirsted for political stability. Many Chinese felt that the disasters of the previous decade were attributable to individuals at the top—if not to Mao personally, then to the pro–Cultural Revolutionaries surrounding him. Cynicism and disenchantment were widespread, but many also derived comfort from the belief that a new set of Communist leaders espousing correct policies would set the country on a proper course. Marxism-Leninism was still seen as germane to the Chinese condition. At the end of the Deng era, not only does the ideological and economic future seem uncertain, but the future direction of the political system is at issue. There is doubt particularly among urban intellectuals that China can surmount the difficulties that have plagued it for a century: factional strife, military intervention, inadequate channels of political participation, disruptive succession struggles and mass movements, and persistent regionalism. Many deeply patriotic members of the elite whose confidence in the party remained unshaken during the Cultural Revolution now despair over its future. Stripped of illusion, they believe the CCP has become irreversibly corrupt and, abandoning hope in the Chinese future, they are encouraging their talented children to go abroad. Few among the intelligentsia adhere to the official ideology; intellectuals have for the most part no confidence in the beliefs propagated by the state, though no competing and comprehensive belief system has yet been articulated. And the profound changes of the Deng era in Chinese society, especially in urban areas, have not been accompanied by political change. Herein lies the foreboding—or hope—about the Chinese future.[3]

Accomplishments, Discontent, and Tragedy

The Deng era can be subdivided into three periods: the time of economic accomplishment until late 1986; a period of growing social discontent, especially in urban areas and particularly in Beijing in 1987–88; and the spring and summer of 1989.[4] During those weeks, the capital became the stage for one of those intense dramas in history that engulf all citizens in a locality, forcing each to be an actor who forever lives with a memory of the part he or she played—or seeks to suppress or alter the memory to conform to subsequent needs. For many residents of Beijing, those days of vividness and their aftermath have assumed a significance equal to the previous ten years. And the battle has just begun to shape the memories of those days, a struggle that will heavily determine how the Deng era will be perceived a decade hence.

Accomplishments

In the decade from late 1978 to late 1988, Chinese society enjoyed its most protracted period of domestic tranquility, sustained economic growth, and politically effective rule in 140 years. The gross national product more than doubled. For an unprecedented ten successive years, peasants in most regions of the country planted and reaped their harvests unencumbered by civil strife, political turmoil, or foreign invasion. With the improvement in Sino-Soviet and Sino-Indian relations as well as the reduction in tensions between Taiwan and the mainland, by early 1989 China faced no immediate military threat. For the first time since the 1830s, no foreign power posed an imminent danger to the nation's security. Negotiations had been completed during the decade to return the last pieces of soil under foreign control—Hong Kong and Macao—to Chinese rule under propitious circumstances. By any measure, China's international stature was at an all-time high. In the council of nations, China's leaders were respected as men of judgment, balance, and credibility. In the cultural and intellectual realm, again until mid-1989, a renaissance was underway. Still living in a constricted and uncertain environment, intellectuals of all sorts—artists, writers, humanists, social scientists, and natural scientists—enjoyed the best conditions that had existed in this century. The results were increasingly bold experimentation and progress in meeting international standards of intellectual attainment. In the social realm, while still bound by village and urban unit (*danwei*) life, the stultifying conformity of the past was yielding to diversity of lifestyles.

China's performance under Deng's aegis from 1978 to 1988, moreover, not only contrasted sharply with the last decade of the Mao era but on balance compared favorably with much of the developing world during the 1980s. Hard hit by the steep rise in energy prices and then by their steep descent, battered by high rates of population increase, and plagued by corrupt rule, ethnic strife, external debts, and capital outflow, many countries in Latin America, Africa, and South Asia seemed mired in poverty and injustice through the 1980s. Only in East and parts of Southeast Asia was the record equally impressive. China under Deng offered the hope that, with wise tutelage and an appropriate set of economic development and national security strategies, the largest of the world's poor countries might solve its most crushing problems. Cautious optimism seemed warranted that within a generation or so, China could be incorporated as a full and constructive member of the world's economic, intellectual, and security communities, and major regions within China—the Pearl River delta, the lower Yangzi, the Beijing-Tianjin area of the North China plain, and the

Manchurian corridor from Mukden to Dalian—would reach the living standards of today's newly industrialized countries (NICs).

Growing Discontent

Most politicians in democratic countries would have been pleased to run for reelection on such a record of accomplishment. Toward the end of Deng's decade as the nation's paramount leader, however, difficulties began to mount. Deng's plans for an orderly succession came unstuck, and dissatisfaction grew rapidly in universities. Soon after his emergence as China's paramount leader in 1978, Deng Xiaoping began carefully to nurture a succession arrangement. By 1982, he had installed the duumvirate of Hu Yaobang as the party leader and Zhao Ziyang as the government leader who would guide the nation as he withdrew from the scene. In 1986, however, this arrangement came under increasing pressure from several of Deng's elderly conservative associates and from sectors of the military, and in early 1987, Deng dismissed Chinese Communist Party (CCP) General Secretary Hu Yaobang. By mid-1987, Deng had patched together another arrangement, transferring Zhao Ziyang from the premiership to the general-secretary position and appointing Li Peng, a protégé of several of the conservative elders, as premier. But this arrangement was tension-ridden and vulnerable to disruption. Student demonstrations in several major cities in late 1986 were followed by periodic indications of discontent on leading campuses in 1987 and 1988. Given the important role that student movements had played in modern Chinese history, the unrest was an ominous sign. The signs of unrest among intellectuals and students caused Deng to abandon political reform in 1987, to the chagrin of numerous intellectuals. The accompanying purge and criticisms of several articulate and appealing proponents of socialist democracy—especially physicist Fang Lizhi—paradoxically served to draw attention to these ideas. In 1988 and early 1989, small groups of intellectuals, including scientists, journalists, artists, novelists, and government economists, began to meet in various forums to assess the Chinese plight, often in disparaging terms, and to discuss ways of improving conditions. A dissident movement was taking shape, and it was establishing links with Chinese abroad.

The domestic critics of the Deng era did not give as positive an assessment of the accomplishments in 1980–86 as that cited above. They felt that at the very beginning of the decade, Deng had compromised with forces of conservatism and darkness. Because of either his own preference or political necessity, Deng had included in his coalition hard-core Leninists who championed ideological dogma, who were opposed to cultural liberation and Western influence, and who at heart disliked Deng's economic reforms. Deng had demonstrated his own rigidities in his harsh crackdown on the democracy wall movement in 1979 and then in a series of campaigns against bourgeois or liberalization trends in the cultural sphere in the 1980s. The continued, strong presence of conservatives in the Deng coalition gave the reforms a tenuous and fragile quality. To the emerging dissident community, then, the disintegration of the succession arrangements and the growing unrest among students and intellectuals in 1987–88 were not new developments but the logical culmination of tensions in Deng's approach to rule: his desire both for reform and conformity.

Other problems pressed upon the leaders in 1986–88. Principal among these in the economic sector were lagging agricultural production, considerable investment in economically dubious projects, government deficits, inflation, some capital flight and undisciplined external borrowing, severe energy shortages, the emergence of a migratory, unskilled work force, increasingly evident problems of pollution and environmental degradation, and a nudge upward in the population growth rate. The leaders divided over how to respond to these crushing difficulties, with some advocating retrenchment, recentralization of economic controls, and reliance upon state planning, while others argued that only the expansion of the market, the introduction of labor and capital markets, price reform, and the creation of effective monetary and fiscal mechanisms for regulating the economy would remedy the ills.

Meanwhile, many in the populace—especially in urban areas—tended to take more note of the consequences of inflation than of the decade-long increase in their purchasing power and improvements in their standard of living. The government bought a measure of urban contentment through heavy subsidies of food, rent, energy, and other daily commodities. This was not enough fully to assuage the public, even though, as in Eastern Europe, a very high percentage of the state budget was devoted to various forms of subsidies.

Inheriting a cynical, disenchanted, and demoralized populace at the end of the Cultural Revolution era, Deng had restored confidence in the regime in the late 1970s and early 1980s by deliberately eschewing ideological appeals and promising, instead, a higher standard of living. And he delivered on his version of goulash communism. Many in the populace responded to their leaders' materialistic appeals, with evident results: a flourishing of personal and bureaucratic entrepreneurship, an increasing avarice among the populace, and increasing family incomes for many. But this course had its inherent risks, as became evident toward the end of the decade. First, a claim to rule on the basis of economic performance is immediately challengeable when the performance falters, as it did somewhat in 1987–88. Second, the expectations of the population soared, fueled by the rapid spread of television, advertising, and exposure to the outside world. The populace appeared to judge their rulers not by the record of a decade but by the immediate past; they judged their welfare not against the past but against their soaring hopes. Third, to intellectuals of diverse stripes—ranging from diehard Leninist ideologues to Marxists seeking a humane and just society outside a Leninist framework—the rampant materialism and the spread of popular East Asian culture were deeply disturbing. Many also perceived their leaders as venal: they resented the evident nepotism, as the children of many leaders received high-level political appointments or prospered in the new corporations.

Thus, growing numbers of intellectuals, civil servants, and the population at large saw their society and political system as increasingly corrupt. Different elements of the populace likened different aspects of the situation to China under the Guomindang. The elder revolutionaries in the party heard echoes of the republican era in cultural and social trends: the worship of things Western, the licentiousness, and the rebelliousness of youth. *Their* China—and the elders considered the country theirs since they and their comrades who died along the way had made heroic sacrifices to create the People's Republic—no longer was imbued with Marxist-Leninist principles. To many aging revolutionaries, China appeared to be for sale to foreigners, overseas Chinese, and even the Guomindang as Taiwan businessmen began to swarm over the mainland. In contrast, many intellectuals who remembered the 1930s and 1940s saw similarities between the CCP of the 1980s and the ineffective Guomindang in its last days on the mainland. Many intellectuals despondently drew the parallels to the attention of visiting Americans: the venality, the abuse of power, the arbitrary efforts to constrain creativity, and the ham-handed efforts to censor and control thought.

Despite the obvious accomplishments of the Deng era, therefore, social tensions toward the end of the era were rising. Tibetans used their improved environment to voice their accumulated, intense grievances against their Han rulers. The urban populace, used to their positions of privilege, resented the capacity of peasants to buy out scarce supplies in the city department stores on the eve of the Spring Festival. Civil servants on fixed salaries resented the new-found wealth of those making profits in the market economy. University students facing bleak employment prospects resented the high incomes of their contemporaries working as taxi drivers, secretaries for joint ventures, or entrepreneurs in the service sector. Many indolent workers and peasants or those saddled with various misfortunes resented the income disparities that separated them from their more industrious, enterprising, and fortunate neighbors. Industrial workers in large state factories worried about the implications for them of the proposed bankruptcy law, which threatened to drive unprofitable and inefficient firms out of business. Since the mid-1950s, many in the populace resented the many privileges that officials enjoyed, and the abuses of power persisted in the Deng era. Moreover, the exposure to the outside world led some intellectuals and students to think that perhaps other, better ways existed to organize their political system. The dissemination of more accurate information about the economic and political progress in Taiwan and South Korea particularly attracted attention, as did the political reforms in the Soviet Union and Eastern Europe. These accumulated grievances and new thoughts meant the leaders confronted an incendiary situation. While retaining raw power, the rulers knew their authority had eroded, and as 1989 began, they feared the possibility of turmoil and protests during the coming year.

Tragedy

A series of events occurring in close proximity plunged the political system into a crisis. The catalytic events were the death of Hu Yaobang on April 15, 1989, and his subsequent funeral, the commemoration of the seventieth anniversary of the May Fourth Movement of 1919, and the arrival of Soviet President and General Secretary Mikhail Gorbachev in Beijing on May 15. Each of these events evoked massive demonstrations in the capital, accompanied by similar outpourings in other cities. There is no easy and balanced way to describe the complex events that unfolded in Beijing from mid-April to early June. Egged on by an octet of octogenarians (Chen Yun, Bo Yibo, Peng Zhen, Deng Yingchao, Yang Shangkun, Song Renqiong, Wang Zhen, and Li Xiannian) and by officials in the Beijing apparatus who were close to Li Peng, Deng Xiaoping concluded that the demonstrations posed a threat to his rule and his policies. He judged the students to be misguided, and he decided that nefarious forces were behind the demonstrations. But the leaders were divided over exactly how to respond. Plaguing their capacity to respond was the rivalry between Zhao Ziyang and Li Peng, as well as, evidently, Deng's widely rumored desire to remove Zhao Ziyang as general secretary after the Gorbachev visit. This disinclined Deng to accept any recommendation Zhao made on how to handle the demonstrations and encouraged Zhao and/or his supporters to attempt to use the demonstrations as a means for securing his political survival. The participants in the demonstrations had a wide range of motivations, goals, and expectations, but they were united by one minimal desire: to give public voice to their grievances and apprehensions over China's future and to express confidence in the essential patriotism of the students. A series of moves by the students, such as the launching of the hunger strike on the eve of Gorbachev's visit and the construction and placing in Tiananmen Square of the statue of the "Goddess of Democracy" helped keep the movement alive in Beijing and prompted its spread to the rest of the country. The leaders responded with an escalating series of measures intended to intimidate the demonstrators, but each one had the opposite effect. The strident April 26 *People's Daily* editorial, publicly televised interviews with student leaders in early May, the declaration of martial law on May 20 and the initial introduction of military force into the Beijing area on June 2 inflamed rather than quelled the populace.

In the week prior to Sunday, June 4, after six weeks of near constant demonstrations, Tiananmen Square was gradually emptying, and life in the city was returning to an unreal order and an eery normality—though this was the result of voluntary behavior rather than a compliant response to authority. By the end of May, it could be said, the leaders of China had lost control of their capital to spontaneous social forces. But, to repeat, the situation was peaceful. For reasons that are still not clearly understood, sometime after mid-morning on Friday, June 2, the decision was made for People's Liberation Army (PLA) units to converge on the square and oust the remaining demonstrators. Several units had gradually been deployed within striking distance in the previous days. Various forays in the subsequent thirty-six hours did not reach the square. Finally, the leaders announced that all necessary measures would be taken to clear the square, warning the populace to stay off the streets. In light of the leaders' vacillation, divisions, and hesitancy during the previous weeks, in which application of force seemed imminent but then was withheld as masses of people swarmed to the streets, the warnings fell on deaf ears. They stimulated a portion of the populace to leave their homes to harass the advancing soldiers. As the situation became more tense, columns of APCs, tanks, and heavily armed soldiers moved toward the square, ultimately firing upon unarmed citizens. A shocked Beijing populace learned of the rough dimensions of the tragedy that had befallen the capital on the night of June 3–4: thousands killed and wounded, vehicles burned on several major thoroughfares, the PLA capturing the city from enemy control. In essence, the order to the PLA to enter the city had provoked a response that the PLA then suppressed. The turbulence in Beijing briefly spread to several other cities.

In the subsequent days and weeks, the leaders launched a harsh crackdown to search out and punish those whom they held responsible for the demonstrations and disorder. The techniques of totalitarian control that had been perfected in the Maoist era but had fallen into disuse in the Deng era were rapidly revived: disseminating patently false accounts of the events, ordering intense study of speeches by major leaders, placing stigmatizing labels upon individuals, purging opponents and dispatching politically reliable personnel to suspect organizations, and in general creating an atmosphere of fear and intimidation. Many in the foreign diplomatic, scholarly, and business communities fled the violence, especially after one of the compounds in which they resided suffered from gunfire, and the outraged and fearful foreigners were understandably reluctant to return to Beijing and elsewhere in the immediate aftermath of the bloodbath. Foreign governments condemned the actions of the Chinese leaders and applied serious economic sanctions against China: suspending concessional interest rate loans, delaying negotiations on Chinese entry into the General Agreement on Tariffs and Trade (GATT), halting military sales, and postponing further relaxation of controls on technology transfers to China.

In that one night of violence unleashed upon his own people before the eyes of the world, Deng Xiaoping did incalculable damage to all that he had sought to achieve in the previous decade. Most importantly, he and his associates, especially Li Peng and Yang Shangkun, were now despised by influential sectors of the populace, and the Chinese leaders had lost their credibility among the world's leaders. A weakened and still divided set of leaders now had to seek to restore their capacity to rule through coercion and propaganda, which meant they had to postpone resolution of the same pressing economic problems that had brought on the crisis. Especially telling was the fury felt among Chinese in Hong Kong and the United States. It is not an exaggeration to say that the events of

June prompted numerous Chinese to commit themselves to the toppling of their leaders; possibly Deng had planted the seeds of the next Chinese revolution.

The weeks from April 15 to June 4 brought two political forms into intense confrontation.[5] On the one hand, despite their revolutionary past, the leaders of China were most comfortable with top-down politics: mobilization, control, at best benevolent authoritarianism. Indeed, their revolutionary experience encouraged them to believe that the masses are incapable of attaining any good purpose without effective and unified leadership from above. On the other hand, in the streets of Beijing, was bottom-up politics, unprecedented in scope for post-1949 China but traceable to various protest movements in the capital in the traditional and Republican eras, as well as to sporadic outbursts in the Communist era. Beijing Spring 1989 was not democracy in action. Mass demonstrations and the occupation of public squares should not be equated with democracy, which after all involves such concepts as the rule of law, a sense of civic obligation, tolerance, and equality of all citizens. But the embryo of democracy existed in the streets of Beijing. The beginnings of a civic society were there—spontaneously formed, orderly, voluntary associations behaving in peaceful and restrained fashion. The Deng era had unleashed the forces producing this new politics, but the leaders did not know how to respond to and incorporate it. A profound uncertainty hung over the capital and China in mid-1989 as a result: which form of politics—or uneasy combination of the two—would characterize the national polity in the years ahead?

Major Political Developments in the Deng Era

Rebuffed in my attempt to identify the Deng political legacy through an assessment of the era's accomplishments, failures, and memorable events, I now pursue another approach. What were the major underlying developments of the era that affected the political system but were not the result of deliberate efforts to reform it? What were the consequences of these changes and which are likely to endure?

A Transition from Revolutionary Rule

The Deng era involved a transition from rule by those who made the Communist revolution to those who grew up within it.[6] At the end of the 1980s, to be sure, a handful of the aging revolutionaries had reassembled themselves and sought to redirect policies away from the reform program that Deng had previously championed. But the death of Mao in 1976 had removed the primary architect of the revolution, and the inexorable passage of time took its toll. While the transition from revolutionary rule neither began nor was completed during the 1980s, it largely occurred in these years. It entailed abandonment of charismatic authority rooted in Mao, of mobilization campaigns to achieve policy objectives, of attempts to achieve a massive and rapid transformation of society, and of policy making based on ideology. The revolutionary approach to governance was yielding slowly, painfully, and with resistance to an era of bureaucratic rule through administrative law, incremental change, and a decisional process involving empirical analysis of policy choices.

But the transition from revolutionary to bureaucratic rule had an inherently problematic quality to it. The revolution had occurred, in part, because China lacked a unifying system of beliefs and an effective organization, and because of the gap between the material conditions and the aspirations and values of the populace. History teaches that revolutions do not necessarily succeed in creating a new value consensus, in forging viable political institutions, or in resynchronizing economic and belief systems. Some revolutions succeed and others fail. As the revolutionary era ends, the polity can either transit into a truly postrevolutionary era, or it can revert to the prerevolutionary situation, driven by competing value systems, contending elite groups, and tensions between the economic and value systems. The early part of the Deng era saw progress toward establishing postrevolutionary rule, but the later years underscored the problematic quality of the transition. The revolutionary era ended during Deng's watch; whether it would be succeeded by postrevolutionary rule or revert to a prerevolutionary condition was uncertain.

Social Change

The sweeping social change in the Deng era is the topic of other chapters in this volume. Suffice it to note here that during the 1980s, the society became more diverse and complex. The decade saw massive urban migration, rapid industrialization, and fundamental changes in the occupational profile even of rural dwellers. Whereas in the 1970s, 70–80 percent of the population earned their income from cultivation of the soil and tending crops, a decade later, the percentage had dropped to 60–70 percent. The communal form of rural social organization had yielded in many places to state-guided family farming. With these changes came an increase in migrant urban workers (many engaged as contract laborers in construction projects) who fell outside the previous channels of state control of the populace. Other significant social developments, many related to rapid economic growth and economic reform, included a weakening of the danwei as the basic work-residential-recreational unit into which the populace was organized; a weakening of the social security net; a steady expansion in university enrollment; and a growth in entrepreneurial households whose income came from private enterprises. The state no longer totally controlled urban-rural linkages, as the spread of peasant free markets in cities gave rural dwellers greater access to urban areas. The intrusive and sometimes harshly administered family planning program, especially the one child per family policy in urban areas, as well as the improved diet and public health system, had yielded an aging population. The partial and superficial recapitulation of societal developments merits emphasis, for in many respects, they outpaced the political trends. In a fundamental sense, the political system did not incorporate and reflect the developments in society.

A Weaker Preeminent Leader

My analysis of the political trends begin at the top, with the power and authority of the preeminent leader Deng Xiaoping. Even in his prime he was a less dominant figure among the top leaders than Mao had been for most of his rule. Mao was the founding father. His thought provided the ideological inspiration for the regime. He cultivated a cult of personality. Mao on several key occasions was able to prevail over widespread initial doubts among the top thirty or forty leaders. Mao's succession arrangements were abandoned because he became disenchanted with them. Deng, in contrast, had to work within shifting coalitions. With perhaps the exception of the 1979 invasion of Vietnam, no case exists of his overwhelming and smothering opposition among the top leaders. His two succession arrangements came unglued in 1987 and 1989, in no small measure because of pressure and opposition from other elders at the apex. Neither his thought nor his charisma served to legitimate the regime. Mao was an inspirational despot; Deng was a ruthless, pragmatic, reform-oriented, strong-armed machine politician. Unlike Mao, Deng leaves no ideological legacy. He wrote not a single memorable political tract that will galvanize future activists. Rather, if any essays were penned in his decade of rule that will motivate future politicians, they were probably written toward the end of the decade by such people as Fang Lizhi in opposition to Deng and his regime. Deng's personal legacy may end up being not only what he did but what he inspired against him.

Political Fragmentation

The top leaders as a group appeared to preside over an increasingly fragmented system at the apex.[7] Party departments and governmental commissions and departments seemed increasingly willing, as the 1980s wore on, to assert and pursue their own interests. In the early 1980s, researchers interviewing middle- and lower-level officials—assistant ministers, bureau chiefs, and section heads—had to dig hard to discover the nature of bureaucratic politics in Beijing, and the top leaders were reluctant to discuss and even denied ministerial recalcitrance. By 1986–87, the top leaders were quick to voice their frustrations in dealing with central-level agencies in Beijing, complaining that coordination in the formulation and implementation of policy had become one of their biggest headaches. The very same middle- and lower-level cadres who earlier in the decade only reluctantly had portrayed their particular organization's distinctive ethos and interests openly discussed the same issues in the late 1980s, identified their principal rivals, and sketched their various stratagems for defending their missions. To some extent, the veil had dropped, and outside observers were able to see what had been transpiring all along. After all, many foreign observers had been arguing for some time that the top leaders were engaged in a process of cajoling and persuasion; as early as 1956, Mao Zedong had complained that the officials in the economic ministries paid insufficient attention to him. Nonetheless, the Deng era witnessed a qualitative, though difficult to prove, change in the frequency, intensity, and duration with which the bureaucratic agencies in Beijing were willing to promote their particularistic causes.

Weakened State Control of the Economy

The top leaders and their central apparatus no longer were in total command of the economy. The 1980s saw an erosion in the capacity of the leaders tightly to control economic activity. It would be difficult, if not impossible, accurately to measure the percentage of gross national product outside the immediate reach of the top leaders and the central-level bureaucracies. If the underground economy and the black market, the productivity of individual entrepreneurs and local enterprises, the off-budget revenue of local governmental agencies, and various foreign commercial activities—not mutually exclusive categories—were included, the total could well have been over one-third and possibly even as much as one-half of GNP.[8] Moreover, the portion not easily amenable to central control was the most vibrant part of the economy. This is one reason the growth rate and inflation were so hard to control in the late 1980s; the leaders were best able to constrain the least dynamic portion of the economy.

From Ideology to Communism

The top leaders no longer had a convincing doctrine or ideology to motivate and orient the populace.[9] Unlike the beliefs that Mao voiced and that appealed to important segments of the population for much of his era, Deng and his associates were unable to articulate ideas, manipulate symbols, and employ propaganda that elicited a mass response. The erosion in their ideological appeals was attributable to the excesses of the Cultural Revolution and the cynicism in the populace toward the regime, especially after the Lin Biao affair. The leaders restored confidence in the regime and reestablished a measure of legitimacy by promising improvements in the standard of living, and as long as the leaders delivered on their promise, the populace responded well.

In the Mao era, economic growth according to plan took place in the heavy industrial sector of the economy—metallurgy, machine tools, energy, and so on—while the consumer sector and individual wages were held down. That changed in the 1980s. Although the heavy industrial sector continued to expand, individual incomes grew rapidly. Supply of consumer goods also expanded swiftly, though not as quickly as income. China for the first time in forty years—and in part of the countryside, for the first time ever—became consumer oriented, with households acquiring a range of durables—starting with bicycles, watches, and radios early in the decade and ending the 1980s with a desire for color televisions, washing machines, and refrigerators. What happened in Zouping County in Shandong Province is probably fairly typical of developments in the rest of China. The first motor vehicles for use by top county officials came in 1973. At the time, the county had only forty kilometers of paved roads. By 1989, automobiles—Jeep Cherokees, Shanghai sedans, Toyotas, Mitsubishis, Volkswagen Santanas, Polish, and Soviet—numbered in the low hundreds. The first television sets came in 1976, and county officials in 1988–89 still vividly remembered one of the first times they saw an event televised live. A TV set was placed in the courtyard of the county party headquarters so a large number could see the funeral of Mao Zedong. By the end of the 1980s, over 70 percent of the households in the county seat had televisions, nearly every village had access to at least one set, and it was not unusual for 30–40 percent of farm households to have a set. Telephone service in the county was still primitive, but new, direct-dial switching equipment was installed in 1989 with a larger capacity, and county officials were planning on installing cellular phones in their automobiles. Two minicomputers were installed in the county, and a large satellite dish had recently been constructed to bring in Central Television from Beijing.

The telecommunications and computer transformations had moved rapidly ahead in China in the 1980s, but the mechanization of agriculture had not. In Zouping, at least, grain was still harvested by sickle and threshed by water buffalo rolling heavy, round stones over the stalks placed on pounded earth; farmers still carried heavy loads on their backs, in wheelbarrows, and by bike. The Chinese path to modernity involves a sequence different from that experienced in the United States and Western Europe. Chinese peasants in the 1980s were experiencing the telecommunications and computer transformation before they underwent mechanization. The Mao era left China with an industrial infrastructure; the Deng era brought an astonishingly high percentage of the populace into contact with Beijing and the world.

The implications of these changes are not easily discerned. What is the legacy that the Deng era leaves in this regard? Are individual Chinese really motivated to comply with government command for different reasons than a decade hence, and if so, what are the implications of the change? Having based their right to rule on promises of improved living standards, have the leaders become particularly vulnerable to economic failures? Have the expectations for a brighter future increased the willingness of the populace to intervene, should their dreams be shattered? Or have the expectations of a better life intensified the desire of many for political stability? It is now easier for the leaders to claim that political turmoil threatens the gains in living standards and the realization of the populace's dreams. Has the spread of television aroused discontent by dramatizing the gap between village and urban living standards? Or has the medium at least temporarily placated the populace and engendered a sense of well-being and participation? These are complicated questions that require social science research to answer accurately, and the responses involve some of the most significant, and at this point uncertain, legacies of the Deng era.

Toward Professionalism, Pluralism, and Internationalism

In a stirring speech to a National Conference on Science and Technology in February 1978, Deng Xiaoping pledged to China's intelligentsia that he would be in their service. He promised to head their Logistics Department, and, in general, until the spring of 1989, he fulfilled this obligation. The professions began to flourish in China. They attended international conferences, joined multinational research projects, and received foreign publications. Gone were the strictures of the Maoist era against specialization and the denigrating of professional values. The telecommunications transformation, coupled with the opening to the outside world, made China's borders permeable. China's growing professional groups—scientists, statisticians, doctors, artists, bankers, philosophers, lawyers, journalists, economists, agronomists, and so on—became aware of and linked to their professional communities around the world, especially to their fellow professionals in Hong Kong, Taiwan, the United States, and Southeast Asia who used the Chinese language as their mode of discourse. Intellectual communities emerged in China that were part of worldwide professions and that participated in international scholarly exchange.[10]

From this 1978 initiative by Deng until the June 1989 crackdown, the leaders tolerated and increasingly encouraged the pursuit of professional and private interests, as long as they did not challenge the structure of authority or the right of the rulers to command. Zhao Ziyang's September 1987 speech to the Thirteenth Party Congress acknowledged the diversity of interests in society and recognized the legitimacy of partial interests. The state, Zhao mentioned explicitly, had a major role to play in reconciling these partial interests. (Significantly, Li Peng's speech to the National People's Congress in March 1989 took a much more restrictive view on this issue.) Herein are the origins of the civic society that expressed itself on the streets of Beijing, rallying to defend the student demonstrators. The state no longer sought totally to penetrate the society and remold the culture, and in their new-found but severely circumscribed areas of autonomy, some in the society began to pursue interests that tested the limits set by the state.

As Harry Harding has phrased it, Deng sought to create a "consultative authoritarianism." Others have termed it a corporate state. No matter the label, in the Deng era, professionals became esteemed for the advice they could offer the policy makers in the areas of their expertise, and they were organized and drawn into the policy process at the leaders' behest. But for the most part, the leaders initiated the process on issues of their choosing; professionals were not consulted in areas outside their competence. Many chafed under the political restrictions; many apparently longed to be involved in the policy process at their volition and on issues of their choosing, possibly outside their areas of expertise. To many in the emerging professional classes, political participation began to be a matter of concern. In a very real sense, the popular support of the student movement in April and May 1989 represented the assertion of these professions against the state. They sought to attain within China the standards of excellence and the same rights that their professions enjoyed elsewhere, especially in the industrialized democracies.

As members of worldwide professions, the Chinese intelligentsia partook of international intellectual currents. Ideas that circulated abroad also spread within China, and political leaders no longer could halt the dissemination of an idea by incarcerating an exponent of it. The same idea still would reach a mainland audience, and the leaders only alienated the individuals involved by preventing them from developing the thought indigenously. In fact, the cases of Fang Lizhi, Liu Binyan, and Yan Jiaqi revealed that the effort publicly to intimidate a particular intellectual increased their audience within China. Enterprising Hong Kong publishers compiled anthologies of Fang's, Liu's, and Yan's writings that were then easily distributed and sold in major Chinese cities. One of the greatest uncertainties among Deng's legacies is which would prevail after him—his commitment to continue a Leninist state or his bolstering of vibrant professions in China linked to the outside world? Probably he did not understand the tension between these two objectives, both of which were important to him.

The Resurgence of the Traditional

Simultaneously with the pulling of China into a technologically advanced future and into the world was the reappearance of customs, style, and practices of ancient vintage. Two major activities of the Zouping County Cultural Bureau capture this strange juxtaposition of past and future. The bureau was sponsoring the revival of the local version of Beijing opera, and its troupe was enjoying considerable success. It also had built a dance hall, with strobe lights, where disco dancing was featured several nights a week. In Shanghai parks in the morning, practitioners of shadow boxing frequently suffered a loss of serenity from the ghetto blasters playing Michael Jackson's hits for the break dancers going through their paces. Villages and families were explicitly encouraged to rediscover and engage in their traditional specialties. In Zouping, for example, villages that grew apricots, raised flowers for distant markets, and manufactured furniture were reviving their old crafts. The periodic markets in rural areas helped to nurture this revival of past practices. Lineages rebuilt their ancestral halls in many South China villages, and traditional burial practices were restored throughout the country. The improvement in relations with Taiwan and the visits to ancestral homes by the mainlanders now on Taiwan further strengthened this trend. The resurgence of traditional values and practices, including familialism, caused deep concern among the revolutionary ideologues, many of whom had joined the CCP in their youth to eliminate many of these traditions, which they blamed for China's backwardness. The simultaneous headlong rush to modernity, which attracted many young Chinese, and the revival of tradition, which was welcomed by many older Chinese, underscored and perhaps intensified the cultural gaps between generations, and between the urban and rural areas.

Conclusion

The major developments of the Deng era yielded a messy China: more unruly than the Mao era; more vibrant with the dynamism that varied from place to place and generally increased as one moved away from Beijing; a country moving in several directions simultaneously. Under Mao, the Chinese populace was forced to live intensely in the present. Under Deng, the people variously resurrected ties to their past, forged links to the outside world, and were pulled into a different technological future. The passing of the revolutionary generation gradually removed from office men of extraordinary will and self-confidence who sought to impose their vision of the Chinese future upon the populace. The reduced power of the preeminent leaders, the fragmentation of bureaucratic authority, the weakened state control of the economy, and the erosion of ideology had diminished the capacity of the leaders to rule the country in a coherent, coordinated, and consistent fashion. What changes did the leaders initiate during the Deng era in their governmental system to reflect and compensate for the broader political, societal and economical changes?

The Political Reforms

Both continuities and changes characterized China's political structure during the Deng decade. The overall design of the system remained essentially unchanged, and therefore its major structural flaws remained. But within the broad framework, major changes did take place.

The Top Elite

The broad contours of the system can be summarized in this fashion: roughly thirty to forty top leaders were at the apex of the system, having the combined functions of the board of directors and the management committee of a large corporation.[11] These leaders consisted of the preeminent leader (Deng Xiaoping); several elders with their independent power bases (Chen Yun, Peng Zhen, Li Xiannian, Ye Jianying, etc.); two to three generalists in charge of day-to-day operations whose responsibilities extended to all functional systems (such as Hu Yaobang, Zhao Ziyang, and Li Peng); and functional specialists clustered into small committees, leadership groups, or "mouths" (*kou*), to use the CCP jargon.

In addition, these top leaders organized themselves into a number of overlapping policy-making bodies that were subject to periodic reorganization and changes in influence and jurisdiction (for example, the CCP's Standing Committee of the Politburo, Politburo, and Secretariat, the government's Standing Committee of the State Council, and the Military Affairs Commission). For most of the Deng era, as in much of the Mao era, the Party Secretariat, State Council, and Military Affairs Commission worked under the guidance of the Politburo and its Standing Committee and separately directed the activities of the party, government, and army. Also as in the Mao era, the new members were pulled into the elite circle by patrons already in it. As before, the arrangements and politics at this level were highly personalistic: power inhered in individuals and the networks of people loyal to them rather than in institutions. The influence of a particular decisional body depended more on who headed it than on the formal role it was assigned by regulations.

The vulnerabilities of this part of the system remained: there were no rules for handling the succession; there was no evident system to introduce new people into the elite based on merit; this patrimonial and patronage system easily led to factionalism at the top; and the privileges and deference given to the top elite soon isolated them from society. Deng Xiaoping encouraged noteworthy efforts to remedy these deficiencies in the early and mid-1980s. He sought to remove the venom that had come to pervade elite politics in the Mao era, and he and his associates also sought to restore a sense of procedure and norms to govern behavior. But all that was swept aside with the purges of Hu Yaobang and Zhao Ziyang, and by mid-1989, elite politics were again rancorous and Byzantine.

Linking Leaders to the Bureaucracy

The top leaders were linked to the bureaucracies through various staff arrangements and membership on coordinating committees that brought them in contact with the heads of party and army departments and government commissions and ministries.[12] In fact, many of the functional specialists among the top thirty to forty leaders simultaneously headed pivotal departments—for example, Yao Yilin as head of the State Planning Commission or Qiao Shi as head of the party's Organization Department. Their performance as head of such an agency frequently was a factor in their promotion to the inner circle.

The Deng era saw major efforts to improve the linkages between the top leaders and the bureaucracies. Staffing procedures were altered to strengthen project planning and evaluation. Efforts were made to improve the capacity of the Zhongnanhai—the party and government headquarters—to deal with the issues that the bureaucracies either passed to the top leaders for decision or sought to hoard or retain. Similar to the situation in Washington between the White House and the departments, bureaucrats had an ambivalent attitude toward this development. To the extent it enhanced their own capacity to influence the top leaders, either through their agency providing the personnel for the Zhongnanhai staff or through an enhanced professional ability of the Zhongnanhai staff to present their agency viewpoint to the top leaders, the bureaucrats welcomed the development. But to the extent that such staff agencies as the Commission on System Restructuring or the Center for Technological, Social, and Economic Development intruded on long-established agency turfs and threatened deeply ingrained ministerial missions, resistance could be expected. Many of these staffing agencies had been cultivated by Hu Yaobang and Zhao Ziyang as their mechanisms for grasping control of the bureaucracies and thereby making them viable successors to Deng. It remains to be seen, with their purges, whether much will be left of this development in the Deng era.

The Party

The Communist party, through its central apparatus and territorial party committees, directed and integrated the various functions of the state. The party secretariat and the party General Office performed this task at the Center, with a chain of command running through party groups (*dangzu*) that directed the work of governmental ministries and through provincial, prefectural, county, and township committees, each of which had its own administrative offices. The territorial committees had their own party groups to direct work in government agencies and they could mobilize party members in all work units through unit party committees and their subordinate branches and cells. This network, drawing on materials prepared by the Propaganda Department, disseminated and organized political study for the nation's roughly forty million party members. The hierarchy of party committees and their offices was badly battered during the Cultural Revolution and its aftermath, but was revived in the Deng era, though the shape of the party apparatus in 1978 and the nature of its rehabilitation were topics that eluded the understanding of foreign observers.

This Leninist system remained essentially unchanged throughout the Deng era—perhaps its most important continuity. On occasion, particularly in 1980–81 and 1986–87, there was much talk about separating the party and government. One step in this direction was the abolition of the party group within most ministries at the central level in 1987–88, but this change was not uniformly implemented at provincial levels and below. The significant developments in this core feature of the Chinese system during the Deng era were not the results of purposeful reform. Rather, the organization lost much of its élan in the 1980s, or perhaps more accurately, it never recovered from the loss of status and morale during the 1966–76 decade. Many of the nation's brightest youth shunned party membership. Its internal system of discipline was weak, and its members found the messages conveyed in political study to be unconvincing. By the end of the Deng era, therefore, the party core faced a crisis of identity and function. What role was it to play in a postrevolutionary, authoritarian regime? Could it survive competition? How could it be made more open and responsive to the opinions of members and nonmembers alike? The questions were the same as those confronting the Communist parties in Eastern Europe and the Soviet Union, and the answers were equally elusive.

The Functional System

Throughout the Mao and Deng eras, the state apparatus was subdivided into major functional systems of organized power: the personnel management bureaucracies and the propaganda hierarchies, both of which were primarily led by territorial party committees; the economic bureaucracies; the coercive hierarchies; the foreign affairs apparatus; and mass organizations. Through mechanisms that Doak Barnett elucidated in his classic *Cadres, Bureaucracy, and Political Power in China*, in many respects the party and government were so intertwined that it did not pay to treat them as clearly separate hierarchies with independent chains of command.[13] Under the direction of the Propaganda Department, party branches supervised the ideological activities of members within government agencies. Territorial party committees, upon recommendation of the CCP Organization Departments at each level, made key personnel appointments within government agencies. CCP discipline and inspection committees monitored the behavior of government agencies, especially during rectification campaigns. Although efforts were made both in the early and late 1980s to separate the party and government and to alter some of the mechanisms of party control, these efforts achieved only limited results.

The major political reforms did not affect the overall design of the state structure. With some minor exceptions, the overall design of the functional systems—personnel management, economics, coercive bureaucracies, and propaganda—remained the same. None of them was dismantled, though their relative importance appeared to change. Mao and his associates relied heavily upon coercive and propaganda bureaucracies to direct the nation, while Deng and his associates assigned greater importance to the economic bureaucracies and reestablished the personnel management bureaucracy after it had been greatly weakened in the Cultural Revolution era. But when Deng and the elders decided to reimpose harsh controls on society in the wake of the Beijing demonstrations and their suppression in spring 1989, the propaganda and coercive systems were still in place and available to implement the top leaders' instructions. Significant administrative changes did take place, however, within each of the broad functional systems.

The Economic System

The once dominant State Planning Commission saw an erosion in its authority vis-à-vis the two other comprehensive agencies in this sphere: the Ministry of

Finance and the People's Bank.[14] This change reflected the effort to develop effective fiscal and monetary instruments and to curtail the role of the plan in directing the economy, a reform that was at best only partially successful. The Ministry of Finance had attempted major changes in the state revenue system, essentially introducing a modern taxation system rather than relying heavily on transfers of profits from state enterprises. The People's Bank was seeking to become a central reserve bank, and new investment and commercial banks were established for deposit and lending purposes. Two other comprehensive agencies that played major roles in the Mao era in directing a command economy—the State Economic Commission and the State Capital Construction Commission—were abolished in the Deng era.

Many line ministries that specialized in specific industries were grouped together into supraministries, and operational corporations were established to direct specific industries. In the energy sphere, for example, a Ministry of Energy was created by amalgamating former ministries of Petroleum, Coal, Nuclear Power, and Electric Power. The intent was to establish corporations to run the various energy industries, with the corporations ultimately independent accounting units, responsible for their profits and losses in a market economy. By 1989, for example, three national petroleum corporations existed, and several provincial exploration companies had begun operations in specific basins. Similar reorganizations were underway in the vast machine tool, automobile, and aviation industries. The organization of foreign trade also underwent massive reforms, and the former Ministry of Foreign Trade lost its near monopoly control over exports and imports. First ministries and provinces and then corporations were able to engage in trade directly, including establishing offices abroad, holding foreign accounts, and even borrowing abroad. So undisciplined did these activities become that additional institutional measures were necessary by the late 1980s to reestablish a measure of central control. New interface organizations arose with the personal involvement of the top leaders and their families to assist foreigners to do business in China, to help finance joint ventures, and even to invest abroad. The most prominent of these was the China International Trust and Investment Corporation.

In short, the institutional landscape in the economic sphere at the end of the Deng decade differed greatly from the late 1970s. In some respects, the structure was more, not less, bureaucratic; certainly it was more complex. Uncertainties surround the structural changes in this sphere, which fostered bureaucratic capitalism rather than a true market economy. How much would be swept away in subsequent reorganizations, and whether the new institutions would ultimately inhibit attaining the goals that their establishment was intended to achieve—a more efficient, guided market economy—are questions that are at the heart of the institutional legacy of the Deng era.

The Propaganda System

Changes also occurred in the propaganda system. Here, the CCP Propaganda Department lost its strong leadership role over major institutions. In the Mao era, a coherent "culture and education system" (*wenjiao xitong*) existed under control of the Propaganda Department until 1966, the Cultural Revolution Small Group until 1970, and then under a succession of leadership small groups (*lingdao xiaozu*). The organization of this sector became much more fragmented in the Deng era. In fact, a *separate* science and technology system, focusing on research and development, emerged on the scene with its own principal spokesmen among the top leaders, Fang Yi (until retirement) and Song Jian. The three key agencies here were the State Science and Technology Commission, the Chinese Academy of Sciences, and the Chinese Association of Science and Technology. In the Mao era, especially during the Cultural Revolution, the party organizations in these bodies reported to the Propaganda Department, while Marshal Nie Rongzhen's early role in this sphere also insured a close liaison with the military. In the Deng era, the science bureaucracies acquired a measure of autonomy, though the extent of that autonomy was never clarified, and the ideologues who previously held sway over the nation's scientific establishment clearly disliked the new arrangement. To a lesser extent, similar trends were observable in the educational sphere, the social sciences and humanities, and the public health sector (which fell within this domain). The State Education Commission, the newly formed and expanded Chinese Academy of Social Sciences (previously a division within the Academy of Sciences), and the Ministry of Public Health all enjoyed greater freedom from Propaganda Department control. Even the areas previously most tightly under the Propaganda Department's leadership—the journalistic and cultural spheres—enjoyed greater latitude.[15] The proliferation of journals and newspapers, the development of markets for art and literature outside the state-controlled commercial outlets, and the emergence of a strong Ministry of Broadcasting, Television, and Film all weakened the Propaganda Department's ability to monitor and direct the nation's cultural life.

In addition, the department never had direct command or a leadership relationship (*lingdao guanxi*) over provincial propaganda departments. Their units were directly led by provincial party committees; the central department only provided professional or functional guidance (*yewu guanxi*) to the provincial departments. When provincial party committees no longer were encouraged to assign priority to propaganda work, this part of the system simply was not as active.

Measured over the decade, the decrease in ideological control exercised by the Propaganda Department over all these areas was considerable; the erosion was due not just to its less compelling message but to organizational changes. The Chinese Association of Science and Technology in particular used its increased autonomy to foster national scientific professional associations, which proliferated in the 1980s. As in the economic sphere, the reforms were in mid-course at the end of the decade. The changes in this sector were crucial in understanding the politics of the late 1980s, from the emergence of Fang Lizhi to the demonstrations of professionals in the streets of Beijing. They were using their new-found autonomy to protest the remaining, considerable fetters upon their life, but without the organizational changes just enumerated, they would not have had the capacity and newly found awareness to press their demands. The questions that remain and that will determine the precise legacy of the Deng era are whether, shaken by the events of April–May 1989, the leaders will restore the old system or whether the organizational changes—and the objective conditions that produced them—will result in even more diverse institutions in this area—perhaps even a set of voluntarily formed, legitimate, pluralistic associations.

The Coercive System: Military and Public Security

Turning to the coercive domain of the state, the Deng reforms were much more limited, though some changes merit mention.[16] The most noteworthy continuity is that the command structure over the Chinese military remained essentially unchanged. Namely, the preeminent leader was commander-in-chief of the military forces. He exercised command through chairmanship of the Military Affairs Commission, a body that reported directly to the Politburo and was equal in rank to the State Council. This critical dimension of the Chinese state since 1949 has been frequently neglected by outside analysts. The two wings of the state—the military and the civilian—came together only at the apex. The Ministry of National Defense remained largely an organization on paper in the Deng era, though some discussion was initiated in the late 1980s to strengthen it. And steps were taken to lodge the MAC within the government. But in reality, both Mao and Deng chose to retain direct control of the military. Put another way, the military enjoyed direct access to the nation's preeminent leader. The operational command then went through the designated person in day-to-day charge of the MAC—either one of its vice-chairmen or its secretary general—and then to the chief of staff of the PLA. The portion of the budget to be allocated to the military was decided at the Politburo level upon recommendation from the MAC. Weapons acquisitions and deployment were decisions made within the military apparatus. As Zhao Ziyang's report to the Thirteenth Party Congress noted, even the issue of military reform was a matter to be decided within the military itself.

Perhaps in part to provide alternative instruments of coercion, and therefore to escape being solely reliant on the main-force PLA units for maintaining domestic order, the top leaders did have alternative forces available to them—the Public Security forces, the People's Armed Police at local levels, and the plain-clothes security forces. These hierarchies underwent considerable reorganization in the Deng era, as did their relationship with the judicial and procuratorial systems. An effort was made to differentiate their functions and create more clearly identified organizational hierarchies. The Ministry of Public Security (MPS) lost many of the functions previously under its domain, such as population enumeration and actual management of the labor camps, but it reacquired command of the public security forces themselves, which had been lodged in the MAC during the Cultural Revolution. The new Ministry of State Security (MSS) brought together intelligence, surveillance, and police functions previously under the party and MPS, but nonetheless the restructured MPS, the new MSS, the courts, and the procuracy all fell under the political-legal "mouth" of the party. Thus, as in the Mao era, the top leaders had two coercive channels to enforce their will: the PLA through the MAC, and the internal security forces through the political-legal group.

Within this framework of continuity, some reforms did occur. Several were aimed at increasing the professionalism of the PLA through changes in recruitment, training, promotion, unit organization, the ranking system, length of service, retirement, weapons, research and procurement, and so on. Perhaps more important was the reorganization of national defense industries, which had previously been under the primary control of the MAC through its subordinate National Defense Industries Commission. In the Deng era, such ministries as the Ordnance and Aviation Industry were substantially reorganized, amalgamated with sister industries in the civilian sector, and transferred to the State Planning Commission and Ministry of Finance for primary supervision. Similarly, in the science domain, many research institutes that had previously looked primarily to the National Defense Science and Technology Commission to define their tasks and provide funds fell under the expanded jurisdiction of the civilian SSTC and the Chinese Academy of Sciences. While the military sector, in short, retained great organizational identity, its sphere of activity or bureaucratic domain shrunk considerably.

Personnel Management

The fourth set of interrelated hierarchies managed personnel assignments.[17] In the absence of a labor market, people and their careers were handled largely administratively in both the Mao and Deng eras, although in this area, the reforms and restructuring were extensive. The Organization Department, which handled personnel work, was not a tightly integrated, vertical hierarchy. Its major directives were approved and disseminated through territorial party committee channels. Nonetheless, until 1966, the control of careers of both party and nonparty members fell very much within the sphere of the CCP, specifically its Organization Department, and the personnel agencies within the government and at the basic levels were staffed largely by party members who looked to the Organization Department for guidance. (However, personnel management within two of the other systems of organized power—the propaganda or *wenjiao* system and the military sector—was handled separately within those systems. Especially within the PLA, the Political Department played the role of the Organization Department in the civilian sector.)

Personnel management become chaotic in the Cultural Revolution era (1966–76), but by 1980, the previous system had been largely restored. Under it, there were separate systems for managing three different types of employees in the party, government, and state-owned enterprises: (1) cadres or administrative personnel; (2) professionals or specialists; and (3) general workers. In addition, agencies existed to perform specific functions in personnel management: assigning high school and university graduates, controlling personnel files, disciplining wayward cadres, transferring personnel from the military to civilian bureaucracies, and easing the retirement of cadres. The agencies responsible for managing the three types of personnel and undertaking the specific functions underwent considerable evolution throughout the Mao and Deng era, merging and splitting apart in various permutations. While interesting, these reforms were not analytically significant from the point of view of system change. These tinkerings were largely aimed at increased efficiency.

More important were these diverse changes in the system of personnel management:

—establishment of a regular system of retirement for administrative cadres;

—reduction in the number of personnel appointments reserved for party committees to decide on recommendation of the Organization Department, and a corresponding increase in the number of personnel appointments made by personnel bureaus within government and basic level units;

—substantial reduction in the number of personnel appointments that had to be approved at higher levels, for example, that a county must refer to the prefecture (*diqu*) or a province must submit to Beijing;

—elimination of appointments that required approval two levels up the hierarchy, such as that top special district officials must be ratified by the center or the top county officials by the province;

—termination of the state's obligation to provide job assignments somewhere in China to all high school graduates, if need be in the interior of China;

—relaxation of class background and lesser use of "labels" and "hats" as criteria in promoting and demoting personnel;

—reduced efficacy of the household registration (*hukou*) and rationing systems and the resultant increase of urban migrants seeking temporary employment.

Many other changes were widely discussed but not implemented. But the cumulative impact of these changes greatly decentralized personnel management, weakened the role of the party and the Organization Department vis-à-vis other agencies of the state, reduced the importance of ideological criteria in the shaping of careers, constricted the role of the state in the allocation of labor, and introduced greater procedural regularity in those areas that remained under state control. However, favoritism, use of *guanxi*, and corruption also remained important dimensions of the personnel system.

Decentralization

Major changes occurred in the distribution of authority among the tiers of the state: center, provinces, prefectures, counties, and townships. Because of the decentralization of the economic, cultural, and personnel systems, the decisional autonomy of the provinces, prefectures, and townships grew enormously. Revenue from enterprises run by each of these levels swelled the coffers of most units at these levels, and the shift to the banking system as the source of local investment funds removed local governments from the discipline of a unified budgetary system. In the Mao era, most investment funds came from the state budget. While this constraint was "soft," local bureaus of finance tended to be under greater vertical controls than local branches of credit banks now are.

The Mao system was highly centralized, though after 1958 and especially after 1970, regional and local levels acquired increased decisional authority and obtained access to more sources of government revenue. The Deng reforms accentuated these trends of administrative decentralization in budgeting, investment banking, personnel management, planning, and material allocation. The Deng reforms also endowed a number of lower units with special economic authority: special economic zones, open cities and open coastal regions, cities still under provincial jurisdiction whose budgets were nonetheless directly negotiated with the center, and so on. In theory, the Chinese state remained under unified control in the Deng era, and the autonomy that provinces enjoyed came at the discretion of central authorities. In reality, by the late 1980s, the top leaders probably could not have retrieved the authority they had granted to the provinces, municipalities, special districts, and counties without waging a major political struggle. Central-provincial relations in essence could not simply be characterized as involving superiors and subordinates; the relationships were intensely political and on most issues involved considerable bargaining and negotiations, although the center was the more powerful of the two. Regionalism—a characteristic of the late Qing and Republican systems as well—had again become an important aspect of the Chinese system.

Rural Local Government and Politics

Considerable controversy now exists among American analysts concerning the consequences of Deng's rural reforms upon local government.[18] This much is known. The previous formal governmental structure below the county of communes, production brigades, and production teams yielded to a system of townships (*xiang*) and administrative villages. Some agencies that previously fell under the command of the communes or brigades were transferred to township authority; others were placed under the direct leadership of the county; and yet other units became independent economic enterprises. The structure of the party, meanwhile, remained the same, and the party committees that previously guided the commune now guide the townships. The introduction of a market economy somewhat weakened the authority of the village (previously brigade) headman, as peasants in many villages were less dependent upon his decisions for the earning of their incomes. But this was a matter of degree, and in many places, the headman remained a dominant figure, as he had been under the commune-brigade system. Perhaps the most significant development affecting rural local government and politics, in addition to changes in the cropping and marketing systems, was the growth of township and village enterprises. Revenue from these activities greatly expanded the financial base at local levels.

Finally, it is clear that there was great variation in both formal structure and behavior below the county. In many counties, other administrative levels were established either between the county and township or between the township and the village. The vitality of the party also varied greatly. In Guangdong and Jiangsu provinces, for example, the party structure below the county existed only on paper in many locales; in reality, the party had ceased to exist as an important part of local affairs. But this was not true in many other regions. The extent of decollectivization also varied. Many villages in Shandong continued to practice a collectivized form of agriculture under a vigorous headman, and one suspects this was true elsewhere as well. Generalities about the consequences of Deng's reform upon local politics should probably be eschewed.

Nonetheless, a useful debate has emerged on one major point. Some argue that the reforms fundamentally altered the nature of local politics and made the peasant more accessible or open to state control by stripping away the buffer that the commune and brigade provided. According to this argument, forcefully articulated by Vivenne Shue, the peasants have lost the protection of their patrons, and they are now vulnerable to market forces and the intervention of the state. Others, however, especially Jean Oi, believe the underlying state structure below the county has not been changed; they argue that the system in most respects remains matrimonial or clientist. My own preference, pending more research, is to opt for a more complex formulation: In some respects, the Deng reforms brought the peasants in direct contact with the state and provided direct access to households, such as in fulfillment of production quotas. But in other respects, such as securing employment in township enterprises or obtaining fertilizer and credit, the local patrimonial system remained unchanged. The Deng legacy in this area left a more complex and varied system than existed at the end of the Mao era.

The Danwei

At the basic levels—industrial enterprises, universities, hospitals, commercial undertakings, rural villages, and so on—the unit (*danwei*) still enveloped the economic, social, and political life of its members. This much-discussed aspect of China continued to be one of its most distinctive political features. The development of individual entrepreneurship, increased geographic mobility, and changes in urban living patterns and political life, however, somewhat weakened the grasp of units upon its members, but only marginally so. The accumulation of tensions within the unit, which Lynn White cites as one of the sources of violence during the Cultural Revolution, remained a source of volatility.[19]

This overview of institutional changes in the Deng era gives less attention to several developments that other analysts might emphasize, particularly the efforts to develop a legal system, to invigorate the minor or democratic parties, and to stimulate the representative assemblies or congresses to play a more active role in supervising the bureaucracy and in drafting legislation.[20] Promising but ultimately faltering steps in the overall scheme of things took place in all these areas, but perhaps these will provide a basis for significant reforms at some later stage.

To summarize, then, noteworthy institutional reforms did occur in the Deng era. The overall Leninist structure remained the same, and the behavioral consequences stemming from the structure remained essentially unaltered.[21] But to varying degrees, each of the functional sectors of organized power underwent internal changes, with the coercive remaining the most centralized and the least altered. In matters difficult both to judge and to measure, it appears that the institutional system in the economic sphere expanded, fragmented, and prospered more than the others. Equally noteworthy were the developments within the wenjiao system, where professional organizations and a separate science-and-technology apparatus began to appear. These changes occurred at the initiative of the top leaders, in accord with their policy preferences. But they also occurred, in part, as a result of dynamics internal to these institutions themselves, and also in response to social and economic developments. One uncertainty at the end of the Deng era concerned the proclivities of the next generation of China's leaders. Would they allow the institutional evolution to continue? Or would they seek to restore the hierarchies to their previous configuration? What solution would they offer to address the problems of the party? Would other developments beyond the top leaders' capacity to affect—the strengthening of lower-level governmental units and the necessary centralization of parts of the coercive sector—be parts of the puzzle of China's political future? Or will China's future reveal that many of the institutional changes were primarily the product of underlying changes in society and be less amenable to reversal than it appeared at the end of the Deng decade? No certain answers existed to these complex questions as the struggle for power in the post-Deng era began.

Lessons Learned by China's Future Leaders

With the advantage of hindsight, one can see that perhaps the greatest impact a particular era had upon modern China's evolution was the lessons it imparted to the subsequent generations of China's leaders. One speaks of China in terms of the searing event that shaped and divided each generation as it came of political age: the May Fourth generation, the December Ninth generation, the Civil War generation, and so on. But no less important were the lessons absorbed by middle-aged aspirants to power in the years prior to their ascent to high position. After all, in no small measure, the Deng era can be seen as a collective response by officialdom to lessons they learned in the Cultural Revolution. The question I probe in this concluding section therefore is not what lasting effect the Deng era generally and Beijing spring 1989 will have upon the youth of the 1990s, the question analysts seem to be fascinated with the moment. After all, those young people are unlikely to lead China until 2010 or 2020 at the earliest, and much will happen in the intervening time. Rather, I ask, what did cadres and military officers in their forties and fifties who will be leading China in the 1990s and beyond absorb during the Deng years?

One can only speculate about this intriguing question. A few lessons probably were rather widely learned, but beyond these important notions, different officials had different experiences and were affected differently. China's next generation of leaders was not welded into a cohesive group through any common lessons they may have learned in the Deng era.

But just as the Cultural Revolution inoculated many officials against the dangers of chaos and the disasters that self-righteous youths can bring about, the Deng era probably did drive home several points. The first was the enormous gap that existed between China and its Asian neighbors. The socialist system of the Mao era had not enabled the nation to keep up with the places with which Chinese compare themselves, and under a different type of rule, the Chinese in Hong Kong and Taiwan had achieved far higher standards of living than on the mainland. No future leader of China can have escaped this message during the Deng era, and through superficial visits to Western Europe, Japan, or the United States, most of China's future leaders were also exposed to the even greater gaps between China and the world's industrialized giants. A poignant conversation with an intelligent and sensitive prefectural party secretary after his month-long tour of the United States summarized this lesson. I asked what was the deepest impression he had gained. He replied, "The United States is such a beautiful country. I didn't realize how many trees existed in your country. And all the greenery." He then sighed, paused, and continued, "You know, before visiting the United States, I thought that with the Four Modernizations, after a number of decades, China would catch up with the developed countries. But since returning home, I have decided that we will never catch up. We have too many people. And we don't have enough land."

There is a second lesson that the 1980s probably hammered home—that the quest for modernity is complex, with no easy path to it, and that its blessings are mixed. I recall a conversation during my first visit to China in 1972. Standing on the trafficless bridge spanning the Yangzi at Nanjing and viewing the city's skyline, I turned to a middle-ranking Jiangsu provincial cadre and said, "I look forward to returning to Nanjing when massive traffic jams will exist on this bridge and factories will so dirty the air that the skyline can't be seen." The Chinese official took my remarks as expressing nothing but the warmest, heartfelt sentiments for China's future, as I knew he would. He could not know what I experienced daily at that time as a commuter to Columbia University from New Jersey across the George Washington Bridge. But seventeen years later, while still yearning for modernity, China's second generation of leaders had become more sensitive to the costs of environmental degradation. By the late 1980s, they would have understood the wryness of my 1972 remarks.

Third, China's next generation of leaders, working in staff positions or at the intermediate levels of the bureaucracy either in Beijing or in the provinces, probably had become aware of the difficulties and dangers of reforming their economic and political system. The transition from a planned to a guided market economy involved many more problems and presented far more challenges than the initiators of the reform had anticipated. During the 1980s China's future leaders probably were responsible for giving specificity to the reform programs and responding to the dislocations they caused. One suspects the result was an enhanced understanding of both the opportunities and the limitations of reform.

Some lessons also probably were not learned by the next generation of leaders. As Andrew Walder's writings have stressed, they probably did not learn new ways of doing business or getting things done. Energizing the network of social relations in which an official was embedded was the leadership skill that successful officials still perfected. And while many officials in their forties and fifties were exposed to Japan and the West, few, if any, acquired in-depth understanding of how their key components actually worked and how they reflected underlying values in Western societies. Fascinated by institutions ranging from stock markets to courts to legislatures, few studied these in sufficient depth to understand the sources of their success. It is almost a certainty that the leaders of China through the 1990s and early into the next century did not come really to comprehend Western economic and political systems. That means they probably learned very little about democracy and its requisites. This is not to imply that these lessons were beyond their reach or could not be acquired under new circumstances. I make a more limited point: the next generation of China's leaders had only a limited exposure to the West in the 1980s.

Beyond these generalities, the lessons varied according to place, bureaucracy, educational background, and personality of the individual involved. Some in the 1980s acquired additional technical competencies, while others continued to nurture political skills. Some had extensive exposure to Westerners in China, while others had little contact with the outside world. Some reacted positively to the foreigners they met while others could barely hide their disdain. Some compared their Western exposure of the 1980s with their extensive Soviet exposure of their youth, while others did not have this basis of comparison.

This cursory review of the experiences in the Deng era of the next generation of leaders again points to the uncertainty of the Chinese future. They are likely to have become realistic about modernization and the process of reform, but on other key issues—understanding of the West, the desirability of economic reform, and their attitudes and understanding of what I earlier labeled the new or "bottom up" politics—there is no reason to believe the proclivities of the whole age group were pushed in a similar direction. To the contrary, there are good reasons to conclude that their experiences nudged them in different directions. Therefore we should expect the underlying and bitterly fought divisions among the top leaders which have prompted such volatility and uncertainty in Chinese politics of the past century to persist in the decades immediately ahead. In this respect, the Deng era's major legacy is likely to be a bittersweet one. It has kept alive and not terminated certain core issues and features of the Chinese political system for a century. But early sections of this chapter sketched major trends and transitions that the era accelerated. The Deng era was both conservative and progressive; it entailed continuities and bold departures. Herein lies the greatest uncertainty of its legacy. What balances will be struck in the post-Deng era among the sharply contending forces in China? And, therefore, how will the Deng era be remembered for its shaping of the outcome? The tensions evident in Beijing in the spring of 1989 and after suggest it is far too early to answer these questions.

Notes

1. A. Doak Barnett, *Uncertain Passage* (Washington, DC: Brookings Institution, 1974).

2. Lucian Pye, *The Spirit of Chinese Politics* (Cambridge: MIT Press, 1968); *The Dynamics of Chinese Politics* (Cambridge: Oelgeschlager, Gunn, Hann, 1981); and *Mandarins and Cadres: China's Political Cultures* (Ann Arbor: University of Michigan Center for Chinese Studies, 1989).

3. See Perry Link, paper presented to Columbia University Seminar on Contemporary China, 1989.

4. A more extensive and balanced assessment of the Deng era is provided by John Woodruff, *China in Search of Its Future* (Seattle: University of Washington Press, 1989), and Harry Harding, *China's Second Revolution* (Washington, DC: Brookings Institution, 1987).

5. I thank Melanie Manion for this information.

6. The classic formulation of this transition is Richard Lowenthal, "Development vs. Utopia in Communist Policy," in *Change in Communist Systems*, ed. Chalmers Johnson (Stanford: Stanford University Press, 1970), pp. 33–116.

7. This theme is elaborated in David M. Lampton, ed. *Policy Implementation in Post-Mao China* (Berkeley: University of California Press, 1987); and Kenneth Lieberthal and Michel Oksenberg, *Policy Making in China: Leaders, Structures, and Processes* (Princeton: Princeton University Press, 1988).

8. I have discussed this with a number of American specialists on the Chinese economy, who concur in the estimate. It is derived from adding together the value of each of

the known above categories and estimating the value of the underground economy at about 10–15 percent of GNP.

9. The transition from ideology to communism is particularly well captured in Orville Schell, *Discos and Democracy* (New York: Pantheon, 1988). This section also draws upon my research in Zouping County.

10. For an interesting analysis of pluralization in the Deng era that attributes the trend to the consequences of economic reform and to student movements for democracy rather than to the emergence of professions as I do in this section, see Nina Halpern, "Economic Reforms and Democratization in Communist Systems: The Case of China," *Studies in Comparative Communism* 22, 2 and 3 (Summer/Autumn 1988): 139–52.

11. This section draws upon Lieberthal and Oksenberg, *Policy Making*, chapter 2.

12. This section draws on ibid.; and Carol Hamrin, "The Party Leadership System," in *Bureaucracy, Politics and Policy Making in Post-Mao China,* ed. Kenneth Lieberthal and David M. Lampton (Berkeley: University of California Press, 1991).

13. A. Doak Barnett, *Cadres, Bureaucracy, and Political Power in China* (New York: Columbia University Press, 1965). This section draws on my interviews in Zouping and Beijing.

14. Economic developments have best been tackled during the decade in *China Business Review*, a journal published by the US-China Business Council (formerly the National Council on US-China Trade), and *China Newsletter*, a journal published by the Japan External Trade Research Organization.

15. The process of state censorship is traced in Perry Link's "Introduction," in Liu Binyan, *People or Monsters* (Bloomington: Indiana University Press, 1983), and his introduction to Perry Link, ed., *Stubborn Weeds* (Bloomington: Indiana University Press, 1983).

16. This section draws on extensive conversations with Chinese military officials. See also Jonathan Pollack, "Structures and Process in the Chinese Military System," in *Bureaucratic Behavior in China*, ed. Lampton and Lieberthal.

17. This section draws on Melanie Manion, "The Cadre Management System, Post Mao," *China Quarterly*, no. 102 (June 1985): 203–33; and John Burns, "China's *Nomenklatura* System," *Problems of Communism* 34, 5 (September–October 1987): 36–51.

18. This section draws on my Zouping research; Vivenne Shue, *The Reach of the State* (Stanford: Stanford University Press, 1988); and Jean Oi, *State and Peasant in Contemporary China* (Berkeley: University of California Press, 1989).

19. Lynn White, *Policies of Chaos* (Princeton: Princeton University Press, 1989).

20. For these developments, see Richard Baum, "Modernization and Legal Reforms in Post Mao China," *Studies in Comparative Communism* 19, 2 (Summer 1986): 69–103; Brantley Womack, "Modernization and Democratic Reforms in China," *Journal of Asian Studies* 43, 3 (May 1984): 417–39; and Kevin J. O'Brien, "China's National People's Congress: Reform and its Limits," *Legislative Studies Quarterly* 13, 3 (August 1988): 343–67.

21. These are particularly well developed in Andrew Walder, *Communist Neo-Traditionalism* (Berkeley: University of California Press, 1986).

14

THE LASTING EFFECT OF CHINA'S ECONOMIC REFORMS, 1979–1989

DWIGHT H. PERKINS

What will last of China's extraordinary economic performance during the 1980s? Have the events of June 3–4, 1989, undone China's hoped for escape from the poverty of a peasant economy? Or were these events a temporary interruption of China's sustained march toward an industrial society?

Only the coming years will provide the definitive answers to these questions. China in the first decades of the twenty-first century either will or will not be a newly industrialized economy. What can be done now is to look back at the fundamental forces at work on the Chinese economy over this past decade and try to understand why the policy reforms begun in the late 1970s had the impact that they did. With an understanding of what was accomplished and why, to the extent that such an understanding is possible, one is on a firmer if still uncertain foundation when talking about the future.

China's Economic Performance, 1979–89

The first point to note about China's economic performance since the Third Plenum in December 1978 is the rapid rate of increase in the gross national product. Throughout the ten-year period beginning in 1979, China's GNP grew at 9.2 percent per year.[1] By the beginning of 1989, per capita GNP was 120 percent higher than was the case in 1978. We do not have reliable estimates of China's GNP for the years before 1978, but the Net Material Product figures are close enough to GNP performance to tell us more or less what happened in those earlier years. If one converts the official Chinese estimates of NMP into constant 1980 prices, the average rate of growth of China over the entire twenty-six-year period was 4.8 percent a year. If one excludes 1977 and 1978 which in a certain sense marked the beginning of the reform period, growth in those two years averaging 10 percent a year, the average for the twenty-four years between 1952 and 1976 was 4.4 percent per year. Put in another way, the total increase in per capita income between 1977 and the end of 1988 (a rise of 165 percent) was nearly as much as what was accomplished in the twenty-four years ending in 1976 (a rise of 180 percent). Taking the two periods together, China's per capita income was seven or eight times what the Communist party inherited once recovery from war was more or less accomplished in 1952.

What is the significance of these various growth rate figures? To begin with, they indicate that under some circumstances China's economy is capable of achieving rates of growth comparable to those of other rapid developers in the post–World War II era. Until the latter half of the 1980s and not even then in some cases, most analysts of China's economy felt that such a high-level performance was impossible or highly unlikely. When I suggested in 1980 and 1981 that China's economic policy reforms were likely to lead to growth rates of 6 to 8 percent per year, I was considered to be an extreme optimist, a polite way of saying I was slightly deranged. As it turns out, these earlier forecasts were wrong, understating the growth potential in China's economy.

What made possible this 1980s' performance? Some of the specific features of the 1980s that contributed to growth will be dealt with below. At the most general level, what China was doing in the 1980s was taking full advantage of the growth potential open to a wide variety of developing countries that met certain factor endowment and policy reform preconditions. Before World War II growth rates of 10 percent a year were unheard of. After World War II, and particularly by the 1960s and 1970s, a tremendous amount of technology and development experience had built up in the more advanced industrialized nations that follower developing nations could exploit if they were prepared to do so. A nation with an educated population, with national unity and a government capable of providing a stable and supportive environment for investment, and a nation willing to import whatever useful equipment and knowledge there was to be imported, was likely to experience rapid growth, with 10 percent a year on a sustained basis appearing to be the upper limit.

It would take an essay on China too far afield to explain why so many developing nations have been unable to take advantage of this opportunity. Among the small number of economies that did take full advantage were the now famous cases of Japan, South Korea, and Taiwan plus the city-states of Hong Kong and Singapore. China before 1977 had many features in common with its East Asian neighbors, but it also had certain critical differences. China, for example, did not provide a stable and supportive policy environment for investment, public or private. The investment climate was seriously disrupted by both the Great Leap Forward and the Cultural Revolution, and the longest periods of policy stability were the five years of the First Five-Year Plan (1953–57) and the four years of recovery from the Great Leap Forward (1962–65). Nor did

China take much advantage of the accumulated backlog of technology and development knowledge that existed abroad. The Chinese did draw on this backlog up to 1957 and grew fairly rapidly as a result, but the Soviet reservoir of technology and knowledge to which China turned was nowhere near as full as that of Japan and the West.

What China did in the 1980s was fundamentally to change the investment climate and to turn to Japan and the West for technology and development-related knowledge. China also began to change the very nature of its economic system, and much more will be said about this effort below. Which of these new policies had the greatest impact on the growth rate is anyone's guess. Most likely these fundamental changes interacted with each other, and together they produced accelerated development. Future research now underway on the sources of growth in the 1980s and before may allow one to be more precise about what caused what, but major areas of uncertainty will remain. At this point we do know that a major rise in total factor productivity was part of the high-growth story. Accelerated development was not brought about by a rise in the rate of capital formation. In fact, the rate of capital formation first fell in the early 1980s and then began to rise back to previous peak levels in the latter half of the decade. If rising rates of capital formation had been the main growth story of the 1980s, one would have to look for an explanation of accelerated growth that was rooted in the mechanisms that made increased capital investment possible. But the difference between growth in the 1980s and that in the 1960s and 1970s appears, as already stated, to be brought about by rising productivity broadly defined. That in turn is the best evidence that policy changes or reforms that led producers to use their inputs more efficiently and to buy better inputs, from abroad among other places, were at the heart of the differences between the pre- and post-1978 periods.

These reform efforts potentially could have an influence on China's growth indefinitely into the future. But there were also elements in the 1980s' growth equation that were more in the nature of short-term, one-shot stimuli to growth, stimuli not likely to be repeated in later years.

First and foremost among these one-shot stimuli was the spurt in agricultural development that commenced with the agricultural reform experience of the 1979–83 period. There were two key elements in these agricultural reforms. The first freed up market forces in rural areas gave farmers the opportunity to make profits by producing for the market. Initially the market was freed up for subsidiary production only, but over time more and more rural products were brought onto the market. The second reform, begun in 1981 and completed by 1983, was the return to household-based farming by dismantling the production teams. This reform made it much easier for rural producers to respond to the new market forces. Under collectivization, farms were run by team and commune leaders who were at least as responsive to the commands of higher-level government bureaucrats as they were to concerns for the profitability of their units. Freeing up the market by itself, therefore, would not have stimulated as much response if the behavior of the primary producers had not been changed in fundamental ways through decollectivization.

These agricultural reforms raised agricultural output in two ways. First, there was the general improvement in incentives that accompanied reforms that tied individual or family material reward to individual or family performance. In theory the workpoint system of the production teams also related income to performance, but egalitarian pressures in the villages were very strong, rooted as they were in notions about social peace and stability, as much as in a concern with Communist ideology. The impact of improved individual incentives can be seen from the fact that even the growth rate of grain output accelerated for a time, from around 3.5 percent a year to 5 percent a year. The acceleration took place despite the fact that production team cadres in the prereform period were told to take "grain as the key link," and after reform the amount of acreage devoted to grain declined year after year. This acceleration in grain output growth, however, came to an end in 1984. Some of the subsequent stagnation in grain output can be attributed to poorer weather and delayed effects of farmers shifting into more lucrative crops. Again, more careful analysis of this period's agricultural performance will allow one to be more precise about the causes than is now possible.

There is little doubt, however, that China will not soon again experience sustained 5 percent a year growth rates for grain. What occurred in the early 1980s was a one-shot move to the production frontier. Having arrived at the frontier, growth of grain output returned to the long-term trend line. What exactly that long-term trend growth rate is, is unclear. It may be the rate of 3 or more percent of the 1960s or 1970s, or it may be lower. Grain output growth among China's East Asian neighbors over the past decade has been zero or negative. China must do better than this in the future, but how much better is really feasible?

The other impact of the agricultural reforms was to encourage farmers to shift their resources into higher-value cash crops and out of agriculture altogether into rural industry and services. Most of the high growth rate of agricultural output in the 1980s can be explained by this change in rural decision making. Between 1980 and 1987, the total increase in gross value of rural grain output valued in current prices accounted for only 14 percent of this increase, while rural enterprises outside of agriculture (such as industry, transport, and construction) accounted for 59 percent.

There is less reason to believe that this acceleration in nongrain rural output is a one-shot phenomenon. Some of China's major cash crops, such as cotton and oil seeds, are affected by the fact that China's arable land area is declining slowly, and there are limits on how fast yields can be increased. But there is no comparable limitation on subsidiary production or rural industry caused by the lack of arable land. Someday much of today's rural industry in China will give way to more efficient plants, some of which will be located in urban rather than rural areas. But there is no cap on the pace of industrialization comparable to that for grain and other crops that depend on China's poor land endowment.

A one-shot phenomenon of less importance than agriculture was the expansion of services that occurred in the 1980s. From the 1950s through the 1970s, China's attitude toward the service sector, which included everything from restaurants to retail shops fit within the traditional Soviet-style mode. The service sector was "unproductive" if not downright exploitative. Middlemen in particular were looked on as parasites, even when they were helping large-scale enterprises to find critical inputs so they could meet their production targets.

In the 1980s, in contrast, individuals and small groups were encouraged to open restaurants and shops, and farmers streamed into the cities to sell their produce directly. Construction companies and repair facilities sprung up on a collective basis. Much of the initial tolerance for these service trades arose from the fact that China's urban areas in the early 1980s faced a serious unemployment problem. The return of sent-down youth from the countryside was the major reason for this unemployment, and the political implications of having a large cadre of educated youth with little to do were potentially serious. As time passed, this growth in the service trades changed from being merely tolerated to being an integral part of China's development strategy. Not everyone was happy with this new strategy. Those on fixed incomes, such as government employees, used to thinking of themselves as the privileged elite, often resented the higher incomes earned by some traders and taxi drivers.

The expansion in these services at a pace faster than the growth of GNP was not something that could continue indefinitely. Most services, notably wholesale and retail trade and transport, are tied to and closely correlated with the development of the physical goods sectors. Once the artificial shortages created by earlier policies had been eliminated, the service sector growth would slow down, and such a slowdown probably did occur in the late 1980s.

When the one-shot gains from accelerated agricultural and services sector growth were exhausted, however, China's GNP growth rate did not also slow down. China in 1987 and 1988 actually grew somewhat more rapidly than in earlier years. But this more rapid growth put considerable strain on the economic system. There was, for example, a considerable drain on China's foreign exchange reserves in 1985 and 1986. The foreign exchange problem was ameliorated by tight controls over imports and the accelerated growth of exports together with borrowing from abroad. These measures in turn probably exacerbated another growing problem, the increase in inflationary pressures. By 1988 China's rate of inflation officially hit an annual rate of 20.7 percent, and the true rate, if repressed inflationary pressures are taken into account, was probably higher. There was more to the sources of inflation than the high growth rate, but there is little doubt that that growth rate was a major contributing element. In economic terms alone, an inflation rate of this magnitude was probably tolerable.

In political terms it was a major danger to the regime and undoubtedly contributed to urban unrest in early 1989.

China's economy, therefore, was not capable of sustaining 10 percent growth rates of GNP on any long-term basis for a combination of economic and political reasons. But in early 1989 there were no substantial reasons why China would have to return to the prereform GNP growth rate of 4 to 5 percent a year either. Whether the sustainable rate was 6 percent or 8 to 9 percent annually was partly a question of how well China learned to control its macroeconomic variables. It was also a question of whether the long-term trend rate for agriculture was 1 percent or 3 percent. Whatever the precise answers to these questions, the Chinese economy was clearly capable of sustaining a pace of development substantially above what had been achieved in the prereform period.

Implications of High GNP Growth

The GNP growth of the 1980s had a profound impact on China's economy and society that went well beyond the political strains described above. To begin with, there was a major increase in nonfarm employment. Workers and employees in the state and urban collective and individual sectors rose from 95 million in 1978 to 132 million in 1987, a rise of 37 million employees at a rate of nearly 4 percent a year. This figure, however, understates the full magnitude of what was happening because it does not include the large numbers of people who were still resident in rural areas but no longer involved in a major way with agricultural work. The numbers of people actually working in agriculture, including fishing, animal husbandry, forestry, and water conservancy work, more or less stagnated after 1982. Those in nonfarm occupations rose from 117.8 million people in 1978 to 210.6 million in 1987, a rise of 6.7 percent a year. The big increases were in construction workers, up 15 million; commerce, up 14 million; and industry, up 32 million persons. By 1987 the percentage of the work force in agriculture had fallen from 71 percent to 60 percent, a dramatic drop for such a short period.

Much of this increase, as pointed out, took place outside of formally designated urban areas. But the rural areas in which this employment off the farm was growing were less and less traditional farming communities. Small- and medium-scale industrial plants dotted the countryside in the agricultural areas near large cities. In effect, China's economy was becoming in one sense more urbanized. Formally, in fact, China's urban population rose from 172.5 million in 1978, 17.9 percent of the total population, to 503.6 million in 1987, 46.6 percent of the national total. There was no migration of 331 million people into the rural areas in this period, however, as these figures seem to imply. Instead it was the boundaries of the cities that were moving out to encompass more of the surrounding countryside and rural market towns that were getting reclassified as urban areas. The employment figures, therefore, are probably a better guide to the magnitude of the change underway than the urban population estimates. Either way, the transformation in process was huge. In nine years, for example, employment in nonfarm occupations in China rose by an amount roughly equivalent to the entire work force of the United States.

If China was not yet a primarily urban, nonfarm society by the end of the 1980s, it was well on its way. Another decade of comparable growth would place over half of the working population outside of agriculture. The implications of this kind of a shift in occupation and residence are profound. Politically, urban people behave differently from rural people, as the events of May and June 1989 clearly demonstrated. Economically, a shift in population of this magnitude puts great strains on the urban infrastructure.

China's urban infrastructure was badly neglected throughout the two decades leading up to the 1978 reforms. Housing was the most neglected part of the urban infrastructure. In 1978 the average urban resident lived in an area of only 4.2 square meters. Put differently, a family of four people was typically crowded into a space 12 feet by 15 feet, about one small bedroom in the average American house.

In the 1980s the Chinese government invested large sums in urban apartment construction. In cities such as Beijing, literally hundreds of tall cranes punctuated the skyline. Throughout the 1980s an average of nearly 900 million square meters of new housing was built each year. The average urban living space per person doubled to 8.5 square meters according to the household surveys, and the average rural living area per capita also doubled, from 8.1 to 16.0 square meters. In the early 1980s this investment in housing was costing thirty to forty billion yuan a year, and the figure rose to 87 billion yuan by 1987. Throughout the 1980s about a quarter of all fixed capital investment was devoted to housing construction. Over half of this money came from individuals, but in the cities the contribution of individuals to total housing construction costs was more like one-quarter. The state had to take the lead in the building of most large apartment complexes. If the official figures are roughly accurate, China in the 1980s built as much housing as had been built in the previous three decades combined.

Of equivalent importance was the consumer durable revolution that accompanied the rise in rural and urban incomes in the 1980s. Before 1978 the typical consumer durables of the Chinese household were bicycles, radios, wrist watches and sewing machines. The possession of these items expanded in the 1980s, particularly in the rural areas. In 1978, for example, only one-third of rural families owned a bicycle, whereas by 1987 there was roughly one bicycle for every family, although some families possessed more than one bicycle and others none. The per capita rural ownership of radios, sewing machines, and watches also tripled or quadrupled in the 1980s. In the urban areas, in contrast, bicycles, radios, sewing machines, and watches were possessed by most families before the reform period, and further expansion in their numbers was modest.

The major change in the urban areas was in the increase in use of the new consumer durables, television sets, washing machines, refrigerators, and recorders. Television sets basically did not exist in China in the early 1970s except perhaps for a privileged few. As late as 1975, China produced only 170,000 television sets a year, and production did not pass one million a year until 1979. By 1987, in contrast, the production of television sets approached twenty million a year, and virtually every urban household had a set. In fact, a third of urban households had color sets. Even in the rural areas there were twenty-four sets for every hundred households by 1987. Since many of these sets were owned by collective units or shared in other ways, it is likely that at least half of the rural population had regular access to television.

It is difficult to overstate the impact of this expansion in television across China. When this medium was used to increase the Chinese people's knowledge of the outside world, for example, as was the case prior to the events of June 1989, its impact could be dramatic. The influence of pictures of Japan's economy and society that were a backdrop to the coverage of Chinese state visits to Japan fundamentally altered how Chinese people saw themselves relative to their neighbors. No longer could Chinese believe articles to the effect that China and Mao had led the rest of the world in creating a better material life. Japan and even Taiwan had not only kept up with China; starting from a higher base, they had steadily widened the gap.

It is likely that television had as much to do with China's revolution of rising expectations as all other influences put together. Certainly, there was such a revolution in expectations, particularly in the urban areas where incomes did not rise as rapidly as in the rural areas after the reform process began. How else except for rising expectations can one explain the building discontent of the urban populace in the late 1980s despite the fact that their real incomes had increased by anywhere from 50 to 80 percent over the previous decade—less than in the rural areas to be sure, but still a major increase in the real standard of living? Some urban residents benefited more than others, and that was also a source of discontent, but most urban people gained during the period. And these estimates of increases in real income do not include the benefit of not having to wait in as many long lines because of the expansion in retail services or the much wider range of cultural entertainment available to them now that Jiang Qing was no longer able to monitor what the people would be allowed to see.

The point of reciting these facts is to underline that the Chinese economy and society was undergoing a rapid transformation in the period after reform began, whether one dates the reform period from the end of 1976 or the end of 1978. The GNP growth rates of the subsequent ten or twelve years were not a technical phenomenon of interest only to economists. The changes had a profound affect on the way of life of most Chinese people. Not only did these people have more material goods and services, they were increasingly doing different kinds of work than their parents and grandparents before them.

The increase in material goods, including food, meant that subsistence and survival were largely questions for those farmers who remained in the more remote mountainous areas of the country. Most of the nation, perhaps as much as three-quarters of the population, could have had its income cut in half without coming close to the kind of poverty that carries with it malnutrition and the numerous other problems of those on the edge of subsistence.

Relatively few of China's youth could look forward to a university education. That was still a privilege for a narrow elite. But a majority of those born in the 1960s and 1970s could contemplate a job outside of farming and the realistic prospect of being able to move to an urban area if they were not already there.

There was nothing unique to China about this transformation. These are the kind of changes that accompany rapid economic growth wherever it occurs. China's experience in this respect was different from that of Europe in the nineteenth century mainly in the pace with which change was occurring. In that respect China was much like its East Asian neighbors. South Korea and Taiwan had been transformed from rural peasant societies into urban industrial societies in the course of roughly three decades. China by the end of the 1980s had had only one decade of such rapid change and growth, enough for the impact to be readily apparent to anyone prepared to open their eyes and look, but not nearly enough to complete the transition to an urban industrial society. The question raised by the events of June 1989 was whether China would be allowed to complete that transition or whether the whole process had somehow been derailed.

The Nature of Chinese Reforms

The importance of the economic reforms to China's accelerated growth in the 1980s has already been mentioned. The task here is to go in more depth into the nature of those reforms to attempt to discern just how far China has moved from the economic system the reformers inherited in 1978. With an understanding of how far China is along the path to a fundamentally different kind of economic system, it then becomes possible to speculate about what might or might not survive of the economic system that existed at the end of the 1980s.

There were three central elements in China's reform process. One, the decollectivization of agriculture in favor of a return to family farming, has already been discussed, if only briefly. The other two central elements were the promotion of closer economic ties with the outside world and the attempt to replace the Soviet-style system of central plans and bureaucratic commands with a system that placed greater reliance on market forces. Each will be taken up in turn.

It is difficult to overstate the pace with which China abandoned earlier policies of turning its back on the outside world in favor of measures that embraced foreign trade and even foreign direct private investment. In 1965, for example,

Chinese exports plus imports were only 8.5 percent of net material product in that year (about 7.4 percent of GNP). By 1970, under the impact of the Cultural Revolution, that ratio had fallen to 5.9 percent. In the early 1970s, presumably under the influence of Zhou Enlai and Deng Xiaoping, China had already begun quietly to move away from the extreme autarchic policies of the late 1960s, and the trade ratio rose to 11.6 percent by 1975. The trade ratios that prevailed in the 1974–78 period were roughly the same as those that existed in China during the later years of the First Five-Year Plan period (1953–57).

Beginning in 1979, however, China's foreign trade ratio began to climb dramatically. By 1980 it was at 15.3 percent of NMP (13 percent of GNP), by 1985 it had hit 29.4 percent of NMP (24.8 percent of GNP), and it was still climbing in 1987 at 33 percent of NMP (27.9 percent of GNP). There are serious methodological problems with these percentage estimates, but the basic story they tell of a rapidly rising foreign trade share is not in question.[2]

To those not immersed in the quantitative analysis of economists, what do these figures imply? One indication of how far China had moved by 1987 and 1988 can be obtained by comparing these ratios with those of China's neighbors. In 1985 in Japan, for example, the ratio of exports plus imports to gross domestic product was 23.1 percent, slightly less than was the case in China. In South Korea, by way of contrast, the same ratio in 1985 was 71.8 percent, and in Taiwan it was 97.7 percent. To a substantial degree, the difference between these very high ratios for Korea and Taiwan and the lower figures for China and Japan reflect the influence of country size. Nations with large populations, for a variety of mainly economic reasons, trade less internationally than do those with smaller populations. Given China's huge population and large geographic area, one would expect China's trade ratio to be below not only Taiwan but also Japan, but that apparently was not the case.[3]

How critical was this expansion in China's foreign trade to the country's high growth rate in the 1980s? A full answer to this question would require a simulation of various alternative growth paths and assumptions about the impact of these different paths on productivity growth. An exercise of that scope is well beyond what is feasible for this essay, but an analysis of China's foreign trade patterns will provide some clues about what might have occurred if foreign trade had stayed at the levels of the early 1970s.

The breakdown for China's exports and imports for 1987 is presented in table 1. One can begin with exports because it is export-led growth that is often argued to be the major reason for the high growth rates achieved by China's neighbors. In Korea and Taiwan, most industries produced in part, often in large part, for the external market. To meet fierce competition in those external markets, Korean and Taiwanese manufacturers had to keep costs low and meet international quality and style standards. Those who were able to achieve these goals grew rapidly and prospered. Those who did not dropped out of the race.

Table 1

Structure of China's Foreign Trade (1987)

	Exports	Imports
Food and tobacco	12.56	6.26
Nonfood raw materials	9.26	7.68
Mining and fuels	11.52	1.25
Chemical products	5.67	11.59
Steel	—	11.08
Textiles and metal products	21.73	11.43
Clothing	9.51	—
Machinery and transport equipment	4.41	33.80
Misc. manufactures and other	25.34	16.91
Total	100.00	100.00

Source: State Statistical Bureau, *Zhongguo tongji nianjian 1988* (Beijing: Tongqi chubanshe, 1988), pp. 722–23.

Chinese manufacturers, in contrast, produced mainly for the domestic market even in 1987. The major exception was textiles and clothing, which together accounted for nearly one-third of all Chinese exports. These exports in turn accounted for roughly one-third of all textile production in China. China was also an exporter of significant quantities of electronic products, chemicals, ferrous and nonferrous metals, and machinery, but in all of these cases exports were a small share of total output, which was destined mainly for China's domestic market. One suspects that Chinese manufacturers learned a great deal about how to improve their products from the need to export, but we don't know enough to measure the impact of this learning on growth.

A bit more can be said about the import side of the ledger again referring to table 1. Many of China's imports provided essential inputs for Chinese industry and construction. Most of these inputs were also produced within China, but not in sufficient quantity to meet domestic demand requirements. China in 1987, for example, imported 12 million tons of steel, down from 18 million tons in 1986, while domestic crude steel output was 56 million tons and finished steel output was 44 million tons. If China had been unable to import steel in these quantities, it is likely that sharp cutbacks in construction and some kinds of machinery would have followed. China imported 90,000 motor vehicles of various kinds, also down from 1986, while domestic production of cars and trucks was 472,000 vehicles. Clearly China's economy could have managed without the imported 90,000 vehicles but at some cost to an already clogged transport system. Similar statements could be made about such other major imports as chemical fertilizer, paper products, and much else.

The most difficult imports to assess are those often categorized as high technology imports. Many forms of machinery and other specialized equipment fall into this category. Some of these items are ones that cannot be produced in China at all or can only be produced at extremely high cost. In these cases, if China were unable to find the foreign exchange to pay for such imports, the cost in lost productivity growth could be large. In other cases, such as commercial aircraft, a drop in imports would have an impact similar to a decline in motor vehicle or steel imports. It would be inconvenient for tourism and business travel, but the impact on overall GNP growth would be modest.

Taking exports and imports together, there is little doubt that if China in 1988 had only been able to pay for imports of $15 to $20 billion instead of the $55 billion of goods that was actually imported, China's growth rate would have fallen. The $35 to $40 billion difference between these two figures is basically what was achieved by China's turn outward. Simply maintaining the trade ratios for the early 1970s into the 1980s would have produced less than $20 billion of either exports or imports. How far would growth have fallen if these lower trade ratios had been maintained? There is no real way of knowing without much more analysis than is possible here, but one suspects that the growth rate would have dropped by two or three percentage points. Certainly there is no reason to expect a drop of four or five percentage points that would have taken China back to the rates of the prereform period.

Those who are inclined to punish China for the events of June 1989 would do well to keep the above reasoning in mind. Even a massive embargo on much of China's trade with the Western industrial nations including Japan, something that is not remotely realistic, might lower China's growth rate by 2 or 3 percent by forcing China to turn back inward. What is realistic, selective trade embargoes on a few items by several countries, will have a very limited impact on either trade or growth unless it provides political ammunition to those within China who want to turn inward for their own reasons.

Where does China's foreign investment boom of the 1980s fit into this picture? Prior to the reforms, China had rejected all forms of foreign capital for nearly twenty years. In the 1950s the nation had received loans from the Soviet Union, but these were paid back in the 1960s. Immediately after the Third Plenum in December 1978, the government reversed its earlier policies and began receiving both loans and foreign direct investment. China took its seat with the International Monetary Fund and the World Bank, promulgated a joint venture law, and created special economic zones in Guangdong and Fujian. The latter were modeled on export-processing zones found elsewhere in Asia and were designed to free foreign investors from the red tape of doing business in China's planned economy.

Initially, the sums China actually received as loans or foreign direct investment were in the $300 million a year range, but the figure reached $4.6 billion in 1985 and $8.5 billion in 1987. Loans provided the bulk of the funds. The World

Bank alone by the latter half of the 1980s was lending China $1.5 billion a year, and cumulative World Bank lending came to $9 billion. China's total foreign debt may have reached $40 billion, but debt service payments remained below 15 percent of exports, an easily managed level as long as new credit remained available.

Foreign direct investment was also sizable, at least in comparison with the experience of most other developing countries. In 1987, foreign direct investment actually realized passed $2 billion for the first time. This figure, for example, was several times the level of foreign direct investment in Taiwan and ten or twenty times more than what Taiwan received annually in the 1960s and 1970s. Most of this direct investment came from Hong Kong (69 percent in 1987) and was used to establish small enterprises in Guangdong. The only other major sources of direct investment were the United States (11 percent in 1987) and Japan (9 percent).

Direct investment came mostly from Hong Kong because other investors had difficulty making money on investments in Chinese enterprises. The majority of foreigners were lured to China by the promise of a billion new customers. Others were attracted by China's offshore oil potential. Hong Kong investors were more attracted by China's cheap labor, which could be used to keep Hong Kong exports competitive despite the high wages prevailing in the colony. The Chinese government's own view of the role of foreign investment was much closer to that of Hong Kong than to that of investors from the United States and Japan.

What has been the economic impact of these loans and direct investments? In the latter half of the 1980s these two sources of foreign exchange were equivalent to 20 percent of the total value of exports in those years. Put differently, these sources allowed China to import 20 percent more goods and services each year than would otherwise have been the case. But foreign investment, particularly direct investment, involved more than an additional source of foreign exchange. Foreign investors in some cases brought technology that was not otherwise available, and they brought improved management practices and knowledge of how to deal with foreign markets. To the extent that this knowledge was passed on to the Chinese, the gain from foreign investment was more than the 20 percent gain in available foreign exchange.

Given the large favorable impact on the economy of rising foreign trade and increased foreign investment in the 1980s, is there reason to believe that these trends will continue beyond the 1980s, or are forces at work that could reverse these trends? Conceivably, the events of June 3–4, 1989, could make the 1990s significantly different in the foreign trade and investment area from the 1980s. The most plausible scenario would be one where a conservative leadership decided that the political risks entailed in maintaining an open economy weren't worth the economic gains. As many in the Chinese leadership realize, opening the economy has brought in forces over which that leadership has only limited control. It is impossible to run an open economy and a closed society in all other respects. Effective operation of an open economy requires extensive contact with the outside world.

If politics could have led China's leadership to turn away from an outward-oriented economic policy, there is no evidence to date that they are moving in that direction. In his June 9, 1989, speech to army commanders, for example, Deng Xiaoping reiterated support for the open economy in general and for continuing to receive foreign loans in particular.

If the leadership sticks with the open policy, will events in the outside world make such a policy viable? The suppression of the students will not by itself deter foreign investors from returning to China for long. The fall of Deng's designated successor, Zhao Ziyang, however, and the implied future instability that appears almost inevitable given that power in the government now rests almost entirely on men in their eighties are likely to discourage foreign investment. Reduced foreign investment, as indicated above, will not only reduce the foreign exchange available to China but will also limit China's access to some kinds of technology and advanced management practices. Creeping world protectionism may also pose some danger for Chinese export growth, but doomsayers have been predicting the end of opportunity for export-oriented development for several decades. So far the countries that have paid the price in lowered growth have been those that have followed the doomsayers' advice.

Will foreign trade and investment sanctions imposed by the outside world slow China's turn outward? Will any sanctions at all outlast the shock effect of television coverage of the night of June 3–4? And if sanctions are applied, will they have much impact? The probable answer to each of these questions is no. People and nations have shot themselves in the foot before, but in this case *both* China and the West would have to shoot themselves in the foot. That is possible, but it is more likely that China will maintain an open-economy policy and that the West will accommodate that openness. Some of the reforms that accompanied openness may disappear, particularly those that carried the highest political price for the conservative leadership. But the general thrust of the policy will probably continue.

Markets versus Commands

The choice between an open and closed economy is a simple one compared to the question of how to introduce market forces into a system dominated by Soviet-style central plans and bureaucratic commands. Economists in the West seldom grasp the full complexity of the task because they take for granted certain kinds of behavior that in a command system one cannot take for granted.

The Chinese economic system that existed in industry and commerce prior to the reforms of the 1980s was as pure a bureaucratic command system as that of the Soviet Union after which it was patterned. The main difference was that the Chinese system was quite decentralized, the commands emanated often from provincial- and even county-level planners rather than only from Beijing. Enterprises in this system had almost no autonomy from higher-level government organs. These enterprises received output and input targets that they were expected to obey. Key inputs when required could not be purchased on the market but were obtained by making an application to the authorities in charge of materials allocation. Even an enterprise's bank account was monitored by the People's Bank. If a major expenditure of funds was consistent with the state plan, the bank allowed the expenditure. If the funds were not in accordance with the plan, the bank could disallow the expenditure.

The reality was never as rigid as this system in its pure form would imply. It could not be and still operate. Instead, informal arrangements between enterprises were commonplace and essential to efficient operations. The "back door" deal was not something invented by the reformers after 1978, it was an inherent part of a centrally planned system. In essence, the problem is that plans are always going to be riddled with errors and distortions. Blind obedience to the plan, therefore, will lead to economic paralysis. Since no one wants paralysis, the central authorities overlook many informal efforts to get around errors in planning so long as the individuals involved are adhering broadly to the spirit of the plan. Needless to say, the ambiguity of what constitutes adherence to the spirit of the plan lends itself to abuse.

China's decision to move away from this system was prompted by rising awareness in the early 1970s that the system was increasingly wasteful of resources. If China were to achieve more rapid growth, the country would have to do better. The energy crunch that hit in 1979 reinforced the point. After a decade and a half of rapid development, output growth of petroleum ground to a halt, and coal production was not in a position to pick up the slack.

There were many experiments with enterprise reform in the early 1980s, but the issue over whether to move toward a more market-oriented system was still open. Chen Yun, for example, saw the market as something that could supplement a system run primarily by central plans. Others, notably Zhao Ziyang, were prepared to go much further. By 1984 the pendulum had swung toward the all-out reformers, and a thorough-going policy of reform in industry was announced in October of that year.

When the reformers decided to move away from central planning toward the greater use of market forces, they had no blueprint to follow. The Hungarians and others in East Europe provided some guidance, but the Hungarians were still in the middle of the reform process and lacked a clear blueprint themselves. The years that followed the October 1984 directive were years of vigorous debate between proponents of one or another reform view. A wide range of ideas received a hearing, and many were tried out in practice.

To understand how far the reforms in industry had or had not gone, one needs a clearer picture of what it takes to make a market system work. There is some danger that by bringing clarity to the analysis of the reforms in industry, one will give the impression that the reform process was itself systematic. The reality was quite different. The whole approach was ad hoc and highly experimental, with many forward movements and reversals in one area or another.

There are five elements to making a market system work: four are essential in all countries, and the fifth is essential in any country with a low tolerance for inflation. To begin with, intermediate inputs as well as final goods must be made available for purchase and sale on the market rather than allocated by administrative means. In China, final goods destined directly for consumers had always been available in part through the market and in part through various systems of rationed allocation. In the 1980s there was a steady progression away from rationing, and by 1986 and 1987, before inflationary pressures became severe, most consumer goods were sold through the market.

Making intermediate inputs available to the market presented a more difficult challenge, for reasons that will be elaborated on below. Despite the difficulties, there was a steady expansion in the scope of the market for intermediate goods, with the total of such goods available on the market in 1985 rising to 27 percent, up from 16 percent in 1984.

One of the beneficiaries of marketed intermediate goods was the small-scale industry sector. There were hundreds of thousands of enterprises in this sector, and there was no way that the central authorities could systematically control their inputs and output. Some inputs could be obtained through subcontracting arrangements with large enterprises; others could sometimes be obtained by county-level planners. But there was no substitute for the enterprise being able to go out and purchase required inputs on their own as needed.

Partly as a result of the easier availability of inputs, but even more because of the decentralization of investment financing authority to the localities, there was a boom in the small- and medium-scale collective industry sector. Growth of the collective industry sector throughout the 1980s was more rapid than in the state-owned industry sector. As a share of total industrial output, the collective proportion rose from 19.5 percent in 1980 to 22.5 percent in 1984 and 25.6 percent in 1987. It does not seem likely that this small-scale industry boom was really planned. Early in the post-Mao era, the government had been cutting back and consolidating many of the rural small-scale industries on the grounds of inefficiency. Later, when the boom in this sector was well underway, it was cited as one of the gains from reform, which it was, but there was considerable ambivalence about the desirability of so much dynamism in this sector. In particular, there were steady complaints about the diversion of resources from high-priority central tasks to lower-priority local ones. By 1988 the dynamism of the local economies, including local industry, was also seen, with some reason, as a source of the inflationary pressures sweeping the country. Despite those qualifications, however, collective industry contributed in important ways to the overall economic boom of the 1980s. As the sector grew in size it also created an increasingly important group with a vested interest in continued decentralization and reform.

Making intermediate and final goods available on the market will lead to greater efficiency only if a second component of reform is also in place. Prices must reflect real scarcities in the economy or goods and services will end up in the hands of the wrong people. But in China, prices had been frozen prior to the 1980s often for as long as twenty years. During a period when industry had grown from 15 percent of China's gross domestic product to around 45 percent and the OPEC countries had increased the price of world energy sources severalfold, China's price structure continued to reflect the world of the mid-1950s, when China was a rural agriculture-based economy and oil was cheap.

From early on, Chinese reformers recognized that price reform had to be part of any package that involved an increasing role for market forces. The hard part was actually carrying out price reform. Since the state had held the responsibility for setting the prices of most important products over the previous two decades, it seemed to follow that the state should take the lead in changing prices to reflect the new situation. But for every change in price there is a winner and a loser. The winner is the person or enterprise that receives a higher price for its output or pays a lower price for an input. The loser is the one who faces the reverse situation, and in most cases the loser will be well aware of the fact that he has been made worse off. Every change in a state-set price, therefore, becomes a political tug of war. In the United States, the tug of war is confined to farm prices and utility rates since these are controlled to a large degree by government. In China, the battles were across the board because the state was involved in setting most prices.

The major breakthrough on price reform came in 1985 and 1986 when the state created the dual-price system. State-set prices continued to be changed slowly if at all, but now goods sold on the market, as contrasted to being allocated through the plan, would have prices set by market forces. While not all prices of goods sold on the market were completely free of state control, the price changes that did occur were dramatic enough. For critical inputs in short supply such as steel or gasoline, the market price was often several times the state allocation price.

In the years immediately following the introduction of the dual-price system, the debate among reformers was over whether dual prices should be continued indefinitely or whether the share of goods subject to state-set prices should be phased out entirely over time. In the interim, the decisions at the margin by many enterprises were being increasingly made on the basis of market prices. In these cases the main role of state-set prices was to provide subsidies to favored firms.

Freeing up prices had two other predictable but less desirable effects as well—one was inflation. Given the chronic shortage of some goods and the price distortions of the past, some inflation is inevitable when a command system begins to shift over to a market system. When Vietnam freed up prices as part of a reform movement begun in 1986, for example, price increases by 1988 reached a rate of 700 percent a year. In China the rate of price increase was more modest, but still high enough to cause considerable political tension in the urban areas.

The other undesirable effect of the dual-price system was on the spread of corrupt practices in the allocation of critical industrial inputs. Individuals with political influence could get large allocations of these goods at low state-set prices and then turn around and sell those same goods at high market prices. The profits involved could be very large, and some of these profits ended up in the pockets of influential individuals. In some cases, new enterprises were created that were little more than an address that could be used to accumulate and resell goods allocated by the state.

The third element in making a market system work is the least well understood and the hardest to reform. The essence of the problem is that enterprises under a centralized command system behave in ways quite different from what is required in an efficient market system. Simply removing the central planning apparatus does not lead automatically to the required change in enterprise behavior. In fact, as the Hungarians have demonstrated, the old ways can hang on even after compulsory central-plan targets have been abolished altogether.

The key issue is how to make the enterprise fully independent of government authorities so that enterprise success is driven by the ability of managers to cut their costs, raise product quality, and increase sales. In practice in China, as well as in other countries where government is heavily involved in the economy, success is more often driven by enterprise managers' ability to extract subsidies and other favors from governments. Part of the problem is known as the "soft budget constraint." Enterprises facing a soft budget constraint know they won't be allowed to fail. If they consistently run losses the state will step in to bail them out with grants or low-interest loans that do not have to be paid back.

Another element of the lack of autonomy derives from the fact that managerial appointments and promotions are determined by higher government authorities in China, not by independent boards of directors concerned mainly with enterprise profits. As a result, managers are deeply concerned with doing what they think higher-level government authorities want them to do. These higher-level authorities have various agendas of their own, and only rarely will those agendas be to achieve complete enterprise autonomy. Thus, Chinese enterprises were still subject to a high degree of bureaucratic control throughout the 1980s.

While bureaucratic commands from central and local government officials continued to play a role, there were significant changes. Profits became the principal enterprise objective instead of gross value output. Government grants were phased out and replaced by bank loans carrying interest rates, although inflation often meant that the real interest rate was negative. There were experiments with alternative forms of ownership, including outright private ownership in the small-scale sector. But even in the small-scale sector in provinces such as

Jiangsu, government authorities continued actively to guide industrial investment and some ongoing operations.

The fourth element in making markets work efficiently involves the introduction of competition. Under central planning competition interferes with the orderly carrying out of the plan so it is usually done away with. In China in the early 1970s, for example, even small-scale enterprises were awarded monopoly control over their local market, usually a countywide market. From the outset of the reform movement that began with the Third Plenum in 1978, China's leaders began to increase the level of competition in the system. At first it was mainly confined to commerce and services. Small shopkeepers were allowed to compete with the large state department stores, and the result was a marked improvement in customer-service orientation. Afterward industrial enterprises were freed up to sell anywhere in the country they could find a market. Local authorities sometimes subverted efforts to bring in goods that competed with local products. It is difficult to assess how widespread and quantitatively significant were these regional blockades. Where such blockades were pervasive, competitive pressures to raise productivity were largely absent. A probably more serious problem was that products in chronically short supply were never subject to meaningful competitive pressures. By definition one could always sell whatever one produced.

The existence of chronic shortages, of soft budget constraints, and of high and rising free-market prices were all symptoms or causes of the fifth element interfacing with the effective operation of market forces—inflation. For markets to work smoothly, China either had to bring inflationary pressures under control or had to learn to live with whatever inflation rate that prevailed. China in the late 1980s was not able to do either. The official urban consumer cost-of-living index in the 1985–87 period rose by an average rate of nearly 10 percent a year and then jumped by 20 percent in 1988. Free-market prices rose at much higher rates.

Inflation existed basically for two reasons. One was the pent-up demand caused by past efforts to freeze prices at well below market-clearing rates. When goods became available on markets with flexible prices, this pent-up demand was released and drove up prices. The other source was clearly related to the soft budget constraint. When enterprises were given greater autonomy in setting wages and in the prices they could pay for inputs, they were free to raise wages and pay higher prices in order to get what they needed. If they ran out of money to pay higher wages and prices, they went to the banking system for a loan, which they might or might not have to pay back. Local governments wishing to invest in new plant capacity also could go to the banks for soft loans. The banks in turn knew that the government would normally increase the money supply so that deposits and bank capacity to lend would not be restricted.

Effective control of inflation, therefore, involved a willingness to let prices soak up past accumulations of excess demand together with an ability to eliminate new sources of excess demand by hardening the soft budget constraint. The former involved tolerating very large increases in prices on a one-shot basis. The latter involved fundamental enterprise reform, something, as pointed out above, that was extremely difficult to accomplish. Neither step was probably politically feasible in the late 1980s even if the leadership had fully understood what was required. Instead, the government temporized by freezing some prices but not others, and by periodic efforts to restrict bank credit by administrative means.[4]

The Political Consequences of Economic Reform

Politics has clearly played a role in determining the pace and nature of economic reform in China, just as politics plays a central role in most economic policy decisions elsewhere. Bureaucratic desires to hold onto power, for example, have much to do with why it is difficult to break the ties that bind enterprise management to higher levels of the government. The decision to decollectivize agriculture must have involved a calculation, perhaps by Deng himself, that the Chinese Communist Party could afford the loss of control over the farm households that decollectivization implied. And the political events of June 3–4, 1989, have limited some of the economic policy options open to China, such as whether to import weapons for the army or produce them at home.

But how did the economic reforms affect politics? Were the reforms themselves directly responsible for the political developments in the spring of 1989 and the repression that followed? Could a different set of economic policies have led to a different outcome?

One can begin by pointing out that major economic policy changes generally do have political consequences. Devaluations of the national currency and removal of food price subsidies are frequent causes of urban riots and successful coups d'etat. Industrialization in Argentina led to the rise of a labor movement that brought Juan Peron to power. In turn, Peron initiated policies that undermined Argentina's long-term growth prospects. Closer to China, low prices of imported rice from Taiwan and Korea in the early twentieth century helped depress the income of Japanese farmers, whose resentment spilled over into the Japanese army and contributed to the increasingly dominant role played by the army in Japanese domestic politics.

There is little doubt that many of the political developments in China would not have occurred in the absence of the economic reforms. Two of the most dominant influences on politics came from the opening of the economy to the outside world and the devolution of power away from the center and toward localities and even to individual firms and households.

The influences of the opening to the outside world are straightforward. Except for the top leadership, the people of China had little idea what life was like in the world outside of China prior to the death of Mao Zedong. The growing gap in standards of living between China and its East Asian neighbors was certainly unknown. Even Chinese enterprise managers knew little of the technological developments occurring elsewhere except when the foreign trade corporations occasionally supplied them with new pieces of high-technology equipment.

The turn outward after Mao's death was clearly motivated mainly by economic considerations, by Deng and others' search for wealth and power. Students were sent abroad to learn about technology. Scientists and engineers came to China to teach about science and technology. Tourists were allowed in to provide foreign exchange. Foreign investors were allowed in both for foreign exchange and technology. The decision to allow foreign investment became a powerful impetus to write new business law so that foreign business would not fear entry into China. Dealing with foreigners and with foreign information became a powerful impetus to learn the English language. A steady flow of information from abroad was essential if Chinese enterprises were to keep up with foreign markets as well as foreign technology. This need for information and technology from abroad was particularly acute given the damage done by the Cultural Revolution to China's domestic research and development capacity.

Once turned outward, however, the influences brought in could not be contained narrowly within the economic sphere. Students abroad learned much more than just technology. Information flowing in included material on different lifestyles and political developments as well as economics. The decision to integrate more closely with Hong Kong leading up to 1997 meant increasing contact with all aspects of the colony's way of life. Those who could read English did not confine themselves to engineering textbooks and translations of *Das Kapital*. Tourists, foreign businessmen, and exchange scholars brought with them more than just their money and their technical specialty.

It will take intellectual historians a long time to sort out just what the Chinese people, particularly the educated urban youth, absorbed of all these influences. There is little doubt that the world view of a twenty-year-old Chinese was very different in 1989 from what it had been in 1969 at the height of the Cultural Revolution, or even in 1979. Expectations of what was possible both in terms of a higher standard of living and a more open pluralistic political system appear to have raced well ahead of what was realistic in a society that was still relatively poor, rural, and ruled by a highly centralized political party.

The other fundamental influence on politics of economic change was brought about by the nature of the domestic economic reforms. As already suggested, agricultural decollectivization had a profound affect on the power of the Chinese Communist Party in the countryside. No longer did rural cadres have the authority to determine who worked on what task on a given day, or how income was to be divided among consumption, investment, and the welfare fund. Rural cadres still had far more power than what is found in the rural parts of Western nations, over family planning, for example, but far less than they had in the prereform period.

The increasing role of market forces, the rapid rise of collective industrial and service enterprises, and the decentralization of much financial authority to the localities had a similar effect. In some cases, local party authorities gained at the expense of the center. In others, enterprises grew up that were not subject to effective government or party control of any kind. Before 1978 an individual of working age had a choice between working in a state bureaucracy or going to a commune. By the late 1980s, tens of millions of workers had chosen other paths over which labor bureaus and the other elements of the control apparatus had much less influence.

These various forms of decentralization of authority also led to a situation where some people did better than others. Growth along the coast was greater than in the interior. It was the coastal provinces, for example, that gained the most from the opening to foreign trade. Reforms of the economy designed to increase the role of market forces had also proceeded much farther than in the interior. In some interior provinces, price reform and a greater role for market forces in industry existed more on paper than in reality. There were also a few individuals who became conspicuously rich. It was not that national inequality, as measured by a gini coefficient, was on the rise. In their first phase in the early 1980s, reforms had probably reduced inequality by reducing the large rural-urban gap in incomes. Whether inequality in this sense rose after agricultural growth slowed down in the latter half of the 1980s remains to be studied.

What is clear is that people in the urban areas became much more aware of differences between their own incomes and those of their immediate neighbors. The fact that shopkeepers and suburban farmers were making more money than many government officials and intellectuals was observed and resented at least by the officials and intellectuals. One could hear the same kinds of complaints in Korea when the differential impact on incomes of rapid economic growth began to be felt in the 1970s.

On top of these fundamental long-term trends was the rising rate of inflation and the increase in corruption. The political impact on inflation also hit government officials and intellectuals hardest. They were the ones on fixed salaries, and even when the government raised salaries to offset the impact of inflation, they tended to see those increases as raises for merit that were being eaten away by inflation.

Corruption was mostly of the petty bribe variety. There are no Marcoses in China, although a few individuals have used their positions to make income manyfold what they could have earned legitimately. The dual-price system in particular probably made a few people millionaires. Given the continued prevalence of regulations over all aspects of daily life and business, however, the opportunities for petty graft were almost infinite, even with the apparent decision to eliminate dual prices. After June 3–4 the temptation of those in power was to increase enforcement of these regulations and police surveillance of those carrying them out, measures that will probably increase both the amount of corruption and the penalties for getting caught. A reduction in the level of corruption would probably require fewer, more transparent regulations and an open society free to criticize those who abuse their positions of authority. Given the political realities of China after June 3–4, 1989, corruption is likely to remain a stick that can be used against those in power, just as it was used against those in power in the late 1980s.

China's economic growth and reforms, therefore, had a great deal to do with the political developments at the end of the decade. Could the economy have been managed in a way that lessened the dangers and enhanced the possibility of a smoother transition to a more open political system? China could have kept the economy closed and the growth rate low. But then China's leaders would have faced a difference set of problems, notably a growing number of educated and unemployed youth. Between 1979 and 1987, China's work force grew by over 107 million persons, or 13 million persons a year. Was it a viable strategy to keep sending these people back to the rural areas? And where would China have obtained the foreign exchange to pay for rising food imports if the country had neither decollectivized agriculture or turned outward? Would tight rationing of grain have been a viable substitute for rising imports? Slower growth in personal incomes would have reduced the increase in demand for grain, but would this have led to higher morale in the work place?

These and many other questions like them would have to be answered before one could reach a judgment about what alternatives the reform-minded leadership of the 1980s really faced. They are the same kinds of issues that will face whoever leads China in the 1990s, but with one difference. Having once exposed the Chinese people to the outside world, it will be difficult to cut them off again. Mao Zedong managed to close down an open society four decades ago, but he was dealing with a nation of peasants, low incomes, and limited education. Would the much smaller rural base and the spread of education and higher incomes provide a sufficient base of power to sustain another turn inward? Will the leadership of the 1990s want to try to do so?

Notes

1. Chinese growth rates in the 1980s may be slightly inflated by the apparent tendency to include some data that are not properly deflated to remove the impact of inflation. There is no doubt, however, that GNP growth in the 1980s was much higher than in earlier years. The data for the pre-1980 period would not be affected by this problem, because there was little or no inflation in those earlier years. All data used in this essay are based on official figures of the Chinese government.

2. The essence of the methodological problem is that NMP is calculated in Chinese domestic prices while the value of exports and imports is calculated at world prices and converted into Chinese currency at the prevailing exchange rate. The ratio of trade to NMP, therefore, can move for reasons other than real increases (or decreases) in foreign trade relative to NMP.

3. The statement made in note 2 and in the text concerning the uncertainties surrounding Chinese trade ratios applies to these international comparisons as well.

4. Those interested in delving further into these issues of urban/enterprise reform in China are referred to the text and bibliography in Dwight H. Perkins, "Reforming China's Economic System," *Journal of Economic Literature* 26, 2 (June 1988): 601–45.

15

THE RENEGOTIATION OF CHINESE CULTURAL IDENTITY IN THE POST-MAO ERA
An Anthropological Perspective

JAMES L. WATSON

> The Red Guards will sweep dirty old water from the earth. The Red Guards will destroy the old world and create a new world.
>
> —1966 middle school slogan

> Cultural accumulation and advance demand that we build first and destroy later—creating the new while *not* destroying the old. When we build a new building, it is not necessary to tear down an old one; so it is with our cultural legacy.
>
> —Wang Meng, "The Principal Contradiction in Culture"

This essay was written in May 1989 while the drama of Tiananmen Square was being played out in full view of a world audience. The television images of Chinese students demonstrating in Beijing were so riveting they gave viewers the vicarious thrill of participating in a momentous historical "event." The live broadcasts were multivariant in their symbolism—and irony. Twenty-two years ago the same square was the venue for another set of demonstrations representing an earlier generation of students who also hoped to change the nature of China's political system. The goals and public rhetoric of the two historical movements were radically different, but one important symbol remained constant: the enigmatic portrait of Mao Zedong still looms over the square. When vandals attacked the portrait on May 23, students reacted with anger and expressed great concern that this act might be used as a pretext for troops to clear the square. Said one, "Mao was a good guy. There was no need to abuse him like that."[1]

Here, in the heat of a political movement, we witness the process by which history is reconstructed. For many Chinese that same image conjures up unpleasant memories of the Cultural Revolution. During my first trip to China in the late 1970s, Mao's portrait was everywhere. Today, aside from Tiananmen Square, one is hard pressed to find depictions of Mao displayed in public. Two gigantic statues of Mao were removed from the campus of Peking University only twelve months prior to the spring demonstrations.[2] The statues had become an embarrassment for a generation of teachers and administrators who had participated—some as persecutors, others as "bad class" victims—in the Cultural Revolution. On May 23, 1989, however, a new generation of students too young to remember the 1960s had appropriated the memory of Mao for their own purposes. He had been transformed into a symbol of selflessness and rectitude in an era characterized by corruption, alienation, and self-doubt. One wonders whether this reinterpretation of Mao as an emblem of protest will be pursued and developed by student leaders. Stranger things have happened in the representation of public personalities since 1949.

The public suffering of the hunger strikers (*jueshizhe*) was another powerful image that television made immediate and tangible. And this, of course, is precisely the point: Fasting is a political act that conveys an unmistakable message to the world at large. In fact, given their expectation that the state-controlled media in China would deny them access to the Chinese people, it seems likely that the Beijing students chose consciously to appeal to an international television audience. The news of young people courting death through fast could then be sent back to China, literally over the heads of party authorities, by the Voice of America and BBC. As it turned out, both Chinese print media and, to a limited extent, local television broadcast the news of the hunger strike.[3] But there can be little doubt that satellite broadcasts of the fasting, complete with howling sirens and fainting students, by CNN, CBS, and other foreign networks had much to do with the creation of an international media event—which, in turn, helped student leaders convert the small-scale demonstrations into China's most serious political crisis since the death of Mao and the subsequent arrest of the Gang of Four in 1976.

Foreign Symbols in a Chinese Political Drama

Why fasting? Why did Beijing students choose a form of political protest that is essentially foreign? There are, of course, parallels in Chinese history. During the Ming-Qing transition an exemplary official, Liu Zongzhou (1578–1645), fasted for twenty days, killing himself to protest the rise of Manchu authority. The *Shiji* records two legendary heroes of the Zhou dynasty, Boyi and Shuqi, who starved to death in a protest against political injustice.[4] In more modern times, however, hunger strikes have not been a standard feature of the Chinese cultural repertoire. According to Chinese colleagues, there were no celebrated precedents during the May Fourth Movement, the anti-Japanese protests, or the civil war era. Fasting plays a central role in the modern political history of Korea but not, apparently, in China.[5]

Judging from the visual images and from the verbal messages conveyed by students in the square, it seems likely that the cultural models for the Beijing actions were Gandhi's anti-imperialist fasts and the hunger strikes associated with the American civil rights movement—both of which are often depicted in the Chinese media. I have not been able to determine whether news of Irish Republican Army prisoners fasting to the death in Northern Ireland made an impact in China during the 1970s. I will return to the question of foreign symbols and Chinese cultural identity in the conclusion of this paper.

By attempting to ignore the demonstrations, party authorities all but conceded the manipulation of the media to the students. After gaining the attention of the world's television audience through the drama of the fast, student leaders could concentrate on presenting their messages. Slogans were simplified (corruption in high places, intransigent leaders, the promise of democracy). Earlier complicating issues such as inflation, job placement, and student living conditions were dropped. Viewed from the outside, it is obvious that the students were far more sophisticated in their ability to *use* the media than were their opponents who remained behind closed doors, conducting politics in the time-tried but increasingly outdated mode that has characterized Communist parties since the early twentieth century.

The Pursuit of Chinese Cultural Identity in the Post-Mao Era

Few who have lived or worked in China during the past five years can fail to notice the high level of alienation and despair that characterizes intellectual life, particularly in the universities. This is partly a consequence of frozen salaries and rising inflation. Meanwhile, the entire society seems to have plunged headlong into the pursuit of personal affluence. Intellectuals have had to join the scramble for new sources of income (e.g., by marketing their foreign language and management skills) or stand aside and watch their standard of living fall below that of workers with minimal education. Financial problems are obviously important, but teachers, writers, and researchers are also deeply concerned about the evolution of Chinese culture in the post-Mao era. The self-sacrificing ethic of the early Communist movement (1949–57) appealed to many intellectuals who participated in the construction of a new socialist culture. Having seen these dreams shattered during the late 1950s and 1960s, they had high hopes for the reforms instituted in the late 1970s. After ten years of reform, however, there is still no agreement on what kind of society China is to become. The Communist party has lost credibility, and its leaders are incapable of enlisting mass support for a new vision of the future. Equally alarming to many intellectuals is the prospect that China has abandoned its past in an effort to join the modern world.

It is unclear whether ordinary Chinese workers and farmers share the intellectuals' sense of despair about the future or the present. In my own research among rural peoples of Guangdong and Jiangsu quite the opposite impression emerged, namely that farmers were delighted with the economic reforms.[6] In most areas I visited, living standards had doubled and tripled in the past five years; the responsibility system in agriculture was welcomed by everyone, save a few diehard cadres who obviously longed for the days when they controlled the destiny of local residents.[7] It is true, of course, that my field research has concentrated in two of China's wealthiest areas (the Pearl River delta and the Jiangnan region); the same sense of buoyancy may not prevail in the North China plain. Myron Cohen's recent research suggests, however, that the reforms have also generated a new sense of optimism about the future in rural Hebei.[8]

In the past, prior to the reforms, to be sent to the countryside was equated with lifelong exile and poverty. Today, ironically, certain rural areas (e.g., Guangdong's Zhongshan and Xinhui xian) are attracting illegal migrants from northern cities; these itinerants do not speak Cantonese and work for wages that no self-respecting Guangdong farmer would even consider accepting. In some parts of China, therefore, the countryside is losing its stigmatized image.

What does this growing split between rural and urban mean for China's future? Martin Whyte has suggested that two cultural systems may be emerging, one in the cities and another in the countryside.[9] I am convinced that Whyte is correct. Before pursuing this argument, however, more needs to be said about the nature of cultural identity in Chinese society.

In what sense is post-Mao Chinese culture "Chinese"? This essay examines the question from an anthropological perspective. "Culture" in this context is not a reflection (exclusively) of the arts, literature, and philosophy. Rather, the term culture as employed here is intimately related to perceptions of appropriate lifestyle—this, in turn, is incorporated into one's sense of personal identity. Culture is embedded in family patterns, religious beliefs, political attitudes, and in the rituals of everyday life. Furthermore, culture, like one's sense of identity, is constantly changing.

Contemporary definitions of culture have been adapted to fit the fluid, boundary-defying expectations of the postmodern world. Most anthropologists now see culture as a set of symbolic representations and expectations that people must *construct* for themselves.[10] It is no longer perceived as a list of traits inherited passively from ancestors in preordained or immutable form, as earlier Tylorian notions would lead us to expect.[11] Culture in today's world has to be negotiated, transacted, and achieved. This approach thus stresses the active participation of people who cooperate—some willingly, others not—to create an acceptable culture. State authorities are, of course, directly involved in this creative process but, in the end, it is the acceptance and routinization of cultural forms by ordinary people that matter most.

Since 1949 the Chinese people have experienced two or three traumatic attempts to destroy key elements of their "traditional" (i.e., presocialist) culture.

Closely associated with these movements have been state-sponsored campaigns to construct competing versions of a new socialist culture—the most notable being the Great Proletarian Cultural Revolution launched in 1966. An earlier and in some respects more far-reaching campaign to obliterate the old and fabricate the new occurred during the Great Leap Forward (1958–60). China's pre-socialist culture was, and to a certain extent still is, a very difficult nut to crack.

Cultural Identity in Late Imperial and Republican Era China

In comparison to other premodern, agrarian societies there can be little doubt that late imperial China exhibited a high degree of cultural integration. Serious divisions based on kinship, ethnicity, and regional loyalties did, of course, exist in China but—unlike Europe or South Asia—the dominant historical theme is one of ever-increasing incorporation and cooptation. One need only read Eugen Weber's *Peasants into Frenchmen* (1976) to appreciate just how integrated China was during its late imperial era. Weber's account of the period immediately preceding World War I (1870–1914) makes it clear that the idea of "France" as a modern nation-state, with a shared culture and a corporate identity that tied all citizens together, did not exist until it was consciously created by Parisian social engineers for the purposes of national mobilization. Benedict Anderson's speculations on the origins of modern nationalism are also relevant here: The Chinese at the turn of the twentieth century could not "imagine" the state as an integral part of their personal identity, but they had no difficulty identifying with the abstraction we call Chinese culture.[12]

In China the notion of a unified culture predated, and made possible, the fabrication of a modern Chinese state following the collapse of the imperial order in 1911. People of all stations in life—peasants, workers, landlords, merchants, officials—already related to China's grand tradition with its ancient history. For ordinary Chinese, this abstraction was made concrete and represented in everyday discourse as the "civilized" way of life; those who did not follow accepted norms were defined as "uncivilized" (*meiwenhuade, yemande*). Notions of civility, conformity, and order are thus at the heart of what all Chinese accepted as the irreducible basis of their cultural identity. The point I wish to emphasize is that the vast majority of Chinese, irrespective of class background, life experience, or education, shared this vision of the acceptable way of life during the late imperial era (there were, of course, dissenters, such as the Taiping rebels and members of various Daoist sects). The notion of a shared culture began to unravel during the late nineteenth and early twentieth centuries, culminating in the May Fourth Movement (see chapter 6), but it survived for most people until the political campaigns of the Communist era.

What were the key elements in this vision of a shared culture? Some have stressed the role of an ideographic[13] (i.e., nonphonetic) script that cuts across speech communities, thereby allowing educated people from different regions to share a common literary/philosophical tradition.[14] Others have argued that it was the autocratic power of the Chinese state, projected through a complex bureaucracy, that held the society together.[15] Still others point to China's elaborate hierarchy of commercial centers and marketing communities as the key to cultural unity.[16] All of these explanations are, of course, correct. One cannot conceive of "China," or the abstraction we call Chinese culture, without a common script, a centralized state, and a complex hierarchy of central places.

My own approach to the problem of cultural identity stresses two interrelated features of everyday life: a shared oral tradition, and the central role of ritual. During the late imperial era everyone—from the emperor in Beijing to the lowly duckherd in the Pearl River delta—celebrated important life transitions with the same set of rites. They also shared essentially the same oral tradition, expressed in folk tales, myths, and legends.

Shared Oral Traditions and Visions of History

David Johnson has argued that it was drama, or more precisely the stories and emotions communicated in popular opera, that helped forge a shared sense of "Chineseness" among all strata of people.[17] As Johnson notes, the audiences of opera varied greatly but the stories remained basically similar over time and space. The essential feature of Chinese opera was that everyone was exposed to the performances at one time or another in their lives. The poor stood in the back or watched from the sides while local worthies occupied the more expensive seats in front. Future magistrates and ministers of state sat with their amahs learning about intrigue, honor, and duty. In the process, according to Johnson, all parties in this audience came to share certain key values and modes of emotional expression. This approach to cultural construction is an elaboration of Johnson's earlier analysis of literary audiences.[18]

Opera was only one of many performance media that served to communicate and inculcate shared values. Perhaps the most obvious were folk tales and oral epics told to the young by elders, or by professional storytellers.[19] This feature of culture is the most difficult for non-Chinese to penetrate. Even after decades of experience in China and fluency in the language, foreigners cannot hope to master the enormous corpus of folklore that—until recently—most Chinese shared as a matter of course.[20] In my own research among the Cantonese I have always been handicapped by this cultural gap; village friends grow weary of my constant, child-like refrain: "What's that all about? Who is Yeung Hau?" A somewhat similar situation confronts American citizens who were reared outside the United States (or who have not raised children here). Who is Paul Bunyan? What is an Easter Bunny? Why do we encourage our children to dress like ghosts and beg for food on October 31? In any culture, I would argue, one learns such things through the inimitable processes of childhood socialization and peer-group communication.

The early phases of elementary education are also critical for generating and perpetuating a sense of cultural or national identity, particularly in respect to history. The sequence of dynasties, the names of emperors, sages, and villains, and the great myths of cultural longevity ("We have two/three/four thousand years of unbroken history") were all taught as part of the curriculum—formal and informal—in China during the late imperial and Republican eras.[21] This received, sanitized vision of history is still taught in Taiwan and, to a limited extent, in Hong Kong today, but not, it would appear, in the People's Republic. More will be said about the erosion of historical consciousness later in this essay.

The Role of Ritual in the Construction of "Chineseness"

Another way to address the problem of cultural identity in China is to ask the question: What makes Chinese culture "Chinese"? What, in other words, are the basic elements of the cultural equation that allowed some residents of that vast country to call themselves Chinese (*Han*) and be accepted as such, while other peoples were labeled "barbarian" (*fan*, or more politely *xiaoshu minzu*, minority peoples). The set of cultural attributes that made one Chinese appears to have little to do with a shared creed or set of prescribed religious beliefs. There was never a unified clergy in China charged with the responsibility of dispensing truth, as in Christendom. The closest parallel to the Western church hierarchy in China was the imperial bureaucracy, but Chinese officials were relatively few in number and were preoccupied with the practical aspects of governance, not religious beliefs.

In examining the processes of cultural construction, it is perhaps best to begin with the distinction between Han and non-Han. Chinese ordinarily present this as a straightforward dichotomy: One either is or is not Han. The key diagnostic feature here is whether a set of people are deemed to have *wen*, variously translated as civilization, learning, or elegance. Han Chinese by definition perceived themselves as civilized whereas non-Han peoples (such as the Miao, Yao, and Zhuang) were categorized, by Han, as uncivilized.[22] In historical terms, however, the distinction between Han and non-Han was never so simple, particularly in the South.[23] Over the centuries, whole populations, on the order of European states, have made the transformation from non-Han to Han.[24] More recently, in the wake of post-Mao reforms, certain groups that had been recognized as Han are seeking to reclaim—and, in the process, reconstruct—earlier non-Han identities.[25] These labels, therefore, are purely cultural and are not racial or biological in any obvious sense.

To be Chinese in this context meant that one played by the rules of the dominant culture and was judged to be a good performer by those who took it upon themselves to make such judgments—neighbors, local leaders, imperial officials. What, then, were the rules of the game? How did one *become* Chinese and maintain one's "Chineseness"? From the perspective of ordinary people, to be Chinese was to understand and accept the view that there was a correct way to live one's life. This was reflected most directly in the enactment of public rituals associated with the life cycle—namely, the rites of birth, marriage, death, and ancestorhood. Correct performance of these rites was one clear and unambiguous method of distinguishing the civilized from the uncivilized or, when considering marginal peoples, the cooked from the uncooked.[26] Put another way, practice rather than belief was what made one Chinese in the eyes of others.

As an example of the principles involved, one can cite the complex rituals surrounding death in China. Based on a survey of ethnographic evidence, I have elsewhere concluded that the basic form of funeral rites is (or was) similar throughout the empire.[27] There were, of course, interesting regional variations, but, in general, all Chinese performed the same sequence of ritual acts at funerals—from the poorest farmer to the emperor himself.[28] This sequence of acts might be called the elementary structure of Chinese funerary ritual; the proper performance of the sequence distinguished civilized from uncivilized rites.

Orthopraxy versus Orthodoxy in the Ritual Context

After much discussion with Cantonese villagers, and observation of hundreds of rites associated with death, it became obvious that correct practice (orthopraxy) and not correct belief (orthodoxy) was paramount in the ritual arena. Cynics, agnostics, and active nonbelievers participated in funeral rites along with those who professed strong faith in the efficacy of the acts. Those who would refuse to follow accepted procedure were consciously isolating themselves from the community and, hence, withdrawing from the dominant culture. It is interesting in this regard that many Cantonese Christians managed to perform the rites according to accepted sequence, even though the oral/textual part of the funeral conformed to Christian expectations.

By emphasizing orthopraxy, I do not mean to imply that beliefs are somehow irrelevant to the construction of "Chineseness." This is obviously not the case. For instance, key elements of the funeral sequence were (and in some areas still are) supported by an underlying belief system that the majority of Chinese no doubt shared. One of the professed goals of funeral rites was to keep corpse and soul together; separation prior to the ritualized expulsion from the community was thought, by many, to bring disaster. The rites were also deemed to have a controlling and placating effect on the deceased's soul, which was portrayed as volatile and disoriented—potentially dangerous to the living. Closely associated with these beliefs was the idea that the living and dead were linked in a network of exchange, as symbolized by the transfer of food, money, and goods to the otherworld.[29] In return, the living expected to receive benefits in this world, including luck, wealth, and progeny.

Important as these beliefs were, it was anxiety over the practice of the rites, in the correct sequence, that took precedence over discussions of meaning or symbolism in the everyday discourse of ordinary people. This does not mean, however, that there was no variation in performance. As long as the acts were accomplished in the approved sequence, there was room for infinite variety in ritual expression.

Herein lies the genius of the (presocialist) Chinese approach to cultural construction: The system allowed for a high degree of variation within an overarching structure of unity. The rites associated with the final disposal of the corpse constitute an excellent example of this principle (variation within unity). Once the sealed coffin is removed from the community in the accepted fashion (by a procession marking the last of the prescribed funeral acts), mourners are free to dispose of the corpse according to local custom. There was, in other words, no elementary structure of disposal that applied to China as a whole (i.e., funeral rites were carefully prescribed, burial rites were not).

In Guangdong, Fujian, and Taiwan, secondary burial—the storage of exhumed bones in pots—was common.[30] On numerous occasions I have witnessed northern cadres recoil in absolute horror when the purpose of Cantonese bone pots is explained to them. Until recently, northerners did things that revolted southerners, such as storing coffins above ground, sometimes for decades, awaiting an auspicious burial date.[31] A survey of ethnographic records makes it obvious that, in contrast to funeral rites, there were no uniform rites of disposal in late imperial and Republican era China.

The secondary burial complex found among southern Han peoples (Cantonese, Hakka, Hokkien) tells us something important about the construction of a shared cultural identity among Chinese. There can be little doubt that the custom is historically linked to close interactions with non-Han (or, more precisely, pre-Han) cultures of the region. The pattern of burial and reburial, which plays on the distinction between flesh and bones, is found throughout the highlands of Southeast Asia and extends down the peninsula into Borneo and New Guinea.[32] Somehow, during the long history of sinification in South China, indigenous burial practices appear to have been transformed and incorporated into the local versions of Han culture.[33] This is not to say that secondary burial is simply a survival from an earlier era of interethnic exchange. Mortuary rites are deeply embedded in the political economy of local subcultures throughout China; they are, for instance, intimately related to notions of property and rights to land. Accordingly, changes in burial practices automatically implied a threat to the legitimacy of regional power structures.

Given their political centrality, it is surely significant that rites of disposal were never subject to renegotiation and modification in the pursuit of a unified cultural identity. The exclusion of burial rites from the roster of prescribed rituals can thus be seen as an implicit concession to ethnic and regional sensitivities. This may well have been the consequence of a conscious policy by imperial officials and educated elites, given that any attempt to control burial practices would have been disastrously expensive and impossible to enforce—as Communist authorities were to discover during the 1950s and 1960s. Following the standard funeral sequence, by contrast, did not challenge local elites who for centuries had verified territorial claims by "placing" the remains of ancestors in the landscape.[34] As long as disposal was not affected, the funeral rites (which are performed inside the community) could easily be adapted to suit "Chinese" norms. Those who chose not to perform funerals according to the standard procedure were marked as non-Han or, worse, dangerous sectarians.

The Chinese cultural system thus allowed for the free expression of what outsiders might perceive to be chaotic local diversity. The domain of ritual, in particular, gave great scope to regional and subethnic cultural displays. The system was so flexible that those who called themselves Chinese could have their cake and eat it too: They could participate in a unified culture while at the same time celebrating their local or regional distinctiveness.

Imperial officials were, of course, intimately involved in the standardization of funerary ritual, but it would never have been possible to impose a uniform structure of rites on a society of such vast size and complexity. More subtle means were required. There is good evidence that imperial officials were engaged in the promotion of a standardized set of funeral and mourning customs throughout the empire; the same is true for marriage rites.[35] Accepted norms were enshrined in manuals available in even the smallest towns of the realm.[36] Given what we know about the distribution of power in late imperial China it is probable that local elites subscribed to the accepted customs and encouraged a kind of ritual orthopraxy in the communities under their control: they led by example. Unacceptable practices were gradually suppressed or modified to conform to centralized models.[37]

This may have been the mechanism for the superimposition of a standard ritual structure, but we know little about the process of acceptance. Is the standardization we now perceive a consequence of government-sponsored social engineering carried out over many centuries, or is it the result of voluntary adoption by the general populace? Need we assume that these processes were mutually exclusive? It is obvious that there must have been strong incentives for people of all classes and regional backgrounds to cooperate in the cultural construction of a standardized set of rites. Much more work needs to be done before we can answer these questions. What is clear, however, is that the preoccupation with ritual practice—rather than religious beliefs—made it possible for imperial authorities, local elites, and ordinary peasants to agree on the proper form for the conduct of key rituals.

Thus, the process of becoming Chinese did not involve any kind of conversion to a received dogma; it did not require professions of belief in a creed or set of ideas. One became Chinese, in effect, by acting Chinese—by behaving like Chinese. Perhaps the clearest indicator that this cultural transformation had been accomplished was the performance of key rituals in the accepted manner.

Orthopraxy in Everyday Life

One can find the origins of what I take to be the unique (presocialist) Chinese approach to the construction of cultural identity as far back as the Confucian *Analects*, and perhaps earlier.[38] By many interpretations, the central theme of Confucianism is harmony in thought and action; correct ideas follow from proper behavior.[39] In this sense orthopraxy is primary to, and takes precedence over, orthodoxy. At the core of Confucian notions of order is the principle of *li*, defined by Benjamin Schwartz as "all those 'objective' prescriptions of behavior, whether involving rite, ceremony, manners, or general deportment."[40] The Confucian approach to li is relevant to cultural construction: Following correct form ensured that one was playing the game of culture by civilized rules, and in so doing, one reaffirmed one's "Chineseness."

It will come as no surprise to learn that the vision of Chinese culture presented in this essay derives from my highly personalized experience of having lived among Cantonese villagers.[41] My cultural instructors knew little of the formal teachings of Confucius or Zhuxi, but they knew a great deal about li, or *laih* as it is pronounced in colloquial Cantonese. Villagers used the term in ordinary speech; one heard it dozens of times each day. To them it was not an abstract, philosophical concept but, rather, an ordinary, mundane idea that had concrete associations. Constant references were made to funeral li, wedding li, and the li of ancestral rites; the term permeated their discourse on social activities. One of the worst things to be said of someone was that he or she is "without li" (*mouh laih* [*meiyou li*]), meaning oblivious to proper behavior, impolite, and uncivilized.

In the Cantonese village context, li is best translated as "proper form," associated closely with correct performance. To perform a ritual properly, in the local view, was to follow its li. A funeral or a wedding had a recognized form (li), and deviations from that form caused great concern. Older people often stood on the sidelines of funerals, watching like hawks to make certain proper form was followed. They did not hesitate to shout advice and dissent when they saw (what they perceived to be) departures from standard ritual practice. Cantonese funeral priests were choreographers of public ritual: They told people where to stand, how to sit, when to wail, what to eat, whom to greet, when to leave. If the ritual went wrong or was not completed in the appointed time, disaster was certain to follow, not just for the bereaved but for the entire community.

Thus, the villagers' concern for proper form (li) was not simply a matter of aesthetics or personal predilections. It was the glue that held the cosmos together. Without li there would be chaos (*luan*), another concept that had concrete associations for most ordinary Chinese. Among rural Cantonese, luan conjured up visions of banditry, famine, and that ultimate symbol of social breakdown—cannibalism. Villagers in the Pearl River delta have a rich corpus of folklore focusing on (mythic) massacres carried out by imperial troops who intervened to reestablish order when local society collapsed.[42] The message is clear: Those who depart from accepted norms of ritual and action invite retribution of the most terrifying kind.

But this is not to say that Cantonese villagers were social automatons, rotely performing rituals over which they had no control and little understanding. Nor should they be seen as puppets dancing on strings of convention held by agents of the state. Stressing orthopraxy rather than orthodoxy had profound consequences for all social classes. It allowed China to attain a level of cultural integration that was never possible in other large-scale agrarian societies.[43] The processes of cultural construction outlined in this essay involved the active participation of all Chinese—not just scholar-bureaucrats but farmers, artisans, merchants, and workers. There is evidence, for instance, that imperial officials were forced to accept, adapt, and coopt mortuary customs that first emerged among the peasantry.[44] The standard Chinese funeral that one still sees in Taiwan, Hong Kong, and rural areas of the PRC appears to be timeless, but it is, in fact, an amalgamation of ancient and modern rites.[45] Ordinary people, such as the ancestors of my Cantonese consultants, had as much to do with creating and promoting this amalgamation as anyone else in the realm, including the emperor himself.

Ritual Form and Cultural Identity in Socialist China

As those who have followed developments in post-1949 China well know, traditional rituals of the sort discussed above were rigorously attacked by Communist party officials during the late 1950s and the late 1960s.[46] Funeral and burial rites were obvious targets of social engineering, especially in South China where activists objected to the "feudal" implications of the ancestral cult. Ancestor worship was intimately related to the political activities of powerful lineages that owned great stretches of double-crop rice land in Guangdong and Fujian. The land was held as corporate property by the descendants of key ancestors; in some parts of Guangdong, over 50 percent of the best paddy was controlled by ancestral estates.[47] One of the first things land reform cadres did in the early 1950s was confiscate and redistribute rights to cultivate the corporately owned land that financed ancestral rites. They also introduced a cremation campaign that struck at the very heart of the ancestral cult: If the bones of key ancestors are not exhumed, preserved in ceramic pots, and reburied in horseshoe-shaped tombs, the exchange relationship between living and dead cannot take place.[48]

Besides attacking the foundation of traditional mortuary rites, Communist authorities attempted to introduce a new set of socialist rituals, based roughly on Soviet models.[49] Although field research on this problem has yet to be done, it would appear that these new rites have had most influence in the larger cities, among the professional classes. The state-sponsored modifications involve the promotion of cremation and the abolition of burial; frugal memorial services replace banquets and ostentatious mourning displays; eulogies extolling the deceased's contribution to the building of socialism are substituted for traditional religious observances.

In the countryside, by contrast, there is considerable evidence that late imperial-style funerals and burials are still common and that, since approximately 1980, rural peoples have begun to invest heavily in mortuary rituals of all kinds.[50] Martin Whyte (1988) has argued that there is a growing cultural gap between urban and rural lifestyles in post-Mao China, reflected most clearly in life-crisis rituals. Whyte's study focuses on funeral rites, but his analysis could be applied equally well to wedding ritual.[51] He notes that urbanites, due partly to the exigencies of city living, have embraced state-sponsored models for funerals and burials. Rural peoples, by contrast, have been less willing to adopt socialist rites, especially those involving cremation and "thrifty" mourning customs.[52]

Interviews with Chinese students living in the United States confirm Whyte's views: Urbanites aged thirty-five or under rarely have any direct experience of traditional wedding or funeral rites, and they consider such performances to be "feudal," even humorous, vestiges of a rural past. In response to my questions about traditional funeral ritual, one Beijing student replied: "Why are you interested in these ancient customs? In China no one cares about such things anymore." Another said that she once saw a traditional funeral portrayed in a film but, other than that, she knew nothing about "feudal" rites. Older students who were sent out to the countryside during the Cultural Revolution, by contrast, had witnessed a wide array of traditional-style rituals and did not use the term "feudal" (*fengjian*) in describing them.[53]

Does the fact that China no longer has an agreed-upon set of rites (to mark birth, marriage, elderhood, death, ancestorhood, etc.) mean that it no longer has a unified culture? In the past, as I have argued, one of the central experiences of life that helped hold China together was the fact that people of all social stations—rich and poor, rural and urban, official and commoner—performed life-crisis rituals according to the same basic form. The disappearance of a unified cultural tradition is something that concerns many Chinese, particularly of the older generation. The physical destruction of the "four olds"[54] during the Cultural Revolution is paralleled by an erosion in knowledge about the past.

Historical Consciousness and Cultural Change in Post-Mao China

During several visits to China during the 1980s I have often been surprised to discover that younger people know very little about their own history and folkloric traditions. This is not simply a matter of misunderstanding the significance of ancient monuments or the inability to read historical plaques (in full-form characters). The problem I am concerned with here goes beyond the high arts, philosophy, and ancient history. Rather, it is a nearly complete void of knowledge regarding traditional folklore: heroic tales, popular sayings, biographies of

void of trad. knowledge

famous people, dynastic myths, religious symbolism, popular arts and crafts.

The disappearance of folk knowledge appears to be most common among urban, educated people who were born after 1955 and, hence, were raised in the aftermath of the antisuperstition campaigns that characterized the 1950s and 1960s. This is the same cohort that considers traditional funeral rites to be "feudal" vestiges of the past (see above). On numerous occasions in China I have been given tours of temples and religious shrines by young urbanites who know almost nothing about the history, symbolism, or social background of the institutions involved. While teaching anthropology at Sun Yat-sen (Zhongshan) University in Guangzhou in 1985, I discovered that my students did not know even basic *chengyu* (popular sayings reflecting ancient wisdom), and that the majority had no conception of traditional Chinese symbolism in folk arts and crafts. This void is all the more remarkable when one compares young people in the People's Republic with their counterparts in Taiwan and Hong Kong. It is obvious that the childhood experiences and early education of PRC urbanites no longer include large doses of traditional folklore.

The Chinese countryside is quite another matter: Rural people of all ages may be (generally) less sophisticated in their knowledge of science, world affairs, and literature, but they are more attuned to presocialist popular culture than are urbanites. Folk tales, religious symbolism, festivals and celebrations, taboos and proscriptions, calendrical observations, and other aspects of "traditional" folk knowledge are still considered relevant to the conduct of everyday life.

This does not mean, of course, that rural people are unaffected by forty years of socialist cultural reconstruction. The contract farmer of the 1980s is very different from the tenant/smallholder peasant of the prerevolutionary era. It is a mistake to see the emergence of religious celebrations and ostentatious displays as a simple "revival" of presocialist cultural forms.

Socialism has transformed rural culture in complex and, as yet, little understood ways. For instance, the Chinese kinship system has been altered to suit socialist production patterns, first by the influences of collectivization and more recently by the requirements of contract farming (i.e., the responsibility system). As a consequence of these political changes, the family—or, more precisely, the household—has been greatly strengthened as a meal/budget/labor-sharing unit.[55] In certain regions the family may now be even more central to the livelihoods of rural peoples than it was during the prerevolutionary period, given the absence of alternative institutions that once served as the organizational framework for economic or social activities (e.g., voluntary associations, religious cults, and irrigation societies).

Corporate lineages and clans do not appear to have reemerged as viable social institutions even in those parts of rural Guangdong where they dominated social life prior to the 1950s. Private worship of domestic (i.e., recently deceased) ancestors is evident everywhere in Guangdong, but corporate worship of more remote, lineage ancestors (at Ming/Qing era tombs) has not been tolerated in most xian. Local party officials have encouraged the renovation of selected ancestral halls as a means of attracting funds from émigrés and overseas Chinese, but collective worship in these halls is discouraged. Temples dedicated to important deities have also been rebuilt in the rural areas of Guangdong, Fujian, and Jiangsu. There are many reports of local peoples worshipping in these renovated tourist attractions, much to the embarrassment of party officials.[56]

An interesting problem for future research is the emergence of a new, *socialist* body of folklore, such as exists in the Soviet Union and Eastern Europe (in conference discussions Paul Pickowicz noted that this should really be described as "postsocialist" folklore). In arguing that Chinese urbanites no longer find traditional sayings, epics, songs, and symbols relevant to their lives, I certainly do not mean to imply that this sector of the society is devoid of folklore. As anyone who has lived or worked in urban China knows, there is a rich (and rapidly growing) tradition of stories, witticisms, ditties, and deliciously vicious metaphors that enliven the speech of ordinary people. Much of this emerging folklore takes the form of subtle (and not so subtle) commentary on the rigors of life under socialism. For the past year I have been collecting material on political metaphors that draw on the symbolism of food and eating, notably the "iron rice bowl" (*tiefanwan*) and *daguofan*, eating from the common pot (literally, "great wok"). These metaphors represent, respectively, unassailable job security and state-supported egalitarianism. Nearly everyone in China's major cities can recite the following ditty:

Mao Zedong gave us the iron rice bowl.
Deng Xiaoping punched a hole in it.
Zhao Ziyang came along and smashed it.

The significance of such lore (much more could be cited) is difficult to determine at present. The thrust, however, seems to be an emerging tradition of political criticism that uses humor and metaphor as a means of saying the unsayable, much as jokes are used in the Soviet Union. Based on limited observations in China and interviews of PRC visitors in the United States, it appears that the new tradition of political folklore is most common among Chinese urbanites.

The Construction of New Cultural Identities in China

The bifurcation of culture into rural and urban forms as outlined in this essay may be part of a general trend toward the renegotiation of "Chineseness" among people in the People's Republic. One wonders whether a new notion of collective identity, based on a new set of standardized rites and unifying symbols, will emerge from the old.

It is possible to interpret the Cultural Revolution as a state-sponsored movement in that direction, shifting from an emphasis on outward behavior and practice to a central concern with inner beliefs and purity of thought. The political campaigns of that era were designed to break the traditional mold, in a shift from form to content. "Redness," judged by inner conviction, was stressed above all else; Red Guards and other activists did not allow people to fall back on ritual form or standardized behavior. This new, revolutionary approach required public confession, conversion, and wholehearted acceptance of Maoist doctrine. Richard Madsen calls this a system based on "rituals of struggle," constituting a departure from older notions of ritual as a means of maintaining community cohesion.[57]

No one, in effect, knew how to act during the early years of the Cultural Revolution. Behavioral conventions and norms of public etiquette were not only challenged, those who adhered to the "old" forms were deemed to be ideologically deficient. By the 1970s, however, routinization began to set in and people learned techniques of distancing, thereby reritualizing political activity.[58]

The results of the Maoist preoccupation with orthodoxy are by now universally recognized: disruption, disintegration, and anomie on a massive scale. It would appear that the construction of a new cultural identity through the imposition of a centrally controlled ideology was an unmitigated disaster for China. This, at least, is one way to read recent history.

What dare one say about the post-Mao reform era? It would be a gross simplification of recent political developments to argue that the reforms of the late 1970s and 1980s constitute a total repudiation of Maoist doctrine, returning the society to a system based on performance rather than ideology. Admittedly, some of the public rhetoric emanating from Beijing does seem to echo such concerns. Deng Xiaoping himself set the tone of the reform era with his famous axiom: "It doesn't matter whether a cat is black or white, as long as it catches mice."

Rural people interpreted this and other pronouncements as a sign that the ideological heat was off and that performance (read production) would henceforth be rewarded, irrespective of class background or inner conviction. The much heralded campaign to "Let a Few Lead the Many to Wealth" was also aimed primarily at rural peoples. In fact, it is safe to say that the post-Mao reforms have had the most *economic* impact in the countryside, and that urbanites—save for a relatively small number of entrepreneurs and independent contractors—have been reduced to the role of disgruntled spectators. The resentment felt toward *nouveau riche* farmers has become a serious social problem in some regions, with urbanites freely commenting on the unfairness of economic policies.

Meanwhile, the cultural gap between rural and urban may be growing wider each year. To be "Chinese" no longer implies that one shares the same sense of cultural identity. The key symbols that helped hold China together (shared rites, folkloric traditions, a common notion of proper lifestyle) no longer have the same meaning that they once did.

The fact that university students used what are essentially foreign (or international) symbols in their Tiananmen Square demonstrations (i.e., fasting, slogan-bearing headbands, V for victory signs, a version of the Statue of Liberty) is revealing and significant. These internationalist forms of political expression have been incorporated into the urbanite culture that is emerging in China's central cities. Thus, in terms of the symbolic reconstruction of a new sense of cultural identity, the activists in the square and their supporters probably have more in common with their Chinese compatriots in Hong Kong, Taipei, and New York than they do with their remote kin in the rural districts of Anhui and Guangdong. We have little idea, at this writing, how the new symbols of democracy have been interpreted in the countryside or in provincial urban centers. It does seem likely, however, that the 1989 spring movement to match economic reforms with political reforms is destined to have more influence on the creators of China's emerging urban subculture. What this means for the future of "Chineseness" as a general construct remains to be seen.

Postscript

The Beijing massacre occurred after this essay had been completed. Another set of political dramas dominated the world's media after June 4: the roundup of "counterrevolutionaries," a sister turning in her "renegade" brother, memorial services for "martyred" soldiers killed by dangerous "thugs." We are presented with one of the century's most blatant (and transparent) efforts by party officials to rewrite recent history.

The crackdown appears (at this writing) to be concentrated in China's major urban centers. The sense of despair that characterizes Chinese intellectual life can only get worse in the immediate future.[59]

Inevitably, the massacre will have a profound effect on the current generation of educated youths and their attempts to reconstruct an acceptable notion of Chinese cultural identity. By mid-June 1989, PRC students and visiting scholars of my acquaintance are asking themselves some deeply troubling questions: "What kind of people are ruling our country?" "How could this happen in the 1980s, with the whole world watching?" One twenty-one-year-old student from Beijing told me during the week following the massacre: "My friends and I have talked all night. We have concluded that this is not just a problem of one man or one party. The blame is more general. We think there is something fundamentally wrong with our society. Everything has to be changed, especially the mentality of the Chinese people. This will take at least fifty years, maybe one hundred years."

The echo of voices from the May Fourth era are all too obvious. Until the very day of the massacre, many Chinese intellectuals were engaged in a movement to reexamine the foundations of Chinese cultural identity. The television epic, *He shang* (River elegy, literally "early death on the river"), is perhaps the best-known product of this movement. It was shown on Chinese Central Television in June 1988 and sparked a major controversy. The series builds on the Yellow River as a symbol of Chinese culture and history; the yellow waters are tyrannical and unpredictable, both life-giving and life-destroying. The river never changes and yet is always changing. To many Chinese, the message of the film was clear: Only by rejecting the past and rebuilding a new political culture can China hope to enter the modern world.

It is significant that the principal writer of *He shang*, Su Xiaokang, was included on the June 23 list of seven top intellectuals wanted by the state for "counterrevolutionary crimes." The authorities were sending a clear message by this act: Henceforth, the Communist party intends to control the redefinition of Chinese cultural identity. This is too important a matter to be left to "unreliable" intellectuals and ordinary people. Thus, for the third time in forty years, the party propaganda apparatus appears to be gearing up for yet another attempt to dominate the ongoing debate regarding the future of "Chineseness." In the meantime, those intellectuals and young people who are preoccupied with such questions have been given a disastrously violent reminder that the Chinese past is still very much alive in the present.

Notes

1. *New York Times*, May 24, 1989.
2. For a description of the demolition, see *Far Eastern Economic Review*, November 17, 1988.
3. See also the extraordinarily detailed and sympathetic account of the student movement in *Beijing Review* 32, 22 (May 29, 1989).
4. K. C. Chang and Hao Chang discussed the historical background of Chinese fasting with me and provided the above information.
5. Kim Kwang-ok, personal communication; but see William Hinton, *Hundred Day War: The Cultural Revolution at Tsinghua University* (New York: Monthly Review Press, 1972), p. 91, for hunger striking as a political tactic during the Cultural Revolution. There have also been reports of hunger strikes among Shanghai textile workers in the 1930s. I am grateful to Paul Cohen and Elizabeth Perry for this information.
6. James L. Watson, "Standardizing the Gods: The Promotion of T'ien-hou ('Empress of Heaven') along the South China Coast, 960–1960," in *Popular Culture in Late Imperial China*, ed. David Johnson, Andrew Nathan, and Evelyn Rawski (Berkeley: University of California Press, 1985); "The Structure of Chinese Funerary Rites: Elementary Forms, Ritual Sequence, and the Primacy of Performance," in *Death Ritual in Late Imperial and Modern China*, ed. James L. Watson and Evelyn S. Rawski (Berkeley: University of California Press, 1988).
7. Kathleen Hartford, "Socialist Agriculture Is Dead; Long Live Socialist Agriculture! Organizational Transformations in Rural China," in *The Political Economy of Reform in Post-Mao China*, ed. Elizabeth Perry and Christine Wong (Cambridge: Harvard University Press, 1985).
8. Myron Cohen, "Family, Society, and the State in a North China Village," paper presented at the 1987 annual meeting of the American Anthropological Association.
9. Martin K. Whyte, "Death Ritual in the People's Republic of China," in *Death*

Ritual in Late Imperial and Modern China, ed. Watson and Rawski.

10. The construction of culture approach is, by now, one of the dominant themes in American anthropology; it draws on the work of Clifford Geertz (*Negara: The Theatre State in Nineteenth Century Bali* [Princeton: Princeton University Press, 1980]); Marshall Sahlins (*Culture and Practical Reason* [Chicago: University of Chicago Press, 1976]); David Schneider (*American Kinship: A Cultural Account*, 2d ed. [Chicago: University of Chicago Press, 1980]); and a host of others who emphasize the creative rather than the passive aspects of culture.

11. See Elvin Hatch, *Theories of Man and Culture* (New York: Columbia University Press, 1973), pp. 20–24.

12. Benedict Anderson, *Imagined Communities: Reflections on the Origin and Spread of Nationalism* (London: Verso, 1983).

13. John DeFrancis, *The Chinese Language: Fact and Fantasy* (Honolulu: University of Hawaii Press, 1984), p. 201, has debunked this argument and attacks the whole notion that Chinese script is ideographic and nonphonetic. His approach, however, is not generally accepted.

14. See e.g., Ho Ping-ti, "The Chinese Civilization: A Search for the Roots of Its Longevity," *Journal of Asian Studies* 35, 4 (1976): 547–54.

15. Karl Wittfogel, *Oriental Despotism: A Comparative Study of Total Power* (New Haven: Yale University Press, 1957).

16. G. William Skinner, "The Structure of Chinese History," *Journal of Asian Studies* 44, 2 (1985): 271–92.

17. David Johnson, "Actions Speak Louder than Words—the Cultural Significance of Opera in Late Imperial China," paper presented at the Conference of U.S.-Japanese Historians, Occidental College and the Huntington Library, 1987; and Barbara E. Ward, "Regional Operas and Their Audiences," in *Popular Culture in Late Imperial China*, ed. Johnson et al.

18. David Johnson, "Communication, Class, and Consciousness in Late Imperial China," in ibid.

19. See e.g., Vena Hrdlickova, "The Professional Training of Chinese Storytellers and the Storytellers' Guilds," *Archiv Orientalni* 33 (1965): 225–48; and David Johnson, "The Wu Tzu-hsu *Pien-wen* and Its Sources: Parts I & II," *Harvard Journal of Asiatic Studies* 40 (1980): 93–156, 465–505.

20. See e.g., Wolfram Eberhard, *A Dictionary of Chinese Symbols* (London: Routledge, 1986); Arthur H. Smith, *Proverbs and Common Sayings from the Chinese* (New York: Dover, 1914).

21. See Evelyn S. Rawski, *Education and Popular Literacy in Ch'ing China* (Ann Arbor: University of Michigan Press, 1979); and Rawski, "Economic and Social Foundations of Late Imperial Culture," in *Popular Culture in Late Imperial China*, ed. Johnson et al., on the unified curriculum.

22. In recent decades, central authorities have discouraged the use of terms such as barbarian (*fan*) and uncivilized (*meiwenhuade, weikaihuade, yemande*) when speaking of non-Han. Nonetheless, one still hears these terms in Taiwan and in many parts of the People's Republic.

23. See David Faure, "The Lineage as a Cultural Invention: The Case of the Pearl River Delta," *Modern China* 15, 1 (1989): 8–14, on Han/Yao interactions in Guangdong.

24. Wolfram Eberhard, *China's Minorities: Yesterday and Today* (Belmont, CA: Wadsworth Publishing Company, 1982), pp. 105–47; Herold J. Wiens, *Han Chinese Expansion in South China* (Hamden, CT: Shoestring Press, 1954), pp. 130–226.

25. See, e.g., David Y. H. Wu, "Minority or Chinese? Ethnicity and Culture Change among the Bai of Yunnan, China," *Human Organization* (1989).

26. The metaphor of cooking is frequently employed by ordinary Chinese when discussing non-Han communities (see, e.g., Susan Naquin and Evelyn S. Rawski, *Chinese Society in the Eighteenth Century* [New Haven: Yale University Press, 1987], pp. 127–28). The dichotomy between "cooked" and "uncooked" is still common in today's Taiwan and is used to designate the degree to which Taiwan's original inhabitants have been assimilated into Han culture.

27. Watson, "The Structure of Chinese Funerary Rites."

28. See Evelyn Rawski, "The Imperial Way of Death," in *Death Ritual in Late Imperial and Modern China*, ed. Watson and Rawski, on imperial rites.

29. See Emily M. Ahern, *The Cult of the Dead in a Chinese Village* (Stanford: Stanford University Press, 1973); Stuart E. Thompson, "Death, Food, and Fertility," in *Death Ritual in Late Imperial and Modern China*, ed. Watson and Rawski.

30. See, e.g., Ahern, *The Cult of the Dead*, pp. 163–219; Ling Xunsheng, "Dongnanyade xiguzang qi qihuan taipingyangde fenbu" (The bone-washing burial custom of Southeast Asia and its circum-Pacific distribution), *Zhongguo minzuxuebao* (Bulletin of the Ethnological Society of China) 1 (1955): 25–42; and James L. Watson, "Of Flesh and Bones: The Management of Death Pollution in Cantonese Society," in *Death and the Regeneration of Life*, ed. Maurice Bloch and Jonathan Parry (Cambridge: Cambridge University Press, 1982).

31. Patricia Ebrey, "State Response to Popular Funeral Practices in Sung China," paper presented at the Symposium on Religion and Society in China, 750–1300, University of Illinois, Urbana; Susan Naquin, "Funerals in North China: Uniformity and Variation," in *Death Ritual in Late Imperial and Modern China*, ed. Watson and Rawski.

32. See, e.g., Robert Hertz, *Death and the Right Hand*, translation of 1907 original by Rodney and Claudia Needham (New York: Free Press, 1960); Peter Metcalf, *A Borneo Journey into Death: Berawan Eschatology From Its Rituals* (Philadelphia: University of Pennsylvania Press, 1982).

33. It is obvious that the burial practices of the modern Cantonese and Hokkien are not mere duplications of the pre-Han forms that once existed in Guangdong and Fujian. The Chinese pattern of secondary burial has, no doubt, undergone numerous changes over the past thousand years—just as modern non-Han cultures have been transformed. One cannot, in other words, expect to find Cantonese-style pot burials among extant minority peoples in Guangdong. For the origins of this burial complex one must look to the pre- and proto-Han cultures that fostered both of these modern populations. W. L. Ballard, "Aspects of the Linguistic History of South China," *Asian Perspective* 24, 2 (1981): 163–85, proposes a similar line of analysis for understanding the origins of southern Chinese dialects.

34. Cf. Maurice Bloch, *Placing the Dead: Tombs, Ancestral Villages, and Kinship Organization in Madagascar* (London: Seminar, 1971).

35. See Patricia B. Ebrey, "The Early Stages in the Development of Descent Group Organization," in *Kinship Organization in Late Imperial China*, ed. Patricia B. Ebrey and James L. Watson (Berkeley: University of California Press, 1986); Evelyn Rawski, "A Historian's Approach to Chinese Death Ritual," in *Death Ritual in Late Imperial and Modern China*, ed. Watson and Rawski; Susan Mann, "Grooming a Daughter for Marriage: Brides and Wives in the Mid Ch'ing Period," in *Marriage and Inequality in Chinese Society*, ed. Rubie S. Watson and Patricia B. Ebrey (Berkeley: University of California Press, 1991); and Susan Naquin, "Marriage in North China: The Role of Ritual," paper presented at the Conference on Marriage and Inequality in Chinese Society, Asilomar, California, 1988.

36. See, e.g., the list of ritual handbooks discovered in Hong Kong bookshops by James Hayes, in "The Popular Culture of Late Ch'ing and Early Twentieth Century

China: Book Lists Prepared from Collecting in Hong Kong,'' *Journal of the Hong Kong Branch of the Royal Asiatic Society* 20 (1980): 174. Most of these texts were published during the late Qing and early Republican periods. Handbooks of this nature were often modeled on a famous text called *Jiali* (Family ritual), usually attributed to the Neo-Confucian scholar Zhuxi (1130–1200); on this text see Patricia Ebrey, ''Education through Ritual: The Formulation of Family Rituals in the Sung Dynasty,'' in *Neo-confucian Education: The Formative Stage*, ed. John Chaffee and Wm. Theodore de Bary (Berkeley: University of California Press, 1990). Written guidelines for proper funeral and mourning rites have a long history in China, beginning with the *Liji* (Book of rites), produced between the fifth and second centuries B.C.E. and the writings of Xunzi (*Hsun tzu [Xunzi]: Basic Writings*, trans. Burton Watson [New York: Columbia University Press, 1963], pp. 96–111), dating from the third century B.C.E. See also Naquin, ''Funerals in North China,'' pp. 63–65, on funeral manuals in North China.

37. Rubie S. Watson, *Inequality Among Brothers: Class and Kinship in South China* (Cambridge: Cambridge University Press, 1985); see also Naquin, ''Funerals in North China,'' pp. 53–66, on the standardizing role of ritual specialists.

38. See, e.g., K. C. Chang, *Art, Myth, and Ritual: The Path to Political Authority in Ancient China* (Cambridge: Harvard University Press, 1983), pp. 101, 108; David N. Keightley, ''Archaeology and Mentality: The Making of China,'' *Representations* 18 (1987): 166.

39. Cf. Herbert Fingarette, *Confucius: The Secular as Sacred* (New York: Harper and Row, 1972).

40. Benjamin I. Schwartz, *The World of Thought in Ancient China* (Cambridge: Harvard University Press, 1985), p. 67.

41. Residence in the villages of San Tin (1969–70) and Ha Tsuen (1977–78), Hong Kong's New Territories, plus frequent return visits in the 1980s. I also conducted ethnographic surveys among Cantonese-speaking farmers in Guangdong's Pearl River delta during the summers of 1985, 1986, and 1988.

42. James L. Watson, ''Waking the Dragon: Visions of the Chinese Imperial State in Local Myth,'' *Journal of the Anthropological Society of Oxford* (1989).

43. Perhaps the clearest contrast is India (South Asia). Prior to the British Raj, South Asia was not dominated by a centralized state system; indeed, according to David Washbrook the very notion of ''India'' as a political/cultural entity did not emerge until relatively late in the colonial era. It was fostered first by the British and later by Western-educated South Asians who were interested in nation building. (Washbrook, ''Gandhi and the Creation of 'India,' '' paper presented at the India-China Seminar, Fairbank Center for East Asian Research, Harvard University, 1987.) See also Bernard S. Cohn, ''Representing Authority in Victorian India,'' in *The Invention of Tradition*, ed. Eric Hobsbawm and Terrence Ranger (Cambridge: Cambridge University Press, 1983).

In China, by contrast, the political reality of state power was reflected in the acceptance of *Zhongguo*, the Central Kingdom, as a meaningful concept by everyone who lived within the boundaries of that state from a very early (and much debated) date. The Chinese peasantry did not need educated elites to remind them that they shared a grand cultural tradition and were subjects of a centralized state.

The problem of national identity is reflected in ritual: Unlike China, the Indian subcontinent does not have a standardized set of rites to mark important life crises. Even if one restricts the analysis to the Hindu population, the contrast with China is striking. In funerary ritual, for instance, Hindu performances do not follow a standard set of acts that distinguishes this tradition from other ethnic or religious traditions. There is, in other words, no elementary structure of Hindu life-crisis rites; various communities (*jati*, subcastes) perform funerals in different ways, and there are more differences between these performances than there are similarities (personal communications with Jonathan Parry, Stanley Tambiah, Chris Fuller, and others).

Thus, it is not orthopraxy that holds Hindu India together as a unified culture. What, then, of orthodoxy? Here too there are serious questions, given that the subcontinent did not have a standardized set of religious beliefs nor a uniform creed. There was, of course, a generally recognized assemblage—as opposed to state- regulated pantheon—of goddesses and gods that were worshipped in various ways by Hindus. (See, e.g., Gerald D. Berreman, *Hindus of the Himalayas* [Berkeley: University of California Press, 1963], pp. 80–120; C. J. Fuller, *Servants of the Goddess: The Priests of a South Indian Temple* [Cambridge: Cambridge University Press, 1984]; McKim Marriott, "Little Communities in an Indigenous Civilization," in *Village India: Studies in the Little Community*, ed. McKim Marriott [Chicago: University of Chicago Press, 1955]; M. N. Srinivas, *Religion and Society among the Coorgs of South India* [Oxford: Clarendon Press, 1952].) But beliefs regarding these Hindu deities were diverse in the extreme; furthermore, there was no state apparatus charged with the responsibility of regulating belief.

Louis Dumont and his followers have proposed that the unity of Indian society is to be found in the realm of ideas and values, specifically those relating to the ideology of pollution, purity, and social hierarchy. (Dumont, *Homo Hierarchicus: The Caste System and Its Implications* [Chicago: University of Chicago Press, 1970].) The first issues of *Contributions to Indian Sociology* carried a revealing exchange on this question: Dumont and Pocock argued that the unity of India is evident in "the existence of castes from one end of the country to the other, and nowhere else." Furthermore, "the very existence, and influence, of higher, sanskritic, civilisation demonstrates without question the unity of India" (Louis Dumont and David Pocock, "For a Sociology of India," *Contributions to Indian Sociology* 1 [1957]: 9). F. G. Bailey replied that is was not, in his view, the task of researchers "to make sense of the 'fragrant contradictions in popular thought' by abstracting out consistent elements" in search of an underlying structure of unity, as Dumont and Pocock had advocated. (Bailey, "For a Sociology of India?" *Contributions to Indian Sociology* 3 [1959]: 90.) Thus, for Bailey, and a host of other critics the ideology of caste is not the universal glue that holds all of Indian society together. (See, e.g., Steve Barrett et al., "Hierarchy Purified: Notes on Dumont and His Critics," *Journal of Asian Studies* 35, 4 [1976]: 627–46; Richard Burghart, "Renunciation in the Religious Traditions of South Asia," *Man* 18, 4 [1983]: 635–53; C. J. Fuller, "The Hindu Pantheon and the Legitimation of Hierarchy," *Man* 23, 1 [1988]: 19–39; Pauline Kolenda, "Seven Kinds of Hierarchy in *Homo Hierarchicus*," *Journal of Asian Studies* 35, 4 [1976]: 581–96.) Viewing this debate from the perspective of China, we are left with the conclusion that India may have the formal apparatus of a modern state, but it lacks the essential ingredients of a unified culture.

44. See, e.g., Ebrey, "The Early Stages in the Development of Descent Group Organization," pp. 20–29.

45. Rawski, "A Historian's Approach to Chinese Death Ritual."

46. See, e.g., Donald E. MacInnis, *Religious Policy and Practice in Communist China* (New York: Macmillan, 1972), pp. 333–34; William L. Parish and Martin K. Whyte, *Village and Family in Contemporary China* (Chicago: University of Chicago Press, 1978), pp. 264–65.

47. See, e.g., R. Watson, *Inequality among Brothers*, pp. 68–69.

48. J. L. Watson, "Of Flesh and Bones."

49. Christopher A. Binns, "The Changing Face of Power: Revolution and Accommodation in the Development of the Soviet Ceremonial System, Part Two," *Man* 15, 1 (1980): 180; Christel Lane, *The Rites of Rulers: Ritual in Industrial Society, the Soviet Union* (Cambridge: Cambridge University Press, 1981).

50. Based on ethnographic surveys conducted by the author in Guangdong, Jiangsu, and Shandong (1985–86); see also Parish and Whyte, *Village and Family in Contemporary China*, pp. 265–66, and William R. Jankowiak, ''The Soul of Lao Yu,'' *Natural History* 97, 12 (1988): 4–11. Myron Cohen (personal communication) reports that late imperial-style funerals were still performed in rural Hebei during his field research in 1986–87. David Wu (personal communication) observed a traditional funeral, complete with full mourning garb, in Zhejiang in the summer of 1987.

51. See, e.g., Martin K. Whyte, ''Rural Marriage Customs,'' *Problems of Communism* 26 (July–August 1977): 41–55; Whyte, ''Revolutionary Social Change and Patrilocal Residence in China,'' *Ethnology* 18, 3 (1979): 211–27.

52. Whyte, ''Death Ritual in the People's Republic of China.''

53. Interviews carried out at the University of Pittsburgh, 1984–88.

54. Old thought, old customs, old culture, and old morals. During the Cultural Revolution, Red Guards destroyed many historical monuments, including graves and tombs (see, e.g., Anita Chan, Richard Madsen, and Jonathan Unger, *Chen Village: The Recent History of a Peasant Community in Mao's China* [Berkeley: University of California Press, 1984], p. 118; Yuan Gao, *Born Red: A Chronicle of the Cultural Revolution* [Stanford: Stanford University Press, 1987], p. 218.)

55. Cohen, ''Family, Society, and the State''; Louis Putterman, ''The Restoration of the Peasant Household as Farm Production Unit in China,'' in *The Political Economy of Reform in Post-Mao China*, ed. Perry and Wong.

56. E.g., Jerry Dennerline, personal communication.

57. Richard Madsen, *Morality and Power in a Chinese Village* (Berkeley: University of California Press, 1984), pp. 22–26.

58. On this latter point, see Whyte, *Small Groups and Political Rituals in China*; and David Zweig, *Agrarian Radicalism in China, 1968–1981* (Cambridge: Harvard University Press, 1989).

59. On this problem see Perry Link's interesting article, ''The Chinese Intellectual and the Revolt,'' *New York Review of Books* 36, 11 (June 29, 1989): 38–41, written just prior to the military intervention.

16

REFLECTIONS ON THE OPENING OF CHINA

JAMES R. TOWNSEND

The popular protests that erupted in China in April 1989, followed by harsh government repression in June, illustrated dramatically the tensions and uncertainties that characterize *kaifang* and make it so difficult to interpret and evaluate. The remarkable scope and spontaneity of these demonstrations, quickly labeled the "democracy movement" because of the salience of demands for democratic reforms, was testimony to the powerful impact of kaifang—the opening or open policy pursued so vigorously by China's leadership over the preceding decade. The forceful closure testified with equal clarity to the fragility of the opening and the speed with which the policy might be altered, if not abandoned. The insurrection was in part a product of kaifang, of that there can be no doubt, but it is less certain how well the democracy movement serves to measure the opening's success or failure, or to predict its future. What one sees depends on one's perspectives on the event, as well as the event itself.

The opening of China has always been a kaleidoscopic event, yielding different images with every twist of the viewer's lens. Most Americans have focused on the recent open foreign policy, seeing a dramatic reversal of China's Maoist isolation followed by rapidly expanding exchanges with the West—especially the United States—with positive benefits on balance for all concerned. The same opening appears different from other vantage points. Observers in Beijing or Guangzhou, Taipei or Hong Kong, Tokyo or Moscow, Seoul or Pyongyang, Hanoi or Jakarta may see an opening that began earlier or later, that looks East as well as West, that has domestic as well as foreign dimensions, and that is less benign in its implications. A turn to a different historical focus reveals another opening in the mid-nineteenth century, to some the *real* "opening of China" and of greater historical import than the present one. The years in between have their openings as well, at the turn of the century, during and after the May Fourth Movement of 1919, and in the 1950s. One can see these as distinct images or let them blur together in a continuous, if erratic, process. Or one can look further into China's past for earlier openings to the non-Chinese world. More questions arise as the images change. Was China ever really closed? Who opened the door and for what purposes? How does the current opening compare to earlier ones? Is it driven by internal or external forces? What goods, ideas, peoples, or even armies have passed or will pass through the opening—in which direction?

This essay can deal with only a few of the many questions raised by such a rich and complex historical phenomenon. It begins with a brief survey of the international and domestic dimensions of the current opening. The next section reviews this material from some historical and comparative perspectives. A third section looks more closely at some forces that have promoted or resisted kaifang. The conclusion reflects on some longer-term trends associated with the opening of China.

Four themes run through the discussion that follows. First, the current opening is significant but not unprecedented, and it draws heavily on earlier openings in modern Chinese history. Although China historically displayed a recurring impulse to restrict exchanges with other nations—an impulse still evident among some Chinese—it was seldom closed to external influences. Since about 1840, it has been part of a global revolution associated with the era of imperialism and the spread of modern technology and ideas. During this century and a half it has remained relatively underdeveloped, immersed for most of the era in a protracted revolution that produced extreme variations in economic performance and international contacts. Nonetheless, although China has not experienced the dramatic transformation experienced by some of its East Asian neighbors, it has slowly expanded its interaction with the global system, particularly during the 1895–1910 reform era, the post-1919 May Fourth era, and the recent period. There was also an important opening toward other socialist countries in the 1950s, but China's primary partners in this long-term opening have been Japan and the West.

Second, although kaifang has strong links to earlier openings of equal historical significance, it also has distinctive features. It has produced a qualitative change in China's *interdependence*, displayed now in unprecedented diversity of international contacts and in the frequency and intensity of China's domestic and international exchanges, with new electronic communications playing a special role. It has been promoted by a truly *sovereign* China—earlier openings were forced on China or found China in a weak bargaining position—thereby signaling China's changing international role and the economic and security challenges that it may pose for others. And it has raised new questions about the meaning of Chinese *nationalism* for the PRC's dominant Han Chinese, for its non-Han minority citizens, and for Chinese living outside it.

Third, the current opening has had a profound but mixed impact on China. It fueled a decade of impressive economic growth and social change, encouraged political reforms that were more erratic but still significant, and underlay the most vigorous cultural flowering in PRC history. Most Chinese and foreigners welcomed these changes, but they produced concern and ultimately reaction among conservative political leaders. Kaifang's links to inflation, corruption, growing economic inequality, and expanding foreign influence created some popular ambivalence as well. The overall impact was extremely varied, both geographically and socially, felt mainly in the southeastern provinces, major cities, and tourist centers, and among officials, intellectuals, and entrepreneurs.

Fourth, this profound yet diverse impact leaves the opening's future uncertain. The historical perspective suggests it must ultimately continue, with primary orientation toward Japan and the West, but the events of 1989 show how controversial it has become. For better or worse, it is now deeply entwined with other key issues in Chinese politics. Several years of intense debate and conflict, possibly even political and social turmoil, may precede the next stage of the opening of China.

The Current Opening

Kaifang refers to policy changes that promoted a decade of opening in politics, economics, and culture, in both international and domestic dimensions. It began in the early 1970s, although the full policy did not emerge until the end of the decade. From the first, it involved issues, concepts, and personalities associated with earlier openings. No brief survey can do justice to all this, but fortunately there are other essays in this volume that provide much richer analysis of the earlier history in general, and of political, economic, and cultural changes in the post-Mao period in particular. The discussion here reviews the origins of the policy in strategic maneuver and the 1978 ''shift of focus'' that transformed its character; it then notes some of kaifang's primary international and domestic features.

Origins and Strategic Maneuver

Contrary to some impressions, China was not ''isolated'' in 1978 or even during most of the years that preceded Nixon's visit in early 1972. Between 1949 and 1966, the PRC developed a modest range of international contacts, largely though not exclusively with socialist countries, that were not totally broken even in the 1966–72 period. China experienced a pronounced closure in those Cultural Revolution years, with varying degrees of disruption in diplomatic relations, foreign trade, and cultural exchange, along with severe doctrinaire limits on domestic expression. The question is when and how the Cultural Revolution closure was reversed. The answer is that the opening began in the early 1970s, and that it was politics that unlocked the door.

The Shanghai Communiqué of February 1972 was the key political evidence that an opening was underway. Several considerations prompted the leaders of the United States and the People's Republic to issue this statement that signified a historic shift in strategic relationships. Although the possibilities for mutually beneficial economic and cultural exchange were evident to them, it was the shared desire to strengthen their strategic position against the Soviet Union and to move toward diplomatic recognition, with initial political agreement on statements about the status of Taiwan, that led the two sides to reverse their two decades of hostility. Strategic maneuver and relaxation of political tension in bilateral relations were the essence of the agreement.

The Nixon invitation and the logic behind it propelled the PRC into the United Nations, initiating a political offensive in China's diplomatic relations that saw the number of countries recognizing the PRC rise from 57 in 1970 to 97 in 1974 and 119 in 1979.[1] Foreign trade also grew quickly in the early 1970s, and the renewal of cultural exchange with capitalist countries got underway. By December 1978, when the United States and China agreed to transform their informal relations through "liaison offices" into formal diplomatic relations, the PRC's international ties had largely regained their pre–Cultural Revolution level and indeed had attained their greatest scope since 1949. This was most evident in international political contacts, reflecting the leading role of politics in this outward push, but the volume of international trade and diversity of partners in trade and cultural exchange also attested to a new level of PRC interaction with the international community.

The Third Plenum of the Eleventh Central Committee of the Chinese Communist Party (CCP) in December 1978 initiated a qualitative change in the opening (see below), but the strategic maneuvering that had started the process remained an important part of it. The political drive for "normalization" continued, with growing international recognition and participation. By May 1989, 137 countries had recognized the PRC,[2] which was continuing to strengthen its role in international organizations. China's foreign relations were by no means free of conflict, some (as with Vietnam and India) involving actual or threatened military force, but the trend of the 1980s was toward peaceful resolution of conflicts through diplomatic means. Beijing practiced a complicated delinkage approach, in which nonrecognition did not prevent restricted economic and cultural relations, and enduring conflicts did not bar normalization of diplomatic relations. The first kind of delinkage was most evident in growing trade and other exchanges with Taiwan and South Korea, despite the apparent impossibility of a diplomatic breakthrough in the near future. Examples of the second version were the February 1989 decision of China and Indonesia to normalize relations, and the normalization of Sino-Soviet relations consummated in Gorbachev's May 1989 visit to China.

The continuation and virtual completion by 1989 of the diplomatic opening begun in 1971 was not a unilinear development, of course. There were many twists and turns in China's bilateral relations, and another important strategic shift in the early 1980s. The initial opening had focused on creation of a "united front'' against the Soviet Union, with China contemplating some type of military cooperation with the United States as it developed its economic and diplomatic relations with the capitalist world as a whole. But after 1980, China and the United States retreated from the notion of an alliance, and the PRC announced its intention to pursue an independent foreign policy that would deal with the two superpowers in an evenhanded way. The effect was to unlock a second door leading toward the Soviet Union, which Gorbachev's efforts pushed open in the late 1980s. With the Soviet Union withdrawing its troops from Afghanistan, reducing them along the Chinese border, and urging the Vietnamese to withdraw from Cambodia, it was making progress on all three conditions that China had specified as necessary for normalization. As this diplomatic process unfolded, Sino-Soviet economic and cultural exchanges resumed, growing at a healthy rate through the late 1980s.

Despite China's avowed stance of equidistance and improved relations with the Soviet Union, it retained its primary economic orientation toward the non-Communist world. Remaining, too, was a tacit understanding (shaken by the events of spring 1989) that China and the United States were potential allies in the event of hostile action by the Soviets toward either of them. The significance of the independent foreign policy lies rather in the evolution of kaifang: what began as a limited strategic maneuver broadened in the 1980s to a more inclusive open foreign policy favoring normal relations, or some approximation thereof when politics barred the way, with all other countries. This evolution not only expanded what was initially only a partial diplomatic opening but also reflected a reformulation of kaifang itself.

The 1978 ''Shift of Focus''

The reformulation, which began to take shape with the Third Plenum of 1978, had two key features. One was the growing importance of economic considerations as the driving force behind the open foreign policy. The other was the linkage of this policy to a broad domestic reform movement, so that kaifang came to mean not simply an opening to the outside world but also a dramatic opening in various spheres of Chinese life—political, social, and cultural as well as economic. It was this reformulation that gave the current opening its special character, significance, and complexity.

The Third Plenum announced a ''shift of focus to socialist modernization,'' rejecting the ''politics in command'' orientation of the Cultural Revolution era and terminating the 1976–78 preoccupation with criticism of the Gang of Four. Henceforth, into the twenty-first century, China's mission was to be the ''development of productive forces'' through attainment of the ''four modernizations'' (of industry, agriculture, national defense, and science and technology). Assignment of highest priority to material goals did not mean abandonment of political concerns, but for the next decade economics was generally in command. Although the CCP insisted that all must adhere to the four cardinal principles of socialism, the people's democratic dictatorship, Communist party leadership, and Marxism–Leninism–Mao Zedong Thought, this commitment took the form of periodic campaigns to check what some leaders saw as violations of the principles, or it simply meant foot dragging on political reforms. Economics had the initiative, while politics and ideology played a more reactive or defensive role.

An ominous development in the aftermath of the government's June 1989 assault on the Beijing demonstrators has been a reversal of this relationship. Only time will tell how long this reassertion of the primacy of political orthodoxy will endure. In any case, for the decade of 1979–89, kaifang was driven by economic goals that were only partially restrained by political orthodoxy and that encouraged proponents of political and cultural reform to push their ideas as well. The result was sweeping changes in both international and domestic spheres.

International Opening

The external "shift of focus" brought accelerated growth of foreign trade that continued, with only minor slowdowns, throughout the decade. Equally striking was the expansion of foreign investment. Initially limited to a few development loans and credits, and to joint ventures in which the Chinese side kept a controlling interest, the efforts to attract foreign capital and technology soon included a range of options including full foreign ownership and operation. The opening of four small "special economic zones" along the Guangdong-Fujian coast offered concessionary terms to foreign investment. The later designation of several cities, mainly along the eastern seaboard, as sites for intensive economic development further expanded such opportunities. With increased international borrowing in the late 1980s, China's transition from a relatively "self-reliant" stance in the late 1960s, through a modest growth of international economic activity in the 1970s, and on to a significant degree of interdependence in the 1980s was complete.

Cultural exchange had a modest place in the opening from the first. The Shanghai Communiqué coincided with China's emergence from the worst turmoil of the Cultural Revolution, permitting some foreign students, teachers, and delegations to return to China. The flow remained weak, however, and for Americans was mainly in the form of highly routinized and restricted exchanges of delegations. Foreign traders continued to conduct most of their business at the semiannual trade fairs in Guangzhou. The "shift of focus" transformed this situation, initiating a decade of rapid growth in China's tourist industry and in its academic, technical, and cultural exchanges with other countries. Tourism quickly severed its earlier links to "people's diplomacy" and became a commercial enterprise. China and foreign investors poured money into facilities that would service the flow—and keep increasing it. More and more cities and sites opened for tourism, which by the mid-1980s included independent travelers as well as tour groups. The number of foreign residents in China grew slowly as students, teachers, researchers, technical advisers, journalists, and diplomatic personnel joined their business counterparts.

Chinese were also going abroad, at first in delegations, then in smaller informal groups, and by the end of the decade even as individual travelers. Longer-term Chinese residence abroad grew along with expanded diplomatic and commercial contacts. Perhaps most importantly, it included tens of thousands of students and scholars. Despite financial and political obstacles to foreign study, more and more Chinese found ways to secure it, in a greater variety of fields, and increasingly in the company of spouses and even children. Although few Chinese went abroad as tourists, some did so to visit relatives, and those living abroad might engage in tourism when their work and study permitted it.

The primary justification for all this was access to foreign goods, capital, technology, and exchange that would contribute to China's overall material modernization. The leadership had little interest in transactions that failed this instrumentalist test. It warned repeatedly that modernization must be socialist, that the opening was not to admit nonsocialist ideology or culture. In practice the warning was not consistently observed. The domestic reforms were the main flaw in the formula, as they soon exposed the lack of a rigorous definition of socialism or ideological rationale for revising the concept; the reforms also provided too many incentives and opportunities for experimentation with nonsocialist things. But the international opening itself proved difficult to control. It operated mainly on market principles that had no place for socialism as a value. Foreign buyers insisted that Chinese goods match the tastes of international consumers, foreign capital needed incentives and safeguards, foreign residents wanted better communications and other comforts of home, and so on. Reciprocity forced China to give on some issues to gain on others. The volume of transactions became increasingly difficult to monitor, let alone police. There was simply no way to open the door wide enough for what China wanted without admitting some unwanted influences. Foreign films, modern art, discos, tapes from Taiwan and Hong Kong, rock groups from Britain and the United States, new clothing styles and fads—on and on in an endless barrage of challenges to the principle that kaifang must serve the cause of socialist modernization. The authorities could and did draw the line at times; more often, they defaulted as the opening continued to widen.

Communications were a critical element in this erosion of the opening's orthodox forms. The CCP cherished its virtual monopoly of internal communications, but kaifang made it impossible to maintain. The flow of international travelers, correspondence, and telecommunications defied control over information. Foreigners brought materials with them, maintained contact with home, and wanted more news in China. Chinese officials exchanged information with foreign contacts, including growing numbers of foreign journalists who could also draw on foreign residents scattered about the country. Chinese media began to modify their style in the face of this competition, and Chinese journalism and mass communications became more professional. As more Chinese studied English, they gained access to English-language materials increasingly available in stores, hotels, or libraries. The significance of this gradual opening in communications became clear in 1989 when many Chinese got news of urban demonstrations and government repression from international sources, including radio broadcasts, telephone calls, fax reports, and visits from Chinese abroad, that often contradicted the official Chinese media. In effect, kaifang had eroded part of the foundation of CCP political control. The government's desperate efforts to rebuild its communications monopoly, in asserting its own version of the spring 1989 events, can only be partially effective.

Domestic Opening

Unlike the external opening that developed gradually over the 1970s, domestic kaifang came with surprising speed. It began with the arrest of the Gang of Four in October 1976, just a month after Mao's death. Observers reported a literal opening of doors as people poured into the streets to discuss and welcome the event. A general relaxation of social tension followed with the waning of the ideologically charged standards of discourse, cultural forms, and social relationships that the Maoists had prescribed. Although major reforms came only after the Third Plenum, they were preceded in 1977 and 1978 by more open political debate, a revival of academic standards and opportunities in higher education, and better treatment of intellectuals. Hence, the two years between Mao's death and the Third Plenum witnessed a modest opening that was largely internally generated.

From 1979 on, however, domestic and international kaifang interacted with and reinforced each other. Both rested after 1979 on economic objectives broadly defined, yet both required supportive political, social, and cultural adjustments, or in some cases brought unanticipated changes in these other areas. This panorama of reforms and related changes was making China a more open society, with a growing range of choices for Chinese citizens in their economic activities, social mobility, intellectual and cultural life, and politics.

At the core of the economic reforms, and hence of the overall strategy of kaifang, was the effort to build a more productive and efficient economy through a mixture of mechanisms, including relaxation of rigid state planning and direction, use of material incentives, and improved technological inputs. One cumulative effect was the growth of entrepreneurial and occupational options. Farmers regained some choice about what they would grow and how they would market the product. Many shifted into commercial farming or other specialized forms of production. Agriculture also released workers for other occupations, as in the construction industry or in unskilled and semiskilled manufacturing. Individual entrepreneurs or small-scale enterprises proliferated, especially in the service and retail trades. Often these entrepreneurs capitalized on the growing tourist industry, which also provided new jobs in hotels and tourist-related activities. These options and incentives, coupled with a decade of strong economic growth, gave many Chinese consumers a degree of affluence previously reserved for the political elite or a few other favored groups. The range of products available to satisfy this consumer demand also expanded significantly, despite some severe problems of supply and quality.

Social mobility went hand in hand with this diversification of economic opportunities. Occupational change often meant residential changes, evident in the growth of cities and rural towns. Two important features of new-found mobility were the growth of Chinese tourism and the emergence of an army of roving workers and transients. Most travel by Chinese citizens was job-related, but affluence plus the spirit of kaifang led to an explosion of recreational travel for vacations, visits to relatives, and standard sightseeing. The transient population consisted of at least three groups, not always easy to distinguish. Some were workers moving from site to site, while maintaining residence in one (usually rural) place; construction crews and farmers regularly selling produce in the cities were examples. Others were job-seekers, going mainly to the large coastal cities and special economic zones in hopes of finding a job, or better job, and settling down in these more desirable areas. Finally, there were vagrants sleeping in train stations or the street, often supported by theft or begging. By 1989 this floating population had reached massive proportions. One survey estimated that about fifty million Chinese were on the move, and that Beijing and Shanghai each had about one million to two million people entering and leaving each day.[3]

The intellectual and cultural opening kept pace. For most Chinese, the spread of television was the centerpiece of a changing popular culture, but books, newspapers, magazines, and films also proliferated. There were changes in content as well as volume, mostly in the direction of a more entertaining, depoliticized style. The advance of market principles created pressures for commercial success, especially evident in the Chinese film industry, that necessarily reflected popular tastes in entertainment. But much more was going on here than a popularization of culture. Educational reforms increased opportunities for advanced academic study, vocational training, and adult education. Offerings in the social sciences and humanities increased, although remaining far behind the scientific, technical, and professional fields that had highest priority for China's modernization. Professionalism was on the rise, with the emergence of associations, publications, exhibitions, and conferences that served to promote various artistic, academic, professional, or even avocational interests. All this was tied closely to the external opening, drawing freely on what Chinese observed abroad or learned from foreigners in China. Debate and experimentation naturally followed, raising questions about the relationship between the scholar's or artist's standards, on the one hand, and those of state or society, on the other. In short, the intellectual and cultural opening was moving toward engagement with fundamental questions about what an open society is and what purposes it should serve. In doing so, it also faced the question that had been there from the first: how wide was the political opening to be?

A standard assessment of the late 1980s was that Chinese economic reforms were well ahead of those in the Soviet Union, whereas the reverse was true in political reform. The CCP leadership's smashing of the 1989 democracy movement, as the USSR was democratizing the Supreme Soviet, confirmed this assessment. Nonetheless, we must not overlook the significance of the political opening that occurred in China between 1976 and 1989. Just as the open foreign policy initially focused on strategic and diplomatic issues, so domestic kaifang began with politics: Hua Guofeng's purge of the Gang of Four, followed quickly by his removal at the hands of Deng Xiaoping and his reform faction. To some extent, this was simply an elite political struggle, not an opening. But Hua and especially Deng supported a modest political liberalization to gain supporters and counter the Maoist dogmatism that had prevailed during the 1966–76 Cultural Revolution era. When Deng took charge at the Third Plenum, he had already committed himself to more professional autonomy for intellectuals, more open debate within the party, and political reforms that might correct some of the worst abuses of Mao's last years.

After the Third Plenum, as noted earlier, kaifang began to serve economics in both domestic and foreign policy. In the international arena, these new economic goals were mainly compatible with a continuation of the strategic realignment and diplomatic offensive that had got it all started. But at home, things were much more complicated. Deng's coalition was loosely united on the need for economic reforms, but its fragile unity did not extend to political reform. Deng's own conception of the latter was quite restricted, as shown by his crackdown on the 1978–79 "Democracy Wall" movement (not to mention his earlier political career), and many of his senior colleagues were clearly more cautious than he. The progress of economic reforms was shaking the party's grip on things, making many party leaders wary of further dilution of their political prerogatives.

On the other hand, the spirit of the times (pro-modernization and anti–Cultural Revolution) and new policy processes emerging from economic reforms, decentralization, and the intellectual-technical revolution made some political opening inescapable. Promotion of "socialist law and democracy" strengthened local congresses and the electoral system, removed adverse class labels from many targets of earlier campaigns, urged officials as well as citizens to observe the law, and encouraged more open political debate and criticism. New policies gave more voice to technical advisers, lower-level officials, and even entrepreneurs, producing a more consultative and competitive decision-making style. The changing intellectual and cultural climate, especially the spread of television and other media with their expanded coverage of domestic and international affairs—including democratic tendencies in the Philippines, Taiwan, the Soviet Union and Eastern Europe—encouraged supporters of political reform to keep pushing.

In the face of such political pressures, a divided CCP leadership gave ground at times and then reasserted its authority by suppressing dissent. Democracy Wall of 1978–79, literary dissent in the early 1980s, and nationwide student demonstrations in December 1986 marked periods of rising political activism followed by CCP reprisals. Over the decade as a whole, a degree of political liberalization took place, but in a climate of uncertainty and under the threat of recurring repression. In retrospect it is clear that this pattern was building toward a major confrontation. It came in the spring of 1989 with the strongest demands for democratic reforms in post-1949 history, followed by a counterattack that threatened to destroy most of the political opening achieved over the previous decade.

Even this cursory account shows that kaifang had a dramatic impact on China's internal and external affairs. Other essays in this volume analyze and evaluate that impact more carefully. In evaluating an episode so complex, it is important to remember the limits to kaifang—not simply the political limits displayed so forcefully in June 1989, but the social and spatial ones as well as those that distributed the impact unevenly among different Chinese groups and regions. These limits remind us that China had earlier openings and closures, and that other countries have experienced similar processes. To get a better grasp of kaifang's significance, the next section considers briefly the question: how wide is the current opening compared to earlier ones in modern China, and to those of other countries today?

Historical and Comparative Perspectives

One could argue that the Opium War and its ensuing treaties marked the real opening of China as they launched China's irrevocable engagement with the forces of the modern world and led to cataclysmic upheavals (the Taiping Rebellion) and changes (the fall of the imperial order) of a magnitude the current opening is unlikely to match. At a minimum, one should recognize that China's opening is a process that "took off" in the mid-nineteenth century and has gone through several phases marked by different emphases and interrupted by phases of relative closure. The earlier phases of most interest here are the "reform" phase of 1895–1910, when foreign activity in China accelerated and led to a variety of Chinese reform proposals; the "May Fourth" phase of 1919–37, when China's intellectuals turned more directly toward the West and foreign influence in China peaked; and the Soviet phase of 1949–60, when China reoriented its external contacts toward the Soviet bloc.

Three points emerge from a comparison of the current opening with these earlier ones. First, each phase has distinctive features that involve dramatic shifts from what went before, and none is unmistakably greater or more significant

Table 1

Estimates of China's Foreign Trade as Percentage of the National Economy

Pre-1949 China

Period	Percentage
Pre-1949	"probably never exceeded 10% of national product"[a]
1925–27	17% of national income[b]
1928–29	12% of national income at the "peak level" of pre-1949 trade[c]

Post-1949 China[d]

(1) Year	(2) Total trade (in RMB 100 mil.)	(3) National income (in RMB 100 mil.)	(4) (2) as percentage of (3)
1952	64.6	589	11.0
1957	104.5	908	11.5
1959	149.3	1,222	12.2
1962	80.9	924	8.7
1966	127.1	1,586	8.0
1970	112.9	1,926	5.9
1975	290.4	2,503	11.6
1980	563.8	3,688	15.3
1985	2,067.1	6,822	30.3

Sources:

aAlbert Feuerwerker, *The Chinese Economy, 1912–1949* (Ann Arbor: University of Michigan, Center for Chinese Studies, 1968), p. 69.

[b]Robert Dernberger, "The Role of the Foreigner in China's Economic Development 1840–1949," in *China's Modern Economy in Historical Perspective*, ed. Dwight Perkins (Stanford: Stanford University Press, 1975), p. 27.

[c]Chi-ming Hou, *Foreign Investment and Economic Development in China, 1840–1937* (Cambridge: Harvard University Press, 1965), p. 189.

[d]State Statistical Bureau, *Statistical Yearbook of China 1986* (Hong Kong: Economic Information Agency, 1986), p. 40.

than the others. Second, the current opening appears more as a continuation or resumption of earlier ones than a departure from them, and in some respects it has still not attained the degree of openness that prevailed in the past. Third, these linkages suggest that some longer-term trends may be operating here and ought to be incorporated in efforts to assess kaifang's prospects as well as its significance. These generalizations are not based on thorough research, but partial evidence suggests they are hypotheses worthy of discussion. To illustrate how such historical comparison illuminates our image of the current opening, I present some illustrative data, admittedly loose and fragmentary, on foreign trade and investment, the foreign presence in China, Chinese study abroad, and the growth of Chinese communications.

China's foreign trade grew rapidly during the 1980s, reaching a total value of U.S. $102.8 billion in 1988.[4] As the political trauma of 1989 seems likely to

Table 2

Estimate of Foreigners Resident in China

Year or period	Number	Category
1903	20,404[a]	
1921	240,769[a]	
1936	370,393[b]	
1950s	11,000[c]	Soviet technicians, teachers, and other experts
	1,600[d]	Foreign students in 1957 (plus a modest number of non-Soviet technicians, teachers, and experts)
1987–88	36,000[e]	Foreign experts and staff
	6,000[f]	Foreign students

Sources:

[a]Albert Feuerwerker, *The Foreign Establishment in China in the Early Twentieth Century* (Ann Arbor: University of Michigan Center for Chinese Studies, 1976), p. 17.

[b]H. G. W. Woodhead, ed., *The China Year Book 1936* (Shanghai), p. 2.

[c]R. F. Price, *Education in Communist China* (New York: Praeger, 1970), p. 102.

[d]Ghanshyam Mehta "The Politics of Student Protest in China," Ph.D. dissertation, University of Washington, 1971, p. 105.

[e] *Renmin ribao*, overseas edition, April 14 1989.

[f]Leo Orleans, *Chinese Students in America* (Washington, DC: National Academy Press, 1988) p. 81.

have some negative effect on trade, the 1988 figure probably represents at least a temporary peak in foreign trade as a percentage of the national economy. Table 1 suggests that this share in the late 1980s had surpassed its pre-Communist peak of the 1920s, but for most of PRC history it apparently remained below that earlier peak. Until the spurt of the late 1980s, the post-1949 peaks were in the 1970s and the Soviet phase of the 1950s. PRC foreign trade was relatively strong in the 1950s and experienced very rapid growth in the 1970s, before Third Plenum policies took effect. The 1950s' trade, largely with the Soviet bloc, grew faster than either China's GNP or total world trade for those years, leading one authority to observe that the Chinese economy of the 1950s in a sense "experienced trade-led growth."[5]

Foreign investment in China is obviously now at its post-1949 peak, a phenomenon due to kaifang. Here is a distinctive feature of the current opening and a sharp reversal of Maoist policies. It is less striking in historical perspective, however, as it is doubtful if the volume of foreign investment in China today is significantly greater relative to GNP or population than it was in the May Fourth phase. Certainly the actual influence of foreign capital and management is less now than it was in that earlier opening. Generally, then, one might say that kaifang has restored foreign trade and investment to levels approximating those of the pre-1937 years, and that even the rapid post-1978 growth of foreign trade has counterparts in the Soviet phase and the 1970s. It is important to note that the post-1970 trade expansion has been largely with capitalist countries, whereas the expansion of the 1950s was with Soviet bloc partners, but the actual realignment of trade from Soviet to capitalist blocs took place in the early 1960s, long before kaifang.

The foreign presence in China is now considerably greater and more varied than it was in the Soviet phase, not to mention the 1960–78 years. On the other hand, it remains modest compared to what it was in the May Fourth phase. Table 2 offers some estimates of foreigners resident in China.

The 1987–88 total omits diplomatic and possibly other categories, but it may be a relatively high figure given the decline one expects after June 1989. In any case, it is far below the 370,000 foreigners estimated for 1936. The Soviet and other foreign presence of the 1950s was not far below that of the mid-1980s as a percentage of population. Needless to say, the foreign presence in China before 1937 included other elements, such as military and missionary personnel, that made it a more intrusive one. It is doubtful that the foreign presence in China will attain anything like its pre-1937 level in the foreseeable future.

Study abroad has been a prominent feature of modern China's education and politics and has created influential personal and institutional links between Chinese and foreign societies. It probably strikes most Americans as one of the central features of China's open door, and so it is. It was also prominent in earlier phases of the opening of China. The first wave, of Chinese students to Japan in 1895–1910, was perhaps the most significant. As table 3 indicates, study in Japan competed even in absolute numbers with higher education in China. The Chinese student and intellectual community in Japan (including many training as military officers) played an absolutely crucial role in the development of Chinese political movements of the times. During the May Fourth phase, the United States replaced Japan as the main provider of foreign education, and the impact shifted toward Chinese academic and professional fields. In this period, and down to 1949, returned students from the United States and Europe occupied many leading positions in Chinese universities and administrative agencies.

Figures for the two more recent phases are more precise in some ways but still problematic. The three figures for study in the Soviet Union no doubt count different types of study or training (the larger estimates including shorter-term or technical training). For the current period, the "over 60,000" figure refers to regular students and visiting scholars, under both state and private sponsorship, whereas the 150,000 estimate for 1983–88 refers to Chinese departures on student visas, including many going for remedial language study who might never

Table 3

Estimates of Chinese Students Abroad

(1) Year or period	(2) Number abroad	(3) Chinese enrollments in higher education	(4) (2) as percentage of (3)
ca. 1870–1949	100,000 (long-term)[a]		
1900–1937	34,000 to Japan (long-term)[b]		
to 1940s	100,000 to Japan (including short-term)[b]		
1854–1953	21,000 to U.S. (long-term)[b]		
1906	15,000 in Japan[c]	40,114 in 1912[h]	37
1950–1959	14,000 to USSR[d]	403,000 in 1956–57[i]	3.4
1949–1959	36,000 to USSR (based on Soviet sources)[e]		
1949–1960s	61,000 to USSR (based on Soviet sources)[f]		
1979–1989	over 60,000 (regular students, public or private sponsors)	2,066,000 in 1988[j]	2.9
1983–1988	150,000 (all Chinese departures on student visas)[g]		

Sources:

[a]Y. C. Wang, *Chinese Intellectuals and the West 1872–1949* (Chapel Hill: University of North Carolina Press, 1966), from foreword by C. Martin Wilbur, p. v.

[b]Ibid., pp. 119–20.

[c]Ibid., p. 64.

[d]Leo A. Orleans, *Professional Manpower and Education in Communist China* (Washington, DC: National Science Foundation, 1961), p. 79.

[e]R. F. Price, *Education in Communist China* (New York: Praeger, 1970), p. 103.

[f]*Beijing Review* 32, 11 (March 13–19, 1989): 19.

[g]*Renmin ribao*, overseas edition, (January 24, 1989).

[h]Orleans, *Professional Manpower*, p. 10.

[i]Ibid., p. 66.

[j]*Beijing Review* 32 10 (March 6–12, 1989): vi.

become regular students in accredited universities.[6] However flawed the data, it suggests that neither of the PRC openings has relied so heavily on foreign study as the earlier ones, and that China's relative reliance on foreign study was at least as great in the 1950s as it is today. The Soviet-trained specialists of the 1950s were also better utilized than their counterparts today.[7] This is a difficult judgment to make, of course, because relatively few of the current cohort have returned, but the 1989 crackdown seems certain to create further defections, delayed returns, or damaged prospects for those who do return. In sum, current study abroad is indeed an important element in kaifang, distinctive mainly because it now centers on the United States (roughly two-thirds of all regular students abroad) rather than on the Soviet Union as in the 1950s or Japan as in the first part of the twentieth century. But it has a very long way to go before it influences Chinese education and politics as heavily as did earlier cohorts, and even the current emphasis on training in the United States, Japan, and other capitalist countries is a resumption of the primary pattern of the past one hundred years.

Table 4 presents a few data as a reminder that the domestic opening of Chinese society has also been underway for a long time. The table focuses on the post-1949 expansion of the communications infrastructure, an expansion that continued rather steadily over the years in question. Feature film production, showing the impact of the Cultural Revolution on this medium, is a reminder that the growth of infrastructure says nothing about political content and restrictions. There is no doubt that Chinese communications in almost every sense expanded greatly and became much more open and diverse during 1979–89—as they did to a lesser extent in the Soviet phase. The pre-1949 openings, not represented here, would also show long-term growth of infrastructure and periods of more or less diversity and freedom in intellectual and political dialogue. The current opening in communications contrasts most dramatically with the Cultural Revolution, less so with the 1950s. Although it is difficult to compare periods of such different social and political systems (and infrastructural capabilities), it seems reasonable to suggest that the long intellectual and political opening of 1895–1937, despite its recurrent political turmoil and repression, was a wider one than that of 1979–89.

How does China's current "openness" compare to that of other countries, especially the PRC's neighbors and other large Third World countries? A few illustrative data suggest that the opening appears less exceptional in this comparative light. By the late 1980s, a decade of rapid economic growth coupled with strong efforts to attract foreign investment had made China a leading Third World site for such investment and had given it the aura of a budding international economic power. The events of 1989 may tarnish this image but, even without them, some qualifications might be in order. China's clearest gain has been in foreign trade, with over 16 percent annual increase in value in 1979–87, the highest in a group including the United States, Japan, Canada, South Korea,

Table 4

A. Growth of Communications in the PRC

Item	Unit	1952	1965	1978	1980	1985
Passenger traffic:						
Railways	100 million person-km	201	479	1,093	1,383	2,416
Highways	100 million person-km	23	162	521	729	1,573
Civil aviation	100 million person-km	0.2	2.5	28	33	47
Letters delivered	100 millions	8	22	28	33	47
Newspapers issued	100 million copies	16	47	128	140	200
Magazines issued	100 million copies	2	4	8	11	26
Books published	100 million copies	8	22	38	46	68
Sales of radio sets	10,000s	2	84	1,389	2,722	2,517
Sales of TV sets	10,000s	—	0.2	55	364	2,157

B. Feature Film Production

Year	Number
1949	10
1954	24
1958	101
1965	43
1967–69	0
1972	5
1978	45
1980	83
1985	127

Sources: Part A is from State Statistical Bureau, *Statistical Yearbook of China 1986* (Hong Kong: Economic Information Agency, 1986), pp. 16–17. Part B is from Paul Clark, *Chinese Cinema: Culture and Politics since 1949* (Cambridge: Cambridge University Press 1987), pp. 185–86.

Brazil, and India; this spurt raised the PRC share of world trade from 0.8 percent in 1978 to 1.6 percent in 1987. Even so, its total trade in 1987 surpassed only India and Brazil in the group named and was only modestly greater than Taiwan's. Its 1986 trade as a percent of GDP was 27, surpassing India (14) and Brazil (18) but less than Egypt (35), South Korea (68), Taiwan (87), Thailand

(43), Malaysia (89), Indonesia (37), and the Philippines (33).[8] China's share of world trade before 1949 has been estimated at 1.3 percent in 1871–84, 1.5 percent in 1901–14, and 2.3 percent in 1925–29.[9] China has thus become one of Asia's most significant traders, but it has not yet regained its pre-1949 peak share of world trade, and its economy remains less dominated by foreign trade than are those of many of its peers.

The substantial flow of foreign investment into China in the mid-1980s came after several years of only modest success in this effort. Much of the total investment comes from Hong Kong, or other ethnic Chinese investors, and the sum is less impressive if calculated in per capita terms or as a share of GNP. China was also borrowing more heavily in the late 1980s, but its total long-term debt in 1986 was about half that of India, Indonesia, Poland, and Korea; somewhat less than that of the Philippines, Malaysia, and Yugoslavia; and, of course, only a fraction of that of Brazil and Mexico. Its long-term debt service as a percentage of both GNP and exports was by far the lowest of all these countries.[10] China is currently quite open to international capital but not unusually dependent on it, and its long-term success in attracting it has not yet been proven.

Comparing the PRC's openness on foreign study yields further insights. China is not exceptionally attractive to foreign students. In 1986 it had 4,343—somewhat more than Taiwan and less than the Philippines; about 30–40 percent of the number hosted by Brazil, Egypt, India, and Japan; and a small fraction of those in the USSR (62,942 in 1980), not to mention the United States (349,610).[11] The number of foreign students in China was rising in the late 1980s but has fallen, at least temporarily, since 1989. By the late 1980s, China was the world's largest exporter of students, a point that deserves emphasis because it is indeed central in kaifang, yet if one calculates students abroad as a percentage of college students, its ratio is less than Taiwan's or Nigeria's and close to some other Third World countries; if one uses total population as a base, China's ratio is less than that of Japan, South Korea, Taiwan, Thailand, Malaysia, Indonesia, and the Philippines.[12] So far as foreign study is concerned, kaifang looks outward more than inward, but even its study abroad program is not unusually large relative to its population or enrollments in higher education.

Tourism yields similar conclusions. China tourist arrivals have mushroomed from about 1.8 million in 1978 to 31.7 million in 1988, the latest figure possibly making China the world leader in this industry. The figure is misleading, however, as only 1.8 million of the 1988 total were "foreign" tourists—the rest were overseas Chinese or "compatriots" from Hong Kong, Macao, and Taiwan. Of 115 million total arrivals between 1979 and 1987, less than 9 million were "foreign" and over 106 million were in the other category. The number of foreign arrivals is in a standard range for many attractive tourist destinations. Again, if one calculates tourists as a percentage of population, China's ratio is very modest if one counts only foreign tourists, and not exceptionally high even if one counts all arrivals.[13] Here, too, 1989 will probably produce at least a temporary decline.

The data suggest that the current opening is a striking reversal of the Cultural Revolution closure and of the Soviet orientation of the 1950s' opening. It cannot claim distinctly greater significance than earlier openings as in many ways it has essentially resumed earlier patterns or regained earlier peaks. China is now (or once again) fairly open to international transactions, but the overall opening is not great compared to many other countries. It is also instructive to note that the current opening may now be retreating, as the earlier ones did at some point, and that ethnic Chinese have played a prominent role in transactions associated with kaifang. These are clues to some important points for later discussion.

Forces Promoting and Resisting Kaifang

In late 1989, the prospects for kaifang appeared worse than at any time in the decade. The main obstacle is politics, the victory of the hardliners in the struggle over how to deal with the democracy movement and their determination to resist political change. Although they insist the open foreign policy and domestic economic reforms will continue, these areas, too, will surely suffer from the domestic and international tensions generated by the crackdown. Politics aside, China faces formidable economic and social problems that might frustrate the efforts of hardliners and progressives alike—inflation, corruption, deficits, weakened governmental regulatory power, an inadequate educational infrastructure, higher population growth rates, restive national minorities, and so on. Kaifang's results now look ambiguous, its prospects uncertain. What can be said in a brief assessment about this issue?

One approach to understanding the opening's prospects is to ask what historical forces have promoted or resisted it, and how the balance is likely to develop in the future. These forces include long-term trends or structural forces that set the context of policy choices and the actors or agents who participate in the choices that are made. The argument here is that structural forces are the best guide to long-run prospects, whereas the relative strength and character of agents determines kaifang's short-run fluctuations; and that structural factors favor the continued opening of China, as they have in general for a century and a half, even though the balance among agents promoting or resisting it currently resists a wider version of kaifang.

The primary structural influence on the opening is the desire for modernization and the growth of new social forces produced by the introduction of modern technology and organization. This desire for modernity rests on the pursuit of "wealth and power," the drive to improve the material well-being of the Chinese people and to provide the state with the power to defend its interests and enhance its domestic and international standing. The modernizing impulse among Chinese elites grew slowly after the Opium War, accelerated in the reform and May

Fourth phases, and ultimately captured the programs of both the Chinese Nationalist and Communist parties. It was a difficult program to realize, of course, due to civil war and other domestic turmoil, global wars, and the strange episode of the Cultural Revolution—strange because Maoism in most of its forms was not antimodern—but the long-term trend has increased Chinese desires to enlist the power of modern technology in addressing China's problems. This is why it is essential to look at earlier phases of the opening to understand that the current orientation toward Japan and the West continues a long-term structural pattern. Leaning toward the USSR in the 1950s was in part a substitute for a West that was not receptive at the time (and a Japan that was disqualified by wartime behavior and defeat); the Cultural Revolution was a short-term exception to the pattern. Bear in mind that Mao led the reopening to the West in 1971, after only a few years of relative isolation from both Soviet and Western technology.

The interests of global powers are a second powerful structural promoter of kaifang. Initially, of course, they were the dominant one, opening China by force against Chinese resistance. They remained dominant until early in the twentieth century, when global wars sapped their capacity to coerce China (Japan being an exception) just as indigenous Chinese desires for opening were rising along with resistance to externally imposed integration. From May Fourth on, the Chinese drive for modernization has probably been stronger than the world's desire, or ability, to impose it. Nonetheless, one must not underestimate the power of global interests to promote the continued opening of China. These interests are both strategic and economic, supported by a mix of intellectual, cultural, and ethical concerns. They cannot now open China against its will, as they did in earlier phases, but they are still a powerful force on the side of kaifang. In the aftermath of June 4, 1989, they are using their control of international resources to show their desire that the opening resume.

A final structural promoter—a specific part of the international system—is the example and competition of the NICs, which intensify China's modernization impulse and demonstrate that the old debate about having to choose either modernization Western style or stagnation Chinese style is outdated. It is understandable that some Chinese believed that was the choice they faced; after all, many others, including Westerners, have thought modernization meant the end of their traditional culture. It was a belief easier to hold when only the West looked modern, but now the evidence is quite different. Japan was the great example, now joined by Hong Kong, Taiwan, and Singapore—to name only the most compelling examples because they display a modernizing Chinese culture. To be sure, the culture in question changes with modernization, as these examples attest, but the changes do not obliterate cultural distinctiveness or links to the past. It is possible to be a NIC and Chinese, too. Other examples around the world show that it is possible to modernize without becoming Western, and, perhaps most importantly, that it is possible for authoritarian systems to democratize, or at least "open" internally in significant ways.

Structural forces have also resisted kaifang, of course. One such factor is the size of China and the relatively slow progress that has been made in building the infrastructure of a modern society, particularly in agriculture, communications, and education. China entered the twentieth century as one of the world's poorest countries, despite the fact it had once been the wealthiest. Although it experienced periods of impressive development both before and after 1949, recurring disruptions kept it in the least-developed cohort of the world's economies. Enormous resources are now required to realize the opening's potential, and foreign contributions of substantial magnitude may have only a modest impact. Large volumes of trade, investment, and tourism by global standards may be small relative to China's needs and population. The PRC may send sixty thousand students abroad, but it educates over two million in its own universities—and the most important figure of all remains the extremely low percentage of Chinese who attend college, a figure low even for a Third World country.[14] The comparative perspective was introduced to underscore the point that China's size reduces some of kaifang's impact. As a huge, continental country, China will probably never attain a high degree of global interdependence. Perhaps a better way to make this point is to say that China's future rests more with the quality of its domestic opening than with its external one.

A second structural restraint has been the ideological legacy of imperialism and the Cold War. As earlier essays on the May Fourth era show, the Chinese interest in socialism grew rapidly after the Bolshevik Revolution, feeding on resentment of the capitalist powers. Intensifying Japanese aggression left a deep imprint, as did the post-1945 Cold War. The Cold War may be over now, but it shaped PRC institutions and attitudes at a formative stage and continues to affect older Chinese leaders' perceptions of the risks of kaifang. More generally, Chinese interpretations of their modern history encourage continuing caution about relations with Japan and the West, restraining to some degree the obvious attraction those countries hold for Chinese modernizers.

Finally, two Chinese cultural patterns may contribute to structural resistance to kaifang: one, a Chinese tendency to distinguish firmly and often unsympathetically between Chinese and foreigners; the other, a Chinese style of social behavior that seems to some to discredit the opening. Historically, Chinese saw the possession or nonpossession of Chinese culture as the mark of civilization or barbarism, and today many continue to think that foreigners are properly treated differently and kept separate from Chinese. This distinction, and the assumption of mutual incapacity to adapt fully to the other's culture, need not involve antiforeign sentiment. On the other hand, there have been many outbursts of xenophobia in China's modern history, which is not surprising given foreign activities in China. Some Chinese continue to view foreigners and their cultures as incompatible or disruptive, a view that may harden into more intense suspicion or hostility. But one must reject emphatically the notion that Chinese nationalism opposes kaifang, because many Chinese favor it precisely on nationalistic grounds. The main point is this: there is in China a way of thinking about China's relations with other peoples and nations that impedes full acceptance of the opening to the outside world. Although it has yielded over time to the dominant logic of kaifang, it has slowed and complicated the process of opening.

The problem in social behavior is the importance of *guanxi*, or connections, in all kinds of transactions, and the dominance of kinship or other personalized networks over broader associations. These deeply rooted cultural patterns sometimes seem to promote corruption, nepotism, and factionalism, or disregard for the public good coupled with unprincipled pursuit of selfish interest. Because kaifang relaxed political controls that restrained such practices and created abundant opportunities for their exercise, with many of these opportunities tied to foreign activities, there is some correlation in Chinese eyes between the opening and the rampant corruption of recent years. This may be offered as evidence that Chinese society needs a strong political authority to set the proper moral tone or that "bourgeois" contacts inevitably lead to corruption. Needless to say, these negative phenomena are not unique to Chinese culture, nor is there any evidence that Chinese societies cannot modernize without succumbing to them. Like the compartmentalization of foreigners, guanxi and kinship loyalties are elements of Chinese culture that complicate the opening and Chinese attitudes toward it without actually blocking it.

On balance, structural forces favor the opening of China, as they have since the turn of the century, and this push is likely to continue and intensify in the coming decades. The formation of agents of kaifang is much more complicated and volatile, however, with a small group of veteran party leaders holding a restricted view of kaifang, in effect restraining a continuation of the broader opening, while more numerous but less powerful groups inside and outside the CCP want to push ahead. How is it that agents promoting the opening generally carried the day from the early 1970s to the mid-1980s, only to see the balance shift the other way in the late 1980s?

The opening began with the strategic realignment of the early 1970s, a decision made behind closed doors by a few top leaders, but it soon developed a wider clientele and rationale. The residual influence of earlier openings should be noted here, as the PRC political and intellectual elite included many who had been trained in Western or Soviet institutions. Even the limited economic and cultural exchange that developed between China and the West in 1972–78 was sufficient to demonstrate to Chinese who participated in it how far behind global standards China had fallen. By the late 1970s, vigorous intellectual arguments for wider opening and deeper reform were filling the elite media. When this pressure became too public and politicized—as it did in the Democracy Wall movement of 1978–79 (preceding the new academic exchanges, hence demonstrating the residual influence of earlier openings)—the leadership suppressed it; but the advice and arguments of specialists were critical in persuading the more reform-minded leaders to push ahead.

The decisive agents in extending the opening were still party leaders who seized the initiative after Mao's death and the purge of the Gang of Four to advance reforms that would restore China to a more stable path of development. Their goal was to reverse the damage of the Cultural Revolution, with kaifang as an instrument in the effort. This reform coalition under Deng's leadership was not united but it held together for about a decade. From the first, its conception of kaifang was limited by a desire to avoid social instability, challenge to party leadership, and excessive foreign influence. In practice, the opening progressed further and faster than the leaders expected as other agents entered the process, pushing the reforms well beyond the wishes of the more conservative members of the coalition. These new agents were diverse: peasants and rural cadres who extended the responsibility system so rapidly; enterprises that capitalized on new domestic or international market opportunities, often with official cooperation; provincial leaders, as in Guangdong, who made kaifang a vehicle for rapid development of their areas; academics, researchers, and traders who found ways to push international exchanges far beyond the initial idea. Often these agents acted on their own initiative, making kaifang anything central authorities failed to prohibit. But all had their advocates at the center, too, the higher officials and think tanks that encouraged the most reformist leaders to keep the opening going. A new political process was taking shape in which the leading coalition was losing its control.

As kaifang progressed, with its attendant inflation, corruption, social differentiation, political stirrings, and growing foreign presence, conflicts within the leading coalition came to the fore. By 1986–87 the balance at the top was shifting to more conservative leaders, thoroughly alarmed by fears of economic problems, social disorder, and challenges to CCP dominance. For this more cautious group, the democracy movement of 1989 was a clear sign that their fears were becoming reality. After considerable delay, reflecting their own divisions as well as recognition of the gravity of the crisis, they cracked down on the demonstrators, ended all immediate hopes of political reform, and compromised many other aspects of kaifang. They were able to do this only by calling military agents into active service as they sacrificed the support of other agents who had helped push the opening so far over the preceding decade.

The current situation is one in which structural forces favor ever-wider kaifang, many loosely defined and poorly organized agents also support it, while the most powerful political agents—the new leading clique in the CCP, its military backers, and bureaucratic elements who fear loss of power and privilege—resist its continued expansion. In shifting from promotion of kaifang to this more ambiguous stance, the CCP leadership has set itself against forces that are likely to grow as its own base contracts. It cannot sustain this position indefinitely because the opening's long-term consequences make it increasingly difficult to govern China without broader domestic and international support. The concluding section reflects on some of these long-term consequences.

Conclusion: Interdependence, Sovereignty, and Nationalism

It is too early for a conclusive evaluation of kaifang's successes and failures, and its future is highly uncertain. This concluding section turns, therefore, to some broader themes that permeate the history of the opening of China. The discussion rests on an assumption that should be explicit. Despite the current setback, the long-term opening is likely to continue, especially in its efforts to acquire the international goods, technology, and capital necessary for China's modernization. Some degree of domestic economic and cultural openness must also continue to accommodate the external opening, although these areas will remain very vulnerable to political fluctuations. The current uncertainty stems from a political closure, one sure to have some restrictive effects on other areas so long as it endures. Because prospects for the resumption of political kaifang are so crucial for the opening as a whole, some comments on them accompany these final reflections on the changing character of interdependence, sovereignty, and nationalism in the course of the opening.

Interdependence

This essay has argued that kaifang is significant but not unprecedented, that it has resumed patterns of opening familiar from earlier phases, and that its magnitude is no greater in some respects than in those other phases. It is most dramatic in its reversal of Cultural Revolution policies and of the 1950s' opening toward the Soviet bloc. Its significance lies mainly in the fact that China's size makes its development and political-strategic orientation of utmost importance in world affairs. Size also limits China's interdependence, as its external transactions remain modest relative to domestic ones. However, there are important ways in which kaifang accelerated the long-term growth of interdependence.

First, Chinese awareness of the realities of global interdependence has increased over the course of the opening, especially in the latest phase. The search for wealth and power continues to dominate the CCP elite's rationale for kaifang, as it did the thinking of the first Chinese sponsors of opening, but there is a growing understanding among educated Chinese that China cannot simply extract what it needs to enrich and strengthen itself but must participate more fully in the give and take of the international system. With this goes a stronger awareness of China's dependence on and responsibilities toward the global economy and ecology, and a stronger appreciation of the value of international norms.

Second, China is now more interdependent in the sense of more frequent and intense interactions with the rest of the world. By some measures kaifang has not matched, or at least not greatly exceeded, earlier openings, but this is not to say nothing has changed. Transactions take place with greater speed, are dispersed more widely in the interior, and are more crucial for the operation of the Chinese economy. For example, the global revolution in communications has greatly increased the speed, volume, and immediacy of messages exchanged between China and other countries. The way in which knowledge of the democracy movement spread outward, and in which external reporting and reaction became part of the Chinese understanding of events, is an excellent example.

Third, today's interdependence is more inclusive than in the past. That is, it involves transactions with more of the world's states and peoples—capitalist and socialist systems; first, second, and third worlds; and diverse groups of people. The latest opening is more truly international than its predecessors.

Finally, China is now more interdependent in the sense that its government needs both domestic and international support. We should not let current official statements deceive us about long-term trends. These statements suggest that China does not need the approval and support of foreign countries and disaffected elements of its own society. This is true only if China is willing to pay the price of this kind of "independence," as it is an independence of action for political elites that will push the country toward a deeper economic and political crisis. Deng and his colleagues were probably right in thinking that a crackdown on their opponents was necessary to maintain their position. The alternative was a dilution of the concentrated power they exercise in the name of socialism and the CCP dictatorship. This kind of power is becoming an anachronism. China's economy and society have become too complex, too dependent on the compliance and initiative of various sectors of its population as well as on the trust and cooperation of its international partners, for a political elite that denies this dependence to govern effectively. The current leadership may be able to hold its position for a while, but only at substantial cost. Its older members will soon be gone, its younger members more vulnerable, and its following within the party at large less certain about the wisdom of upholding the four cardinal principles. As these trends unfold, major changes in Chinese politics will ensue.

What these changes will be is uncertain, and there is no guarantee they will be for the better. Dreadful scenarios of political stalemate, economic decline, or even civil war are possibilities. But if our assessment of the long-term opening is valid, more optimistic forecasts are not unrealistic. The future of political kaifang does not lie with Western-style democracy, at least in the foreseeable future. "Democracy" is really a code word for other kinds of openings that are more attainable—more freedom of association, more freedom of the press, more meaningful consultation between the elite and representative bodies, and some degree of accountability on the part of elites. The political opening of 1979–89 produced demands for, and some experimentation with, all of these goals. All represent revivals of demands heard in earlier phases of the opening as well. Three models of incorporating these demands exist. One is the Gorbachev model, in which a vigorous party leader (or group of leaders) reforms existing institutions from the top. Another is the Polish model, with a truly independent, popular association fighting a long battle, involving bitter and possibly bloody confrontation, to gain legitimacy and wrest a share of power from the ruling party. The third is the Taiwan model, in which the ruling party allows its opposition to form a political party and gives it enough legal guarantees to offer some hope that a competitive party system might eventually emerge. None of these models promises a smooth or painless transition, but all involve recognition of the Chinese state's dependence on societal and international supports.

Sovereignty

Another theme in the opening of China has been a recapture and consolidation of its sovereignty, the transition from a status in which foreign powers forced concessions from China, often by military action, to one in which these concessions have been reclaimed and China negotiates its international agreements on an equal basis. The opening's earliest phases reflected the foreign powers' initiative and hegemony, although Chinese soon began to pursue the opening for their own purposes, often in conflict with the interests of the powers. The Nationalist Revolution of 1925–27 brought a government in Nanking that regained some lost rights, only to suffer the Japanese invasion and occupation of 1937–45. By 1949, formal sovereignty was largely restored, although the PRC's weak bargaining position gave the Soviet Union some privileges reminiscent of earlier concessions. Kaifang stands out in this history as the one phase of the opening unmistakably pursued on Chinese initiative by a truly sovereign Chinese state.

The relationship between sovereignty and interdependence is complex. No state, however sovereign, is free from external restraints or is wholly effective in controlling its territory and frontiers. Interdependence requires recognition of such restraints and willingness to accept the increased difficulties of control that go with more intensive international transactions, but it does not require a state to yield its right to regulate such transactions or to change its policy on them. Kaifang has granted concessions to foreigners, especially in the special economic zones, complicated Chinese control of the increased transactions that flow across its borders, and made the PRC party to more international agreements that involve some limits on its actions. None of this involves any renunciation of sovereignty, which China insists be duly recognized as it remains extremely sensitive to any actions that smack of interference in its internal affairs. This jealously guarded sovereignty was a precondition for kaifang, not an obstacle to it. Without the confidence that it could control the process and its impact on Chinese territory and citizens, thereby avoiding the externally dominated patterns of earlier openings, China would not have promoted it. Kaifang has become more vulnerable to its critics since about 1986 in part because of some evident erosion in this control. Outsiders might prefer this combination of kaifang promoted by a weakened Chinese state, but China's choice is kaifang backed by a strong state. If the world wants a more open China, it has to deal with a stronger China.

China's current sovereign concerns focus most sharply on territorial jurisdiction over areas the PRC claims but does not administer, the most important ones being Hong Kong, Macao, Taiwan, and various islands in the East and South China Seas, especially the Spratly or Nansha Islands. Part of the political incentive for U.S.-China rapprochement was an accommodation on the vexing issue of Taiwan. For China, this was a first step toward securing by diplomatic means what it had no hope of securing by force; there was never any ambiguity about the PRC's claims to sovereignty over the areas mentioned. Kaifang was not to sacrifice China's sovereignty but to assist in realizing it, so there was an explicit linkage, from the Shanghai Communiqué on, between the open foreign policy and the ultimate goal of reunification.

PRC sovereign claims raise monumental problems, however, because neither the peoples nor the governing authorities of Hong Kong, Macao, and Taiwan have welcomed the mainland formula for reunification. Although Hong Kong and Macao had no real choice but to accede to PRC pressure, the 1984 Sino-British Joint Declaration on Hong Kong that provides for resumption of Chinese sovereignty in 1997 produced great uneasiness in Hong Kong. This concern reached crisis proportions as Hong Kong witnessed the violent suppression of the democracy movement in June 1989. After 1989, there is no prospect at all that Taiwan will rejoin the mainland under anything like the terms the PRC offers, and there will be strong pressure to renegotiate or resist the agreements returning Hong Kong and Macao to the PRC. As for the Spratlys and other islands, there are competing claims from neighboring states that make PRC sovereignty a highly controversial issue here as well.

Sovereignty is an ambiguous theme in the opening of China. Its pursuit required reversal of patterns established in earlier openings, its consolidation by the PRC permitted and even encouraged kaifang, and now it appears to some observers as evidence of a dangerous assertiveness and insensitivity in Chinese foreign policy. The majority of the international community does not challenge the claim that Taiwan, Hong Kong, and Macao are part of China, but this community also observes that the PRC's pursuit of its sovereign claims has shown minimal recognition of and deference to the views of the people most directly concerned. Inescapably, the assertion of Chinese sovereignty not only poses immediate threats to the interests of the territories in question but also stimulates fears about the longer-range implications of rising Chinese power. Although that subject is beyond the scope of this essay, projections of kaifang's future impact must address the possibility that it will be a threat to some of China's neighbors.

Nationalism

Chinese nationalists have opposed foreign intervention in China, both undue influence and outright occupation of Chinese territory, and favored unification of China under a single government. They have professed patriotism and the need for all Chinese to sacrifice for the national cause. At times they have made nationalism something like the religion of modern China, and scholars have invoked it to explain most of the key events of the era. But Chinese nationalists have still disagreed on specific issues like the opening. Some have favored the fullest possible opening, in culture and politics as well as economics; some have taken a more cautious view, seeking to admit only critical techniques or instruments that China can put to use for its own purposes; and some have been suspicious of foreign influence in general, seeing it as a threat to Chinese values. Today proponents of different degrees of kaifang continue to justify their positions on nationalist grounds and accuse their opponents of being unpatriotic. This is not surprising as nationalism and patriotism have always been slippery terms, in both scholarship and politics. Despite this confusion, there are some important connections between nationalism and kaifang that are worth exploring.

One way to start thinking about Chinese nationalism is to ask what nation we have in mind. There are several candidates, the most obvious and powerful being the Han Chinese who live in the People's Republic, the people one usually means when one talks about Chinese nationalism. A second Chinese nation is defined by PRC citizenship and includes over one billion Han citizens plus about seventy million non-Han national minorities. A third Chinese nation consists of all ethnic Chinese (that is, Han Chinese) wherever they live, in China, Hong Kong, Taiwan, Singapore, Indonesia, the United States, and so on; we usually refer to all such people as "Chinese" unless we want to emphasize the non-Chinese citizenship held by those outside the PRC. Finally, the largest grouping of Chinese is divided into subgroups that might be thought of as nations in themselves, most obviously Singaporeans or Taiwanese, although linguistic groups such as Cantonese or Hakka may also be considered ethnic groups or subethnic groups within the larger Chinese nation. Kaifang has had quite different effects on these different nations.

Despite the fact that kaifang is often justified in nationalist terms, that unfulfilled sovereign claims produce a lot of nationalist rhetoric from the state, and that we have become accustomed to thinking of the Chinese as peculiarly open to nationalistic if not overtly antiforeign appeals, Chinese society has experienced little nationalist mobilization over the past decade. There have been some antiforeign demonstrations or incidents, but none has gained much momentum. The principal effect of kaifang has been to free Chinese citizens from demands for profession of political loyalties, allowing them to pursue their private lives and economic interests as best they can. This encouragement of privatization seems to have been one source of kaifang's popular appeal. Response to it has been so pervasive, among bureaucrats and even top leaders as well as ordinary citizens, that state regulatory capacities have begun to suffer. Whatever the nationalist rhetoric one hears from state and citizen alike, kaifang seems to have disaggregated the nation more than it has unified it.

Kaifang is also building new links and associations among Chinese across the country, which is a form of nation building. There is no doubt that the nation can be mobilized in a formidable nationalist movement if the proper cause comes along, but what might that cause be? The enemies of the imperialist era, and of the succeeding conflicts with the United States, Soviet Union, and Vietnam, seem less threatening. There are still conflicts, and lingering grievances and resentments, with some of these former enemies, but none that seems to justify national mobilization. The most likely future cause would be a direct challenge to Chinese sovereignty over the territorial issues (e.g., Taiwan), so there indeed lies fuel for a nationalist fire. It is still worth noting that the strongest popular mobilization since the Cultural Revolution was the democracy movement in Beijing, supported by activities in other major cities, in April–June 1989. Despite its professed patriotic character, it proved to be a divisive movement, hence vulnerable to countercharges of violating national interests. The salient political issues for Chinese citizens seem to be domestic ones. Movements having a clearer nationalist character could rise rapidly, especially in the event of external crisis, but it is not certain that Chinese would be united by them.

Turning to the nation that includes the national minorities, the most striking impact of kaifang has been to encourage Tibetan nationalism. The causes of this lie much deeper, of course, but the timing of recent Han-Tibetan conflicts is related to the opportunities provided by more open policies. There have been stirrings in Xinjiang as well, among the Uighur minority there. As in the USSR, it seems that political openings, the airing of old grievances, and the knowledge that national and international attention can now be captured are a stimulus for expression of ethnic nationalism among minorities. Although the problem in China is less acute than in the Soviet Union, we should anticipate that continuation of the open policies will produce more conflicts among the nationalities that make up the larger PRC nation.

Finally, there is the larger Chinese nation that extends outside the PRC, including the "compatriots" of Taiwan, Hong Kong, and Macao; the overseas Chinese of Southeast Asia; and the ethnic Chinese citizens of other states. Mingled among them now are hundreds of thousands of PRC students, scholars, sojourners, and emigrants fresh from China who may be on the road to citizenship elsewhere. There has always been a vague sense of common cultural identity among the Chinese diaspora, although some have fully assimilated, too, and perhaps denied their Chinese heritage at times. Since 1949 some have maintained close ties with the mainland, but there have also been serious political disputes and other barriers between the People's Republic and many of these external Chinese. Kaifang has breached these barriers with remarkable ease and speed, as if the nation were waiting to reclaim itself as soon as politics could be put aside. The leading participant here, in trade, investment, and tourism, is Hong Kong. By 1989 Taiwan was also becoming a leading provider of trade and tourism for the PRC, offering more and more investment funds, receiving some mainland visitors and (illegal) workers, and opening up other communication links with the PRC. Ethnic Chinese from the non-Chinese states have also been very visible and important in managing kaifang's foreign transactions. In short, much of what passed through the open door was based on the ethnic Chinese connection.

The democracy movement had a stunning impact on this larger Chinese nation, galvanizing it as few events have done before. Everywhere outside China it seemed other Chinese were demonstrating in support of a mainland movement. There has been nothing like this since Sun Yat-sen mobilized overseas Chinese support for his revolutionary activities early in the twentieth century. Suppression of the democracy movement widened the gulf between the CCP and the "compatriots" of Taiwan and Hong Kong, making reunification under PRC auspices even more implausible for Taiwan and more controversial for Hong Kong, yet it created a stronger bond at the popular level—among all Chinese, anywhere, who supported the movement—than anyone could have imagined.

As the initial reaction to June 4 yields to questions about long-run response, divisions have begun to appear among the external Chinese. Just as on the mainland, common nationalist bonds and aspirations are no guarantee of consensus on political tactics. The episode remains significant for two reasons, however. It demonstrated how rapidly kaifang had bridged or moderated older divisions among mainland and external Chinese; and it revealed that the sentiments of the external Chinese are solidly in support of kaifang. Because we are accustomed to thinking of Chinese nationalism as an actual or potential threat to the opening, it is important to note this developing connection between kaifang and Chinese nationalists at home and abroad, which may become one of the stronger forces supporting the continued opening of China.

Notes

Part of this essay draws on research assisted by a grant from the Joint Committee on Chinese Studies of the Social Science Research Council and the American Council of Learned Societies with funds provided by the Ford Foundation and the National Endowment for the Humanities. An-jen Chiang assisted in preparation of the tables. Conference participants, especially Kenneth Lieberthal, offered valued suggestions for corrections and revisions, as did George Brown, Peter Cheung, Gao Ming, and Lin Zhimin. The author gratefully acknowledges all this assistance but remains solely responsible for the content of the essay.

1. James R. Townsend and Richard C. Bush, comps., *The People's Republic of China: A Basic Handboook*, 2d ed. (New York: China Council of the Asia Society, 1981), p. 70.

2. Li Jiaquan, "Taiwan's New Mainland Policy Raises Concern," *Beijing Review* 32, 21 (May 22–26, 1989): 23–24.

3. *Beijing Review* 32, 12 (March 20–26, 1989): 11.

4. *Beijing Review* 32, 10 (March 6–12, 1989): vi.

5. Alexander Eckstein, *China's Economic Revolution* (Cambridge: Cambridge University Press, 1977), p. 245.

6. Problems of calculating the number of Chinese students abroad are discussed in Leo A. Orleans, *Chinese Students in America* (Washington, DC: National Academy Press, 1988), esp. pp. 77–86.

7. See ibid., pp. 57–73, for a discussion of contemporary problems in the utilization of returned students. The comparison is imbalanced because the Soviet-trained cohort is now old enough to assume high positions. In June 1989, for example, the PRC's premier and the CCP's general secretary were both products of Soviet training in the 1950s. One wonders if American training of the 1980s will ever be able to make this claim.

8. *MOR China Letter* 2, 11 (December 1988): 7, citing World Bank data. Trade for 1986 as percentage of GDP calculated from World Bank, *World Development Report 1988* (New York: Oxford University Press, 1988), pp. 226–27, 242–43; the Taiwan figure is from Directorate-General of Budget, Accounting and Statistics, *Statistical Yearbook of the Republic of China 1987* (Taibei, 1987), pp. 97, 192.

9. Robert Dernberger, "The Role of the Foreigner in China's Economic Development, 1840–1949," in *China's Modern Economy in Historical Perspective*, ed. Dwight Perkins (Stanford: Stanford University Press, 1975), p. 27.

10. World Bank, *World Development Report 1988*, pp. 256–57.

11. UNESCO, *Statistical Yearbook 1988* (Paris, 1988), table 3–11. See *Statistical Yearbook of the Republic of China 1987*, p. 254, for the Taiwan figure.

12. Calculated from the sources cited in note 11 and World Bank, *World Development Report 1988*, pp. 222–23.

13. Data on Chinese tourism are from *Beijing Review* 31, 41 (October 10–16, 1988): 31, and 32, 7–8 (February 13–26, 1989): 38. International tourist data are from United Nations, *Statistical Yearbook 1983–84* (New York, 1986), table 169.

14. For details on this and other current problems in Chinese education, see "Chinese Education in Crisis," *China Exchange News* 17, 1 (March 1989): 2–14.

INDEX